ROMAN
but Not
CATHOLIC

ROMAN
but Not
CATHOLIC

What Remains at Stake

500 Years *after the* Reformation

Kenneth J. Collins and Jerry L. Walls

Baker Academic
a division of Baker Publishing Group
www.BakerAcademic.com

© 2017 by Kenneth J. Collins and Jerry L. Walls

Published by Baker Academic
a division of Baker Publishing Group
PO Box 6287, Grand Rapids, MI 49516-6287
www.bakeracademic.com

Printed in the United States of America

Library of Congress Cataloging-in-Publication Data
Names: Collins, Kenneth J., author.
Title: Roman but not Catholic : what remains at stake 500 years after the Reformation / Kenneth J. Collins and Jerry L. Walls.
Description: Grand Rapids : Baker Academic, 2017. | Includes bibliographical references and index.
Identifiers: LCCN 2017015992 | ISBN 9780801098932 (pbk. : alk. paper)
Subjects: LCSH: Theology, Doctrinal—History—Modern period, 1500– | Protestant churches—Relations—Catholic Church. | Catholic Church—Relations—Protestant churches. | Reformed Church—Doctrines—History—Modern period, 1500–
Classification: LCC BT27 .C65 2017 | DDC 280/.042—dc23
LC record available at https://lccn.loc.gov/2017015992

Scripture quotations are from the Holy Bible, New International Version®. NIV®. Copyright © 1973, 1978, 1984, 2011 by Biblica, Inc.™ Used by permission of Zondervan. All rights reserved worldwide. www.zondervan.com

17 18 19 20 21 22 23   7 6 5 4 3 2 1

To the memory of Roger Reynolds
KJC

To all my friends from the Dulles Colloquium, with fond
memories of those many spirited discussions in the Union
League Club, led by Father Neuhaus and Cardinal Dulles
JLW

CONTENTS

ACKNOWLEDGMENTS

I am grateful to the board of trustees and the administration of Asbury Theological Seminary for giving me the sabbatical that helped to make writing this book possible.

Thanks go to Dr. William Abraham of Southern Methodist University, who read much of the manuscript and offered many very helpful and insightful suggestions. I am also grateful to John Bugay, Reformed apologist, who read the work and offered well-received and much-appreciated counsel. Thanks also to Drs. Edwin Tait and Anthony Joseph, who read part of the manuscript and had several interesting observations and comments. A word of praise, of course, goes out to our friend and colleague, Dr. Ben Witherington III, New Testament scholar, who kept us grounded in Scripture. I am also appreciative of the faithful service of Rev. Andy Newman, who assisted in the research for this work, and of the advice of my fall 2016 Church History class who contributed to the process of naming the book.

Finally, I would like to express gratitude to my family: Marilyn; Brooke, Aaron, Kyla, and Darah; Lauren, Cody, and Gwenyth. They make all that I do a pleasure.

KJC

I want to thank several people who helped in various ways in the writing of this book, and made my chapters much better than they would otherwise be. First, I am grateful to several colleagues at Houston Baptist University who have discussed these issues with me over the past year or two and patiently endured my raising these topics at "pub night" more times than they would probably like to remember. They have also read some of the chapters and offered helpful criticism. In particular, I thank Dave Davis, Josh Farris, Bruce Gordon, Russ Hemati, Anthony Joseph, Tyler McNabb, Jeremy Neill, and Nancy Pearcey.

A number of other people have read chapters or parts of chapters and given helpful comments: Brandon Addison, John Behr, Petey Bellini, Al Howsapien, Peter Leithart, Paul Manata, David Opderbeck, and Glenn Peoples.

I am very grateful to Brian Hall, Timothy McGrew, and Josh Rasmussen, who gave expert advice for formulating my argument in chapter 13.

A special word of thanks to Billy Abraham, Brian Hall, Alan Rhoda, and Luke Van Horn, all of whom read several (in some cases all) of my chapters and provided insightful criticism.

Finally, I want to thank my family: Timothy and Angela Amos, Madelyn Rose, Mackenzie Grace and Abigail Joy; and Jonathan and Emily Walls. They always provide inspiration and encouragement, both directly and indirectly, for everything I write.

JLW

ABBREVIATIONS

Bibliographic

ANF *The Ante-Nicene Fathers: Translations of the Writings of the Fathers down to A.D. 325.* Edited by Alexander Roberts, James Donaldson, and A. Cleveland Coxe. 10 vols. New York: Christian Literature, 1885–1887. Reprinted, Peabody, MA: Hendrickson, 1994.

Catechism *Catechism of the Catholic Church.* 2nd ed. Mahwah, NJ: Paulist Press, 1994.

JDDJ *Joint Declaration on the Doctrine of Justification* (1999)

LW Martin Luther. *Luther's Works.* Philadelphia: Fortress; Saint Louis: Concordia, 1958–86, 2008–.

NABRE New American Bible, revised (2010) edition

NIV New International Version (2011)

NPNF¹ *A Select Library of Nicene and Post-Nicene Fathers of the Christian Church.* 1st series. Edited by Philip Schaff. 14 vols. New York: Christian Literature, 1886–1889. Reprinted, Peabody, MA: Hendrickson, 1994.

NPNF² *A Select Library of Nicene and Post-Nicene Fathers of the Christian Church.* 2nd series. Edited by Philip Schaff and Henry Wace. 14 vols. New York: Christian Literature, 1890–1900. Reprinted, Peabody, MA: Hendrickson, 1994.

NT New Testament

OT Old Testament

PG Patrologia Graeca. Edited by J.-P. Migne. 162 vols. Paris, 1857–86.

Miscellaneous

§ section

AD anno Domini, year of our Lord

art. article

b. born

BC before Christ

c. circa

can.	canon	n(n).	note(s)
cf.	*confer*, compare	n.p.	no place
chap(s).	chapter(s)	n.s.	new series
d.	died	par(s).	paragraph(s)
ed(s).	editor(s), edited by, edition	r.	reigned
e.g.	*exempli gratia*, for example	RCC	Roman Catholic Church
EKD	Evangelische Kirche in	repr.	reprinted
	Deutschland	rev.	revised
esp.	especially	sec.	section
etc.	*et cetera*, and so forth	s.v.	*sub verbo*, under the word
i.e.	*id est*, that is	trans.	translator, translated by
n.d.	no date	v(v).	verse(s)

INTRODUCTION

As a historian/theologian with a particular passion for the field of Wesley studies, I (Ken) came to this work reluctantly. Producing materials that help to communicate the genius of the Wesleyan theological tradition to the spiritually hungry around the world, I have witnessed countless testimonies of genuine salvation and radical transformation of persons who now both know and love God as revealed in Jesus Christ by the power of the Holy Spirit. Why then should I leave this very positive and enormously satisfying work, even for a season, to take up the task of what initially looked to me like polemics?

As Jerry Walls walked the halls of Asbury Theological Seminary, at first he said, "Collins, you should write this book," knowing, as he did, something of my background. Yes, I am a product of twelve years of Roman Catholic education. My aunt was a Mercy nun, and my older brother a Xaverian Brother for a time. However, I fled the church—that's the right word—as a junior in high school after a particularly emotionally wrenching experience. Earlier, while I was in grammar school, I had often been physically abused by Roman Catholic brothers who had been quite creative here and even made a sport of inflicting physical and emotional pain. Though I was serious, an excellent student, and even won the religion medal in my graduating class, I, like other students at the school, received an inordinate number of blows throughout my grammar school career. One beating, for example, was so severe (on the hands with a very thick composite "ruler") that I couldn't even hold anything in my hands for several days. I often walked to class in fear, not knowing what would set off the brother on that particular day. By the time I was sixteen and feeling some of my teenage pushback oats, I had had enough. My thought at the time was simply this: "I need to get away from these people."

Today, I have not the slightest twinge of resentment toward Roman Catholicism or its clergy. How can that be? Indeed, I myself often marvel at this. In fact, I am in some sense even grateful for this particular theological tradition. Again, how can that be? The answer here has much to do with grace. That is, it was no one less than the Holy Spirit, orchestrating providential grace, who not only changed my heart but also used my early, negative experiences in Roman Catholicism to bring great good out of them. In particular, the Spirit of the living Christ ultimately led me into the church that is known as the Wesleyan theological tradition, in which I have flourished for more than four decades now. If I live to be a thousand years old, I would still not have enough time to express all the gratitude in my heart for this wonderful, life-transforming journey. The riches of the Wesleyan tradition are so very considerable. In the end, I must energetically confess, it's all good, for God's grace is sufficient, and God's love is over all!

Knowing something of this history (though certainly not all its earlier gory details), Jerry Walls kept coming at me, urging me to write this book. He repeated this entreaty again and again. I politely replied, "No" in every creative way I could imagine. I thought we were finally done with the matter, but no, I was wrong. Years later when he was well ensconced at Houston Baptist University as a scholar in residence in the Department of Philosophy, Jerry asked me over the phone if I would join him in writing this book. This would be something we could do together. Again I said, "No." However, after several more efforts he was ultimately persuasive—as usual.

What changed my mind? The simple answer is that by this point Jerry had convinced me that I could help a large population of Christians who are currently struggling with the issues we discuss in this book. Many of these folk are evangelicals—though some are not—who have begun to look at their own communions of faith in greatly diminished ways precisely due to errors in historiography (how they read the history of the church and their own place within it) as well as in ecclesiology, that is, with respect to a proper understanding of what constitutes the church, the body of Christ. Properly motivated now to take up the cause by love for my brothers and sisters, some of whom are suffering, I came to view this whole enterprise much differently and very positively. I had this change of heart even though I realized that writing such a book would open up both Jerry and me to much criticism, even to personal attack (did I really want a round 2?). However, that also comes with the lay of the land here and reveals, once again, precisely why such a book must be written.

This work is preeminently about Roman Catholicism; it is not about Protestantism, at least not directly. Accordingly, we can save some of the Roman Catholic apologists, authors, and bloggers much wasted effort in pointing out that we are humbly, honestly, and forthrightly aware of many of the faults and missteps of Protestant theological traditions. However, that is not our topic. Therefore, to point out repeatedly the weaknesses of Protestantism in the face of serious reflection on Roman Catholicism, as some apologists are wont to do, is in our judgment just another way of changing the conversation, even shutting it down, so that the very real problems of the Roman Catholic tradition are never actually faced. We avoid such an egregious error. Thus Roman Catholicism (and its many claims) is after all the topic of this book, and we unswervingly pursue this throughout. To be sure, this subject is well worth the focus and effort, as the unfolding of the book will clearly demonstrate. It constitutes much of why neither of us is a Roman Catholic even today.

Moreover, this book is about the official teaching of Roman Catholicism; it is not, by and large, about what contemporary Roman Catholic theologians or even what laypeople at times think. Indeed, in several instances these last two groups can differ, sometimes markedly and confusedly so, from the official doctrine of the Roman Catholic Church. Therefore, we pay particular attention to valuable resources such as the *Catechism*; Vatican II materials; historic documents of the church such as Scripture, creeds (Apostles', Nicene, Athanasian), rules of faith, and councils (Lateran, Trent, Vatican I, etc.); canons; papal encyclicals; and various practices that together make up the formal teaching of the Roman Catholic theological tradition.

Beyond this, considerable care was taken in terms of the order of the chapters and what issues would be addressed. First, this effort is by no means a systematic treatment in the sense that the book flows from the doctrine of God to eschatology and takes every step along the way. Instead, the work proceeds by essays (largely historical and philosophical) along key themes that highlight the distinct claims of the Roman Catholic Church, especially those that set it apart from other theological traditions such as Eastern Orthodoxy and Protestantism. Second, due to space limitations, even in terms of what topics are in fact treated (such as the sacraments, the priesthood, and the papacy) we could by no means be exhaustive. Indeed, entire books could be written in each one of these areas. Third, by the perspective of the Protestant Reformation, which is part of the book's vantage point, we understand this terminology very broadly to refer at times to the historic leaders and materials of the sixteenth century (to which there are many references throughout the book), but also to how Reformation Christians today participate in these living Christian traditions that are being passed along from century to century.

Authors who take three years out of their lives to dedicate themselves to a worthy writing project such as this would, no doubt, like to reach the widest audience possible. However, this goal cannot be the only consideration. Added to this must be the concern to contextualize the essays, so that they will be carefully understood and therefore more effective in achieving their larger purpose, illumination, which means that this effort moves in a decidedly different direction than a popular account does. In the face of such a dilemma, we have tried to hold both of these considerations in tension, though we have no doubt leaned, almost by necessity (given the demands of the task), toward a more scholarly treatment.

Though Roman Catholics, of course, are likely to think otherwise, our larger argument in the book does not impugn any essential or nonnegotiable teaching of the Christian faith, but only those later additions that for many today serve as obstacles, stumbling blocks, to the proper Christian witness. Indeed, the case that we make throughout the book richly affirms what C. S. Lewis called "mere Christianity," the classic trinitarian orthodoxy of the historic creeds. This judgment, of course, represents a Protestant perspective, as our critics will no doubt claim, but we receive such criticism as an opportunity to articulate the importance not only of perspective in the life of the church but also of the ongoing vitality and integrity of many Protestant theological traditions. We never have to apologize for being Protestant.

Rejecting the extreme polemics of some Protestant apologists (claiming that Roman Catholics are not Christians, and the pope is the antichrist), we affirm Roman Catholicism as a distinct Christian theological communion, though we recognize that some of the traditions and practices it has developed over the centuries may at times detract from both the power and the clarity of the gospel. Our argument then is broadly ecumenical and generous, especially since it not only acknowledges the theological differences of distinct traditions (such as Roman Catholicism and Eastern Orthodoxy) in an open and forthright way but also has the good sense not to make any one of these traditions the heart of the church. Indeed, since each Christian tradition has been a part of a prior schism (the one in 1054 readily comes to mind), no one tradition can ever be the center. Those days are long gone.

We recognize that the word "Catholic" is employed today by Roman Catholics and Protestants in much different ways than in previous centuries, and these differences reflect distinct theological traditions and ecclesiastical locations. In fact, the differing renderings of this common word epitomize a fair portion of our major argument throughout the book. Since speaking out of our respective theological traditions might, given the disputed nature of the term, appear to be triumphalism or cause a gross misunderstanding, we suggest taking the principal meanings (historically and etymologically speaking) of the unabridged and highly reputable *Oxford English Dictionary* (OED) as a common ground and as an authoritative resource in this disputed area.

The *OED* points out that the word "Catholic" means "general" or "universal" or even "whole," and it was expressed much earlier in Greek by the word καθολικός and in Latin by *catholicus*.[1] The term "catholic church" was never used by either Jesus or the apostles; it made its first appearance in the writings of Ignatius during the early part of the second century, when it referred to "the *whole body* of believers."[2] Much later, after the Great Schism in 1054, the word "Catholic" was used as a "descriptive epithet by the Western or Latin Church,"[3] whereas the Christian East much preferred the designation "Orthodox." It was during the Reformation in the sixteenth century that those under "the Roman obedience"[4] began to claim the word as "its exclusive right . . . in opposition to the 'Protestant' or 'Reformed.'"[5]

This brief history, along with some etymological considerations, suggests that today's usage of the term "Catholic" by those under the authority of the bishop of Rome (which includes Roman Catholics, of course, as well as other "Catholic" communions, that is, those bodies of differing rites)[6] actually has its origin in the polemical context of the sixteenth century, when it began to take on a *particular* meaning, one that rendered the Roman tradition itself distinct from other Christian communions. In this heated and troubled context, the word "Catholic" no longer referred, as it once had in charity and grace, to "the whole body of believers."[7] The realities of the second-century (ancient ecumenical) church were by now long gone. Rome, no doubt, felt justified in shifting this definition simply because, in its estimation at least, Protestants had left the "holy mother church." Protestants, for their part, chafed under such restrictive and, in their estimation, newfangled usage.

In light of these basic historical truths, we demonstrate in considerable detail the theological and ecclesiastical trouble that emerges when any one communion insists on being the center. For one thing, the Roman Catholic

1. *Oxford English Dictionary*, 3rd ed. (Oxford: Oxford University Press, 2010), s.v. "catholic."
2. Ibid. (emphasis added).
3. Ibid.
4. Ibid.
5. Ibid.
6. See the discussion of this issue in Richard P. McBrien, *Catholicism* (New York: HarperOne, 1994): "In addition to the Latin, or Roman tradition, there are seven other non-Latin, non-Roman ecclesial traditions: Armenian, Byzantine, Coptic, Ethiopian, East Syrian (Chaldean), West Syrian, and Maronite. Each of these is a Catholic church in communion with the Bishop of Rome; none of these is a *Roman* Catholic Church" (5). Our use of the term "Roman Catholic" does not ignore the reality that there is a small minority of Catholic churches in communion with Rome that are not Roman, strictly speaking. See Ignatius, *Spiritual Exercises of St. Ignatius of Loyola*, trans. Elder Mullan, SJ (New York: P. J. Kenedy & Sons, 1914), http://www.ccel.org/ccel/ignatius/exercises.xix.v.html.
7. McBrien, *Catholicism*, 5.

Church has no greater claim to catholicity or universality than does Eastern Orthodoxy. And when these two traditions make the same or similar claims simultaneously, that's a prescription for historical and ecclesiastical confusion. The unfortunate reality, substantiated throughout the pages of church history, is that the ancient ecumenical church broke up into distinct theological traditions. We fully and unabashedly recognize this historical truth. Therefore, we most often refer to the Roman Catholic Church (instead of simply the Catholic Church) in order to avoid the confusing wordplay that does not fully acknowledge the significance of Eastern Orthodoxy, much less that of other equally Christian theological traditions such as those that make up Protestantism. Moreover, for the sake of style and also to avoid tedium, we employ the term "Rome" to refer to the Roman Catholic Church (instead of repeating RCC), recognizing, of course, that this particular tradition is in no way limited to Europe but is a global communion of faith.

Though we affirm that Jesus Christ and the apostolic testimony to him are the foundation of the church, and though we celebrate the first-century church, especially in its proclamation at Pentecost, we are not making a primitivistic argument here. We fully recognize that the church develops over time under the authority of the Holy Spirit. Such development, in the best sense of the term, is consonant with the basic truth of Scripture and with the interpretive traditions (expressed in thought and practice) that Scripture has stimulated among the faithful, such that the church is equipped by Word and Spirit to bear its testimony from age to age. Thus our chief concern, especially as we face the Roman Catholic tradition, is not to engage in primitivism but to avoid the error of anachronism, such as reading back into the first-century church later historical products (e.g., the papacy) as if they had always been there.

Finally, our approach is biblical, historical, theological, and philosophical, not dogmatic. We are open to learning from all Christians, including those who fundamentally differ from us. Accordingly, we read and learn even from Roman Catholic dogmatists, that is, from those authors who have already made up their minds that whatever Rome affirms is the gospel truth. This mind-set, which seems to be prevalent among many Roman Catholic apologists and bloggers, was evidenced much earlier in the writings of Ignatius of Loyola himself, who declared: "To be right in everything, we ought always to hold that the white which I see, is black, if the Hierarchical Church so decides it."[8] Our argument is not addressed to the contemporary exemplars of this mind-set, and we are under no illusions that it would be heard by them even if it were.

KJC

8. Ibid.

My (Jerry) religious background is quite different from that of my good friend Collins. Whereas he was raised in Brooklyn, New York, I was born and raised in Knockemstiff, Ohio. Whereas he was baptized as an infant and confirmed as a Roman Catholic, I accepted Christ as an eleven-year-old in an emotional conversion experience during a revival in a small country church and was later baptized in a creek across the road from my house. Whereas he has painful memories of his religious instruction in his Roman Catholic schools, which led him to lose his faith for a time, I have warm memories of loving nurture from those formative years when I attended Bethel Chapel Christian Union Church, and my faith has never seriously wavered since my conversion experience.

I say this to emphasize that I came to my interest in the issues in this book from a very different direction. I knew very little about Roman Catholicism while growing up, and I don't recall having any particular opinions about it. Looking back, I have no distinct memories of interacting with Catholics until I went to Princeton Theological Seminary from 1977 to 1980—during which time, by the way, I first met Collins, who was a fellow student at Princeton. No doubt I had met Catholics before then, but my world was very much a Protestant evangelical one. At Princeton, there were several Roman Catholic students, and one of my professors was a Roman Catholic. Those were balmy post–Vatican II days (though I did not know much about the details of Vatican II at the time), and on the front burner was the growing sense of unity among Christians, not the issues that divided us from Rome. I do not recall any discussions or debates about the doctrines that divided us or any concern from Catholics to make an issue of them.

My first serious engagement with Roman Catholicism came when I enrolled as a graduate student in the philosophy department at the University of Notre Dame in the fall of 1984. My years there were some of the best of my life; not only am I a proud graduate of that great university, but I also recall my years there with both fondness and gratitude. During this period Notre Dame was in the process of building a great Christian philosophy department with an ecumenical composition, and the excitement was palpable. In addition to a number of serious Catholics, Notre Dame had attracted some noted Protestants, including the great Alvin Plantinga and Tom Morris, who had recently completed graduate school at Yale and was already off to a roaring start in his academic career by the time I arrived.

While I was getting a great philosophical education at Notre Dame, I was also acquiring an informal education of another sort, namely, about Roman Catholicism, at least of the American variety. In addition to faculty members, several of my fellow graduate students were committed Roman Catholics, and my conversations with them were the first I can recall in which I ever discussed at length the differences that divide Protestants from Catholics; they not only took those issues seriously but also were eager to defend their side of the matter. Indeed, I came to realize that many conservative Roman Catholics view evangelicals as Catholics just waiting to happen, and they would love to help push us over the edge. I had numerous conversations about these issues with my Catholic friends and teachers, and I distinctly recall the parting words of one of my professors, Fred Freddoso, when I left Notre Dame: "I'm disappointed as hell you did not become a Catholic."

But I was not done with these sorts of conversations. Several years later I had the good fortune to meet Richard John Neuhaus and to get to know him a bit. We hit it off, and he was intrigued to learn that I was a Protestant who was defending a version of the doctrine of purgatory in the book I was then writing about heaven.[9] Shortly thereafter he invited me to join the Dulles Colloquium, an ecumenical theology discussion group hosted by him and Avery Dulles, after whom it was named. The Dulles Colloquium met once or twice a year in New York, usually at the Union League Club, and the official business of the day was to discuss a paper that had been sent to us several weeks earlier.

My participation in this group for several years was one of the great blessings and privileges of my life, for which I remain deeply grateful. One of my lasting regrets is that personal circumstances caused me to miss the last meeting to which I was invited in the spring of 2008, not knowing it was my last chance to see both Father Neuhaus and Cardinal Dulles in this life. Through the years when I was involved in the colloquium, I got to discuss matters of vital importance with some remarkable people: Gary Anderson, Jody Bottum, Shalom Carmy, Chuck Colson, Robert George, Timothy George, Paul Griffiths, Thomas Guarino, David Hart, Stanley Hauerwas, Russ Hittinger, Robert Jensen, George Lindbeck, Bruce Marshall, Gilbert Meilaender, David Novak, Michael Novak, James Nuechterlein, Tom Oden, Rusty Reno, Steve Webb, George Weigel, Robert Wilken, and many others. The group was composed of persons from a number of traditions, including Lutherans, Roman Catholics, Anglicans, Orthodox, Methodists, and evangelicals, as well as a few Jews.

The paper topics covered a wide range of theological and moral issues and often dealt with matters of ecumenical concern. After the formal session, conversation continued more casually over dinner. Then we usually retired to the bar to continue to talk until bedtime. Occasionally a few of us were invited to Neuhaus's apartment for drinks and conversation. Not infrequently these

9. Jerry L. Walls, *Heaven: The Logic of Eternal Joy* (New York: Oxford University Press, 2002). I report that Collins does not share my views about the viability of a Protestant doctrine of purgatory. He rejects the doctrine.

more informal talks centered on issues dividing Protestants and Catholics, with Neuhaus leading the way in making the case for Rome with his characteristic wit, charm, and ecumenical sensibilities. In these discussions with Neuhaus and other members of the group, I regularly defended the Protestant view.

In retrospect, I suspect that the unofficial agenda of the Dulles Colloquium— and I say this with all due affection—was to be a Catholic Conversion Club, particularly with the aim of converting Protestant intellectuals to Rome. (Indeed, I cannot help but wonder if part of the reason I was invited to join the group was that Neuhaus thought I might be ripe for conversion to Rome since I was defending the doctrine of purgatory.) In any case, when I joined the colloquium, a number of the members of the group were evangelicals, Anglicans, Lutherans, and so on who later converted to Rome. I cannot read their minds, and I cannot speak for them, so I will not presume what role, if any, their participation in the Dulles Colloquium might have played in their conversion. But I will say that in my experience, the dynamics of the group encouraged conversion to Rome. Indeed, the same might be said for the highly regarded magazine *First Things*, which Neuhaus founded. Rusty Reno, a convert from the Episcopal Church and the current editor of *First Things*, commented playfully on the matter as follows in an issue of the magazine featuring two articles by Protestants.

> On the topic of Catholic triumphalism: Not a few Protestant friends complain that *First Things* is a Catholic party with a few Protestants and Jews invited. That always makes me wince, because it's not altogether false. After all, the magazine was begun by a man who had just published a book titled *The Catholic Moment*. But I hope the two forceful essays about Protestantism in this issue convince readers that it's not altogether true. . . . There's no requirement that one kowtow to Catholicism.[10]

Reno's somewhat whimsical comment accurately conveys my experience as a participant in the Dulles Colloquium for several years. Certainly there was no requirement to "kowtow to Catholicism," but the claim of Rome to be the one true church was promoted, sometimes in subtle ways, sometimes in humorous flourishes, but always with urbane sophistication. But then, what else should one expect in a group named after, and attended by, a distinguished Roman Catholic cardinal and led by a famous Lutheran convert to Rome?

So in one sense the experience was deeply and richly ecumenical, but it also vividly showed the limits of Roman ecumenism. A few times the Protestants among us attended Mass with our Catholic friends, and it always struck me

10. Reno, "While We're At It," *First Things*, August/September 2014, 69.

how odd it was that we had more genuine Christian unity and fellowship around the dinner table than we did at the table of the Lord. The welcome that was extended to those of us who did not regard Rome as the one true church only went so far: we watched from a distance when our Roman Catholic brothers shared the sacrament of Communion.

These sorts of experiences have generated my interest in the issues of this book and led me to think that it needed to be written. I also share these experiences to emphasize that my experiences and interactions with Roman Catholics have been overwhelmingly positive for the most part. In the past several years, I have had further positive interactions with Roman Catholics, partly because of further work I have done on purgatory. (Indeed, because of this work, not infrequently it has been assumed that I *am* a Roman Catholic!) Since my earlier discussion of the doctrine in my book on heaven, I have written a whole book defending an ecumenical version of the doctrine, the first book-length defense of purgatory ever by a Protestant, so far as I know.[11] I hope this also shows that I am not automatically critical of a doctrine just because of its Roman Catholic pedigree or associations. To the contrary, it is always my aim to weigh doctrinal claims on their biblical, theological, and rational merits, regardless of their ecclesial connections.

I should frankly say that I have never been seriously tempted to convert to Rome, although I have obviously pondered it, as indicated by the experiences described above. Somewhat ironically, that is part of why I wanted to write this book with Collins. In recent years we have heard from lots of evangelicals who have converted to Rome. (Most of them, it seems, feel they need to write a book or at least contribute an essay to one of those collections of conversion narratives that are so popular among Catholic apologists.) I thought it might be helpful for the many persons who are struggling with these issues to hear from persons who have thought about them carefully but have not converted to Rome. We have heard from lots of people who have read John Henry Newman's famous essay on doctrinal development and found his arguments compelling. I thought it might be helpful to hear from persons who have read Newman but found his arguments deeply confused and his conclusions badly overstated.

I also want to reiterate that this book aims to be ecumenical in the best sense of the word. We very much agree with Kevin Vanhoozer that the "only good Protestant is a catholic Protestant—one who learns from, and bears

---

11. Walls, *Purgatory: The Logic of Total Transformation* (New York: Oxford University Press, 2012); see also Walls, *Heaven, Hell, and Purgatory: Rethinking the Things That Matter Most* (Grand Rapids: Brazos, 2015).

fruit for, the *whole* church."[12] Indeed, we believe that challenging the exclusive claims of Rome is essential to true catholicism and for advancing deeper unity in the body of Christ. While committed Roman Catholics no doubt believe that promoting their exclusive claims is necessary to their very identity, we aim to show a better way forward.

JLW

For any curious souls who want to know, as well as our critics, this is how the authors cooperated: They cowrote the introduction. Kenneth Collins wrote chapters 2, 3, 6, 7, 9–12, 15–19, and the conclusion. Jerry Walls wrote chapters 1, 4, 5, 8, 13, 14, and 20.

12. Kevin J. Vanhoozer, *Biblical Authority after Babel: Retrieving the* Solas *in the Spirit of Mere Protestant Christianity* (Grand Rapids: Brazos, 2016), 33 (emphasis original).

1

What We Have in Common

Despite what our title may suggest, we intend this to be a deeply ecumenical book that will ultimately serve the cause of Christian unity. True ecumenism requires forthright and respectful acknowledgment of differences, but even more important, it proceeds from a hearty recognition and appreciation of the more important common ground we share by virtue of our common commitment to classic creedal Christianity. While this book is concerned primarily with exploring honest differences, we never want to lose sight of that common ground. So although this will be the shortest chapter in the book, it is only so because there is no need to belabor points where we agree. Still, we want not only to recognize but also to celebrate the profound fellowship that unites all persons whose hearts and minds have been captured by the incomparably beautiful truth definitively revealed through the life, death, and resurrection of Jesus Christ.

The Creeds and the Hierarchy of Christian Truth

Let us begin by declaring that we share a commitment to the classic creeds: the Apostles', the Nicene, and the Athanasian. The core doctrines summarized in these classic creeds provide the fundamental framework for the Christian faith as professed by Eastern Orthodox churches, Roman Catholic churches, and the churches of the Protestant Reformation.[1]

1. The *filioque* clause of the Nicene Creed is not accepted by Eastern Orthodox churches.

Our agreement with the classic creeds is only one aspect of our shared heritage of classic patristic theology. With Roman Catholics, we look to the early centuries of the church and the fathers for seminal theology and doctrinal guidance. Indeed, we also find much to agree about in classic medieval philosophers and theologians, to whom we also look for inspiration and Christian wisdom.

The pivotal role of the creeds is reflected in part 1 of the *Catechism of the Catholic Church*, which deals with "the profession of faith" and articulates that profession by expounding the Apostles' Creed, supplemented by numerous references to the Nicene Creed. As the *Catechism* states, "Communion in faith needs a common language of faith, normative for all and uniting all in the same confession of faith."[2]

The exposition of the Apostles' Creed in the *Catechism* is powerful, demonstrating the fact that orthodox Christians of all traditions are indeed united "in the same confession of faith." This is hardly to suggest that evangelicals and other Christians in the Reformation tradition will agree entirely with part 1 of the *Catechism*. They surely will not, and Protestants who read through it will likely find it an ambivalent experience, for they will disagree at a number of points while profoundly resonating at many others.

Indeed, where they disagree, they will often judge that points of dispute represent instances where the Church of Rome has overreached and made claims that have greatly harmed the cause of Christian unity. For instance, when it expounds the Nicene affirmation "We believe in one holy catholic and apostolic Church," the *Catechism* advances claims for the Church of Rome that are at the heart of some of the most fundamental differences separating Rome not only from Reformation Christians but also from Eastern Orthodox Christians. Moreover, the modest, clearly biblical, and creedal claim that Christ was "conceived by the power of the Holy Spirit and born of the Virgin Mary" occasions in the *Catechism* a statement and defense of Marian doctrines that Reformation Christians typically reject because they see no support for them in Scripture. Protestants will be similarly skeptical of the attempt to situate within the affirmation "I believe in the holy catholic Church, the communion of saints" the doctrine of Mary's bodily assumption. Most will find it extravagant, to say the least, to claim that she has been "exalted by the Lord as Queen over all things, so that she might be the more fully conformed to her Son, the Lord of lords, and conqueror of sin and death."[3]

2. *Catechism of the Catholic Church*, 2nd ed. (Mahwah, NJ: Paulist Press, 1994), par. 185.
3. Ibid., par. 966.

These and many other issues and points of disagreement will be taken up in more detail below, but for now they are not our concern. Here is what we want to emphasize now. Despite these differences, which indeed are significant, as we shall argue, the common ground we share is far more important than any disagreements that distinguish and even divide us. As C. S. Lewis observed, the convictions we share are so profound and far reaching that they divide us "from all non-Christian beliefs by a chasm to which the worst divisions inside Christendom are not really comparable at all."[4] Indeed, compared to the chasm that separates us from non-Christians, we might even say that our differences are a mere gully. To be sure, some gullies are fairly wide and difficult to cross, but they are nothing compared to the chasm that separates orthodox Christians from non-Christians.

Consider the core of beliefs we share and how these beliefs are radically at odds with various non-Christian beliefs, starting with the fundamental confession "We believe in God, the Father almighty, creator of heaven and earth." The notion that we and our world are creatures, that we owe our very existence to an almighty God who sovereignly chose to give us life and being, separates us profoundly from various atheistic and secular views contending that we are the product of entirely accidental, natural causes that did not intend for us to be here. The conviction that God almighty is a Father, not merely a powerful Lord, is an immediate indication that the purpose for which we exist is full of meaning and positive significance.

So the difference between belief in such a God and unbelief is far from a merely theoretical issue. Rather, it is deeply practical and has enormous existential implications. The *Catechism* summarizes these implications in a series of pithy statements: "It means coming to know God's greatness and majesty. . . . It means living in thanksgiving. . . . It means knowing the unity and true dignity of all men. . . . It means making good use of created things. . . . It means trusting God in every circumstance, even in adversity."[5]

We can hardly exaggerate the difference in worldview between believing that all existing things are here by virtue of the purposeful actions of a Father almighty and believing that the blind forces of nature somehow generated us. This fundamental difference of conviction, moreover, is at the heart of many national as well as global conflicts in our world today. Protestants stand firmly united with Roman Catholics in sharing a worldview that starts with belief in God the Father almighty.

4. Lewis, *Mere Christianity* (New York: HarperSanFrancisco, 2001), xi.
5. *Catechism*, pars. 223–27. Each statement is supported by a passage from Scripture or a quote from a classic theological source.

But much more is involved in the fact that the creeds call God "Father," and this brings us to the very heart of distinctively Christian doctrine. The doctrine that God is the creator of all that exists besides himself is shared by Jews and Muslims and many other theists. But for Christian theists, the Father is the First Person of the Trinity, and this extraordinary doctrine divides them from other theistic believers. The *Catechism* comments on the absolutely pivotal nature of this doctrine as follows: "The mystery of the Most Holy Trinity is the central mystery of the Christian faith and life. It is the most fundamental and essential teaching in the 'hierarchy of the truths of faith.' The whole history of salvation is identical with the history of the way and the means by which the one true God, Father, Son, and Holy Spirit, reveals himself to men and 'reconciles and unites with himself those who turn away from sin.'"[6] The doctrine of the Trinity is singled out as "the most fundamental and essential teaching" in a hierarchy of truths. That some doctrines have this status is significant in terms of highlighting common ground between Roman Catholics and Reformation Christians. It is particularly these doctrines that are essential to Christian identity, and it is these doctrines that ground genuine fellowship.

The shared commitment to the doctrine of the Trinity is a common faith in the story of human salvation. Again, certain differences of understanding cannot be ignored, but more important is this central fact: we agree that Jesus Christ is the incarnate Son of God who was born of the virgin Mary and who died and rose again to provide salvation for the human race.

So agreement that God is a Trinity is far more than a matter of agreeing on a speculative theological claim. It is agreement on the fact that human beings are sinners estranged from their Creator, who stand desperately in need of salvation. It is agreement that faith in Christ is necessary for our sins to be forgiven, but that we cannot exercise that faith by our own power. Here we rely on the Third Person of the Trinity, the last of the three to be revealed in the history of salvation, yet the one whose saving action in another sense is first. "Through his grace, the Holy Spirit is the first to awaken faith in us and to communicate to us the new life, which is to 'know the Father and the one whom he has sent, Jesus Christ.'"[7]

We share, moreover, a common hope for the ultimate end of the human story. We anticipate the resurrection of all persons and the final judgment, after which all persons will either enter eternal joy in the presence of God along with others who have been redeemed or experience eternal separation from God if they have rejected his offer of salvation.

6. Ibid., par. 234, quoting *General Catechetical Directory*, pars. 43, 47.
7. *Catechism*, par. 684.

In short, we share convictions that profoundly unite us in heart and mind against the secular worldview that predominates in much contemporary culture. We share a distinctive version of the human story, and we agree that the central events that illumine the story are found in the self-revelation of the Triune God and his acts to provide salvation to his fallen children through the death and resurrection of his Son. And we anticipate a future that will bring the story to a glorious end.

It would be incomplete, if not misleading, however, to leave the impression that what Reformation Christians and Roman Catholics share is only theological or doctrinal. We also share important moral and social commitments, many of which are under pressure in contemporary culture from the forces of secularism. Roman Catholics have consistently been outspoken advocates for justice issues, the right to life, and traditional views of marriage, and we deeply appreciate the important role they have played in these matters. Evangelicals and many other Protestants gratefully join hands with Roman Catholics in support of these vital spiritual and moral values.

Mere Christianity and the Center We Share

Many evangelicals and other Reformation Christians will instinctively respond positively to these lines of thinking in no small part because they have been schooled to think of ecumenical relationships in terms of what C. S. Lewis famously called "mere Christianity." Lewis was likely the most influential Christian writer of the twentieth century, and his appeal shows no sign of waning as we move well into the twenty-first century. Lewis, of course, was a Protestant from Northern Ireland and a loyal member of the Church of England, but his influence is hardly confined to his fellow Protestants. Certainly he has been, and remains, especially popular in evangelical circles, but he also has a wide following among Roman Catholics.

We think the enormous ecumenical appeal of Lewis is another telling way to see the fundamental core of agreement between Protestants and Roman Catholics.[8] Indeed, it is not uncommon for Roman Catholics and Protestants to come together and work on various projects under the banner of "mere Christianity," and both of us have participated in such efforts.

Lewis clearly wrote his classic book with the goal of articulating an account of the faith that Roman Catholics could identify with, even though the book

8. We could have made the same point by examining any of the classic Protestant confessions of faith and highlighting the fundamental doctrines they all share. We chose to look at Lewis because of the wide familiarity with his book among Roman Catholics as well as Protestants.

does not in any way affirm a Roman account of authority, the sacraments, Marian dogmas, and the like. In the preface Lewis reports that he sent the original manuscript of book 2, *What Christians Believe*, to four clergymen, one of whom was a Roman Catholic. (The other three were Anglican, Methodist, and Presbyterian.) Although it is obvious that no single ordinary clergyman can claim to speak for his entire church, Lewis took it as evidence that he had succeeded in his goal when only two of the clergymen had minor quibbles. The Methodist thought he had not paid enough attention to faith, and the Roman Catholic thought he had gone a bit too far in playing down the importance of particular theories of the atonement. Still, what is remarkable is the fact that millions of Christians of various traditions have recognized in Lewis's pages a faithful account of the heart of the faith they confess.

Although Lewis is by far the most famous person to use the term "mere Christianity" to refer to the heart of the faith, he did not invent the term. As he states in his preface, he borrowed the language from Richard Baxter, a Puritan theologian who lived in the seventeenth century (1615–91). In the eighteenth century, one of Lewis's earlier Anglican compatriots attempted to spell out common ground with Roman Catholics, namely, John Wesley, in "A Letter to a Roman Catholic."[9] But the more important point here is not merely who coined the term but rather that the notion of a core of common ground that is the very essence of the faith is something Christians have recognized for generations. Indeed, Lewis emphasizes that it long antedated him and that there is something objective about it, explaining, "For I am not writing to expound something I could call 'my religion,' but to expound 'mere' Christianity, which is what it is and what it was long before I was born and whether I like it or not."[10]

We can also see this reality in the often-observed fact that orthodox Christians of different denominations and theological traditions recognize more real fellowship and unity with each other than they do with liberal members of their own churches. Conservative Presbyterians and Roman Catholics, say, have much more in common with each other than they do with members of their own churches who play fast and loose with the creedal doctrines. Again to cite Lewis: "It is at her centre, where her truest children dwell, that each communion is really closest to every other in spirit, if not in doctrine. And this suggests that at the centre of each there is a something, or a Someone, who against all the divergencies of belief, all differences of temperament, all memories of mutual persecution, speaks with the same voice."[11]

---

9. *The Works of John Wesley*, 3rd ed. (1872; repr., Grand Rapids: Baker, 1979), 10:80–86.
10. Lewis, *Mere Christianity*, ix.
11. Ibid., xii.

Lewis made a similar point in a letter to one of his Roman Catholic correspondents from America. "I believe we are very near to one another, but not because I am at all on the Rome-ward frontier of my own communion. I believe that, in the present divided state of Christendom, those who are at the heart of each division are closer to one another than those who are on the fringes."[12]

Notice particularly Lewis's point that the center of Christian faith is recognized and defined by a "Someone" who is at the heart of true faith, namely, the trinitarian God whose Son became incarnate to save us from our sins. Those who have faith in Christ discern the essential truth of their faith because they have encountered him and have learned how to recognize him. As Jesus said, "My sheep listen to my voice; I know them, and they follow me" (John 10:27). Those who know Christ because they are known by him instinctively gravitate to the center where his voice is most distinctly heard.

By now it will be apparent that we reject the attitude of some evangelicals who do not consider Roman Catholics true Christians or doubt that they have genuine faith. We forthrightly affirm our Roman Catholic brothers and sisters as full members of the body of Christ, and we celebrate our common convictions that unite us as the family of God. While "the memories of mutual persecution" that Lewis references can hardly be swept under the rug or ignored, we rejoice in the fact that believers in our respective churches have repented of many of these sins of the past and seek to move forward in love as fellow believers whose agreements matter far more than our disagreements.

To be sure, this "mutual persecution" of the past has even included mutual anathemas. Official Roman Catholic teaching in the past has taught that Protestants cannot be saved, and many Protestants have returned the favor. In contrast with this unhappy history, official Roman Catholic teaching today takes a more ecumenical stance toward Christians in other traditions. While lamenting and condemning schism, that teaching now recognizes Protestants as brothers and sisters in Christ.

> However, one cannot charge with the sin of the separation those who at present are born into these communities [that resulted from such separation] and in them are brought up in the faith of Christ, and the Catholic Church accepts them with respect and affection as brothers. . . . All who have been justified by faith in Baptism are incorporated into Christ; they therefore have a right to be

12. Lewis, *Yours, Jack: Spiritual Direction from C. S. Lewis*, ed. Paul F. Ford (New York: HarperOne, 2008), 190.

called Christians, and with good reason are accepted as brothers in the Lord by the children of the Catholic Church.[13]

While Reformation Christians may regret that this acknowledgment is still qualified, the fact remains that the recent changes in Roman Catholic thought have helped to engender much true ecumenism and mutual respect among believers in these different traditions.

The *Catechism* goes on to acknowledge: "'Furthermore, many elements of sanctification and of truth' are found outside the visible confines of the Catholic Church: 'the written Word of God, the life of grace; faith, hope and charity, with the other interior gifts of the Holy Spirit, as well as visible elements.'"[14] Again, these "elements of sanctification and of truth" are the telltale signs that one has encountered true Christianity. When these are present, those who follow Christ will distinctly hear his voice.

In short, then, whether we talk in terms of beliefs that are "most fundamental and essential" in the hierarchy of truth, or whether we talk about a core of doctrines popularly called "mere Christianity," believers on both sides of the Reformation divide properly discern a common faith that unites them around a common center. Protestants who read part 1 of the *Catechism of the Catholic Church* will discern in those pages the essence of the faith they profess for the same reason that many Roman Catholics who read *Mere Christianity* see in those pages a true account of the heart of their faith. While Protestants will see things in the *Catechism* that they think are unbiblical, and Roman Catholics will see things missing in *Mere Christianity* that are important to them,[15] it is nevertheless remarkable that members of each group discern a common faith that transcends disagreements.

So Why Did We Write This Book, and for Whom?

Given what we have written in this chapter, some readers may think there is something ironic, perhaps even inconsistent, in our writing a book spelling out where we think Roman Catholicism goes wrong. Is this book not inevitably an assault on the very ecumenism and unity we profess? We recognize the potential danger here. In a letter to one of his Roman Catholic correspondents,

---

13. *Catechism*, par. 818. This paragraph comes from the 1964 Vatican II document titled *Unitatis Redintegratio: Decree on Ecumenism*.

14. *Catechism*, par. 819.

15. This is also true for most Protestants. Lewis intended not to spell out the fully developed faith of any Christian tradition or denomination but only to present what he thought was common to all.

C. S. Lewis wrote: "The question for me (naturally) is not, 'Why should I not become a Roman Catholic?' but 'Why should I?' But I don't like discussing such matters, because it emphasizes differences and endangers charity. By the time I had really explained my objections to certain doctrines which differentiate you from us (and also in my opinion from the Apostolic and even Medieval Church), you would like me less."[16]

In our introduction, we gave some reasons why we thought this book needed to be written, despite the potential hazards Lewis identified. As we commented there, the most basic reason is that many people are concerned with these issues and are struggling with them. A number of evangelicals have converted to Rome, and many Roman Catholics have converted to evangelicalism and other Protestant traditions, including Pentecostalism.[17] Part of this is due to aggressive apologists on both sides who have taken as their mission the "conversion" of fellow Christians to their church. They unsettle the faith of fellow Christians, and frankly, many people seem to be confused and are pressured to "convert" because of claims that their faith is deficient, or somehow inconsistent or lacking in full integrity, unless they join a particular church or denomination. To be sure, many who have "converted" have done so only after careful study, consultation, and prayer for discernment. But many others, we suspect, have done so under the pressure of dubious reasons, spurious arguments, and misinformation. And some of these persons who have "converted" are having serious second thoughts about their decision.

We have written this book for all persons grappling with these issues who want to think about them honestly and carefully, as well as for those who minister to such persons. Our concern in this book is as much pastoral as it is theological.

So this book is not aimed at faithful Roman Catholics. We do not write to unsettle the faith of fellow believers, and we say to all our Roman Catholic brothers and sisters with whom we share an active faith in Christ as described above, there are probably other books you should be reading. We recognize you as full members of the body of Christ, as affirmed above, and we have no interest in converting you to our church.[18] Your time would likely be better spent reading a book by C. S. Lewis or G. K. Chesterton rather than this one.

---

16. Lewis, *Letters of C. S. Lewis*, ed. W. H. Lewis (New York: Harcourt Brace Jovanovich, 1975), 230. For a detailed exploration of why Lewis was not a Roman Catholic, see Stewart Goetz, *A Philosophical Walking Tour with C. S. Lewis: Why It Did Not Include Rome* (New York: Bloomsbury, 2015).

17. Indeed, Pentecostalism has grown dramatically in many traditionally Roman Catholic countries, especially in the Global South.

18. There are many nominal Christians in all traditions. There is certainly a viable ministry of introducing such persons to a vital faith in Christ. That, we believe, should be our focus, not getting them to join our particular church.

But if you have an interest in the issues that divide evangelicals and other orthodox Protestants from Rome, and particularly if you are struggling with whether you need to cross the Tiber to practice your faith with full integrity (or if you have already done so but are rethinking the matter), we have written this book to explain why you need not do so. The chapters that follow are straightforwardly critical, sometimes pointedly so. Still, we emphasize that we are dealing with family issues. Sometimes families are divided and face conflict. We do not shy away from that reality even as we aim to speak the truth in love. And ultimately, we aim to serve the cause of true Christian unity in the common faith we profess.

2

Tradition and the Traditions

The first chapter has clearly demonstrated that Protestants and Roman Catholics share much in common. As fellow Christians who believe in Jesus Christ and who seek to love their neighbors through the great theological traditions that have emerged in the long and variegated history of the church, they realize the importance of speaking truth to one another, even if this worthy goal is sometimes deflected by prejudice, sectarianism, or even party spirit. Indeed, to see the Christian faith as others view it, for the sake of genuine and at times painful understanding, is in most cases a challenge that is beyond even some of the best representatives of the distinct theological traditions that exist in Christianity. Take the case of John Henry Newman, for example, a principal leader of the high church movement in Anglicanism during the nineteenth century and eventually a Roman Catholic cardinal. His statement "To be deep in history is to cease to be a Protestant"[1] perhaps tells us more about Newman's own social location, his Roman Catholicism, for instance, than it does about the living body of Christ represented by the magisterial Reformation that bears its witness from age to age. Operating within a particular tradition, without fully recognizing this, Newman was apparently baffled by the "other" Christian enough that he failed to recognize in a forthright way that Protestants could after all actually read the lengthy history of the Christian church in ways that did not immediately undermine their own existence! Indeed, the celebrated cardinal seemed to be unaware that for many informed Protestants historical

1. As quoted in Christian Smith, *How to Go from Being a Good Evangelical to a Committed Catholic in Ninety-Five Difficult Steps* (Eugene, OR: Cascade, 2011), Kindle edition, locations 697–98.

understanding actually undermines the claims of Rome[2]—and at times in very decisive ways. The mistake of Newman here, his basic historiographical error in reading and misreading the history of the church as he did, is unfortunately repeated in a burgeoning literature of Roman Catholic apologetics, now taken up even by former evangelicals such as Christian Smith, who actually quotes Newman on this very matter quite favorably.[3]

A principal way of repeatedly misunderstanding Protestantism, so that it never really emerges as a viable conversation partner, is to misrepresent what it teaches concerning the vital doctrine of *sola Scriptura*, with the result that Protestantism's ongoing recognition of the importance of early oral tradition, the rule of faith, the church fathers, and the councils of the church, for example, is hardly affirmed and in the worst instances is outright repudiated. To be sure, we know of few Protestants, except for some radicals who are a part of any movement, who would affirm, much less defend, the kind of things that are so often attributed to them in recent Roman Catholic apologetic literature.[4] Misconstruing sola Scriptura as understood simply in an exclusive sense (whereby it is the only authority appealed to) rather than in the more appropriate normative sense (whereby it norms whatever other authorities have emerged in the life of the church, such as the church fathers) can only result in stripping Protestantism of some of its more important theological contributions. To be sure, such a move renders this grace-filled church virtually naked by an overweening apologetics that is so eager to criticize that it has failed to meet the very first requirement of the fairness required for genuine ecumenical dialogue, namely, accurate description.

Accordingly, in the material that follows, one of our goals is to take great care in the description of both Roman Catholicism and Protestantism, such that each communion of faith will see its own tradition carefully reflected in an account largely sustained by careful citations from the primary literature and important secondary materials. Clearly, it does not serve our larger purpose in writing this book to misrepresent, distort, or caricature Roman Catholic teaching in any way. Instead, it is nothing less than a rich acquaintance with the actual teachings of the Roman tradition

---

2. This has certainly been my own experience (Collins). Reading Roland Bainton's biography of Martin Luther, *Here I Stand*, as a young man not only was a wonderfully liberating experience but also set me on a graciously led course to become a church historian.

3. For examples of this type of literature, see Smith, *How to Go*, Kindle ed., locations 697–98; Devin Rose, *If Protestantism Is True* (n.p.: Unitatis Books, 2011). This latter book is on very shaky ground if it would like to suggest, as the title apparently does, that Protestantism and truth are two very different things.

4. For an example of this, see Robert Sungenis, *Not by Scripture Alone: A Catholic Critique of the Protestant Doctrine of Sola Scriptura* (Goelta, CA: Queenship, 1997), esp. 1–26.

as propounded by the magisterium, not their misconstrual, that forms the substance of why neither of us is a Roman Catholic today. No one, however, can accomplish this descriptive task perfectly. Our views will always contain something of our own ecclesiastical setting, our Protestantism, our rich Reformation heritage. We fully acknowledge that. It is therefore more a matter of approximation or, better yet, of more accurate interpretations and descriptions than anything else, but we always aspire to be informed by goodwill even when we differ sharply from Roman Catholic views. To be sure, we both fully recognize Roman Catholics as our brothers and sisters in Christ and vigorously reject any Protestant apologetic approaches that revel in misrepresentation or that in the end are needlessly disruptive. This careful approach, as valuable as it is, will of course not eliminate all the problems that are likely to emerge. One such difficulty is that the very same elements of the history of the church will at times be viewed quite differently by the respective traditions: this difference can be perceived as a challenge, and at times even as a threat, to what the "other" Christian communion holds dear. This can result in great pain for both in the midst of the conversation, as each grapples with the other's own self-understanding in Christ. Such frankness and honesty, though it may sometimes lead to more than a little discomfort, is necessary for the sake of speaking truth to one another in holy love as we are best able.

Oral Tradition and the Rule of Faith

In large measure, the differences between the Roman Catholic and the Protestant communions have to do with how the history of the church is properly understood. Historians call this whole area of concern historiography, and this domain of knowledge indicates that the story of the church can be understood in several ways, not just one. In a real sense, the central question of church history for both is posed: How does the body of Christ go through time, from age to age, and yet maintain the integrity of the revelation of God manifested in Jesus Christ by the power of the Holy Spirit? There is a content, the very substance of revelation, that has to be transferred faithfully to subsequent generations across the vagaries of time, a process that can lead to modification and even to a significant transformation of the original message, the *kerygma*. Moreover, in this "traditioning" process the substance of revelation must be distinguished, at least in some sense, from the means or mechanisms employed by the church to communicate that rich deposit of faith in the form of catechisms, sermons, hymns, liturgies, and so on.

We begin our topic with the frank acknowledgment that the head of the church is Jesus Christ. He is the authority above all others; his voice is unlike all other voices because not only is he the Word incarnate, in distinction from all other human beings, but also his words constitute revelation in the best sense of the term, a content that we could not have told ourselves. Oral tradition, then, has its very fount in Jesus Christ, who spoke much but never wrote a single book. The authority of the apostles, then, in distinguishing it from that of Christ, is in some sense derivative in that it points to the Son of God. Nevertheless, the apostolic testimony is itself undoubtedly revelation, for it amplifies, for example, the larger meaning of the person and work of Christ. Put another way, this apostolic testimony, richly informed by some of those who actually knew Christ, communicates both the words and the powerful deeds of the Messiah, the very substance of revelation as well as its larger meaning, to the next generation.

The first-century church was well aware of the value of such gifts, and it therefore passed along the words of Christ as well as the apostolic testimony by means of both oral and written forms. That is, before the Gospels were even written, the very heart of the good news was already being communicated by oral means through the ritual of baptism, the regularity of preaching, the celebration of the Lord's Supper, and the necessity of instruction or catechesis. In terms of specific written forms, Paul's writings played an important part in this larger process, as did the Gospels, all of which had been written before the close of the first century. Indeed, as D. H. Williams points out, "The language and earliest content of the Christian tradition were first articulated by the apostle Paul, who encouraged the Thessalonians to 'stand firm and hold on to the traditions we passed on to you' (2 Thess. 2:15)."[5]

As the church entered the second century, Irenaeus of Lyons underscored the importance of receiving "this tradition from the apostles."[6] Moreover, as J. N. D. Kelly points out, Tertullian, whose witness crossed from the second to the third century, referred to the entire body of apostolic teaching, "whether delivered orally or in epistles, as *apostolorum traditio* or *apostolica traditio*,"[7] a sacred deposit of faith. In the fourth century Athanasius of Alexandria

---

5. D. H. Williams, *Evangelicals and Tradition: The Formative Influence of the Early Church* (Grand Rapids: Baker Academic, 2005), 32–33. See also Matthew Levering, *Engaging the Doctrine of Revelation: The Mediation of the Gospel through Church and Scripture* (Grand Rapids: Baker Academic, 2014), in which he argues, "Tradition involves two aspects: an enduring doctrinal and moral content ('the word of God') and the mediation of divine revelation (entrusted to the apostles by Christ the Lord and the Holy Spirit)" (172).

6. Irenaeus of Lyons, *Against Heresies* 9.1, in *The Apostolic Fathers with Justin Martyr and Irenaeus*, ANF 1:369.

7. Kelly, *Early Christian Doctrines* (San Francisco: Harper & Row, 1960), 36.

pointed out that the faith of the church, the teachings it held dear, "were not novel but Apostolical."[8] During this same century, Eusebius of Caesarea began to describe the apostolic testimony as "the living and abiding voice,"[9] suggesting something of the high valuation that the church attached to this witness, which, precisely because of its importance, must endure through time.

One of the ways the early church communicated the essentials of the revelation of Christ, in order to pass it down from generation to generation, was through the rule of faith (Greek κανὼν τῆς πίστεως [*kanōn tēs pisteōs*]; Latin *regula fidei*). Growing out of the need both for a pithy public confession by candidates for baptism and for a readily teachable content for catechetical instruction,[10] the rule of faith can be understood as a "doctrinal summary of Christianity or a compend of the faith of the church."[11] Both Irenaeus and Tertullian used the rule of faith as one of their principal instruments to refute the teachings of false prophets and heretics. Although the NT canon was yet to be recognized by the church, during the second century Irenaeus understood the connection between the rule of faith and the Scriptures as primarily dialogical; that is, the oral tradition and the Scriptures gave rise to the rule, and in turn the rule of faith suggested the proper interpretation of the Scriptures. Our reading of Irenaeus, especially in terms of this last point, is once again confirmed in the observation of Kelly, who maintains that "the *regula* points the way to the correct exegesis of Scripture."[12] In fact, during the second and into the third century, Tertullian in his *Prescription against Heretics* argued that "wherever it shall be manifest that the true Christian rule and faith shall be, *there* will likewise be the true Scriptures and expositions thereof, and all the Christian traditions."[13]

A somewhat different estimation of the rule of faith, however, can be found in the writings of the great Reformation scholar Heiko Oberman. He suggests, citing recent scholarship, that the regula fidei as employed by Irenaeus, Tertullian, and Clement of Alexandria is best understood not as a rule *for* faith but as the rule constituted *by* faith or truth, that is, as "the historical acts of God's action in creation and redemption."[14] This means, then, that the regula

8. Athanasius of Alexandria, *On the Councils of Ariminum and Seleucia* 5, NPNF[2] 4:453.

9. Eusebius of Caesarea, *The Church History of Eusebius* 3.39, in *Eusebius: Church History, Life of Constantine the Great, and Oration in Praise of Constantine*, trans. Arthur Cushman McGiffert, NPNF[2] 1:171.

10. Philip Schaff and David Schley Schaff, *History of the Christian Church* (New York: Scribner, 1910), 2:529.

11. Ibid.

12. Kelly, *Early Christian Doctrines*, 40.

13. Tertullian, *Prescription against Heretics* 19, in *Latin Christianity: Its Founder, Tertullian*, trans. Peter Holmes, ANF 3:251–52.

14. Heiko Oberman, *The Dawn of the Reformation* (Grand Rapids: Eerdmans, 1992), 273.

fidei is not simply the means or the mechanism to communicate revelation, but what is more important, it also constitutes revelation itself since it is made up of both faith and truth. "The rule of faith," Oberman observes, "is not to be regarded as authoritative interpretation of Holy Scripture. . . . [Rather] the rule of faith is revelation itself, the backbone and structure of Holy Scripture."[15] Here, then, is a clear indication that Protestants are fully aware of the value of oral tradition in the early church, specifically in the form of the rule of faith, whose harmony and essential unity with Scripture can be seen in terms of forming its very backbone and structure. Indeed, there is nothing in the proper understanding of sola Scriptura that prevents such recognition.

Beyond this, the early church in its struggle against heresy composed a number of creeds that not only can be distinguished in some sense from the regula fidei but also set the parameters within which the orthodox faith would thrive. Arising out of the kinds of questions, once again, that would be asked of baptismal candidates in the early church, the Old Roman Creed, for example, was apparently "the baptismal creed of the early Roman church,"[16] as well as a prototype of the later Apostles' Creed. The essence of this early creed can be discerned in the baptismal questions of Hippolytus at the beginning of the third century, though the Old Roman Creed (Romanum) may actually be earlier. Indeed, the dating of this particular creed is difficult, and though some scholars suggest an origin as early as the beginning of the second century,[17] others contend that since the baptismal questions that emerge in this creed are not well attested "before the end of the second century,"[18] this date must represent the terminus a quo, the earliest time of composition. A similar creedal development can be seen in the early third century in the work of the author just noted above, that is, *The Apostolic Tradition of Hippolytus*, which contains a prior form of the Apostles' Creed, and in the Caesarean Creed, composed around 250, which became the basis for the preeminent Nicene Creed.

Early Church Fathers

The history of the church can be read differently depending upon the location of one's theological tradition. This is not an invitation to relativism

15. Ibid.

16. Dietmar Wyrwa, "The Old Roman Creed," in *The Encyclopedia of Christianity*, 5 vols., ed. Erwin Fahlbusch and Geoffrey William Bromiley (Grand Rapids: Eerdmans; Leiden: Brill, 1999–2003), 3:828.

17. Susan Lynn Peterson, *Timeline Charts of the Western Church* (Grand Rapids: Zondervan, 1999), 19.

18. Wyrwa, "Old Roman Creed," 242.

but is the frank recognition that the body of Christ today exists in different communions of faith. One such way of reading the tradition of the church, taking its cues from the experience of the apostle Paul, is to recognize that each person or community of faith is equally distant from the reality of Jesus Christ, and the length of time from his ascension to the present (however defined) does not really make an existential or separating difference. Thus, this immediacy of Christ made present by the Holy Spirit within the fellowship of the saints suggests that the history of the church can be understood not simply in a linear chronological way, whereby current believers become farther and farther removed from Christ of the first century, but also as an arc along a circle. On this latter view, we can picture current believers as the segment of a circle along its circumference that, on the one hand, indicates the linear passage of time in its forward direction but that, on the other hand, suggests that each point along the circumference is immediately related to the center of the circle, which is none other than Jesus Christ, the One who proclaimed, "And surely I am with you always, to the very end of the age" (Matt. 28:20).

Such an approach, looking at familiar things in slightly different ways, a favorite of those Protestants who view the church as a living tradition, as "reformed and always reforming,"[19] underscores the reality that Jesus Christ is alive, not dead, and that his presence therefore cannot be exhausted by the reference to and remembrance of the historical figure of Jesus who lived, died, and rose from the dead in the first century. Clearly the apostle Paul is no less an apostle than Peter or John even though Paul did not know the historical Jesus. Such a vantage point, helpful in many ways, also highlights the basic equality, the essential fellowship, of all segments of the church throughout history under the lordship of Christ while ever yet being mindful of the considerable value of those who have gone on before, especially the apostles and disciples, who after all did know the historical Jesus.

When one reads the documents of the early church carefully, a basic linear conception of the life of the body of Christ does indeed emerge (indicated by the arc along the circle in our model), and such a conception gives evidence even of a "chain of command," if you will, in terms of the specific issue of authority, as is evident in figure 2.1.

The Apostolic Fathers,[20] branching out beyond the apostolic testimony, represent a body of literature composed by authors from both the East and the

19. For the careful development of such an approach, see Roger E. Olson, *Reformed and Always Reforming: The Postconservative Approach to Evangelical Theology* (Grand Rapids: Baker Academic, 2007).

20. We use the title "Father" as did the early church in order to communicate more effectively with a readership, both Roman Catholic and Protestant, that has grown accustomed to its usage

Figure 2.1

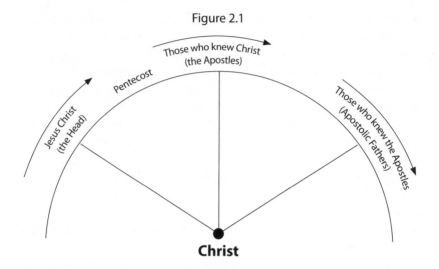

Those who knew Christ
(the Apostles)

Pentecost

Jesus Christ
(the Head)

Those who knew the Apostles
(Apostolic Fathers)

Christ

West, some of whom supposedly knew an apostle who in turn knew Christ. For example, it was believed that Polycarp, an early Eastern writer, was acquainted with the disciple John. However, the writing *Pseudo-Barnabas* is far more problematic in this area, simply because the lines to one who actually knew an apostle (in this case Paul) are not at all clear in this composition. Indeed, the author of this work was *not* thought to be the Barnabas of the NT. At any rate, these early writings of the church, ranging from the late first century to the mid-second century, included materials, counsels, and exhortations that were enormously helpful in terms of the thought and practice of the primitive church.

Moreover, the Apostolic Fathers were so treasured by the early church that some of these writings were actually thought to be on par, or nearly so, with the writings eventually recognized in the fourth century, through the power and illumination of the Holy Spirit, to be nothing less than the NT canon. Accordingly, though the *Shepherd of Hermas* was not a part of the Muratorian Canon, the "New Testament" used by the church in Rome in 200, it nevertheless was a document that was at least disputed in terms of its status during the time of Origen in 250. Again, by the fourth century, judging in light of the

---

through the centuries, though we also must recognize that the title does after all directly reject the counsel of Jesus (Matt. 23:9) and for that reason may issue in a different understanding of the church than Christ had in mind. We must at the very least be open to that possibility. We also want to be second to none in our appreciation of the church fathers, though their chief value must be seen insofar as they are faithful exegetes and communicators of both the early oral tradition and Scripture. Simply put, the authority of the "Fathers" is an achieved one and not ascribed, and even their constructive theology, the doctrine of the Trinity, e.g., must be viewed in this way as well—as a faithful reflection upon sacred Scripture.

"New Testament" employed by Eusebius, it was generally acknowledged by the church that the *Shepherd of Hermas*, *Pseudo-Barnabas*, and the *Didache* were not part of the "New Testament," even though the canon had not been more formally recognized by this point, for the *Thirty-Ninth Festal Letter* of Athanasius (367) was not yet written and the Council of Carthage (Synod of 397) had not yet met.

Early Ecumenical Councils

The church began the fourth century by suffering persecution under the rule of Diocletian, especially during 303 to 305, but in just a few short years, in 313 to be exact, the church's fortunes began to change considerably as Constantine and Licinius promulgated the Edict of Milan, which led to more favorable treatment. It was not, however, until much later, in the latter part of the fourth century and under the rule of Theodosius I, that Christianity was eventually preferred by the state and paganism was greatly weakened. The rise of Constantine, after his defeat of Licinius, had enormous impact upon the church, for this leader saw himself not simply as a temporal ruler but also as a spiritual one. Indeed it was Constantine, the successful military general and emperor, and not any bishop—certainly not Sylvester I, the bishop of Rome at the time—who called the First Ecumenical Council. Interestingly enough, this action by Constantine set a pattern of authority that would continue in the eastern part of the empire for centuries in which the emperor himself was considered to be a vital leader of the church.

The principal task of the First Ecumenical Council, at Nicaea in 325, was to turn back the low Christology of Arius, which had reduced Christ to a mere creature and thereby undermined the clear teaching of the Prologue to the Gospel of John. Constantine—this erstwhile pagan general who had worshiped the sun, Sol Invictus, even placing this image on his coins—did something perhaps even more monumental than calling this first council, because beyond this he sought to establish nothing less than the divine authority of *all* such councils that are rightly called by the emperor and are properly constituted of bishops. Such an approach to authority in the life of the early church was, in some sense, new. Constantine exclaimed: "Whatever is decided in the holy councils of the bishops must be attributed to the divine will."[21]

After the First Ecumenical Council had expressed its judgment on the Arian controversy as well as declared that the bishop of Jerusalem, not Rome, was

21. Leo Donald Davis, *The First Seven Ecumenical Councils (325–787): Their History and Theology* (Collegeville, MN: Liturgical Press, 1983), 57.

to have precedence, still reflecting the earlier Jewish origins of the church, a second council was likewise called by the emperor; this time, however, it was Theodosius I. Meeting in Constantinople in 381, the Second Ecumenical Council, like so many of the early ones, was dominated by Eastern bishops. Indeed, Bishop Damasus of Rome did not even send delegates![22] This second assembly reaffirmed the Nicene Creed and thereby gave the church the carefully crafted Niceno-Constantinopolitan Creed, which is still with us even today. By the fifth century a new emperor, Theodosius II, called the Third Ecumenical Council, which met at Ephesus in 431, and it condemned the teaching of Nestorius, who denied the suitability of referring to Mary as "*theotokos*," or "the bearer or mother of God." The successor of Theodosius II, the emperor Marcian, brought together the fourth general council, which met in Chalcedon in 451, and this body not only condemned the teaching of Eutyches—who had confused the natures of Christ in an overreaction to the earlier Nestorianism—but also affirmed, in canon 28, that "the bishop of New Rome [meaning Constantinople] shall enjoy the same honor as the bishop of Old Rome,"[23] demonstrating once again at this point the basic equality as well as the fellowship of grace and love that existed between Western and Eastern Christians.

The Recognition of the New Testament Canon

The emergence of the NT as canon, as the church's sacred Scripture, entailed a lengthy process that issued in a common recognition, by both Eastern and Western Christians, that our current twenty-seven books, and only these, were God-breathed and therefore made up, in part, the Christian Bible. In other words, the church as a community of saints was involved in a process of increasing awareness in terms of the very nature of this literature, but not in the way suggested by historical criticism, which maintains that the canon is "a fundamentally human construct that can be adequately accounted for in purely natural terms."[24] In such a view, "canon" is not "something that describes the quality of a book, but is something that is done to a book."[25]

22. Christopher M. Bellitto, *The General Councils: A History of the Twenty-One Church Councils from Nicaea to Vatican II* (Mahwah, NJ: Paulist Press, 2002), 22.
23. This quotation represents the summary of the canon by H. J. Schroeder. See his *Disciplinary Decrees of the General Councils: Text, Translation, and Commentary* (St. Louis: Herder, 1937), 125.
24. Michael J. Kruger, *Canon Revisited: Establishing the Origins and Authority of the New Testament Books* (Wheaton: Crossway Books, 2012), Kindle edition, locations 667–68.
25. Ibid., Kindle ed., locations 671–72.

With its naturalistic presuppositions, what the historical-critical approach leaves out, then, is the proper discernment of the Holy Spirit's role with respect to the inspiration of these writings. Accordingly, a more balanced view will be able to hold together the activity of the community in its gracious recognition of remarkably distinct writings, along with the generous role of the Holy Spirit in terms of the very inspiration of these same writings, that is, their God-breathed nature (2 Tim. 3:16). In his very helpful work *Canon Revisited*, Michael Kruger quotes J. I. Packer on this score: "The Church no more gave us the New Testament canon than Sir Isaac Newton gave us the force of gravity. God gave us gravity. . . . Newton did not create gravity but recognized it."[26] Historians usually point to the *Thirty-Ninth Festal Letter* of Athanasius as the time (367) when this process bore its considerable fruit. Later councils, such as the Synod Hippo Regius in North Africa (393) and the Council of Carthage (397), simply reaffirmed a reality that had already existed in the ancient church. The canon emerged independently about the same time in the East, the West, and northern Africa. Simply put, Rome did not give us the Bible.

The rise of the NT canon, as well as its broader significance in terms of both the question of authority and the value of the ongoing tradition of the church, is often conceived differently by Roman Catholics and Protestants. The larger issue here, once again, is clear: How does the church deliver without modification the substance of revelation that could be undermined by the transforming elements entailed in the passage of time itself? In this context, for the sake of clarity, a distinction must be made between the traditions that emerged before the recognition of the NT canon and those that followed it. Thus, in terms of this first sense of tradition, most Protestants wholeheartedly affirm the broad coinherence of "kerygma, Scripture and tradition."[27] Moreover, this first understanding of tradition, again embraced by both Protestants and Roman Catholics alike, is clearly dynamic; that is, the oral traditions will now, at least in some sense, be understood in terms of the canon, while at the same time the oral tradition, as in the rule of faith, will point to the proper interpretation of Scripture.

The second sense of tradition, however, that is, the traditions that grew up in the life of the church after the recognition of the NT canon, will also be understood somewhat differently by Roman Catholics and Protestants, in large part due to the different ways in which they recognize Scripture as a standard. In other words, the normative value of Scripture has to be

26. Ibid., Kindle ed., locations 881–82.
27. Oberman, *Dawn of the Reformation*, 270.

comprehended not simply in terms of the affirmation that the NT is nothing less than the Word of God, representing a distinct categorical difference
from all other writings, but also in the acknowledgment that the very form
of Scripture itself, as written language, represents a fixity and a stability that
subsequent oral traditions (esp. in terms of Mary, for example) as well as
emergent ecclesiastical practices simply cannot match. As Karl Barth observed
in the early twentieth century: "'Unwritten tradition' is an elusive thing,
which in practice coincides with the inner life of the church."[28] Scripture
then is a most suitable form that is especially poised to meet the challenges
of the traditioning process, to communicate the Word of God from age to
age, unfettered by the continual rise of all-too-human traditions or undermined by the vicissitudes of history. To be sure, for many Protestants the
recognition of the NT canon thus represents nothing less than a watershed
in the history of the church since at the point of textualization, and later of
canonization, the very notion of tradition is given new and lasting meaning. In short, a distinction can now be made with deep understanding and
justification, for example, between 1 Corinthians and 2 *Clement*, between
the apostolic testimony and an apostolic father.

The Unity of the Ancient Ecumenical Church

Though Ignatius of Antioch, as a representative of the Eastern tradition and
writing his letter to the Smyrnaeans in the early second century, was the first
to employ the phrase "the Catholic Church" to describe the body of Christ[29]
(Rome once again was a latecomer here), nevertheless, given the subsequent
history of the church, especially the schism that occurred between East and
West in 1054, no one theological tradition can now accurately maintain that
the "Catholic Church" subsists in its own particular communion of faith.[30]
Indeed, to continue such usage fails to reckon with the basic facts of church
history, troubling as they are at times, and it always results in the diminishment
of other theological traditions, especially, in this case, Eastern Orthodoxy.
Thus, in order to avoid this confusion, which entails considerable "wordplay"
in which the part is repeatedly offered as the whole, we shall employ the

28. As quoted in Avery Dulles, "Scripture: Recent Protestant and Catholic Views," *Theology Today* 37, no. 1 (1980): 7–26.
29. Ignatius of Antioch, *To the Smyrnaeans* 8, in *The Apostolic Fathers with Justin Martyr and Irenaeus*, ANF 1:90.
30. Rome does not deny that other theological traditions have emerged in the church, such as Eastern Orthodoxy, which is but one prominent example. It's just that Rome sees itself as the central tradition to which all others (including Protestant ones) must be properly related.

phrase "the ancient ecumenical church"[31] to refer to that early time up until the mid-fifth century, that is, the time of the Fourth Ecumenical Council at Chalcedon in 451, when the Christian faithful were marked by considerable and broad unity. We will therefore reserve the language of Roman Catholic to describe the discrete theological tradition that distinguished itself, especially from the East, and later emerged out of this prior unity,[32] such as during the Third Synod at Toledo in 589, by departing from the earlier consensus of the ancient ecumenical church (see below).

Ever mindful of the great tradition of the early church, in which both a proper Christology and the doctrine of the Trinity had been carefully articulated, Lancelot Andrewes, an Anglican theologian and bishop during the reigns of Elizabeth I and James I, reflected deeply upon the matter of how this early history of the church should be properly valued in both a foundational and a formative way. Indeed, Bishop Andrewes expressed the enduring significance of this common inheritance, shared by Roman Catholics, Eastern Orthodox, and Protestants alike, in the pithy statement: "One canon [the Bible] reduced to writing by God himself, two testaments, three creeds, four general councils, five centuries and the series of fathers in that period."[33] Indeed, Martin Luther, in the *Smalkald Articles*, essentially maintained, in the words of David Steinmetz, that "Protestants had no quarrel with Catholics over the doctrines of the Trinity and the two natures of Christ."[34] Moreover, the Reformed tradition in its *Westminster Catechism* vigorously embraced the theological substance of both the Nicene and the Apostles' Creeds, demonstrating in a very tangible way just how significant the great tradition was to Protestants as well.[35] Furthermore, in terms of the authority of the early councils of the church, Calvin pointed out, "We willingly embrace and reverence as holy the early councils, such as those of Nicaea, Constantinople, Ephesus I, Chalcedon,

31. We could not employ the language of "Old Catholic Church" to refer to this ancient period because the Roman Catholic tradition has repeatedly spawned other theological traditions throughout its long history, in this case, the "Old Catholic Church," a theological tradition that coalesced around 1870 and affirmed all the Christian doctrines accepted as essential before the East-West schism of 1054.

32. Some Roman Catholics will maintain that the term "Roman Catholic" itself comes out of the Anglican church to buttress the latter's claims to catholicity, yet the terminology is appropriate simply because the bishop of *Rome* has played and continues to play such an enormous role in defining this discrete theological tradition. See D. H. Williams, *Retrieving the Tradition and Renewing Evangelicalism* (Grand Rapids: Eerdmans, 1999), 222.

33. Stephen Sykes and John Booty, eds., *The Study of Anglicanism* (London: SPCK, 1988), 267.

34. David Steinmetz, "Unsettled Issues: The Protestant-Catholic Impasse," *Christian Century*, May 16, 2012, 33.

35. Philip Schaff, *The Creeds of Christendom*, vol. 3, *The Evangelical Protestant Creeds, with Translations* (Grand Rapids: Baker, 1983), 821.

... which were concerned with refuting errors."[36] And Luther, for his part, observed: "I hold, after the four principal councils, all the others to be of lesser value, even though I would regard several (understand me rightly), I say several, as equally good."[37]

Beyond this, for D. H. Williams, a contemporary Protestant scholar, the faith expressed in the first five centuries can be seen in the "two pillars of authority" on which Christians stand: "(1) an apostolic canon of Scripture (the Bible) and (2) a theological canon of apostolicity (cardinal doctrines and confessions of the Trinity, Christology, etc.)."[38] It is therefore simply mythic, in light of the preceding evidence, to contend that Protestants reject tradition in toto in the name of sola Scriptura. In fact, we will be so bold as to make the claim, speculative as it is, that if no significant theological changes had been made after the Council of Chalcedon in 451, some of which affected how the good news of the gospel was understood by both clergy and laity alike, then the Protestant theological traditions would have never likely emerged. The Reformation would not have happened, simply because there would have been little to reform. Indeed, the agreement of Protestantism with Roman Catholicism is considerable, though not exact, through the fifth century. We do share so much in common—enough for both to be considered part of the true Christian church.

The Roman Catholic Understanding of Tradition

A key difference, then, between Roman Catholics and Protestants is not only how they read the history of the church, as noted earlier, but also how they understand tradition and precisely what content deserves to be passed along to subsequent generations bearing the sacred title of "revelation." For Rome revelation is made up of both sacred Scripture and sacred tradition as articulated in the *Catechism of the Catholic Church*, which states: "Sacred Tradition and Sacred Scripture, then, are bound closely together and communicate one with the other. For both of them, *flowing out from the same divine well-spring*, come together in some fashion to form one thing and move towards the same goal."[39]

Even more emphatically, the *Catechism* maintains that Scripture and tradition are of equal value, as displayed in the following observation: "Both

36. As cited in James R. Payton Jr., *Getting the Reformation Wrong: Correcting Some Misunderstandings* (Downers Grove, IL: InterVarsity, 2010), 155.

37. Martin Luther, *Church and Ministry III*, LW 41:48.

38. Williams, *Evangelicals and Tradition*, 56.

39. *Catechism of the Catholic Church*, 2nd ed. (Mahwah, NJ: Paulist Press, 1994), par. 80 (emphasis added).

Scripture and Tradition must be accepted and honored with equal sentiments of devotion and reverence."[40] Remarkably enough, this last phrase, "accepted and honored with equal sentiments of devotion and reverence," was drawn—no doubt, in a slightly modified form—from the pages of the Council of Trent (1545–63) itself. Indeed, as the late Richard John Neuhaus and the late Charles Colson pointed out in their book, *Your Word Is Truth*, "Trent further asserted that both Scripture and Tradition were to be received and venerated 'with the same sense of loyalty and reverence.'"[41] Furthermore, although the late Avery Dulles (and contemporary Roman Catholic apologists) has tried to soften this observation, drawn from Trent, by claiming that "the 'two sources' theory of Counter Reformation Catholicism [is] . . . unsatisfactory,"[42] nevertheless this same language emerged yet again at the Second Vatican Council, which declared in its *Dogmatic Constitution on Divine Revelation*, "Thus it comes about that the Church does not draw her certainty about all revealed truths from the holy Scriptures alone. Hence, both Scripture and Tradition must be accepted and honored with equal feelings of devotion and reverence."[43] Again, this same document from Vatican II insists, "Sacred Tradition and Sacred Scripture make up a single sacred deposit of the Word of God, which is entrusted to the church."[44] However, what is needed in light of these judgments is a suitable typology that will not only offer a number of different senses of tradition but also see the canon of Scripture, the Word of God, at the very center of these different meanings.

Heiko Oberman's Typology of Tradition

Well aware of the early history of the church, in which Tertullian, for example, postulated a distinction between "the tradition of God, preserved in

40. Ibid., par. 82.

41. Colson and Neuhaus, eds., *Your Word Is Truth: A Project of Evangelicals and Catholics Together* (Grand Rapids: Eerdmans, 2002), 23.

42. Dulles, "Scripture," 25. See also Oberman (*Dawn of the Reformation*, 286), who contends that "while the Reformation understood the coinherence of Scripture and Church in terms of Tradition I, the Council of Trent in its fourth session gave its sanction to the coinherence of Scripture and Church in terms of Tradition II."

43. Pope Paul VI, *Dei Verbum: Dogmatic Constitution on Divine Revelation*, sec. 9, in *The Conciliar and Post Conciliar Documents*, vol. 1 of *Vatican Council II*, ed. Austin Flannery (Northport, NY: Costello, 1998), 755; see also the Holy See, http://www.vatican.va/archive/hist_councils/ii_vatican_council/documents/vat-ii_const_19651118_dei-verbum_en.html.

44. Pope Paul VI, *Dei Verbum*, sec. 10, in Flannery, *Conciliar and Post Conciliar Documents*, 755.

the canon, and the *traditions* of man (*consuetudines*),"[45] Heiko Oberman in his own age discerned several senses in which tradition must be rightly understood. Thus, for example, he affirmed: "For clarity's sake we call the single exegetical tradition of interpreted scripture 'Tradition I' and the two-sources theory which allows for an extra-biblical oral tradition 'Tradition II.'"[46] In this setting, then, Scripture as the Word of God is at the heart of this differentiation, and Oberman as a Protestant scholar clearly acknowledges the considerable value of tradition in the form of various interpretations of the Bible that will be transmitted from age to age such that the church, in a certain sense, becomes a hermeneutical community, distinguishing itself rightly over the course of time from Jews, Muslims, and heretics.

In addition, Oberman's typology of "Tradition I" and "Tradition II" allows for the frank recognition of the sense of tradition championed by Roman Catholics and developed early on by Basil the Great (330–70) in the East and by Augustine (354–430) in the West, in which the Christian "owes equal respect and obedience to the written *and* to the unwritten ecclesiastical traditions, whether they are contained in the canonical writings or in the secret oral tradition handed down by the Apostles through succession."[47] Much later, during the Middle Ages, the nominalist William of Ockham (1288–1347) began to invest "the unwritten traditions with the same apostolic authority as the Scriptures"[48] (Gabriel Biel, the last of the medieval scholastics, did this as well) and thereby prepared the way for the response of John Wycliffe (ca. 1330–84) in England, Jan Hus (1369–1415) in Prague, and Wessel Gansfort (1419–89) in the Netherlands, all of whom maintained the normative supremacy of what in effect was Tradition I over Tradition II. To be sure, only some of the Reformers who were a part of the Radical Reformation, not the magisterial Reformers, denied tradition altogether, even in the sense of an ongoing interpretive deposit that must be passed on from generation to generation. So then, the great debate between Protestants and Roman Catholics over the authority of Scripture and tradition is actually in the end a dispute, to use Oberman's own language, over "two concepts of tradition."[49] The typology employed here, as well as its broader significance for the discussion at hand, can now be outlined as follows:

45. Oberman, *Dawn of the Reformation*, 274 (emphasis added).
46. Ibid., 280.
47. Ibid., 277 (emphasis original).
48. Ibid., 281–82. Indeed, Oberman points out that "such nominalists as Occam, Gerson, d'Ailly and Biel had prepared the way for Trent's reception of Tradition II."
49. Ibid., 270.

Different senses of tradition	Judgment on and source of tradition	Different theological communions
Tradition 0	No place for tradition; sola Scriptura (the Bible is the *only* authority)	Radical Reformation
Tradition I	Single source of tradition (the Bible is the only unquestioned authority for faith and practice)	Protestant Reformers Luther and Calvin and precursors of the Reformation (Wycliffe, Hus, and Gansfort)
Tradition II	Dual source of tradition (Scripture and tradition are of equal value)	The Council of Trent, Vatican II, and *Catechism of the Catholic Church*

The preceding table, though it goes a long way in expressing our judgments, nevertheless does not encompass our entire view. The issue here is one of clarity, not contrast. We affirm the value of the oral traditions in the form of the words of Christ as well as the apostolic testimony that preceded the NT canon, testimony that eventually became a part of that canon. We also recognize, as a further example, the tradition of the rule of faith, which, though it can be distinguished from Scripture in some sense, nevertheless is consonant with it. We are arguing for the generous and "proleptic" use of Oberman's Tradition I so that it is readily able to affirm revelation in the form of oral tradition prior to the recognition of the canon of Scripture. With these caveats in mind, we acknowledge the suitability of Oberman's typology for distinguishing what is implied by revelation, and is in essential continuity with it, from what is not.

Traditions: Getting to the Heart of the Problem

One of the chief challenges that the church faces with regard to the deposit of faith is the very tension recognized by Plato as he thought through the perspective of Heraclitus (b. 535 BC) that all is change and of Parmenides (b. before 500 BC) that permanence is real and therefore change is an illusion. This broader philosophical problem, resolved in an adept way in Plato's philosophy, is a window on the predicament that historians know all too well: the question of permanence and change across the sands of time, mirrored also in the question of what is essential and what is unessential. Moreover, Vincent of Lérins (d. AD 445) is well remembered for his pithy phrase identifying "that faith which has been believed everywhere, always, by all,"[50] thus seeing nothing but permanence and unity; yet this phrase is perhaps far more

---

50. Vincent of Lérins, "The Commonitory of Vincent of Lérins" 2.6, in *Sulpitius Severus, Vincent of Lérins, John Cassian*, trans. C. A. Heurtley, NPNF[2] 11:132.

descriptive of the ancient ecumenical church before the year 451, before the Fourth Ecumenical Council, for instance, than it is of the church after that significant date.

To be sure, the Latin-speaking Roman tradition began to be more sharply distinguished from the tradition of its Greek-speaking Eastern brothers and sisters after Constantine moved the capital to Constantinople in 330 and when the Roman Empire was permanently divided into East and West in 395 after the death of Theodosius I. Differences in culture, language, and geography were augmented by variations in general theological perspective (more of style than of substance) in which the East was largely philosophical (and at times speculative) in its approach to theology, whereas the West was by and large far more pragmatic, focusing on issues of polity and ethics. Despite these disparities, both of these traditions shared early on in the broader unity of which Vincent of Lérins wrote, thereby valuing in unison the rule of faith, the church fathers, the ancient creeds and councils, and, of course, Scripture itself. This unbroken unity was to last until Rome finally expressed itself more fully on a fourth-century creed of the early ecumenical church.

Emerging as a distinct theological tradition in the sixth century, Rome added the *filioque* clause (that the Holy Spirit proceeds from the Father *and from the Son*) to the Niceno-Constantinopolitan Creed at the Third Synod at Toledo in 589. This theological interpolation in the creed was one of the factors that eventually led to schism much later, in 1054. However, while we affirm the importance of the early unity of the ancient ecumenical church, the universal faith that was in place before 500, broadly speaking (as Lancelot Andrewes had pointed out in his own age, noted earlier), we are not laying all the blame for this theological diversity on the back of Rome itself. In fact, by the sixth century the Eastern tradition was already distinguishing itself by basically misprizing the major theological contributions of one of the most important church fathers, Augustine (354–430), although this relative neglect was eventually reversed much later.[51]

Our point, then, is far subtler than what often arises in the usual Protestant apologetics and polemics. Indeed, we believe that given a significant length of time (centuries in this case), it was virtually inevitable that the West and the East would emerge as distinct theological traditions precisely because of the theological drift that had occurred in the sixth century. The key question then arises: Can Christian orthodoxy exist in theological traditions that interpolate the Nicene Creed or that essentially neglect an important church father, perhaps

51. See George E. Demacopoulos and Aristotle Papanikolaou, *Orthodox Readings of Augustine* (Yonkers, NY: St. Vladimir's Seminary Press, 2008).

the most important Latin father of all? We believe the answer to that question is, interestingly enough, "Yes." After all, such a response is theologically appropriate and can be substantiated with numerous arguments, especially by the claim, for example, that the faith of both Western and Eastern Christians, at least at this point in history, was yet in basic harmony with the Word of God, the apostolic testimony as well as the rule of faith. Simply put, orthodoxy can exist in distinct theological traditions (East and West) so long as the very substance of the faith (in terms of its core beliefs) is shared. The *filioque* addition to the Nicene Creed does not overthrow the gospel, the doctrine of the Trinity, or proper Christology, though it does indeed result in distinct theological traditions.

Once Rome started down this path of doctrinal innovation, making doctrinal declarations that disrupted a prior consensus (esp. in the eyes of the East), momentum carried it further, and it simply could not stop. Emboldened by an understanding of tradition that at times spawned theological novelties, some of which not even the East could accept (e.g., purgatory), Rome began to assume, especially during the Middle Ages, that whatever *is* (emerging from the ongoing tradition) is *right*. Indeed, Tradition II came into full swing once the medieval canon lawyers and theologians concluded that "all the truths actually held by the Church could not be found explicitly or implicitly in Holy Scripture."[52] Since an appeal to the canon of Scripture was not in the offing in this setting, the tradition itself necessarily became somewhat separate, isolated from the Bible, at times acquiring the second-source feel of Tradition II. Moreover, even Terrence Tilley, a Roman Catholic theologian, had to admit that some traditions could not even be sustained by an appeal to the earlier history of the church. "Certain beliefs and practices deemed 'traditional' by the church hierarchy,"[53] he wrote, "are not found in the previous ages of the church in their present form or have no precedent at all."[54] To rectify this considerable deficit in terms of both earlier church history and generous scriptural support, a deficit that was at times embarrassing, medieval theologians such as Rabanus Maurus (on the doctrine of purgatory) simply appealed to the tradition itself or, by implication, to the Holy Spirit as the guarantee of the tradition, thereby placing a sacred canopy—to borrow a phrase from Peter Berger[55]—over some of what, in effect, was simply all-too-human teaching. How do we know that such is merely human teaching? It is at variance with the clear teaching of sacred Scripture.

52. Oberman, *Dawn of the Reformation*, 294.
53. Williams, *Evangelicals and Tradition*, 21.
54. Ibid.
55. As drawn from the title of Berger's celebrated book *The Sacred Canopy: Elements of a Sociological Theory of Religion*, repr. ed. (New York: Anchor Books, 1990).

Part of the difficulty here, no doubt, is that Rome failed to recognize in a frank way that the term "tradition" as employed in the Bible is sophisticated, indicating several different meanings, not just one, and is at times actually negative. Thus, as John G. Stackhouse points out, Jesus Christ was "openly critical of certain *human traditions* within Judaism that [were] in conflict with the Word of God."[56] We encounter this negative sense of tradition in the pages of the NT as Jesus rebukes the Jewish religious leaders (who are at the helm of the tradition-making process): "You have let go of the commands of God and are holding on to *human traditions*" (Mark 7:8, emphasis added). This sense of tradition, however, was clearly comprehended by Protestants, as revealed in the following: "The Reformers almost always used the word *tradition* in the plural to refer to those 'human traditions (*Menschensatzungen*), instituted to placate God, to merit grace, and to make satisfaction for sins,' as the Augsburg Confession puts it."[57]

Below, then, are a few of the more important (and controversial) subsequent traditions of Roman Catholicism. Some of them are affirmed by Eastern Orthodoxy; others are not. Again, some of them are affirmed by Protestantism; others are not. More to the point, when the rejections of both Eastern Orthodoxy and Protestantism are added up, so to speak, it becomes remarkably clear that Roman Catholicism represents not the universal church, as is so often claimed, but instead a distinct theological tradition, one among *others*.

Roman Catholicism	Eastern Orthodoxy	Protestantism
High valuation of the theological emphases of Augustine	Augustine not affirmed early on (his theology is deemed "too philosophical and speculative")	Augustine affirmed
The *filioque* clause	Rejected	Affirmed
Priestly celibacy	Affirmed for higher orders, bishops; yet priests may marry	Rejected (as a requirement)
Veneration of the saints, icons, and relics	Affirmed	Rejected (with cautions)
The papacy	Rejected	Rejected
Purgatory	Rejected	Rejected
Transubstantiation	Specific language rejected as "Scholastic"; yet the reality of the real presence localized in the elements is affirmed as a "mystery"	Rejected, yet the reality of the real presence localized in the elements is affirmed by some Protestant traditions

56. Stackhouse, *Evangelical Futures: A Conversation on Theological Method* (Grand Rapids: Baker Books, 2000), 141 (emphasis added).
57. Colson and Neuhaus, *Your Word Is Truth*, 16.

Roman Catholicism	Eastern Orthodoxy	Protestantism
The immaculate conception	Rejected	Rejected
The assumption of Mary	Affirmed (Dormition)	Rejected
The treasury of merits	Rejected	Rejected

Though some of the traditions enumerated above were present in early forms before the middle of the fourth century, yet one of the basic errors that Rome has committed with respect to the proper estimation of Scripture and tradition, from the perspective of Protestants, is that it has failed to take into account what significance the recognition of the canon holds for the understanding of tradition itself. At the very least, the traditions that predate sacred Scripture and are now integral to it, such as the apostolic testimony, must be distinguished from those that follow it and are not integral to it. Put another way, it is important to rightly divide the Word of God from the words of human beings, and in many instances from the pronouncements simply of later clerics. Indeed, when the latter resource is unduly elevated to the status of revelation, this constitutes nothing less than a categorical error. We will therefore take up a biblical and theological estimation of these numerous all-too-human traditions in subsequent chapters.

3

Scripture

No Greater Authority?

Surprising as it may seem, the *New York Times Book Review* is often wrong when it lists the number one nonfiction book of the week. In terms of sheer numbers, it's not some political screed (whether from the right or the left) or a biography of the latest cultural icon (which after all will appear at the top of the list in a genuinely ersatz manner) that is *actually* number one in sales. Rather, it's a book that's been around for a very long time, was centuries in the making, has been translated into more languages than we have time to list here, and not surprisingly remains a smashing best seller. What book is that? It's the Bible in one of its more popular versions (e.g., the NIV or the NAB), though this fact will hardly grace the pages of this weekly cultural barometer. Indeed, according to Guinness World Records, the Bible is clearly the champion here: "There is little doubt that the Bible is the world's best-selling and most widely distributed book."[1] In fact, it weighs in at over five billion copies! Indeed, the Bible today is read all around the world by clergy and laity, men and women, young and old, white and black, rich and poor, conservatives and liberals. It appears on apps, iPads, and Kindles; it is listened to on the train, memorized in the classroom; studied in both the church and the academy; it is the center of attention globally in numerous Bible studies, north and south, east and west. Moreover, in the wake of Vatican II, its pages

1. "Best-Selling Book of Non-fiction," Guinness World Records, accessed December 1, 2016, http://www.guinnessworldrecords.com/world-records/best-selling-book-of-non-fiction.

are marked up, tabs and bookmarks are inserted, by those layfolk, both Roman Catholic and Protestant, who have learned to estimate Scripture properly by cherishing its very words. But it was not always so.

Earlier Attitudes toward Bible Reading

During the time of the Reformation and the Council of Trent, the Vatican feared that Roman Catholics would not be able to read the Bible with proper understanding, in line with the magisterium,[2] so it generally discouraged the practice of Scripture reading among the laity, often viewing it as the seedbed for many forms of individualism and error. That is, wary of the variety of interpretations of Scripture that could emerge beyond the public teaching of the church, the council in its fourth session declared in the *Decree concerning the Canonical Scriptures* as follows: "Furthermore, in order to restrain petulant spirits, it [the council] decrees, that no one, relying on his own skill, shall,—in matters of faith, and of morals pertaining to the edification of Christian doctrine,—wresting the sacred Scripture to his own senses, presume to interpret the said sacred Scripture contrary to that sense which holy mother Church,—whose it is to judge of the true sense and interpretation of the holy Scriptures, . . . hath held and doth hold."[3]

This same fear was directed toward not only the laity in general but also scholars in particular, who were not permitted to "publish any work relating to the interpretation of Scripture, unless it had first been vetted by [their] superiors and declared that publication had been approved."[4] Due to these restrictions, which were not suffered by Protestants, "it would be centuries," Alister McGrath reports, "before Roman Catholic scholarship recovered from this setback."[5] In fact, later Pope Leo XIII (r. 1878–1903) essentially condemned the scholarly, higher-critical approach to the Bible in his encyclical *Providentissimus Deus*, propounded in 1893. A cloud therefore hung over serious critical biblical scholarship in the Roman church until around 1943, when Pope Pius XII, in his encyclical *Divino Afflante Spiritu*, recognized the

2. Readers will see a difference in capitalization with respect to the word "magisterium" throughout this book. Since the Roman Catholic Church understands the word "magisterium" as a reference to its own teaching authority for the universal church, the word is often, though not always, capitalized in Roman Catholic materials. But since Protestants (and the Eastern Orthodox) deny that the Roman magisterium speaks for the universal church, we lowercase the term outside of quotations.

3. Philip Schaff, *The Creeds of Christendom*, vol. 2, *The Greek and Latin Creeds, with Translations* (Grand Rapids: Baker, 1983), 83.

4. McGrath, *Reformation Thought: An Introduction*, 2nd ed. (Oxford: Blackwell, 1993), 156.

5. Ibid.

helpful fruit that could indeed emerge even from a rigorously academic approach to the Bible (what Pope Leo before had considered to be "secular"); thus Pope Pius offered far more encouragement to Roman Catholic scholars than had his predecessor. What Rome had learned in the interim, well before the pronouncements of Vatican II (which took a more generous view of the use of Scripture), was that scholars and laity alike, though of course in different ways and in different degrees, invariably brought the major teachings of the hierarchy to the text as a basic orientation or presupposition. Roman Catholics, regardless of translation, in the end read Roman Catholic Bibles. They too, like everyone else in the broader ecumenical church, are a part of an interpretive tradition. Earlier fears now proved to have been groundless.

In light of this history, it therefore is not difficult to appreciate that in some sense Roman Catholics and Protestants embrace different Bibles due to the significant import of the distinct interpretive communities in which they participate. In other words, differing theological traditions naturally lead to dissimilar interpretations of the very same passages of the Bible. For example, when many Roman Catholics read Matthew 16:18, they may discern the wherewithal to make a claim for the papacy; for Protestants, however, this passage suggests nothing of the sort. Such salient interpretive differences that make up the respective traditions, at least in part, could be cited again and again. Yet there is another significant sense in which Roman Catholics and Protestants do, after all, read different Bibles: they *literally* read different Bibles, not only in terms of the various translations that correspond to each tradition (The Jerusalem Bible versus the New International Version, for instance), but also and more significantly in terms of the dissimilar content of the Scriptures read, specifically in terms of the composition of the OT canon itself.

The Old Testament Canon

The terminology of "Old" and "New" Testaments did not arise in the early church until the latter part of the second century in the writings of Justin Martyr, Irenaeus, and Clement of Alexandria.[6] Moreover, that class of writings known as the OT Apocrypha, which marks the difference between the Roman Catholic and the Protestant OT canons, was made up of Jewish religious literature whose dates range from 300 BC to AD 70.[7] All these apocryphal

---

6. Walter A. Elwell and Barry J. Beitzel, *Baker Encyclopedia of the Bible* (Grand Rapids: Baker, 1988), 300–301.

7. James H. Charlesworth, "Apocrypha: Old Testament Apocrypha," in *The Anchor Yale Bible Dictionary*, ed. David Noel Freedman (New York: Doubleday, 1992), 292.

writings were composed in a Semitic tongue with the notable exceptions of the Wisdom of Solomon and 2 Maccabees, which were written in Greek, most likely in Alexandria, Egypt.[8] Though these writings were included in the Septuagint, a third- to second-century-BC Greek translation of the OT that was produced in Egypt for Jews who no longer knew Hebrew, a canonical status for the Apocrypha was ultimately rejected by the Jews (by Philo and Josephus, for instance) in a complicated process that some historians unduly simplify by pointing to the judgments of the Council of Jamnia in AD 90.[9] Indeed, scholars have begun to cast doubt upon the historicity of this council.[10] Of the larger issue of the competence of the Jews to recognize their canon, their own Bible, one Roman Catholic apologist writes as follows: "The Jews at Jamnia had rejected Christ as God, let us not forget. Those who had accepted Christ had already become Christians. The remainder certainly had no rightful authority to decide anything about divine truth."[11] This statement suggests that not only is Christian revelation essential to understanding the OT aright, but also the Jews themselves, oddly enough, are not even fit to recognize their own canon. Such a Roman Catholic apologetic foray is hardly required or even implied by affirming the authority of the NT revelation.

At any rate, many of the apocryphal writings, though not all,[12] were taken up into the Roman Catholic OT canon most likely because of their appearance in the Septuagint (of which many first-century Christians were well aware) and because Jerome included them in the Latin Vulgate edition of the Bible, whose OT section was completed in 405. Though Jerome had incorporated the Apocrypha into his translation, nevertheless he specifically cautioned against receiving this literature as sacred Scripture. To illustrate, in his preface to the Vulgate, Jerome wrote as follows: "As, then, the Church reads Judith, Tobit, and the books of Maccabees, but does not admit them among the canonical Scriptures, so let it read these two volumes for the edification of the people, not to give authority to doctrines of the Church."[13] For one thing, Jerome was

8. Ibid.

9. Jack P. Lewis, "Jamnia, Council of," in *Anchor Yale Bible Dictionary*, 634.

10. E.g., Michael W. Holmes argues that "the consensus supporting this view (still defended in various forms) has largely collapsed, undermined primarily by (a) the recognition that the idea of an authoritative 'council' dealing with matters of canon at Jamnia is largely a myth." Holmes, "The Biblical Canon," in *The Oxford Handbook of Early Christian Studies*, ed. Susan Ashbrook Harvey and David Hunter (Oxford: Oxford University Press, 2010), 409.

11. Devin Rose, *If Protestantism Is True* (n.p.: Unitatis Books, 2011), 72.

12. Though 13 writings make up the *Apocrypha* found in the Septuagint, *The Catechism of the Catholic Church* (as well as *The Catholic Study Bible*) embraces only a part of this collection. See *Catechism of the Catholic Church*, 2nd ed. (Mahwah, NJ: Paulist Press, 1994), par. 120.

13. Jerome, "Prefaces to the Books of the Vulgate Version of the Old Testament," in *St. Jerome: Letters and Select Works*, trans. W. H. Fremantle, G. Lewis, and W. G. Martley, NPNF[2] 6:492.

likely well aware of some of the theological oddities of this literature. Take the book of Tobit, for example. Its observation found in 12:9, "For almsgiving saves from death, and purges all sin,"[14] is no doubt theologically confused, for it not only contradicts the clear teaching of the apostolic testimony of Paul found in Romans 4–5, for example, but also detracts from the unique and glorious atoning work of the Son of God incarnate, Jesus Christ.

Not surprisingly, Jerome's judgment regarding the Apocrypha was shared by a veritable litany of church fathers, by those before him such as Melito of Sardis (d. 180), Origen (182–254), Eusebius of Caesarea (263–339), Athanasius (296–373), Hilary of Poitiers (300–368); Hilary's contemporaries such as Epiphanius (310–403) and Rufinus (340–410); and those after him such as the venerable Cyril of Alexandria (378–444). Furthermore, as late as the eighth century, John Damascene embraced the Hebrew canon and thereby excluded such apocryphal books as Wisdom and Ecclesiasticus (Sirach) from the Bible.[15] For their part, the Protestant Reformers of the sixteenth century were well aware of the fruits of the groundbreaking scholarship of the Northern Renaissance, especially in terms of biblical studies and humane letters, and they therefore readily affirmed the appropriateness of the conclusion of Jerome. The Reformation motto *Ad fontes* (back to the sources), in terms of the OT, must surely mean going back to the Hebrew, not to the Greek.

Perhaps, then, one of the keys to Rome's decision about the constitution of the OT canon can be found in the observation that "Augustine, . . . whose influence in the West was decisive, made no distinction between them [apocryphal books] and the rest of the Old Testament."[16] However, since we judge ongoing dialogue about the OT among Roman Catholics, Protestants, and even Jews to be a valuable project, it is best perhaps to begin the conversation in terms of what is common rather than what is different, working with the specific content of the Hebrew Bible, which after all is affirmed by Roman Catholics, Protestants, and Jews. For that reason, this content, and not any other, should be the focus of ongoing attention and conversation.

Inspiration and Authority

The Roman Catholic *Catechism* clearly affirms the Bible to be nothing less than the Word of God in the following observation: "In Sacred Scripture, the

14. Donald Senior, John J. Collins, and Mary Ann Getty, eds., *The Catholic Study Bible: The New American Bible*, rev. ed. (New York: Oxford University Press, 1990), 592.

15. J. N. D. Kelly, *Early Christian Doctrines* (San Francisco: Harper & Row, 1960), 55.

16. Ibid., 55–56.

Church constantly finds her nourishment and her strength, for she welcomes it not as a human word, 'but as what it really is, the word of God' [1 Thess. 2:13]."[17] Recognizing that the Scriptures came into being under the inspiration of the Holy Spirit, the *Catechism* carefully observes that "Sacred Scripture must be read and interpreted in the light of the same Spirit by whom it was written."[18] However, in underscoring the preeminent role of the Holy Spirit in the generation of and reflection upon the Bible, Rome goes on to declare that the Word of God is "not a written and mute word, but the Word which is incarnate and living," and that the Christian faith, then, "is not a 'religion of the book,'"[19] a formulation that may give at least some pause to Protestants.

The deeper sense of this last observation is revealed by Charles Colson and Richard John Neuhaus in their writings: they point out that "because the Catholic reading of Scripture is founded on event, it is close to Liturgy and is also, instinctively, a development of the understanding of the *res* [thing] and not merely the *verba* [word]."[20] Sensitive to other views on this matter, these authors quickly added: "Admittedly this is disconcerting to Protestants."[21] Since "the Eucharist sacrifice," in the words of Pope Paul VI in his *Lumen Gentium*, promulgated in 1964, "is the fount and apex of the whole Christian life,"[22] it is therefore at the heart of the interpretive context in which Scripture is properly read and understood. This liturgical orientation to the Word of God, in which the *res* of the sacrament is ever foremost, may in turn bring to the interpretive process of Scripture certain sacramental accretions that have emerged in the liturgy of the Mass over time, especially during the Middle Ages (more on this in chap. 9), and as a whole have issued in a sacerdotal understanding (highlighting the distinct role and authority of priests) of both the Eucharist and in turn, interestingly enough, now the Word of God itself. This is yet another way in which Roman Catholics and Protestants read different Bibles.

It may surprise some Protestants, especially evangelicals, that on the topic of the authority of Scripture Rome employs a vocabulary that is remarkably familiar, though in the end it remains distinct.[23] Thus the *Catechism* declares,

17. *Catechism*, par. 104.
18. Ibid., par. 111.
19. Ibid., par. 108.
20. Colson and Neuhaus, eds., *Your Word Is Truth: A Project of Evangelicals and Catholics Together* (Grand Rapids: Eerdmans, 2002), 167.
21. Ibid.
22. Pope Paul VI, *Lumen Gentium: Dogmatic Constitution on the Church*, sec. 11, the Holy See, 1964, http://www.vatican.va/archive/hist_councils/ii_vatican_council/documents/vat-ii_const_19641121_lumen-gentium_en.html.
23. Indeed, David F. Wells has pointed out instances of ambiguity on the topic of inerrancy as found in Vatican II documents. He wrote: "The frustrating element for the interpreter of the

"We must acknowledge that the books of Scripture firmly, faithfully, and without error teach that truth which God, for the sake of our salvation, wished to see confided to the Sacred Scriptures."[24] Earlier, in his encyclical *Divino Afflante Spiritu*, Pope Pius XII affirmed: "For as the substantial Word of God became like to men in all things, 'except sin' [Heb. 4:15], so the words of God, expressed in human language, are made like to human speech in every respect, except error."[25] Moreover, some of the language of this encyclical was employed later at Vatican II, but this council focused the issue on redemption itself: "It follows that the books of Scripture must be acknowledged as teaching solidly, faithfully and without error that truth which God wanted put into sacred writings for the sake of salvation."[26] Though some Protestants, especially Reformed evangelicals, may discern in these words the substance of their own understanding of the authority of Scripture, nevertheless the late Avery Dulles offered a word of caution: "In Roman Catholicism, many prominent theologians still assert inerrancy, but only in a very qualified manner."[27] In fact, as the late cardinal also pointed out, "The term 'inerrancy,' though present in the original 1962 schema [of Vatican II], was dropped in the final text of *Dei Verbum*."[28]

In light of these observations of Dulles, it may be helpful for Rome to be more clear in its employment of the language of "without error" and "except error" in its documents by understanding the referent here specifically in terms of faith and practice. That is, henceforth it should prefer the language of Vatican II to that of the earlier pronouncements of Pius XII. In a more ecumenical vein Rome could even make common cause with the careful articulation of the Lausanne Movement on this very issue. In fact, Neuhaus and Colson cited this organization quite favorably in their own efforts to support the broader project of Evangelicals and Catholics Together: "In the words of the Lausanne Covenant (1974), . . . the Scriptures are 'the only written word of God . . . and the only infallible rule of faith and practice.'"[29]

Vatican II documents is that the new approach to inerrancy can apparently be *justified* or *denied* from the same statement." *Revolution in Rome* (Downers Grove, IL: InterVarsity, 1972), 33.

24. *Catechism*, par. 107.

25. Pope Pius XII, *Divino Afflante Spiritu*, par. 37, the Holy See, 1943, http://www.vatican .va/holy_father/pius_xii/encyclicals/documents/hf_p-xii_enc_30091943_divino-afflante -spiritu_en.html.

26. Pope Paul VI, *Dei Verbum: Dogmatic Constitution on Divine Revelation*, sec. 11, in *The Conciliar and Post Conciliar Documents*, vol. 1 of *Vatican II*, ed. Austin Flannery (Vatican City: Libreria Editrice Vaticana, 2011), 757; see also the Holy See, http://www.vatican.va/archive/hist _councils/ii_vatican_council/documents/vat-ii_const_19651118_dei-verbum_en.html.

27. Dulles, "Scripture: Recent Protestant and Catholic Views," *Theology Today* 37, no. 1 (1980): 20.

28. Ibid., 13.

29. Colson and Neuhaus, *Your Word Is Truth*, 11.

The Problem of Interpretation

The larger problem of interpretation of sacred Scripture can be focused in two major questions: First, what does the Bible actually mean to current readers? Second, who or what authority determines and declares this meaning? These two questions, essential to the ongoing life of the church, are remarkably illuminated by what the Protestant Reformers meant by the language of sola Scriptura. Though this Protestant affirmation has often been misprized as celebrating a wanton individualism,[30] it actually does nothing of the sort when it is carefully assessed. In essence the doctrine of sola Scriptura is made up of three subsidiary claims that get at the heart of our two principal interpretive questions: (1) the clarity of Scripture (in its basic affirmations), (2) the sufficiency of Scripture (doctrines not found or implied in its pages cannot be required for salvation), and (3) the normative power of Scripture as canon (it is the only unquestioned standard of faith and practice).[31]

In terms of the first claim of the clarity of Scripture, whose more technical name is the perspicuity of the Bible, Luther acknowledged that the Scriptures could be understood unto salvation by all, from common folk to scholars. In his treatise *The Bondage of the Will*, for example, he observed: "The notion that in Scripture some things are recondite and all is not plain was spread by the godless Sophists."[32] In fact, when the Reformer was translating the Greek text of the NT into German, he would sometimes go among the common folk to determine how a word should be rightly translated into the German of the day for broad understanding. However, the perspicuity of Scripture in this setting does not mean that the average person will not encounter difficult or perplexing passages. It's simply an affirmation that the basic story of redemption, the good news of the gospel, can be comprehended by all in light of two basic conditions: first, that the meaning of passages must be assessed in the context of community, and in this case it's the Lutheran interpretive tradition that will be attentive not only to the current setting (synchronic) but also to the flow of the history of the church that has preceded it (diachronic);[33] second, that difficult passages are to be

30. Christian Smith, *How to Go from Being a Good Evangelical to a Committed Catholic in Ninety-Five Difficult Steps* (Eugene, OR: Cascade, 2011), Kindle edition, location 517.

31. We have added to McGrath's two points and have reversed his order for the sake of the flow of the argument. See Alister McGrath, *Christianity's Dangerous Idea: The Protestant Revolution—a History from the Sixteenth Century to the Twenty-First* (New York: HarperOne, 2007), 203.

32. John Dillenberger, ed., *Martin Luther: Selections from His Writings* (New York: Knopf Doubleday, 1958), 172.

33. McGrath, *Christianity's Dangerous Idea*, 210.

seen against the backdrop of clearer ones: "Scripture is the interpreter of Scripture (*Scriptura Scripturae interpres*)."[34]

The second subsidiary claim of sola Scriptura affirms the sufficiency of Scripture in the sense that only teachings found among its pages or grounded therein (such that they make explicit what is implicit in the Bible, the doctrine of the Trinity, for example) can be required of the faithful. Here, then, is not only a clear expression of Oberman's Tradition I but also a reasonable critique of these various traditions, spawned throughout history, that in essence constitute not the Word of God or revelation, as is mistakenly supposed, but merely human teachings and contrivances. The historic *Thirty-Nine Articles* of the Anglican communion expresses this concern succinctly. To illustrate, article 6, "Of the Sufficiency of the Holy Scriptures for Salvation," reads as follows: "Holy Scripture containeth all things necessary to salvation: so that whatsoever is not read therein, nor may be proved thereby, is not to be required of any man, that it should be believed as an article of the Faith, or be thought requisite *or* necessary to salvation."[35]

The last subsidiary claim fully acknowledges the normative power of Scripture in that the Bible constitutes nothing less than a canon, a rule or standard, as recognized in the ancient ecumenical church in the fourth century, by which the faithful community throughout history can rightly order its life, under the power and authority of the Holy Spirit. In this context, then, *sola Scriptura* does not mean *nuda Scriptura*;[36] instead, this key phrase, championed during the Reformation and its aftermath, underscores that in its unquestioned normative role the Bible will rightly order, and thereby render capable of proper assessment, those elements such as church tradition, reason, and human experience that are also a part of any viable interpretive context.

Sola Scriptura then, properly understood, fully recognizes the watershed event in the history of the church, a genuine before and after, when the Holy Spirit, in the larger providence of God, helped the ancient ecumenical church to recognize a canon that was fixed in specific texts, so that the church would be equipped to go through time, facing its ongoing vicissitudes, while preserving the precious deposit of the faith. Observe, however, that we are not making some form of the "primitivism argument" here in our historiographical judgments. That is, we fully acknowledge the ongoing role of the Holy Spirit in the life of the church, especially in terms of guiding theological traditions (East and West) as well as interpretive communities. However, with the canon

---

34. Robert Newton Flew, *The Catholicity of Protestantism* (Cambridge: Lutterworth, 1950), 120.

35. Schaff, *Creeds of Christendom*, 3:489 (emphasis original).

36. Colson and Neuhaus, *Your Word Is Truth*, 4.

now in place, those subsequent traditions must not only be in harmony with sacred Scripture but also have clear biblical grounding.

The Roman Catholic Interpretive Difference

In terms of Protestantism, as we have just seen, the important work of understanding the Bible is a function of the entire community of the respective tradition, not merely of a single individual. To argue otherwise is the stuff of which caricatures are made. Consequently, if one offered an idiosyncratic reading of Scripture that contradicted the published doctrinal materials of the respective tradition (let's say the *Book of Concord* for Lutherans, or the *Book of Discipline* for United Methodists), then that view would not likely become a part of that tradition. There are, after all, checks in this process, to be sure. More important for the task at hand, we must make comparisons appropriately and compare apples with apples and oranges with oranges, so to speak. Accordingly, the official teachings of the Roman Catholic Church as propounded by the hierarchy should be seen in relation to the official, public doctrinal teachings of Protestants. Given such a judgment and for the sake of fairness, two situations should readily be avoided: first, comparing the official teachings of Roman Catholicism with the quotidian pronouncements of Protestants, both laity and scholars alike, some of which may not represent the official teaching of the Protestant church; second, comparing the official teachings of Protestantism with the quotidian pronouncements of flesh-and-blood Roman Catholics, both laity and scholars alike, some of which, again, may not represent the official teaching of the Roman Catholic Church.

Clearly, Rome offers a number of official resources (*Catechism*, Vatican II documents, papal encyclicals, etc.) that help to address the two major interpretive questions before us: What does the Bible mean? And, who or what is the competent authority to declare such meaning? With respect to this second question, the *Catechism*, for example, declares: "The task of giving an authentic interpretation of the Word of God, whether in its written form or in the form of Tradition, has been entrusted to the living, teaching office of the Church alone."[37] The *Catechism* then goes on to explain that this office actually is "the Magisterium of the Church,"[38] and more specifically that such teaching authority has been entrusted "to the bishops in communion with the successor of Peter, the Bishop of Rome."[39]

37. *Catechism*, par. 85.
38. Ibid., par. 100.
39. Ibid., par. 85.

Though the proper interpretation of the Scriptures according to the *Cate-chism* has been limited to the Roman Catholic tradition *apart from* Eastern Orthodoxy and Protestantism[40]—another example of Rome alone as an unmatched authority—it nevertheless makes provision at least for Roman Catholics beyond the magisterium, even for laypeople, to be involved in this process. Thus Peter Williamson, in his *Catholic Principles for Interpreting Scripture*, affirms that "various special roles in interpretation belong to clergy, catechists, exegetes and others, . . . [though] the Magisterium exercises a role of final authority if occasion requires it."[41] In fact, according to Rome, the authority of the magisterium is so great, a truly awe-inspiring power, that not even Scripture can stand on its own two feet, so to speak, but it ever needs the support of this particular Roman authority. The *Catechism* elaborates: "It is clear therefore that, in the supremely wise arrangement of God, sacred Tradition, Sacred Scripture, and the Magisterium of the Church are so connected and associated that one of them cannot stand without the others."[42]

Though we do not for a moment make light of the interpretive community that constitutes the magisterium, the teaching authority of the church, that worldwide fellowship of bishops in communion with the bishop of Rome, nevertheless we must also recognize the structure of the Roman Catholic hierarchy in general and more specifically the declaration of papal infallibility propounded at the First Vatican Council by Pope Pius IX in 1870. As Christopher M. Bellitto, a Roman Catholic scholar, puts it, "The pope could make infallible statements [when he speaks ex cathedra] on faith and morals on his own authority."[43] Again, Bellitto writes: "The pope had the final say, he could judge all things and all persons, but he himself could be judged by no one."[44] Thus if the pope, for whatever reason, corrects, adds to, or even dismisses the judgment of the magisterium, his voice and his alone in the end is decisive as to what Scripture actually means. The irony here is noteworthy:

40. One author offers a critique of this Roman Catholic practice in light of the perspective of the Old Catholic Church. See Petrus Johannes Maan, "The Meaning and Significance of Tradition: According to the Old Catholic Conception," *Ecumenical Review* 1, no. 4 (Summer 1949): 393–98. Maan writes: "The reason for the disavowal of tradition by reforming groups was the development which the Roman conception of tradition had brought about. Tradition, that is to say, which should have been linked beyond question to the *Church*, was linked to one branch of the church" (394).

41. Williamson, *Catholic Principles for Interpreting Scripture: A Study of the Pontifical Biblical Commission's "The Interpretation of the Bible in the Church,"* Subsidia Biblica 22 (Roma: Pontificio Istituto Biblico, 2001), 109.

42. *Catechism*, par. 95.

43. Bellitto, *The General Councils: A History of the Twenty-One Church Councils from Nicaea to Vatican II* (Mahwah, NJ: Paulist Press, 2002), 119.

44. Ibid.

having started out with the claim that Protestants are roundly "individualistic" in their reading of the Bible, Roman Catholic apologists now must confront, in an evenhanded way, the embedded individualism that is part and parcel of the ascending powers of the hierarchy itself. In fact, the divisions of competing interests at Vatican I were so great that when the bishops proposed that it was "the papal magisterium, not the person of the pope, that was infallible,"[45] Pius IX angrily shot back: "I am the church! I am the tradition."[46] It's hard to get more individualistic (or self-centered) than that.[47] In fact, this dogma was so disruptive to the peace and good order of the church (especially in the eyes of Eastern Orthodoxy) that Rome, once again, spawned yet another new theological tradition at the time, a new schism, known simply as the Old Catholic Church.

The Rise of Tradition III

Oberman noticed the rise of so many new doctrines in the Roman Catholic Church that are not grounded in Scripture, especially during the nineteenth and twentieth centuries (the immaculate conception and papal infallibility among them), as pointed out in chapter 3; he reasoned that with respect to the sources of revelation the magisterium must now be viewed as an "active tradition."[48] "The weakness of proofs from Scripture and tradition," he wrote, "gave the teaching office of the Church as the *regula proxima fidei*, a primary position which had of course its repercussion on the concept of dogma as such."[49] In other words, the doctrinal germinating power of Tradition II over the course of the centuries eventually enabled the Roman hierarchy to view itself as a living tradition (now in the sense of Tradition III): its authority extended not only to the interpretation of Scripture but also to all prior tradition, especially when that tradition (such as the Council of Trent) proved to be problematic in a contemporary setting. Oberman explains: "Nevertheless, so long as the Roman Catholic Church was committed to Tradition II, it stood under the authority of its past decisions among which the Council of Trent formed a major barrier in the ecumenical dialogue. The Tradition III concept gives the

---

45. John W. O'Malley, "The Beatification of Pope Pius IX," *America: The National Catholic Review*, August 26, 2000, http://americamagazine.org/issue/378/article/beatification-pope-pius-ix.
46. Ibid.
47. For a work that suggests a larger role for bishops in relation to the pope in the outworking of the magisterium, see Michael J. Buckley, *Papal Primacy and the Episcopate* (New York: Crossroad, 1998).
48. Heiko A. Oberman, *The Dawn of the Reformation* (Grand Rapids: Eerdmans, 1992), 290.
49. Ibid., 292.

Church a new and a large measure of freedom, not only over against Holy
Scripture but also over against its own doctrinal past."[50]

This line of reasoning, no doubt, informed the observation of Michael
Horton, a leading Reformed theologian, who argued to the effect that at the
end of the day, given the considerable power of the hierarchy, what is evident in
the Roman Catholic Church is not the primacy of Scripture or even tradition
for that matter, but the primacy of the magisterium itself, of which the pope
is ever the head, a veritable *solum magisterium*.[51] Eduardo J. Echeverria, a
Roman Catholic apologist, tried to counter this argument and brought forth
some of those same thoughtless stereotypes of the past by claiming that contemporary Protestant theology, lacking magisterial authority,[52] is "tossed to and
fro and carried about with every wind of doctrine" (Eph. 4:14),[53] separating
Protestants once again not only from their historic documents and creeds but
also from their interpretive communities.

The more positive and substantive side of Echeverria's argument consisted
in maintaining that Horton had failed to distinguish "the magisterial authority
of the Word of God from the ministerial authority of the Church's teaching
office,"[54] the ground of faith from "the means through which [one assents] to
divine truth."[55] Apparently Echeverria thought that the mere mention of this
distinction would carry the day; unfortunately for his sake it did not. Indeed,
what this Roman apologist had failed to take into account in a straightforward
way is precisely what Horton, as a gifted Reformed theologian, was already well
aware of: the context in which such a distinction must be properly understood.
Though the Roman hierarchy *should* simply play a ministerial rather than a
magisterial role in terms of the Word of God, for example, the magisterium
with a *pontifex maximus* as its head has been invested with such considerable
power that it is a virtual leviathan in the eyes of the laity. Even Peter Kreeft,
a Roman Catholic apologist, took note of these issues of power early in his
career and thereby raised the matter of *sola Roma* once again in the form of
authority: "Most Catholics believe such things as purgatory, the immaculate
conception, and the seven sacraments not because they have thought through
each issue separately and have come to the Catholic position by theological

---

50. Ibid., 295.

51. Michael Horton, *Christian Faith: A Systematic Theology for Pilgrims on the Way* (Grand
Rapids: Zondervan, 2011), 189, cited in Eduardo J. Echeverria, "Revelation, Faith and Tradition: Catholic Ecumenical Dialogue," *Calvin Theological Journal* 49, no. 1 (April 2014): 27.

52. Translation: Protestantism does not have the structure or polity of the Roman Catholic
Church.

53. Echeverria, "Revelation," 46.

54. Ibid., 33.

55. Ibid., 32.

reasoning, but because the church teaches them and they accept all the teachings of Christ simply because they accept the Church's authority."[56]

Moreover, Echeverria failed to observe that Rome has taken great efforts to inculcate docility among the laity at almost every turn, from affirming the custom of addressing a priest as "father" to declaring that certain topics (such as the ordination of women) are no longer even to be discussed.[57] Offering what proper attitudes should be instilled among the laity, the *Catechism* today declares: "Mindful of Christ's words to his apostles: 'He who hears you, hears me' [Luke 10:16], the faithful receive *with docility* the teachings and directives that their pastors give them in different forms."[58] Or as the *Catechism of the Council of Trent* puts it: "This knowledge, however, is nothing else than faith, by which *we yield our unhesitating assent to whatever the authority of our Holy Mother the Church teaches us* to have been revealed by God."[59] So, if Horton is correct, if the postulation of Tradition III by Oberman is accurate, then the question of Scripture and tradition for Rome may in the end turn out to be not a question of revelation per se but a question of ecclesiology: What is the proper place and authority of "Holy Mother Church"?

56. Kreeft, "Toward Uniting the Church: Is Reunion without Compromise Possible?," *Reformed Journal* 29, no. 1 (1979): 10–11.

57. B. A. Robinson, "Roman Catholicism and Female Ordination: Recent History of the Debate," Ontario Consultants on Religious Tolerance, last updated July 10, 2005, http://www.religioustolerance.org/femclrg10.htm.

58. *Catechism*, par. 87 (emphasis added).

59. Theodore Alois Buckley, *The Catechism of the Council of Trent* (London: Aeterna, 2014), Kindle edition, locations 173–74 (emphasis added). See also Echeverria, "Revelation," 31.

4

Rome or Nothing?

In chapters 2 and 3 we explored the foundational issues of tradition and Scripture. There we observed that the Protestant view of sola Scriptura is often the subject of caricature by Roman Catholic apologists, who contend that the notion cuts Protestants off from the historic roots of Christianity and leaves them with no secure place to stand amid the many winds of doctrine that continually blow about.

Indeed, it is worse, for the claim is often pressed that Protestants are hopelessly inconsistent, that their view lacks objective authority and reduces to subjective individualism. For the church, it is argued, gave us the Bible, so Protestants cannot consistently appeal to the authority of Scripture without acknowledging the prior authority of the church. Consider these lines from Peter Kreeft, a former evangelical, who is now a Roman Catholic. "If Scripture is infallible, as traditional Protestants believe, then the Church must be infallible too, for a fallible cause cannot produce an infallible effect, and the Church produced the Bible. The Church (apostles and saints) wrote the New Testament, and the Church (subsequent bishops) defined its canon."[1] This argument is confused at a number of levels, but for now we simply want to highlight the claim that "a fallible cause cannot produce an infallible effect." Suppose this is true. Does it follow that an infallible cause cannot employ a fallible instrument to produce an infallible effect? Cannot God as an infallible cause inspire and direct fallible human beings to infallibly convey his truth?

1. Cited by Gregg R. Allison, *Roman Catholic Theology and Practice: An Evangelical Assessment* (Wheaton: Crossway, 2014), 95n62.

Does Paul need to be infallible for God to use him to write, say, epistles that have infallible authority to teach doctrinal and moral truth? It seems clear that Paul need not be infallible for an infallible God to inspire him in this fashion.[2]

Claims similar to those made about the Bible are made about the classic creeds. Protestants who reject the claims of the Roman church, it may be argued, have no principled reason to insist that the Nicene Creed is correct or to appeal to its authority to fend off heretical claims about Christ.

This basic line of argument is often employed to unsettle evangelicals and other Protestants and to pressure them to convert to Rome. On one level, it is not surprising that these lines of argument are so effective with many such believers. After all, evangelicals love Scripture, and their faith in Christ is the very heart of what gives meaning and direction to their lives. If they become convinced that the only way they can preserve their faith in Christ and the authority of the Bible is by going to Rome, well, they will go to Rome.

But while the appeal of this line of argument, not least its emotional appeal, is undeniable in a number of ways, its rational credentials are another matter altogether. In this chapter and the next, we want to build on the preceding chapters on Scripture and tradition (chaps. 2 and 3) and advance our argument that Reformation Christians can heartily affirm the authority of the Bible and the classic creeds with full intellectual integrity while rejecting the claims of the Roman magisterium. In chapters 2 and 3, we looked at these issues from a historical and theological standpoint. Now we want to focus more on philosophical and epistemological issues involved in revelation, biblical authority, and the status of classic creeds.

So let us begin to do so by looking at this passage from the *Catechism of the Catholic Church*, which spells out the Roman Catholic claims about the magisterium and its teaching authority. "'The task of giving an authentic interpretation of the Word of God, whether in its written form or in the form of Tradition, has been entrusted to the living teaching office of the Church alone. Its authority in this matter is exercised in the name of Jesus Christ.' This means that the task of interpretation has been entrusted to the bishops in communion with the successor of Peter, the Bishop of Rome."[3] The first thing we particularly want to underscore here is that the magisterium

---

2. As Gregg Allison states, no one ever claimed that Israel had to be infallible to produce the OT Scriptures. Ibid.

3. *Catechism of the Catholic Church*, 2nd ed. (Mahwah, NJ: Paulist Press, 1994), par. 85. The sentences quoted in this paragraph come from the Vatican II document by Pope Paul VI, *Dei Verbum: Dogmatic Constitution on Divine Revelation*, 1965, sec. 10; for a translation, see http://www.vatican.va/archive/hist_councils/ii_vatican_council/documents/vat-ii_const_196 51118_dei-verbum_en.html.

is identified with "bishops in communion with the successor of Peter, the Bishop of Rome." So this clearly gives distinctive, if not exclusive, interpretive authority to the pope and those bishops in communion with him. The magisterium *alone* has the task of "giving an authentic interpretation of the Word of God."

Consider now this passage, cited earlier, which is particularly significant for our concerns because it encapsulates the issues we will consider in this chapter and the next: "It is clear therefore that, in the supremely wise arrangement of God, sacred Tradition, Sacred Scripture, and the Magisterium of the Church are so connected and associated that one of them cannot stand without the others. Working together, each in its own way, under the action of the one Holy Spirit, they all contribute effectively to the salvation of souls."[4] This paragraph is a paraphrase of a paragraph from the 1965 Vatican II document *Dei Verbum*, which reads as follows: "It is clear, therefore, that sacred tradition, Sacred Scripture and the teaching authority of the Church, in accord with God's most wise design, are so linked and joined together that one cannot stand without the others, and that all together and each in its own way under the action of the one Holy Spirit contribute effectively to the salvation of souls."[5]

A few things are worth noting here. First, notice that the phrase "teaching authority of the Church" from the 1965 document is replaced by the phrase "Magisterium of the Church." That magisterium, recall, is composed of bishops in communion with the pope. So the teaching authority of the church appears to be identified with the Roman Catholic magisterium. Second, notice the claim that one of these three factors, sacred tradition, sacred Scripture, and the magisterium, "cannot stand without the others." Now it is worth asking whether this also means that no two of them can stand without the third. That is not explicitly stated, but it appears to be the claim.

Third, notice the claim that these three factors, working under the direction of the Holy Spirit, "all contribute effectively to the salvation of souls." So the ultimate aim is soteriological, not merely intellectual or rational. However, we should not in any way draw a contrast between justified dogmatic belief and the salvation of our souls. Indeed, dogmatic belief is essential to our spiritual formation and final salvation: "There is an organic connection between our spiritual life and the dogmas. Dogmas are lights along the path of faith; they illuminate it and make it secure. Conversely, if our life is upright, our intellect and heart will be open to welcome the light shed by the dogmas of

4. *Catechism*, par. 95.
5. Pope Paul VI, *Dei Verbum*, sec. 10.

faith."[6] Clearly, then, a lot is at stake in the matter of discerning "authentic interpretation of the Word of God" and the dogmas that should bind our minds and hearts.

So here is the important claim we want to examine, that there is some sort of necessary connection or linkage between Scripture, tradition, and the Roman magisterium. Consequently, anyone who wants to affirm any one of them must also affirm the other two, or anyone who affirms any two must also affirm the third. Clearly, this claim is a frontal challenge to Christians in other traditions who do not acknowledge the authority of the Roman magisterium and the claims of papal authority. To consider and assess this claim, we need to get clear on just what is meant by the claim that no one or two of these factors can "stand without the others."

Just what is involved in failing to stand? Are these three factors like the legs of a three-legged stool, so that if any one of them is removed, the stool cannot stand even for a moment, let alone bear any weight?[7] Is the claim that anyone who attempts to maintain or rationally accept the authority of Scripture and traditional creedal orthodoxy while rejecting the claims of the Roman magisterium will inevitably fail? Does it mean that all such efforts will suffer from inconsistency or other rational defects? Is it actually a weaker claim to the effect that any one or two of the factors is less effective without the others? Is it a prediction or a claim about historical inevitability? Does it mean that any effort to maintain the authority of one or two of these factors without the magisterium will fizzle out and eventually come to nothing? Are such efforts inherently unstable and bound to disintegrate?

Exactly what the claim is here is not altogether clear. So we shall proceed by considering and assessing various options as to what it might mean. We shall not, however, attempt to settle which one of these options is the correct interpretation of this claim, since that is up to Rome. We shall begin with a rather strong version of the claim that would entirely discredit Protestant (and perhaps Eastern Orthodox) Christianity. While versions of this strong interpretation are common with popular apologists and bloggers, we shall take as our representative of this view John Henry Newman, a famous convert to Rome who has been very influential in converting others to his view. Indeed, Newman is the patron saint of many contemporary Roman Catholic apologists. In particular, we shall examine his argument in his celebrated book *An Essay on the Development of Christian Doctrine*.

6. *Catechism*, par. 89.
7. Gregg Allison uses this image to explain the claim of the *Catechism*. See *Roman Catholic Theology and Practice*, 80.

It's All or Nothing!?

In his famous book Newman's project is to resolve a serious difficulty we have identified several times in this book, that many of Rome's essential doctrinal claims have scant support at best in the explicit teaching of Scripture as well as the early patristic sources. Indeed, they were articulated much later, often after centuries of development from many historical factors and influences. It is important to be clear that Newman's whole theory is premised on the reality of this problem. If it were not recognized as a serious problem, there would be no need for his famous theory.

Newman's ingenious solution, in short, is to argue that these doctrinal developments of later centuries were in fact present from the beginning, albeit in embryonic form. The later development simply brought to maturity the various seeds that were planted in the original revelation given to the apostles. The very heart of Christian orthodoxy, after all, was not formulated in dogmatic terms until the Nicene Creed in 325/381. In a parallel way, Newman argues, later Roman doctrinal developments were simply making explicit and filling in the details of what was there all along in Christian revelation.

The claim that these developments are parallel is not only at the heart of Newman's overall argument; it is also crucial to his version of what I call the all-or-nothing argument, one that has convinced a number of Protestants to migrate to Rome. So let's take a careful look at Newman's rather ambitious argument.

After making his case for development, Newman proceeds to the heart of his argument for the rational necessity to accept the authority of Rome.

> If the Christian doctrine, as originally taught, admits of true and important developments, as was argued in the foregoing Section, this is a strong antecedent argument in favor of a provision in the Dispensation for putting a seal of authority upon those developments. The probability of their being known to be true varies with that of their truth. The ideas indeed are quite distinct, I grant, of revealing and of guaranteeing a truth, and they are quite often distinct in fact. . . . If then there are certain great truths, or duties, or observances, naturally and legitimately resulting from the doctrines originally professed, it is but reasonable to include these true results in the idea of the revelation itself, to consider them parts of it, and if the revelation be not only true, but [also] guaranteed as true, to anticipate that they too will come under the privileges of that guarantee.[8]

8. Newman, *An Essay on the Development of Christian Doctrine* (Notre Dame, IN: University of Notre Dame Press, 1989), 79–80.

Notice a few things about this passage. First, he distinguishes revealing a truth from guaranteeing it. What exactly is involved in this guarantee that goes beyond revelation itself? Second, he describes "certain great truths" that "naturally and legitimately" result from the original revelation; he claims that these are part of the revelation and consequently share in whatever guarantees pertain to that revelation itself. Now the crucial question here is how we shall identify natural and legitimate development, and whether everything that might be called natural can be guaranteed to be true. Just what qualifies a development as legitimate? We shall come back to these questions, which we now raise in a preliminary way.

Next, it is important to emphasize that Newman advances his argument for an infallible guarantor of revelation in terms of what seems probable or reasonable. Indeed, dozens of times throughout his book he appeals to judgments of antecedent probability, of what seems likely, and so on. Here is how he casts his argument for an infallible guarantor of revelation: "A probable infallibility is a probable gift of never erring; a reception of the doctrine of probable infallibility is faith and obedience towards a person founded on the probability of his never erring in his declaration or commands."[9]

He also takes care to point out that infallibility is often confused with certitude and insists that the argument for probable infallibility is not an attempt to achieve certitude.[10] Probabilities remain just that: probabilities. Technically, probabilities range anywhere from 0 to 1, and impossibilities have a probability of 0, while necessary truths have a probability of 1. Newman appears to think that his argument for the probability of an infallible guarantor of revelation lies somewhere between 0 and 1, but much closer to 1 than to 0.

Now, with this in mind, we can turn to Newman's all-or-nothing argument. He proceeds toward this argument by reiterating that the intellectual content of the Christian faith inevitably grew and developed as it was reflected on by many generations of people, and as its implications were applied to various matters and situations. He then writes:

> Next, that, if development must be, then, whereas Revelation is a heavenly gift, He who gave it virtually has not given it, unless He has also secured it from perversion and corruption, in all such development as comes upon it by the necessity of its nature, or, in other words, that the intellectual action through successive generations, which is the organ of development, must so far as it can claim to have been put in charge of the Revelation, be in its determinations infallible.[11]

9. Ibid., 81.
10. Ibid., 81n1.
11. Ibid., 92.

A number of things are worth highlighting here. First, he reiterates the point that revelation has virtually not been given unless it is secured from perversion and corruption. But notice here the specific sort of developments to which this pertains: "such development as comes upon it by the necessity of its nature." Now the language of necessity is interesting and considerably stronger than his earlier language about developments that "naturally and legitimately" result from Christian revelation. Indeed, necessity is typically understood along the lines of logical necessity of some sort. So is Newman here limiting his claim to developments that follow with logical necessity from the original revelation?

Although the answer to this is not entirely clear, in the second part of this passage Newman goes on apparently to restate, "in other words," what he claimed in the first part of it. But notice what he is saying in the second part. For one thing, he identifies the "organ of development" as "the intellectual action through successive generations." Again, development occurs through reflection on revelation over the course of many generations and even centuries. So here are two accounts of development that Newman takes to be equivalent and to have the stamp of infallibility (D = development):

D1 All such development as comes upon the original revelation by the necessity of its nature

D2 All development that occurs as the product of intellectual action upon revelation through successive generations

Now the notion that these two accounts of development are equivalent is very important. But here is another more significant point: Newman claims that the development in D2 is infallible in its determinations "so far as it can claim to have been put in charge of the Revelation."

This claim, too, raises a number of questions. What is entailed in being "put in charge of the Revelation"? Is there a clear answer to who can *rightfully* claim to be in charge of revelation, as opposed to who *merely* claims to be? And does the responsibility of being put in charge of the revelation really warrant anything more than faithfully preserving and passing it on?

But most fundamentally, here is the question that must be pressed: is it really true that D1 is essentially the same as D2? Newman, of course, is arguing that the Church of Rome, particularly the Roman magisterium, rightfully claims to be in charge of the revelation, and thus that the deliberations resulting from its intellectual action are infallible. So we can rephrase the question as follows: can the claim plausibly be made that all the official deliberations of the Roman magisterium represent developments of revelation that are due to the "necessity of its nature"?

Consider now this passage, which comes shortly after the one above. New-man reiterates his argument, in slightly different language: "And if again, Christianity being from heaven, all that is necessarily involved in it, and is evolved from it, is from heaven, and if, on the other hand, large accretions actually do exist, professing to be its true and legitimate results, our first impression naturally is, that these must be the very developments which they profess to be."[12] Notice again the language of necessity, but here the claim pertains to "all that is necessarily involved in" the revelation as well as what "is evolved from it." Again, it is far from clear what this means. Is Newman claiming that everything necessarily involved in revelation will necessarily evolve from it?

The notion of evolution period, let alone evolution in terms of ideas and religious practices, is not one easily stated in terms of necessity, for things evolve over a long process, typically involving countless subtle changes caused by numerous historical and other causal factors.[13] Moreover, beliefs and prac-tices that evolve this way can result in changes so dramatic that the product evolved in later stages is altogether unrecognizable in comparison to earlier ones. Newman contends that if Christianity is from heaven, everything neces-sarily involved in it, and evolved from it, is also from heaven.

The results of this evolution, Newman is saying, are as much guaranteed as the original revelation. This is what he is claiming when he says that "large accretions" professing to be true and legitimate developments are likely what they claim to be. So again, we have two accounts of development that New-man takes to be equivalent:

D3 All that is necessarily involved in Christian revelation, or evolved from it

D4 Large accretions on the Christian revelation that profess to be its true and legitimate developments

Now the assumption that all the "large accretions" to the Christian revelation in Roman Catholic theology are likely to be true developments is rather gen-erous, to put it mildly, but let us continue to examine how Newman expands his argument. Several lines later in the same paragraph, he writes as follows: "These doctrines are members of one family, and suggestive or correlative, or confirmatory, or illustrative of each other. One furnishes evidence to another, and all to each of them; if this is proved, that becomes probable; and if this

---

12. Ibid., 93.
13. Physical evolution could be thought necessary on the assumption of all-encompassing physical determinism. It could be claimed that all physical events and states of affairs are de-termined by laws of nature and previous states of the universe.

and that are both probable, but for different reasons, each adds to the other its own probability."[14] Now this passage is interesting because of the various ways Newman thinks the doctrinal developments can gain rational support and credence. His claims here range from metaphorical suggestions, as when he says the doctrines are "members of one family," to modest claims that some doctrines illustrate others or correlate with them, to rather general claims about how one or more doctrinal claims may render others more probable.

But then Newman immediately continues as follows. Here I quote him at length to show how strong and wide ranging are his claims about doctrinal development.

> The Incarnation is the antecedent of the doctrine of Mediation, and the archetype both of the Sacramental principle and the merits of the Saints. From the doctrine of Mediation follow the Atonement, the Mass, the merits of Martyrs and Saints, their invocation and *cultus*. From the Sacramental principle come the Sacraments properly so called; the unity of the Church, and the Holy See as its type and centre; the authority of Councils; the sanctity of rites; the veneration of holy places, shrines, images, vessels, furniture and vestments. Of the Sacraments, Baptism is developed into Confirmation on the one hand; into Penance, Purgatory and Indulgences on the other; and the Eucharist into the Real Presence, adoration of the Host, Resurrection of the body and the virtue of the relics. Again, the doctrine of the Sacraments leads to the doctrine of Justification; Justification to that of Original Sin; Original Sin to the merit of Celibacy.[15]

This is an extraordinary passage, and any moderately attentive reader can hardly help but notice how extravagant the claims are that it advances. Although Newman does not even begin to explain, let alone demonstrate, how all these doctrines "follow" or "come" from the doctrines they allegedly follow or come from, he proclaims that they do with a sense bordering on infallible authority. The number and range of complex issues that Newman pontificates on is nothing short of stunning.

But as extraordinary as this passage is, Newman's conclusion to this paragraph is even more so: "You must accept the whole or reject the whole; attenuation does but enfeeble, and amputation mutilate. It is trifling to receive all but something which is as integral as any other portion; and on the other hand, it is a solemn thing to accept any part, for, before you know where you are, you may be carried on by a stern logical necessity to accept the whole."[16]

14. Newman, *Essay*, 93.
15. Ibid., 93–94.
16. Ibid., 94.

Recall that earlier in this very paragraph, Newman mentioned a number of relatively modest support-relations that may obtain between various doctrinal claims, ranging from suggestion and illustration to one or more claims making others more probable. Here, all those modest claims are left behind, and Newman insists that one must accept all these claims or none of them, that they are connected by nothing less than "stern logical necessity." Probability has miraculously been transformed into logical necessity, though to all appearances his actual argument rests entirely on various probability judgments and alleged connections between different doctrines, many of which are highly contestable.

Whoever accepts any part must beware, for before realizing what is happening, that person may be led inexorably to accept the whole. It will not help Newman to defend him against his extraordinary exaggeration to notice that he says only that one "may" be carried on in this fashion. For it would not even be possible that one could be carried on by stern logical necessity to accept the whole unless such logical necessities actually held among these various claims. If Newman is right, then, a Christian apparently cannot coherently accept the Nicene Creed while rejecting the Roman view of the Mass, the see of Rome as the center of the church, the merits of the saints, indulgences, and so on. It's all or nothing. And thus by a sort of magisterial wave of the wand, all Protestants who want to be coherent are transformed into Roman Catholics.

Conflation, Confusion, and Caricature

This long paragraph we have examined in some detail above encapsulates in many ways both the charm and the deep flaws of Newman's classic book. On the one hand, he appeals to a number of plausible principles and mounts an argument that, at best, gives us a result with some degree of rational probability. On the other hand, he not infrequently gets carried away with his own rhetoric and makes claims that far outstrip his evidence and arguments. Moreover, he conflates and equates his more plausible claims with his more ambitious ones, as observed in some of the examples above, and the former lend a false and confusing sense of credibility to the latter.

We see him doing the same sort of thing at the beginning of his next chapter, after the one we have just considered. After reiterating the notion that the entirety of Roman Catholic dogma and practice goes back to the apostles, at least in nascent form, he writes as follows about that body of doctrine:

> Moreover, they are confessed to form one body one with another, so that to reject one is to disparage the rest; and they include within the range of their

system even those primary articles of faith, as the Incarnation, which many an impugner of the said doctrinal system, as a system, professes to accept, and which, do what he will, he cannot intelligibly separate, whether in point of evidence or of internal character, from others which he disavows.[17]

Notice again how the all-or-nothing claim is articulated. If one accepts the incarnation, one must accept the whole Roman panoply of dogmas and practices, and it is impossible for "impugners" of Roman theology to "intelligibly separate" the incarnation from that larger body of claims. As Newman puts it a few lines later, "We have to choose between this theology and none at all."

Before concluding this section, it is worth recognizing how Newman tries to bolster his claim by suggesting that Protestantism will inevitably end in some sort of heresy.[18] The essence of Protestantism, he seems to think, is private judgment, so it is doomed to come to a bad end. For instance, here is his take on Calvinism: "Calvinism has changed into Unitarianism; yet this need not be called a corruption, even if it is not, strictly speaking, a development; for Harding, in controversy with Jewell, surmised the coming change three centuries since, and it has occurred not in one country, but many."[19] Newman likely would be surprised to see the resurgence of Calvinism in the contemporary church and the vitality it enjoys not only in America but in other parts of the world as well.

For another instance of his treatment of Protestants, consider his comments on John Wesley: "One of the chief points of discipline to which Wesley attached most importance was that of preaching early in the morning. That was his principle. In Georgia, he began preaching at five o'clock every day, winter and summer. 'Early preaching,' he said, 'is the glory of the Methodists; whenever this is dropt, they will dwindle away into nothing, they have lost their first love, they are a fallen people.'"[20] One would never guess that Wesley was an Oxford don whose works fill over thirty large volumes, or that he was one of the great preachers and practitioners of scriptural holiness, or indeed that he had any other principle besides preaching early in the morning. No, Wesley is reduced here to a cartoon figure to advance Newman's narrative that Protestant Christianity is destined to "dwindle away into nothing." Newman would likely be surprised to see Pentecostal Christianity, which has roots in

17. Ibid., 99–100.
18. Recall that one proposed interpretation of the claim that Scripture, tradition, and the magisterium stand or fall together was a claim about this sort of historical inevitability.
19. Newman, *Essay*, 175.
20. Ibid., 184–85.

Wesleyan theology, flourishing worldwide, especially in South America, which has historically been dominated by Roman Catholicism.

In any case, throughout his book are numerous similarly tendentious accounts, as well as utter caricatures of other Christian traditions, including the Eastern Church.[21] To be sure, Newman could be more ecumenical in other contexts, but not in this book. His accounts of other Christian traditions here are designed to discredit them and to serve his larger contention that Rome alone can coherently maintain orthodoxy, so we must embrace Rome or be left with no viable place to stand.

If these really are our only options, it is altogether understandable why many lovers of Jesus, the Son of God incarnate, will choose to go to Rome. But this claim that we cannot have Jesus without Rome is a classic case of rhetorical overreach as well as deeply confused thinking, and Newman's argument does not even come close to demonstrating it.

Leaner Versions of the All-or-Nothing Argument

But perhaps, it might be suggested, Newman was on the right track, even if his particular all-or-nothing argument was far too ambitious and bloated with excess. After all, not everything Newman cites as part of the body of Roman Catholic doctrine has the official stamp of infallible dogma. Not everything he includes is the product of an infallible conciliar determination or something the pope declared ex cathedra. So perhaps there might be a more promising argument along the lines Newman attempted if we restrict our claims to infallible dogma.

Recall the passages from the *Catechism* we quoted at the beginning of this chapter, which assert a connection between Scripture, tradition, and the Roman magisterium such that no one of them can stand without the others. Recall too the claim that "the task of giving an authentic interpretation of the Word of God, whether in its written form or in the form of Tradition, has been entrusted to the living teaching office of the Church alone." The claim that the magisterium *alone* has the authority of "authentic interpretation of the Word of God" is a far-reaching one with large implications. Consider now this claim: "The Church's Magisterium exercises the authority it holds from Christ to the fullest extent when it defines dogmas, that is when it proposes, in a form obliging the Christian people to an irrevocable adherence of faith, truths contained in divine Revelation or also when it proposes, in a

---

21. See ibid., 54, 96, 181, 192–93, 198, 205, 306, 353–54.

definitive way, truths having a necessary connection with these."[22] And here is one more passage with large implications for the role of the magisterium in Christian knowledge. Here the *Catechism* is expounding the Roman view that revelation comes to us both in the form of Scripture and in the form of tradition, including oral tradition. "As a result, the Church, to whom the transmission and interpretation of Revelation is entrusted, 'does not derive her certainty about all revealed truths from the Holy Scriptures alone. Both Scripture and Tradition must be accepted and honored with equal sentiments of devotion and reverence.'"[23]

Notice here in particular the claim that the church "does not derive her certainty about all revealed truths from the Holy Scriptures alone." To the contrary, according to Rome, the church also derives its certainty about some revealed truths from tradition. Indeed, the claim appears to be that the truths derived from tradition are as certain as those derived from Holy Scripture, since both "must be accepted and honored with equal sentiments of devotion and reverence."

Now these various claims from the *Catechism* give us the material to construct a more rigorous all-or-nothing argument. Think about the implications of these claims for Rome in relation to other Christian traditions. The Roman magisterium allegedly has exclusive authority to provide "authentic interpretation of the Word of God," whether in the form of Scripture or tradition, including oral tradition. Moreover, dogma, which is defined "in a form obliging the Christian people to an irrevocable adherence of faith," is equal in authority and certainty whether derived from Scripture or tradition. These binding truths, again, may either be contained in revelation or have a "necessary connection" with such truths.

So consider the Nicene Creed, the paradigmatic instance of a conciliar dogmatic determination that not only Roman Catholics but also many other believers, including many Reformation Christians, would accept not only as an authentic interpretation of Scripture but also as having binding authority. Now consider another dogma that Roman Catholics believe has the same sort of authority: the immaculate conception of Mary, a dogma the pope has declared ex cathedra to be infallible truth, but is typically rejected by Christians in the Reformation traditions.[24] The question is whether one can coherently affirm the creed as a true interpretation of Scripture while rejecting the dogma of the immaculate conception. A closely related question is whether it is a

---

22. *Catechism*, par. 88.
23. Ibid., par. 82. The passage quoted is from *Dei Verbum*, par. 9.
24. It is, however, accepted by some Lutherans, who find some support for the doctrine in Luther himself.

coherent position to affirm the creed but deny immaculate conception *given Roman Catholic claims about magisterial authority.*[25]

As we have noted, Roman Catholics often argue that Protestants cannot consistently accept or believe in the authority of the Bible and the classic creeds if they reject the authority of the Roman magisterium. So consider the following argument as a more rigorous version of this sort of all-or-nothing argument.

1. We can consistently believe that the Nicene Creed is a true interpretation of Scripture only if we believe that the Roman Catholic magisterium (RCM) has infallible teaching authority.
2. If we believe that the RCM has infallible teaching authority, then we believe that what the pope proclaims ex cathedra is infallible truth.
3. If we believe that what the pope proclaims ex cathedra is infallible truth, then we believe that the dogma of the immaculate conception of Mary is infallible truth.
4. We can consistently believe that the Nicene Creed is a true interpretation of Scripture only if we believe that the dogma of the immaculate conception of Mary is infallible truth.
5. If we do not believe that the dogma of the immaculate conception of Mary is infallible truth, then we cannot consistently believe that the Nicene Creed is a true interpretation of Scripture.[26]

This argument is valid, so its conclusion does in fact follow from its premises with "stern logical necessity." The more interesting question, obviously, is whether all its premises are true, and whether it is thus a sound argument, as well as a valid one. The key premise, upon which the entire argument turns, is the first one. The other premises (2 and 3) are straightforward propositions that must be accepted by anyone who understands the teaching authority Rome claims for itself, and knows the pope has declared ex cathedra that the dogma of

---

25. Apparently Pope Pius IX, who dogmatically defined the doctrine of the immaculate conception in 1854, did not think so, as indicated by these words that followed that definition: "Hence, if anyone shall dare—which God forbid!—to think otherwise than as has been defined by us, let him know and understand that he is condemned by his own judgment; that he has suffered shipwreck in the faith; that he has separated from the unity of the Church; and that, furthermore, by his own action he incurs the penalties established by law if he should dare to express in words or writing or by any other outward means the errors he think in his heart." Pope Pius IX, *The Immaculate Conception,* 1854, Papal Encyclicals Online, http://www.papalencyclicals.net/Pius09/p9ineff.htm.

26. Thanks to Kyle Blanchette for suggesting this more efficient version of my argument, which has fewer steps than my original construction.

the immaculate conception is infallible truth. Premise 4 follows from 1 through 3 (by extended hypothetical syllogism), and 5 follows from 4 (by contraposition).

Protestants will deny premise 1, and in chapter 5 we will show why Protestants have excellent reasons to affirm the truth and authority of the Nicene Creed on their own principles. But the question remains whether this premise fairly states what Roman Catholics are committed to. Is this what is entailed in the claim that Scripture, tradition, and the magisterium are so connected that one cannot stand without the others?

I will not attempt a definitive answer to that question: that is up to Rome. But here I want to identify some other variations on the argument that might be suggested instead of the one above. Another, slightly weaker claim would be the following:

1a. We can be rationally certain that the Nicene Creed is a true interpretation of Scripture only if we believe that the Roman Catholic magisterium has infallible teaching authority.

The argument would be rephrased accordingly, and the conclusion would be the following:

5a. If we do not believe that the dogma of the immaculate conception of Mary is infallible truth, we cannot be rationally certain that the Nicene Creed is a true interpretation of Scripture.

Notice that the claim here pertains to rational certainty, not consistency. That is, it might be argued that one is not, strictly speaking, inconsistent in rejecting the claims of the Roman magisterium while believing that the Nicene Creed is a true interpretation of Scripture. But one does not have solid grounds for rational certainty.

Another, stronger version would be the following.

1b. We can *know* that the Nicene Creed is a true interpretation of Scripture only if the Roman Catholic magisterium *has* infallible teaching authority.

Again, the argument would be rephrased accordingly, and the conclusion would be as follows:

5b. If the dogma of the immaculate conception of Mary is not infallible truth, we cannot know that the Nicene Creed is a true interpretation of Scripture.

This version is stronger because it claims that the very possibility of knowing that the creed is a true interpretation of Scripture hinges on the Roman magisterium having infallible authority. The issue here is not whether one can be consistent or rational or rationally certain in believing that the creed is a true interpretation of Scripture if one does not believe that the magisterium has infallible teaching authority. What is at stake in this claim is not the consistency or rationality of anyone's beliefs but *the very possibility* of having knowledge about the true interpretation of Scripture.

Before moving on, it is worth noting that these various all-or-nothing arguments so beloved by Roman Catholic apologists are strikingly similar to certain arguments sometimes deployed by conservative, usually fundamentalist, Protestant apologists. Consider this argument and the ways it is parallel to the ones above.

1. We can consistently believe in the bodily resurrection of Jesus only if we believe that the Bible is the infallible Word of God.
2. If we believe that the Bible is the infallible Word of God, then we believe what it teaches in every detail.
3. If we believe what the Bible teaches in every detail, then we believe that the earth is only thousands of years old.
4. We can consistently believe in the bodily resurrection of Jesus only if we believe that the earth is only thousands of years old.
5. If we do not believe that the earth is only thousands of years old, then we cannot consistently believe in the bodily resurrection of Jesus.

While the parallel is not exact, the fundamental similarity is that this argument, like the ones preceding it, appeals to a far-reaching claim about infallible authority, and on this basis it tries to establish that certain doctrines are equally supported by this authority.[27] Those doctrines are consequently on an epistemic par, and we have no rational right to accept one without accepting the other. To do so is to fall into irrationality or inconsistency of some sort.

The fundamental similarity of these arguments explains why many Roman Catholic apologists, like their fundamentalist counterparts, are so driven to try to demonstrate some glaring contradiction in the views of the persons they have targeted for conversion to their position, or to claim that their

27. Claiming the Bible teaches that the earth is only thousands of years old depends on a rather literalistic reading of the OT chronologies. Yet the young-earth view probably has more direct biblical support than the immaculate conception. On such a literal reading, Archbishop Ussher's famous chronology dated creation at 4004 BC.

position alone is fully consistent. (It is perhaps telling that many of the most zealous Roman Catholic apologists are former Protestant fundamentalists.) Although this argumentative strategy unsettles many people who naturally want to maintain their cherished beliefs, and many convert under the pressure of thinking they need to do so in order to preserve their faith, the sense of settledness gained by such "consistency" is fragile. Indeed, we suspect that those who employ these all-or-nothing arguments, by insisting that one cannot affirm the creed without affirming these distinctive claims of Rome, realize those distinctive claims are on tenuous grounds otherwise. Unfortunately, this strategy for shoring up those beliefs puts the whole faith in jeopardy.

Consider, again by way of comparison, the young persons who are convinced that their basis for believing in the bodily resurrection of Jesus has the same ground as their belief that the world is only thousands of years old. When confronted with powerful scientific evidence that the earth is in fact much older, their faith in the resurrection of Jesus is thereby threatened. They face the unsettling choice of rejecting that scientific evidence or having their faith in the resurrection of Jesus undermined. The same situation is faced by those who are convinced by Newman's all-or-nothing argument. To doubt anything is to begin to doubt it all, to reject any of that panoply of claims he listed in that remarkable passage quoted above is to reject it all. The same problems face the leaner, more rigorous versions of the argument, and this may be true for any substantive claim holding that Scripture, tradition, and the magisterium are so connected that none can stand without the others.

So I conclude this section with key questions: Can a person who accepts the Roman claims of authority question the immaculate conception of Mary without raising corresponding doubts about the doctrines affirmed in the classic creeds? Are these doctrines so connected that the incarnation cannot stand without the immaculate conception? If one doubted transubstantiation, would doubts about the Trinity inevitably follow? If one looked into the historical foundations of the papacy and found them wanting, would that person's faith in Christ crumble as well?

It is important to emphasize that more is at stake here than an intellectual debate about logical consistency. This is a pastoral issue as well as a philosophical and theological one. Believers who think their right to believe in the resurrection of Jesus depends on their believing that the earth is only several thousand years old, or who think their right to believe in the incarnation and atonement of Jesus requires them to believe in the immaculate conception— such Christians are caught up in a position that is not only intellectually dubious but also spiritually precarious as well. The "right" to believe the saving truths of the gospel should never be held hostage by other beliefs that are peripheral at best. Those who press such arguments on vulnerable believers in order to pressure them to "convert" to their church or theological position are setting them up not only for intellectual implosion but for spiritual shipwreck as well.

5

Revelation, Biblical Authority, and Creed

How to Affirm Catholic Faith
without Affirming the Claims of Rome

In chapter 4 we examined various all-or-nothing arguments that try to support the conclusion that there are no principled grounds for accepting the authority of Scripture or classic creedal Christianity for those who reject the claims of Rome. In this chapter we want to show that there are perfectly good Protestant reasons to accept the authority of the Nicene Creed and indeed that biblical and creedal authority stand together but do not require us to accept the claim that the Roman magisterium is the exclusively authorized interpreter of Scripture. Before making the case for creedal authority, we want to sketch our reasons for accepting the NT canon as Scripture, and to point out the basic rationale that is common for accepting both scriptural and creedal authority.

Revelation and the New Testament Canon

What is fundamentally at stake here is what is involved in the basic concept of a divine revelation. In short, a divine revelation is by definition a *successful* undertaking on the part of God to reveal himself, his truth, his intentions, his purposes, and so on. Or to put it another way, "reveal" is an achievement verb. It only applies when revelation is actually achieved or accomplished.[1]

Consider another example, the verb "communicate." Suppose Calvin said that Hobbes was a great communicator, but upon being asked to identify the main points of Hobbes's speech, Calvin could not do so. Would that not undercut the claim that Hobbes was a great communicator? Assuming that Calvin is a competent recipient for the message of Hobbes's speech, we could conclude that Hobbes did not in fact communicate his key points. He perhaps attempted to communicate but failed to do so.

"Reveal" is an achievement verb in the same sort of way. William Abraham sums the matter up concisely: "Divine speaking and human sensitivity together bring about divine revelation."[2] Human sensitivity is itself a gift of God. It is due not only to the fact that apostles are made in God's image as knowers but also to the fact that the Holy Spirit illumines their hearts and minds to faithfully understand and record God's revelation.

So if the Christian revelation is in fact from God, we have every reason to think that the recipients of that revelation understood what God intended to reveal. For a paradigmatic instance of this, consider Paul's words defending his apostleship to the Galatians. "I want you to know, brothers and sisters, that the gospel I preached is not of human origin. I did not receive it from any man, nor was I taught it; rather I received it by revelation from Jesus Christ" (Gal. 1:11–12). To receive a revelation from Christ is to receive a communication from a supreme authority, warranting the claim that Paul, as the recipient, knows what he is talking about. Or consider Luke's account of Jesus appearing to the disciples after he was raised from the dead to explain to them from the OT Scriptures the meaning of his death and resurrection (Luke 24:25–49). Given the risen Jesus as the source of this revelation, we have reason to believe that the disciples correctly understood the meaning and significance of Jesus's death and resurrection. Finally, in the Gospel of John, consider Jesus's promise to the disciples that the Holy Spirit would speak to them and guide them into truth (John 14:26; 15:26; 16:12–14). The point is the same. Given the guidance of the Holy Spirit upon the apostles, we have every reason to believe that they would accurately communicate what God intended.

Thus far Protestants and Roman Catholics can agree. But how, it will be asked, can we know which books are precisely the books that contain

---

1. For more on the notion of "reveal" as an achievement verb, see William J. Abraham, *Divine Revelation and the Limits of Historical Criticism* (Oxford: Oxford University Press, 1982), 11–12.

2. Abraham, *The Divine Inspiration of Holy Scripture* (Oxford: Oxford University Press, 1981), 89.

authoritative revelation for the church? The answer to this question is a major point of contention between Roman Catholics and Protestants. We think the notion of revelation itself provides us with resources to answer this question. So let us turn now to consider the NT canon in light of these observations about the nature of revelation.

Discerning the Canon

The whole notion of canon is a very controversial and deeply contested notion, and we can hardly delve into the details of that debate here. But for our purposes, we want to sketch some of the central insights of an account of canon that we think has considerable promise, and one that is most pertinent to our concerns in this chapter, namely, that of Michael J. Kruger.

Kruger's project is to develop an epistemological account of how Christians can be rationally justified in believing that the twenty-seven books in the NT are indeed the only ones that belong there. His project is modeled after Alvin Plantinga's account of Christian knowledge in his landmark book *Warranted Christian Belief.*[3] One of the most impressive aspects of Kruger's account is that he incorporates into his view the strengths of a number of competing accounts of canon, while taking pains to steer clear of their weaknesses.

His model is classically Protestant since it rests on the claim that Scripture is ultimately self-authenticating. However, he understands this claim more broadly than is often the case in Protestant theology. The essence of what he means by this claim is that one cannot authenticate the canon without appealing to the canon itself and allowing it to set the terms by which it will be validated. "A self-authenticating canon is not just a canon that claims to have authority, nor is it simply a canon that bears internal evidence of authority, but one that guides and determines how that authority is to be established."[4]

To understand what is meant by the self-authenticating authority of Scripture, compare some of our basic sources of belief such as reason, sense experience, and memory. How, for instance, do we know that reason is reliable, that we can trust the basic laws of logic? The answer is that we just "see" them to be true. For instance, one cannot argue for reason without assuming its basic reliability, because the very act of arguing consists of giving reasons

3. Plantinga, *Warranted Christian Belief* (New York: Oxford University Press, 2000).

4. Kruger, *Canon Revisited: Establishing the Origins and Authority of the New Testament Books* (Wheaton: Crossway, 2012), 91.

for a conclusion.[5] To defend reason we must use reason! In a similar way, to account for the authority of Scripture, we have to appeal to Scripture itself.

Kruger offers an illuminating angle on the self-authenticating nature of Scripture by reflecting on the question of how we can recognize God himself. He writes: "After all, how does a person know when he has encountered God? Does God need some external authority to confirm his identity? When men encounter God, they are vividly aware of his beauty, majesty, and perfection and need no further 'evidence' that he is God (Pss. 27:4; 50:2; 96:6; Isa. 6:1–7; Rev. 1:12–17; 4:3). In addition, Scripture itself is described over and over again throughout the Bible as bearing these very same attributes."[6] When God is encountered, the evidence for this is in himself, so to speak, and Scripture, as the Word of God, is self-authenticating in a similar way.

At first glance, it might be objected that Kruger is begging the question against potential critics, but in fact he is not. To see why this is not begging the question, it is important to be clear about what Kruger is and is not attempting to do. He is *not* trying to give an account of why anyone comes to believe the gospel or accepts the authority of Scripture in the first place. Nor is he presenting an argument to skeptics to try to convince them that the twenty-seven books of the NT are canonical. If he were arguing with such persons, his case might be question-begging. "Instead, the issue that concerns us here is not about our having knowledge of the canon (or proving the truth of the canon) but *accounting* for our knowledge of the canon. It is about whether the Christian religion provides sufficient grounds for thinking that Christians can know which books belong in the canon and which do not."[7]

In terms of the concerns of this book, the issue can be stated as follows: Can Protestants deploy these grounds and resources to account for the authority of the canon without appeal to the Roman magisterium? Indeed, do they have an account of the authority of the canon that is a satisfactory and indeed preferable alternative to that of Rome?

Kruger answers the question he has raised by pointing to three crucial components that ground and provide adequate warrant for Christians to claim that they know the twenty-seven books of the NT are the books God intended for the canon.[8] Let us look at each of these to see how they bear on our concerns.

---

5. For the similarity between the self-authentication of Scripture and basic sources of belief, see Plantinga, *Warranted Christian Belief*, 260–62.

6. Kruger, *Canon Revisited*, 127. Kruger also cites Pss. 19:7–8; 119:103, 129.

7. Ibid., 21; cf. 91–92.

8. Kruger puts this claim in terms similar to Plantinga's account of warranted Christian belief: "God has created the proper epistemic environment wherein belief in the New Testament canon can be reliably formed." Ibid., 94.

The first of these components is "providential exposure." The idea here is fairly straightforward. If God intended for the church to recognize certain books as canonical, then God would preserve those books and make sure they were exposed to the larger church, not merely the body of believers who originally received them. For instance, if God intended Paul's Letter to the Galatians to be in the canon, it is reasonable to think he would preserve that letter and expose it to the larger church for its discernment.

The second of these components that warrant our knowledge of the canon consists of three "attributes of canonicity" that distinguish canonical books from all other books. The first of these attributes is the divine qualities of canonical books, such as their beauty, their spiritual power, and their harmony. By exhibiting such marks, the canonical books bear the imprint of the Holy Spirit. Next, there is the attribute of apostolicity, a traditional condition that a canonical book must be the result of the redemptive activity of the apostles. The third attribute is corporate reception, which means that a canonical book must be accepted by the church as a whole, not merely as a segment of it.[9]

Now this third attribute is of particular interest for our concerns in this chapter, and it points to a matter of conflict that often divides Roman Catholics from Protestants. On the one hand, Roman Catholics have often emphasized the authority of the church as either the primary or the sole factor to determine the canon. Recall the quote from Kreeft at the beginning of chapter 4, in which he contends that accepting the authority of Scripture requires a prior commitment to the infallibility of the church, since the church has defined the canon. On the other hand, Protestants have sometimes downplayed or denied the role of the church in determining the canon in their concern to defend the self-authenticating authority of Scripture.

One of the strengths of Kruger's account is that he offers a distinctively Protestant view of the canon that strongly emphasizes the essential role of the corporate reception of canonical books. "The books received by the church inform our understanding of which books are canonical not because the church is infallible or because it created or constituted the canon, but because *the church's reception of these books is a natural and inevitable outworking of the self-authenticating nature of Scripture.*"[10] He continues a few lines later, further distinguishing his view of corporate reception from the Roman Catholic account of this matter.

9. I have reversed the second and third attributes. Kruger has apostolic origins as the third attribute.
10. Kruger, *Canon Revisited*, 106 (emphasis original).

In the self-authenticating model, however, the church's reception of these books proves not to be evidence of the church's authority to create the canon, but evidence of the *opposite*, namely, the authority, power, and impact of the self-authenticating Scriptures to elicit a corporate response from the church. Jesus' statement that "my sheep hear my voice, . . . and they follow me" (John 10:27) is not evidence for the authority of the sheep's decision to follow, but evidence for the authority and efficacy of the Shepherd's voice to call. After all, the act of hearing is, by definition, derivative not constitutive. Thus, when the canon is understood as self-authenticating, it is clear that the church did not choose the canon, but the canon, in a sense, chose itself. . . . In this way, then, the role of the church is like a thermometer, not a thermostat. Both instruments provide information about the temperature in the room—but one determines it and one reflects it.[11]

Now, having considered the three attributes of canonicity (which together compose the *second* of Kruger's components that warrant rational belief in the canon), we come to the third crucial component in his account, which is the illumination and witness of the Holy Spirit. This component is involved not only with the first component of providential exposure but with the second as well, for it is the work of the Holy Spirit that leads the church to discern the divine attributes of Scripture. Moreover, the three attributes of canonicity mutually support and imply each other. Divine qualities can be expected to belong to a book if it is the product of an inspired apostolic author. "In addition, any book with divine qualities (and apostolic origins) will impose itself on the church and, via the work of the *testimonium*, be corporately received."[12]

It is important to understand the role of the illumination and witness of the Holy Spirit in this larger context to avoid subjectivism and individualism. Indeed, it is the work of the Holy Spirit in the corporate church, the discernment of the church at large, that gives us reason to believe that the twenty-seven books of the NT do indeed compose the canon God intended us to receive.

Moreover, this account of why we are justified in accepting the NT canon does not give us Cartesian certainty, nor does it give us a simple answer to the question "What is the correct date for the origin of the canon?" Indeed, this account of canon recognizes that a historical process was involved in the formation and recognition of the canon. How we define the canon will determine how we date its origin. If we define the canon *ontologically*, we can say that the canon existed in its entirety the minute after the final book of the NT was written, likely sometime in the first century. If we define the canon *functionally*, we could date it sometime in the mid-second century, if

---

11. Ibid. (emphasis original).
12. Ibid., 115.

not before, when most of the books were being used as Scripture in the early church. If we define it *exclusively*, we would date it in the third or fourth century, when a consensus was reached about the twenty-seven books of the canon. Kruger sums this up as follows:

> When these three dates are viewed as a whole, they nicely capture the entire flow of canonical history: (1) God gives his books through the apostles; →(2) the books are recognized and used as Scripture by early Christians; →(3) the corporate church achieves a consensus around these books. The fact that these three dates are linked in such a natural chronological order reminds us that the story of the canon is indeed a *process*, and therefore it should not be artificially restricted to one moment in time. Put differently, the story of the canon is less like a dot and more like a line.[13]

Let us now bring this discussion of the canon back to the larger issue we raised at the beginning of this chapter: What is involved in the very idea of revelation? Recall that revelation is an achievement verb, implying something about the recipients of revelation as well as about the one who gives the revelation. For revelation actually to be achieved, those who receive it must grasp or understand what the revealer intended to be revealed. But Protestants will disagree with Roman Catholics concerning what this implies about the authority of the church, particularly the Roman magisterium.

Recall again Kruger's point that for the self-authenticating model, "the church's reception of these books proves not to be evidence of the church's authority to create the canon, but evidence of the *opposite*, namely, the authority, power, and impact of the self-authenticating Scriptures to elicit a corporate response from the church." Here it is important to see how both views agree that the corporate church plays an essential role, but they disagree in how they understand the relationship between the authority of Scripture and the authority of the church. Again we cite that earlier passage from Kruger: "After all, the act of hearing is, by definition, derivative not constitutive." So we have good reason to believe that the church heard correctly and got the canon right, but that is primarily a statement about the authority and power of the canonical books and ultimately the One who inspired them.

Biblical Authority Implies Creedal Authority

We now want to argue that the same basic points we made about the nature of revelation lead us to the conclusion that the classic creeds are faithful

---

13. Ibid., 119.

summaries of biblical revelation, particularly the most ecumenical of these, the Nicene Creed.[14] It may be objected that it is one thing to believe the apostles faithfully wrote and recorded what God intended to reveal, and that a self-authenticating canon was correctly discerned by the corporate church, but it is another matter to take postapostolic creeds as authoritative. At this point many Protestants may instinctively appeal to the slogan "No creed but the Bible" and even pit the authority of Scripture against the authority of the classic creeds. Indeed, they may even think that the Protestant principle of sola Scriptura requires them to do so.

But this is a profound distortion of that principle, and indeed one that actually undermines biblical authority. As Michael Allen and Scott R. Swain have argued, the Reformers themselves insisted that Scripture could not be read alone but rather must be read in the larger Christian community, and particularly in light of Christian tradition. "The Bible itself calls for the exercise of pastoral authority, confessional authority, and what we could call ecumenical authority. . . . *To be more biblical, then, one cannot be biblistic. To be more biblical, one must also be engaged in the process of traditioning.*"[15] This will entail, they recognize, a certain fixed content to the Christian faith. "God has spoken in Holy Scripture, and the church by God's grace has made a faithful confession. In this regard, 'dogmas'—the church's public and binding summaries of scriptural truth—stand as 'irreversible' expressions of the rule of faith, expressions with which all later summaries of the rule of faith must cohere and which all further summaries of the rule of faith must exhibit."[16] We very much agree with these sentiments and concur with the judgment that a proper understanding of sola Scriptura will make one more catholic, not less so.[17] Indeed, we want to argue that a sound understanding of biblical authority implies the dogmatic authority of the Nicene Creed, the very heart of catholic orthodoxy.

The *Catechism of the Catholic Church* underscores the significance of this classic statement of faith as follows: "The *Niceno-Constantinopolitan*

14. Here I revisit issues I discussed in my first book several years ago. See Jerry L. Walls, *The Problem of Pluralism: Recovering United Methodist Identity* (Wilmore, KY: Good News Books, 1986), 87–98.

15. Allen and Swain, *Reformed Catholicity: The Promise of Retrieval for Theology and Biblical Interpretation* (Grand Rapids: Baker Academic, 2015), 84–85 (emphasis original). For more on this, see esp. chaps. 2–3.

16. Allen and Swain, *Reformed Catholicity*, 112. The word "irreversible" in the quote comes from Robert Jenson, *Systematic Theology* (New York: Oxford University Press, 1997), 1:36.

17. Here we very much agree with the emphasis on "Mere Protestant Catholicity" in Kevin J. Vanhoozer, *Biblical Authority after Babel: Retrieving the Solas in the Spirit of Mere Protestant Christianity* (Grand Rapids: Brazos, 2016); and the emphasis on "Reformational Catholicity" in Peter J. Leithart, *The End of Protestantism: Pursuing Unity in a Fragmented Church* (Grand Rapids: Brazos, 2016).

or *Nicene Creed* draws its great authority from the fact that it stems from the first two ecumenical councils (in 325 and 381). It remains common to all the great Churches of both East and West to this day."[18] As such, the Nicene Creed represents something as close to a doctrinal consensus among all Christians as anything. While we agree that this creed has "great authority," we think the reason this is so is slightly different from what the *Catechism* claims. It is precisely the authority of Scripture as the definitive written revelation of God that leads us to this conclusion.

The basic thrust of our argument is very similar to Newman's, particularly his more modest claims discussed in chapter 4. Recall, for instance, his claim that "whereas Revelation is a heavenly gift, He who gave it virtually has not given it, unless He has also secured it from perversion and corruption, in all such development as comes upon it by the necessity of its nature."[19] What we particularly want to underscore here is his notion of "development as comes upon it by the necessity of its nature."

Consider now his similar claim that "there is a high antecedent probability that Providence would watch over His own work, and would direct and ratify those developments of doctrine which were inevitable."[20] An inevitable development is perhaps not as strongly implied or required by the original revelation as a development that follows by the necessity of its own nature, but it is still rather strong. But the main point we are driving at is that these forms of development indeed seem likely to be true if the original revelation was given by God.

This is not to say that everything in that revelation will be clear or immediately apparent. God may have reasons for some of his revelation to be difficult to understand or even to remain debatable. But if something follows from that revelation by some sort of necessity or inevitability, it is reasonable to think that the recipients of the revelation would correctly discern it if it concerns something that is essential or central to the revelation.[21]

Now let us consider the Nicene Creed and its famous affirmation that Jesus Christ is "begotten, not made, being of one substance with the Father, through whom all things were made." This is the very heart of the Christian faith, the conviction that Jesus is nothing less than the fully divine Son of

---

18. *Catechism*, par. 195.

19. John Henry Cardinal Newman, *An Essay on the Development of Christian Doctrine* (Notre Dame, IN: University of Notre Dame Press, 1989), 92.

20. Ibid., 100.

21. This qualification is worth noting for the simple reason that countless things follow from the Christian revelation that are not theologically significant. For instance, from the simple claim "God has revealed himself," a number of things immediately follow, such as that there is a word "revealed," that it has eight letters in English, that there is more than one word, and so on.

God who became incarnate and died to save us. Is it possible that the church could have gotten this wrong? Does a Protestant have a principled reason for insisting that the Nicene Creed got this matter definitively right?

As we reflect on this question, notice also that this issue, raised by Arius, is just the sort of question inevitably raised by the Christian revelation. Given the nature of that revelation and the extraordinary things it teaches us about Christ, this is a question that necessarily demands an answer. Christ is clearly the central character of the NT, and the issue of his identity has to be addressed. And Arius gave one at least plausible reply, one that was held by a number of Christians of his time.

But while it was plausible, the Nicene fathers insisted that it did not accurately reflect what the NT teaches about Christ. Indeed, the affirmation of the full divinity of Christ is a statement not only about the Son of God but also about the trinitarian nature of the entire Godhead. The Nicene Creed is also a landmark in affirming the trinitarian nature of God by its confession of the divinity not only of the Father and the Son but also of the Holy Spirit, "who together with the Father and the Son is worshiped and glorified."

It is precisely insofar as we affirm the authority of the biblical revelation that we have reason to hold that the Nicene fathers correctly and truly defined these fundamental Christian doctrines. Indeed, the Protestant principle of the clarity and perspicuity of Scripture is also at stake here. For if the Nicene fathers were competent readers of Scripture and were making their best effort to correctly interpret what it teaches about matters utterly central to the faith, we have every reason to believe they got it right. To suggest that they may have gotten it wrong not only undermines any substantive claim about the clarity of Scripture, but even worse, it discredits the very claim that Scripture is revelation from God. Again, the claim that Scripture is revelation from God implies that the recipients of that revelation will understand it correctly, at least on its most central and important points. So anyone who wants to make strong claims about the authority and clarity of Scripture should have a firm commitment to catholic Christianity as represented in the Nicene Creed.

Let us recall the significance of this argument as it relates to the larger purposes of this chapter and the previous one, in particular the various all-or-nothing sorts of arguments Roman Catholics often press on Protestants to try to convert them to Rome. We have argued that Protestants have perfectly good reasons on their own principles to accept the authority of Scripture and the doctrines of catholic Christianity. Consequently, they have good reason to reject those arguments that hinge on premises like this:

We can consistently believe that the Nicene Creed is a true interpretation of Scripture only if we believe that the Roman Catholic magisterium has infallible teaching authority.

Reformation Christians can reject such premises and, accordingly, the arguments that hinge upon them. We have excellent reasons to be catholic, reasons that do not commit us to be Roman Catholic.

Incarnation, Trinity, and Marian Dogma

Now we are ready to advance this case by revisiting the Newman-style arguments that try to tie our right to believe in the authority of Scripture and the Nicene Creed to the authority of the Roman magisterium. Let us do so by looking more carefully at a dogma that has the highest dogmatic status possible for Rome: the immaculate conception of Mary, a dogma that has been declared infallibly true ex cathedra by the pope.

Recall that Newman's general strategy is to argue that later doctrinal developments, such as those pertaining to Mary and the pope, are essentially on the same ground as the doctrines of the incarnation and the Trinity. Moreover, he conflates very different kinds of doctrinal developments, namely, (1) those that occur by some sort of necessity or inevitability and (2) those that occur as the result of intellectual action or reflection on the original revelation throughout successive centuries. By this conflation, he attempts to get us to accept the "large accretions" that claim to be legitimate developments of the original revelation.

Recall too that the *Catechism* employs similar language about necessity, particularly in affirming the authority of the magisterium to define dogma. This authority is exercised "when [the magisterium] proposes, in a form obliging the Christian people to an irrevocable adherence of faith, truths contained in divine Revelation or also when it proposes, in a definitive way, truths having a necessary connection with those."[22]

Before proceeding any further, let us ask what is meant by "truths having a necessary connection with those." Here are three different versions of what this might mean.

N1 Every binding dogma not contained explicitly in divine revelation is one that it is necessary to affirm because it is an "inevitable" development from that doctrine.

22. *Catechism*, par. 88.

N2 Every binding dogma not explicitly contained in divine revelation is a truth that necessarily follows from truths that are.

N3 Every binding dogma not explicitly contained in divine revelation is one that is metaphysically necessary by virtue of truths clearly taught in divine revelation.

Now N2 and N3 are obviously much more stringent than N1. Let us consider N2, which is straightforward logical necessity. What sort of example would qualify for N2? Consider the doctrine of the Trinity, a classic doctrine of fundamental significance. It is only implicit in Scripture, but all the components that entail the doctrine are clearly there, such as the full divinity of Christ and the Holy Spirit, as noted above. Once we are clear about these truths, and the fact that the Father is not the Son, and so on, the doctrine of the Trinity follows logically.

Moreover, there is yet another kind of necessity involved here, for Christians typically believe that God is necessarily a Trinity. This is the sort of necessity described in N3. Following Alvin Plantinga's famous account of this matter, we can call this "broadly logical" or a metaphysical necessity.[23] That God is a Trinity is a necessary truth in the same sense that it is a necessary truth that "no prime minister is a prime number" (one of Plantinga's examples of broadly logical necessity).[24] It is a kind of necessity that resides in the very nature of things.

So what about the dogma of the immaculate conception? This doctrine is not explicitly taught in Scripture, so at best it is implicitly taught. In what sense, then, might it have a "necessary connection" with truths that are explicitly part of revelation?

First consider necessity in the sense of N1. Does it appear to be an "inevitable" development in the sense that any thoughtful reader of the NT would ponder this question and have to come to terms with it in the way that the issue of the identity of Christ is inescapably raised? It is highly doubtful that it is inevitable in this sense. Christ says nothing suggesting that he thought his mother was sinless, and indeed at times she seemed, like his brothers, to have misunderstood him and his vocation (Mark 3:20–21, 31–35). It is also remarkable that Mary is not explicitly mentioned *even one time* in the NT epistles, the documents that especially spell out the doctrinal and theological implications of the life, death, and resurrection of Jesus.[25] The fact that there

23. See Plantinga, *The Nature of Necessity* (Oxford: Clarendon, 1974), chap. 1.
24. Ibid., 2.
25. Mary is indirectly alluded to in Gal. 4:4 and perhaps also in 1 Tim. 2:15.

are countless evangelical biblical scholars who have not only a thorough knowledge of the Scriptures but also a deep commitment to their authority, and yet
they do not see the immaculate conception in their pages severely undermines
any suggestion that the doctrine is inevitable in the sense of N1.

What about N2? Does the doctrine perhaps follow by logical necessity from
things that are clearly taught in Christian revelation? Consider this passage
from the *Catechism*: "The angel Gabriel at the moment of the annunciation
salutes her as 'full of grace.' In fact, in order for Mary to be able to give the
free assent of her faith to the announcement of her vocation, it was necessary
that she be wholly borne by God's grace."[26]

Notice particularly the claim that it was "necessary" for Mary to be wholly
borne by God's grace for her to assent to her vocation. The reason for this claim
is far from clear. To be sure, anyone who has a divine vocation requires the
assistance of grace to accept it and carry it out. Indeed, some of the prophets,
such as Jeremiah and John the Baptist, were said to be sanctified or filled with
the Holy Spirit even before they were born (Jer. 1:5; Luke 1:15). But it is another
matter altogether to insist that it necessarily follows from having such a divine
vocation that one must be born without sin and live a completely perfect life.
So it does not seem necessary in the sense of N2. It is not altogether clear
whether this is what the *Catechism* is claiming, but if so, it is highly dubious.

It is worth noting here that Thomas Aquinas rejected the doctrine of immaculate conception as it has been traditionally understood, though he did
affirm that Mary was sanctified in the womb in a sense similar to Jeremiah
and John the Baptist. Still, he rejected the doctrine as it is dogmatically defined
by the Church of Rome.[27]

Nor, finally, does there seem to be a claim of metaphysical necessity in
the sense of N3. Perhaps this is what is actually being affirmed rather than
straightforward logical necessity. But if so, again, this is an extraordinarily
strong claim to assert on such slender grounds. Is it a necessary truth that
Mary had to be immaculately conceived to carry out her vocation in the same
sense that it is necessarily true that God is a Trinity?

The upshot of all this is that there seems to be no strong sense in which
it can plausibly be maintained that the Marian dogmas are "truths having a
necessary connection" to truths clearly contained in the original Christian

26. *Catechism*, par. 490. The biblical text cited ("full of grace"; Douay–Rheims) is from
Luke 1:28.

27. See Francis Beckwith, "The Immaculate Conception, St. Thomas Aquinas, and the Catholic Church," *Return to Rome: Francis Beckwith's Reflections on Faith, Ethics and Culture* (blog),
December 8, 2011, Patheos, http://www.patheos.com/blogs/returntorome/2011/12/the-immac
ulate-conception-st-thomas-aquinas-and-the-catholic-church.

revelation. Moreover, Newman's attempt to argue that such later Roman dogmas are doctrinal developments that parallel the doctrines of incarnation and Trinity badly fails. Neither the quantity nor the quality of material on those later dogmas is even remotely comparable to that supporting the classic creedal doctrines in the original revelation, so there is nothing that logically necessitates those later developments or even makes them inevitable in any sense that commands our assent.

Indeed, there is something obviously wrong when an argument can be mounted that we cannot consistently or rationally believe in classic creedal doctrines without accepting the Marian dogmas and similar claims. Think about it. These arguments claim that we cannot rationally believe doctrines that are utterly central to the Christian revelation, doctrines that have enormous biblical support, unless we believe certain doctrines that have only the most tenuous, if any, biblical support and even little grounding in early tradition.[28] Any theology that advances this claim is fundamentally off-center.

There is, to be sure, an inner coherence and logical relationship between those classic creedal doctrines that compose the heart of our faith. Everything starts, in the order of *knowing*, from the bodily resurrection of Jesus. "If Christ has not been raised, your faith is futile; you are still in your sins" (1 Cor. 15:17). The resurrection was the explosive event that eventually propelled and gave shape to the historic Christian faith. It is the definitive evidence for the deity of Jesus, which leads us straight to the doctrines of atonement and incarnation.[29] And these doctrines, along with the revelation of the Holy Spirit at Pentecost, lead to the doctrine of the Trinity.[30] There are, moreover, logical relations among these doctrines and an inner coherence that weaves them together as a single garment. Denying any of these doctrines begins to unravel the whole.

But here is the question: Can it seriously be maintained that the Marian dogmas have a similar relation to these doctrines? Is denial of the immaculate conception really tantamount to denying the incarnation and the Trinity? Does rejection of this doctrine unravel classic creedal Christianity?[31]

28. Mary is named only four times in the Apostolic Fathers, the patristic sources closest to the original apostles. All four references are in Ignatius of Antioch, and none even hint at the claims asserted by the later Marian dogmas: immaculate conception, bodily assumption, and perpetual virginity. See Ignatius, *To the Ephesians* 7.2; 18.2; 19.1; *To the Trallians* 9.

29. This is not to insist that any particular *theory* of atonement is essential. The creed does not settle that.

30. The order of *being* is exactly the opposite of the order of *knowing* these central Christian doctrines. God was a Trinity from all eternity; the Son of God became incarnate, then atoned for our sins, and then was resurrected.

31. Recall the claim of Pius IX; after defining the dogma in 1854, he declared: "Hence, if anyone shall dare—which God forbid!—to think otherwise than as has been defined by us, let

Protestants, we have argued, have principled reasons for affirming the authority of Scripture and the Nicene Creed while rejecting the claims of the Roman magisterium. The coherence of catholic Reformation Christianity in no way depends on accepting the Marian dogmas or other claims of Roman Catholicism such as papal infallibility and transubstantiation.

For Roman Catholics, however, it is far from clear that their faith in classic creedal doctrines can coherently stand without the Marian dogmas. Again, the basic logic is straightforward: If the immaculate conception is not infallibly true, the doctrine of papal infallibility is not true; and if the doctrine of papal infallibility is not true, the claims of the Roman magisterium to have exclusive authority to define dogma are not true. And the claim to such exclusive authority by Rome is apparent in the claim we have been examining in this chapter that "sacred Tradition, Sacred Scripture, and the Magisterium of the Church are so connected and associated that one of them cannot stand without the others." In short, the credibility of the entire Roman Catholic authority structure hinges on the infallible truth of the immaculate conception. Those who are not dogmatically committed to Rome may see here a house of cards waiting to fall. And that is a good reason to think Roman authority claims are fundamentally mistaken.

Deep Disagreement despite Deeper Agreement

As we conclude this chapter, let us consider some comments on the nature of revelation from contemporary Roman Catholic theologian Matthew Levering. His recent book on revelation is deeply informed not only by biblical exegesis but also by broad ecumenical sympathies. We find ourselves in the interesting position that we largely agree with Levering's account of revelation, even as we profoundly disagree with him about a number of particular doctrinal claims. Near the end of his book he writes as follows: "Against all ecclesiastical fall narratives, I have argued in this book that the Church truthfully mediates God's revelation to us, due to the efficacious missions of the Son and the Holy Spirit. . . . The Holy Spirit's inspiration of Scripture and the Holy Spirit's guidance of the people of God are inextricably bound together."[32] By "ecclesiastical fall narratives," Levering means those

---

him know and understand that he is condemned by his own judgment; that he has suffered shipwreck in the faith; that he has separated from the unity of the Church." *The Immaculate Conception*, Papal Encyclicals Online, http://www.papalencyclicals.net/Pius09/p9ineff.htm.

32. Levering, *Engaging the Doctrine of Revelation: The Mediation of the Gospel through Church and Scripture* (Grand Rapids: Baker Academic, 2014), 286.

accounts of the history of the church that view it as the story of one long departure from the purity of the apostolic age. By contrast, Levering insists on the continuing guidance of the Holy Spirit in the church. Yet what he means by the church here is a bit ambiguous. Does he mean the Church of Rome? Or does he mean the larger church as composed of all those who have faith in Christ and have been baptized into his body? In any case, we agree with Levering on this: the very claim that God has revealed himself in the Christian revelation entails that the church has faithfully mediated that revelation; indeed, that has been one of the central convictions driving this chapter. But what one means by "the Church" will determine what one means by the claim that "the Church" truthfully mediates God's revelation.

Several pages later, Levering reiterates this crucial claim about revelation and elaborates on it as follows:

> In my view, however, Christians should be loath to grant that the Holy Spirit has not ensured the fidelity of the Church's doctrinal development. Indeed, Christians are generally agreed about the truthfulness of the doctrinal developments of the first few centuries. For persons who deny that the Holy Spirit has ever guided the Church (or, for that matter, that the Holy Spirit has ever existed), it makes sense to reject a consistent Tradition or doctrinal development. But it does not make sense for the Christian to do so, especially once one recognizes that doctrine develops in ways that reflect historical vitality rather than a strict logical unfolding.[33]

This passage is reminiscent of some of those passages from Newman that we analyzed earlier. It begins with a claim that is not only highly plausible but should be readily accepted by most orthodox Christians (again, depending on what one means by "the Church"). But it concludes with one that is much more dubious, which the author seems to think should follow for anyone who accepts the earlier claim about the work of the Holy Spirit in ensuring the fidelity of doctrinal development. Notice the claim that "doctrine develops in ways that reflect historical vitality rather than a strict logical unfolding."

And here is where fundamental differences once again emerge between Reformation Christians and our Roman brothers and sisters. As Levering declares, we can agree with the "truthfulness of the doctrinal developments of the first few centuries," and we have good reason to believe that the same Holy Spirit who inspired Scripture also granted discernment and insight to the church as it gave formal definition to those central doctrines revealed in Scripture. But it is another matter altogether to suggest that later Roman

33. Ibid., 296.

Catholic claims are equally warranted by the observation that "doctrine develops in ways that reflect historical vitality." Despite the positive, dynamic connotations of this phrase, it is far too vague and open-ended to provide a satisfactory criterion for legitimate doctrinal development. Indeed, it is quite reminiscent of Newman's appeal to the "intellectual action through successive generations, which is the organ of development."

Recall from chapter 4 that Newman not only conflated this view of doctrinal development with more restrained and modest ones but that he also used this more expansive view to defend the whole Roman panoply of doctrinal claims and to argue that consistency requires accepting all or accepting none. But Reformation Christians will insist that there are principled reasons for accepting those earlier doctrinal developments while rejecting those that appeal to "intellectual action through successive generations" or "historical vitality" to warrant them.

Those principled reasons stem from the Reformation principle of sola Scriptura, rightly understood. As we have noticed, this principle is misrepresented not only by its critics but also sometimes by its advocates as well. Michael Allen and Scott R. Swain provide a timely caution against contemporary distortions of this principle.

> Indeed, *sola Scriptura* has served for some moderns as a banner for private judgment and against catholicity. In so doing, however, churches and Christians have turned from *sola Scriptura* to *solo Scriptura*, a bastard child nursed at the breast of modern rationalism and individualism. Even the Reformational doctrine of perspicuity has been transformed in much popular Christianity and some scholarly reflection as well to function as the theological equivalent of philosophical objectivity, namely, the belief that any objective observer can, by the use of appropriate measures, always gain the appropriate interpretation of a biblical text.[34]

Again, insofar as we truly have reason to believe in biblical authority, we have reason to believe the doctrines of catholic Christianity. But the principle of sola Scriptura is essential to providing the proper constraints on any theological developments that result from "intellectual action through successive generations" or from "historical vitality" if they are rightly to demand our assent.

This is not to say, as Levering suggests it might, that the only legitimate doctrinal development is development that occurs by "strict logical unfolding." But it is to say that any dogma that can claim to bind the Christian conscience must have substantial support from clear biblical teaching. In this connection

---

34. Allen and Swain, *Reformed Catholicity*, 85.

it is significant and quite telling that Newman insistently rejected this sort of scriptural constraint in his account of doctrinal development.

> It may be objected that its [the Church's] inspired documents at once determine the limits of its mission without further trouble; but ideas are in the writer and reader of the revelation, not the inspired text itself; and the question is whether those ideas which the letter conveys from writer to reader, reach the reader at once in their completeness and accuracy on his first perception of them, or whether they open out in his intellect and grow to perfection in the course of time. Nor could it surely be maintained without extravagance that the letter of the New Testament, or of any assignable number of books, comprises a delineation of all possible forms which the divine message will assume when submitted to a multitude of minds.[35]

Several things are worth noticing here to underscore the crucial role of sola Scriptura in legitimate doctrinal development. First, Newman suggests that the only alternative to his view is to believe that "those ideas which the letter conveys from writer to reader, reach the reader at once in their completeness and accuracy on his first perception of them." As is often the case, his rhetoric is grossly misleading, for those who reject Newman's account of development obviously need not assume anything as absurd as the notion that the full meaning of Scripture is instantly understood at first sight. Second, Newman suggests that on his view, the truths in Scripture only "grow to perfection in the course of time." Now it is one thing to say that our understanding of Scripture grows closer to perfection over the course of time and reflection, but it is another matter altogether to say the message itself grows to perfection. Third, notice Newman's claim that the ideas in the Christian revelation are not in the text but "in the writer and reader of the revelation." This is a telling observation in its own right, but it also leads to the fourth point, which we particularly want to emphasize. Newman apparently wants to legitimize "all possible forms which the divine message will assume when submitted to a multitude of minds."

This is the sort of claim that Newman recognizes he must make to support his contention that the whole Roman panoply represents authoritative doctrinal development. He is keenly aware that the express teaching of Scripture will not support those "large accretions," nor will the early history of the church. But he thinks they can be legitimized if one accepts as true development "all possible forms which the divine message will assume when submitted to a multitude of minds."

35. Newman, *Essay*, 56–57.

Later in the same chapter, Newman advances a similar claim: "It is in point to notice also the structure and style of Scripture, a structure so unsystematic and various, and a style so figurative and indirect, that no one would presume at first sight to say what is in it and what is not. . . . Of no doctrine whatever, which does not actually contradict what has been delivered, can it be peremptorily asserted that it is not in Scripture."[36] Again, Newman is highly tendentious in his rhetoric when he speaks of presuming "at first sight" to know what is in Scripture or of "peremptorily" determining what is not. We can agree with this while insisting that his observation does not rule out that a community of well-informed, thoughtful, patient readers can determine what is and what is not in Scripture. Notice also Newman's appeal to the "figurative and indirect" style of Scripture. The reason for this is obvious: the Marian dogmas have little if any "direct" support from Scripture, so any viable claim to biblical support must come by way of various figurative interpretations of Scripture.

But most significant, notice how difficult it is on Newman's terms to show that a doctrine is not in Scripture: no doctrine can be ruled out if it "does not actually contradict what has been delivered." We cannot determine that a doctrine is not in Scripture by showing that it lacks express biblical support or by showing that it is not in any substantial sense necessarily connected with doctrines that do have such support. For Newman, one cannot show that a doctrine is not in Scripture unless it actually contradicts what clearly is in Scripture.

Given Newman's project of providing an account of doctrinal development that warrants all the claims of Rome, these sorts of moves are altogether understandable. But for those who are not committed to Rome, they have little to commend them.

Indeed, precisely the sort of extravagance that Newman defends is what the principle of sola Scriptura intends to guard against. It is our minds (and imaginations) that must be submitted to the revelation, and not the revelation submitted to our minds. We are not warranted in thinking that any idea that might be generated by a "multitude of minds" reflecting on Christian revelation is a viable candidate for a binding dogma. Again, this does not mean that our minds do not play a key role in the reception and perception of divine revelation, particularly the corporate mind of the church. But it does mean that legitimate doctrinal development is constrained by clear scriptural support.

Such clear scriptural support will be further reflected in the ecumenical sense of the corporate church, a consensus that goes beyond the Church of Rome.

36. Ibid., 71.

The *Catechism* recognizes the sense of the faithful as a crucial indicator of doctrinal truth because this sense is produced by the anointing of the Holy Spirit. "The whole body of the faithful . . . cannot err in matters of belief. This characteristic is shown in the supernatural appreciation of faith (*sensus fidei*) on the part of the whole people, when from bishops to the last of the faithful, they manifest a universal consent in matters of faith and morals."[37]

It is precisely this sort of "universal consent" that is enjoyed by the doctrines of the Nicene Creed. These doctrines are shared among all branches of the church: Eastern, Roman, and Reformation. By contrast, the doctrines of papal infallibility and the doctrines that have been declared infallible ex cathedra enjoy no similar universal consent. They are therefore hardly catholic in the classic sense of the word. To the contrary, they have occasioned, exacerbated, and sustained division within the church, separating Rome from other Christians. Commenting on this reality, C. S. Lewis makes this telling observation: "In a word, the whole set-up of modern Romanism seems to me to be as much a provincial or local *variation* from the central, ancient tradition as any particular Protestant sect is."[38] The fact that Rome is provincial in significant ways is another reason to think there are principled grounds for accepting the catholic faith while rejecting certain claims of the Roman magisterium. In short, ironic though it is, the Church of Rome is not sufficiently catholic.

37. *Catechism*, par. 92, quoting Pope Paul VI, *Lumen Gentium: Dogmatic Constitution on the Church*, sec. 12 (ellipsis original), the Holy See, 1964, http://www.vatican.va/archive/hist_councils/ii_vatican_council/documents/vat-ii_const_19641121_lumen-gentium_en.html.
38. C. S. Lewis, *The Collected Letters of C. S. Lewis*, vol. 2, ed. Walter Hooper (New York: HarperSanFrancisco, 2004), 647.

6

The Church, Part I

Excavating Rome's Exclusive Ecclesial Claims

One of the pieces of technology that helped to foster the Reformation was the Gutenberg printing press, which was up and running by the middle of the fifteenth century and issued a rapid advance in the dissemination of knowledge. Taking advantage of this newfangled resource, Luther published a German translation of the NT in 1522, shortly after his excommunication *from* Rome, using the text of Erasmus (*Novum instrumentum*) as a foundation, and the entire Bible was produced in German by 1534. The fresh text of Erasmus (Luther had employed the second edition of 1519) not only represented the best scholarship of the day but also ushered in a much-needed advance over the earlier translation of Jerome known as the Latin Vulgate. Consider Matthew 3:2 ("Repent, for the kingdom of heaven has come near") as rendered by this Latin church father: "et dicens paenitentiam agite adpropinquavit enim regnum caelorum."[1] The problem here was that the Latin *paenitentiam* was often understood in the context of medieval Christianity as "to do penance," a meaning that actually departs from the original Greek word "μετανοεῖτε," which is most suitably translated as "repent" in the sense of "having a change of mind" or even of "turning around to face a new direction."[2]

---

1. *Biblia Sacra Vulgata: Iuxta Vulgatem Versionem*, electronic edition of the 3rd ed. (Stuttgart: Deutsche Bibelgesellschaft, 1969), Matt. 3:2.
2. Vincent points out that μετάνοια (repentance) is therefore primarily an afterthought, different from the former thought: *a change of mind which issues in regret and in change of*

Mindful of the earlier work of Wycliffe, who had produced an English translation of the Bible from the Vulgate by the latter part of the fourteenth century, Henry VIII, though he broke from Rome, actually opposed the efforts of William Tyndale in his own day; his opposition was partly due to what he deemed to be the inordinate influence of Luther, and of doctrinal reform in general, upon the gifted translator.[3] During much of the sixteenth century the Roman Catholic Church, for its part, was likewise reluctant to support the broad vernacularization of the Bible, placing it in the hands of common people as championed by the Protestant Reformers, Luther and Calvin among them. Though Rome eventually produced an English New Testament in 1582 at Rheims, France, and the full Bible in 1609 to 1610, known as the Douay–Rheims translation, these works must be distinguished from Protestant efforts in two key respects. First, the Roman Catholic version was much later than William Tyndale's New Testament which was printed in about 1525, Myles Coverdale's Bible in 1535, and Thomas Cranmer's Great Bible in 1539. Second, Tyndale, along with other Protestant translators, worked with a Greek text, not the Latin Vulgate, for the New Testament.

One of the hierarchy's likely concerns, given the late appearance of the Douay–Rheims version, was that if the laity of the time (this term "laity," by the way, is foreign to the pages of the NT) read the sacred Scriptures for themselves in their own tongue, they might discern, among other things, a jarring difference between the church as depicted in the Bible and the church as they had come to know it in daily life, largely through the teaching of priests.

Despite this initial, salient observation, we are by no means suggesting that this dissonance between the church as displayed in the pages of the Bible and the church in current understandings is merely a Roman Catholic problem. Indeed, it is a *Christian* issue that includes the different theological and liturgical locations of both Eastern Orthodoxy and Protestantism as well. The key element here that is common to all these traditions, posing this problem afresh, is simply the passage of time, the flow of history, by means of which earlier understandings of the church can subtly, and sometimes not so subtly, be transformed into new meanings. From our reading of the history of the church, no contemporary tradition faithfully reproduces NT

---

conduct. See Marvin Richardson Vincent, *Word Studies in the New Testament* (New York: Scribner, 1887), 1:23.

3. Henry VIII was very conservative theologically and much preferred the theology of the *Six Articles* to anything of the reform that was being produced on the continent. In fact, there was a planned purge of the evangelicals in England on the basis of the *Articles* that fortunately was halted by Henry himself. See Derek Wilson, *A Brief History of the English Reformation* (London: Running Press, 2012), Kindle edition, locations 4051–53.

Christianity in its entirety (although some have tried), simply because these same communions of faith invariably judge later articulations of doctrine, order, and practice (christological judgments and the doctrine of the Trinity readily come to mind) to be essential to "the faith." We therefore certainly agree that historical development is necessary in order to render explicit what is implicit in NT Christianity or in the canon of Scripture, for example, as well as to offer the gospel in a way that will be heard from age to age. We are not, after all, primitivists, unaware of the importance and necessity of historical development and the importance of tradition. Perhaps, then, the key distinction, given the passage of time, is between what is essential (*diaphora*) to the faith and what is unessential (*adiaphora*) to it, or, to express the issue more strongly, what preserves the heart of the Christian faith, in the midst of change, and what in reality distorts or even at times undermines it.

The Strange New World of the Bible

During the early twentieth century Karl Barth, in his engaging essay "The Strange New World within the Bible," highlighted the difference between modern realities and the world that is actually revealed in the Bible.[4] If rightly perceived by readers, this difference can be unsettling in a good way by presenting key insights into the mystery of the kingdom of God as well as offering possibilities for transformation and renewal. However, in order to see that world aright, we may have to shuck off some traditional teachings that have been heard again and again and are no doubt popular but that are actually nowhere to be found in that remarkable world and may in the end even distort it.

To be sure, the early church that is evident in the pages of Scripture can in three principal ways challenge much later understandings of the church, many of which are historical products. First of all, readers cannot help but be impressed by the generous and embracing unity of the early church. From the birthday of the church at Pentecost, where diverse populations each heard the message of that day in their own native tongue, to the unity expressed by Paul in his Letter to the Ephesians, "There is one body and one Spirit, just as you were called to one hope when you were called; one Lord, one faith, one baptism; one God and Father of all, who is over all and through all and in all" (4:4–6), the clear and preeminent message is that the church is one. Observe that this oneness is not sustained by the church looking to any of its human leaders in a horizontal way, so to speak—"One of you says, 'I

---

4. See Barth, "The Strange New World within the Bible," in *The Word of God and the Word of Man* (Gloucester, MA: Peter Smith, 1978), 28–50.

follow Paul'; another, 'I follow Apollos'; another, 'I follow Cephas'" (1 Cor.
1:12a)—but precisely by looking beyond them with vertical lift, if you will, to
Christ the Lord and to God the Father, who transcend the church in beauty,
power, and holiness. Simply put, the unity of the church is *in* Christ, the
Son, and in God the Father; it is not in any member of the church, however
exalted or celebrated.

Second, the first-century church has no life apart from the Holy Spirit of
the risen Christ, the Spirit of God given in miracle-working splendor and
power at Pentecost. Indeed, from the perspectives of the apostles it is simply impossible to be a Christian apart from the Holy Spirit. Accordingly,
the church as the living body of Christ is animated by no one less than the
Spirit of God. Paul makes this point decisively in his observation, "If anyone
does not have the Spirit of Christ, they do not belong to Christ" (Rom. 8:9).
Indeed, the guidance, correction, and care through the Holy Spirit in terms
of the members of the body of Christ were so richly appreciated in the early
church that the author of 1 John highlights this superintending role of the
Holy Spirit by directing believers to the Spirit as their principal teacher and
guide: "As for you, the anointing you received from him remains in you, and
you do not need anyone to teach you. But as his anointing teaches you about
all things and as that anointing is real, not counterfeit—just as it has taught
you, remain in him" (2:27).

Third, the unity of the church is understood in terms of genuine *transcen-
dence*, going beyond all-too-human divisions to be *in* Christ, who is over
all; and the *immanence* of the Holy Spirit animates the body of Christ in
an abundance of chrisms now properly appreciated, whereby believers are
anointed with that gracious presence in holy love for service; hence it is not
surprising to learn of the repeated emphasis of the first-century church on the
fellowship of the saints, on the basic equality of all believers in the church.
On this point Jesus was emphatic: "But you are not to be called 'Rabbi,' for
you have one Teacher, and you are all brothers. And do not call anyone on
earth 'father,' for you have one Father, and he is in heaven. Nor are you to be
called instructors, for you have one Instructor, the Messiah" (Matt. 23:8–10).
In each case, Jesus points in a transcending way either to himself as Lord or to
his Father, who is in heaven. Thus, no human power can substitute for what in
reality is a divine role. Moreover, the apostle Paul, for his part, also thought
through the implications of the revelation of God as revealed in Jesus Christ,
through the power of the Holy Spirit, in a way that disrupted some human
structures: the common, sinful hierarchies of the day that kept the "other"
in its subordinate, "proper" place: "There is neither Jew nor Gentile, neither
slave nor free, nor is there male and female, for you are all one in Christ Jesus"

(Gal. 3:28). To be a member of the body of Christ in the first century, then, was nothing less than a taste of heaven.

The Church as Understood by Rome

When the *Catechism* or Vatican II documents or even encyclical letters are consulted, it is readily apparent to historians, at least, that the basic definition of the church as found in these materials gathers up historical products, some of which were literally centuries in the making. To illustrate, embedded in the Roman Catholic understanding of the church, in a way that does not characterize first-century Christianity, is the notion of "hierarchy," of ascending and graded distinctions within the church. Thus the *Catechism* defines the body of Christ, in part, as a "society structured with hierarchical organs,"[5] and asserts that the Holy Spirit "bestows upon the Church varied hierarchic and charismatic gifts."[6] Much earlier, Robert Bellarmine, in his attempt to refute Protestant divines, argued that the church is a "specific type of community (*coetus hominum*)"[7] that is marked by three leading traits: "The one and true Church is the community of men brought together by the profession of the same Christian *faith* and conjoined in the communion of the same *sacraments*, under the *government* of the legitimate pastors and especially the one vicar of Christ on earth, the Roman pontiff."[8] The emphasis on this same troika of faith, sacraments, and hierarchical governance can be found more recently in the encyclical *Ut Unum Sint*, proclaimed in May 1995 by John Paul II. On the unity of the church, the late bishop of Rome wrote as follows: "It is a unity constituted by the bonds of the profession of faith, the sacraments and hierarchical communion."[9]

We do not disagree that later elements, beyond first-century Christianity, will no doubt be necessary in order to comprehend the church aright in the fullness of its witness. Our chief concern, however, is that any elements identified by later theological traditions must be in utter harmony with the gracious realities of the primitive church, especially in terms of its most basic posture of union in Christ, a genuine fellowship of the saints, by means of the superintending and ever-present Holy Spirit. In the following analysis we will

---

5. *Catechism of the Catholic Church*, 2nd ed. (Mahwah, NJ: Paulist Press, 1994), par. 771.
6. Ibid., par. 768.
7. Avery Dulles, *Models of the Church* (New York: Random House, 2002), 16.
8. Ibid. (emphasis added).
9. Pope John Paul II, *Ut Unum Sint: On Commitment to Ecumenism*, sec. 9, the Holy See, 1995, http://w2.vatican.va/content/john-paul-ii/en/encyclicals/documents/hf_jp-ii_enc_25051 995_ut-unum-sint.html.

lift up the marks or characteristics of the church that hail not from the first century but from the fourth century, the time of Theodosius I and the Second Ecumenical Council, held at Constantinople in 381. More to the point, in its reflections this second great council not only modified, in some sense, the earlier work of Nicaea in 325 in order to produce the Niceno-Constantinopolitan Creed, but it also highlighted the four leading attributes of the church (one, holy, catholic, and apostolic), which are as helpful today as they were then.

The Church Is One

Citing the very same passage noted above, the authors of the *Catechism* maintain that the church is one in that "she acknowledges one Lord, confesses one faith, is born of one Baptism, forms only one Body, is given life by the one Spirit, for the sake of one hope (cf. Eph. 4:3–5), at whose fulfillment all divisions will be overcome."[10] In subsequent observations, however, this unity is not explored in terms of the entirety of the church in its historic fullness under the lordship of Christ, but instead everything is referred to and devolves upon a particular theological tradition, that of Rome. The *Catechism*, for example, declares: "This Church, constituted and organized as a society in the present world, subsists in (*subsistit in*) the [Roman] Catholic Church, which is governed by the successor of Peter and by the bishops in communion with him."[11] In this judgment, which was literally centuries in the making, Rome is at the very center of things, in which a part of the church has unfortunately been mistaken for the whole (e.g., where is Eastern Orthodoxy?). Subtle but no less significant has been this shift of attention: from Christ, in whom all union rightly subsists, to a particular theological tradition, the Roman church. What is more, Rome as the center of unity, so the documents of Vatican II go on to claim, is something that can never be lost: "This unity, we believe, dwells in the [Roman] Catholic Church as something she can never lose, and we hope that it will continue to increase until the end of time."[12] However, a unity that is found only in Rome and that it can never lose regardless of its moral and spiritual behavior (think of the lives of some of the popes, for instance) or regardless of what doctrinal innovations it eagerly embraces in the name of ongoing tradition—all of this suggests not the proper grounding

10. *Catechism*, par. 866.
11. Ibid., par. 816.
12. *Reflections and Suggestions concerning Ecumenical Dialogue*, sec. II.2.d, in *The Conciliar and Post Conciliar Documents*, vol. 1 of *Vatican Council II*, ed. Austin Flannery (Collegeville, MN: Liturgical Press, 1996), 541.

of any theological communion but the claim of a particular one that ever seeks to maintain a monopoly of ecclesiastical power and privilege. Indeed, it is the pretense to such power and the attempt to hold it unswervingly within the broader Christian community that invariably leads to the diminishment of all other theological traditions, at least in some sense, such as Eastern Orthodoxy and, of course, Protestantism.

The shift from the proper grounding of Ephesians 4 to an understanding of the unity of the church centered on the Vatican has, ironically enough, proved to be remarkably disruptive with respect to the fellowship of the saints, that is, when the broader body of Christ is considered. As noted in chapter 5, it was not Rome's stance at the Third Synod of Toledo in 589 that was actually the spark of schism, though it did create a distinct theological tradition. Other elements would have to be brought into play before such a rupture of fellowship would occur. Indeed, the ancient ecumenical church of the time, in our view, was more than capable of maintaining unity even in the face of some the theological differences between the Latin and Greek traditions. However, relations between Rome and Constantinople, so to speak, continued to be strained in the sixth and on into the seventh century. Gerald Bray, for example, observes that "the two parts of the Christian world were becoming strangers to one another, a fact that was confirmed after the Council in Trullo (691–92), when the Eastern churches sorted out the rules by which they were to be governed."[13] By the ninth century, relations had soured and love was lost, especially during the Photian schism (863–67), when Nicholas I, the bishop of Rome, insisted on making claims to authority and governance over lands that were rightly overseen by the Orthodox. Greatly overstepping his authority, Nicholas even declared Photius, the Eastern patriarch, deposed.[14]

Not surprisingly, theological accusations flew back and forth during this fray such that by 870 the pope and the patriarch of Constantinople had excommunicated each other.[15] Moreover, the East was indeed claiming that Rome was theologically deficient precisely because of its interpolation (of *filioque*) into the historic Nicene Creed, but the schism at its root, at its very heart, also appears to have been about the broader issue of power and its repeated abuse. Indeed, it was precisely the Roman understanding of the oneness of the church, once again centered on Rome, that was at the heart of all the trouble.

13. Bray, *The Church: A Theological and Historical Account* (Grand Rapids: Baker Academic, 2016), 104.

14. Earle E. Cairns, *Christianity through the Centuries: A History of the Christian Church*, 3rd rev. ed. (Grand Rapids: Zondervan, 2009), Kindle edition, location 3647.

15. Susan Lynn Peterson, *Timeline Charts of the Western Church* (Grand Rapids: Zondervan, 1999), 75.

Therefore it was inevitable, in our judgment, that a misplaced center, one that celebrated the particular over the universal, the human (pope as head) over the divine (Christ as head), and at times to the exclusion or diminishment of others, would in the end be disruptive. Remember that from the Roman perspective, then as now, the unity of the church must be understood in terms of three principal things: right faith, valid sacraments, and proper governance, understood as being under the hierarchical authority of the bishop of Rome. Twentieth- and twenty-first-century popes have maintained the very same things: not even Vatican II has changed this.

Schism One: East and West

The formal schism between East and West erupted in 1054, when Michael Cerularius condemned the Western church for its use of unleavened bread in the Eucharist. Such a practice was not at the heart of the various differences between the East and the West; it was simply its most recent and not-all-that-important expression. Sensing broader difficulties, Pope Leo IX sent Cardinal Humbert as his ambassador to resolve the dispute with the East, but in the end the cardinal placed a decree of excommunication on the high altar of the historic church of Saint Sophia, thereby giving public expression to a schism in the Christian church that was literally centuries in the making. Efforts were made to overcome this breach of holy love on a few occasions, most notably at the Council of Ferrara-Florence in the fifteenth century, but in the end discussions broke down. Once again the Eastern bishops left a council with issues of governance and power on their mind, and in frustration they exclaimed: "Better the turban of the Prophet than the tiara of the pope."[16]

Though schism is rightly defined as a breach, a rupture, or a separation in the church, and though doctrinal differences are clearly important, it must also be borne in mind that schism represents a loss of communion, at least in some sense, and therefore it marks a deficiency in love, which should overcome such differences for the sake of the larger good of a common Lord. Such a holy love, marked by the unifying bonds of filial affection and care, should have been the very emblem of the body of Christ to the world, as Jesus himself had proclaimed: "My prayer is . . . that all of them may be one, Father, just as you are in me and I am in you. May they also be in us so that the world may believe that you have sent me" (John 17:20–21). Thus schism is so serious not only because it represents a fault in terms of how the church is to

16. Ibid., 120.

be rightly understood in its very grounding, often confusing *adiaphora* with *diaphora*, but also because it strikes at the substance of the church's mission, its witness to the world.

Yet another consequence of Rome's misplaced center is its failure to recognize, in a factually accurate and forthright way, its own involvement in the Great Schism of the eleventh century. "When East and West split apart, for example, the Western Church spoke of the 'Eastern schism,'" as Bray points out, "but to the Eastern church it was the 'Western (papal) schism—as it still is today."[17] To be sure, not even Vatican II documents fully acknowledge the culpability and responsibility that should have been freely acknowledged and that, by the way, is so readily seen by others both within and without the church. For example, in the *Decree on Ecumenism* the Roman church lays the lion's share of the blame for separation and for the impulse to schism itself not on Western Christianity but on developments in the East. Indeed, this document maintains that "the first divisions occurred in the East,"[18] though it is likely referring to the earlier schisms in the wake of the Councils of Ephesus, in which Nestorianism was condemned, or perhaps even the later disruption at Chalcedon, when the Coptic Orthodox Church was effectively alienated by Pope Leo's Tome (doctrinal letter *To Flavian*). At any rate, even though Rome does not apply the exact language of "Churches and ecclesial communities came to be separated *from* the Apostolic See of Rome" to Eastern Orthodoxy as Rome does to Protestantism, the implication, when broader teachings are considered, is nevertheless much the same. Rome still insists that the Orthodox, like Protestants, must find their way to obedience and to being properly related to "the one vicar of Christ on earth, the Roman pontiff."[19] What is more, entertaining a traditionalist viewpoint (for the sake of argument) that apparently still lingers among some, even in the face of Vatican II, William Thompson-Uberuaga points out that "the Orthodox churches are both in a state of schism with the Roman Catholic Church as well as formal heresy."[20] See figure 6.1 for a comparison between the Roman view and the Protestant view on the schisms of the church.

Beyond this, the Roman Catholic Church has also tried to mute the seriousness as well as the extent of its own involvement in the schism by claiming that the mutual excommunications of 1054 simply entailed "the Patriarch

17. Bray, *Church*, 115.

18. *Unitatis Redintegratio: Decree on Ecumenism*, sec. 13, in Flannery, *Conciliar and Post Conciliar Documents*, 463.

19. Dulles, *Models of the Church*, 16.

20. Thompson-Uberuaga, "Continuity amidst Disruption: The Spirit and Apostolic Succession at the Reformation," *Horizons* 29, no. 2 (2002): 293.

Figure 6.1

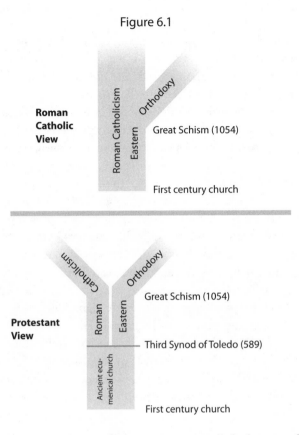

Michael Cerularius and two other persons, . . . [and] the legates of the Roman See led by Cardinal Humbert."[21] The limitation of the censure here simply to the immediate people involved (with tempers flaring, by the way, and angry denunciations in the air) appears to be the later perspective of a more irenic, ecumenically minded church that now feels compelled to approach some of the ugly facts of church history with "new understandings." Though Vatican II did at least recognize that events in the eleventh century "eventually led to the effective rupture of ecclesiastical communion,"[22] it nevertheless, once again, did not take its fair share of the blame.

In light of this last observation consider this: the failure of the Roman Catholic Church to acknowledge fully its part in the Great Schism of 1054

21. *The Common Declaration of Pope Paul VI and Patriarch Athenagoras*, par. 2, in Flannery, *Conciliar and Post Conciliar Documents*, 471.
22. *Common Declaration of Pope Paul VI and Patriarch Athenagoras*, par. 4.c, in Flannery, *Conciliar and Post Conciliar Documents* , 472.

is like a divorced man who tells his friends that he has never been divorced because he feels that he was not at fault and that it "was done to him." It seldom works that way. Almost always when there is division in the face of a prior unity, both parties are involved, and ample evidence shows that to be the case here. Furthermore, though the unity of the ancient ecumenical church (though not its formal unity) was long gone by the time of this Great Schism, as the theological traditions of the East and the West had increasingly distinguished themselves—and at times in contrarian ways, especially after the sixth century—the events of 1054 demonstrated that every theological tradition today, not excluding Roman Catholicism or Eastern Orthodoxy, has been a part of a prior schism. In short, there are no unsplit churches any longer. Indeed, when John Paul II was asked about the lasting separations that characterize the contemporary church (which, of course, includes Protestantism as well), he not only attributed this to human sin and failure (a point on which we believe all can agree) but also went on to state something remarkable, given his own understanding of the church, by conjecturing that perhaps the current separated situation was "a signal that the Spirit wants to bring us to a greater appreciation of pluralism and diversity."[23] For our part, we believe that the unity, the oneness of the church, can be affirmed and that orthodoxy can be maintained in the face of differing theological traditions (in which the essential is affirmed and the unessential is not mistaken for the essential), so long as just one of these traditions is not itself made the center.

The Church Is Holy

The Holy One of Israel as revealed to the world in Jesus Christ through the power of the Holy Spirit is expressed in the Bible so simply and yet so ably in the pithy statement "God is love" (1 John 4:16). That love is not just any love; it is uncanny and distinct. Moreover, if that love is not defined properly, in accordance with the humble, sacrificial love displayed at Calvary, it can easily be misunderstood by the substitution of some human value (e.g., pride) that fails to appreciate the divine splendor and glory. Accordingly, the love of God that is celebrated in the church from age to age is not just any love; it is holy love, a love that bespeaks the radiance and beauty of the divine being.

The church, then, as the living body of Christ, is holy precisely because the Holy Spirit has been given at Pentecost. That is, the Holy Spirit animates the body corporately in its mission to the world and personally in the

23. Thompson-Uberuaga, "Continuity amidst Disruption," 295.

depths—however unfathomable they are—of those who believe in God's only begotten Son. The church, enlivened by the Spirit, has been washed "with water through the word" so that it may be "without stain or wrinkle or any other blemish, . . . holy and blameless" (Eph. 5:25–27). Furthermore, the apostle Paul's prayer for the community of faith is, "May God himself, the God of peace, sanctify you through and through. May your whole spirit, soul and body be kept blameless at the coming of our Lord Jesus Christ" (1 Thess. 5:23). The *Catechism of the Catholic Church* expresses these same truths in the following observation: "The Church is holy: the Most Holy God is her author; Christ, her bridegroom, gave himself up to make her holy; the Spirit of holiness gives her life."[24]

This giving of the Holy Spirit, whereby believers are made holy, is so vital to the life of the church that it marks a genuine before-and-after reality, as revealed in the words of Jesus: "Truly I tell you, among those born of women there has not risen anyone greater than John the Baptist; yet whoever is least in the kingdom of heaven is greater than he" (Matt. 11:11). Again, Jesus proclaimed to his followers: "'Whoever believes in me, as Scripture has said, rivers of living water will flow from within them.' By this he meant the Spirit, whom those who believed in him were later to receive. Up to that time the Spirit had not been given, since Jesus had not yet been glorified" (John 7:38–39). Furthermore, when Jesus taught Nicodemus, a key Jewish religious leader, about the quickening power of the Holy Spirit in the new birth, he underscored the abiding truth that the Spirit is sovereign and that human beings are not in control, especially in this special area. "The wind blows wherever it pleases. You hear its sound, but you cannot tell where it comes from or where it is going. So it is with everyone born of the Spirit" (John 3:8).

These pungent observations of Jesus underscore the precious truth that holiness, apart from the person and work of the Holy Spirit, is not a human possibility; it is not a human work or achievement; it is not something that people could ever bring about by themselves through their own resources but indicates a dependent relationship whereby they receive the gift of the lordship of Christ with the accompanying Holy Spirit, a gift that marks all the children of God. Again, holiness is not a human prerogative in the sense that undertaking serious studies or taking up some moral-improvement program will necessarily result in or require the Spirit's presence. The new birth, then, resplendent in Spirit-created holiness, cannot be brought about even by human will, as the apostle John declared: "But to all who received him, who believed in his name, he gave power to become children of God, who were born, not

---

24. *Catechism*, par. 867.

of blood or of the will of the flesh or of the will of man, but of God" (John 1:12–13 NRSV). In addition, the Spirit most assuredly cannot be controlled, manipulated, or bought (remember Simon Magus, Acts 8:9–24). The Spirit makes the church holy as a distinct community, a peculiar people, and whoever testifies to Jesus Christ as Lord does so through a sheer gift, to be received by grace through faith. Martin Luther expressed the ongoing dependence of the Christian believer upon a transcendent God: "[The believer] lives in Christ through faith, in his neighbor through love. By faith he is caught up beyond himself into God. By love he descends beneath himself into his neighbor."[25]

Though the church militant is holy, it is not utterly so. Sin, evil, and failure, at least in part, are also characteristics of the church on earth, in contrast to the church triumphant, which reigns with Christ in heaven. However, the theologically naïve among us, both Roman Catholics and Protestants, have a difficult time discerning, much less acknowledging, the self-interest, the shortsightedness, and even the genuine harm at times done by the "saints" in the name of God. Christ, however, was not so deceived and offered an eye-opening parable to his followers, that of "the wheat and the tares," in which he cautioned against the attempt to utterly remove the tares, an action that, though apparently well intentioned, nevertheless would result in the genuine evil of the destruction of at least some of the wheat as well. Again, consider the mystery of iniquity that found its way into the hearts of Ananias and Sapphira, members of the early church, who, in the very midst of an act of charity, nevertheless lied to the Holy Spirit (Acts 5:1–11), with tragic results. Moreover, bear in mind the Corinthian church that gave the apostle Paul so much trouble with its disorderliness, its challenge to his authority as an apostle, and even its scandalous affairs: "It is actually reported that there is sexual immorality among you, and of a kind that even pagans do not tolerate: A man is sleeping with his father's wife" (1 Cor. 5:1).

Contrary to what our postmodern age suggests, evil does not simply run within the politically incorrect side of the following group divisions: male/female, white/black, rich/poor, and believer/unbeliever. Instead, upon serious reflection the wise, like Isaiah the prophet before them, will be faced, if they are humble and honest enough, with the reality of their own evil: "'Woe to me!' I cried. 'I am ruined! For I am a man of unclean lips, and I live among a people of unclean lips'" (Isa. 6:5). Thus the dividing line between good and evil does not run neatly or conveniently between various groups; instead it runs smack through every human heart, including everyone: clergy, women, laity, men, cardinals, whites, popes, blacks, Protestants, Roman Catholics.

25. Luther, *Career of the Reformer I*, LW 31:371.

All have fallen short of the glory of God. Therefore the subtleness and the extent of evil, even within the church, as a mixed community, means that not even holding an office in the church, as is sometimes mistakenly supposed, can guarantee the holiness of the officer and utterly eliminate sin, as Jesus Christ himself recognized by way of analogy in the caution he offered to his followers: "The teachers of the law and the Pharisees sit in Moses' seat. So you must be careful to do everything they tell you. But do not do what they do, for they do not practice what they preach" (Matt. 23:2–3). Again, the church on earth is holy, to be sure, but not entirely so. The frank recognition of such surely means that the church should ever be in a spirit of humility and therefore open to ongoing repentance and reform. To be sure, if an institutional church does not have the proper mechanisms in place to come to terms with its own evil, in all its various forms, then this deficit (a genuine *privatio boni*, "absence of good") will surely prove to be troubling.

The Church Is Catholic

The third mark of the church, its catholicity, is often confused with the first mark, that is, the oneness of the body of Christ. The two terms, however, are not the same. In fact, the proper synonyms for the word "catholic," especially in an ecclesiastical context, include all the following: universal, comprehensive, ecumenical, global, extensive, and whole. The *Catechism*, for its part, points out that this leading attribute is to be understood in a double sense:

> First, the Church is catholic because Christ is present in her. "Where there is Christ Jesus, there is the [Roman] Catholic Church." In her subsists the fullness of Christ's body united with its head; this implies that she receives from him "the fullness of the means of salvation" which he has willed: correct and complete confession of faith, full sacramental life, and ordained ministry in apostolic succession.
>
> Secondly, the Church is catholic because she has been sent out by Christ on a mission to the whole of the human race.[26]

In the definition above notice that the authors of the *Catechism* have defined the universality of the church in terms of the particular form that the church has taken in the Roman Catholic tradition and in its own understanding of the same three elements encountered earlier: (1) the faith (with the addition of the *filioque* clause), (2) sacramental life (which took centuries to develop),

26. *Catechism*, pars. 830–31.

and (3) particular polity expressed in an apostolic succession (under the authority of the bishop of Rome). The second element, sacramental life, will be treated more extensively in chapter 9; the third element, apostolic succession, in the material below.

For now, however, observe the wordplay as well as the irony entailed in the use of the term "catholic" above, a term that should, in a genuine universal and encompassing way, embrace the entire reality of the church but that instead here simply refers, once again, to Rome. The Roman employment of this much-misunderstood word entails a confusing and, in the end, contradictory twofold process: first, it maintains that the word "catholic" refers to the universal, comprehensive church; second, it then identifies that universal, catholic church specifically with itself in a move of generalization in which a part, that is, a particular theological tradition, is mistaken for the whole. These two steps, each of which suggests a very different meaning for the word "catholic," are at times switched in and out as needed, given the apologetic requirements of the time, where one meaning is emphasized and the other is not, and all of this to considerable confusion and historiographical error. It seems, then, that equivocation, one of the first logical errors that Aristotle cautioned against,[27] lies at the very heart of the Roman Catholic definitional posture. Oddly enough, the following much-touted claim of the *Catechism*—which will be judged by those beyond the Roman communion as excessive, unreasonable, and again as historically inaccurate, especially in light of the larger history of the church—is actually brought forth as the very basis of unity! This move is simply stunning in its reach and in its assertion of power. The *Catechism* declares: "Particular Churches are fully catholic through their communion with one of them, the Church of Rome 'which presides in charity.' 'For with this church, by reason of its pre-eminence, the whole Church, that is the faithful everywhere, must be in accord.'"[28]

Furthermore, in order to buttress these contrived ecclesiastical claims, the *Catechism* harkens back to the glory days, so to speak, before the Great Schism and lifts up a snapshot from the words of Maximus the Confessor, who died in 662: "All Christian churches everywhere have held and hold the great Church that is here [at Rome] to be their only basis and foundation."[29]

---

27. For an excellent article on Aristotle's understanding of the error of equivocation, see Christopher Kirwan, "Aristotle and the So-Called Fallacy of Equivocation," *Philosophical Quarterly* 29, no. 114 (January 1979): 35–46.

28. *Catechism*, par. 834, quoting Ignatius of Antioch, *To the Romans* 1.1, and Irenaeus, *Against Heresies* 3.3.2.

29. *Catechism*, par. 834. See Maximus the Confessor, *Opuscula theologica et polemica* (PG 91:137–40). See also *The Formula of Hormisdas*, propounded in 519, in which the pope claims that Rome is the center of the church. "The Formula of Pope St Hormisdas," The Byzantine

However, if the snapshot were taken earlier, at the First Ecumenical Council (325), for example, it would be the bishop of Jerusalem, and not Rome, who is preeminent. Citing canon 7 of that first council, H. J. Schroeder observes: "Since custom and ancient tradition show that the bishop of Aelia (Jerusalem) ought to be honored, he shall have precedence, without, however, infringing on the rights of the metropolis."[30] However, if the snapshot were taken later, such as after 1054, then Rome once more would by no means be the center. Wordplay and the equivocation it breeds always lead to confusion.

At any rate, this broader claim as applied to the present means, then, that the Eastern Orthodox Church—which has in place (1) the historic orthodox faith (and without the interpolation, the innovation, of the *filioque* clause in the Nicene Creed), (2) proper sacramental life, and (3) a supposed valid ministry in the apostolic succession (though not under the authority of the bishop of Rome)—is judged to be not completely catholic simply because this historic church is not in full communion with the Vatican. However, if this be the case, then the same argument, from the Orthodox side, could be equally applied to Rome itself, though of course in a slightly different way. The Vatican, so to speak, cannot "outcatholic" the Eastern Orthodox Church. This is a basic fault in both ecclesiology and historiography that the Roman tradition insists upon and has therefore repeated again and again. However, a repetition of this fundamental error, even by many, does not make it any more likely. That this spurious claim has been championed now for centuries does not add in the least to its truthfulness.

So then, in order to proceed in such a way as to avoid the diminishment of other vital Christian theological traditions, as well as to put aside this unnecessary rending of the body of Christ, we have restricted the language of "catholic" to the actual universal church, which exists under the power, authority, and sovereignty of Christ, the head of the church, and not simply to one part of it, that is, the Roman Catholic communion. In a real sense, the Roman view is an ideational abstraction, divorced from what the church *actually is* today and from what it has been for quite some time well beyond the sixth and eleventh centuries. Therefore, when the term "catholic" is employed in this work with respect to the Western tradition that was a part of the Great Schism of 1054, we will always refer to it, most properly and accurately, as the *Roman* Catholic Church, and therefore in a way that does not do harm to our brothers and sisters in Christ in other theological traditions,

---

Forum, last updated July 28, 2002, http://www.byzcath.org/forums/ubbthreads.php/topics/12 2063/The%20Formula%20of%20Pope%20St%20Hormisd.

30. Schroeder, *Disciplinary Decrees of the General Councils: Text, Translation, and Commentary* (St. Louis: Herder, 1937), 33.

especially those in Eastern Orthodoxy.[31] Simply put, Jesus Christ is the center of the church, to whom all must be properly related, not the papacy, not a particular theological tradition.

Excursus: A Much Quoted and Often Misunderstood Passage

The following controversial passage from Irenaeus's *Against Heresies* has been used to buttress the Petrine claims of Rome and its ecclesiastical power, especially during the fourth century and thereafter.

> I say, by indicating that tradition derived from the apostles, of the very great, the very ancient, and universally known Church founded and organized at Rome by the two most glorious apostles, Peter and Paul; as also [by pointing out] the faith preached to men, which comes down to our time by means of the successions of the bishops. For it is a matter of necessity that every Church should agree with this Church, on account of its preeminent authority, that is, the faithful everywhere, inasmuch as the apostolical tradition has been preserved continuously by those [faithful men] who exist everywhere.[32]

This material, from the mid-second century, has posed a number of challenges for historians who seek to contextualize it within that temporal framework. First, as Eric Osborn has pointed out, this text, though composed by Irenaeus originally in Greek (only a few fragments remain), has come down to us as a full manuscript only in a later Latin translation composed around 380.[33] This translation was likely overseen by Damasus I, bishop of Rome, who was also superintending a revision or rewriting of the history of the imperial city in order to include key ecclesiastical events. Is there similarity between the statements of Irenaeus and the ecclesiastical realities of Rome during the fourth century? Can historians even pose such a question?

Second, the passage from Irenaeus above indeed contains factual error, as Oscar Cullmann noted in his own day: "The Roman church in any case was not *founded* by Paul. That is entirely clear from his letter to the Romans."[34] Beyond this, as one judges the content of Paul's Epistle to the Romans,

---

31. Rome rejects this reasoning: "Let us be very careful not to conceive of the universal Church as the simple sum, or . . . the more or less anomalous federation of essentially different particular churches." *Catechism*, par. 833.

32. Irenaeus of Lyons, *Against Heresies* 3.2, in *The Apostolic Fathers with Justin Martyr and Irenaeus*, ANF 1:415–16.

33. Eric Osborn, *Irenaeus of Lyons* (Cambridge: Cambridge University Press, 2005), 1.

34. Cullmann, *Peter: Disciple, Apostle, Martyr* (New York: Living Age Books, 1958), 116 (emphasis original).

especially those to whom the apostle sends greetings at the end of his letter (he does not greet Peter), it is clear that the church was already well established before Peter arrived. Together, these errors detract from the historical accuracy and therefore from the credibility of this material, raising further doubts for any interpreter.

Third, J. B. Lightfoot observes that the language of "the succession of bishops" is employed by Irenaeus in the second century in a much different way than by the later church, that is, as the bricks and mortar of a far more developed hierarchical structure. "In other words, though he [Irenaeus] views the episcopate as a distinct office from the presbytery," Lightfoot argues, "he does not regard it as a distinct order in the same sense in which the diaconate is a distinct order."[35] In fact, Lightfoot continues, Irenaeus "seems to be wholly ignorant that the word bishop had passed from a lower value since the apostolic times."[36]

Fourth, in the nineteenth century Alexander Roberts, James Donaldson, and A. Cleveland Coxe questioned how the Latin phrase *Ad hanc enim ecclesiam propter potiorem principalitatem necesse est omnem convenire ecclesiam* ("For it is a matter of necessity that every church should agree with this church, on account of its preeminent authority") should be translated and interpreted. They maintain, "It is impossible to say with certainty of what words in the Greek original 'potiorem principalitatem' [preeminent authority; literally, preferential prominence] may be the translation."[37] In the face of such ambiguity they conclude, "We are far from sure that the rendering given above is correct, but we have been unable to think of anything better."[38]

Finally, regarding the last phrase of this much-debated paragraph (*hoc est eos qui sunt undique fideles, in qua semper ab his qui sunt undique conservata est ea quae est ab apostolis traditio*, or "the faithful everywhere, inasmuch as the apostolic tradition has been preserved continuously by those [faithful men] who exist everywhere"), J. N. D Kelly offers a rendering that views Rome as neither the source nor the guardian of proper doctrine but instead as its exemplification. He reasons: "Hence it seems more plausible to take *in qua* with *omnem . . . ecclesiam* [the faithful everywhere] and to understand Irenaeus as suggesting that the Roman church supplies an ideal illustration."[39] Kelly, therefore, concludes his analysis of this pericope, drawn from the writings

35. J. B. Lightfoot, *The Christian Ministry* (New York: MacMillan, 1901), 73.

36. Ibid., 72.

37. Roberts, Donaldson, and Coxe, *Apostolic Fathers with Justin Martyr and Irenaeus*, ANF 1:415–16.

38. Ibid.

39. Kelly, *Early Christian Doctrines* (San Francisco: Harper and Row, 1960), 193.

of Irenaeus, by affirming, "There is therefore no allusion to the later Petrine claims of the Roman see."[40] Indeed, given the doubts and the ambiguity that surround this passage, it is difficult to find a solid basis for the considerably broader claims to ecclesiastical power and privilege that came later.

The Church Is Apostolic

In making the vital affirmation that the church is apostolic because "she is founded on the apostles,"[41] the magisterium, however, immediately adds to this assertion a number of elements that not only favor Roman ecclesiology and polity but also separate the Roman communion, at least in some senses, from every other theological tradition. Thus the *Catechism* fills out what is entailed in the notion of apostolicity in the following way: "[The church] continues to be taught, sanctified, and guided by the apostles until Christ's return, through their successors in pastoral office: the college of bishops, 'assisted by priests, in union with the successor of Peter, the Church's supreme pastor.'"[42] Imbedded in this last assertion of what Rome means by apostolicity, and found elsewhere throughout the *Catechism* as well as in Vatican II documents, are a number of declarations that can be parsed out as follows:

1. Bishops have been distinguished from elders from the time of the apostles and are their superiors (monarchical episcopacy).

2. The authority of the apostles was directly and immediately passed on to monarchical bishops.

3. Apostolic succession means that current Roman Catholic bishops are in a line of bishops, an unbroken chain or connection, that goes all the way back to the first (monarchical) bishop of Rome.

4. The pope is the apostolic successor of Peter, the first (monarchical) bishop of Rome.[43]

40. Ibid.
41. *Catechism*, par. 857.
42. Ibid.
43. Bryan Cross, a popular Roman Catholic apologist, defends all of these theses in what can only be termed, as Brandon Addison puts it, "dogmatic sophistry." Cross does not take up the arduous task of historical reasoning nor use a suitable methodology, but proceeds in an utterly dogmatic way (whatever Rome teaches is correct), and then he interprets the facts and artifacts of history to fit this preconceived and vigorously defended view. See Bryan Cross's *Called to Communion* blog at http://www.calledtocommunion.com/2014/06/the-bishops-of-history-and -the-catholic-faith-a-reply-to-brandon-addison/. See also Brandon Addison's contribution to

We will initially consider the first three claims and then explore some of their more important consequences for every Protestant tradition. Only after this work is done will we then take up the fourth claim in terms of the authority of the papacy itself, in chapter 11.

Rome's Claim: Bishops Were Ever above Elders

Though Rome maintains that Jesus Christ founded the hierarchy of the Roman Catholic Church ("Christ . . . established . . . a society structured with hierarchical organs"),[44] the pages of the NT prove otherwise. Indeed, in describing virtually the same attributes of an elder, 1 Timothy employs the language of *episkopos* (ἐπίσκοπος), as in 3:1, where this Greek word is suitably translated as bishop *or* elder. Simply put, the language of bishop and the language of presbyter, in terms of their Greek equivalents, both describe the same reality of an elder in the early church. The interchangeability of these two terms, ἐπίσκοπος and πρεσβύτερος (*presbyteros*) in their various forms, is underscored, ironically enough, in 1 Peter 5:1–2, for example, in which the words *episkopountes* (ἐπισκοποῦντες) and *presbyterous* (πρεσβυτέρους) are utilized to refer to the very same leaders.

Beyond this, in the writings of the apostolic fathers of the late first century, such as those of Clement of Rome, the basic equivalence of bishop and presbyter (both understood as elders or overseers) is similarly maintained.[45] However, toward the end of the first century and into the second, thus beyond the time of the apostles, a shift (which was likely simply a local expression at first) is indeed evident in the writings of Ignatius of Antioch, who begins to distinguish the bishop from the presbyter in a judgment that will lead to the rise of what is called the monarchical episcopate. In this move the office of bishop is viewed as "above" that of the presbyter or elder, and it forms the basis of local unity in the church. Ignatius writes: "Be ye subject to the bishop as to the Lord, for 'he watches for your souls, as one that shall give account to God' [Heb. 13:17]."[46] Despite the shift that has occurred in the

this debate, "The Quest for the Historical Church: A Protestant Assessment," guest post on *Called to Communion*, March 24, 2014, https://reformation500.files.wordpress.com/2014/05/brandon-addison-ctc-article-20140501.pdf, and his reply to Cross's criticism of "The Quest for the Historical Church": "Brandon Addison's Complete Response to 'Called to Communion' regarding 'the Nonexistent Early Papacy,'" *Triablogue* (blog), May 14, 2016, http://triablogue.blogspot.com/2016/05/brandon-addisons-complete-response-to.html.

44. *Catechism*, par. 771.

45. Clement of Rome, "The First Epistle of Clement to the Corinthians" 44, in *The Apostolic Fathers with Justin Martyr and Irenaeus*, ANF 1:17.

46. Ignatius of Antioch, *To the Trallians* 2, in *The Apostolic Fathers with Justin Martyr and Irenaeus*, ANF 1:66.

writings of Ignatius, where the seeds for the monarchical episcopacy were planted in the East, in Antioch in particular, our basic point remains: the rise of bishops as monarchs, in which bishops and elders are sharply distinguished, is a later development, perhaps as late as 107,[47] and this distinction is therefore not descriptive of either the pages of the NT or of first-century Christianity. Therefore the rise of the bishop as a monarch, as one who oversees the presbyters and the deacons, is a later historical development that is beyond the time of the apostles. Peter and Paul, for example, knew nothing of it.

Rome's Claim: The Apostles' Authority Was Passed On to Monarchical Bishops

The strong form of this claim can be found, once again, in the *Catechism*: "So also endures the office, which the apostles received, of shepherding the Church, a charge destined to be exercised *without interruption* by the sacred order of bishops. Hence the Church teaches that 'the bishops have by divine institution taken the place of the apostles as pastors of the Church.'"[48] The problem with this claim, however, is that the apostles passed along this authority not to bishops ruling their flocks as monarchs, a later development well beyond their time, but apparently to the entire body of elders, whether the term *episkopos* or *presbyteros* was employed to describe them. As Lightfoot puts it, "The episcopate was formed not out of the apostolic order by localisation but out of the presbyteral by elevation: and the title, which originally was common to all, came at length to be appropriated to the chief among them."[49] Moreover, Rome's language of "without interruption" is likewise problematic and represents factual error by reading the much later local reality of Ignatius back into the sixth, fifth, and even fourth decades of the first-century church, where it simply does not belong. Accordingly, that monarchical bishops can be traced back to the apostles in an uninterrupted manner, in which all the dots are connected, is a myth that is required for Rome's (and Constantinople's) self-understanding, but it is one that never touches the ground, so to speak, of the apostolic age. It's left hanging in the air somewhere in the early second century. It therefore is hardly a proper foundation for the massive hierarchical infrastructure that Rome eventually built.

47. Martin Hein, Hans-Gernot Jung, and Marlin Vanelderen, "Bishop, Episcopate," *The Encyclopedia of Christianity*, 5 vols., ed. Erwin Fahlbusch and Geoffrey William Bromiley (Grand Rapids: Eerdmans; Leiden: Brill, 1999–2003), 1:262.

48. *Catechism*, par. 862 (emphasis added).

49. Lightfoot, *Christian Ministry*, 25.

Rome's Claim: An Unbroken Chain of Bishops Centered in Rome

Since so many elements of this third claim are predicated on the first two claims, which have already been shown to be faulty, this additional claim is likewise without warrant, especially when the details of church history are taken into account. Nevertheless, this third claim does indeed deserve some treatment because it goes beyond the first two by specifically appealing to the notion of apostolic succession (throughout history) and by grounding such an understanding in a supposed monarchical episcopacy specifically in the city of Rome during the first century.

First of all, the notion of apostolic succession can and must be distinguished from that of the monarchical episcopacy, in which the bishop is elevated above the elder. The two ideas are not the same. One cannot simply move from one framework to the next as if they were equivalent. For example, although we affirm that there is a basis for the monarchical episcopacy in the writings of Ignatius of Antioch, there is no such grounding of apostolic succession in these same writings. Thus, for example, a monarchical episcopacy could exist without a clearly defined apostolic succession in place. As William R. Schoedel explains, "Still missing in Ignatius is any convincing evidence of the idea of apostolic succession, for episcopal authority is seen as derived directly from God or Christ."[50]

So then, the idea that the episcopal office itself is the basis of authority (though an appeal is made to the Holy Spirit through the laying on of hands) is a later development that came about as the church began to grapple more seriously with heresy in general, and gnosticism in particular. Such a configuration must therefore be distinguished from the earlier and proper form of authority as "derived directly from God or Christ."[51] Observe, then, the subtle shift in this setting (though it has enormous consequences) from a charismatic understanding of authority (where Christ or the Holy Spirit is preeminent) to a more institutional one (where the office itself is in reality the focus of attention). Once again, in his focus on the communication of proper doctrine from age to age, Lightfoot points out that "succession . . . does not consist in an identity of office."[52] Moreover, if Roman Catholic critics will contend that the episcopal office conceived in the framework of apostolic succession is really a charismatic understanding, underscoring the freedom and sovereignty of the Holy Spirit, and not a more institutional one, it must be borne in mind

---

50. Schoedel, "Ignatius, Epistles of," in *The Anchor Yale Bible Dictionary*, ed. David Noel Freedman (New York: Doubleday, 1992), 386.

51. Ibid.

52. Lightfoot, *Christian Ministry*, 24.

that in this view the Spirit is, after all, limited to working within the line of office and authority as articulated by Rome—an authority, so it is claimed, that it can never lose. The Roman view, at least in this context, appears to be well in line with what the late Avery Dulles referred to as the "institutional model" of the church. He observed: "By institutionalism we mean a system in which the institutional element is treated as primary. From the point of view of this author [Dulles], institutionalism is a deformation of the true nature of the Church—a deformation that has unfortunately affected the Church at certain periods of its history, and one that remains in every age a real danger to the institutional Church."[53]

Second, the idea that an apostolic succession of monarchical bishops can be traced back to Rome of the first century is simply false. Consider initially the temporal problem entailed. Such a view of succession represents a later understanding of authority within the church that has been read back into the past. Here again is the familiar problem of anachronism. For while we affirm an Ignatian monarchical episcopacy by the early second century, as stated earlier, the point is that such a model was local, at least in the beginning. It took time for the structure of the monarchical episcopacy to develop such that it eventually became the universal polity of the church, at least for a season. Indeed, some scholars maintain that this happened late in the second century;[54] others in the third century.[55] Consider also the difficulty entailed specifically in terms of the city of Rome itself. To illustrate this issue, Behr has argued that when Ignatius addressed his letter to this imperial city, he wrote "to the Church . . . in the country of the land of the Romans,"[56] apparently "unsure whom he was addressing,"[57] a statement that would be quite odd if there were indeed a monarchical bishop (or a supposed pope) in that city. Moreover, this temporal problem is compounded in the realization that when the church in Rome confronted the heresy of Marcion around the middle of the second century, it was not any monarchical bishop who took a leading role here but the presbyters themselves.[58] Behr explains: "Christian communities in Rome, though clearly having a unified sense of their own faith sufficient not to accept Marcion's teaching, had not yet coalesced into a body organized enough to take upon itself the action of collectively excluding a figure such as Marcion."[59]

53. Dulles, *Models of the Church*, 35.
54. Peterson, *Timeline Charts*, 29.
55. Hans-Gernot Jung and Marlin Vanelderen, "Mary," in *Encyclopedia of Christianity*, 3:439.
56. John Behr, *Irenaeus of Lyons* (New York: Oxford University Press, 2013), 22.
57. Ibid.
58. Ibid., 26.
59. Ibid.

Beyond these temporal considerations, there is a "geographical" problem as well, having to do with the actual layout of the Christian community in Rome, which has been revealed by archaeological studies of the city. This geographical problem and its connection to the rise of the monarchical episcopacy in Rome are ably treated in the careful scholarship of Peter Lampe, who has developed the "fractionation thesis" to illustrate the house-church-decentralized flavor of the city along with its various Christian districts. He argues that even well into the second century, Rome had a polity that matched the Christian layout of the city. Such a polity was characterized not by an elevated bishop but by presbyters or elders under the larger authority of the Holy Spirit. Lampe observes: "The fractionation in Rome favored a collegial presbyterial system of governance and prevented for a long time, until the second half of the second century, the development of a monarchical episcopacy in the city."[60] Moreover, Lampe maintains that in the letter of Paul to Rome and later that of Ignatius as well, there is simply no mention of a monarchical leader, "even though Ignatius knew of a monarchical bishop's office from his experience in the east."[61] Beyond this, Clement of Rome's letter 1 Clement assumes "the same presbyterial governance"[62] in this urban area. In light of such evidence, the development of the office of the bishop in Rome was clearly gradual, given the Roman church's early decentralized ecclesiastical geography. The presbyter in this key city who had been entrusted with "external affairs,"[63] largely ministering to the poor, eventually gained prominence "until at the latest with Victor (c. 189–99) a powerful monarchos developed."[64]

Although the work of Clement of Rome has been cited as "proof" of an early apostolic succession—a succession, by the way, that is itself contingent on the notion of the monarchical episcopacy—the preceding evidence indicates otherwise. The classic text in support of this oft-repeated claim, drawn from the writings of the Apostolic Fathers, is as follows: "The apostles have preached the Gospel to us from the Lord Jesus Christ; Jesus Christ [has done so] from God. Christ therefore was sent forth by God, and the apostles by Christ."[65] We grant that the general idea of succession is found here: from

60. Lampe, From Paul to Valentinus: Christians at Rome in the First Two Centuries (Minneapolis: Fortress, 2003), 397.

61. Ibid., 399. Lampe (399n5) even casts doubt on the nature of the episcopacy evident in the writings of Ignatius: "Whether the monarchical episcopacy was established in the east is, however, questionable. Ignatius (Phil. [To the Philadelphians] 7–8; cf. Magn. [To the Magnesians] 6–8) presupposed Christians who do not wish to be under a bishop."

62. Ibid.

63. Ibid., 402.

64. Ibid., 401.

65. Clement of Rome, "The First Epistle of Clement to the Corinthians" 42, in The Apostolic Fathers with Justin Martyr and Irenaeus, ANF 1:16.

God to Jesus Christ, from Jesus Christ to the apostles. However, observe also that there is no mention at all in this setting of the kind of succession that Rome wants (and needs), that is, from the apostles to the monarchical bishops.

Beyond this, when Lampe addresses this same issue, but this time in terms of the writings of Irenaeus, he observes, "The list of Irenaeus (*Haer.* [*Against Heresies*] 3.3.3) is with highest probability a historical construction from the 180s."[66] Thus, if we were to fill in the blanks in this context and thereby continue the line of succession, it would have to be from the apostles to the *presbyters*! In addition, the purpose of this list was evidently not to ground a succession of office but to "anchor the present *doctrine*"[67] with a line of authorities that went back to the first century. In fact, when Hegesippus, upon whose work Irenaeus in some sense depended, visited Rome in 160, Hegesippus merely observed that "Anicetus stood in the succession of correct doctrine."[68] Moreover, as pointed out by Daniel O'Connor, Hegesippus was working not with an already-existing list but with one that he had compiled himself,[69] a fact that underscores its mid-second-century context and origin.

Nevertheless, at this point those who favor the Roman Catholic view may argue that Clement of Rome did point to an apostolic succession linked from age to age by the office of the bishop by citing material from *1 Clement* 44, which reads: "Our apostles also knew, through our Lord Jesus Christ, that there would be strife on account of the office of the episcopate. For this reason, therefore, inasmuch as they had obtained a perfect fore-knowledge of this, they appointed those [ministers] already mentioned, and afterwards gave instructions, that when these should fall asleep, other approved men should succeed them in their ministry."[70] However, *1 Clement*, like 1 Timothy and Titus, employed the terminology of ἐπίσκοπος (*episkopos*) and πρεσβύτερος (*presbyteros*) interchangeably and in a manner typical of a first-century setting: "For our sin will not be small, if we eject from the episcopate those who have blamelessly and holily fulfilled its duties. Blessed are those presbyters who, having finished their course before now, have obtained a fruitful and perfect departure [from this world]."[71] That this judgment is accurate, having greater explanatory power than the Roman view, can be seen in the further observation that Clement of Rome's earlier passage, as in chapter 42, mentions only

66. Lampe, *From Paul to Valentinus*, 406.
67. Ibid., 404 (emphasis added).
68. Ibid., 405.
69. O'Connor, *Peter in Rome: The Literary, Liturgical, and Archeological Evidence* (New York: Columbia University Press, 1969), 27.
70. Clement of Rome, "The First Epistle of Clement to the Corinthians" 44, in *The Apostolic Fathers with Justin Martyr and Irenaeus*, ANF 1:17.
71. Ibid.

overseers (ἐπίσκοπος, *episkopos*) and deacons (διάκονος, *diakonos*) and not the hierarchical order of deacon, presbyter, and bishop.[72] The clear implication of such usage is that Clement sees the overseers functioning as elders within the church and not as monarchical bishops in a threefold order.

Furthermore, the list of Roman church leaders composed by Irenaeus late in the second century is also at times cited as "proof" of apostolic succession. However, there are a couple of problems with such an assertion. First of all, in developing his list of twelve leaders—which runs backward from Bishop Eleutherus around AD 180, when the monarchical episcopacy was a reality in Rome, to Linus (not Peter, by the way) in the first century, when it was not—Irenaeus depends upon the prior construction of Hegesippus, who in confronting the gnostics of his day underscored, once again, a succession not of office but of doctrine.[73] In fact, Hegesippus saw himself as the "guardian of apostolic tradition,"[74] not of a particular office.

Moreover, to view the list of Irenaeus as focusing on a monarchical succession that goes back to the apostle Peter presupposes, in the words of Allen Brent, "that his model is that of a chronographer charting the succession of kings, consuls, high priests,"[75] in which exact dates become very important. However, the larger context behind this list once again suggests a looser, didactic purpose in that Irenaeus and Hegisippus put their lists together "on the basis of a 'succession' of philosophers and a 'succession' of apostles."[76] So by the latter part of the second century, the office of the bishop was viewed as "the counterpart to the president of a philosophical school, like the *diadochoi* [successors] of Plato, Aristotle, Stoics, and Epicureans."[77] Such a construal resulted in an emphasis, once again, on proper teaching and not on an episcopal monarch who supposedly paralleled a high priest or king. In light of such considerations, Brent concludes: "The model for Irenaeus's succession list was therefore quite different from that which was to inform Fabian's Episcopal monarchy. It was, as we have argued, scholastic. To prove that there was a coherence in philosophical or theological teaching, you needed only to show that the school of the philosophers or of the apostles simply had an orderly succession of one philosopher or bishop to another: dates were not essential."[78]

72. Ibid., 16.
73. Lampe, *From Paul to Valentinus*, 404.
74. Ibid., 403.
75. Brent, "How Irenaeus Has Misled the Archaeologists," in *Irenaeus: Life, Scripture, and Legacy*, ed. Sarah Parvis and Paul Foster (Minneapolis: Fortress, 2012), Kindle edition, locations 1337–39.
76. Ibid., Kindle ed., locations 1415–16.
77. Ibid., Kindle ed., locations 1479–80.
78. Ibid., Kindle ed., locations 1810–13.

Second, treating the list of Irenaeus found in *Adversus haereses* (*Against Heresies*) as a succession of monarchical bishops—from Eleutherus, who was one, to Linus, who was not—means considering these twelve leaders as a class, something that on some level even Irenaeus apparently does,[79] the members of which supposedly all contain the same characteristics of office that mark the last few of the succession: Anicetus, Soter, and Eleutherus. Part of the problem here concerns Irenaeus himself and his construction or, better yet, his reconstruction of the early history of the church to match his late-second-century apologetic intent. Such an approach, for the sake of argument—that is, if Irenaeus were to argue for a succession of office rather than of teaching (and we believe he does not)—would immediately encounter the problem of a confusion of time frames in which the later reality of monarchical episcopacy would be attributed to each and every member of the class of twelve, whether accurate or not. Indeed, the focus of Irenaeus on the particular number of twelve is "fictive," according to Lampe.[80] One could have easily, for example, included Peter in such a list, but then the number would be an awkward thirteen. At any rate, many of the persons on the list of Irenaeus "would never have understood themselves as monarchical leaders—especially Pius at the time of Hermas."[81]

So then, the picture that has emerged—in light of the careful work of Behr, Lampe, and Brent, along with our own observations—is that the Roman claim of an apostolic succession going back to a monarchical bishop of Rome (Peter?) during the first century ("the chief place, according to the witness of tradition, is held by the function of those who, through their appointment to the dignity and responsibility of bishop, and in virtue consequently of the unbroken succession, going back to the beginning are regarded as transmitters of the apostolic line")[82] is clearly without grounding.[83] It is a claim that

79. Irenaeus writes: "The blessed apostles, then, having founded and built up the Church, committed into the hands of Linus the office of the episcopate. Of this Linus, Paul makes mention in the Epistles to Timothy. To him succeeded Anacletus; and after him, in the third place from the apostles, Clement was allotted the bishopric." See Irenaeus of Lyons, *Against Heresies* 3.3, in *The Apostolic Fathers with Justin Martyr and Irenaeus*, ANF 1:416.

80. Lampe, *From Paul to Valentinus*, 406. Oscar Cullmann notes a historical error that Irenaeus made, dependent as he was on Papias, in claiming that the Roman church was founded by Peter and Paul. Cullmann states: "Here, too, occurs at least *one* error: the Roman church in any case was not *founded* by Paul. That is entirely clear from his letter to the Romans." See Oscar Cullmann, *Peter: Disciple, Apostle, Martyr* (New York: Living Age Books, 1958), 116.

81. Lampe, *From Paul to Valentinus*, 406.

82. Pope Paul VI, *Lumen Gentium: Dogmatic Constitution on the Church*, sec. 20, in Flannery, *Conciliar and Post Conciliar Documents*, 371–72; see also the Holy See, http://www.vatican.va/archive/hist_councils/ii_vatican_council/documents/vat-ii_const_19641121_lumen-gentium_en.html.

83. In addition, Eamon Duffy explains, "Nor can we assume, as Irenaeus did, that the Apostles established there a succession of bishops to carry on their work in the city, for all the

has been repeated by many throughout the centuries; however, its veracity can neither be helped in the least by such a repetition nor by any length of time. Therefore the notion of apostolic succession, especially in terms of how Rome employs it, is a well-worked "myth" whose truth coheres with other Roman Catholic self-understandings but not with those that must embrace, in a careful and evenhanded manner, in grace and charity, the entire history of the church, and the first century in particular.

---

indications are that there was no single bishop at Rome for almost a century after the deaths of the Apostles. In fact, wherever we turn, the solid outlines of the Petrine succession at Rome seem to blur and dissolve." Eamon Duffy, *Saints and Sinners: A History of the Popes*, 4th ed. (New Haven: Yale University Press, 2015), 2.

7

The Church, Part II

Are Other Traditions Ecumenically Understood?

In the sixteenth century a second great schism shook the church, breaking the unity of Western Christianity into two and more theological traditions. Again Roman Catholicism, as well as its critics, played a part. This ecclesiastical disruption can be understood in two key ways: first, in terms of the specific issues of doctrine, polity, and practice that led both Protestants *and* Roman Catholics to call for reform; second, in terms of the subsequent relations between Rome and large segments of the Western church, composed now of several theological traditions that had embraced the necessity of reform in the sixteenth century precisely in order to preserve the grace and beauty of the apostolic faith.

In the following chapters the first issue will be treated in considerable detail in terms of such matters as justification by faith, the new birth, the priesthood, sacraments, the papacy, and the doctrine of Mary. This chapter will focus on the second issue: how Rome now relates to its brothers and sisters who are heirs of the Reformation, raised up by no one less than the Holy Spirit. Indeed, it is that relation which so deeply indicates the basic doctrine of the church, especially in terms of ongoing ecclesiological assumptions and commitments. That relation, however, is by no means exhausted in ecclesiological concerns. Rather, it also expresses Rome's ongoing theological posture, especially as it faces the Christian other, and it even entails such things as moral and spiritual judgments, the last of which are seldom considered. We will therefore take up that task as well in this present chapter.

How Rome Views Protestantism Today

When the Roman Catholic Church looks in the direction of the broader church, beyond its Vatican walls, so to speak, it does so from the vantage point of the same three standards identified earlier as championed by both Bellarmine during the Reformation and its aftermath and by Pope John Paul II more recently in his encyclical *Ut Unum Sint* (1995): right faith, valid sacraments, and proper governance under the authority of the pope. In this specific context, with these standards well in mind, Rome engages in yet another round of wordplay by distinguishing the church (the [Roman] Catholic Church) from churches (plural) and then again the church (the [Roman] Catholic Church) from what are called ecclesiastical communities. Remarkably enough, in this schema not only will the Protestant so-called ecclesiastical communities be found wanting, but the Orthodox Church as well. Notice, however, that the "deficiency" of Eastern Orthodoxy surely cannot consist in a lack of valid sacraments or even in a lack of proper governance, since this church likewise affirms the myth of apostolic succession in a way similar to Rome, a succession that supposedly grounds the validity of both its ministry and sacramental life. What the Orthodox lack, then, is submission to the authority of the bishop of Rome, an aspect of proper governance. However, this deficit alone is apparently enough to cause and keep in place an ongoing separation such that there does not exist even today, except on rare occasions, intercommunion (where the Lord's Supper is freely and jointly celebrated) between Roman Catholicism and Eastern Orthodoxy. In handling this awkward situation, the *Catechism of the Catholic Church* needs to walk a very tight line: on the one hand it underscores the similarity of these two theological traditions; on the other hand it refers to the lack, the deficiency, that yet remains within Orthodoxy: "*With the Orthodox Churches* [notice the plural], this communion is so profound 'that it *lacks* little to attain the fullness that would permit a common celebration of the Lord's Eucharist.'"[1] However, in the face of that lack, a common celebration is indeed prohibited. Here once again Rome is alone and hardly catholic.

The picture, however, is very different with respect to Protestantism. In fact, Reformation Christians, the sons and daughters of reform, those who

---

1. *Catechism of the Catholic Church*, 2nd ed. (Mahwah, NJ: Paulist Press, 1994), par. 838, quoting Paul VI in a "discourse" of 1975 (emphasis original, except emphasis of "*lacks*" is added).

responded to the gentle leading of the Holy Spirit in the sixteenth century and those who do so even today, are judged by Rome to participate in communions of faith deficient in all three areas: faith, sacraments, and governance. For example, difficulties in terms of the first and third areas were lifted up by Vatican II in its *Lumen Gentium: Dogmatic Constitution on the Church*, which states: "The Church knows that she is joined in many ways to the baptized who are honored by the name of Christian, but who do not however profess the [Roman] Catholic faith in its entirety or have not preserved unity or communion under the successor of Peter."[2] Again, but this time in terms of the second and third areas, Vatican II in its *Decree on Ecumenism* declared:

> Although the ecclesial communities separated from us lack the fullness of unity with us which flows from baptism, and although we believe they have not preserved the proper reality of the eucharistic mystery in its fullness, especially because of the absence of the sacrament of Orders, nevertheless when they commemorate the Lord's death and resurrection in the Holy Supper, they profess that it signifies life in communion with Christ and await his coming in glory.[3]

In these judgments Rome neither denies that "'many elements of sanctification and of truth' are found outside the visible confines of the [Roman] Catholic Church,"[4] nor contends that the Spirit of Christ is unable to use "the separated Churches and communities . . . as means of salvation."[5] What Rome does insist upon, however, to use its own idiom, is that the means of salvation, which are found within the Protestant church, "derive their efficacy from the very fullness of grace and truth entrusted to the [Roman] Catholic Church."[6] This last claim, however, is deeply flawed in its handling of the issue of the means of salvation, on the one hand, and the ends of redemption, on the other hand, especially with respect to the various theological traditions that exist today. To illustrate, the means of salvation in the Protestant church such as preaching, prayer, reading Scripture, fasting, baptism, and the Lord's Supper derive their efficacy not from a particular theological tradition such as Rome but from no one less than the Holy Spirit. It is the end or goal of

2. Pope Paul VI, *Lumen Gentium: Dogmatic Constitution on the Church*, sec. 15, in *The Conciliar and Post Conciliar Documents*, vol. 1 of *Vatican II*, ed. Austin Flannery (Vatican City: Libreria Editrice Vaticana, 2011), 366; see also the Holy See, http://www.vatican.va/archive/hist _councils/ii_vatican_council/documents/vat-ii_const_19641121_lumen-gentium_en.html.

3. *Unitatis Redintegratio: Decree on Ecumenism*, sec. 22, in Flannery, *Conciliar and Post Conciliar Documents*, 469.

4. *Catechism*, par. 819.

5. *Unitatis Redintegratio*, sec. 3, in Flannery, *Conciliar and Post Conciliar Documents*, 456.

6. Ibid.

religion, the Holy Spirit reigning in the heart in the community of faith, that informs the means and validates them. Indeed, Roman Catholicism as a distinct tradition, involved as it was in earlier schisms, is limited to ministering only its own means of grace, not those of other communions, and not even then does it have any power to manage the very ends of salvation to which all such means of grace point: a sovereign and free Holy Spirit reigning in the hearts of believers as the Spirit wills.

Moreover, such an observation is further substantiated in the realization that grace is not a commodity whereby Rome is the alleged principal broker, through its hierarchy, for the entire church. Rather grace, in terms of both divine favor and empowerment, is nothing less than the presence of the Holy Spirit within the church, whose members faithfully proclaim the apostolic testimony from age to age. Surely those members include believers who look to the much-needed reform of the body of Christ that took place in the sixteenth century. Again, since grace *is* the presence of the Holy Spirit, a presence that is without lack in the Protestant church (as in Eastern Orthodoxy), there is, after all, no deficiency here, despite Rome's protestations to the contrary. This abiding truth of the larger and more ecumenically minded church becomes convincingly clear once it is recognized that the Holy Spirit of the risen Christ, reigning in the hearts of confessors and present in every Protestant orthodox theological tradition and not the Roman hierarchy itself, is ever at the center.

In light of the preceding observations, the deficiency argument championed by the Roman Catholic Church, especially at Vatican II, can now be expressed in its simplest form: since Protestant churches or ecclesiastical communities have not maintained the apostolic succession, the ordination of their clergy is improper, and as a consequence such churches cannot offer a valid Eucharist. Yet before we point out what harm, in our judgment, the Roman Catholic Church has done to the gracious unity of the body of Christ by such a line of reasoning, we must first of all observe that the very foundation of this argument is faulty since it is predicated on the mistaken notion, the much-touted myth, that in the Roman Catholic Church there currently exists a succession of bishops that can be traced back to the apostles of the middle of the first century (see chap. 6).

What Rome does with this specious reasoning and improper foundation, however, is to turn around and use them as an instrument to cause a division at the Lord's Supper, a disruption, a schism, precisely at a place where there should be Christian love and unity in abundance, resplendent in fellowship, as a witness to the world: one Lord, one faith, one baptism. While many Protestants would welcome a joint celebration of the Eucharist with their Roman Catholic brothers and sisters, Rome insists that such communion, animated by holy love and the Spirit of Christ, must not take place. Indeed, Protestants are actually prohibited from receiving the elements of the Lord's Supper except under very rare circumstances.[7] These Protestant members of the body of Christ, sanctified by the Holy Spirit, are likewise banned from receiving the sacrament of penance and the anointing of the sick, or what used to be called last rites or extreme unction,[8] even if they so desired. Not surprisingly, given such judgments, Rome also forbids its own members, in an atmosphere of fear and threats, from receiving the Lord's Supper at the hands of Protestant clergy. Thus Roman Catholics may not ask for this sacrament "except from a minister who has been validly ordained."[9] So if it is wrong (spiritually? morally?) for Roman Catholics to participate in Protestant Communion services, then is it similarly wrong, on some level, for Protestants themselves to participate in their own services?

Readers who don't have a dog in this fight, so to speak, especially those of gracious and moderate sensibilities, may be asking themselves, "What in the world is going on here?" To answer this fair and eminently reasonable question, a little church history is necessary. Bear in mind that to elevate the office of bishop to a monarchical role in the church and then to view that same office in terms of an apostolic succession was one of the chief vehicles employed by Irenaeus and others in their ongoing struggle with heretics in general and the gnostics in particular during the late second century. Given this reality, it is therefore highly inappropriate, a genuine rending of the body of Christ, almost as if the immune system were attacking the body itself, to apply this same heretic-repulsing approach to Protestant believers, some of whom live holy and exemplary Christian lives, and then to find them wanting. Jesus gave the bread to Judas; Roman Catholic priests will not give it to Protestant saints!

Is Roman Catholicism an Ecumenical Church?

In the wake of Vatican II, many Protestant leaders as well as Roman Catholics assumed that the Roman Catholic Church had taken on a genuinely ecumenical

7. *The Declaration on the Celebration of the Eucharist* states: "This may be permitted in danger of death or in urgent need (during persecution, in prisons) if the separated brother has no access to a minister of his own communion, and spontaneously asks for a Catholic priest for the sacraments—so long as he declares a faith in these sacraments in harmony with that of the Church, and is rightly disposed." See *Eucharist in Common*, par. 6, in Flannery, *Conciliar and Post Conciliar Documents*, 504–5.
8. *Eucharist in Common*, par. 6, in Flannery, *Conciliar and Post Conciliar Documents*, 504.
9. Ibid., 505.

stance in its recognition of "the separated brethren." While relations between Roman Catholics and Protestants did in fact improve after the council, nevertheless several old patterns of Roman triumphalism and ethnocentrism remained, carried along by the notion that the Roman Catholic tradition itself is once again at the very heart of the church, to which all other communions of Christian faith must therefore be properly related. It is this basic fault, one of a mistaken ecclesiology, that mars the ecumenical context even today, especially when we consider the specific issue of moving from one tradition to the other: from the Protestant church to the Roman Catholic Church, or from the Roman Catholic Church to the Protestant church. Undoubtedly most readers will be quite surprised to learn what both the *Catechism* and Vatican II actually teach on this important topic.

Numerous examples can be cited of popular Protestant leaders who eventually entered the Roman Catholic Church: Thomas Howard, Richard John Neuhaus, Scott Hahn, and more recently Christian Smith. In the eyes of Rome there was nothing either ecclesiastically problematic or theologically troubling about these transitions, or "conversions," if you will. Given Rome's understanding of the church, this is precisely how things ought to be. But what about the other side of the equation, so to speak, of popular Roman Catholics who made their way into the Protestant church? Marie Cavallier, the princess of Denmark, became a Lutheran; Tim Pawlenty, governor of Minnesota, became a nondenominational Protestant, as did Sarah Palin, along with her entire family, when she was a child; and Vice President Mike Pence, though he was raised in the Roman Catholic Church, used to worship in an evangelical church in Indianapolis when he was governor of Indiana.[10] Was all of this, too, okay in the eyes of Rome? Was the same gracious judgment that was applied to Richard John Neuhaus, for instance, to be applied to Sarah Palin, Tim Pawlenty, Mike Pence, and those like them, as well?

The Condemnation Argument Laid Out

Contrary to popular misunderstandings, among both Roman Catholics (principally laity) and Protestants, the Roman church apparently does not consider the two distinct kinds of conversions to be equal: it is fine for a Protestant to become a Roman Catholic, but it is not okay for the reverse to occur. The *Catechism* states: "Basing itself on Scripture *and* Tradition, the

10. For a helpful list of these, as well as other kinds of conversions, see "List of Former Roman Catholics," accessed December 23, 2016, http://en.wikipedia.org/wiki/List_of_former _Roman_Catholics#Protestantism.

[Second Vatican] Council teaches that the Church, a pilgrim now on earth, is necessary for salvation. . . . Hence they could not be saved who, knowing that the [Roman] Catholic Church was founded as necessary by God through Christ, would refuse either to enter it or *to remain* in it."[11] Attempting to soften the blow somewhat, Rome makes an important distinction between those who are born and raised in Protestant communions of faith and those who willfully enter them of their own accord later, after being baptized in the Roman Catholic Church. To illustrate this last point, the "Directory concerning Ecumenical Matters," propounded in 1967 in the aftermath of the Second Vatican Council, declares:

> The Decree on Ecumenism makes clear that the brethren born and baptized outside the visible communion of the [Roman] Catholic Church should be carefully distinguished from those who, though baptized in the [Roman] Catholic Church, have knowingly and publicly abjured her faith. According to the decree (n. 3) "one cannot charge with the sin of separation those who at present are born into these communities and in them are brought up in the faith of Christ." Hence, in the absence of such blame, if they freely wish to embrace the [Roman] Catholic faith, they have no need to be absolved from excommunication, but after making profession of their faith according to the regulations set down by the ordinary of the place they should be admitted to the full communion of the [Roman] Catholic Church. What Canon 2314 prescribes is only applicable to those who, after culpably giving up the Catholic faith or communion, repent and ask to be reconciled with mother Church.[12]

There are a number of oddities in the preceding passage, one of which is the salient reference to the pre–Vatican II *Code of Canon Law* (citing canon 2314), promulgated in 1917, which declares: "§1. All apostates from the Christian faith and each and every heretic or schismatic: 1. Incur by that fact excommunication. . . . §2. Absolution from the excommunication mentioned in §1, sought in the forum of conscience, is specifically reserved to the Apostolic See."[13] Why is this particular canon of 1917 even mentioned in 1967, since it refers to the *Christian* faith and not the (Roman) Catholic faith? Was the presumption in the early twentieth century that the (Roman) Catholic faith equals the Christian faith? We hope not. Why then refer to this canon at all? Indeed, although this specific passage, canon 2314, was not, after all, reproduced in its entirety in the 1983 revision of the *Code of Canon*

---

11. *Catechism*, par. 846 (emphasis added).
12. *Unitatis Redintegratio*, par. 19, in Flannery, *Conciliar and Post Conciliar Documents*, 490.
13. Edward N. Peters, ed., *The 1917 or Pio-Benedictine Code of Canon Law* (1917; repr., San Francisco: Ignatius Press, 2001), 735.

Law, it was nevertheless referred to specifically in the "Directory concerning Ecumenical Matters," drafted in 1967, in the wake of Vatican II, as if somehow this particular canon still mattered. This is quite surprising. In addition, when the two codes of canon law are compared, the 1917 and 1983 editions, the substance of canon 2314 does indeed reemerge, though in an abbreviated form, in canon 1364 in the later edition. The language employed in this subsequent rendition is hardly ecumenical: it is not at all appreciative of the integrity and soundness of other theological traditions beyond Rome. Indeed, they are judged to be little more than schismatic: "§1. Without prejudice to the prescript of can. 194, §1, n. 2, an apostate from the faith, a heretic, or a schismatic incurs a *latae sententiae* [sentence already passed] excommunication; in addition, a cleric can be punished with the penalties mentioned in can. 1336, §1, nn. 1, 2, and 3."[14]

So then, in light of these judgments, and bearing in mind the distinction noted earlier in terms of Protestants who are born into the Protestant church and those who leave Roman Catholicism to enter a Reformation church, the situation looks something like this: since Ulrich Zwingli and John Calvin both left the Roman Catholic Church, whereas John Wesley did not, having been born into the Church of England and baptized as an infant, Zwingli and Calvin are both schismatics and therefore likely lost (bearing in mind Rome's earlier language of "Hence they could not be saved . . ."), though Wesley may yet be in heaven since he is by no means personally chargeable with the sin of schism!

Does the Roman Catholic Church Believe in Religious Liberty?

The condemnation argument is predicated on the mistaken foundation that Rome is supposedly "The Church" with a capital "C," or "The Christian faith," as canon 2314 puts it. This same argument keeps emerging in different contexts even today, and in some places where one would hardly expect it, especially in the area, for example, of religious freedom. Two senses of religious liberty can be distinguished at the outset: the first concerns the freedom in the political realm—as in various nation-states—to practice religion in accordance with one's best judgments unfettered by the state. Clearly the documents of Vatican II affirm this first, basic understanding of religious liberty. A second sense

---

14. *Code of Canon Law* 6.2.1, "Delicts against Religion and the Unity of the Church," the Holy See, http://www.vatican.va/archive/ENG1104/__P52.HTM. Since Rome has maintained that the church of Christ subsists in the Roman Catholic Church, to be excommunicated from it is to be lost—so argue some.

of liberty, however, concerns the spiritual and moral freedom to practice religion freely even if such liberty entails rejecting a hitherto-embraced Roman Catholicism for the Protestant faith. Despite appearances to the contrary, Vatican II has not been a champion of religious liberty in this second sense, for it can only rightly be exercised if it points to Rome, not to Wittenberg (Lutheranism), Geneva (Calvinism), Canterbury (Anglicanism), or Epworth (Wesleyanism).

One of the more important documents of Vatican II on this topic is the *Dignitatis Humanae: Declaration on Religious Liberty*, which was drafted in December 1965. In this writing, after a general declaration that "the one true religion continues to exist in the [Roman] Catholic and Apostolic Church,"[15] Rome then teaches that "religious liberty is in keeping with the dignity of man and divine revelation," and that the church therefore "gives [religious liberty] her support."[16] However, these two statements may actually be at odds with each other such that what is given with one hand is taken away with the other. Thus the magisterium does affirm in this document that "the human person has a right to religious freedom," which should not be denied either on a social or a political level, through "coercion in civil society,"[17] or on a personal level, through repudiating the operations of conscience;[18] nevertheless all of this liberty must in the end be understood in a second sense against the larger backdrop that in the eyes of the magisterium in general and Vatican II in particular, the Roman Catholic Church is and remains the one true church. Such an affirmation implies obligations as well as restrictions that actually result in a delimitation of freedom precisely when religious liberty is comprehended in the spiritual or moral sphere. Rome declares:

> The sacred Council likewise proclaims that these obligations bind man's conscience. Truth can impose itself on the mind of man only in virtue of its own truth, which wins over the mind with both gentleness and power. So while the religious freedom which men demand in fulfilling their obligation to worship God has to do with freedom from coercion in civil society, *it leaves intact the traditional [Roman] Catholic teaching on the moral duty of individuals and societies towards the true religion and the one Church of Christ.*[19]

What is that moral duty? It is the irrevocable obligation to enter and remain in the one true church established by Jesus Christ, which Rome identifies as

15. *Dignitatis Humanae: Declaration on Religious Liberty*, sec. 1, in Flannery, *Conciliar and Post Conciliar Documents*, 799.
16. Ibid., sec. 12, in Flannery, *Conciliar and Post Conciliar Documents*, 809.
17. Ibid.
18. Ibid., sec. 3, in Flannery, *Conciliar and Post Conciliar Documents*, 801.
19. Ibid., sec. 1, in Flannery, *Conciliar and Post Conciliar Documents*, 800 (emphasis added).

itself. Protestants, then, who were baptized as Roman Catholics are seemingly not so free after all. They certainly do not enjoy the same religious liberty as others, not even by means of the gentle leading of conscience. It thus is abundantly evident, given the declarations above, that no one is so free as to be able to leave the Roman Catholic Church in order to become Protestant. Such an action would constitute not religious liberty but its abuse. Rome simply refuses, at all costs, to be viewed as just a different theological tradition. In its own self-understanding it is nothing less than "The Church" with capital letters. What Zwingli and Calvin did, then, was not a bold and judicious exercise of religious liberty but simply to sin, to wallow in the darkness of schism, to which no person, then as now, has any right.

Giving Rome the Benefit of the Doubt

Though Roman Catholicism does make its own tradition the center of the church to the diminishment of both Eastern Orthodoxy and Protestantism, perhaps the condemnation argument explained above is not as harsh or as unecumenical as we have imagined. Thus, in a spirit of Christian grace and charity, we are willing to give Rome the benefit of the doubt. In passages drawn from both the *Catechism* and *Canon Law* that are fraught with ambiguity, perhaps other interpretations should be in the offing. We will consider at least two more. At any rate, let Rome speak for itself in light of our arguments; let its scholars and apologists think through and state their own case in light of the following two scenarios that suggest additional interpretations of the condemnation argument. Perhaps things are better than we have supposed, but then again perhaps they are even worse.

Scenario 1: First of all, recall the specifics of the condemnation argument: "Hence they could not be saved who, knowing that the [Roman] Catholic Church was founded as necessary by God through Christ, would refuse either to enter it or *to remain* in it."[20] In light of this passage, it may be that Protestants, even those who have left the Roman church, are yet in a state of salvation and remain so simply because they do not meet the criterion of the second clause since they do not know that "the [Roman] Catholic Church was founded as necessary by God through Christ." That is, they do not comprehend this for all sorts of reasons, one of which is that they reject the wordplay entailed in confusing the Roman church with the catholic or universal church (in our language, the ancient ecumenical church). Thus Christ did not and could not have founded

---

20. *Catechism*, par. 846 (emphasis added).

the Roman Catholic Church as necessary. Such a claim would be an ecumenical nonstarter. In this first instance Protestants are not damned precisely because they are "invincibly ignorant" of the true state of affairs that Christ, in Rome's view at least, did indeed establish the Roman Catholic Church as necessary.

Scenario 2: Roman Catholics who eventually make their way to the Protestant church may indeed acknowledge that Christ established the Roman Catholic Church as necessary to salvation at the beginning of things (meeting the criterion of the second clause for condemnation) but that the subsequent history of the church has abundantly demonstrated that the Roman communion is no longer necessary (certainly not in an exclusive or myopic sense). Due to its corruptions, many of which emerged in the Middle Ages, and due also to the schisms, the disruptions of fellowship and love, in which it was involved as a divorced partner, so to speak, especially during the Great Schism of 1054 and that of the sixteenth century, the Roman Catholic Church quite simply is no longer necessary in the way it has imagined. Vibrant scriptural Christianity also exists beyond its walls (in the form of Eastern Orthodoxy and Protestantism, for instance), for the church has moved from a monological understanding of unity to a more dialogical and historically accurate one whose chief characteristic is unity in a diversity of vibrant theological traditions. This unity is expressed in the many members and yet the one body of Christ, of which even the apostle Paul wrote. However, observe in this second scenario that such "reformist" Protestants cannot be saved since they strike at the very heart of Rome's own self-understanding: they challenge this particular tradition at the deepest level of its myths.

Let's shift the framework a bit in order to entertain how this matter is viewed by those who have been labeled by Rome as "the other." How does this second scenario look to those baptized Roman Catholics who have become Protestants today? From their perspective, within the broader ecumenical church, these vibrant Christians (who are obviously very intentional about their religion) have had a life-changing encounter with Christ outside the Roman communion. Indeed, they have experienced the witness of the Holy Spirit that they are the children of God and are fully members of the body of Christ as they participate in other theological traditions. Indeed, they enjoy an abundance of gracious gifts from God and are growing in holiness and Christian maturity. For its part, Rome apparently cannot accept this Protestant conversion at its face value without responding with the language of heresy, schism, excommunication, and condemnation simply because such a movement decenters Rome's own authority. It is simply an intolerable challenge to embrace the reality of what the church has been for ages: different theological traditions under the one lordship of Christ.

If this condemnation of some Protestants is real, an accurate interpretation, then it is important to consider at least some of its theological implications for the body of Christ. Again, from the perspective of erstwhile Roman Catholics who have now become Protestants, it is no one less than the Holy Spirit who has regenerated them and witnessed to them of the fullness of salvation in other theological traditions, a vibrancy and a life of which they hitherto had not known. From the vantage point of Rome, however, since such a transition apparently results in condemnation and the loss of redemption, it cannot have been a true work of the Holy Spirit. This is exactly where the Roman Catholic insistence upon being the center of the church, apart from a full and complete acceptance of other Christian communions, gets into so much trouble, theologically speaking. To illustrate, consider the same elements here, but now in one last way: Protestants profess that the Holy Spirit has assured them of salvation and the fullness of Christian experience as they actively practice their faith as members of the Protestant church. Rome, it seems, must doubt that the Holy Spirit has done this since the result, entailing the loss of salvation, is a great evil. From the Protestant viewpoint, however, Rome's erroneous judgment—mistaking the part for the whole, or the part for its fullness and center—has now revealed its very bitter ethnocentric fruit: evil, at least in some sense, has now been attributed to the gracious and blessed work of the Holy Spirit.

Observe, once again, that this is merely a hypothetical scenario, though the conclusion we have suggested seems to follow if the public claims of Rome are taken seriously. Let Rome speak for itself. Let it clear up any misunderstanding in terms of those former Roman Catholics who are now born-again Protestants, for example. Let it resolve any ambiguity in terms of the salvific status of those many former Roman Catholics in Latin and South America, for instance, who are now exuberant Pentecostal Protestants and appear to be anything but lost. Does Rome really believe that all such folk—whether from Guatemala, Ecuador, or Brazil—who have become Protestants are invincibly ignorant, or worse yet, schismatics who may be damned? If not, then Rome should forthrightly acknowledge that many former Roman Catholics are being faithfully led by the Holy Spirit, who witnesses to them in Spirit and in truth that they are nothing less than children of God (Romans 8), even as they practice their faith in various Protestant traditions. Indeed, though we affirm that Roman Catholics are our brothers and sisters in Christ, we must also acknowledge in a clear and forthright way that former Roman Catholics make wonderful Christians, indeed, some of the best around.

In the end, Rome not only has a problem with the church, the living body of Christ well beyond its walls, but also has a problem with reality, a reality that is right in front of its eyes. Within the broader Christian community, vibrant in its witness to the truth and beauty that is Jesus Christ, it is never a sin not to be a Roman Catholic. Indeed, the Eastern Orthodox have known this basic truth all along, and so have Protestants since the sixteenth century. Such a recognition, with grace and abundant charity, fosters the true spirit of Christian ecumenism.

8

"You Are Your Own Pope"

The Tu Quoque *Objection*

The phrase *tu quoque* literally means "you too"; it is the Latin name for the informal fallacy that occurs when someone accuses a critic of the same thing of which the critic is accusing that person. *Tu quoque* is thus in one sense a diversionary tactic that aims to turn the tables on one's critic instead of answering a criticism. "I'm a scoundrel, huh? Well, so are you!"

While it is recognized as an informal fallacy, those who deploy the *tu quoque* move sometimes have a point. For instance, if one is accused of lying, the charge loses at least much of its force if the person making the accusation is a known liar. Although it does not show that you are not a liar, it does at least show that you are on the same level as your critic, who thus loses the high moral ground if guilty of the same thing you are.

It is in this sense that Reformation Christians may make the *tu quoque* move in response to certain criticisms from their Roman colleagues pertaining to authority. In this chapter, I will examine a statement of the argument by the Roman Catholic philosopher and apologist (and former evangelical) Bryan Cross, who tries to show that Roman Catholics are not in the same boat as they contend their Protestant friends are, and thus that the *tu quoque* argument against Roman Catholics has no force.

Cross prefaces his response to the *tu quoque* objection by summarizing an argument about the nature of authority that he thinks poses problems for Protestants. Here he reiterates the familiar claim that those who do not accept

Roman claims about apostolic succession are bereft of any principled reason to accept the authority of creeds and confessions. This is another variation of the all-or-nothing arguments we examined earlier. As Cross puts it, each individual is left to "pick" the confession that most closely resembles their own personal interpretation of Scripture. But believers are not bound by a chosen confession: if their interpretation of Scripture changes, they can simply pick another one that lines up better with their new perspective.

The important principle Cross wants to emphasize is that if we submit to an authority only when we agree with it, we are really only submitting to ourselves. "In other words, agreement with oneself cannot be the basis for authority over oneself. Therefore a creed or confession's agreement with one's own interpretation of Scripture cannot be the basis for its authority. And this is why without apostolic succession, creeds or confession have no actual authority."[1]

Or, put another way, if you do not accept Roman claims about apostolic succession and the authority of the magisterium, you are your own pope, as one of my Roman Catholic friends insisted to me![2] So the charge is that every Protestant elects himself to the office of pope over the domain of his own personal interpretation of the faith.

Oh Yeah? You Too!

Here is where Reformation Christians want to lodge the *tu quoque* objection. Aren't persons who embrace Rome in the same boat? Aren't they choosing the denomination or church that best fits their own understanding of Scripture, history, and tradition?

> But if picking a confession on the basis of its agreement with one's own interpretation of Scripture entails that this confession has no authority over oneself, then picking the Catholic Church on the basis of its agreement with one's own interpretation of history, tradition, and Scripture entails that the Catholic Church has no authority over oneself. In short, the conclusion of the *tu quoque* objection is that either the Catholic Church likewise has no authority, or the Protestant confessions can truly have authority.[3]

Cross, however, denies that Reformation and Roman Christians are in the same boat in this regard. Indeed, as he apparently sees things, Reformation

---

1. Cross, "The *Tu Quoque*," sec. 1, *Called to Communion* (blog), May 24, 2010, http://www.calledtocommunion.com/2010/05/the-tu-quoque.
2. This came from Mike Allen, a former student of mine.
3. Cross, "*Tu Quoque*," sec. 2.

Christians are buffeted about in a leaky little sailboat, whereas Roman Christians are aboard a majestic ocean liner. His reply to the *tu quoque* objection is given in three key points, which we summarize in the next section.

Not Us, Just You!

First, he spells out the course of study that should be followed by those who seek to join the Church of Rome and explains what he believes will be the outcome of that study. "Apart from a supernatural experience, ideally, an adult would come to seek full communion with the Catholic Church only after careful study of the motives of credibility, Church history, the Church Fathers, and Scripture."[4] The "motives of credibility" are the external proofs of the Christian revelation such as "the miracles of Christ and the saints, prophecies, the Church's growth and holiness, and her fruitfulness and stability."[5]

The study of church history would be a decade-by-decade exploration, starting with the time of the apostles and continuing down to the present day. The study would pay particular attention to schisms; in each case the prospective Roman Catholic would notice the criteria by which it was determined that the party in schism was guilty of dividing the church. Now here is the expected outcome: "By such a study, and by the help of the Holy Spirit, he would discover that the Catholic Church is the one, holy, catholic and apostolic Church that Christ founded in the first century, and that has continued to grow throughout the world over the past two millennia."[6]

The key word here is "discover," a word that Cross continues to employ over and over. In particular, he thinks his prospective convert "discovers" the Catholic Church, whereas the Protestant only "discovers" a confession that agrees with his personal interpretation of Scripture. And that, he alleges, explains why the former can have real authority, while the latter cannot. "The difference lies fundamentally neither in the discovery process nor in the evidence by which the discovery is made, even though these may be different. The difference lies fundamentally in the nature of that which is discovered."[7]

Second, Cross highlights why there is a difference between the authority of Scripture and that of Protestant confessions. Whereas Scripture has intrinsic, binding authority because God himself is its source, all confessions are "merely" human interpretations of Scripture and thus do not bear the same

---

4. Ibid., sec. 3.A.
5. *Catechism of the Catholic Church*, 2nd ed. (Mahwah, NJ: Paulist Press, 1994), par. 156.
6. Cross, "*Tu Quoque*," sec. 3.A.
7. Ibid.

authority. He reiterates this claim over and over, using some form of the word "mere" at least nine times in the course of making this second point in order to underscore the contrast he wants to draw between Roman Catholic "discovery" and Protestant "interpretation." There is no "guarantee of protection from error" for Protestants, since these confessions are "essentially human opinion" that has no more authority than a systematic theology written by a theologian. "This is why a Protestant confession has its 'authority' only on the basis of the individual's agreement with its interpretation of Scripture, not because of who wrote that confession."[8]

This puts Protestants in a rather precarious position, according to Cross, for if the only basis for the authority of a confession is the individual's agreement with its interpretation of Scripture, that authority could shift at any time. The individual may agree with it now, but perhaps not tomorrow. "This shows that the confession has no intrinsic authority; it is not the confession that is authoritative over his beliefs; rather, his present beliefs make the confession to be 'authoritative,' by containing the interpretation he presently believes to be required of himself. . . . He picks this particular confession because it conforms to his interpretation; it does not oblige him to conform to it, or, once picked, to remain conformed to it."[9]

Third, Cross draws a contrast between what he takes to be the authority of the Church of Rome and the authority of Protestant confessions. And here his case hinges crucially on his claim that the convert to Rome "discovers" something that is not a mere interpretation. What the convert finds through study of history, tradition, and Scripture is the true church.

> He finds the one, holy, catholic and apostolic Church and its magisterial authority in succession from the Apostles and from Christ. He does not merely find an interpretation in which the Church has apostolic succession; he finds this very same Church itself, and he finds it to have divine authority by a succession from the Apostles. In finding the Church he finds an organic entity nearly two thousand years old with a divinely established hierarchy preserving divine authority.[10]

And this he takes to be the crucial difference between the church that the Roman convert finds and any church united around a Protestant confession. Whereas Protestant confessions have "mere" human authority, "the Church" is of divine origin and authority and consequently can bind the conscience.

8. Ibid., sec. 3.B.
9. Ibid.
10. Ibid., sec. 3.C.

Indeed, Cross compares the discovery of the church through study of Scripture, tradition, and history to the discovery of Christ himself through reading the Scriptures. The reader who discovers Christ in the Scriptures has discovered a divine Person, someone who has authority over him. To discover Christ in this fashion is not to "pick" him as an authority, so this discovery is nothing like adopting a Protestant confession. "Just as discovering Christ through the study of Scripture is not subject to the *tu quoque* objection, so for the same reason discovering the Body of Christ through the study of Scripture, tradition and history is not subject to the *tu quoque*. In both cases, it is the same Christ he has discovered, in His physical body which has ascended into Heaven, or His mystical body, the Church."[11] Now this is a remarkable claim: discovering Christ in Scripture is essentially the same as discovering the Church through Scripture, tradition, and history. Indeed, immediately after these lines, he cites the following quote from Joan of Arc that he thinks sums up the faith and good sense of both the holy doctors and ordinary believers: "About Jesus Christ and the Church, I simply know they're just one thing, and we shouldn't complicate the matter."[12]

By contrast, he alleges that Protestants define the church not in terms of divine authority that is handed down in succession from the apostles but rather in terms of agreement with one's personal interpretation of Scripture. This undercuts any meaningful ecclesial authority "because for each disputant, if 'the Church' rules against his interpretation, for him she ceases to be 'the Church,' and hence, he need not submit to her." This, moreover, amounts to "nothing less than an implicit denial of a visible catholic Church."[13]

Thus according to Cross, Protestants cannot claim that they have "discovered" the church in any sense like Roman Catholics can. The only worth of their claim is "that they have discovered other persons who have faith in Christ, a faith in Christ that is sufficiently similar to their own."[14]

To make matters even worse, Protestants cannot appeal to the fact that they have discovered the gospel to solve their individualistic-authority problem. While Scripture surely has authority, any interpretation of Scripture that goes beyond repeating the exact words of the Bible is a merely human product and has no conscience-binding authority. "So for that reason, what Protestants refer to as 'the gospel,' insofar as it is not an exact re-statement of Scripture, has no more authority than a systematic theology text, being a merely human opinion."[15]

11. Ibid.
12. This quote is from *Catechism*, par. 795.
13. Cross, "*Tu Quoque*," 3.C.
14. Ibid., sec. 3.Q1A.
15. Ibid., sec. 3.Q2A.

An Utterly Impractical Ideal

Cross mounts an impressive effort to stave off the *tu quoque* objection, but unfortunately for him, his case has numerous problems. First, consider what his "ideal" convert to Rome must study before conversion: the "motives of credibility," Scripture, the church fathers, and church history. The problem here is that if he means serious study of all these matters to the point that one has any sort of sound understanding of the controverted issues, of the arguments and counterarguments, then he is asking for something that is utterly unrealistic.

Take Scripture for a start. If prospective converts are to intelligently weigh in on disputed issues of biblical interpretation, must they learn Greek and Hebrew? Must they at least read the best Protestant and Eastern Orthodox biblical scholarship, along with the best Roman Catholic scholarship, and master this material well enough to render an informed judgment? Doing this with anything approaching even competence, let alone expertise, would require years of intensive study.

Then there are two thousand years of church history to examine. Recall that Cross envisions a decade-by-decade study of the history of the church from the apostles to the present day. That's a lot of decades. Such a study that would be anything beyond the most superficial survey would be far beyond the competence of most persons. Consider the issues involved in patristic scholarship and the controverted issues that separated Roman Catholics from Eastern Orthodoxy. Or consider the exquisitely detailed and often technical nature of Peter Lampe's analysis of the church in early Rome. Most prospective converts are hardly equipped even to begin to grasp these issues in any sort of depth, let alone to pronounce upon them. Another set of extraordinarily complex issues are involved in the medieval period of church history, ranging from penance to indulgences to purgatory to transubstantiation. Then there are the issues of the period of the Reformation. Again, is the prospective convert really to become an expert in Reformation history? Skipping over a few centuries, we come to the difficult issues that arise with the modernist controversy and the rather significant changes of Vatican II. What we have mentioned here represents just a few of the bare bones of church history, and even to understand these issues with anything approaching competence would require massive time and effort.

We have not even mentioned the complex philosophical and historical issues involved in exploring with real insight the "motives of credibility" or the issues surrounding tradition and the various ways it is understood in the three major branches of the Christian church. But the point for now is clear: Cross's "ideal" convert is just that, an ideal that seldom if ever exists.

Scripture's Not Clear, Yet Church History Is Clear?

Here is the deeper problem with Cross's suggestion. Roman Catholics are sharply critical of the Protestant principle of sola Scriptura and the attendant claim about the clarity of Scripture. Roman apologists love to point out that commitment to the authority of Scripture is no guarantee of orthodoxy, that groups ranging from fundamentalist Baptists to a number of cults affirm the Bible as their sole authority. Moreover, evangelicals of different stripes disagree about various issues, such as the sacraments, predestination, church polity, and so on. If Scripture is clear, the question is pressed, how can all these groups differ so much, since they all claim to accept the authority of the Bible?

In response to this question, it is important to remember that the clarity of Scripture is not a claim that everything in Scripture is clear or equally clear. As Peter observed about the Letters of Paul, "His letters contain some things that are hard to understand" (2 Pet. 3:16). But the fact that some things are hard to understand suggests that much is not hard to grasp. And the principle of the clarity of Scripture pertains to those things. *The Westminster Confession* puts it as follows: "All things in Scripture are not alike plain in themselves, nor alike clear unto all; yet those things which are necessary to be known, believed, and observed for salvation, are so clearly propounded and opened in some place of Scripture or other that not only the learned but the unlearned, in a due use of ordinary means, may attain unto a sufficient understanding of them."[16] Now here is the point. While Cross apparently denies the Protestant principle of the clarity of Scripture, he appears to believe clarity is to be found in something vastly more complex: the motives (motifs) of credibility plus church history plus the church fathers plus Scripture. In other words, while appeal to the authority of Scripture is not adequate to provide Protestants with a sufficiently clear source of doctrinal authority, appeal to the fourfold criterion cited above is.

Now if this is what Cross is claiming, it is not only a remarkable claim but also a highly implausible one. The clarity that Scripture lacks as a doctrinal authority is to be supplied by the far more extensive body of material that adds to Scripture the motives of credibility, the church fathers, and two thousand years of church history. All of that is supposed to generate clarity in a way that Scripture does not! Really?

Indeed, the utter impracticality of trying to understand, let alone master, this massive body of literature can actually be a strategic ploy for Roman

---

16. *The Westminster Confession of Faith*, 1.7, in *The Constitution of the Presbyterian Church (U.S.A.), Book of Confessions, Part 1* (Louisville: Office of the General Assembly, 2014), 151, available at https://www.pcusa.org/site_media/media/uploads/oga/pdf/boc2014.pdf.

apologists. If prospective converts are convinced that they need to master all this material, if they have even a remote idea what that involves, they will be completely overwhelmed. In this condition, they may welcome any answers that purport to make sense of this enormous welter of material they are not qualified to assess. And all the more so if those "answers" invoke infallible authority.

Now, by contrast with such utterly unrealistic ideals, let us turn to the book of Acts and the famous example of the Bereans. When they heard the preaching of Paul and Silas, they "received the message with great eagerness and examined the Scriptures every day to see if what Paul said was true" (Acts 17:11). Only after examining the Scriptures did they believe. But more important for our concerns, this implies that they could understand the meaning of Scripture well enough to render this judgment. This examination, moreover, was done communally, not merely as individuals, and it is clear that their response to Paul and Silas is described approvingly.

Examining the Scriptures in this fashion, while a demanding task, is at least reasonably practical. Testing a claim that purports to be God's ultimate good news against the standard of Scripture is within the reach of ordinary seekers who diligently study Scripture, especially as they do so in community. But it is hard to imagine an equivalent story where prospective converts would be expected to examine not only the Scriptures but also two thousand years of church history and theological controversy as well before rendering a judgment.

Trivializing Protestant "Authority"

Next, Cross's account of Protestant authority is highly tendentious and misleading. Recall his charge that Protestants have no real authority because each person "picks" the confession or church that matches their current interpretation of Scripture. Consequently, the confession has no authority since their "present beliefs make the confession to be authoritative." If they change their mind or their interpretation varies, they are not bound and can simply "pick" another church or confession.

There are a number of problems with these claims. First, Cross's account of individuals "picking" their beliefs is hardly true to how Protestants typically come to affirm a confession or church. Despite the common caricature, Protestants do not typically arrive at their beliefs by going into the desert with their Bible so they can be alone to figure out its meaning for themselves. Rather, they are more typically reared in churches where they are taught the Scriptures in the context of Christian community and hear biblical preaching, often for years, before they embrace the faith for themselves. In this sort of context Protestants are formed and, not unlike the Bereans, discern a match between what Scripture teaches and what their church teaches. They do not simply "pick" a church or confession after constructing their own personal version of the faith.

At the heart of Protestant preaching and teaching is the gospel, which Paul summed up as the wonderful news that Christ died for our sins in accordance with the Scriptures, that he was buried and on the third day was raised from the dead and appeared to numerous witnesses, starting with Peter and the other disciples (1 Cor. 15:1–7). It is this straightforward message that Paul says he received and in turn passed on to the Corinthians. This is the gospel that has been passed down from generation to generation to the present day. It is not mere opinion but the very word of salvation in which we stand and through which we are being saved (see esp. vv. 1–2).

Moreover, core creedal orthodoxy, abundantly attested in Scripture, is affirmed not only in magisterial Protestantism but also in other evangelical churches. Thus Protestants are in fact schooled and formed by apostolic truth that has been affirmed for over two thousand years, and it is with this sort of formation that they "pick" their confession/church. It would be far more accurate to say, however, that the truth of the gospel has gripped them, and their acceptance of it is simply a matter of acknowledging that reality.

Here we come to one of the fundamental problems in Cross's article. It is completely misleading, if not outright caricature, to say that a Protestant's present beliefs "make" a confession authoritative. This is to confuse (1) what makes a claim authoritative and (2) the mental act of recognizing or discerning an authority. What makes a theological truth claim authoritative is that it is either a direct revelation from God, or a faithful statement of that revelation, or a clear inference from it. My beliefs do not make any of these authoritative. However, my belief can reflect that authoritative truth when I recognize it and assent to it. But that hardly means that my belief is what makes that truth authoritative. It is completely the other way around. The truth elicits our belief, but our belief does not create or establish truth.

An Extreme Claim and a False Dilemma

Here Cross may protest that any element of human judgment undermines authority and renders it a matter of "mere" human opinion. Indeed, any claim that goes beyond stating the exact words of Scripture must be a matter of mere human authority.

Once again, this is an extreme claim that leads to some rather dubious implications. Recall that Scripture was originally written in Hebrew, Aramaic, and Greek. So if Protestants cannot take anything as authoritative except the exact words of Scripture, then we are confined to the original languages. Every translation involves some degree of human judgment, and indeed, this even goes for the Hebrew and Greek text, for we do not have the original autographs, and the copied manuscripts in our possession have suffered some degree of corruption, however slight. So once again, Cross is demanding something that is utterly unrealistic.

Consider the common Christian practice of sharing our faith with unbelievers. Are we restricted to citing the exact words of Scripture when we do so? Or may we explain the meaning of Scripture, paraphrase it, and so on? Surely we may do this, and we can be faithful to Scripture in doing so.

Even more, it is certainly reasonable to believe that Bible translations can accurately, even if imperfectly, communicate God's revelation to us in authoritative form. God did not intend his Word only for the original recipients, and it is certainly reasonable to accept human language as an adequate medium to convey God's revelation in Scripture to different ages and cultures. Again, confidence in the essential clarity of Scripture and the more foundational belief that God has successfully revealed himself in Scripture lead us to this conclusion.

In view of this, Cross presents us with an altogether misleading picture when he insists that "every interpretation of Scripture that is made by men-without-divine authorization is the product of mere-man, and thus has no divine authority over man."[17] It is a false dilemma to suggest that any authority must be either (1) utterly free of any sort of error or imperfection or (2) a mere human interpretation with no real authority. A more realistic picture recognizes a range of authorities, beginning with the authority of Scripture as absolute. Next, Protestants also have reason to affirm the classic creeds as normative summaries of core biblical teaching precisely because they believe Scripture succeeds as revelation and is essentially clear, as we argued in chapter 5. Moreover, they may recognize pastors and teachers as having authority insofar as they faithfully study and preach the Scriptures in a way that is consistent with those essential truths. Authority to interpret Scripture is also enhanced by appropriate training and spiritual maturity, and again, not all interpreters are equally authoritative.

Again, consider the Bereans. Who authorized them to interpret Scripture and to judge the preaching of the apostles by the standard of Scripture? Or

17. Cross, "*Tu Quoque*," sec. 3.C.

think about Paul's word to Timothy: "But as for you, continue in what you have learned and have become convinced of, because you know those from whom you learned it, and how from infancy you have known the Holy Scriptures, which are able to make you wise for salvation through faith in Christ Jesus" (2 Tim. 3:14–15). It is the sacred writings themselves "that are able to make you wise for salvation through faith in Christ Jesus." Of course, Timothy had some human teachers, including his mother, Eunice, and his grandmother, Lois (2 Tim. 1:5). Did their teaching lack authority because they were not formally authorized interpreters of Scripture? It seems clear that the authority here resides in the power of Scripture itself to instruct, and even merely human teachers may be "authorized" by Scripture itself to pass on its message to all those who are willing to learn.

There is no guarantee of infallible perfection here, but again, there is no need for infallible clarity on every issue. Indeed, a vital part of Christian discipleship and sanctification is ongoing study of Scripture, including wrestling with those parts of Scripture that are "hard to understand."

Degrees of Authority and Room for Disagreement

Protestants will not agree on everything, but neither do Roman Catholics. Consider one of the most famously contested issues among Protestants: the issue of how predestination relates to free will and responsibility. Calvinists and Arminians have sharply disagreed on that issue for centuries and vigorously debate it to this day.

It is less well known, but highly instructive, that Roman Catholics have their own version of this same dispute, particularly the historic controversy between the determinist Dominicans and the libertarian Molinists. This controversy was hotly contested, and the opponents of Molina pressed for his condemnation, and in fact when Molina died there were numerous rumors that his views would be condemned by Rome. The pope declined to condemn Molinism, but he did issue a decree forbidding the contending parties from calling each other heretics and promised to resolve the matter at an opportune time. Alfred Freddoso, who translated Molina into English, wryly observed: "It stands as a tribute to the prudence of Paul V and his successors that this 'opportune' time has yet to arrive."[18]

While we may agree with Freddoso in admiring the pope and his successors in one way, in another way we might wonder what the alleged advantage of

---

18. Luis de Molina, *On Divine Foreknowledge: Part IV of the Concordia*, trans. with an introduction and notes by Alfred J. Freddoso (Ithaca, NY: Cornell University Press, 1988), viii.

having a pope amounts to if controversies like this one are left unresolved. Clearly the issue is important and both sides cannot be right. One might wonder why the pope did not pronounce more definitively on the matter, unless perhaps it shows that such disagreements and disputes are altogether legitimate and maybe even integral to a growing understanding of biblical truth, whether in Roman Catholicism or Protestantism.

Here it is worth underscoring that infallible proclamations are relatively few and far between. To be sure, Roman Catholicism makes more claims to infallible teaching than Orthodoxy and Protestantism, and this is part of its appeal to many people. Many of these doctrines are shared by Protestants, such as the classic creeds and the repudiation of Pelagianism. Even if Protestants do not typically identify these creeds as infallible, the central doctrines they affirm are normative for most in a way that is functionally the same.

Other pronouncements that have been elevated to the level of infallibility by Rome are more dubious, however. The doctrine of transubstantiation and the post-Reformation decrees on justification were the product of a divided church and do not carry the authority of truly catholic consensus. The same can be said of the Marian dogmas, which represent the only two occasions when the pope has spoken ex cathedra. The Marian dogmas have no clear basis in Scripture or the earliest sources, and they do nothing to settle disputed issues of biblical interpretation, like the Molinist-Dominican controversy.

In view of all this, the initial appeal of a larger body of infallible doctrine claimed by Rome loses much of its luster. Indeed, given that Roman theology elevates dubiously grounded, if not extrabiblical, doctrine to the same level of authority as central christological teaching and tends to generate an all-or-nothing mentality, Protestants have good reason to think that the Roman claim to infallibility is actually a serious liability rather than an asset.

In any case, the reality is that in their day-to-day Christian discipleship, Roman Catholics do not have infallible pronouncements to guide them but have to make do with what is called the "ordinary magisterium." This "ordinary magisterium" is nondefinitive teaching from popes, bishops, and priests that the faithful are expected to follow. Aidan Nichols, a contemporary Roman Catholic theologian, explains that the faithful should give allegiance to this teaching even though it makes no claim to be the last word.

As Nichols recognizes, "The Second Vatican Council itself considerably modified certain elements in the ordinary papal teaching (faithfully echoed by the wider episcopate) of the last hundred years."[19] In view of this reality, Nichols contends that the guidance of the Holy Spirit in the church "justifies

---

19. Nichols, *The Shape of Catholic Theology* (Collegeville, MN: Liturgical Press, 1991), 250.

our confidence in the general reliability of the ordinary magisterium, even though we cannot deny a priori that some particular aspect of its teaching may eventually be perceived as needing mulching or pruning, cultivation or cutting back." Now here is the practical upshot of recognizing this reality.

> From these considerations there derives the duty of Catholics to make a sincere, sustained effort to give ex animo assent to the teachings of the ordinary magisterium—teachings that are always more likely to be right than not. However, in a given case, they may find that, nevertheless, they are not convinced. . . . More than this, they find themselves in a state of moral certitude on some point in a manner that they could not leave the magisterial teaching intact.[20]

Notice: these teachings are "more likely to be right than not." That is far from a guarantee of truth, let alone infallible truth. Indeed, as Nichols acknowledges, conscientious Roman Catholics my find themselves in a "state of moral certitude" that would be incompatible with some of this teaching.

So here are the questions: Does the magisterium have authority, even when it is recognized that its teaching is not infallible and may well require "pruning" of various kinds? Or does the magisterium function as "mere men" in such cases? Presumably Cross would want to say it has genuine teaching authority despite the fallible nature of its pronouncements and directives. If so, then it is hardly a problem for Protestant confessions and other teaching that they are not the final, infallible word on matters they address.

"Discovering" the Church

Cross's central contention is that the difference between the Roman convert and the Protestant lies fundamentally in the nature of what is discovered. What he thinks the prospective Roman convert discovers is that the (Roman) Catholic Church is identical with the church that Christ founded, and that it has maintained its magisterial authority ever since. "The Church he finds in history and in the present has its divine authority from Christ through the Apostles and the bishops by way of succession. Herein lies the critical difference between the Church the inquirer finds in the centuries following Christ, and a Protestant confession."[21]

But Cross's claim is profoundly question-begging. The issue at stake here is precisely whether the Roman Catholic Church is in fact what it claims to be.

20. Ibid., 251.
21. Cross, "*Tu Quoque*," sec. 3.C.

For Cross simply to state that this is what the inquirer will find is to presume what is very much at issue. This is not to say that he needs to make his case from history in his brief article, yet that does not warrant him in a polemical article simply to take it as a given that the inquirer will "discover" what he, Cross, believes to be the case.

Indeed, what Cross professes to "find" or "discover" involves numerous interpretations of historical evidence, and he cannot validate his judgment simply by labeling it a "discovery." What makes his interpretations even more precarious is that what he claims about the origin of the Roman Catholic Church, including the papacy and so forth, flies in the face of the consensus of serious scholarship, both Protestant and Roman Catholic.

Cross is obviously aware that many church historians, historical theologians, biblical scholars, and others, who have given years to careful study of the evidence, have not "discovered" the Roman Catholic Church to be what he claims it to be. We will not reiterate what we have already detailed in earlier chapters: there we have laid out some of the evidence and lines of argument that lead us to reject the claims of Roman Catholicism. The notion that Peter was the first pope is an anachronism, entirely lacking historical evidence (see chap. 11). Likewise, the claims about unbroken lines of apostolic succession going back to the apostles do not hold up under critical historical investigation (see chap. 6). Moreover, the Church of Rome is hardly blameless in the schisms that have occurred: it must shoulder a portion of responsibility in these tragic events that have divided the church.

The Clarity of Christ and the Visible Church

This brings us to Cross's claim that discovering Christ through the study of Scripture is tantamount to discovering the church, the body of Christ, through the study of Scripture, tradition, and church history. We think this is a dubious claim and even misleading at best. Consider what we come to see when we discover Christ in Scripture. We see that he is the very Son of God, and that he came to provide salvation and eternal life. We see perfect humanity as well as deity. "No one has ever seen God, but the one and only Son, who is himself God and is in closest relationship with the Father, has made him known" (John 1:18).

Consider again the luminous splendor of Christ as revealed in the pages of Scripture. He is the spotless Lamb of God, who could ask his critics, "Can any of you prove me guilty of sin?" (John 8:46). Every word he spoke, as well as every action performed with his body, demonstrated God's holy love. We see a man who was never compromised by corruption or sinful motives and who expressed God's character perfectly.

Can anyone honestly say that the body of Christ in any of its manifestations shows forth God's holy character in a comparable way? Indeed, specify this question to the Roman Catholic Church. Does the history of the Church of Rome display the "same" Christ with the same sort of clarity and luminous splendor with which Christ is displayed in the pages of Scripture? The answer, we think, is apparent. We do not discover a church that is distinctly holy even by comparison with other churches, but one that has its own unsavory history marred by zeal for political power and other forms of scandal and moral corruption, continuing into the twenty-first century.[22] The reality of the morally ambiguous history of the Church of Rome further undermines Cross's claim that "the Church" can be discovered in Scripture/history in a way that parallels how Christ is discovered in the pages of Scripture.

Now if the church cannot be identified in Scripture/history with the sort of clarity that Cross believes it can, does that mean we deny a visible catholic church, as he contends? Is an invisible church the only alternative to securing the true identity of the church through demonstrating an "unbroken" magisterial succession from Christ and the apostles?

It is a false dilemma to insist that our only alternative to an invisible church is a demonstrable episcopal succession going back to Christ and the apostles. We can believe that the church catholic is visible without insisting that it can be identified through magisterial succession. Consider an analogy. Imagine a first-time visitor to Oxford who wants to see the university for which that city is famous. "Where is the university?" he asks. Now anyone who is familiar with Oxford knows there is no simple answer to this question, since Oxford University is composed of a number of different colleges, some of which go back to medieval times, while others were founded much more recently. There is no one of these colleges to which one can point and say, "*That* is Oxford University," in the sense that that particular college is identical with Oxford University. If our visitor has a preconceived notion of what a university is or insists on a more definite answer to his question, he will be disappointed.

However, the fact that we cannot simply point to one college or one part of Oxford University to answer the question of that visitor does not mean that Oxford University is invisible or that there is anything particularly mysterious about its identity. Nor does it undermine the essential unity of purpose common to every college that is part of Oxford University, nor the fact that the

---

22. The sex scandals depicted in the Academy Award–winning movie *Spotlight* are only the most notorious of recent examples of moral corruption.

university was founded in 1096. Every college, moreover, can trace its roots back to that date insofar as it is part of Oxford University. Likewise, the catholic church that was founded by Christ is composed of a number of churches, some ancient, some more recent, but all of them united by commitment to the gospel and rooted in classical Christian faith as expressed in the ecumenical creeds. All of them are now products of historical splits and divisions, but all can also trace their roots back to Christ and the apostles. There is, no doubt, ambiguity with respect to some of these churches and some members of all these churches. But the ambiguity does not override the impressive unity that runs through the various branches and parts of the church.

Given this ambiguity, it is inevitable that our judgment will sometimes be mistaken about the extent and location of the church. But the main point remains that we need not resort to the notion of an invisible church if we reject the claims of Rome.

Sustaining the Objection: Inescapable Individual Judgment

Our argument running through this chapter can perhaps be summed up like this: Cross not only exaggerates the individualism of Protestants but also downplays the individualistic aspect of conversion to Rome. There are places in his article, however, when he acknowledges this issue. One of them is in response to this question: "But isn't the person who becomes Catholic using his own private judgment just like the Protestant?" Here is his reply:

> We cannot but use our intellect and will in interpreting evidence, drawing conclusions, discovering truths, and making decisions. In that respect, inquirers who eventually become Protestant or Catholic start in the same epistemic situation. . . . With the help of the Holy Spirit, the inquirer who uses his intellect and will to examine history, tradition and Scripture, discovers this divinely founded entity bearing divine authority, and at that point submits to it. His own interpretation has no divine authority. But he discovers something beyond his own interpretation, something to which his interpretation points, and which **does** have divine authority. He discovers the Church. The Protestant can understand this in some sense, because in discovering Scripture the Protestant too has discovered something having divine authority, even while using his own intellect and will.[23]

The rhetorical force of Cross's essay very much depends on the contrast he continually attempts to draw between the Protestant's individual, personal

---

23. Cross, "*Tu Quoque*," sec. 3.Q4A (emphasis original).

"interpretation" and the Roman Catholic's "discovery" of objective, divine authority. In this quote, however, he broaches a crucial point that must be kept squarely in view in discussing these issues: all of us start in a similar epistemic situation and rely on the same fallible faculties as we render our judgment on these vital matters.

This is particularly important to keep in mind because of the extraordinary range and complexity of issues that Cross thinks the ideal inquirer should investigate and presumably master to the point of rendering an informed judgment. Clearly Cross's view makes remarkable demands for individual judgment on a vast body of literature and issues.

And even though his ideal is utterly impractical, it is not hard to see why he suggests that the inquirer must consider all this material in rendering a personal decision. The inquirer who focuses on Scripture is not likely to be impressed with the claims of Rome. This is why Roman Catholic apologists want to convince inquirers that later extrabiblical sources and traditions represent "developments" that have authority equal to clear scriptural teaching. In saying this, we want to be clear that we do not believe subsequent historical developments support the claims of Roman Catholicism. Our point is simply that Roman apologists need to shift the debate outside the pages of Scripture to give their claims any sort of plausibility.

But the main point to emphasize here is that an inescapable element of individual judgment is involved for all persons who join any church or convert to one of them. This is true for Roman Catholics no less than Protestants. We do not deny or downplay the reality that all such individual choices and judgments take place in community and are formed and shaped by our participation in various communities. Our judgments and decisions may be very much influenced by other persons, but when we join a church or convert, we are exercising an element of personal judgment and doing what seems right to us (assuming we do so sincerely with even a modicum of thought). Both the individual and the communal aspects of these decisions need to be frankly recognized by all sides. In *this* sense, all of us are "our own pope."

It is also worth recognizing here, in response to one of Cross's related claims, that a decision to accept the authority claims of Rome is no guarantee that converts will not later change their minds. Cross seems to think that it is a particular tendency of Protestants to reject the authority of the church they join if they come to disagree with it. The fact is, however, that converts to Rome, as well as "cradle Catholics," may also come to reject the authority of that church. Many have in the past, and many continue to do so in the present. On the other hand, many Protestants faithfully submit to the authority and discipline of their church even when they find it unpleasant or difficult. They do so because they recognize the church as a legitimate authority, even when it is inconvenient.[24] Such submission is a moral act of the will, but it depends on the prior judgment that the church is a legitimate authority. Likewise, faithful Roman Catholics will submit to their church even when it is hard to do so. Yet some Roman Catholics may come to believe that their church does not have the authority they once thought it did. And if they do, they may join another church.

In short, there is no escaping personal responsibility here. And in this regard, Roman Catholics are no more exempt from individual judgment than Protestants are. Indeed, the reality is that they are *far* more dependent on such judgment if they have to study and render judgment on the massive literature and range of issues that Cross invokes.

Sustaining the Objection: Parallel Discoveries

This reality cannot be evaded by insisting that Protestants are trusting only in their "interpretation" while Roman Catholics have truly "discovered" divine authority. The fact is that both sides judge that they have discovered divine truth and authority, and both have plausible claims to having done so. Notice the quote above: Cross concedes that Protestants "have discovered something having divine authority" in their discovery of Scripture. Recall, too, his claim that discovering Christ in Scripture is not subject to the *tu quoque* objection.

Here again we have parallel claims, despite Cross's denial. Discovering something having divine authority in Scripture amounts to grasping the central claims of Scripture and their truth. To find Christ in Scripture, as Cross observes, is to discover "the second Person of the Divine Trinity."[25] It is important to emphasize that this discovery is not merely a formal one about divine authority but a substantial one that involves discernment of the truth that we must acknowledge, believe, and obey. If Scripture is not essentially clear in its central claims, the claim that we discover divine authority in it is effectively vacuous. On the other hand, if it is not vacuous, if we do in fact

24. According to recent data from the Pew Research Center, Protestants keep their faith at a higher rate than do Roman Catholics. Sarah Eekhoff Zylstra, "Cradle Christians: Protestants Keep the Faith Better Than Catholics or Nones," *Christianity Today*, October 26, 2016, http://www .christianitytoday.com/gleanings/2016/october/protestant-parents-kids-keep-faith-catholics -nones-pew.html; Michael O'Loughlin, "Pew Survey: Percentage of US Catholics Drops and Catholicism Is Losing Members Faster than Any Denomination," *Crux*, May 12, 2015, http:// www.cruxnow.com/church/2015/05/12/pew-survey-percentage-of-us-catholics-drops-and -catholicism-is-losing-members-faster-than-any-denomination.

25. Cross, "*Tu Quoque*," sec. 3.C.

discover "the second Person of the Divine Trinity" in Scripture, this supports the Protestant conviction that we find in its pages a stable core of divine truth, by virtue of Scripture's essential clarity.

Furthermore, and for similar reasons, Protestants believe they have discovered that these central truths represent a broad consensus among all the main branches of the church, including the various evangelical churches. It is not a matter of enormous historical complexity beyond the reach of ordinary believers to discover classic creedal Christianity, or what C. S. Lewis identified as "mere Christianity," as a matter of essential agreement among Christians of different traditions. The enormous appeal of Lewis's account across denominational and international lines is a telling indicator that this essential truth is accessible and readily recognized by Christians throughout the world.

This point underscores the fact that Protestants do not have to determine the truth of each doctrine on a case-by-case basis by using personal judgment. They do not construct the faith from the ground up by employing individual interpretation. Rather, they discern essential Christian truth not only in the pages of Scripture but also in the consensus of the church catholic, understood as a reality that is more expansive and inclusive than the Church of Rome.

A Discovery or an Encounter?

We have been using the language of "discovery" in this discussion, language that may suggest an intellectual quest in which we play the primary active role. The reality, however, is that coming to see Christ in Scripture is better described as a personal encounter than as a "discovery." Indeed, we come face-to-face with Christ himself. As Paul put it, those who read the Scriptures have a veil over their minds, one that is removed only by those who turn to Christ. "For God, who said, 'Let light shine out of darkness,' made his light shine in our hearts to give us the light of the knowledge of God's glory displayed in the face of Christ" (2 Cor. 4:6; for the larger context, see 3:12–4:6).

Paul reminds us here that we do not merely discover an abstraction called divine authority; we are encountered by a Divine Person! Indeed we are encountered by Three Persons who take the initiative to reveal themselves to us and make their word clear to us. In seeing "the glory of God in the face of Jesus Christ," we encounter the Father of the Son who is "the radiance of God's glory and the exact representation of his being" (Heb. 1:3).

This encounter is mediated by the Holy Spirit, whom Jesus also called the Spirit of truth, who would glorify him and lead us into all truth (John 16:12–15). Jesus taught that the testimony of the Holy Spirit along with that of the apostles would convince us of the truth about Jesus. "When the Advocate comes, whom I will send to you from the Father—the Spirit of truth who goes out from the Father—he will testify about me. And you also must testify, for you have been with me from the beginning" (John 15:26–27). The apostles also invoked this twofold testimony when they gave witness to the resurrection of Jesus: "We are witnesses of these things, and so is the Holy Spirit, whom God has given to those who obey him" (Acts 5:32).

The witness of the Holy Spirit to Christ and the gospel has been essential to Reformation accounts of the authority of Scripture.[26] Again, what this highlights is the illuminating power of the Holy Spirit and the crucial role the Spirit plays in grounding biblical authority and the clarity of its central message. The clarity of Scripture is not merely a matter of the verbal or grammatical features of a document but one of the truth, beauty, and power of the God who is revealed as we personally encounter him through his inspired Word.

It is noteworthy that Cross appeals to the "help of the Holy Spirit" in his description of how his inquirer "discovers" the Catholic Church. It is not clear if he means to suggest that the Holy Spirit witnesses to the truth about the church as discovered in the fathers plus church history plus Scripture in the same sort of way the Bible clearly teaches that the Holy Spirit witnesses to the truth about Christ and the gospel. Perhaps he does, given that he identifies Christ as revealed in Scripture with the body of Christ as revealed in history and tradition. Recall, moreover, his quotation of Joan of Arc: "About Jesus Christ and the Church, I simply know they're just one thing, and we shouldn't complicate the matter."

With all due respect to Joan of Arc, it's not that simple. To insist otherwise is to distort the truth about both Christ and his church. Christ should not be identified with his church in any way that makes our knowledge of him and of the way of salvation hinge on any particular ecclesial or theological tradition.

We conclude, then, that the *tu quoque* objection is sustained. Roman Catholics are not above the fray, and they cannot seize the high moral or epistemic ground by insisting that they have "discovered" objective authority, while their Protestant counterparts are mired in "mere" subjective "interpretations."

---

26. Alvin Plantinga has developed this in philosophical detail in his epistemology of Christian belief. Plantinga contends that essentially the same view was held by both Aquinas and Calvin. See his *Warranted Christian Belief* (New York: Oxford University Press, 2000), esp. chaps. 6–9. More recently Plantinga has published a more concise version of his account of Christian epistemology: *Knowledge and Christian Belief* (Grand Rapids: Eerdmans, 2015).

9

Sacraments

Baptismal Unity and Separated Suppers

Several theologians from the time of the Reformation and forward have noticed the shift in the understanding of the church that took place between the earliest centuries and a later age. This is a transition that is reflected, fossil-like, in the later (and current) sacramental practices of Roman Catholic priests. Thus the very word "sacrament," which literally means "holy thing," has a story, an etymology, a family history, so to speak. As J. N. D. Kelly has pointed out, "While the technical terms for sacrament were to be μυστήριον in Greek and *sacramentum* in Latin, there are no absolutely certain instances of their use before the Alexandrian fathers and Tertullian respectively."[1] Indeed, the employment of this term, *sacramentum*, since it is not, after all, found in the pages of the NT, marks a considerable transformation from the first century to the institutional church of later centuries, changing from a charismatic conception of the body of Christ marked by gifts and charisms, as the Holy Spirit willed in sovereign freedom, to an institutional body that ever underscored the significance of *office*. For example, reflecting on the difference between conceiving the Lord's Supper as a rite and as a sacrament, Emil Brunner during the early twentieth century observed: "[This] Sacrament belongs just as much to the institution of the Church as the fellowship-meal

1. Kelly, *Early Christian Doctrines* (San Francisco: Harper & Row, 1960), 193.

belongs to the Ekklesia."[2] The transition from the Lord's Supper understood as a fellowship meal to the reality of the *sacrament* of the Mass, a much later development, marks a world of difference.[3] Brunner went on to point out that "the Lord's Supper is never brought together with Baptism under [the] one co-ordinating concept [of sacrament]"[4] in the NT.

This initial observation, however, is not offered to deny the significance of the sacraments in the life of the church, an employment that is affirmed by both Protestants and Roman Catholics alike, but simply to underscore the ongoing problem of anachronism in this area, especially when Rome repeatedly reads back later historical realities into the first century in confusing and inaccurate configurations. To cite just one example, it is clear that Christ established not the "sacrament of the Mass" and all that this entails, as the *Catechism* would have it, but rather the fellowship meal of the Lord's Supper, which is quite a different thing. This last point is doubly important once it is realized that the development of the early rites of the church (which were indeed established by Jesus) into its later sacramental life is strongly associated with the change in framework—again from a more charismatic to a more institutional model—that likewise marks the transition from elder or presbyter to priest.

At the outset it is also helpful, for the sake of the clarity of the following discussion, to distinguish between the larger category of "the means of grace" and the more particular subset of sacraments (e.g., of the Lord's Supper and baptism) through which grace, in the form of the presence of the Holy Spirit, can be communicated to believers. Thus the broader class of the means of grace would also include such things as praying, attending church, hearing the Word of God preached, fasting, having fellowship with other Christians, and engaging in works of charity and mercy, especially among the poor, the least of all. In this mix of the means of grace, sacraments would still, of course, have a special place since the early practices that eventually resulted in their later institutionalization over time were indeed established by Christ. What is more, the sacraments have a sign (as well as a significance) associated with them (water for baptism; bread and wine for the Lord's Supper), and they

---

2. Brunner, *The Christian Doctrine of the Church, Faith, and the Consummation* (Philadelphia: Westminster, 1962), 64.

3. Andrew McGowan understands this process somewhat differently but not in sharp contrast to the meaning suggested by Brunner. McGowan writes: "These assemblies [meal fellowships] . . . were of course the forerunners of what Christians have known as the Eucharist, the Lord's Supper, Holy Communion or Mass." See McGowan, *Ancient Christian Worship: Early Church Practices in Social, Historical, and Theological Perspective* (Grand Rapids: Baker Academic, 2014), 19.

4. Brunner, *Christian Doctrine*, 64.

carry nothing less than the very promises of the gospel expressed in concrete and tangible ways, and which are received in grace, as Luther himself well understood.[5]

Baptism

Baptism is well attested in the earliest periods of the church. Jesus Christ himself, for example, not only was baptized by John the Baptist but also, in submitting to this ritual, affirmed John's call for both repentance and a genuine washing and renewal among the Jewish people. Therefore the Roman Catholic Church is surely correct in declaring the necessity of baptism for all Christians, especially in light of Peter's response to the question posed to him at Pentecost, "Brothers, what shall we do?" (Acts 2:37). To this the leading apostle replied, "Repent and be baptized, every one of you, in the name of Jesus Christ for the forgiveness of your sins. And you will receive the gift of the Holy Spirit" (2:38). Beyond this, the necessity of baptism (surely a challenge to both Quakers and Salvationists) is further attested through the voice of Jesus present in the Gospel of Mark: "Whoever believes and is baptized will be saved, but whoever does not believe will be condemned" (Mark 16:16).

Even today, as the *Catechism* puts it, "Baptism constitutes the foundation of communion among all Christians."[6] Baptism, which has such a rich and deep history, is shared by nearly all Christians regardless of theological tradition. Baptism is therefore rightly the basis upon which to affirm the broad unity of the body of Christ regardless of differing parts or members, as the apostle Paul himself declared in his own day: "For we were all baptized by one Spirit so as to form one body—whether Jews or Gentiles, slave or free—and we were all given the one Spirit to drink" (1 Cor. 12:13). In this last verse, Paul underscores the transcendent unity of the gospel (as he did also in Gal. 3:28), which is grounded precisely in one Lord and one Spirit. Such a liberating understanding, going beyond all tribalism or provincialism, is likewise reflected in Paul's call to harmony with respect to the Ephesian church: "There is one body and one Spirit, just as you were called to one hope when you were

---

5. See Martin Luther's treatise *The Babylonian Captivity of the Church*, in which he lays out the elements that constitute a sacrament, in Luther, *Word and Sacrament II*, LW 36:68. The Roman Catholic understanding of a sacrament, somewhat different, can be seen in the observations of Peter Lombard (1100–1160) who wrote as follows: "Something can properly be called a sacrament if it is a sign of the grace of God and a form of invisible grace, so that it bears its image and exists as its cause." Cited in Alister McGrath, *Christian Theology: An Introduction*, 6th ed. (Hoboken, NJ: Wiley-Blackwell, 2016), Kindle edition, locations 13043–47.

6. *Catechism of the Catholic Church*, 2nd ed. (Mahwah, NJ: Paulist Press, 1994), par. 1271.

called; one Lord, one faith, one baptism; one God and Father of all, who is over all and through all and in all" (Eph. 4:4–6).

Given the very nature of baptism, as articulated by the apostles Peter and Paul, it remains the sacrament that even today holds enormous promise for a genuine ecumenism, marked by filial affection, holy love, and generous care, in the abiding recognition of a common Lord and Spirit. Accord at this level is one of the most broad-based unities of all. Indeed, the *Catechism* rightly affirms these realities, on one level, in its recognition that "Holy Baptism is the basis of the whole Christian life, the gateway to life in the Spirit."[7] Nevertheless, immediately after citing this salient material, which does indeed celebrate the genuine unity already present in baptism and among the baptized, the *Catechism* then adds to this language, making a move that once again marks not the oneness of the church but bespeaks its particularistic, all-too-Roman divisions: baptism is "the door which gives access to the other sacraments."[8] The problem with this last statement, however, is that baptism, this emblem of unity, is in fact only the gateway to the other sacraments for Roman Catholics, not for the Eastern Orthodox and certainly not for Protestants, as chapter 8 has already clearly demonstrated. Roman provincialism once again rules the day, even at this basic and very gracious level. Indeed, for many baptized, professing, holy Christians, who acknowledge one Lord and one Spirit (sometimes even in the midst of suffering and persecution), the way to giving formal and public expression to such a unity, *precisely* at the Lord's table, is now barred. What is this, then, but to turn Peter and Paul's very good counsel on its head? Indeed, by the time the Roman ecclesiastics and canon lawyers are done with the codes that are now applied to those "other" baptized Christians, such restrictions must necessarily *reflect back upon the nature of baptism itself*—precisely as a purported genuine door, a gateway to the Lord's Supper, for example—and thereby leave it now in a very distorted state. Baptism has thus been caught up in a larger, alien structure in which its proper unifying voice cannot be heard. What has been given with one hand has been quickly taken away by the other.

Moreover, some Protestants, due to their ongoing fear of formalism that they discern in the Roman church, are concerned with the matter of an *ex opere operato* (literally, "by the work worked") understanding, at least on some level, as it pertains to the relation between baptism and the new birth. That is, some take exception to Rome's language that the sacrament of baptism, to quote the *Catechism*, "signifies and *actually brings about* the birth of water

7. Ibid., par. 1213.
8. Ibid.

and the Spirit without which no one 'can enter the kingdom of God.'"[9] Can we then assume, with sound biblical and theological justification, that anyone being baptized is at that point born of God? The biblical reference of this catechetical observation is John 3:5, in which Jesus taught Nicodemus, "Very truly I tell you, no one can enter the kingdom of God unless they are born of water and the Spirit." As a first-century Jew, Nicodemus would have likely understood the reference to being born of water (though he was baffled by the reality of being born in the Spirit) as pointing to natural birth[10] (which is indeed very watery!) and not to *Christian* baptism, as the *Catechism* would have it. Another option would be that Nicodemus may have had in mind the Jewish ritual of baptism for gentile converts.

At any rate, the Roman Catholic Church may actually be on more solid biblical ground than some Protestants have imagined. In a few important passages the NT does indeed assume that when people are baptized, they are renewed through the reception of the Holy Spirit. In Romans 6:3–4, for example, Paul strongly associates baptism and regeneration: "Or don't you know that all of us who were baptized into Christ Jesus were baptized into his death? We were therefore buried with him through baptism into death in order that, just as Christ was raised from the dead through the glory of the Father, we too may live a new life." Add to this Peter's pointed observation, "In it [the ark Noah built] only a few people, eight in all, were saved through water, and this water symbolizes baptism that now saves you also" (1 Pet. 3:20–21), and the picture that begins to emerge is that baptism is intimately associated with the renewal of regeneration in the biblical materials, as the Roman tradition has claimed all along. Though Luther essentially shared this judgment as well, he nevertheless cautioned in his own day, in his *Lectures on Genesis*, for instance, lest there be misunderstanding: it is not the sacrament itself that brings new life but the Holy Spirit who works through it as a suitable means of grace.[11]

A far more controversial area has to do with Roman claims (shared by some Protestants, by the way) regarding infant baptism as the preferred way of becoming a part of the body of Christ. The Roman hierarchy claims that "the practice of infant Baptism is an immemorial tradition of the Church."[12]

---

9. Ibid., par. 1215 (emphasis added).

10. Edwin A. Blum argues that one interpretive option is as follows: (1) The "water" refers to the natural birth, and (2) the "Spirit" to the birth from above. Blum, "John," in *The Bible Knowledge Commentary: An Exposition of the Scriptures*, ed. J. F. Walvoord and R. B. Zuck (Wheaton: Victor Books, 1985), 2:281.

11. Martin Luther, e.g., wrote: "Baptism has the promise that it, together with the Holy Spirit, brings about the new birth." See Luther, *Lectures on Genesis: Chapters 1–5*, LW 1:228.

12. *Catechism*, par. 1252.

However, if this last statement accounts infant baptism as the normal practice of first-century Christianity, as readily practiced by the apostles themselves, then this claim is surely mistaken unless one commits the fallacy entailed in eisegesis. To be sure, the NT nowhere mentions that infants were baptized unless one reads one's own assumptions and preferences with respect to this issue (actually indicative of a later date) into those biblical accounts that are of a very general nature, as found, for example, in Acts 18:8, where it is reported: "Crispus, the synagogue leader, and his entire household believed in the Lord; and many of the Corinthians who heard Paul believed and were baptized." Indeed, it is difficult to find evidence of infant baptism before the time of Tertullian. This practice, eventually taken up by the church, came into its full stride during the fourth century, especially during and after the time of Constantine, when large numbers of people (and for all sorts of reasons) were flooding into the church. Here, as in so many other areas, Rome actually favors not the earliest practices of the church but those that have developed during a later period of time. That is, Rome prefers what historians can only recognize as an innovation.

In making infant baptism the usual way that one enters the church, well suited to an institutional understanding of the body of Christ, the Roman tradition, like so many others (some Protestant traditions included here as well), runs the risk of fostering nominal Christianity, whereby the very heart of the Christian faith, at least in its earliest phases, is mistaken for the priestly rituals that are performed at times regardless of the will, the knowledge, and even the faith of the recipient. As Gerald Bray points out, "Baptism was like vaccination; it worked whether the recipient was aware of what was happening or not."[13] In order to justify this practice, Rome advances two principal arguments.

First, the baptism of infants underscores the sovereignty of God. The grace of baptism is an utter gift to be received. Such an understanding is reflected once again in the words of the *Catechism*: "The sheer gratuitousness of the grace of salvation is particularly manifest in infant Baptism."[14] However, this theological observation may actually be more in line with the monergism (emphasizing the work of God *alone*) of the magisterial Reformation than with the ongoing synergistic (divine and human cooperation) theological emphases of Rome. Moreover, if monergism is indeed operative here, then why not elsewhere in Roman Catholic theology?

13. Bray, *The Church: A Theological and Historical Account* (Grand Rapids: Baker Academic, 2016), 120.
14. *Catechism*, par. 1250.

Second, in order to justify the practice of infant baptism, Rome offers a comparison between the OT ritual of circumcision and the alleged NT practice of infant baptism.[15] At first glance this analogy may seem to be apt (if one already assumes that infant baptism is scriptural), and even Protestant scholar Alister McGrath contends that "Paul treats baptism as a spiritual counterpart to circumcision (Col. 2:11–12), suggesting that the parallel may extend to its application to infants."[16] However, upon further examination this association of circumcision and infant baptism quickly falls apart, especially when the larger Pauline corpus is taken into account. It is, therefore, not descriptive of apostolic intent and judgment. Consider this: circumcision as practiced by the Jews (the heirs of the covenantal promises of Abraham, Isaac, and Jacob) flowed along familial, racial lines indicative of a chosen people. Not only was circumcision a "sign of the covenant," as Genesis 17:11 puts it, but it was also the mark that literally and physically distinguished this chosen people from the gentiles. To be a member of a particular family in effect made one an heir of the covenant. One was born into a favored, privileged relationship with the Most High. This is not, however, how Christian believers, both Jews and gentiles today, are related to Christ.

To be sure, these relations between families, signs, and covenantal people are not descriptive of how a gentile stands with respect to the new covenant, as the apostle Paul so clearly explained in Romans 11:17–21. In this passage, gentiles are not the "natural branches" of the tree of redemption, so to speak; rather the Jews as the chosen people are. While it is true, as Paul observes, that natural branches have been broken off to make room for "a wild olive shoot" that has been grafted in, the latter stand only "by faith" and not by any sort of natural relation. Accordingly, being born into a Roman Catholic family, and almost immediately baptized, does not function in the same way as being born into the family of Israel and then circumcised. Paul makes an important distinction between the two covenants as well as between the standing of Jews and that of gentiles, as revealed in the following: "After all, if you were cut out of an olive tree that is wild by nature, and contrary to nature were grafted into a cultivated olive tree, how much more readily will these, the natural branches, be grafted into their own olive tree!" (Rom. 11:24). Hence infant baptism, as practiced by the Roman church as the nearly exclusive way to become a member of the body of Christ, must by necessity draw increasing

15. Ibid., par. 1150. The *Catechism* states: "Among these liturgical signs from the Old Covenant are circumcision, anointing and consecration of kings and priests, laying on of hands, sacrifices, and above all the Passover. The Church sees in these signs a prefiguring of the sacraments of the New Covenant."

16. McGrath, *Christian Theology*, Kindle ed., locations 13569–98.

attention to belonging to particular families ("the pious desires of parents and elders"), and even at times to distinct ethnic groups, in a way that improperly shadows the OT practice of circumcision. Such a practice, therefore, does not sufficiently celebrate the only possible standing for gentiles (and Jews as well in the new covenant) in the eyes of the apostle Paul, that is, by faith.[17] The apostle reasoned: "You will say then, 'Branches were broken off so that I could be grafted in.' Granted. But they were broken off because of unbelief, *and you stand by faith*. Do not be arrogant, but tremble. For if God did not spare the natural branches, he will not spare you either" (Rom. 11:19–21).[18]

The Lord's Supper

The Lord's Supper is the sacrament in which such great change is to be observed from the meanings of the original ritual to the accretions that bit by bit have been added over time by a priestly class that was determined, with all manner of supposed justifications, to transform the Supper in accordance with its own self-ascribed role. Martin Stringer has described this process as "a product of a long series of gradual changes."[19] For one thing, the Lord's Supper, judging from its first occurrence, was not the reworking of the Levitical sacrifices in a new setting in which altar, office, and human action were some of the overriding themes. Instead, the Supper was quite literally a meal, a Passover, to which new meanings were added by Christ himself, suggesting that a much different covenant relation was now in effect.

Remarkably, some scholars have raised the question whether the meal over which Jesus presided shortly before his death was in fact a Passover, since there are problems of chronology here. Though the three Synoptic Gospels all agree that the Last Supper was a Passover, there is evidence in the Gospel of John to suggest, as I. Howard Marshall points out, that "the Jews had not yet celebrated the Passover at the time when Jesus had already concluded his meal."[20] Then Marshall goes on to make the case that since the meal which

---

17. Not surprisingly, then, even the *Catechism* points out that infant baptism "requires a post-baptismal catechumenate." See *Catechism*, par. 1231.

18. Karl Barth wrote at length of the difficulties entailed in infant baptism and he cautioned theologians: "To all concerned: to theologians, for unfortunately even theology has not yet realized by a long way that infant baptism is an ancient ecclesiastical error; . . . whether they can and will continue to bear responsibility for what has become the dominant baptismal practice, whether they might not and must not dare to face up to the wound from which the Church suffers at this genuinely vital point with its many-sided implications. . . ." Karl Barth, *Church Dogmatics* IV/4, ed. G. W. Bromiley and T. F. Torrance (London: T&T Clark, 2004), 194.

19. Stringer, *Rethinking the Origins of the Eucharist* (London: SCM, 2011), 193.

20. Marshall, *Last Supper and Lord's Supper* (Carlisle, UK: Paternoster, 1980), 57.

the disciples were sent to prepare is "clearly stated to be the Passover," and also since Jesus presided in this setting because "he wished to celebrate the Passover,"[21] it may be reasonably concluded that the Last Supper held by Jesus was "a Passover meal, probably held in advance of the official date."[22]

Since the Lord's Supper can, after all, be suitably described as a meal, even a Passover[23] (which included the element of sacrifice by means of the slaughtered lamb), this fact clearly indicates that the actions of Jesus, in presiding, must in some sense be comprehended in terms of the rich salvific history of the Jewish people, which includes sacrifice, deliverance, and exodus. Indeed, the Passover in its historic setting was a common meal, celebrated by the Hebrew people, in remembrance of the mighty saving acts of God on their behalf. Everyone reclining around the table (though some in Exod. 12:11 were apparently standing) was equally the recipient of such mighty acts, ever mindful of the common heritage, and the meal therefore was marked by an atmosphere of praise, gratitude, and thanksgiving for the deliverance brought about by the Holy One of Israel.

The setting of the Lord's Supper itself is likewise noteworthy and has often been depicted by artists throughout the centuries; Leonardo da Vinci's *The Last Supper*, produced in the latter part of the fifteenth century, is perhaps the most famous. Yet the disciples were probably *not* gathered around the table, as Leonardo would have it, with all facing the eye of the beholder. At any rate, this supper, judging from the Gospel accounts, is clearly marked by the love of Christ for those gathered and by the very strong theme of fellowship.[24] Again, Marshall indicates that Jesus transformed this particular Passover in some sense: "He saw it as an occasion of *fellowship* with his disciples, . . . and thus it took on the character of a farewell meal."[25] Luke's account of the supper (22:14–21) reveals that the direction in which Jesus moves the elements as he grasps them and speaks of their new-covenant significance is not with great vertical lift,[26] a priestly move, offering them up to the Father, for example, but a horizontal one in which they are divided and shared among those around the table, with Jesus saying of both the bread and the cup that they are literally "for you" (vv. 19–20).[27] The direction was not upward but outward toward the disciples, suggestive of both giving and gift. Indeed, the setting of an upper

21. Ibid.
22. Ibid., 76.
23. McGowan, *Ancient Christian Worship*, 24.
24. Marshall, *Last Supper*, 107.
25. Ibid. (emphasis added).
26. The elements were likely lifted a hand's length above the table.
27. The change that came with Vatican II allowing the priest to face the people is but a small move in the direction of what the Lord's Supper originally was.

room, the gathering around a table, reclining, the face-to-face interactions, the voices heard, the givenness of the elements, the "for you" language spoken by Jesus—all of this bespeaks fellowship, even communion, as the disciples shared an intimate, not public, setting with their Lord.

Before we chronicle how the early church understood the Lord's Supper, beyond the Gospel accounts, it may be helpful (in order to see the significant contrast in one of its sharpest forms) to compare the original setting of the Lord's farewell meal, with its strong theme of fellowship, with how the Roman Catholic Church understands the Supper today. We particularly want to highlight how that understanding is caught up in the much-later supervening structures of what the Mass had become over time, with its sharp distinction of roles as well as with its priestcraft and sacerdotalism. Thus, for example, in a way that basically repudiates the key element of the *fellowship* of the Supper, even today Rome still insists, after having been criticized by the magisterial Reformers,[28] that "every priest retains the right to celebrate *alone.*"[29] Yet in his own age, Luther insisted, "We can nonetheless readily abandon the private mass as something that we have not been commanded to do and that is a purely individual, fabricated, self-chosen, human doctrine and invention."[30] Indeed the priest by himself, off at some side altar while saying such a Mass, is not able, despite what priestly powers he supposedly possesses, to express in a very real and bodily way (only possible in the assembly of flesh-and-blood people who will both participate and consume, in a ministry at the very least for the church militant) one of the leading and undoubtedly necessary elements of the first Lord's Supper, namely, fellowship. In this case priestcraft has driven fellowship away—or worse yet, the priests think that physical and bodily fellowship, a genuine assembly, is at times unnecessary. Inattention to the community of the faithful is spawned by a focus on priestly powers themselves, as reflected in Anthony Kenny's observation on the anticipation and even the exhilaration that those same powers often bring to the minds of priests: "I have no clear memory of this celebration [of his first Mass], but I do recall most vividly the exaltation of the first months

28. In his treatise *The Private Mass and the Consecration of Priests*, Martin Luther observed: "Because you have been consecrated for no other purpose than for the private mass, that is, to act contrary to the word and ordinance of Christ, contrary to the intention and faith of the church, you are more desecrated than consecrated, and your consecration is much more futile and worse than the baptism of a bell and the consecration of a stone." See Luther, *Word and Sacrament IV*, LW 38:156.

29. *Instruction on the Worship of the Eucharistic Mystery*, par. 47, in *The Conciliar and Post Conciliar Documents*, vol. 1 of *Vatican II*, ed. Austin Flannery (Vatican City: Libreria Editrice Vaticana, 2011), 128 (emphasis added).

30. Luther, *Word and Sacrament IV*, LW 38:170.

during which I had the power to say Mass. Normally a slow and sluggish riser, I would leap early out of bed, fully awake and full of excitement at the thought of the momentous act I was privileged to perform."[31]

Second, the fellowship of the Lord's table is likewise disrupted, at least in some sense, by the later ecclesiastical narrative that Rome prefers, which once again represents an innovation, one that celebrates not the equality of fellowship (in which no one is called teacher or master, as Jesus required) but the inequality of rank, of graded hierarchical distinctions, and of exclusive priestly roles. What some Protestants find so amazing, given the grace and beauty of the first Lord's Supper, is that Rome must see itself as in a mirror, with all its preferred polity and hierarchical structures that took so much time to develop, even here at this special, sacred place. Accordingly, a document from Vatican II declares: "The people of God, when assembled for Mass, has an organic and hierarchical structure which is manifested in the various actions and different functions performed during Mass."[32] Moreover, in case the Roman Catholic faithful are not yet sufficiently informed concerning the attitudes and roles they are to embrace at this meal before their ecclesiastical "superiors," Vatican II documents make this explicit: "The unity of this community, having its origin in the one bread in which all share (cf. 1 Cor. 10:17), is arranged in hierarchical order. For this reason it is necessary that 'each person, performing his role as a minister or as one of the faithful, should do all that the nature of the action and the liturgical norms require of him, and only that.'"[33]

Again, this same council declared: "The hierarchical structure of the liturgy, its sacramental power, and the respect due to the community of God's people require that the priest exercise his liturgical service as a 'faithful minister and steward of the mysteries of God' [1 Cor. 4:1]."[34] Rome reads its own hierarchy into the Lord's Supper so strongly as to insist that "the Pope is associated with every celebration of the Eucharist, wherein he is named as the sign and servant of the unity of the universal church."[35]

This language of "hierarchical fellowship"[36] employed by Vatican II may be considered an oxymoron by some of the Christian faithful today, especially

31. Anthony Kenny, *A Path from Rome: An Autobiography* (London: Sidgwick & Jackson, 1985), 101.

32. *General Instruction on the Roman Missal*, par. 257, in Flannery, *Conciliar and Post Conciliar Documents*, 190.

33. *The Eucharist*, par. 16, in Flannery, *Conciliar and Post Conciliar Documents*, 113.

34. *Third Instruction on the Correct Implementation of the Constitution on the Sacred Liturgy*, par. 1, in Flannery, *Conciliar and Post Conciliar Documents*, 212.

35. *Catechism*, par. 1369.

36. *Third Instruction on the Correct Implementation*, par. 1, in Flannery, *Conciliar and Post Conciliar Documents*, 212.

when they have in mind the reality of the first Lord's Supper. In his own early twentieth-century setting, Emil Brunner declared that when the Lord's Supper is refashioned in this manner—such that the original rite has now become the sacrament of the institutional hierarchical church, intent upon reading its preferred structure and its particular polity into everything, even into the earliest of times—then this move can only mark a fundamental and not insignificant modification of what the church is in its essence or nature. As Brunner observed, "When the Lord's Supper is conceived of as Sacrament, there takes place a fundamental sociological change in the structure of the Ekklesia."[37] This is a transition from soteriological equality (one Lord, one faith, one baptism) to hierarchical difference.[38] This, then, is a hierarchy that actually transforms the Supper.

The Early Church Weighs In

If our reading of the Lord's Supper during its rise is accurate, then we should see the early church continuing this practice in what one scholar calls "a meal fellowship."[39] Indeed, when the evidence of the early church is consulted, in both the NT and some material from the Apostolic Fathers, this is precisely what is found. The practice of the first-century church was to meet in houses around a table to celebrate the Supper. By the time of the *Didache* (mid- to late first century) and of Ignatius (d. AD 107), the term Eucharist (literally, "thanksgiving") was beginning to be used to describe the meal and to under-score the church's vibrant gratitude and praise for having received the gift of the Son from the Father. However even before this later period, the Gospel of John affirmed that God the Father is the giver of the bread, that the direction of giving is *from the Father to us*: "Jesus said to them, 'Very truly I tell you, it is not Moses who has given you the bread from heaven, but it is my Father who gives you the true bread from heaven. For the bread of God is the bread that comes down from heaven and gives life to the world'" (John 6:32–33). The proper liturgical response, then, to the Father's offer of the gift of the

37. Brunner, *Christian Doctrine*, 64.

38. In these observations we are not making the case that there cannot and should not be distinct roles in the church. Affirming the "priesthood of believers" in a way similar to Luther, we fully acknowledge that various members will be called to differing roles in the church. Such difference, however, does not constitute a hierarchy as Rome would have it. See Martin Luther's treatise *That a Christian Assembly or Congregation Has the Right and Power to Judge All Teaching and to Call, Appoint, and Dismiss Teachers, Established and Proven by Scripture*, in *Church and Ministry I*, LW 39:305–14.

39. Gordon W. Lathrop, "The Reforming Gospels: A Liturgical Theologian Looks Again at Eucharistic Origins," *Worship* 83, no. 3 (2009): 194.

Son was and remains thanksgiving and adoration. Accordingly, Garry Wills describes the early Eucharist as "initially a literal meal, held most likely in the evening within a domestic 'house church' setting, with the contents of the meal provided by members of the assembly."[40]

The strong emphasis on the Supper as a meal, with its eating and drinking, is easily discerned in Paul's rebuke of the Corinthian church, some of whose members were engaged in "private" meals when they came together as the church, with the result that some were left hungry and others drunk (1 Cor. 11:20–22). So strong were the overtones of the Eucharist as a meal fellowship that in its earliest practice it often took place in concert with the Agape feast. By the latter part of the first century, however, as Andrew McGowan points out, this conjoined communal banquet was separated into "a morning sacramental ritual [and a] prosaic communal supper."[41] Moreover, with these transitions in place, the church's meal was no longer the Passover meal that it was for Jesus and his disciples, and therefore "it was not bound by the Passover ritual."[42]

One of the more important witnesses of the Apostolic Fathers, the *Didache*, ties together the eucharistic flavor of the Supper—its strong theme of thanksgiving, a commonplace by now—with the elements of a meal fellowship in this observation: "And after you have been satisfied with food, give thanks as follows: We give thanks to you, O Holy Father, for your holy name which you caused to dwell in our hearts and for the knowledge and faith and immortality which you made known to us through Jesus your child; to you be the glory forever."[43] To the criticism offered by some scholars that this chapter describes a "transition to a full eucharistic celebration following the meal,"[44] Paul Bradshaw observes: "What [this criticism] fails to explain . . . is why the author of the *Didache* should provide such detailed instructions and liturgical texts for this purely ancillary rite and yet pass over the Eucharist proper with hardly a word."[45] This fellowship meal that the *Didache* has described, then, was likely the Lord's Supper celebrated during the mid- to late first century.

Beyond this, writing in the middle of the second century, Justin Martyr retains these emphases and begins to stress the role of "the president of the

---

40. Wills, *Why Priests? A Failed Tradition* (New York: Viking Adult, 2013), 248.
41. McGowan, "Rethinking Eucharistic Origins," *Pacifica* 23 (June 2010): 173.
42. Marshall, *Last Supper*, 111.
43. *Didache* 10.1, in *The Apostolic Fathers in English*, trans. Rick Brannan (Bellingham, WA: Lexham, 2012).
44. Bradshaw, *Eucharistic Origins* (New York: Oxford University Press, 2004), 26.
45. Ibid.

brethren" (who, by the way, is clearly not a priest, judging from the contents of this material), who presides at the table and thereby takes responsibility for the proper distribution of the bread and wine. Justin Martyr explains: "There is then brought to the president of the brethren bread and a cup of wine mixed with water; and he taking them, gives praise and glory to the Father of the universe, through the name of the Son and of the Holy Ghost, and offers thanks at considerable length for our being counted worthy to receive these things at His hands."[46] Since the Lord's Supper of the NT and the Eucharist of some of the Apostolic Fathers is so clearly a meal, it seems to follow that "the appropriate setting for the sacrament is a table, and the appropriate posture . . . is sitting."[47]

The Lord's Supper and Sacrifice

The early Eucharist, though clearly a fellowship meal, also embraced the idea of sacrifice, a theme that was present from the beginning and that was implied by the words of Christ himself, used in this special setting: "This is my body given for you" (Luke 22:19), and, "This cup is the new covenant in my blood, which is poured out for you" (22:20). Naturally, the sacrificial nature entailed in the Supper, whose prefiguring type is seen in the Passover lamb, can be variously understood. Thus it can take on a range of meanings depending upon how sacrifice is conceived, especially in terms of who or what is sacrificed (and there are so many options here, judging from the historical record). After this, of course, the question must then be addressed as to how the idea of sacrifice is related to the ongoing, strong theme of fellowship. There are at least three major possibilities: (1) The theme of sacrifice now predominates such that fellowship is in a very real way, despite claims to the contrary, subsumed under it. Tables are transformed into altars even though the language of tables is retained, and "presidents of the assembly" become full-blown priests. (2) The Lord's Supper is not a sacrifice but is simply a fellowship meal that offers the gospel promises through the tangible signs of bread and wine. Tables do not become altars, and priests never emerge. (3) Sacrifice is a distinct theme (describing the reality of the paschal lamb and Golgotha); however, it emerges within the context of the fellowship meal (though it is temporally distinct from it) in that the food and drink consumed symbolize the sacrifice on the cross, which forms the basis not only for the "for you"

46. Justin Martyr, *First Apology* 65, in *The Apostolic Fathers with Justin Martyr and Irenaeus*, ANF 1:185.
47. Marshall, *Last Supper*, 156.

nature of the meal but also for the Communion, which would be impossible apart from a given (by God the Father), sacrificed Lord.

Though no one theological tradition perfectly fits any of the three options described above, Roman Catholicism does resonate in many respects with the first. Observe, for example, how Rome in its public documents employs the language of both altar and table, though a clear preference is given to the former: "The altar, around which the Church is gathered in the celebration of the Eucharist, represents the two aspects of the same mystery: the altar of the sacrifice and the table of the Lord."[48] The altar represents the two aspects of the mystery and thus does this double duty, so to speak, and not the table. Indeed, so many elements of the Mass, from the liturgical vessels used, to the words spoken, to the vestments of the priest, all underscore this same reality. However, gathering around an altar, in the ongoing practice of the Mass, is clearly different from the apostolic practice of sitting or reclining at the table. Indeed, these basic postures represent a world of theological difference.

Our view, which is similar to the third option above, does not deny the sacrificial relations or connections of the Lord's Supper but simply maintains that they must be appropriately understood, in line with the nature of the meal itself as instituted by Jesus and with the earliest understandings of the church. In the *Didache*, for instance, the sacrificial language that does emerge is a "sacrifice of thanksgiving,"[49] as is evident in the following: "And coming together on the Lord's own day, break bread and give thanks, confessing beforehand your sins so that your sacrifice may be pure."[50] Moreover, Colin Bulley points out that when Justin Martyr employs the vocabulary of sacrifice in terms of the Supper, he has in mind the "offerings of praise and thanksgiving for blessings received,"[51] and Irenaeus, for his part, has in view "the bread and wine being like the OT offering of the firstfruits."[52] Beyond this, Tertullian viewed the Eucharist "as one Christian sacrifice among many,"[53] Bulley continues, "and probably saw its sacrificial aspects as involving thanksgiving and, less clearly, the gifts the faithful offer when the eucharist is celebrated."[54]

48. *Catechism*, par. 1383.
49. Willy Rordorf, *The Eucharist of the Early Christians* (Collegeville, MN: Liturgical Press, 1976), 17.
50. *Didache* 14.1, in J. B. Lightfoot and J. R. Harmer, trans., *The Apostolic Fathers* (London: Macmillan, 1891), 234.
51. Bulley, *The Priesthood of Some Believers: Developments from the General to the Special Priesthood in the Christian Literature of the First Three Centuries* (Waynesboro, GA: Paternoster, 2000), 132.
52. Ibid.
53. Ibid., 133.
54. Ibid.

The Roman Catholic view does indeed acknowledge the practice of the early church to consider sacrifice in terms of both celebratory thanksgiving and the offerings of the people ("The Holy Sacrifice . . . includes the Church's offering"[55]), but this is a less prominent note, especially after the third and fourth centuries, when the role of the one who presided at the Supper was transformed into that of a priest with all sorts of supposed powers. With these transformations in place, the original meal—which was rich in the meanings of the Passover, as well as the communion that emerged through receiving the gift of the Son, offered directly by the Father—became something remarkably different. A meal and a fellowship that required no priest, in a way similar to the original Passover, by the third century became a reworked Levitical sacrifice (going back to the shadows) in which a priestly class, separated and distinguished from the rest of the body of Christ, took on a sacerdotal role that Jesus had never offered his disciples on Maundy Thursday. Thus in line with this ancient transformation of the Supper, Vatican II declared more recently: "The Church, the spouse and minister of Christ, . . . offers him to the Father and at the same time makes a total offering of herself together with him."[56] Again, "The Church . . . offers the immaculate Victim to God the Father, in the Holy Spirit."[57]

Observe the change in direction with this significant modification of the Supper. Instead of the leading note being *from* the Father through the Son and *to* the church, a movement that evokes abundant joy and thanksgiving, a veritable Eucharist, it is now a movement *from* the Roman Catholic priest who offers Christ *to* the Father as a sacrifice. So stark is this shift from the divine sovereign action in the one framework to the human, priestly action in the other that even Rome must quickly modify it and not allow this particular meaning, though repeatedly affirmed, to stand alone. Accordingly, the human priestly role is seen in concert with that of the divine Jesus. In other words, the claim is quickly made (but upon what basis?) that the priestly role of Christ is shared by Roman Catholic clergy: "The Church, the spouse and minister of Christ, performs *together with him* the role of priest and victim."[58] In the Mass, then, the Roman priest offers up Christ to the Father. But if the

55. *Catechism*, par. 1330.
56. *Instruction on the Worship of the Eucharistic Mystery*, par. 3.c, in Flannery, *Conciliar and Post Conciliar Documents*, 103.
57. *General Instruction on the Roman Missal*, par. 55.f, in Flannery, *Conciliar and Post Conciliar Documents*, 176.
58. *Instruction on the Worship of the Eucharistic Mystery*, par. 3.c, in Flannery, *Conciliar and Post Conciliar Documents*, 103 (emphasis added).

Father has already given the gift of the Son, which is abundantly evident at Golgotha ("*God presented Christ as a sacrifice of atonement*, through the shedding of his blood—to be received by faith. He did this to demonstrate his righteousness," Rom. 3:25a, emphasis added) and celebrated in the Supper with thanksgiving, then why is the gift returned?

Though the Lord's Supper is not itself a sacrifice, nevertheless we do not deny that the once-and-for-all oblation of Christ at Calvary, with its rich meanings of propitiation and atonement, is indeed proclaimed *through* this meal. Like Marshall and other Protestants, we affirm that "no sacrifice takes place in the Lord's Supper, but the sacrifice of Jesus in dying on the cross is proclaimed to sinners"[59] by means of the Supper. This is a crucial distinction that Rome repeatedly obscures. If such is the case, then it seems to follow, as Luther argued in his own day,[60] that the Lord's Supper offers the new covenant in a very tangible way, as a sacrament, through the signs of bread and wine, and this is precisely what the bold proclamation of the gospel, animated by the Holy Spirit, offers in an invisible way through the Word. Therefore, to make a sharp distinction between these two ways the gospel is presented depends on affirming that a clear, distinct priestly role was given by Christ to some in the church and not to others, a claim that constantly begs for what evidence could possibly sustain it. Indeed, McGrath cautions against creating a New Testament priesthood out of Old Testament materials:

> Whereas the Old Testament used the term "priest" (Hebrew: *Kohen*) to refer to an official who was set apart from the rest of the community in order to carry out certain duties associated with worship and sacrifice, this specific term is not used to refer to Christian ministers in the New Testament. Rather, the term "priest" is used to refer to Jesus Christ, who is seen as the fulfillment of the Old Testament ideal of a priest or to the church as a whole exercising a "priestly" ministry. Christians as a group are referred to as "a royal priesthood" (1 Pet. 2:9).[61]

This significant issue will be addressed, though in a slightly different way, in chapter 10, in which the claim that the Roman Catholic priest during the Mass acts *in persona Christi* will be thoroughly examined. If this role falters, then that failure will, no doubt, have considerable implications for the very notion of the Roman priesthood as well.

---

59. Marshall, *Last Supper*, 149.
60. See Luther, *Babylonian Captivity*, esp. 28–58.
61. McGrath, *Christian Theology*, Kindle ed., location 12878.

Transubstantiation

The Roman Catholic Church teaches that "from the beginning Christians have celebrated the Eucharist and in a form whose substance has not changed despite the great diversity of times and liturgies."[62] However, for the sake of a proper chronology in this area, informed by the intricacies of historical development, it must be pointed out that the manner in which the elements of the Supper have been understood, specifically in terms of the bread and the wine, has changed considerably over time. Put another way, Rome's view of the elements today, surely a liturgical innovation, is by and large best comprehended against the backdrop of the developments that took place from the ninth century onward. To illustrate, in AD 831, Paschasius Radbertus, a monk at the monastery in Corbie, produced a liturgical work, *On the Body and Blood of the Lord*, that reified the presence of Christ in the Supper by localizing the Savior in the elements. Earlier some of the church fathers, such as Ambrose in the West ("Before it is consecrated, it is bread; but when Christ's words have been added, it is the body of Christ")[63] and Cyril of Jerusalem in the East ("We beseech the merciful God to send forth His Holy Spirit upon the gifts lying before Him, that He may make the bread the Body of Christ, and the wine the Blood of Christ"),[64] had little difficulty, for their part, in referring to the elements of the Supper as the body and blood of Christ. Paschasius, however, developed this idea to such an extent, underscoring its miraculous nature ("so that as from the Virgin through the Spirit true flesh is created without union of sex, so through the same, out of the substance of bread and wine, the same body and blood of Christ may be mystically consecrated"),[65] that he sparked a spirited response from his fellow monk Ratramnus of Corbie. Others who disagreed sharply with Paschasius's twist on things included John Scotus Eriugena and Rabanus Maurus, both also in the ninth century, and Berengar of Tours in the eleventh century, theologians of no small standing.

Centuries later, with the reintroduction of the works of Aristotle into Europe, the thread developed by Paschasius was given new meaning in light of the philosopher's technical distinctions between substance and accident. Thus an accident, as medieval clerics understood it, exists in another just as the color

---

62. *Catechism*, par. 1356.

63. Gerald Bray, ed., *1–2 Corinthians*, Ancient Christian Commentary on Scripture: NT 7 (Downers Grove, IL: InterVarsity, 1999), 112.

64. Edward Hamilton Gifford, "The Catechetical Lectures of S. Cyril: Introduction," in *S. Cyril of Jerusalem, S. Gregory Nazianzen*, NPNF² 7:xxxvii.

65. William C. Placher, *Readings in the History of Christian Theology*, vol. 1, *From Its Beginnings to the Eve of the Reformation* (Louisville: Westminster John Knox, 1988), 140.

gray exists in a particular stone, apart from which (as its basis or substance) the gray of the stone has no existence. However, a substance, in contrast to an accident, does not exist in another. Now when such a well-worked distinction was applied to a liturgical context, after the pronouncement of Christ's words of institution by the priest, what remained was utterly, substantively the body and blood of Christ, though the elements still appeared to the senses as having all the characteristics or "accidents" of bread and wine in terms of such things as smell, taste, and feel. This form of the teaching was propounded as dogma, required to be affirmed by all the faithful, at the Fourth Lateran Council in 1215, headed up by one of the most powerful popes of all, Innocent III. The first constitution of this council, the confession of faith, stated: "His [Christ's] body and blood are truly contained in the sacrament of the altar under the forms of bread and wine, the bread and wine having been changed *in substance*, by God's power, into his body and blood."[66]

Later, during the sixteenth century, Trent took up this teaching and declared, contrary to the magisterial Reformers, both Luther and Calvin: "There is made a change of the whole *essence* of the bread into the body, and of the whole *essence* of the wine into the blood; which change the [Roman] Catholic Church calls transubstantiation."[67] So controversial was this idea by this point that Trent, in a very defensive posture, thundered eleven decrees of excommunication that were now associated with this *particular* teaching.[68] This view of the elements of the Supper, which would likely surprise many Roman Catholic laity even today if it were explained to them in considerable detail, is nevertheless articulated in the current *Catechism* in the following words: "Under the consecrated species of bread and wine Christ himself, living and glorious, is present in a true, real, and substantial manner: his Body and his Blood, with his soul and his divinity."[69] Simply put, the bread is no longer bread: it simply appears to be so; instead it is utterly *in essence* the body of Christ. Again, the wine is no longer wine: it simply appears to be so; instead it is utterly *in essence* the blood of Christ. Such a teaching is by no means an article of the faith that characterized the ancient ecumenical church. Rather, it is that particular and much-developed doctrine, culled from its distinct historical location, upon which the Roman dogmatic apparatus, for all sorts of reasons, has landed.

66. *Fourth Lateran Council: 1215*, constitution 1, "Confession of Faith," http://www.papal encyclicals.net/Councils/ecum12-2.htm (emphasis added).
67. Philip Schaff, *The Creeds of Christendom*, vol. 2, *The Greek and Latin Creeds, with Translations* (Grand Rapids: Baker, 1983), 208 (emphasis added).
68. Wills, *Why Priests?*, 54.
69. *Catechism*, par. 1413.

The Implications of This Medieval Doctrine

Once the change in doctrine offered by Paschasius and later developed by others became the official view of the Western church, it brought with it a number of implications that were not always clearly thought out by its defenders. First of all, and bearing in mind the original setting of the Lord's Supper, if the elements are substantively the body and blood of Christ, then this can only mean, among other things, that Christ had two bodies. By this understanding, at the original Lord's Supper Christ, with full bodily integrity, was holding the bread, which itself was fully another body of Christ ("Christ is present whole and entire in each of the species").[70] However, the formula of the ancient church, evident at Chalcedon, was one person with two natures, which means that Christ as the God/Human had only one body (even the Monophysites could agree on this last point): "We . . . confess one and the same Son, our Lord Jesus Christ, the same perfect in Godhead and also perfect in manhood; truly God and truly man, of a reasonable [rational] soul and body."[71] Thus this two-body teaching of Rome, which is an unavoidable implication of transubstantiation, is clearly an aberration and shows that the metaphors at the first Supper ("This is my body. . . . This is my blood") have been pressed "to the point at which they cease to be metaphors."[72]

Second, since Rome insists that after the words of consecration what arises is "the real and *permanent* presence of Christ under the Eucharistic species,"[73] such a view is fraught with a number of troubling implications. Gary Wills, for example, has posed the predicament in this way: "The first miracle, how the wafer became Jesus, was to be followed by an obscure second miracle, how the wafer had to be 'de-consecrated' before it became an excretion."[74] Along these lines, Wills quotes Edward Schillebeeckx in observing that "there had to be a 'reverse transubstantiation' to separate Jesus from the 'accidents' of bread and wine before they were excreted."[75] And for those Christian thinkers who had raised this admittedly uncomfortable issue in the past, Rome responded once again with a bout of name-calling and branded such inquirers as heretics, as

70. Ibid., par. 1377.
71. Schaff, *Creeds of Christendom*, 2:62.
72. Marshall, *Last Supper*, 151.
73. *Instruction on Facilitating Sacramental Eucharistic Communion in Particular Circumstances* (par. "Piety and Reverence towards the Blessed Sacrament When the Eucharist Is Placed in the Hands of the Faithful"), in Flannery, *Conciliar and Post Conciliar Documents*, 232 (emphasis added).
74. Wills, *Why Priests?*, 23.
75. Ibid.

"Stercorantis from *stercus*, meaning 'feces.'"[76] It may be tempting to dismiss such questions as frivolous. The reality, however, is that such questions are perfectly serious if the doctrine of transubstantiation is taken as a sober truth claim.

Though the Roman Catholic Church understands the presence of Christ in four key ways—(1) "in the assembly of the faithful," (2) "in the word when the Scriptures are read," (3) "in the person of the priest," and (4) "above all he is present under the eucharistic species"[77]—it has emphasized this last way, the claim of transubstantiation, especially by means of the "above all" language just cited. The question of *how* Christ is present in the church is not a minor issue but has all sorts of implications for Christology, revelation, ecclesiology, ministry, Christian discipleship, fellowship, evangelism, and Christian hope.

In emphasizing the fourth way just specified, Rome has unavoidably underscored the presence of Christ in objects—in species, as Rome puts it, with the cultic overtones and priestly associations of that term—and not in the persons, the very members of the body of Christ, assembled at the table. God as revealed in Jesus Christ by the power of the Holy Spirit marks Christian revelation in a magnificent way and gives it a distinct character. That is, the Christian faith has to do preeminently with persons without neglecting the importance of matter. Choosing otherwise here, offering a different emphasis, amounts to taking the wrong fork in the road, so to speak, with its accompanying consequences. The Christian understanding of revelation, via the witness of Scripture in its broadest sense, celebrates the precious truth that God is revealed as nothing less than personal, and the Christian Godhead is expressed best in terms of the relations of love evident among the persons of the Father, the Son, and the Holy Spirit. To turn away, at least in some sense, from this personhood (reflected in a relational way also in the *imago Dei*) and its relations, to face toward the object, the species, which as a metaphor was never intended to be the focus of attention—all this is in some sense to turn away from the by-now "weakened 'mystical' body of Christ."[78] Such a move fails to give sufficient value and attention to that presence of Christ toward which Communion itself ever points: in the assembly and fellowship of the faithful. We therefore heartily affirm the real presence of Christ in the Supper. However, Christ can only reign in the worshiping hearts of believers; he cannot reign in bread.

The additional twists and turns into which the doctrine of transubstantiation leads do not entail a careful exegesis of Scripture but are rather the outworking or the logic of considering the bread to be essentially the body

76. Ibid.
77. *On Holy Communion and the Worship of the Eucharist Mystery outside the Mass*, in Flannery, *Conciliar and Post Conciliar Documents*, 243.
78. Wills, *Why Priests?*, 58.

of Christ. If such is the case, then the body of Christ in this form must now be worshiped. And this is precisely what Rome calls for, as is evident in the following: "The faithful should therefore strive to worship Christ our Lord in the Blessed Sacrament."[79] Not only is the object still very much available to the senses (it looks, smells, tastes, and feels like bread) to be worshiped and adored, but great care must also be taken so that the clergy inculcates the proper attitudes of reverence and docility in the laity. To this end the parishioners are taught to genuflect or to bow deeply as a "sign of adoration of the Lord."[80] They are also instructed to kneel before the presence of the host, "since kneeling is itself a sign of adoration,"[81] though the Anglicans apparently did not think so when they added the black rubric to the Book of Common Prayer during the reign of Edward VI.

At any rate, the worship of the host is ensured by placing it in the liturgical vessel designed for this purpose, the monstrance. This instrument often takes the form of a starburst in a suitable metal and can include precious stones, depending on the wealth of the church. A special, larger host is enclosed in a glass case at the center of this receptacle. The priest then places the monstrance prominently on the altar, and the laity are encouraged to sing, to offer prayers, and to engage in outright adoration and praise. Such liturgical practices that occur, for instance, during the rite of benediction have been more formally organized in a society created for this purpose and suitably called the Nocturnal Adoration Society. Here the Roman Catholic faithful assemble to adore "The Blessed Sacrament" throughout the night.

If the bread is, after all, literally and substantively the body of Christ, then it must be suitably cared for. The priests therefore must make sure that during the distribution of the elements nothing is dropped or spilled. Vatican II cautioned: "What you have allowed to drop, think of it as though you had lost one of your own members."[82] After the Mass the consecrated hosts can be placed in a tabernacle, often embedded atop the altar structure itself. The name "tabernacle" is reminiscent of the OT edifice, though the Roman Catholic structure is considerably smaller. Christ, so it is assumed, is placed in a small, dark, and at times cool or even cold box, depending on the temperature of the church. Given the logic of transubstantiation, it must surely

79. *Instruction on the Worship of the Eucharistic Mystery*, par. 50, in Flannery, *Conciliar and Post Conciliar Documents*, 130.

80. *Catechism*, par. 1378.

81. *Instruction on the Worship of the Eucharistic Mystery*, par. 34.b, in Flannery, *Conciliar and Post Conciliar Documents*, 122.

82. *Instruction on the Manner of Distributing Holy Communion*, in Flannery, *Conciliar and Post Conciliar Documents*, 150.

be asked: "How is such an enclosure appropriate for the Savior, the Lord of Hosts, the King of kings and Lord of lords?" Bishops and popes have retired to better quarters.

This topic is admittedly difficult for Roman Catholic and Protestant relations. What Roman Catholics view as a supreme act of adoration and worship, many Protestants understandably consider to be consummate idolatry, given their rejection of transubstantiation. Consequently, with Roman Catholics and Protestants just being themselves, thinking in accordance with their respective theologies, they will likely and necessarily give grave offense to each other. Protestants call transubstantiation idolatrous; Roman Catholics call that Protestant view sacrilegious. For our part, we believe that such an offense is unavoidable if the ecumenical discussion is open and remains rigorously honest and factual. In this particular area, then, there can be peace only if nothing of substance is discussed.

Furthermore, these significant differences in theological understanding cannot simply be chalked up to the Protestant reluctance to embrace doctrinal development over time, as John Courtney Murray had once implied.[83] We, the authors, being a historian/theologian and a philosopher/theologian, both recognize the essential role of legitimate doctrinal development in the life of the church, an issue we will further explore in subsequent chapters. We affirm, for example, that the Council of Nicaea is as crucial today for the articulation of the proper Christian faith as it was back in the fourth century. This is not the issue. Rather, from our perspective, it is a question of embracing the transitions in doctrine that are clearly in accordance with the early, basic teachings of God's revelation in Jesus Christ and rejecting those that are not. Transubstantiation, in the judgment of most Protestants, quite simply turns Christian revelation on its head. It contains a self-propelled logic that takes the Christian story where it ought not to go. Consider this: whereas the death of Christ caused the temple curtain to be torn in two, from top to bottom, signifying that the way is now open between God and humanity (Matt. 27:51), the very architecture of Roman Catholic (and Eastern Orthodox) churches (with its rails, gates, altars, sanctuary, and tabernacles), put in place by a misunderstanding of the Supper (most notably in the doctrine of transubstantiation, though Eastern Orthodoxy itself does not affirm this exact doctrine, certainly not in its Western form), suggests an ongoing inappropriate separation, though all of this division accords well with a priestly, sacerdotal role. Vatican II

83. Murray, *The Problem of God Yesterday and Today* (New Haven: Yale University Press, 1964), 55.

removed some of the rails, physically if not figuratively, but some of the older thinking lingered.

Again, whereas the death of Christ marked the fulfillment of the Levitical sacrificial system, rendering it obsolete (Heb. 8:13), this very problematic Roman Catholic doctrine, the development of the Middle Ages, places the Son of God in a tabernacle, reminiscent of old-covenant understandings that have been surpassed precisely in this death. Moreover, the apostle Paul clearly made the transition from the shadows of the OT temple to the living temple of the NT in 1 Corinthians: "Don't you know that *you yourselves are God's temple* and that God's Spirit dwells in your midst? If anyone destroys God's temple, God will destroy that person; for God's temple is sacred, and *you together are that temple*" (3:16–17, emphasis added).

Finally, transubstantiation (and its implications) contradicts the dying witness of the first martyr of the church. Indeed, as his blood was being spilled on that special day, after he had recounted so much of salvation history, Stephen, a deacon in the church, uttered the precious truth at the very heart of Christian revelation: "The Most High does not live in houses made by human hands" (Acts 7:48). The death of Christ rendered the tabernacle obsolete; Rome, however, brought it back—because its priests required it.

Protestants Barred from the Lord's Table?

Interestingly enough, the doctrine of transubstantiation has led not to a celebration of the fellowship and unity of all baptized Christians under one Lord but to their ongoing division. To illustrate, although Roman Catholics are welcomed at a Protestant celebration of the Lord's Supper (e.g., at a United Methodist table), that invitation is not returned. Here the body of Christ is visibly rent asunder for all the world to see. Rome's justification for this ongoing exclusion, this schism, at the table of the Lord adopts an odd exegesis of a well-known Pauline passage. Roman Catholics justify the exclusion of Protestants from this sacrament by appealing to Paul's words of warning in 1 Corinthians: "Those who eat and drink without discerning the body of Christ eat and drink judgment on themselves" (11:29). That is, since Protestants do not accept the "true" understanding of the sacrament (in other words, the Roman Catholic view), they fail to recognize or to discern "the body." Indeed, Roman Catholics have even told Protestants that they must be vigorously excluded and separated from the Lord's table in order to protect *them* from danger since they do not correctly discern the body. Schismatic behavior has hardly had such a confused theological grounding.

Indeed, it took literally centuries for the doctrine of transubstantiation to emerge. The early church knew nothing of it.[84] It is troubling then to divide the table over it.

This particular and contrived interpretation of Paul's words is dubious and is therefore rejected by many scholars. In fact, many historians, theologians, and biblical scholars believe the "body" that must be recognized in the Lord's Supper is the community of believers as the one body of Christ. This is what the Corinthian church, with its various divisions and their disregard for one another, failed to recognize. Peter Leithart convincingly argues that, ironically, it is *precisely those who exclude other Christians* from the sacrament of Communion who fail to heed Paul's words of warning:

> Otherwise, though, there are no valid grounds for excluding any believer from the Lord's Supper. Christians of different traditions differ in their understanding of what happens at the Lord's table, but those differences of theological formulation should not separate members of the corporate body from a common share in Christ's eucharistic body. In context, Paul's warnings about "discerning the body" (see 1 Cor. 11:29) do not have to do with the theology of the Supper but with factionalism in the church. Those who exclude other believers because of different beliefs about the Supper *fail* to discern the body.[85]

Since the table is the center of Christian worship and belongs to Christ, it must be open to all his disciples. It is also the center of church discipline, so flagrant, impenitent sinners must be rebuked and cut off from Communion if necessary. But Protestants who are in grace and are seeking yet additional grace, should be welcomed in any celebration of one Lord, one faith, one Spirit.

---

84. Though the early church fathers such as Ignatius, e.g., affirmed that the bread of the Eucharist is the body of Christ, thereby affirming a real presence, much more is needed to propound a full-blown doctrine of transubstantiation, a teaching that took considerable time to develop. See Ignatius of Antioch, *To the Romans 7*, in *The Apostolic Fathers with Justin Martyr and Irenaeus*, ANF 1:77.

85. Peter J. Leithart, *The End of Protestantism: Pursuing Unity in a Fragmented Church* (Grand Rapids: Brazos, 2016), 181 (emphasis original). For scholars who interpret the text similarly, see Gordon D. Fee, *The New International Commentary on the New Testament: The First Epistle to the Corinthians* (Grand Rapids: Eerdmans, 1987), 558–64; Richard B. Hays, *First Corinthians*, Interpretation: A Bible Commentary for Teaching and Preaching (Louisville: John Knox Press, 1997), 200–203. Anthony C. Thistleton rejects this interpretation, as well as the popular Roman interpretation, in his *First Corinthians: A Shorter Exegetical and Pastoral Commentary* (Grand Rapids: Eerdmans, 2006), 186–89.

10

Priesthood

From Presbyter to Priest, from Table to Altar

As the head of the church, Jesus Christ made provision for proper polity or governance so that the faithful body of believers would thrive from age to age. Marked by an abundance of graces, Christ called forth charismatic leaders, who, like the blessed Savior, would be marked by charisms, special gifts that would enable them for service. In deep and abiding wisdom, Jesus called forth twelve apostles out of ordinary life to take up an extraordinary call. As apostles, these disciples were not only called forth out of the world, as a peculiar people, but also called back into that same world for the sake of a mission, one that is the very heart of what an apostle is.

Continuing his charismatic leadership, Christ then called forth, to use the words of the apostle Paul in Ephesians 4:11–13, "the prophets, the evangelists, the pastors and teachers, to equip his people for works of service, so that the body of Christ may be built up until we all reach unity in the faith and in the knowledge of the Son of God." Two things in Paul's observations warrant special attention. First of all, observe that Christ establishes these charismatic offices to equip his people for service so that the church may be built up. Edification, then, is at the heart of ministry. Second, notice that such ministry must not be done in a divisive way by creating artificial separations and divisions. Instead, ministry to Christ, the Lord, should always have the larger goal of reaching "unity in the faith and in the knowledge of the Son of God."

Beyond these charismatic offices established by Christ, others emerged in the early church that were of a more administrative nature, having to do with the governance of an expanding church in the face of a limited number of apostles. "Unlike the apostles and other charismatic officials," Earle E. Cairns points out, "these men, and in some cases women, worked and exercised their authority in the local church or congregation rather than in the church of Christ as a whole."[1] Again, these administrative offices, which were also marked by gifts and graces for service, emerged as the church faced the reality of the necessity of differentiation of function for the sake of the larger good of the body of Christ and its mission. Luke recounts this process along with the rise of the office of deacons, who would wait on tables, in distinction from that of elders, who would proclaim the Word, in the following narrative: "It would not be right for us to neglect the ministry of the word of God in order to wait on tables. Brothers and sisters, choose seven men from among you who are known to be full of the Spirit and wisdom. We will turn this responsibility over to them and will give our attention to prayer and the ministry of the word" (Acts 6:2–4). The offices of deacon and elder, distinguished here, were yet alike in that the standards or qualifications for these two forms of service were significant indeed, as revealed in Acts 6:3 and 1 Timothy 3:8–13 for deacons and in 1 Timothy 3:1–7 and Titus 1:5–9 for elders or bishops.

Deacons

In light of the preceding discussion, it is clear that the first-century church embraced the ministries of deacons and presbyters. Both of these calls to service were marked by the gifts (charisms) of the Holy Spirit for the larger good of the church. In time these roles were viewed as ordained offices such that by the second century they were understood in terms of the threefold structure of deacon, elder, and (monarchical) bishop. As an interesting feature of this early development in the church's life, it is clear from the pages of the NT that women served in this ordained capacity during the early church period. The apostle Paul, for example, observed in his Letter to the Romans: "I commend to you our sister Phoebe, a deacon of the church in Cenchreae" (16:1). The evidence from the early tradition of the church is likewise both strong and compelling. During the first half of the third century, for example, the Didascalia Apostolorum (Teaching of the Apostles) suggested that "male

---

1. Cairns, *Christianity through the Centuries: A History of the Christian Church*, 3rd rev. ed. (Grand Rapids: Zondervan, 2009), Kindle edition, locations 1500–1501.

deacons should be compared to Christ, and deaconesses to the Holy Spirit."[2] Moreover, the Council of Chalcedon in 451 laid down a few counsels as to how and when deaconesses were to be ordained.[3]

Churches stopped ordaining women to the office of deacon, however, during the sixth century in the West and much later in the East.[4] Indeed, in the Byzantine tradition women deacons became scarce not till the twelfth century,[5] a time when Abelard and Heloise in their own European setting were still making the case to revive this ancient ecumenical practice.[6] So why then did the church, in both the East and the West, eventually exclude women from this ordained office? One school of thought lays the blame on the doorstep of the church's reaction to Montanism, a heretical movement in which women—Prisca and Maximilla, for instance—played generous leadership roles.[7] In other words, the seeds of some very troubled views of women began to flower precisely in the wake of the church's energetic reaction to heresy. This climate, which was informed by other streams as well, eventually colored the judgment even of many of the leading church fathers when the topic turned to women. In my earlier book *The Evangelical Moment*,[8] I reported:

> Clement of Alexandria, for instance, once observed that "a woman should properly be shamed when she thinks 'of what nature she is.'"[9] And Augustine, who was sexually dissolute before becoming a Christian, exclaimed that "the good Christian likes what is human, loathes what is feminine."[10] In a similar way, Jerome viewed women more often than not as temptations to male lust and he therefore advised his brothers to associate principally with one another and only with those women who had lost the seductive, female form and therefore looked more like men through rigorous fasting. "Let your companions," this Latin father cautions, "be women pale and thin with fasting, and approved by

2. Alister McGrath, *Christian History: An Introduction* (Hoboken, NJ: Wiley-Blackwell, 2012), 35.

3. Ibid.

4. Susan Lynn Peterson, *Timeline Charts of the Western Church* (Grand Rapids: Zondervan, 1999), 54.

5. Gary Macy, *Women Deacons: Past, Present, Future* (Mahwah, NJ: Paulist Press, 2012), Kindle edition, locations 483–84.

6. Ibid.

7. Christine Trevett, *Montanism: Gender, Authority and the New Prophecy* (Cambridge: Cambridge University Press, 2002), 185.

8. Kenneth J. Collins, *The Evangelical Moment: The Promise of an American Religion* (Grand Rapids: Baker Academic, 2005), 140.

9. Thomas C. Fox, *Sexuality and Catholicism* (New York: George Braziller, 1995), 219.

10. Ibid. For a detailed study of a local Roman Catholic congregation that protests against Rome's diminishment of women, see Jim Naughton, *Catholics in Crisis: The Rift between American Catholics and Their Church* (New York: Penguin Books, 1996).

their years of conduct."[11] Beyond this, Jerome reveals his estimation of women as he champions the cause of "continent" marriage in his observation: "You have with you one who was once your partner in the flesh but is now your partner in the spirit; once your wife but now your sister; once a woman but now a man; once an inferior but now an equal."[12]

Though the atmosphere in terms of women was deeply troubled by the sixth century, rendered so by the ongoing struggle with heresy as well as by the problematic attitudes of some of the church fathers, as just noted above, nevertheless recent scholarship lays the lion's share of the blame for the ordination ban on other considerations. Quoting Theodore Balsamon, a twelfth-century Greek canonist, Gary Macy, for instance, points out: "In times past, orders (*tagmata*) of deaconesses were recognized, and they had access to the sanctuary (*bema*). But the monthly affliction banished them from the divine and holy sanctuary."[13] Put another way, harkening back to OT models in which "menstruation and childbirth were seen as impediments to women serving at the altar,"[14] the medieval church excluded women henceforth from all ordained roles. Again, Macy explains: "It seems that the major reason women stopped being ordained deacons in both the East and West was the gradual introduction of purity laws from the Hebrew Scriptures."[15] However, if the new covenant rendered such things as circumcision, dietary laws, and other Mosaic social and priestly codes obsolete, how then could Rome (and Constantinople) bring them back?

The key point to see here, however, is that Rome's view, once again, does not go all the way to the first century, or even to the early church, for that matter. Instead, the Roman Catholic teaching on this score selects a much later development, an innovation that arose during the early Middle Ages, and then it renders such a judgment normative for subsequent generations with all the power, authority, and force that its exclusive male hierarchy can muster. In fact, so fearful was the hierarchy in terms of the association of women with the ordained office of deacon that the diaconate basically languished in the Roman tradition until most recently, a fact that even Vatican II had to acknowledge.[16] In the renewal of the diaconate, fostered by this council, to whom would this ancient office be offered? On this point Vatican II left no ambiguity and pointedly declared, pouring salt into an old wound: "It will be

11. Jerome, "Letter to Eustochium" 17, in *NPNF²* 6:28.
12. Jerome, "Letter to Lucinius" 3, in *NPNF²* 6:153.
13. Macy, *Women Deacons*, Kindle ed., locations 486–87.
14. Ibid., Kindle ed., locations 503–4.
15. Ibid., Kindle ed., locations 502–3.
16. *Catechism of the Catholic Church*, 2nd ed. (Mahwah, NJ: Paulist Press, 1994), par. 1571.

possible to confer this diaconal order even upon *married men*, provided they be of more mature age, and also on *suitable young men*, for whom, however, the law of celibacy must remain in force."[17] However, during the early church the work of a deacon was never so restricted.

Using Romans 16:1 ("I commend to you our sister Phoebe, a deacon of the church in Cenchreae") to deny that women held ordained office in the early church, Roman Catholic scholar Thomas Lane demarcates two meanings for the Greek word διάκονος: "deacon" as a specific office and "deacon" as simply one who serves:

> Earlier, I pointed out the fluidity in the meaning of *diakonos*, as it can refer to service as well as Christian ministry and on three occasions refers to the office of deacon. The use of *diakonos* in Romans 16:1 is one of the many occasions in the New Testament where *diakonos* does not mean a deacon, but rather someone who serves others.[18]

Though the NT sense of διάκονος embraces these two understandings, it seems arbitrary to conclude that there was a wall of separation between them such that the one role did not include the other, and *specifically for Phoebe*, an important church leader who is actually the first person called "deacon" in the New Testament. Moreover, John Witmer points out, "Use of the word [deacon] with the phrase 'of the church' [in Rom. 16:1] strongly suggests some recognized position, a fact appropriate for a person serving as Paul's emissary."[19] Perhaps, then, Rome refuses to recognize fully the practice of the early church in terms of deacons, preferring much later and more limited understandings, simply because going by early church practice could only open the door to much more leadership by women.

Priests

With the notable exception of Christ himself (e.g., in Heb. 7), it is impossible to find in the pages of the NT a sacerdotal priesthood, marked with all sorts of powers and indelible marks, one that is distinguished from the rest

---

17. Pope Paul VI, *Lumen Gentium: Dogmatic Constitution on the Church*, sec. 29, in *The Conciliar and Post Conciliar Documents*, vol. 1 of *Vatican II*, ed. Austin Flannery (Northport, NY: Costello, 1998), 387 (emphasis added); see also the Holy See, http://www.vatican.va/archive /hist_councils/ii_vatican_council/documents/vat-ii_const_19641121_lumen-gentium_en.html.

18. Thomas Lane, *The Catholic Priesthood: Biblical Foundations* (Steubenville, OH: Emmaus Road, 2016), Kindle edition, locations 3086–88.

19. John A. Witmer, "Romans," in *The Bible Knowledge Commentary: An Exposition of the Scriptures*, ed. J. F. Walvoord and R. B. Zuck, vol. 2 (Wheaton: Victor Books, 1985), 499.

of the church[20] in considerable hierarchical "lift." As Ray Robert Noll points out, "We know that nowhere in the New Testament is the Christian minister considered to be a priest (*hiereus*)."[21] To be sure, Jesus Christ established not priestly offices but charismatic roles—marked by the Holy Spirit—of apostles, prophets, evangelists, pastors, and teachers, as noted earlier, in order "to equip his people for works of service, so that the body of Christ may be built up until we all reach unity in the faith" (Eph. 4:11–13). Accordingly, "above all, this charisma creates no rank, no power of command, no *right* to obedience,"[22] Emil Brunner affirms. "There is no other obedience than that which results from the acknowledgment of the one Lord who through His Spirit allocates to each his service."[23]

Beyond this, the very vocabulary of the NT in terms of deacon/servant/ minister (διάκονος, *diakonos*), presbyter/elder (πρεσβύτερος, *presbyteros*), and overseer/elder/bishop (ἐπίσκοπος, *episkopos*) is ill suited to become the building blocks that make up all that Rome (and Constantinople) mean (and want) by the word "priest" today. Nevertheless, the last term, ἐπίσκοπος, was eventually employed by some of the early church fathers, as by Tertullian, with respect to a high- or chief-priestly role.[24] This last move, however, was a much later development. Indeed, there is no objective evidence that the first-century church, made up of Jesus and his disciples, affirmed the notion of a "priest" within the church other than the general or common priesthood of all believers as reflected in Revelation 1:6; 5:10; 20:6; 1 Peter 2:5, 9, and the priesthood of Christ himself. Again, if any of these three terms above constituted a full-blown priesthood of selected individual leaders in the NT, then there should have been a strong connection with any of them (διάκονος, πρεσβύτερος, or ἐπίσκοπος) to the appropriate Greek word, ἱερεύς (*hiereus*), which does indeed mean "priest." Unfortunately for Rome, this is once again not the case. Instead, ἱερεύς in the NT is associated with either the OT and the ongoing Levitical priesthood (Matt. 12:5), with Melchizedek (Heb. 7:1), or with Christ (Heb. 7:17), but not with Christian deacons or elders. As Garry Wills points out: "Not only is there no mention of a single priest among the Followers and Learners in the NT, there is no

20. Colin Bulley, *The Priesthood of Some Believers: Developments from the General to the Special Priesthood in the Christian Literature of the First Three Centuries* (Waynesboro, GA: Paternoster, 2000), 48.

21. Noll, *Christian Ministerial Priesthood* (San Francisco: Catholic Scholars Press, 1993), 3.

22. Emil Brunner, *The Christian Doctrine of the Church, Faith, and the Consummation* (Philadelphia: Westminster, 1962), 66 (emphasis original).

23. Ibid.

24. Tertullian, "On Baptism," in *Latin Christianity: Its Founder, Tertullian*, trans. S. Thelwall, *ANF* 3:677.

mention of the acts we now associate with the priesthood."[25] Continuing this line of thought, Wills pointedly exclaims: "There were no priests and no priestly services; no male presider at the agape meal, no re-enactment of Jesus' Last Supper, no 'sacrifice of the Mass,' no consecrations of bread and wine; nothing that resembled what priests now claim to do."[26]

What we do find in the pages of the NT is a call to service that is recognized by the elders of the church through the laying on of hands. Even here, however, such a practice was not employed exclusively in the very simple rite of ordination during the first century, for the laying on of hands was also associated with the gift of prophecy (1 Tim. 4:14) and with the new birth itself (Acts. 19:4–7). In fact, in the period immediately following the apostles, the recognition of a call to ministry "involved little in the way of ceremony or protocol."[27]

The Early Church Perspective

The rise of the priesthood, which eventually took place in the church, whereby both presbyters (πρεσβύτεροι, *presbyteroi*) and bishops (ἐπίσκοποι, *episkopoi*) took on a sacerdotal and even a mediatorial role, sharply distinguishing themselves from their fellow church members, is a fascinating story of which only the highlights can be treated here. However, before some of the material from the early church fathers is examined, we need to recognize a strong connection in the literature between how the Lord's Supper is understood on the one hand, and the rise of the priestly role on the other hand. Indeed, such a dynamic can be fleshed out in two key questions. First, did changes in how the Lord's Supper was viewed in the later church give rise to and actually create the Christian priestly role? Second, did modifications in terms of how the offices of presbyter and bishop were later configured result in viewing the Lord's Supper in a remarkably new way? However this dynamic is interpreted, emphasizing one factor or the other, this much at least is clear: once the office of a priest was in place, that perspective by itself colored everything. The priestly role not only affected relations within the body of Christ, especially in terms of fellowship, but also modified how the Lord's Supper itself was understood.

Little evidence of the priesthood can be discerned from the writings of the Apostolic Fathers, though some of these authors were likely aware of it.[28]

25. Wills, *Why Priests? A Failed Tradition* (New York: Viking Adult, 2013), 14.
26. Ibid., 17.
27. Marjorie Warkentin, *Ordination: A Biblical-Historical View* (Grand Rapids: Eerdmans, 1982), 33.
28. Bulley, *Priesthood of Some*, 216.

Clement of Rome, for example, does not apply the "sacrificial terminology of the Old Testament . . . to . . . Christian leaders."[29] Moreover, it cannot be demonstrated from the letters of Ignatius of Antioch that "a separate priestly class"[30] was in place during his time, though he does employ the language of "'the altar of Eucharistic sacrifice' (*thysiastērion*) as a sign and guarantor of church unity."[31] From Polycarp's observations, made later, in the second century, to the church at Philippi, it appears that a presbyterial arrangement was operative, and therefore there is nothing in this letter to suggest "the presence of a separate priestly class."[32] Beyond this, the situation is much the same in the *Shepherd of Hermas*, though by the early second century, in the writings of Justin Martyr, for instance, the language of a priest does emerge, though Justin may have had in mind not a specialized order but the common priesthood in which all believers participate. He taught that all Christians make up, as he puts it, "the true high priestly race of God, as even God Himself bears witness."[33]

A clear shift in the language of priesthood does take place in the writings of Tertullian, during the late second century and into the third. While this Latin father appreciated the general or common priesthood of all Christians, he nevertheless focused not on the office of presbyter or elder in his priestly ruminations (as we might expect) but on that of the bishop. He wrote: "Of giving it [baptism], the chief priest (who is the bishop) has the right: in the next place, the presbyters and deacons, yet not without the bishop's authority."[34] Hippolytus, for his part, viewed the bishop in much the same way as did Tertullian, that is, as a high priest, but he also implied, in a way that Tertullian did not, that the presbyter was "ordained to the priesthood."[35] Origen, writing shortly thereafter, continued these themes and applied the terminology of a priest to both the bishops and the presbyters.[36]

During the third century the theme of priesthood as a specialized sacerdotal role was so developed in the writings of Cyprian that he neglected the clear

29. Noll, *Christian Ministerial Priesthood*, 77.

30. Ibid., 124.

31. Eugene LaVerdiere, *The Eucharist in the New Testament and the Early Church* (Collegeville, MN: Liturgical Press, 1996), 152.

32. Ibid., 151.

33. Justin Martyr, *Dialogue with Trypho* 116, in *The Apostolic Fathers with Justin Martyr and Irenaeus*, ANF 1:257.

34. Tertullian, "On Baptism" 17, ANF 3:677.

35. Bulley, *Priesthood of Some*, 133.

36. Ibid., 134. Bulley points out, "[Origen] likens the bishop to the high priest, and the priest identifies the OT priests and Levites with the presbyters and deacons respectively, and fairly often refers to church leaders as priests in such a way that it is difficult to know whether he has bishops alone, presbyters alone, or both, in mind" (ibid.).

biblical teaching of the general priesthood[37] of all Christians (indeed he was unwilling "to use *sacerdos* of ordinary Christians").[38] Continuing in this vein, he also specifically advanced the notion that the work of the priest (understood preeminently as the bishop but also as the presbyter) is to act on behalf of Christ and thereby to offer a suitable sacrifice to the Father, in which the table of the first Lord's Supper had by now clearly become an altar. Cyprian expressed these themes in a passage that warrants being quoted at length:

> For if Jesus Christ, our Lord and God, is Himself the chief priest of God the Father, and has first offered Himself a sacrifice to the Father, and has commanded this to be done in commemoration of Himself, certainly that priest truly discharges the office of Christ, who imitates that which Christ did; and he then offers a true and full sacrifice in the Church to God the Father, when he proceeds to offer it according to what he sees Christ Himself to have offered.[39]

In this interpretation of earlier historical realities, Christ commands not only that his priestly role be taken up by others but also that they offer a true and full sacrifice to the Father. Even today Rome could not have asked for more.

Limited space does not permit us to describe in detail the development of a sacerdotal understanding of both bishops and elders—both now called priests—in the later church at the hands of Gregory of Nazianzus, Ambrose, Augustine, and Cyril of Alexander, to name a few. Our main point all along has been simply to establish, with suitable evidence, that the conception of a presbyter or bishop as a priest represents a later historical development that did not characterize either the first-century church or that of much of the next century. We conclude, after a careful estimation of the primary sources and in a way similar to the judgments of Bulley, that "the practice of thinking of the ordained as priests grew up in the late second century, becoming widespread at its end."[40] In recognizing that the reality of a Christian priest is, after all, a historical product (whether it was the work of the Holy Spirit or a human creation remains at this point an open question), we must therefore take special care not to read such later developments back into the first century, in which they cannot be properly situated or contextualized. The option remains that this later development of the priesthood does admittedly represent a significant modification, but that such change can be understood

---

37. Ibid., 223.
38. Ibid., 226.
39. Cyprian of Carthage, *The Epistles of Cyprian* 62.14, in *Fathers of the Third Century: Hippolytus, Cyprian, Novatian, Appendix*, trans. Robert Ernest Wallis, *ANF* 5:362.
40. Bulley, *Priesthood of Some*, 136.

as merely rendering explicit what was implicit in the first-century church, as Raymond Brown has claimed.[41] In other words, this historical process that we have described was putatively superintended by the Holy Spirit. However, the reasonableness of such a claim (with its implied argument) will have to be assessed, for the most part, on biblical and theological grounds. That is, do such later developments in the church actually cohere with the theology of the gospel in general, with the nature of the church itself, and with the Lord's Supper in particular?

The Roman Catholic Conception of the Priesthood

Roman Catholic doctrinal materials do indeed commit the error of anachronism by reading back later and well-developed elements—in the form, for example, of what the sacraments had eventually become—into the apostolic age itself. In this way, nothing less than the authority of the apostles is supposedly given to, and a legitimizing canopy is draped over, all those later realities, those transformations and innovations that Rome actually prefers. Indeed, the *Catechism* makes the following claim, which is greatly in need of a substantiating argument: "The criterion that assures unity amid the diversity of liturgical traditions is fidelity to apostolic Tradition, i.e., the communion in the faith and the sacraments received from the apostles, a communion that is both signified and guaranteed by apostolic succession."[42] Indeed, chapter 6 has already demonstrated how deeply troubled such an allegation is. Moreover, in the material below virtually none of the leading characteristics that Rome wants in its reconfiguring of a first-century presbyter into a priest (e.g., celibacy) can be found during the apostolic period.

After declaring that the apostles established the sacrament of Holy Orders as Rome has reworked it,[43] this particular theological tradition then goes on to contend that ordination to the priesthood "confers a gift of the Holy Spirit that permits the exercise of a 'sacred power.'"[44] What is that sacred power that is not given to all the holy, faithful believers of the church but is reserved only for its supposed priests? It is, as the documents of Vatican II declare, the power

41. Ibid., 320.
42. *Catechism*, par. 1209.
43. See ibid., par. 1576, which states: "Since the sacrament of Holy Orders is the sacrament of the apostolic ministry, it is for the bishops as the successors of the apostles to hand on the 'gift of the Spirit,' the 'apostolic line.'" Such a claim is also compromised since it is predicated in part on the myth of apostolic succession, which was shown to be fraught with difficulties in chapter 9.
44. Ibid., par. 1538.

"of offering sacrifice and forgiving sins."[45] Wills unpacks the first part of this assertion in terms of the "power to effect transubstantiation,"[46] a capability that we have no objective evidence to believe characterized the life of the early church. Indeed, such a view would have undoubtedly come as a surprise to any apostle, whether Peter, James, or John. Beyond this, Rome tries to make sense of the second part of this claim, in light of the NT observation "Who can forgive sins but God alone?" by contending that the priest not only has the "power of sanctifying"[47] but also acts in *figura Christi*, that is, the action of the priest is none other than the very work of Christ himself. That's why, as Wills points out, the priest says, "I baptize you," or, "I absolve you," or, "This is My body."[48] Here the personhood of the priest has in effect been switched out for that of Christ. There will be more on this particular claim toward the end of the chapter.

For now it is sufficient to notice that the Roman Catholic Church does after all go back to the first century in at least one attempt to ground its particular understanding of the priesthood. Unfortunately its reasoning in this case is specious and its consequences for women are outright detrimental. To illustrate, the Roman church argues (e.g., in neglecting the theological wisdom of Gal. 3:28 ["There is neither Jew nor Gentile, neither slave nor free, nor is there male and female, for you are all one in Christ Jesus"] and other broad truths of Scripture, such as the *imago Dei*) that the ordination of women is simply impossible. Interestingly enough, there is a sense in which, judging from the literature, this whole matter is not even to be discussed anymore. Indeed, Pope John Paul II drafted an apostolic letter *Ordinatio Sacerdotalis* in 1994 and cautioned all Roman Catholics along the following lines: "I declare that the [Roman Catholic] Church has no authority whatsoever to confer priestly ordination on women and that this judgment is to be definitively held by all the [Roman Catholic] Church's faithful."[49]

Why has this ban against women, as part of the body of Christ (think through the gender implications of that!), been so energetically proclaimed? It is because, so the argument goes, Jesus chose only males to be his disciples. The *Catechism* explains: "'Only a baptized man (*vir*) validly receives sacred ordination.' The Lord Jesus chose men (*viri*) to form the college of the twelve

45. *Decree on the Ministry and Life of Priests*, par. 2, in Flannery, *Conciliar and Post Conciliar Documents*, 864.
46. Wills, *Why Priests?*, 20.
47. *Catechism*, par. 1087.
48. Wills, *Why Priests?*, 219.
49. Pope John Paul II, *Ordinatio Sacerdotalis* (apostolic letter), sec. 4, the Holy See, 1994, http://w2.vatican.va/content/john-paul-i/en/apost_letters/1994/documents/hf_jp-ii_apl_1994 0522_ordinatio-sacerdotalis.html.

apostles, and the apostles did the same when they chose collaborators to succeed them in their ministry. . . . For this reason the ordination of women is not possible."[50] Really? That's it? That's the substance of the argument? But why simply settle on gender here? Why not focus on race or ethnicity or social class or economic status or even marital status? With this *form* of reasoning in place, then, one perhaps can only conclude that since Jesus chose only Jews to be his disciples, then only Jews and not any gentiles should be eligible for ordination. In response to this objection, if the Roman Catholic Church contends that the universality of the gospel so obviously transcends the Jew/gentile divide such that gentiles are rightly ordained, especially in light of the judgment of Galatians 3:28, then it is fair to ask why the same line of reasoning does not apply to the male/female divide as well.[51]

So then, the preceding "argument" as to why women cannot be ordained in the Roman Catholic Church lacks the marks of a final judgment (theological reasoning so well substantiated and convincing that there would be little point in continuing), and thus we suspect that something else is going on here, that there is a larger subtext that is actually behind the brief, dogmatic, and at times nervous public pronouncements of the all-male hierarchy. For one thing, the vehement response to any opposing views suggests a climate limned with anxiety and fear. If this assessment is accurate, and we believe it is, then the question must immediately be addressed: just what is actually at stake here?[52]

A clue to this puzzle can be found in Pope John Paul II's earlier statement. Observe that he did not declare that *he* lacked the authority to ordain women but that the [Roman Catholic] *Church* "has no authority whatsoever to confer priestly ordination."[53] Given the logic of Roman Catholicism, in a certain sense the pope was right. That is, the whole matter of women's ordination is not simply an isolated issue about gender in which the theological elements of women being equally created in the *imago Dei* as well as the frank recognition of their God-given gifts for service would trump all other considerations. No, the ordination issue bespeaks ecclesiology, as Rome understands it, an ecclesiology of a particular sort. In fact, the hierarchy has celebrated maleness at every step along the way in its conception of a priest, going back to OT Levitical materials, even to the point of maintaining that the male specimen

50. *Catechism*, par. 1577.

51. Some Protestants, such as Southern Baptists, agree with Rome on its ban with respect to women in key ecclesiastical leadership roles.

52. Depending in some sense on the prior thought of Plato, Augustine considered women to be "the weaker sex," a phrase repeated throughout the Middle Ages to the detriment of women. See Augustine, *On the Morals of the Catholic Church* 30.63, NPNF[1] 4:58.

53. John Paul II, *Ordinatio Sacerdotalis*, sec. 4.

must be "intact," so to speak ("Priests must not . . . cut their bodies" [Lev. 21:5]; thus the ordination of Origen, for example, who was castrated, was precluded). According to the most recent edition of canon law, "a person who has mutilated himself"[54] cannot be ordained.

The magisterium then turned around and embedded these very male notions into the *work* of a supposed NT priest by once again reaching back to OT models, especially in terms of the practice of offering sacrifice like a Levite: "The liturgy of the Church, however, sees in the priesthood of Aaron and the service of the Levites, as in the institution of the seventy elders, a prefiguring of the ordained ministry of the New Covenant."[55] With these moves in place, which entailed a process through which the privileged status of maleness was carried over from one covenant to the other, whether appropriate or not, Rome has in the end painted itself into a corner in terms of the role of women in the church. That is, this issue is a remarkably good window on so many others of theological substance, to which it is related by implication. To be sure, to make a change regarding the ordination of women would begin a process that would ultimately lead to nothing less than the unraveling of the Roman Catholic tradition itself—and the hierarchy clearly comprehends this. That's what is behind all the anxiety and fear: Deny that maleness is a necessary characteristic of a priest, and the priesthood as Rome has conceived it begins to topple. If the priesthood falls, then the sacraments, again as Rome has conceived them (e.g., with the proper offering of a sacrifice), begin to unravel along with it. If the sacraments unravel, then the sacramental understanding of redemption itself is at stake. Little wonder that the magisterium has spoken so forcefully on this matter.

Strange Bedfellows: Priestly Celibacy and the Investiture Controversy

In his teaching on marriage, divorce, and adultery, Jesus Christ described that special dedication on the part of some who would *choose* to remain "eunuchs for the sake of the kingdom of heaven" (Matt. 19:12). Moreover, the apostle Paul, himself a bachelor, mindful of that special dedication and thinking that the return of Christ would be imminent ("What I mean, brothers and sisters, is that the time is short. From now on those who have wives should live as if they do not" [1 Cor. 7:29]), advised that those believers who are not married should remain so and not seek a spouse: "Are you pledged to a

54. *Code of Canon Law* 4.1.6.2.3, "Irregularities and Other Impediments," http://www .vatican.va/archive/ENG1104/__P3S.HTM.
55. *Catechism*, par. 1541.

woman? Do not seek to be released. Are you free from such a commitment? Do not look for a wife" (v. 27). Paul quickly added, however, lest his words be misinterpreted, "But if you do marry, you have not sinned" (v. 28), thereby reaffirming the larger basic biblical truth (that many of the Jews, by the way, understood very well) that the God of redemption and the God of creation are not two different gods.

Human sexuality, in the form of marital love, is that great good—a genuine gift from the Creator—that in its best sense mirrors, even if only faintly, the trinitarian love of the Christian Godhead in its radiant beauty.

Admittedly, there is nothing in the teaching of either Jesus or the apostle Paul that requires universal celibacy on the part of the elders of the church. In fact, during the first three centuries most presbyters, both in the West and the East, were married. Around the middle of the second century, for instance, Tertullian, the great Latin church father who himself took a wife, impugned the teachings of Marcion, the heretic, who had renounced the blessed practice of marriage: "We must now encounter the subject of marriage, which Marcion, more continent than the apostle, prohibits."[56] During the fourth century the Council of Nicaea (325) mandated that a priest could not take a wife after ordination, a judgment that helps to explain the Eastern Orthodox practice even today of permitting marriage before ordination but generally not afterward. Furthermore, during this same century the Council of Elvira (306) mandated "continence" for married clergy, though this canon probably did not entail a total rejection of normal marital relations. It was simply a counsel limited to certain periods of time, seasons of sexual abstinence about which even the apostle Paul wrote, since many of the clergy continued to marry and have children.[57] Indeed, during this period both Gregory of Nazianzus and Gregory of Nyssa, leading Cappadocian fathers, were married bishops.[58]

Two significant developments helped to prepare the way for the much-later requirement and strict enforcement of priestly celibacy in the West. First of all, the rise of Neoplatonism in the third century, one of whose chief expositors was Plotinus, brought to bear on the church some strong Hellenistic cultural influences (with their celebration of spirit, mind, and form over the body) and thereby strengthened an already-existing asceticism, though Jesus Christ

---

56. Tertullian, *Against Marcion*, in *Latin Christianity: Its Founder, Tertullian*, ANF 3:443.

57. Canon 33, e.g., states: "Bishops, presbyters, deacons, and others with a position in the ministry are to abstain completely from sexual intercourse with their wives and from the procreation of children. If anyone disobeys, he shall be removed from the clerical office." See "Canons of the Church Council," https://www.csun.edu/~hcfll004/elvira.html.

58. Philip Schaff, *History of the Christian Church—from the 1st to the 19th Century* (n.p.: Delmarva Publications, 2014), Kindle edition, locations 24957–59.

himself was clearly no ascetic: "The Son of Man came eating and drinking" (Luke 7:34). The evidences of this Greek cultural influence or deposit, especially in terms of human sexuality, can be discerned in the writings of Augustine (early fifth century) as they linked the transmission of original sin with normal human copulation.

Second, the rise of monasticism, through the leadership of Antony in the third century and Pachomius in the fourth, as well as the celebration of this way of life by Jerome in the West, brought with it the judgment that the forswearing of all sexual relations in celibacy (and in virginity), this carefully chosen ascetic path, was strongly associated with greater sanctity, a deeper fund of holiness. Not surprisingly, the great monastic houses in the West, modeled after the Benedictine order established at Subiaco in the sixth century, were grounded in the vows of poverty, chastity, and obedience.

Yet none of this early history, as interesting as it is, explains why, once again, the Roman tradition departed from the common and ongoing practice of the East (where priests can be married even today) to chart its own course (once again, Rome alone) and to make this particular spiritual counsel, this innovation, a requirement for all priests and bishops, regardless of their personal constitution and comportment. Significant clues to this riddle can be found in the life and work of Hildebrand, who became Pope Gregory VII in the eleventh century, though there were precursory developments as well. Coming to the papacy in April 1073, after he had increased the powers of the office earlier as a cardinal, Gregory VII had to face two key problems during his pontificate.

First of all, the investiture controversy, the struggle for power and authority between the spiritual and temporal leaders of medieval Europe, was still raging, and the feudal lords and Gregory VII were struggling with the question of who was to confer the symbols of authority upon an ecclesiastical feudal vassal whose allegiances, given the structure of society at the time, went in two different directions. This is the troubled, contentious context in which the Holy Roman Emperor Henry IV was humiliated by Gregory at Canossa. Indeed, the pope left Henry standing outside the castle walls in the snow for three days (January 25–27, 1077) as the emperor sought a papal audience as well as forgiveness. After this humiliation of the temporal power (the memory of which helps to explain the secularism of Europe even today), Henry regained some of his power among the German nobility, such that by 1080 he was in a position and bold enough to march on Rome, remove Gregory from office, and establish Wibert of Ravenna as the bishop of Rome.[59] In the eyes of Rome, however, Wibert was little more than a feckless antipope.

---

59. Cairns, *Christianity through the Centuries*, Kindle ed., locations 3836–39.

Second, the tradition, going back to the first-century church, that "priests" or presbyters could marry was yet alive in the eleventh century even in the West, though Gregory VII did not like it. Uta Ranke-Heinemann observes: "Gregory made it clear what he thought of priestly marriage: He called it a 'crime of fornication.' He called upon the people to boycott married priests. . . . To Gregory, priestly marriage was concubinage."[60] Among other things, the pope feared that some ecclesiastical families, if you will, were becoming inordinately powerful by passing on wealth, power, and privilege from one generation to the next. As Gerald Bray put it recently: "One of the reasons that celibacy was imposed on the Western clergy in the Middle Ages was to ensure that they would not have legitimate children who could inherit their positions."[61] Pope Gregory therefore fought vigorously for reform in the church and inveighed against the practice of simony as well as the moral failure of "open concubinage."[62] This complicated task, as Schaff put it in his own day, was "to restore in a measure the old laws of celibacy."[63] However, such codes proved to be insufficient "to prevent the secret and, to morality, far more dangerous violations of [celibacy]."[64]

Always preoccupied with the ongoing problem of the investiture controversy during his pontificate, and fending off powerful political families such as the Tuscalani,[65] Gregory saw an ingenious way in which to deal with this larger issue of power. Remarkably, he would be able to address simultaneously two difficulties that confronted the authority of the hierarchy: married clergy with powerful families behind them and unmarried clergy who kept mistresses. To put this issue of the sexual behavior of priests, whether licit or illicit, to rest, and also to eviscerate what power strong families held with respect to the will of the hierarchy, he simply required that henceforth all priests must make a sacred promise of celibacy. Thus the vow of chastity (which actually embraced celibacy) that had been taken by monks for centuries would now reappear in the context of "secular" clergy or diocesan priests—no longer as a vow, but simply as a promise.[66] The consequence, however, was much the same.

---

60. Ranke-Heinemann, *Eunuchs for the Kingdom of Heaven: Women, Sexuality, and the Catholic Church* (New York: Doubleday, 1990), 108.

61. Bray, *The Church: A Theological and Historical Account* (Grand Rapids: Baker Academic, 2016), 18–19.

62. Schaff, *History of the Christian Church*, Kindle ed., locations 36674–76.

63. Ibid.

64. Ibid.

65. Alister McGrath, *Christian History: An Introduction* (Hoboken, NJ: Wiley-Blackwell, 2012), 90.

66. Religious order priests, in contrast to diocesan priests, take the vow of celibacy.

Such a move, as Adolf von Harnack pointed out, led to "the estrangement of the priests from secular life"[67] and thereby weakened the familial networks and powers of which priests had been a part. This, in turn, made the clergy utterly dependent on the hierarchy and therefore ready to receive the counsel of "docility" as one of their chief virtues as they faced their "superiors." They were aware, it seems, that the power that gives you everything is also the same power that can take everything away. The clergy quickly got the message. Gregory also ordered that even married clergy were to put away their wives ("priests [must] first escape from the clutches of their wives").[68] This whole shift indeed strengthened the hierarchy, at every rung along the way, up to and including the papacy itself, especially in the form of the later pontificate of Innocent III. This was a bold move by the Gregorians (thinking of the curia, the administrative organ of the Vatican, as well), in which papal decrees, as Karl F. Morrison observes, were set against an earlier tradition of married priests.[69]

Priestly celibacy, then, was not simply about sex. That is a modern misconception. It was also very much about power as it developed over time, and such a consideration remains a part of the equation even today, though it is seldom discussed. Therefore, making either a biblical or a theological argument as to why priests should be "allowed" to marry today will hardly carry the day among the Roman Catholic hierarchy in general and at the Vatican in particular. Rather, what will likely trump all this reasoning to let priests marry, however clear, energetic, or cogent, is yet again a preferred and in many respects privileged ecclesiology, one that continually bleeds into everything.

67. Harnack, *History of Dogma*, trans. Neil Buchanan, 3rd ed. (Seattle: Amazon Digital Services, 2011), Kindle edition, locations 36850–52.

68. "A Brief History of Celibacy in the Catholic Church," FutureChurch, accessed December 24, 2016, https://www.futurechurch.org/brief-history-of-celibacy-in-catholic-church.

69. Morrison, ed., *The Investiture Controversy: Issues, Ideals, and Results* (New York: Holt, Rinehart & Winston, 1971), 67. We recognize that the imposition of celibacy on all presbyters of the church, now known as priests, had developments beyond the forceful actions of Gregory VII. Bray, e.g., points out: "In the twelfth century that tendency to celibacy was formally imposed on all priests (it had been imposed on bishops in 692), something that has remained characteristic of Roman Catholic clergy today." See Bray, *Church*, 123–24. Moreover, clerical marriages, though greatly reduced, continued into the twelfth century. In its canon 21 the First Lateran Council actually decreed not only that clergy must not enter into a marriage contract but also that those who had already done so must simply dissolve such marriages. See *The Canons of the First Lateran Council, 1123*, in Internet Medieval Source Book, part of the Internet History Sourcebooks Project, ed. Paul Halsall, Fordham University Center for Medieval Studies, text excerpted from H. J. Schroeder, *Disciplinary Decrees of the General Councils: Text, Translation and Commentary* (St. Louis: B. Herder, 1937), 177–94, http://sourcebooks .fordham.edu/basis/lateran1.asp.

The Purported Identity of a Priest

During the pontificate of Innocent III (1198–1216), the medieval period in the West was marked by a clericalism expressed in a sharp distinction between the power and prerogatives of the clergy on the one hand, and those of the laity on the other hand. As the roles of priests were expanded, those of the laity were naturally viewed as being more limited both in nature and scope. The exception here was that special and limited population of brothers and sisters who were a part of religious orders but who were not ordained. Their religious lives were quite broad, active, and engaging, to be sure. The contrast here, then, is at its sharpest when priests are compared to those who were not ordained and who were also not a part of any religious order (or monastery) but who were in the workaday world. The attitudes of clericalism in this particular context, which oftentimes did not lead to a more active engagement of the laity, were present even up until the time of Vatican II. Naturally this council took up reform in this area and attempted to correct the problem left in the wake of an earlier clericalism and thereby bridged a previous divide between clergy and laity. The council now trumpeted the language that the church is "the whole people of God"[70] as the proper ecclesiastical expression.

Roman Catholic priests today, nevertheless, remain a very distinct group, separated from the laity by their promise of celibacy as well as in other important ways, so there yet remains a lingering clericalism even in the wake of Vatican II. First of all, as was noted in passing, priests have the supposed special powers of offering sacrifice, effecting transubstantiation, and forgiving sins; laity do not. Priests have a reputed special "sacerdotal dignity, in virtue of Holy Orders";[71] laity do not. Moreover, through the sacrament of Holy Orders priests alone are given an indelible mark on their souls that not even the worst moral failure can remove in such a way that they would, as a consequence, lose their priestly, sacerdotal character and thereby sink to the level (keeping in mind the RCC hierarchical order) of laity. Remarkably enough, the *Catechism* actually explores this admittedly difficult matter in significant detail, as revealed in the following observation: "It is true that someone validly ordained can, for grave reasons, be discharged from the obligations and functions linked to ordination, or can be forbidden to exercise them; but he cannot become a layman again in the strict sense, because the character imprinted by

---

70. *Instruction on the Worship of the Eucharistic Mystery*, par. 42, in Flannery, *Conciliar and Post Conciliar Documents*, 126.

71. *Catechism*, par. 1564.

ordination is forever."[72] Add to this the Roman Catholic Church's insistence
that the laity properly address their priests as "fathers"[73] (a dubious counsel
in light of Jesus's words in Matt. 23:9) as well as Vatican II's declaration that
"the priests of the New Testament are, it is true, by their vocation to ordination, *set apart* in some way in the midst of the People of God,"[74] and the
things that emerge are all the ingredients necessary to reconstitute a (more
modest) form of clericalism.

Clearly, then, the Roman Catholic institution of the priesthood not only
leads to the separation of priests from laity, in some very important senses,
but also results in Roman Catholics' estrangement from the broader church,
as Wills has aptly observed: "I shall be arguing here that priesthood . . . keeps
[Roman] Catholics at a remove from other Christians."[75] Again, Wills asks
the frank and honest question: "How is it Christian to make that priesthood
a means for excluding all Christians but Roman Catholics?"[76] To use the
language of Vatican II itself, when "the Church is most perfectly displayed
in its hierarchic structure in that celebration of the Eucharist at which the
bishop presides, surrounded by his priests and ministers, with the active
participation of the whole people of God,"[77] Protestants are not welcomed
to commune in this setting. Such an exclusion, therefore, casts into doubt
once again whether believers in Reformation churches are really a part of
"the whole people of God."[78] In contrast to this troubled theology, the first
Lord's Supper, established by Jesus Christ, placed a premium on genuine
communion and fellowship. The transformation of that simple fellowship
meal into a sacrifice, as a later historical development, one orchestrated
by priests and bishops with added sacerdotal dignity and powers, has led
to division and lasting separation within the body of Christ. That's an
unavoidable consequence of what the Roman Catholic conception of the
priesthood requires. It rends the garment that the death of Christ had sown
together.

72. Ibid., par. 1583.
73. *Decree on the Ministry and Life of Priests*, par. 9, in Flannery, *Conciliar and Post Conciliar Documents*, 881.
74. Ibid., par. 3, in Flannery, *Conciliar and Post Conciliar Documents*, 866 (emphasis added).
Vatican II insists that such setting apart is "not in order that they should be separated from
that people or from any man" (ibid.), but the claim is hardly convincing given the realities on
the ground, so to speak, especially surrounding the altar.
75. Wills, *Why Priests?*, 4.
76. Ibid.
77. *Instruction on the Worship of the Eucharistic Mystery*, par. 42, in Flannery, *Conciliar
and Post Conciliar Documents*, 126.
78. Ibid.

Do New Testament Priests Actually Exist?

As stated earlier, the Roman Catholic Church reaches back to OT understand-ings in many ways, and it therefore views the priesthood of Aaron and the ministrations of the Levities as "a prefiguring of the ordained ministry of the New Covenant."[79] Accordingly, Willy Rordorf sets up a parallel relation between the two covenants on this issue that is mirrored in Roman Catholic doctrinal materials as well. He declares: "The offering of sacrifices in the Old Testament . . . required the intervention of the Levitic priesthood. So too do the rites of the New Testament require the intervention of a priesthood which is the specific attribute of a hierarchy."[80] In fact, at the ordination of every Roman Catholic priest around the world today, the following words are spoken:

> Lord, holy Father, . . .
> when you had appointed high priests to rule your people,
> you chose other men next to them in rank and dignity
> to be with them and to help them in their task. . . .
>
> You extended the spirit of Moses to seventy wise men. . . .
> You shared among the sons of Aaron
> the fullness of their father's power.[81]

One of several problems entailed in creating a putative NT priesthood using and appealing to OT materials is that the Levitical priesthood (as well as the Mosaic covenant) has been surpassed in important ways by the death and resurrection of Jesus Christ. This basic truth is repeatedly explored in the NT witness. In Acts, for example, Luke reveals that human beings "were not able to obtain [justification, the forgiveness of sins] under the law of Moses" (13:39). Furthermore, the apostle Paul in 2 Corinthians points out that the old covenant, along with its many sacrifices, was a "ministry that brought death," a "ministry that brought condemnation" and as such was "transitory" (3:7–11).

Beyond this, the themes touched upon by Luke and Paul are developed more extensively by the author of the book of Hebrews, who compares the ministry of Jesus to that of the ancient Levitical priests and thereby finds the latter wanting: "But in fact the ministry Jesus has received is as superior to theirs as the covenant of which he is mediator is superior to the old one, since

79. *Catechism*, par. 1541.
80. Rordorf, *The Eucharist of the Early Christians* (Collegeville, MN: Liturgical Press, 1976), 30.
81. *Catechism*, par. 1542.

the new covenant is established on better promises" (8:6). Again, the author of this "liturgical" NT book, fully apprised of the reality of the new covenant and its better promises, poses a basic question to all those who in their understanding of priesthood yet seek to be informed by an Aaronic model: "If perfection could have been attained through the Levitical priesthood—and indeed the law given to the people established that priesthood—why was there still need for another priest to come, one in the order of Melchizedek, not in the order of Aaron?" (Heb. 7:11). In fact, "by calling this covenant 'new,' [Christ] has made the first one obsolete; and what is obsolete and outdated will soon disappear" (Heb. 8:13).

In light of this important biblical evidence, then, the Aaronic priesthood, belonging to the shadows of the Mosaic covenant, if you will, has been transcended in the reality of the superlative priesthood of Jesus Christ, the Mediator, the God/Human who establishes a new covenant in his own blood. With Christ, something genuinely new has come, and it therefore transforms all earlier understandings. There is a sense in which Rome knows all of this, but it continues to appeal to the Levitical priesthood in its own understanding of what a NT priest should be. The magisterium teaches, for example, that the Mass is a holy sacrifice, repeated daily and by many priests, "because it makes present the *one sacrifice* of Christ the Savior and includes the Church's offering."[82]

Thus, in this context, Rome not only reaches out for the ongoing significance of a Levitical conception of the priesthood but also embraces an understanding that pertains to the distinct priesthood of Melchizedek. The appeal to the latter conception of priesthood, however, is largely in an indirect manner, especially when Rome draws the connection to its own priests. In other words, Roman Catholic priests could never directly claim the priesthood of Melchizedek, a sheer impossibility given the unique attributes of this priestly office. What connection they could possibly have to this priestly order, then, could only come by means of either acting through Christ or being a representative of Christ. The *Catechism* explains: "[Christ is] the unique high priest, according to the order of Melchizedek. Christ fulfilled everything that the priesthood of the old covenant prefigured (cf. Heb. 5:10; 6:20). He offered himself once and for all (Heb. 10:14), in a perfect sacrifice upon the cross. His priesthood is made present in a special way in the Church through the ministerial priesthood, conferred through the Sacrament of Holy Orders."[83]

---

82. Ibid., par. 1330 (emphasis added).
83. *Catechism of the Catholic Church*, 2nd ed. (Mahwah, NJ: Paulist Press, 1994), Kindle edition, locations 28148–51. This material is drawn from the glossary (under the heading "The

A major problem emerges in this material, just noted, a genuine nonstarter if you will. It is not, however, the once-and-for-all nature of Christ's sacrifice. Rome publicly agrees with the eternal nature of this offering, though it has a difficult time incorporating this truth into a coherent liturgical theology that remains rooted, in some sense, in Levitical transitory understandings. Consequently, the eternal nature and perfection of Christ's sacrifice is not *directly* at stake here at the moment, though some Protestants will continue to find trouble with the Roman Catholic take on things, that is, that the one sacrifice of Christ is repeated daily by many priests (lingering Levitical understandings) precisely in light of the clear teaching of Hebrews. At any rate our focus, at least for the moment, is elsewhere. Accordingly, observe in the last sentence in the material just quoted above how the Roman Catholic Church tries to connect the priesthood of Leviticus (the many) and of Melchizedek (the one), as well as its own priesthood (the many) and that of Jesus Christ (the one), through the vaunted and ungrounded declaration (found nowhere in the Bible, by the way) that Christ's priesthood "is made present *in a special way* in the Church through the ministerial priesthood."[84]

The first issue to be addressed in the last claim is in focus: How is it that only the Roman Catholic priesthood is the means through which the ordinary ministry of Christ can be rendered special? Is not the adjective "special" here and its relation to mediation and possible agency badly misconstrued? Again, is it only through the Roman priesthood that Christ's priesthood can appear in a special way? Is Christ's priesthood, then, merely ordinary without the help of Rome's priests? And what about the priests of Eastern Orthodoxy? Are they rendered special too? Second, such confusion continues and is unfortunately reflected in the declaration that "the ordained priesthood *guarantees* that it really *is* Christ who acts in the sacraments."[85] Again, how is it that the priesthood (Rome's preferred ecclesiology linked to "apostolic succession" and sacerdotal developments) guarantees—and is therefore the substantiating, foundational authority for the *being* of, for the very reality of—Christ in the sacraments? Is not Christ himself the guarantee of all such things? Are Roman Catholic priests edging out Jesus here? Is the being of Christ also dependent, in some sense, on the hierarchy and its teachings?

Difficult as it is to imagine, there is yet a third, far more serious, problem in this priestly context, and it concerns the claim that in the Mass the priest acts not on behalf of Christ but actually in the person of Christ. To illustrate,

---

Priesthood of Christ") that is a part of the Kindle edition of the *Catechism* but is not found in the print version.

84. *Catechism*, in the glossary under the heading "Priesthood of Christ" (emphasis added).

85. Ibid., par. 1120 (emphasis added).

Vatican II declared: "In the ecclesial service of the ordained minister, it is Christ himself who is present to his Church . . . [as] high priest of the redemptive sacrifice."[86] Even more explicitly, during worship, in the celebration of the Lord's Supper, the priest "presides over them [the people of God] and *acts in the person of Christ*."[87] Therefore the officiant at Mass is an "'icon' of Christ the priest."[88] The *Catechism* expresses this same teaching in a slightly different manner: "In the ecclesial service of the ordained minister, it is Christ himself who is present to his Church as Head of his Body, Shepherd of his flock, high priest of the redemptive sacrifice, Teacher of Truth. This is what the Church means by saying that the priest, by virtue of the sacrament of Holy Orders, acts *in persona Christi Capitis*."[89] In contrast to this reconfiguration of the Lord's Supper, and in thinking through the significance of the transition from the obsolete Levitical priesthood to the surpassing priesthood of Christ as expressed in Hebrews, Franz Hildebrandt reasoned in the following helpful way: "Christ, *because* He is priest *forever* according to the order of Melchizedek, 'admitteth neither partner nor successor' (Cranmer); the office which He holds 'passeth not away' into other hands. . . . None of them ever 'take over' from Him."[90] Thus the NT witness itself affirms the perfection of the Mediator, precisely as the God/Human, and especially along the lines of the eternity of his work: "Because Jesus lives forever, he has a permanent priesthood. Therefore he is able to save completely those who come to God through him" (Heb. 7:24–25).

Furthermore, not only must the kind of issues that Hildebrandt raised with respect to the unique priestly role of Christ be addressed, but the annoying problem of the moral life of Roman Catholic priests themselves must also be factored into any assessment of the claim to such a lofty and distinct role. Well aware of the ongoing and animated criticism of the moral behavior of Roman Catholic priests, especially of late, Rome contends that such objections to its priestly affirmation (*in persona Christi Capitis*) are beside the point. The *Catechism* elaborates precisely on this point:

> This presence of Christ in the minister is not to be understood as if the latter were preserved from all human weaknesses, the spirit of domination, error, even sin. The power of the Holy Spirit does not guarantee all acts of ministers

86. Ibid., par. 1548.
87. *General Instruction on the Roman Missal*, par. 7, in Flannery, *Conciliar and Post Conciliar Documents*, 163 (emphasis added).
88. *Catechism*, par. 1142.
89. Ibid., par. 1548.
90. Hildebrandt, *I Offered Christ: A Protestant Study of the Mass* (Philadelphia: Fortress, 1967), 146 (emphasis original).

in the same way. While this guarantee extends to the sacraments, so that even the minister's sin cannot impede the fruit of grace, in many other acts the minister leaves human traces that are not always signs of fidelity to the Gospel and consequently can harm the apostolic fruitfulness of the Church.[91]

Again, this doctrinal manual affirms: "The sacrament is not wrought by the righteousness of either the celebrant or the recipient, but by the power of God."[92]

Historians and theologians alike will quickly recognize that Rome's teaching in this setting—that is, that the moral unworthiness of the priest, even one in abject sin, in no way affects his capability to act *in persona Christi* during the Mass—is buttressed by an implicit appeal to the church's earlier judgment during the Donatist schism that broke out during the early fourth century. The facts of this earlier controversy can be easily stated in order to assess the propriety of the current claim before us.

The Donatist controversy erupted in North Africa in the wake of the Diocletian persecution, which lasted from AD 303 to 305. During that troubled time several believers succumbed to the threats by the Roman pagan authorities, and they therefore handed over copies of the Scriptures. For that reason these fallen ones became known as *traditores* (the ones who hand over), and the church was divided over their status once the persecution had run its course. This issue came to a head when Donatus refused to recognize the validity of the ordination of Caecilian as the bishop of Carthage simply because that ordination had been performed by Felix, who had been suspected and later accused of being a *traditor*.[93] After careful deliberation, a Roman synod concluded that the validity of a sacrament (and by implication the validity of the ritual of ordination as well) is not a function of "the character of the one administering the sacrament."[94] This judgment was reaffirmed in the West during the Council at Arles in 314 and later in the writings of Augustine, who rightly recognized that the integrity of the church was in the offing.[95]

In light of this Donatist controversy, it will soon be evident that such a judgment cannot, after all, ground the claim that sinful, all-too-human priests can take on the distinct, high-priestly role of Melchizedek as well as be the very presence of Christ himself in the sacrament,[96] or the claim that—to

---

91. *Catechism*, par. 1550.

92. Ibid., par. 1128, quoting Thomas Aquinas, *Summa Theologica* III, 68, 8.

93. Cairns, *Christianity through the Centuries*, Kindle ed., locations 1892–93.

94. Ibid., Kindle ed., location 1897.

95. Ibid., Kindle ed., locations 1897–99.

96. *Catechism*, par. 1088. "Christ is always present in his Church, especially in her liturgical celebrations. He is present in the Sacrifice of the Mass not only in the person of his minister."

repeat Rome's language just quoted above—"the presence of Christ [is] *in* the minister."[97] This would be to confuse matters badly and to apply the proper lessons of church history (we heartily agree with the Donatist judgment) to the wrong situations. Indeed, the consequence—the takeaway, if you will, of the Donatist controversy—was the church's abiding affirmation that *God is able to communicate grace*, that is, the divine presence, through the means of church rituals (e.g., ordination) and sacraments unimpeded by the moral and spiritual standing of the officiant, the minister. In other words, the person and character of the priest cannot frustrate God's will to bless through the means of grace. McGrath points out, "The validity of the sacraments is independent of the merits of those who administer them."[98]

The problem before us, however, is remarkably different. It involves a claim neither about the possibility of frustrating God's will to bless nor about the integrity of the sacrament or ritual itself. The difficulty, rather, is the contention that in the Mass the priest *is* the presence of Christ himself. In this special setting, then, and with this particular claim in place, character and being are after all important, and the person of the priest does indeed matter, for Christ will not reign in any heart where mortal, damning sin is allowed, a point that even Rome itself, at least on some level, seems to acknowledge in its added declaration: "Through the sacrament [of Holy Orders] priests by the anointing of the Holy Spirit are signed with a special *character* and so are configured to Christ."[99] If the character of the priest, so conceived, could never be made void or sullied by serious sin, such that "the presence of Christ in the minister" yet remains, even while officiating at the Mass in mortal sin, then such an affirmation would actually be not a liturgical one but a confused soteriological one.

To be sure, a glimpse of what's actually at stake here, theologically speaking, can be seen in the comparison between the Levitical priesthood of the OT and the priesthood of Jesus Christ, the High Priest of a better covenant, as revealed in the following observations: the Levitical priests were many, Christ is one; the former were temporary, the Messiah is eternal; old covenant priests sacrificed daily, Jesus offered himself once and for all; Levitical priests were sinful, Christ utterly holy; OT priests had to offer sacrifices for themselves, Jesus offered himself only for others.[100] So then, in light of the

97. Ibid., par. 1550 (emphasis added).

98. Alister McGrath, *Christian Theology: An Introduction*, 6th ed. (Hoboken, NJ: Wiley-Blackwell, 2016), Kindle edition, locations 13107–11.

99. *Decree on the Ministry and Life of Priests*, par. 2, in Flannery, *Conciliar and Post Conciliar Documents*, 865.

100. We are dependent for these observations, in part, on the following very helpful chart: Justin Taylor, "Differences between Jesus and the Levitical Priests," Gospel Coalition, April

many elements of this assessment, Roman Catholic clergy, given their moral and spiritual behavior of late, look more like sinful, obsolete Levitical priests than the special, distinct, unique, and eternal priesthood of Jesus Christ. Such a contrast surely underscores that the high-priestly role of Christ, foreshadowed in the priesthood of Melchizedek, the work of making atonement for the sins of all humanity, can be accomplished only by the Mediator, the divine/human Savior who is utterly holy. Consider, then, the abiding truth of Hebrews: "Such a high priest truly meets our need—one who is holy, blameless, pure, set apart from sinners, exalted above the heavens. Unlike the other high priests, he does not need to offer sacrifices day after day, first for his own sins, and then for the sins of the people" (7:26–28).

Although Rome continues to insist that its priests have been "really made sharers"[101] in the priesthood of Christ, the merely human cannot make the grade here precisely in terms of the priesthood of Melchizedek, which has been perfected in Christ. This is a divine, holy, glorious, and marvelously redeeming work that only the Messiah can fulfill. Thus Rome's allegation that every one of its priests, regardless of spiritual condition, can act *in persona Christi* necessarily detracts from the exclusive divine role that only Christ as the God/Human can fulfill: "For there is one God and one mediator between God and mankind, the man Christ Jesus, who gave himself as a ransom for all people" (1 Tim. 2:5–6). Again, Rome's allegation undermines the uniqueness of Christ, in terms of both his person and work as the only high priest who can bring about atonement and reconciliation once and for all.

The magisterium is aware of such a line of reasoning and has responded: "The same is true of the one priesthood of Christ; it is made present through the ministerial priesthood without diminishing the uniqueness of Christ's priesthood."[102] But surely this once again is an empty claim, one that tries to have its cake and eat it too, a claim that the ongoing positive good of the unique priestly role of Christ, which is at the very heart of the gospel, itself ever undermines. In short, this special, exclusive work of reconciling a God of holy love to a sinful humanity, given its very nature, requires nothing less than divinity, a trait that every Roman Catholic priest so obviously lacks. To be sure, divinity cannot be pretended or feigned or playacted without verging on either the blasphemous or the pathetic. Here there can be no fill-ins, no representatives, no substitutes. And if you think there can be, then this

---

26, 2011, http://www.thegospelcoalition.org/blogs/justintaylor/2011/04/26/differences-between-the-jesus-and-the-levitical-high-priests.

101. *Decree on the Ministry and Life of Priests*, par. 10, in Flannery, *Conciliar and Post Conciliar Documents*, 882.

102. *Catechism*, par. 1545.

is simply further evidence that both the person and the work of Christ, precisely as the distinct, unique God/Human, have been deeply misunderstood. Sound soteriology, then, must not be sacrificed on the altar of ecclesiology, for Christ does not reign in a sinfully conquered heart, even if it's the heart of a priest. Again, the high-priestly work of the blessed and most holy Savior Jesus Christ is what only the God/Human can do. Christ alone is our high priest. The church must therefore accept no substitutes or ersatz characters. In this setting, person and character are everything![103]

So then, instead of standing at an altar, it might be better to sit down or recline at the table among the brothers and sisters in deep humility, as it used to be so long ago, appreciating the one Lord, our only high priest, who is not absent but actually presides at the Supper through the presence of his Spirit, at this paschal meal, this Eucharist, which he has so wonderfully established *for you.*

---

103. We are not denying the efficacy of the sacrament. We agree with the Donatist judgment. We simply maintain that a Roman Catholic priest has not taken on the fullness of the lofty role that he has imagined for himself. Nevertheless, grace is communicated despite such mistaken claims. Indeed, not even such a misunderstanding of the priestly role can prevent the flow of grace or God's good purpose to bless.

11

The Papacy

Shaking the Foundations

When many non–Roman Catholics think of the hierarchical structure of this theological tradition, which distinguished itself from Eastern Christianity in 589, they immediately begin at the top of the pyramid, so to speak, with the pope. However, in some respects, though clearly not all, this is a mistake, and it may lead to a distorted view of the day-to-day life of this church. It may be more helpful, then, to see the Roman Catholic Church as hierarchical, first of all, not in the sense of the papacy at the top but in terms of its more local life of parishes and dioceses, which is expressed in and served by the offices of deacons, priests, and bishops. With this lens in place, the Roman Catholic Church will be understood, in one sense, as a communion of bishops, overseeing their dioceses and shepherding their priests, deacons, and laity throughout the world. In other words, the collegiality of bishops, a genuine fellowship of those who have dedicated their lives to the proclamation of the gospel, in both Word and sacrament, must be seen for what it is. This dimension, then, is at the very heart of what Roman Catholicism is in its basic life and polity. We grant that the college or assembly of bishops is under the authority of one particular bishop, the bishop of Rome; no one is denying that. Nevertheless, to begin at the top and to proceed downward may in the end distort; it may miss the very collegial nature of episcopal life and its fellowship among the people of God.

Bishops

Though chapter 6 has demonstrated that the monarchical episcopacy (whereby the bishop, *episkopos*, ἐπίσκοπος, was distinguished from the elder, *presbyteros*, πρεσβύτερος) did not emerge in the church until the early second century, as evidenced in the writings of Ignatius, Rome insists that there is a direct connection, a line of succession, from its bishops today that goes all the way back to the time of the apostles. With this understanding in place, the documents of Vatican II, for instance, affirm that "the order of bishops is the successor to the college of the apostles in their role as teachers and pastors, and in it the apostolic college is perpetuated."[1] Quoting the language of Ignatius, the *Catechism*, for its part, argues that the bishop is "like the living image of God the Father,"[2] an ascription that would more appropriately be applied to Jesus Christ himself. At any rate, the bishop, in the eyes of Rome, is considered to be not only "the High Priest of his flock"[3] but also "Christ's vicar,"[4] who "has the pastoral care of the particular Church entrusted to him, but at the same time he bears collegially with all his brothers in the episcopacy the solicitude for all the Churches."[5]

In Rome's view, then, the bishops as the successors of the apostles (though none of the apostles were monarchical bishops, as the magisterium would have it) play a special role in the liturgical life of the church as an emblem of its purported unity: "The outstanding example of this unity may be seen 'in the full and active participation of the entire people of God . . . ,'" Vatican II documents point out, "'in the same Eucharist, in a single prayer, around the one altar where the bishop presides, accompanied by his priests and ministers.'"[6] The Eucharist being celebrated by the bishop, surrounded by "his" priests and ministers, represents the church as it should be according to Rome. In this view not only is the Eucharist at the very heart of the church's witness, but also the hierarchy is present at the Eucharist's celebration, providing validation and authority. However, as Raymond Brown, Roman Catholic NT scholar, points out, "There is simply no compelling evidence for the classic [Catholic] thesis that the members of the Twelve always presided

1. Pope Paul VI, *Christus Dominus: Decree on the Pastoral Office of Bishops in the Church*, sec. 4, in *The Conciliar and Post Conciliar Documents*, vol. 1 of *Vatican II*, ed. Austin Flannery (Northport, NY: Costello, 1998), 566; see also the Holy See, http://www.vatican.va/archive/hist _councils/ii_vatican_council/documents/vat-ii_decree_19651028_christus-dominus_en.html.
2. *Catechism of the Catholic Church*, 2nd ed. (Mahwah, NJ: Paulist Press, 1994), par. 1549.
3. *The Constitution on the Sacred Liturgy*, par. 41, in Flannery, *Conciliar and Post Conciliar Documents*, 14.
4. *Catechism*, par. 1560.
5. Ibid.
6. *Instruction on the Worship of the Eucharistic Mystery*, par. 16, in Flannery, *Conciliar and Post Conciliar Documents*, 113.

when they were present, and that there was a chain of ordination passing the power of presiding at the Eucharist from the Twelve to missionary apostles to presbyter-bishops."[7]

In any case, the designation of a bishop as a successor of the apostles, surrounded at the Eucharist by the priests under him, whom he considers "his co-workers, his sons, his brothers and his friends,"[8] provides some indication of the esteem in which bishops are held. Among other things, the powers of the bishop include officiating at the rite of ordination for priests, with its imposition of hands, as well as at the rite of episcopal consecration itself, where three bishops are often present. However, as great as the power of the bishop is—and it is considerable—it must be exercised, especially at the consecration of a fellow bishop, "always without prejudice to the power which the Roman Pontiff possesses."[9] To be sure, the proper ordination of a bishop requires nothing less than "a special intervention of the Bishop of Rome."[10] The hierarchy is important, after all.

In employing a historical lens to make sense of the power and authority of that one particular bishop, the bishop of Rome, our approach will entail two movements, and a chapter will be devoted to each. First we will consider the current Roman Catholic conception of the pope in terms of a proper definition of this distinct office as well as its many prerogatives. Then we will explore and along the way critique the so-called Petrine theory, the claim that the current pope, and he alone, sits in the seat of the apostle Peter. In chapter 12 we will consider the pontificates of several key leaders who have demonstrated quite clearly for the historical record the all-too-human nature of the holders of this celebrated office. After this we will offer a few conclusions about the institution of the papacy and the consequences that it has had in terms of the nature of the church, its universal mission, and its ecumenical possibilities, especially in light of the claim of papal infallibility.

Current Roman Catholic Claims with Respect to the Bishop of Rome

The bishop of Rome, otherwise known as the pope, is hailed by Roman Catholics today as "Peter's successor."[11] Thus both the *Catechism* and Vatican II

7. Raymond Brown, *Priest and Bishop* (Eugene, OR: Wipf & Stock, 2004), 41, quoted in Garry Wills, *Papal Sin: Structures of Deceit* (New York: Doubleday, 2000), 139.

8. *Catechism*, par. 1567.

9. Pope Paul VI, *Christus Dominus*, sec. 8, in Flannery, *Conciliar and Post Conciliar Documents*, 567.

10. *Catechism*, par. 1559.

11. Ibid., par. 882.

documents reach back to the time of the apostles and draw a relation between it and the current polity of this church. The *Catechism*, for instance,
observes, "Just as . . . St. Peter and the rest of the apostles constitute a single
apostolic college, so in like fashion the Roman Pontiff, Peter's successor, and
the bishops, the successors of the apostles, are related with and united to one
another."[12] Put another way, the relation of authority that supposedly was
in place between Peter and the rest of the apostles is suitably mirrored in the
relation between the current pope and *his* bishops. The power relations here,
at least as Rome understands them, are especially important: the *Catechism*
goes on to point out that "the *college or body of bishops* has *no authority*
unless united with the Roman Pontiff, Peter's successor, as its head."[13]

The claims of papal power, however, are not limited to the Roman Catholic
Church itself but oddly enough extend over Eastern Orthodoxy and Protestantism as well, that is, over all Christians everywhere. Indeed, in a broad
and encompassing move, Vatican II contended that the pope as the vicar of
Christ is the "Pastor of the universal Church."[14] Bringing forth the notion
that the papacy is in reality a divine institution and not an all-too-human one
that has grown up in the course of history (marked with all its vicissitudes),
the *Catechism* fills out the power and authority of the bishop of Rome by
employing a string of superlatives: "The Pope enjoys, by divine institution,
nothing less than '*supreme, full, immediate, and universal power* in the care of
souls.'"[15] However, as Nigel G. Wright points out, "The claim of the papacy
to universal jurisdiction was denounced especially by Orthodox Churches as
the overweening self-exaltation of the Western Patriarch."[16]

In the Roman Catholic view, then, where a great and inordinate power
exists, a "Holy Father," one that evokes awe, one that is held in place partly
by the social and theological norms pertaining to sacrilege, there must in the
end be submission. Taking Rome at its own word, we must for the sake of
forthrightness point out Vatican II's added declaration that both full obedience
and submission to the pope are necessary: "This religious *submission of mind
and will must be shown* in a special way to the authentic magisterium of the
Roman Pontiff, even when he is not speaking ex cathedra."[17] However, given

12. Ibid., par. 880.

13. Ibid., par. 883 (emphasis added to "no authority").

14. *The Explanatory Note Attached to the "Dogmatic Constitution on the Church,"* par. 3,
in Flannery, *Conciliar and Post Conciliar Documents*, 425.

15. *Catechism*, par. 937 (emphasis added), quoting Pope Paul VI, *Christus Dominus*, preface, sec. 2.

16. Wright, "The Petrine Ministry: Baptist Reflections," *Pro Ecclesia* 13, no. 4 (2004): 454.

17. Pope Paul VI, *Lumen Gentium: Dogmatic Constitution on the Church*, sec. 25, in Flannery,
Conciliar and Post Conciliar Documents, 379 (emphasis added); see also the Holy See, http://

the reality of Christianity in the world today, as a major world religion—that is, one composed of a number of theological traditions, each one no less Christian for its being a distinct, theologically orthodox tradition—such a broad and sweeping declaration made on behalf of a single individual can only be received by Protestants (and perhaps by Eastern Orthodox as well) as both deeply troubled and in the end theologically confused.

It therefore is not without reason that several leaders throughout history have likewise taken note of the excessive claims to power surrounding the papal office. In the seventeenth century, for instance, Thomas Hobbes in his classic of political philosophy, *Leviathan*, declared that "the Papacy is no other than the ghost of the deceased Roman Empire, sitting crowned upon the grave thereof."[18] Moreover, in the nineteenth century, in a quote that is familiar to most people today, Lord Acton quipped: "Power tends to corrupt, and absolute power corrupts absolutely."[19] More to the point, Gary Wills reminds us of the context of Lord Acton's pithy statement in his own pungent observation: "Most people are familiar with Acton's famous axiom. . . . Fewer people remember that he was speaking of papal absolutism."[20]

Officially speaking, the titles that the papacy enjoys today include the following: "Vicar of Jesus Christ, Successor of the Prince of the Apostles, Supreme Pontiff of the Universal Church, Primate of Italy, Archbishop and metropolitan of the Roman province, Sovereign of Vatican City-State, Servant of the Servants of God."[21] Given his undoubted humility, Pope Francis may have found such designations to be far too difficult, even somewhat embarrassing. He therefore may have preferred instead, according to a recent article in the *National Catholic Reporter*, to be listed in the most recent directory, *Annuario Pontificio*, simply as the "Bishop of Rome,"[22] putting aside the pompous titles and the usual string of superlatives. After all, Jesus Christ, the head of the church, was a donkey-riding Savior, and he proclaimed a transformation of values whereby the last would be first and the first would be last (Matt. 20:16). What constitutes greatness, then, is no longer either simple or straightforward.

---

www.vatican.va/archive/hist_councils/ii_vatican_council/documents/vat-ii_const_19641121 _lumen-gentium_en.html.

18. Thomas Hobbes, *Leviathan* (New York: Penguin Classics, 1982), 712, quoted in Frederick Copleston, *A History of Philosophy* (Garden City, NY: Image Books, 1959), 5:44.

19. Quoted in Wills, *Papal Sin*, 2.

20. Ibid.

21. Joshua J. McElwee, "Pope Francis Officially De-emphasizes Papal Titles," *The Francis Chronicles* (blog), May 23, 2013, *National Catholic Reporter*, http://ncronline.org/blogs/ncr -today/pope-francis-officially-de-emphasizes-papal-titles.

22. Ibid.

What then is the papacy? In a real sense it is an office composed of a number of claims that have been made and then repeated throughout the history of the church, distinctly in its Western manifestation. Such claims have accrued over time, being added to by the various popes themselves, and they have been repeated by the faithful and therefore have been brought forward, from age to age, as accepted "truths." The issue of repetition (and the readied assumptions and attitudes it brings) is the key here, simply because it can lead to a situation in which Roman Catholics will simply forget, or at least be reluctant to acknowledge, that at the end of the day and at least in some sense, the papacy is a historical product, which took literally centuries to put into place. This history can and will be viewed differently by Roman Catholics and Protestants. In one interpretation this history entails the superintendence of the Holy Spirit in creating a divine institution. In another account, however, this history gives rise to an office that in reality is a human creation, a product, if you will, which has therefore been marked by not only the vagaries of history but also repeated human sin. At this point, however, regardless of how one reads this history, it must simply be observed at the outset that of this papal office, the supposed Vicar of Christ, the apostles Peter and Paul themselves knew nothing, absolutely nothing.

The Early History of the Presbyters and Bishops of Rome

During the time of Christ and in the immediately following decades, Rome was not well developed ecclesiastically speaking. As Eamon Duffy points out, "There is nothing directly approaching a papal theory in the pages of the New Testament,"[23] especially in terms of the city of Rome. For one thing, though the apostle Paul obviously addressed an important epistle at this time to this capital church, nevertheless its polity and ecclesiastical structure had hardly advanced beyond a "collegial presbyterial system of governance,"[24] so typical of the period. And though the monarchical episcopacy did develop farther to the east in the early second century (and in a limited area at first), as we have argued earlier, such an advanced polity did not appear in Rome, due to its local and presbyterial arrangements (which, you will recall, Lampe has described as the fractionation thesis; see chap. 6), "until the second half of the second

23. Duffy, *Saints and Sinners: A History of the Popes*, 4th ed. (New Haven: Yale University Press, 2015), Kindle edition, locations 225–26.
24. Peter Lampe, *From Paul to Valentinus: Christians at Rome in the First Two Centuries* (Minneapolis: Fortress, 2003), 397.

century."[25] Accordingly, the key leaders in the Roman church during the first century were not monarchical bishops, since there weren't any, but presbyters.

Even though the early history of the church, particularly at Rome, has hardly been considered in our description and analysis up to this point, there is already an insuperable problem for the way the Roman Catholic Church reads this early history, especially as it seeks to legitimize its current authority and structure. Here's the problem: if the pope is equivalent to the bishop of Rome, then the line of apostolic succession to this particular bishop can only go back, once again, to the "second half of the second century."[26] This claim is left hanging in the air of the second century, one that never touches the ground of first-century realities, as we have explained earlier. Thus during the first century a pope did not exist in Rome; indeed, this city didn't even have a monarchical bishop. And if the material of the episcopacy is indeed necessary in order to construct the office of the papacy at Rome, precisely where the magisterium wants it, then such a construction will just have to wait. As with so much in church history, things simply take time to develop.

After a few false starts and halfhearted attempts by Anicetus, Soter, and Eleutherus,[27] Victor eventually emerged as a full-blown monarchical bishop of Rome around the third quarter of the second century; he distinguished himself by exercising the power and authority normally identified with this office. In the following century the bishop of Rome, Stephen I, began to gather up some of the powers and honors attributed to the apostle Peter, and in a bold move he then turned around and applied them all to himself.[28] Indeed, "Stephen's invocation of Matthew 16 is the first known claim by a pope to an authority derived exclusively from Peter."[29] "In effect," as Arlo Nau observes, "[Stephen] became a Peter redivivus, the Peter of Matthew 16:17–19 reborn."[30] Moreover, though Damasus in the fourth century added to the claims of the bishop of Rome, the full aggregate of such was not yet in place, so he himself was not actually a pope. He was, however, the first to claim that his "see" of ecclesiastical governance was in reality the apostolic see, going back in a supposed succession to the first century. Therefore, although Damasus's self-perceived authority at the time does, after all, represent something of a

25. Ibid. See also Brandon Addison's helpful article "The Quest for the Historical Church," guest post on *Called to Communion* (blog), March 24, 2014, http://www.calledtocommunion.com/2014/03/the-quest-for-the-historical-church-a-protestant-assessment/.

26. Ibid.

27. Ibid.

28. Arlo J. Nau, *Peter in Matthew: Discipleship, Diplomacy, and Dispraise* (Collegeville, MN: Liturgical Press, 1992), 17.

29. Duffy, *Saints and Sinners*, Kindle ed., location 540.

30. Nau, *Peter in Matthew*, 17.

transition, he didn't trouble himself either with the proof of his specific claim of jurisdiction or with the details of church history.[31]

All these bishops of Rome whom we have just considered were relatively minor figures; their importance, remarkably enough, grew by leaps and bounds only after their deaths, when the institution of the papacy eventually came into being in a preeminent way. Once that happened, the newfangled papal perspective was vigorously and anachronistically read back into all prior history such that not only did Stephen and Damasus now emerge as full-blown popes, but the apostle Peter did as well. Clearly, Rome continually reads back into the past much-later historical products as if they were ever present. To claim, for example, that the apostle Peter was the first pope, as Devin Rose does,[32] is akin to the error in stating, "In the fourteenth century the United States of America had few people." Such a statement simply doesn't compute. The city that was of such great importance to the Christian faith in the mid-first century was not Rome but Jerusalem—and after that it was Antioch, thus once again not Rome.

The shift from a city that symbolized the Jews to one the epitomized the gentiles was gradual in the life of the early church, and a number of factors played into this development. First, the Roman community of believers as well as its later bishops took on increasing importance as they basked in the shadow of the authority and power associated with this imperial city of great cultural and world significance. Second, the power of the Roman bishop was enhanced in the wake of the vacuum of authority left in place by Constantine's transition in 330 to the city that he founded on the Bosporus bearing his name. Accordingly, by the following century the bishop of Rome functioned not simply as a spiritual ruler, shepherding the flock, but also as a temporal ruler, one to whom the local populace looked in order to get simple, even mundane, things done.

During the fourth century and into the fifth, the Roman bishop eventually became known as a first among equals among the patriarchs. At the outset such a designation was simply a matter of honor and respect, not a statement of formal ecclesiastical authority. The Roman bishop, however, liked to emphasize the "first" element of this statement, though many of the bishops in the East quite naturally underscored the second element, a basic equality. However, the claims to broader powers by Roman bishops increased in

31. For a view that attaches more significance to Damasus, especially in light of his claim to the title of apostolic see, thereby marking a genuine before and after, see Robert B. Eno, *The Rise of the Papacy* (Wilmington, DE: Michael Glazier, 1990; repr., Eugene, OR: Wipf & Stock, 2008), 147.

32. Devin Rose, *If Protestantism Is True* (n.p.: Unitatis Books, 2011), Kindle edition, 31.

number during the fifth century. For example, when Leo I became the bishop of Rome in 440, he began to assert his supremacy over all other bishops. Five years later the emperor Valentinian III, well ensconced in Constantinople, recognized the spiritual supremacy of Leo in the West, but he still left great room for the prerogatives of the patriarchs in the East,[33] and he of course said nothing about Leo's temporal power, precisely what one would expect from an emperor.

Pope Benedict XVI, much more recently, was very critical of this reading of the history of the church in general along with the basic polity celebrated in Eastern Orthodoxy in particular because it undoubtedly eviscerates Roman claims. Indeed, the erstwhile pope believes that the very notion of the "patriarchate" affirmed by Valentinian III in the East, as just noted, can only weaken not only the authority of "the apostolic see" (viewing it largely in an administrative sense) but also the ongoing claims of Roman primacy that ought to be affirmed throughout the church. Benedict explains:

> The idea of the five patriarchates must be regarded as the real evil in the dispute between East and West, an evil that also had its effect upon the West, inasmuch as—despite the retention of the concept of the *sedes apostolica*—a largely administrative and patriarchal concept of the importance of the Roman See developed that could hardly help any outsider to have a clear grasp of the real essence of the Roman claim, as distinct from any other claims.[34]

Rome's never-ending contentions, and even outright arguments, about ecclesiology and polity have to do not simply with Protestantism but with Greek Orthodoxy as well, as the historical record makes abundantly clear.

At any rate, enjoying at least the recognition of his spiritual authority, Leo I in his own age liked to be referred to as *papas* (father), from which the word "pope" is derived.[35] Not content with this, Leo introduced a title drawn from Roman religion, "pontifex maximus," which had referred to "the chief priest of the city in pagan times,"[36] though it was now to have ongoing papal

33. Earle E. Cairns, *Christianity through the Centuries: A History of the Christian Church*, 3rd rev. ed. (Grand Rapids: Zondervan, 2009), 159.

34. Joseph Cardinal Ratzinger, *God's Word: Scripture, Tradition and Office* (San Francisco: Ignatius Press, 2008), Kindle edition, 35.

35. Cairns, *Christianity through the Centuries*, 159. However, in the early church the word "papas" ("pope" or "father") was often used to refer to bishops, such as Cyprian. Eamon Duffy explains: "[Cyprian] himself, like many other bishops in the early Church, used the title 'Pope,' which only came to be confined to the Bishop of Rome from the sixth century." Duffy, *Saints and Sinners*, 21.

36. Alister McGrath, *Christian History: An Introduction* (Hoboken, NJ: Wiley-Blackwell, 2012), 74.

use. A competent leader and an adept administrator, Leo I was successful in persuading Attila the Hun to spare the Eternal City from onslaught and pillage. Though Rome, in appreciating the many gifts of Leo, likes to present him as *the* champion of orthodoxy in light of his famous *Tome*, hailed at the Council of Chalcedon in 451, the careful scholarship of Jaroslav Pelikan reveals a far more complicated and admittedly more modest picture, one in which Leo simply played a part in a much larger drama. Pelikan states:

> The genealogy of this decree [of the Council of Chalcedon] makes clear that "the formula is not an original and new creation, but like a mosaic, was assembled almost entirely from stones that were already available." Specifically, its sources were the so-called *Second Letter of Cyril to Nestorius*, the *Letter of Cyril to the Antiochenes* together with the union formula of 433, and the *Tome of Leo*; the phrase "not divided or separated into two persons" appears to have come from Theodoret.[37]

In light of such a consideration, Leo cannot receive the exclusive or even the lion's share of the credit for what was eventually hammered out, christologically speaking, at the fourth ecumenical council. In fact, initially he was not even pleased with that council's determinations concerning his role. When Chalcedon in its canon 28 reaffirmed the judgment of the earlier ecumenical council held at Constantinople that the patriarch of the new Rome (Constantinople) should "rank next after her,"[38] meaning after ecclesiastical Rome, this affirmation so disturbed Leo that he "delayed his acceptance of Chalcedon for two years on the strength of" his disapproval.[39] Nevertheless, Leo was and remained an important bishop in the West: due to the powers and prerogatives he exercised there, especially in the city of Rome itself, Leo may rightly be referred to as a pope. Indeed, in the eyes of some historians Leo in effect constitutes the first pope simply because he exercises so many of the powers and prerogatives that pertain to what actually constitutes this office, at least in the West.

Despite this line of reasoning, not all have agreed even with this late dating of the papacy. For some it is still simply much too early. For one thing, the bishop of Rome and the patriarch of Constantinople continued to bicker over the whole matter of proper titles well into the sixth century. Ecclesiastical turf was still being carved out, and it was a messy business. Bishop John of

37. Jaroslav Pelikan, *The Emergence of the Catholic Tradition* (Chicago: University of Chicago Press, 1971), 1:264.
38. *The XXX Canons of the Holy and Fourth Synods, of Chalcedon*, in *The Seven Ecumenical Councils*, trans. Henry R. Percival, NPNF² 14:287.
39. Duffy, *Saints and Sinners*, Kindle ed., locations 955–56.

Constantinople, for example, began to refer to himself as the "ecumenical patriarch," a designation that infuriated Gregory I (d. 604) of Rome.[40] Indeed, Gregory was so upset by what he perceived to be a bold, usurping action that he was determined to strip John of any such vaunted title, a cause to which he devoted considerable effort.

To demonstrate just what a difficult matter this is (who, then, was really the first pope?), Martin Luther, for his part, believed that it was neither Leo I nor Gregory I but Boniface III. How did Luther come to this judgment? In the early seventh century it was Boniface who was able to convince Phocas, the emperor of the Byzantine Empire, that the Roman bishop, and he alone, was "the head of all churches."[41] In other words, the kind of claim that Leo I had made much earlier in terms of spiritual authority was now accepted formally by this emperor and without the kinds of qualifications that the earlier emperor had brought to bear, mindful as he was of the authority of his patriarchs.

Though Luther obviously had his own preference here, a strong case can be made for other bishops of Rome as well. This engaging issue will obviously not be resolved here. To be sure, its complexity would require a book-length treatment (it would also make a great question on a doctoral comprehensive exam!) in order to lay out all the pertinent issues (such as what characteristics constitute the papacy and when they were first in place) and to address them properly. So without resolving this difficult matter, we will simply employ the language of "pope" and "papacy" beginning with Leo I in the fifth century. Though significant evidence can be brought to bear for this choice, evidence that is much earlier than Luther's, nevertheless it too is not without its problems. In fact, after Leo, at the end of the sixth century, Gregory I, able liturgist and bishop of Rome, specifically rejected the title of "pope" itself![42] In a letter to Eulogius of Alexandria he exclaimed: "Here at the head of your letter I find the proud title of 'Universal Pope,' which I have refused. . . . Away with these words which inflate vanity and wound charity."[43]

The Petrine Theory

By the time Gregory I became the bishop of Rome in 590, three of the great patriarchates—Jerusalem, Antioch, and Alexandria—had already receded in

---

40. Norman V. Hope, "Church Organization: Its Development and Forms," in *Baker's Dictionary of Practical Theology*, ed. Ralph G. Turnbull (Grand Rapids: Baker, 1967), 246.

41. Martin Luther, *Church and Ministry III*, LW 41:291–92.

42. Cairns, *Christianity through the Centuries*, 167.

43. Duffy, *Saints and Sinners*, Kindle ed., locations 1318–20.

importance. This left Rome and Constantinople, cities that epitomized the two great theological traditions of the church, which were marked by differences in language, populations, and theological approach. Later designated as a doctor of the church, Gregory I was one of the last great ecumenical figures whose sanctity was recognized by both Latins and Greeks. Moreover, for many historians the pontificate of Gregory marks a genuine watershed by ushering in the medieval period. In addition, during his pontificate the so-called Petrine theory was not only in place, in light of the earlier claims of Leo I, but also by now generally accepted. Henceforth it would be further developed, with later popes adding their voices and respective interests to its claims.

The Petrine theory, which represents the theological reflections of simply one particular theological tradition, Roman Catholicism, can be stated simply. It is the affirmation and attempted substantiation of papal primacy over the universal church by an appeal to two key scriptural passages concerning the apostle Peter (hence the adjective "Petrine"). The first is Matthew 16:18: "And I tell you that you are Peter, and on this rock I will build my church, and the gates of Hades will not overcome it." The second is Matthew 16:19: "I will give you the keys of the kingdom of heaven; whatever you bind on earth will be bound in heaven, and whatever you loose on earth will be loosed in heaven."

Recent expressions of the Petrine theory can be easily seen in the documents of Vatican II, along with some papal encyclicals. Attributing to Jesus a number of elements of what is in fact a later ecclesiology, Vatican II declared: "In order that the episcopate itself might be one and undivided, He [Christ] placed Blessed Peter over the other apostles, and instituted in him a permanent and visible source and foundation of unity of faith and communion."[44] What this statement maintains, in effect, is that Jesus Christ himself established the papacy, an institution that is supposedly a visible and permanent source of unity in the church. Again, Vatican II's declaration is "loaded up" with the characteristics that bespeak not the social location of the first century but a much later one. In short, the voice of Jesus is made to sound like that of either Leo or Gregory. However, as Oscar Cullmann has pointed out so ably in his work *Peter: Disciple, Apostle, Martyr*, before the death and resurrection of Christ, Peter's role among the disciples was viewed "merely as that of a representative."[45] Indeed, the notion that Peter was somehow over the universal

44. Pope Paul VI, *Lumen Gentium: Dogmatic Constitution on the Church*, sec. 18, in Flannery, *Conciliar and Post Conciliar Documents*, 370, see also the Holy See, http://www.vatican.va/archive/hist_councils/ii_vatican_council/documents/vat-ii_const_19641121_lumen-gentium_en.html.

45. Oscar Cullmann, *Peter: Disciple, Apostle, Martyr*, 2nd ed. (Waco: Baylor University Press, 1960), 34.

church is unfounded. Cullmann explains: "He himself [Peter] never gave distinction to any Church *except Jerusalem* as the seat of his own leadership of the entire Church. For even if, after his leadership of the Jerusalem church, he temporarily as apostolic missionary was the leader of still other churches, yet so much at least is definite, that when he was there he was only the leader of those single churches, and in no case leader of the entire Church."[46]

Undeterred, John Paul II in his encyclical *Ut Unum Sint* contended that the Roman Catholic Church has preserved "the ministry of the Successor of the Apostle Peter, the Bishop of Rome, whom God established as her 'perpetual and visible principle and foundation of unity.'"[47] In this pointed observation, John Paul II makes clear that the establishment of the "perpetual and visible principle and foundation of unity," which is none other than the language and rhetoric of the papacy, has nothing less than a divine foundation. In John Paul's estimation, the papacy is quite simply a divine institution, not merely a human one. Its establishment is as certain and as sure as the stars of the heavens. Such a declaration is surely a bold move since earlier and properly contextualized meanings that should have come into play here have been switched out for much later dogmatic ones. So intent is Rome in reading its later institutional, hierarchical structure into the first century that it has not only placed such language on the lips of Jesus (through its interpretation of his meaning) but also affixed these words onto the stone at the base of the dome of St. Peter's Basilica in Rome: "Tu es Petrus et super hanc petram aedificabo ecclesiam meam et tibi dabo claves regni caelorum," a Latin sentence that basically constitutes the substance of Matthew 16:18–19. At this point of the argument, we simply notice a few important shifts: Jesus spoke these words in Aramaic; Rome reproduces them in Latin. Jesus uttered them in the Middle East; Rome engraves them in Europe. Jesus proclaimed these words in the first century; Rome inscribes them centuries later.

Before we consider the key passages (Matt. 16:18 and 19) of the Petrine theory in terms of their proper interpretation, we observe that the Petrine theory is actually composed of two key claims, not just one, although one of them has indeed received the lion's share of attention. This theory contends not only that Jesus made Peter himself the foundation of the church (e.g., Vatican II states, "He selected Peter, and after his confession of faith

---

46. Ibid., 229.

47. Pope John Paul II, *Ut Unum Sint: On Commitment to Ecumenism*, sec. 88, quoting Pope Paul VI, *Lumen Gentium*, sec. 23, the Holy See, 1995, http://w2.vatican.va/content/john-paul-ii/en/encyclicals/documents/hf_jp-ii_enc_25051995_ut-unum-sint.html.

determined that *on him* He would build His Church")[48] but also that Peter was the principal church leader not so much in Jerusalem, or even Antioch, for that matter, but in Rome. Indeed, to think immediately of Rome, rather than of Jerusalem or Antioch, whenever the name of the apostle Peter is pronounced is precisely what this second claim is all about. Observe how it almost becomes second nature by sheer repetition through the centuries. In the Petrine theory, with this last claim in view, all roads lead to Rome. But repetition does not always lead to truths that can be substantiated by the historical record. We will therefore explore this second claim as well immediately after considering the first.

Matthew 16:18

The substance of Matthew 16:18 ("You are Peter, and on this rock I will build my church") was never interpreted by the first-century church in terms of claims to preeminence by a nonexistent monarchical bishop of Rome, or even later by the Apostolic Fathers once this office eventually emerged. The time frame for the first period as well as the historical and ecclesiastical setting then in place for the second simply do not allow for this kind of assertion. Indeed, some of the early appeals along these lines were found in the claims of two bishops of Rome much later: Stephen I during the third century and Damasus in the fourth. They both offered a "papal" interpretation of this already-familiar text by strongly associating the apostle Peter with their own ecclesiastical office.[49]

During the fifth century, Theodore of Mopsuestia, an Antiochian exegete, commented on this Matthean passage and emphasized that whatever authority was offered here was common and shared: "This means he [Christ] will build his church upon this same confession and faith. . . . It was from this confession, which was going to become the common property of all believers, that he bestowed upon him [Peter] this name, the rock."[50] In contrast to this view, Vatican II declared: "For our Lord placed Simon *alone* as the rock, and the

---

48. *Unitatis Redintegratio: Decree on Ecumenism*, sec. 2, in Flannery, *Conciliar and Post Conciliar Documents*, 454 (emphasis added).

49. Peter De Rosa, *Vicars of Christ: The Dark Side of the Papacy* (New York: Crown, 1988), 39. De Rosa, in citing the work of Henry Chadwick, mentions only Damasus; yet Stephen I, a century earlier, actually interpreted this material in a similar way. In other words, Stephen I claimed that his office was strongly associated with that of the apostle Peter, a claim that could not be made apart from the distinct interpretation of Matt. 16:18.

50. Manlio Simonetti, *Matthew 14–28*, Ancient Christian Commentary on Scripture: NT 1b (Downers Grove, IL: InterVarsity, 2001), 45–46.

bearer of the keys of the church."[51] In addition, Augustine eventually came to the understanding that the rock of which Matthew 16:18 speaks was actually Christ himself, the true foundation of the church, as is expressed also in the writings of the apostle Paul (e.g., 1 Cor. 10:3–4).[52] Indeed, Chester Hartranft, who introduces this material from Augustine's writings, observes: "Augustine here identified Peter with the rock, on which the Church was to be built; but afterwards he regarded that rock as Christ, who was the subject of the Petrine confession; on Christ was the Church to be built."[53] More recently Ulrich Luz has argued that "Augustine's interpretation expressed his doctrine of grace: Peter, and in him the whole church, is built upon Christ alone."[54] This interpretation of Augustine seems eminently plausible given the following two considerations: first, Peter's confession points not to himself but to Christ, who is "the Messiah, the Son of the living God" (Matt. 16:16b); second, it is once again not Peter but Christ who is the subject par excellence here. Christ is the one who "will build [his] church" (Matt 16:18a). Simply put, Peter basks in a light that is not his own.

If Roman Catholic commentaries on Matthew 16:18 both before Vatican II and afterward are compared, a genuine development in interpretation will be readily discerned, one that moves from an earlier triumphalism, which discerns the institution of the papacy in this verse, to a more historically and exegetically informed approach. Take, for example, *A Catholic Commentary on Holy Scripture*, produced in 1953. After teaching that it was actually the Father who had singled out Peter as "the natural foundation for his Son's society"[55] and that Jesus was simply following the Father's lead, the commentary then contends, apart from any appropriate exegetical evidence, that "Simon is to be the ultimate authority on earth of this society which is itself the *hierarchical body* described in 18:15–18."[56] However, in his commentary on this passage, Luz underscores the importance of both exegetical acuity and historical awareness in coming to terms with a suitable interpretation. He

---

51. Pope Paul VI, *Lumen Gentium: Dogmatic Constitution on the Church*, sec. 22, in Flannery, *Conciliar and Post Conciliar Documents*, 375 (emphasis added); see also the Holy See, http://www.vatican.va/archive/hist_councils/ii_vatican_council/documents/vat-ii_const_196 41121_lumen-gentium_en.html.

52. Chester D. Hartranft, "Augustin: Anti-Donatist Writings; Introductory Essay," in *St. Augustin: The Writings against the Manichaeans and against the Donatists*, NPNF[1] 4:375.

53. Ibid.

54. Luz, "The Primacy Text (Matt. 16:18)," *Princeton Seminary Bulletin* 12, no. 1 (1991): 50.

55. Alexander Jones, "The Gospel of Jesus Christ according to St Matthew," in *A Catholic Commentary on Holy Scripture*, ed. Bernard Orchard and Edmund F. Sutcliffe (Toronto: Thomas Nelson, 1953), 881.

56. Ibid. (emphasis added).

writes: "Historically, we must say that the interpretation of Matthew 16:18 in terms of the Roman primacy is a *new* interpretation from the third century. It is a later 'rereading of scripture,' based on 'historical . . . experiences of faith,' or, put somewhat more sharply, a 'retroactive legitimizing' of a Roman claim to leadership that had developed since the third century."[57] Now compare this "traditional" interpretation from *A Catholic Commentary* with that of the current *Catholic Study Bible*. Indeed, this latter resource is obviously aware of the well-worked Protestant exegetical perspective on this passage, which distinguishes, for example, the masculine form of Πέτρος (*Petros*), which refers to Peter, from the feminine form πέτρα (*petra*), which supposedly concerns his confession: "The presumed original Aramaic of Jesus' statement would have been, in English, 'You are the Rock (*Kepa*) and upon this rock (*kepa*) I will build my church.' The Greek text probably means the same, for the difference in gender between the masculine noun *petros*, the disciple's new name, and the feminine noun *petra* (rock) may be due simply to the unsuitability of using a feminine noun as the proper name of a male."[58]

Though many Protestants believe that they have won the exegetical argument by maintaining that the foundation of the church of which Jesus spoke is expressed in the feminine form of πέτρα, which obviously cannot refer to Peter himself and must therefore point to his confession, others are not so convinced. To illustrate this last point, the late Marvin Richardson Vincent, Presbyterian minister and NT scholar, cautioned his fellow Protestants along the following lines: "Equally untenable is the explanation which refers πέτρα to Simon's confession. Both the play upon the words and the natural reading of the passage are against it, and besides, it does not conform to the fact, since the church is built, not on *confessions*, but on *confessors*—living men."[59] Yes, the church is composed of living members who confess that Jesus of Nazareth is the Messiah, but they are also distinct from the world and indeed are called out of it, given the nature and substance of their confession. In his own estimation of this passage, Craig Keener brings together these two important threads in a helpful observation: "Peter is the rock in his role as *confessor*, and others build on the foundation by their proclamation of the same *confession*."[60] Indeed, Keener's emphasis on development here is surely

57. Ulrich Luz, *Matthew 8–20*, Hermeneia (Minneapolis: Augsburg Fortress, 2001), 372.

58. Donald Senior, John J. Collins, and Mary Ann Getty, eds., *The Catholic Study Bible: The New American Bible*, rev. ed. (New York: Oxford University Press, 1990), 1366.

59. Vincent, *Word Studies in the New Testament* (New York: Scribner, 1887), 1:92 (emphasis original).

60. Keener, *The IVP Background Commentary: New Testament* (Downers Grove, IL: InterVarsity, 1993), Matt. 16:18 (emphasis added).

appropriate, because as the church confronted heresy in the fourth century, for example, "the basic Christian confession of the divine sonship," as Luz once again observes, "really was the rock upon which the church was built."[61] Indeed, after the rise of Islam and the challenge that it posed to the church, this traditional confession "remained the rock of the Christian churches that secured their identity."[62]

Much later, during the sixteenth century, Calvin's observations on this Matthean passage are remarkably instructive, since as a competent exegete of Scripture he rightly recognized that this passage must be comprehended in light of other key ones drawn from the NT. Appealing to 1 Peter 2:5 as a guide, the Genevan Reformer recognized Christ as that "living Stone" chosen by God and rejected by the people. From this basic truth he reasoned that all the disciples of Jesus, all those who believe, are therefore the living stones that make up the temple of God.[63] Even more emphatically, Calvin appealed to the significant christological passages of 1 Corinthians 3:11 ("For no one can lay any foundation other than the one already laid, which is Jesus Christ") and Ephesians 2:20 ("built on the foundation of the apostles and prophets, with Christ Jesus himself as the chief cornerstone") in his commentary on the account found in Matthew. Again, Calvin declared forthrightly that "the Church can have no other *foundation* than Christ alone."[64] The one who was before Abraham, the eternal Word made flesh, and he alone, is "the chief cornerstone."

In a similar fashion, when John Wesley grappled with Matthew 16:18, he believed that Jesus was referring, once again, not to Peter as the focus of attention in this account but to himself. Thus the other key passage that came to mind in Wesley's own reflections was none other than John 2:19, which indicates quite clearly that Christ himself is the temple. "And it is certain, that as he is spoken in Scripture, as the only foundation of the Church," Wesley observed, "so this is that which the apostles and evangelists laid in their preaching."[65]

Beyond this, Matthew 16:18 cannot mean that Peter had authority in an extraordinary way over the other apostles, as Vatican II would have it,[66] and

61. Luz, "Primacy Text," 49.

62. Ibid.

63. John Calvin, *Commentary on a Harmony of the Evangelists Matthew, Mark, and Luke*, trans. William Pringle (Bellingham, WA: Logos Bible Software, 2010), 2:291.

64. Ibid. (emphasis original).

65. John Wesley, *Explanatory Notes upon the New Testament* (1765; repr., Salem, OH: Schmul, 1975), 56, on Matt. 16:18.

66. Pope Paul VI, *Lumen Gentium: Dogmatic Constitution on the Church*, sec. 19, in Flannery, *Conciliar and Post Conciliar Documents*, 370; see also the Holy See, http://www

as popes have claimed throughout the centuries. Such a reconfiguration of the essential meaning of this passage is belied, once again, by the realities of the first-century church in general and by the apostle Paul in particular, especially in his severe, extensive, and public rebuke of Peter for the latter's hypocrisy in terms of a basic truth of the gospel (the Jew/gentile distinction has been transcended in Christ), as recorded in Galatians 2:11–14. Consider that by the time of Pope Boniface VIII in the early fourteenth century, the claims and pretensions of the bishop of Rome had grown so considerably that Boniface himself insisted he could be judged by no one but God alone.[67] The power differential between the pope and the rest of the church had by this point grown so great, due in large measure to an improper interpretation of Matthew 16:18, that if Paul had somehow or other emerged in this medieval papal court, and if he had a "negative" prophetic word to pronounce to the pope, he likely would have been reprimanded for his supposed rudeness ("How dare you speak to the pope in this way!"), quickly shown the door, or perhaps much worse.[68] Moreover, it is both jejune and theologically inappropriate to discount Paul's power here (esp. since he is undergirded by the strength of the gospel itself) as if this demonstrative matter related only to a specific practice and not also to the very real doctrinal consequences of this same deeply troubled practice. Indeed, nothing less than the proper teaching of the gospel, in both thought and action, was at stake here. Peter had gotten it wrong.

Matthew 16:19

The words of Jesus found in Matthew 16:19 ("I will give you the keys of the kingdom of heaven; whatever you bind on earth will be bound in heaven, and whatever you loose on earth will be loosed in heaven") have been interpreted by the magisterium today in terms of the later hierarchy that eventually arose in the Roman Catholic Church. The *Catechism*, for example, states: "The office of binding and loosing which was given to Peter was also assigned to

---

.vatican.va/archive/hist_councils/ii_vatican_council/documents/vat-ii_const_19641121_lumen-gentium_en.html.

67. Boniface wrote: "Therefore, if the terrestrial power err, it will be judged by the spiritual power; but if a minor spiritual power err, it will be judged by a superior spiritual power; but if the highest power of all err, it can be judged only by God, and not by man, according to the testimony of the Apostle: '*The spiritual man judgeth of all things and he himself is judged by no man*' [1 Cor. 2:15]." Boniface VIII, *Unam Sanctam*, 1302, Papal Encyclicals Online, http://www.papalencyclicals.net/Bon08/B8unam.htm (emphasis original).

68. It also appears that Peter did not have authority *over* James, the brother of Jesus, at the Jerusalem Council as recorded in Acts 15. Indeed, it was James and not Peter who was in a key position of leadership at this council.

the college of apostles united to its head. This pastoral office of Peter and the other apostles belongs to the Church's very foundation and is continued by the bishops under the primacy of the Pope."[69]

Luther considered the power of the keys very extensively in his own writings and maintained that since the binding and loosing so described by Jesus entails excommunication, such an authority is one that is held not individually but communally.[70] That is, it belongs not simply to one man in an idiosyncratic way (even if in concert with the bishops) but to the entire church, the people of God. In a similar fashion, Calvin acknowledged that "nothing is here given to Peter that was not common to him with his colleagues."[71] And Wesley, for his part in the eighteenth century, concluded in a slightly different way while still emphasizing the communal dimension of this power: the keys were not given to Peter alone but "to all the apostles at the same time."[72]

The case made by the Protestant Reformers as well as by Wesley is strengthened, exegetically speaking, when due consideration is given to other passages of Scripture that help to illuminate Matthew 16:19. Take, for example, the process of excommunication laid out by Jesus a couple of chapters later, in Matthew 18:15–18, with its famous command to "tell it to the church" (v. 17). Such an authority therefore does not belong, once again, to any individual, certainly not in a self-referential way, but to the entire church. Or consider the postresurrection account found in John 20:19–23, a passage that in many respects parallels the language of Matthew 16:19: "And with that he [Jesus] breathed on them and said, 'Receive the Holy Spirit. If you forgive anyone's sins, their sins are forgiven; if you do not forgive them, they are not forgiven'" (vv. 22–23). Notice that in this context the referent for "you," as in "you forgive," is the Spirit-anointed assembly. Accordingly one interpretation that must be excluded for its lack of plausibility here in John and therefore elsewhere in its parallel in Matthew is that Jesus has an individual in mind when he speaks these words. The grammatical form of the verb in this verse is not the second-person singular but the second-person plural. So then it is a charismatic office that is being explored in this setting, one that is corporately held. Thus the people of God, animated by the Holy Spirit, hold the power of the keys. The divine presence and activity in the entire community must ever be in view.

69. *Catechism*, par. 881.

70. Martin Luther, *Church and Ministry II*, LW 40:359.

71. John Calvin, *Institutes of the Christian Religion*, 2 vols., ed. John T. McNeill, trans. Ford Lewis Battles, Library of Christian Classics 20–21 (Philadelphia: Westminster Press, 1960), 4.6.4 (2:1105).

72. Wesley, *Explanatory Notes upon the New Testament*, 56–57, on Matt. 16:19.

Though this second passage, in conjunction with the first, is employed by the Roman Catholic Church to elevate the apostle Peter in a preeminent way, supposedly taking him and him alone beyond the authority of the remainder of the apostles, such an interpretation is fraught with difficulties, especially in terms of the larger picture that emerges from the Gospel of Matthew itself. In an important work titled *Peter in Matthew: Discipleship, Diplomacy, and Dispraise*, Arlo Nau has put forth the engaging thesis that the author of Matthew employs the rhetorical device of "encomiastic dispraise" as he "seeks to neutralize Peter's traditional prominence within the Antiochian community."[73] The ironic flavor of this subtle literary device is fleshed out in this Gospel as Peter, on the one hand, is praised in a special way on numerous occasions, but on the other hand is dispraised repeatedly, as evident in the following, all of which are listed by Nau:

Peter sinks; "Little-faith, doubt" (14:30)
"Still without understanding" (15:16)
Peter's rebuke; "Satan . . . hindrance" (16:23)
Peter corrected; "70 times 7" (18:22)
Peter sleeps (26:40)
Peter's denials (26:69–74)
Peter weeps bitterly (26:75)[74]

Why, then, did the author of Matthew employ such an approach? For one thing, it suited one of his larger purposes in this Gospel, which was to underscore that "in the end Jesus [would] stand alone, the singular, living, present authoritative focus of the Christian Community's allegiance, obedience and hope."[75] Therefore, to remove Peter from this very realistic context with its encomiastic dispraise and to place him in a "huge hierarchical superstructure known today as the Petrine office," Nau points out, is not only in some sense to displace Jesus but is also "precisely the opposite of what Matthew intended."[76]

The Petrine Theory and the City of Rome

Even if Christ had decided to found his church on Peter himself, a highly unlikely basis in our estimation, this act in itself would not be sufficient to

73. Nau, *Peter in Matthew*, 37.
74. Ibid., 25.
75. Ibid., 143.
76. Ibid., 145–46.

ground all that the Petrine theory of the papacy requires. Beyond the supposed founding on Peter, there would also have to be a shift in continent, land, and city in order to get the job done. Consider that Peter most likely made his confession (to which Jesus responded) in Caesarea Philippi, a city on the edge of the northern part of Israel, about 150 miles north of Jerusalem. More to the point, Caesarea Philippi was well over 1,000 miles from Rome, so any attempt to complete the requirements of the Petrine theory would be forced to engage in considerable geographical gymnastics in order to do so.

Judging from the evidence of the NT, we affirm that Peter is strongly associated with the city of Jerusalem, where the church was first established at Pentecost and where he likely participated in the first council of the church in 50. Moreover, when Paul the apostle wrote the book of Romans about seven or eight years later, he gave no indication in this letter that such an illustrious leader as Peter was then resident in the imperial city. In fact, when Paul offers his greetings to key people at the end of this missive, the name of Peter is not among them. In addition, when the letters written by Paul *from Rome* are taken into account, such as Philippians, Colossians, Ephesians, and Philemon, as J. B. Lightfoot has observed, here also Peter is not mentioned at all.[77] Add to this that Peter is nowhere to be found in 2 Timothy, and the picture beginning to emerge is one in which "*St. Peter's visit to Rome must have been brief, and probably during St. Paul's absence, a period which is not represented either by the Acts or his Epistles.*"[78] After his significant and foundational work in Jerusalem, where the church was born, Peter is largely associated once again not with Rome but with Antioch, the city in which the followers of Christ were first known as Christians. In terms of Peter's own personal journey, then, he is surely a latecomer to Rome, and his stay there did not likely last very long.

Some of the best evidence that Peter was actually in Rome, however briefly, comes from one of his own epistles, which states: "She who is in Babylon, chosen together with you, sends you her greetings" (1 Pet. 5:13). The name Babylon in this context most likely refers to Rome and, interestingly enough, suggests how first-century Jews viewed this gentile city. Beyond this biblical evidence, Clement of Rome, writing toward the latter part of the first century, recounts the martyrdom of Peter in the following fashion: "Peter, through unrighteous envy, endured not one or two, but numerous labors; and when he had at length suffered martyrdom, departed to the place of glory due

77. Lightfoot, *2 Corinthians and 1 Peter*, ed. Ben Witherington III and Todd Sill (Downers Grove, IL: InterVarsity, 2016), 99.
78. Ibid. (emphasis added).

to him."[79] Later tradition added to Clement's account and maintained that Peter died at the hands of Emperor Nero in Rome around 64.[80] Indeed, by the middle of the second century it was generally accepted that Peter had been executed in Rome.[81] This fact of his untimely death, in conjunction with his prior imprisonment, seems to be Peter's strongest link to the city. Such a curious, and in some sense strange, linkage prompted Calvin to observe even in his own day: "And how does he [the pope] prove it [the papal primacy in Rome]? Because Peter died at Rome; as if Rome, by the detestable murder of the Apostle, had procured for herself the primacy."[82]

Despite these traditions that have grown up around the larger-than-life apostle Peter, not all the details of his later life, or his death for that matter, can be so easily confirmed. For example, though Duffy points out that by the second century, church tradition taught that Peter was martyred in Rome,[83] as we have just noticed, yet "on this particular matter,"[84] he adds, "the New Testament, itself, was utterly silent."[85] Moreover, in his own scholarship Daniel O'Conner urges caution in making claims in terms of Peter's relation to Rome: "That Peter founded the Church at Rome is extremely doubtful and that he served as its first bishop . . . for even one year, much less the twenty-five-year period that is claimed for him, is an unfounded tradition that can be traced back to a point no earlier than the third century."[86] A number of extrabiblical legends surrounding Peter did emerge, one of which had Peter struggling with "the magician and father of heresy, Simon Magus."[87] Another account had the apostle meeting his fate crucified "upside down in the Vatican Circus."[88] These stories (Duffy refers to them as "pious romance"[89]) even came to be accepted by Origen, Ambrose, and Augustine,[90] though "we have no reliable accounts either of Peter's later life or of the manner or place of his death."[91]

---

79. Clement of Rome, "The First Epistle of Clement to the Corinthians" 5, in *The Apostolic Fathers with Justin Martyr and Irenaeus*, ANF 1:6.

80. Nau, *Peter in Matthew*, 11.

81. John Julius Norwich, *Absolute Monarchs: A History of the Papacy* (New York: Random House, 2011), Kindle edition, locations 172–74.

82. Calvin and Pringle, *Commentary on a Harmony of the Evangelists*, 297.

83. Duffy, *Saints and Sinners*, Kindle ed., locations 147–48.

84. Ibid.

85. Ibid.

86. O'Connor, *Peter in Rome: The Literary, Liturgical and Archeological Evidence* (New York: Columbia University Press, 1969), 207.

87. Duffy, *Saints and Sinners*, Kindle ed., location 151.

88. Ibid., Kindle ed., location 152.

89. Ibid., Kindle ed., location 154.

90. Ibid., Kindle ed., locations 154–55.

91. Ibid.

Given such difficulties, when it comes to Peter's activities beyond the pages of the NT, it is exceedingly difficult to distinguish fact from fiction. Duffy's claim that "neither Peter nor Paul founded the Church at Rome, for there were Christians in the city before either of the Apostles set foot there" further muddles the interpretive situation surrounding Peter.[92] What then becomes of the specific claim of Irenaeus in the second century that the church was organized and founded in Rome by the apostles Peter and Paul?[93] It is a claim in search of a historically grounded argument, one that therefore was and remains dubious.[94]

By the middle of the second century the transition from the Middle East to Europe, from Jerusalem (or Antioch) to Rome, was beginning to take shape. During this century and into the next, "European and North African proponents recaptured Peter for the western, Latin, Church."[95] By the middle of the third century Stephen I, the bishop of Rome from 254 to 257, began to appropriate to himself "all the accumulated prerogatives of Peter"[96] in a dispute with Cyprian and with Firmilian, bishop of Caesarea, though the latter "not only [did] not accept the claim, he seems never to have heard it before."[97] The following century Constantine himself, very much caught up in the elevation of ecclesiastical Rome, determined "to build a basilica dedicated to Peter on [what is now] the Vatican Hill."[98] The emperor actually thought such a spot held the bones of the apostle himself. And though none of the Apostolic Fathers had ever offered the wherewithal to construct the Roman primacy, Cyprian in the middle of the third century and Jerome in the later fourth and early fifth began to do precisely that (though the former eventually expressed some misgivings),[99] with the result that the mere mention of Peter's

92. Ibid.
93. Irenaeus of Lyons, *Against Heresies* 3.3, in *The Apostolic Fathers with Justin Martyr and Irenaeus*, ANF 1:415.
94. Oscar Cullmann points out the error of Irenaeus, who maintained that the Roman church was founded and organized by Peter and Paul, though Cullmann's focus in the current context is simply on the apostle Paul. See Cullmann, *Peter: Disciple, Apostle, Martyr* (New York: Living Age Books, 1958), 116.
95. Nau, *Peter in Matthew*, 16.
96. Ibid., 17.
97. Eno, *Rise of the Papacy*, 64.
98. Norwich, *Absolute Monarchs*, Kindle ed., locations 176–77.
99. Duffy, e.g., writes: "During Pope Cornelius' lifetime, Cyprian had written a treatise on *The Unity of the Catholic Church*, in which he had bolstered his own authority and that of the Pope against the Novatianist schism by stressing the unique role of the See of Peter as the foundation of unity. He now rewrote the treatise, editing out these passages and denying that the Bishop of Rome had any special claim on Christ's promise to Peter." See Duffy, *Saints and Sinners*, Kindle ed., locations 528–31.

name henceforth began to call up, especially in the West, not Jerusalem or Antioch but, once again, Rome.[100] The myth was now well on its way.[101]

---

100. Klaus Schatz, a Roman Catholic scholar, argues: "It is clear that the Roman primacy was not a given from the outset; it underwent a long process of development whose initial phases extended well into the fifth century." Schatz, *Papal Primacy: From Its Origins to the Present* (Collegeville, MN: Liturgical Press, 1996), 36.

101. In light of this history, the claim of Devin Rose, a popular Roman Catholic apologist ("Regardless of anyone's opinion of the pope or the papacy in general, the historical fact is that the Church has had a pope since the beginning of its existence"), is simply nonsensical. Dogma has apparently beclouded sound historical judgment. See Rose, *If Protestantism Is True*, Kindle ed., 31.

12

Machiavellian Machinations and More

The Later History of the Papacy

It is a blessing to both the Roman Catholic Church and the larger Christian community that the past fifty years or so have been marked by very good popes. The smiling face of Pope Francis, his openness to the poor and downtrodden of Buenos Aires, his affirmation that building walls is not Christian—all of this has made Francis a respected and beloved leader among Roman Catholics and non–Roman Catholics alike. And who can forget the well-traveled, slope-skiing Pope John Paul II, the vigorous traditionalist, who not only was one of the most important spiritual leaders of the twentieth century but also was instrumental in precipitating important political and social changes in his own native Poland and beyond. Indeed, some have claimed that it was the steady leadership of Gorbachev, Reagan, Thatcher, and Pope John Paul himself that led to the breakup of the Soviet Union.

These recent images of smiling, happy, effective leaders, popes who have all the markings of magnificent and generous people, fill the minds of contemporary Roman Catholic laity, who therefore so readily assume, especially in terms of the papal office, that all is well. It is not. Indeed, as historians and philosophers who think in terms of centuries, not decades, we are well acquainted with what can be described as "the dark side of the papacy." Entire books have been written about this. To be sure, the pages of church history, its historical records and annals, are filled with the antics of evil and even wicked popes, some of whom would likely be judged today as insane.

Although Roman Catholic apologists like to lift up one of the major faults of Protestantism, in terms of its apparent fissiparous nature, they should also be mindful of one of the major faults of Roman Catholicism: its hierarchical, docility-inducing, obedience-inculcating structure. Simply put, when things go wrong at the top, things go very wrong.

Given this history, some of which will be detailed below, and given human nature being what it is (the office does not change that), we are in a strong position to make an important prediction. However, before we make this judgment, understand that we are not trying to be polemical, just accurate; not argumentative, just realistic. Naïveté, precisely when it comes to the papacy, not only is unhelpful but also lacks the clarity of truth. At the very least, then, we need to speak truth to one another. And so with those caveats in place we can now make our prediction, which is informed by both historical understanding and anthropological, philosophical, and theological considerations: what once was will be again. It's just a matter of time.

Forgery, Competing Claimants, and Post-1054 Pretensions

Holding the office of the bishop of Rome does not guarantee that one will be good, moral, or even orthodox. Things just don't work that way. To illustrate, the Sixth Ecumenical Council, held in 680, had to set the theological record straight by posthumously condemning the likes of Pope Honorius I, who was a rank heretic, given his aberrant christological views. Confused in his theological reflections, which made him especially dangerous since he held a seat of authority, Honorius espoused the monothelite heresy (that Christ had only one will) and thereby failed to distinguish properly the two natures of Christ and what precisely pertained to each.[1]

Apart from the heresy of Pope Honorius, the subsequent history of the papacy is marked by the attempt to increase the power of this office, both spiritually and temporally. Thus when Pope Leo III on Christmas Day in 800 placed the crown on the head of Charlemagne, who was declared "*Romanorum Imperator*," or Holy Roman emperor, the pope's action suggested, in a way that he understood all too well, that he and he alone could confer such

---

1. The reputation of the bishop of Rome had already been sullied earlier, in the fourth century, due to the well-known cowardice of Marcellinus. Fearing the personal consequences he would suffer in the throes of the Diocletian persecution, Marcellinus not only handed over what Scriptures he had to the pagan Roman authorities but also sacrificed to the gods. As Eamon Duffy puts it, "He died a year later in disgrace, and the Roman church set about forgetting him." Duffy, *Saints and Sinners: A History of the Popes*, 4th ed. (New Haven: Yale University Press, 2015), 20.

authority on the newly crowned emperor. During this same century, Pope Nicholas I insisted on the supremacy of the see of Rome throughout the entire church. Furthermore, this pope added to the ever-growing claims of the papacy by contending that he was the superior of every temporal ruler, even the emperor, in matters both spiritual and moral.[2] Lording it over the church was no longer enough. Nicholas tried to buttress his authority even further by an appeal to two documents (*The Pseudo-Isidorian Decretals* and *The Donation of Constantine*) that subsequent scholarship has ably demonstrated were forgeries. By the way, this is the same pope who had declared the Eastern patriarch Photius deposed and who thereby despoiled an already sour relationship with the East. An Eastern synod, headed by Photius, returned the favor in kind and accused the Western church, once again, of heresy.[3]

In a pontificate characterized by insanity, Stephen VII (sometimes referred to as Stephen VI because of confusion in reckoning the Stephen popes) conducted what has become known as the "cadaver synod" in 896 and thereby took vengeance on the pitiful corpse of a prior pope (Formosus), whose very name represented a living, rival faction that Stephen detested. The gory details of this escapade are as follows:

> Pope Stephen VII set in motion a solemn trial of the late Pope Formosus. . . . The act of judgment was no mere formality. The corpse itself was dragged from the tomb where it had rested for eight months and, dressed again in its sacerdotal robes, was brought into the council chamber. There it was propped up in the throne that it had occupied in life while, in a parody of legal form, the "trial" went its blasphemous way.[4]

There were few good popes from the time of this debacle to the middle of the eleventh century. Taking the papal office, then, did not necessarily increase one's gifts or talents, though it did appear to engender in some men an inordinate desire to amass more: money, preferment, and titles. Furthermore, grasping for the office of the papacy got so out of hand among rival factions during the eleventh century, when it was viewed as something of a prize, that three men at one point all claimed to be the rightful bishop of Rome: Benedict IX, Sylvester III, and Gregory VI. Each of these claimants was eventually cast aside in favor of Clement II, who was appointed pope in 1046 by the Council of Sutri, an assembly held just north of Rome.

2. Earle E. Cairns, *Christianity through the Centuries: A History of the Christian Church*, 3rd rev. ed. (Grand Rapids: Zondervan, 2009), 202.

3. Ibid.

4. E. R. Chamberlin, *The Bad Popes* (New York: Dorset, 1969), 19–20.

After Pope Leo IX and Patriarch Michael Cerularius split the church in 1054 over a squabble that, among other things, included the issue of papal authority, later popes, oddly enough, acted as if this Great Schism had not even occurred. They pretended that Rome itself had not really been a part of or responsible for any such schism (the fault lies with the "other," with those who have separated from the Roman Catholic Church) and that therefore the pope's supreme authority over the entire church remained undiminished and continued apace—again as if nothing had happened. Thus during this same schismatic century Pope Gregory VII insisted that the Roman pontiff yet had the right to be called "universal," a title that Gregory I had repudiated earlier, as chapter 11 has already noted. Some have questioned whether the document from which this claim of universality is drawn, the *Dictatus Papae*, was actually written by Gregory VII himself. At any rate, it was indeed listed in his papal register in 1075, and as a consequence this artifact does appear to represent Gregory's own views. Since the *Dictatus Papae* is a good window on the papacy (as an institution that was made up of numerous claims that slowly emerged and that were repeated over time), it will be cited at length. The relevant articles are as follows:

1. That the Roman church was founded by God alone.
2. That the Roman pontiff alone can with right be called universal.
8. That he alone may use the imperial insignia.
9. That of the pope alone all princes shall kiss the feet.
10. That his name alone shall be spoken in the churches.
11. That this is the only name in the world.
12. That it may be permitted to him to depose emperors.
16. That no synod shall be called a general one without his order.
17. That no chapter and no book shall be considered canonical without his authority.
19. That he himself may be judged by no one.
22. That the Roman church has never erred; nor will it err to all eternity, the Scripture bearing witness.
26. That he who is not at peace with the Roman church shall not be considered catholic.[5]

Observe that the content of this document touches upon both temporal and spiritual matters. Thus the effects of the article that the pope would be

5. Ernest F. Henderson, *Select Documents of the Middle Ages* (London: George Bell & Sons, 1910), 366–67.

permitted to depose emperors was fleshed out, in a certain sense, in 1077 at Canossa, where Gregory VII left Emperor Henry IV, along with his family, out in the snow for three days humbly seeking a papal audience and reconciliation, as we have noted in chapter 10. Such a humiliating action, ironically enough, led to the weakening of the papacy much later as the temporal powers of Europe, kings and queens among them, were eventually able to free themselves from the yoke of such power-grasping claims. However, until that time the course set by Gregory remained in place and constituted the mindset of popes like Innocent III and Boniface VIII of the thirteenth century. Indeed, "by the end of the twelfth century," as E. R. Chamberlin points out, "the emperor had become a shadow and the pope stepped forward to claim dominion over all the world."[6]

Notice also that the final article cited above touched upon spiritual matters and essentially denied the Orthodox East the title of "catholic," a judgment that once again failed to take into account, in a historically accurate and evenhanded way, Rome's own complicity in the Great Schism. Indeed, the pretense that the (Roman) Catholic Church had remained undivided (though some "schismatic" traditions obviously separated from it) and that the very catholicity of the church had therefore been unaffected and uninterrupted by events like that of 1054 was a part of Gregory's own misreading of the history of the church, views that he would pass along to other popes. From this point on, then, an air of unreality marks the papacy, especially as popes continue to pretend they are at the helm of a universal church. In short, they repeatedly forget about the East and its own well-substantiated claims to catholicity. The church henceforth exists not in one grand institution but in distinct theological traditions.

Expanding Papal Prerogatives and Political Power

Pope Innocent III reveled in the power and prerogatives of the papacy and brought them to their height. Claiming that he was "the Vicar of Christ,"[7] with "supreme authority on earth,"[8] in 1215 Innocent called the Fourth Lateran Council, which not only codified the obscure teaching of transubstantiation, with all its theological and sophistic missteps, but also issued a number of

6. Chamberlin, *Bad Popes*, 74.
7. William H. W. Fanning, "The Vicar of Christ," in *The Catholic Encyclopedia: An International Work of Reference on the Constitution, Doctrine, Discipline, and History of the Catholic Church*, ed. Charles G. Herbermann (London: Catholic Way, 2014), Kindle edition, locations 673035–36.
8. Cairns, *Christianity through the Centuries*, 213.

directives against the Jews, who, due to their relatively small numbers in Europe at the time, were increasingly being singled out for attention by a nearly exclusively gentile church. To illustrate, in a statement that no doubt caused anxiety among the Jewish community, canon 68 declares: "We decree that such Jews and Saracens of both sexes in every Christian province and at all times shall be marked off in the eyes of the public from other peoples through the character of their dress."[9]

Hardly content with what spiritual power he had amassed, Innocent erroneously believed, in what looks like the beginnings of megalomania, that "God had given the successor of Peter the task of 'ruling the whole world' as well as the church."[10] Such papal claims, such pretenses, just kept on coming, with each pope trying to outdo the previous one, as each continually sought new and ever-widening forms of power, supposedly all laid out in Matthew 16:18. Never has a verse of the Bible been so fruitful for the discovery of ecclesiastical claims. Mindful of the earlier history of Henry IV and Pope Gregory VII, Innocent III was determined to exercise his will over King John of England and bring him into submission. Not liking very much Innocent's own choice for the archbishop of Canterbury, Stephen Langton, the king refused to accept him. Such a refusal no doubt angered Innocent, who then turned around and effectively brought John Lackland (King John) into submission by excommunicating him and by placing England under an interdict (the normal sacramental life of the church was by and large disrupted). As part of the eventual settlement that was worked out between the Crown and the Vatican, John agreed, among other things, that henceforth he would rule his kingdom of England as "the feudal vassal of the pope."[11] This was the English Canossa (humiliation), and King John had been so put in his place that he even agreed to pay the bishop of Rome one thousand marks of very good English coin each year. This practice lasted until the sixteenth century, when Henry VIII, thinking very differently of the whole matter, finally put an end to this humiliating tax.

During this same thirteenth century, Pope Gregory IX vied with Emperor Frederick II for power throughout Europe in what became one of the normal and more tedious scripts of the later Middle Ages, competition fraught

---

9. *The Canons of the Fourth Lateran Council, 1215*, in Internet Medieval Source Book, part of the Internet History Sourcebooks Project, ed. Paul Halsall, Fordham University Center for Medieval Studies, text excerpted from H. J. Schroeder, *Disciplinary Decrees of the General Councils: Text, Translation, and Commentary* (St. Louis: B. Herder, 1937), 236–96, http://legacy.fordham.edu/halsall/basis/lateran4.asp.

10. Cairns, *Christianity through the Centuries*, 214.

11. Ibid., 215.

with considerable trouble. This was the same Gregory who in feeling his oats, so to speak, declared out of all sense of proportion that he was "the lord and master of the universe, *things as well as people.*"[12] For the time being, however, Gregory would simply have to content himself with the far more mundane task of dealing with the Holy Roman emperor. At one point in their remarkably turbulent relationship, the pope even went so far as to excommunicate Frederick just as the emperor set out to regain Jerusalem from the Muslims. Wanting to add some muscle to his spiritual authority (beyond forcing all bishops to take an oath of obedience to him),[13] especially as he looked toward his theological enemies, the Cathari among them, Gregory IX developed the papal inquisition in France and thereby enlisted the Dominicans and the Franciscans as his agents. The early phase of this troubled institution, however, is not to be confused with either the Spanish Inquisition in 1478 or the Roman Inquisition of the latter half of the sixteenth century, whose target was often Protestants, who, unlike the Cathari, were hardly heretics.

As with any phase of an inquisition, each manifestation of which always had connections with Rome, the inquisitors could investigate, but they could not punish. Thus, in the thirteenth century under Gregory IX, the spiritual estate in the form of these two inquisitorial religious orders, the Dominicans and the Franciscans, lacked the authority to execute their judgments, a task that was therefore left to the civil authorities. Sadly enough, it is one of the ironies of papal history that the very same pope who canonized the humble and peaceful Francis of Assisi in 1228 was also at the heart of the papal inquisition with all its mischief. For one thing, the humble and saintly Francis, who was kind even to animals, would almost certainly have taken issue with how the order he founded was used. Good things can indeed be put to bad uses. All that's needed is the will to do so.

After the abdication of Pope Celestine V in 1294, and with rumors flying, Benedetto Caetani was elected as Pope Boniface VIII. Declaring that he held both broad spiritual and temporal powers, Boniface eventually struggled with Philip IV of France, who thought otherwise on these matters. Indeed, in response to the alleged temporal power of Boniface, a pope who considered himself to be, for want of better language, a "papal monarch," King Philip wryly declared: "Let your stupendous fatuity know that in temporal matters we are subject to no man."[14] Undeterred by this insult, Boniface retorted to

12. Peter De Rosa, *Vicars of Christ: The Dark Side of the Papacy* (New York: Crown, 1988), 74 (emphasis original).

13. Paul Enns, *Moody Handbook of Theology* (Grand Rapids: Moody Press, 1989), 530.

14. Chamberlin, *Bad Popes*, 118.

the king: "Our predecessors have deposed three kings of France. Know—we can depose you like a stable boy if it prove necessary."[15]

The ultimate response of Boniface to Philip and others came in the form of the papal bull *Unam Sanctam*, promulgated in 1302, which articulated the pope's spiritual and temporal authority, at least according to the liking and vision of Caetani. In terms of the first set of claims, Boniface observed in the opening lines of the bull: "Urged by faith, we are obliged to believe and to maintain that the Church is one, holy, catholic, and also apostolic. We believe in her firmly and we confess with simplicity that outside of her there is neither salvation nor the remission of sins."[16] At this point the statement by itself is ambiguous and therefore open to different interpretations. Thus the "one, holy, catholic, and apostolic" church may refer to all who, like Peter, confess that Jesus Christ is the Son of God (Matt. 16:16).

Boniface, however, made his meaning far clearer in a later declaration that not only focused on the Latin church as the center of all but also cast aspersions on Eastern Orthodoxy: "Therefore, if the Greeks or others should say that they are not confided to Peter and to his successors, they must confess not being the sheep of Christ, since Our Lord says in John 'there is one sheepfold and one shepherd.'"[17] Put another way, unless the Greek Orthodox view themselves as under the authority of the bishop of Rome ("to Peter and to his successors"), they are not part of the one sheepfold that Boniface clearly identifies with the Roman Catholic Church. Such a confused ecclesiological judgment, which once again mistakes the part for the whole and is based upon the considerable mistakes of the Petrine theory, would continue even into the nineteenth century, when its substance would be repeated by Pope Pius IX in 1863 in his encyclical *Quanto Conficiamur*.[18]

Not content with what spiritual authority over others he had cobbled together (and the Eastern Orthodox, by the way, remained resistant to his designs), Boniface broadened his privileges in *Unam Sanctam* to include temporal authority as well. This second move was accomplished concisely in the declaration that the "two swords" (both spiritual and temporal power) belonged to the church and preeminently to the pope as its head. In a move that would baffle competent exegetes today of whatever theological tradition, Boniface

15. Ibid.
16. Boniface VIII, *Unam Sanctam*, 1302, translated in a doctoral dissertation written in the Department of Philosophy at the Catholic University of America, published by Catholic University of America Press, 1927, here quoted from Halsall, Internet Medieval Sourcebook, http://legacy.fordham.edu/halsall/source/B8-unam.asp.
17. Ibid.
18. Cairns, *Christianity through the Centuries*, 217.

in commenting on Luke 22:38 reasoned as follows: "Certainly the one who denies that the temporal sword is in the power of Peter has not listened well to the word of the Lord commanding: 'Put up thy sword into thy scabbard' [Matt. 26:52]. Both, therefore, are in the power of the Church, that is to say, the spiritual and the material sword."[19]

Interestingly enough, after making these sweeping temporal claims, the bull reverts to issues pertaining to spiritual authority in the closing line of the proclamation, which with the usual air of unreality so typical of the papacy at this time, will once again fail to take into account, in a realistic and judicious way, the ongoing vitality and catholicity of the Greek church. Boniface affirms: "Furthermore, we declare, we proclaim, we define that it is absolutely necessary for salvation that every human creature be subject to the Roman Pontiff."[20] Dante thought so little of this power-grasping man, who had further alienated the Eastern church while he hid behind title and office, that the gifted Italian poet apparently reserved a place in the *Inferno* for him:

> He [Pope Nicholas III] shouted: "Ha! already standest there?
> Already standest there, O Boniface!
> By many a year the writing play'd me false.
> So early dost thou surfeit with the wealth,
> For which thou fearedst not in guile to take
> The lovely lady, and then mangle her?"[21]

Lines equally suited to Boniface are the following:

> Were separate those, that with no hairy cowls
> Are crown'd, both Popes and Cardinals,
> o'er whom Av'rice dominion absolute maintains.[22]

A number of irregularities weakened the papacy's status and authority in the common people's eyes during the early fourteenth century. Troubles with the growing power of France (Boniface VIII had hardly been successful here) resulted in the papacy eventually being transferred to Avignon in 1309 by Clement V. Thus began the "Babylonian Captivity of the Papacy," a period of dominance by French kings that lasted until 1377, when Catherine

19. Boniface VIII, *Unam Sanctam*, 1302, in Halsall, Internet Medieval Sourcebook, http://legacy.fordham.edu/halsall/source/B8-unam.asp.

20. Ibid.

21. Dante Alighieri, *The Divine Comedy by Dante, Illustrated, Hell, Complete*, trans. H. F. Cary (Seattle: Amazon Digital Services, 2011), Kindle edition, locations 1183–85.

22. Ibid., Kindle ed., locations 448–49.

of Siena persuaded Gregory XI to return to Rome.[23] Unfortunately Gregory, despite his good intentions, died the following year, setting the stage for a conflict between the people of Rome, who wanted the pope to remain in their city, and the college of cardinals, a body dominated by French interests.[24] Nevertheless, due in part to pressure from the people of Rome, Urban VI was chosen pope, and he was determined to remain in the Eternal City. However, not all was well: the college of cardinals, not liking Urban very much, due to his inattention and contentious personality, proceeded to elect Clement VII as the pope. What was one of the first things that the newly elected Clement did? He moved the papacy to Avignon once more. Now there were two popes: one in Rome, the other in Avignon.

Three Concurrent Popes, a Lost Opportunity, and Machiavelli's Inspiration

From the time of the election of Clement VII (whom Roman Catholics consider to be an antipope) to the Council of Constance, which began in 1414, papal history is downright chaotic, marked by a whirligig of claims and counterclaims, of Roman and French interests, of popes and antipopes, of struggles between the Roman populace and the college of cardinals, of papal machinations and conciliar misgivings—and all this dysfunction (which is a kind and gracious way of putting it) was served up in the preceding feckless Council of Pisa, which met in the spring of 1409. Ostensibly the work of this assembly was to resolve this morass, but it ended up aggravating matters by producing not two claimants to papal authority but three (Benedict XIII in Avignon, Gregory XII in Rome, and Alexander V, whom the council itself elected)! To be sure, when an office this powerful is created over time, increment by increment, claim on top of inordinate claim, it will eventually produce, given human nature with its sin and self-centered desires, precisely the kind of struggle, both political and ecclesiastical, that played out during this very troubled period.

But this dark hour in the history of the Western church was also one of enormous opportunity—if such opportunity could be seen for what it was and then seized. Earlier in the fourteenth century, in 1324 to be exact, Marsilius of Padua and John of Jandun had already envisioned the kind of problems that the Latin church would invariably stumble into, given its preference for a polity that was in effect (and often in practice) an absolute monarchy. The brilliance of Marsilius's *Defensor Pacis*, whose counsels could be applied to the church as easily as to the state, consisted in its careful recommendations,

---

23. Cairns, *Christianity through the Centuries*, 247.
24. Ibid.

which avoided all the excesses of an apex-driven hierarchy, a rule by Caesar, so to speak. It offered a way of thinking about polity and governance that was conciliar in nature and thus far more appropriate for the body of Christ, with its various members.[25]

No doubt aware of this earlier reforming literature, the Council of Constance, in resolving the multifarious and conflicting claims to the papacy, threw off the hierarchical yoke and put in place a conciliar polity, a gracious means of governance more in accord with the nature of the church militant. Thus in its decree *Sacrosanct* the Council of Constance tried to ensure that the Western church would henceforth be governed not by the wisdom of one but by that of many. It substituted "conciliar control of the Church of Rome for papal absolutism."[26] Indeed, this reforming council not only took the power of electing the pope away from the college of cardinals, placing it in a general council, but also provided for the ongoing conciliar governance of the Western church in its decree *Frequens*.[27]

The Council of Constance, then, not only rightly diagnosed the ills that had so plagued the Latin church for centuries due in large measure to the misbehavior of its popes but also chartered a suitable way forward. Unfortunately the conciliar governance of the church, despite the best efforts at Constance, lasted for only a brief time. When Pius II became pope, he continued in the well-worked papal habit of making excessive, unrealistic claims for his own office as well as engaging in denunciations in terms of the power of others. After only two years on the papal chair, he issued the bull *Execrabilis* in 1460, which undid all the conciliar work of the Council of Constance in one fell swoop. As one scholar put it, "The papacy reverted to the system of papal despotism that it had followed for so many centuries."[28] The great opportunity for the Western church was simply squandered away.

Pope Sixtus IV, a member of the Franciscan order, enmeshed himself in the political troubles of Ferdinand and Isabella of Spain during the fifteenth century as they targeted their enemies: among them were heretics, Jews, and Muslims, the usual suspects. Though in many respects the Spanish Inquisition was conducted by the Spanish Crown with many political ends in mind, nevertheless Sixtus aided in its founding in November 1478 and therefore gave

25. For a helpful and informative examination of this classic, see Ephraim Emerton, *The Defensor Pacis of Marsiglio of Padua* (Seattle: Amazon Digital Services, 2012), Kindle ed.; first published as *The Defensor Pacis of Marsiglio of Padua: A Critical Study* (Cambridge, MA: Harvard University Press, 1920).

26. Cairns, *Christianity through the Centuries*, 256.

27. Ibid.

28. Ibid.

it the papal seal of approval. Moreover, support for this institution was further strengthened when Sixtus issued a bull in October 1483 that put the soon-to-be-feared Torquemada in place as the inquisitor general of "Aragon, Valencia and Catalonia."[29] This proclamation of the pope, then, not only renewed the earlier ecclesiastical approval but also helped to place "the Inquisitions of the Spanish crown under a single head,"[30] thereby making this enterprise more unified and efficient in the cause of persecution. This was hardly the proper work of any supposed Vicar of Christ.

It was not until the following pontificate of Innocent VIII in 1484, however, that the two German Dominican inquisitors Heinrich Kram and James Sprenger rose to power—the latter known as the "Apostle of the Rosary"[31]—who together produced the ungodly *Malleus Maleficarum* (The witches' hammer), which, according to some, "led to more misery and deaths than any other book."[32] One of the early questions of this oddly composed manual is as follows: "*By which Devils are the Operations of Incubus and Succubus Practised?*"[33] It's very much downhill all the way after such a troubled start; indeed, the book is steeped in ignorance and superstition. What Kram and Sprenger in their witch-hunting, evil-seeking zeal failed to realize, and what a world-class sociologist like Stanley Cohen understood all too well, is that the instrument employed to ferret out witches may actually lead to their very feigned creation.[34] Such tools spawn an artfully constructed fantasy, driven by the fearful imaginations of the powerful as they lord it over the weak and innocent. In a real sense these instruments are a function of the phobias and the "moral panic" of their creators. Here women, now perceived as an ongoing sexual threat by a celibate male clergy, evoke deep-seated, ongoing anxieties, and they therefore emerge as targets.[35] If the precepts of the Universal Declaration of Human Rights, promulgated in 1948, were applied to the likes of the *Malleus Maleficarum*, this Dominican creation during the pontificate of Innocent VIII could only be deemed an engine for crimes against humanity.

29. Henry Kamen, *The Spanish Inquisition* (London: Folio Society, 1998), 52.
30. Ibid.
31. De Rosa, *Vicars of Christ*, 184.
32. Ibid.
33. Kram and Sprenger, *Malleus Maleficarum*, ed. Wicasta Lovelace, trans. Montague Summers, Internet Sacred Text Archive, accessed December 27, 2016, http://www.sacred-texts .com/pag/mm.
34. See the treatment of Cohen's analysis in terms of the European witch craze in Ian Marsh and Gaynor Melville, *Crime, Justice and the Media* (New York: Routledge, 2009), 61. See also Stanley Cohen, *Folk Devils and Moral Panics* (New York: Routledge, 2002).
35. Cohen, *Folk Devils and Moral Panics*, xix–xx. Cohen's context is obviously affected by time and place, but some of the dynamics that pertain to "moral panic" appear to suit different contexts as well.

Though popes have boasted that they could be judged by no one but God alone, nevertheless even the very secular minded today are competent enough to make a proper judgment in this area.

After Innocent, Vatican politics continued their descent with the election of Rodrigo Borgia as Pope Alexander VI by the college of cardinals. The British historian Edward Gibbon, in his *Decline and Fall of the Roman Empire*, referred to this Borgia pope as "the Tiberius of Rome."[36] To prepare the way for his election, which with its ugly politics seemed to have little to do with the Holy Spirit, Rodrigo approached the cardinal of Venice and quickly bought him off to the tune of five thousand ducats. Upon ascending to the papacy, Rodrigo boisterously proclaimed, "'I am pope, I am pope,' . . . and hastened to robe himself in the gorgeous vestments."[37] Not liking the promise of celibacy very much, Pope Alexander VI had several mistresses and fathered numerous children, whom he preferred in blatant acts of nepotism.[38] His favorite sexual partner was the aristocratic Roman Vannozza Catanei,[39] who gave birth to Juan, Lucrezia, Goffredo, and the infamous Cesare Borgia, the last of whom served as an exemplar for the wily statesmanship displayed in Niccolò Machiavelli's *The Prince*.[40]

Living peacefully in his native Florence, in which he was both a respected spiritual and civic leader, Girolamo Savonarola was well apprised of the moral turpitude into which the papacy had sunk under Alexander VI. Preaching prophetically, marked by the Holy Spirit, and pointing out several papal abuses, Savonarola soon attracted the attention of Alexander VI—but it was the wrong kind of attention. After a period of widening disagreement, Savonarola was eventually excommunicated by the pope in 1497, though the Florentine was clearly no heretic. His chief crime in this morally inverted world of the Borgia

36. Gibbon, *The Decline and Fall of the Roman Empire*, ed. Hans Friedrich Mueller (New York: Modern Library, 2003), quoted in De Rosa, *Vicars of Christ*, 105.

37. Chamberlin, *Bad Popes*, 171.

38. In his *Essay on the Development of Christian Doctrine*, John Henry Newman believed he had discerned in the annals of church history a "divinely bestowed" institution in the papacy. However, this abstracted reading of the history of the church, in which the considerable evil of the popes is either minimized or repudiated, from Damasus I in the fourth century to Stephen VII in the ninth and to Alexander VI in the fifteenth, is hardly what one expects of a divine establishment. John Henry Newman, *An Essay on the Development of Christian Doctrine* (Westminster, MD: Christian Classics, 1968), 153–54.

39. J. N. D Kelly, *The Oxford Dictionary of Popes* (Oxford: Oxford University Press, 1989), 253.

40. Machiavelli writes: "Of each of these methods of becoming a Prince, namely, by merit and by good fortune, I shall select an instance from times within my own recollection, and shall take the cases of Francesco Sforza and Cesare Borgia." See Niccolò Machiavelli, *The Prince* (Mineola, NY: Dover, 1992), 15.

papacy was that he had the audacity to point out the very real evils well ensconced at the Vatican. For his efforts, Savonarola was tortured in the midst
of a rigorous examination and then finally executed the following year. Alexander VI would simply not tolerate any criticism. In his own estimation,
perhaps mindful of the pretentions of the earlier *Dictatus Papae*, the pope
considered himself to be, once again, above it all.

Fortunately, there have been some rumblings in the Roman Catholic
Church of late in terms of repairing the reputation of Savonarola. In 1998
the archbishop of Florence appointed a commission to look into the possible beatification of this godly man.[41] While this is certainly a step in the
right direction, it is clearly not enough to set the record straight. Not only
must the good name of this prophetic and gifted preacher be restored, but
the church must also acknowledge the evil perpetrated by Alexander VI in
a full and forthright way. The Holy Spirit, after all, is the Spirit of Truth, as
Scripture so clearly attests. Indeed, to falter in this last task, to fail to recognize the egregious wrong done in Florence *and* at the Vatican during the
fifteenth century is to remain morally complicit. In short, the evil that you
don't confess (and that the rest of the church so clearly sees) is one that's
still to your debit.[42]

Leo, Luther, and Rejecting the Reformation

As a member of a powerful family situated in Florence, Giovanni de Medici
was elected Pope Leo X in 1513. With a page out of the playbook of Alexander VI, upon his election as the bishop of Rome, Leo exclaimed in a letter
to his brother: "God has given us the Papacy—let us enjoy it."[43] Again, like
Alexander, Leo succumbed to the siren song of nepotism in quickly appointing
his cousin Giulio a cardinal.[44] Considered to be a Renaissance pope, Leo X
was an avid patron of the arts and liked to surround himself with beautiful
things. Due to his ever-expanding tastes and with a desire to acquire some of
the best art in the world for the Latin church, Leo was constantly in need of

---

41. Francis X. Rocca, "Saint Savonarola?," *Wall Street Journal*, last updated July 10, 1998,
http://www.wsj.com/articles/SB89986872420390000.

42. Matthew Levering, well aware of the troubled history of the papacy, observes: "Given
that there have been many bad popes (and even a period when three rivals each claimed to be
pope), can anyone hold that the Church, in its definitive teaching, has continued to be the 'pillar
and bulwark of the truth'?" Levering, *Engaging the Doctrine of Revelation: The Mediation of
the Gospel through Church and Scripture* (Grand Rapids: Baker Academic, 2014), 293.

43. Chamberlin, *Bad Popes*, 210.

44. Ibid., 228.

money. His grand design was the continued construction of St. Peter's Basilica in Rome, and he had the good judgment to enlist no one less than Raphael to take over its construction.

Around the same time that Leo was forming his plans for St. Peter's, Archbishop Albert, a prince of the House of Hohenzollern—who already, by the way, held two episcopal sees—set his eyes upon yet another, the bishopric of Mainz in Germany.[45] Holding three bishoprics at the same time was exceptional, to be sure, but not impossible if the proper fees for a dispensation were paid to the Vatican. Albert negotiated with Leo, and they finally came to an agreement. The archbishop would pay the pope ten thousand ducats for the exception he desired. The problem was that the sum of money involved was simply astronomical, far beyond the resources even of a well-situated and prominent archbishop. At this juncture the pope suggested a plan that would involve the banking efforts of the Fuggers, a Jewish financial powerhouse, which would float the loan to Albert. So that he would be able to repay the debt, the archbishop was given permission by Leo to announce the sale of indulgences in his territories. A portion of the funds raised would go to the Fuggers, the rest to Pope Leo, and some no doubt found its way into the stones of St. Peter's.

This issue of Albert's indulgence selling, though hardly anyone realized it at the time, represented a clash of values between those on the one hand who equated the splendor of the church with remarkably expensive *things* in the form of extravagantly constructed basilicas, a theology of glory, if you will—and those on the other hand who saw true splendor in a far more humble and realistic fashion, in the grace and wonderful mercy of God abounding in the forgiveness of sins and in the renewal of the heart, a theology of the cross. Just imagine for a moment the lowly, no-place-to-lay-his-head Jesus in the midst of St. Peter's in order to get a sense of the enormous difference, the considerable contrast, here. In that opulent building Jesus, the donkey-riding Savior, would be lost.

Now, in terms of the theology of indulgences, there is a significant difference between the official teaching of the Roman Catholic Church in the fifteenth century and the folk theology that emerged around this theologically disruptive issue. To illustrate, Tetzel, the Dominican monk who was put in charge of selling indulgences in Germany (though the elector Frederick the Wise would not allow him to do so in Wittenberg), conducted the sale by departing from the doctrine of the Western church in his excessive and ill-founded claims.

---

45. Justo L. Gonzalez, *The Story of Christianity*, vol. 2 (San Francisco: HarperOne, 2010), Kindle edition, locations 521–22.

Justo Gonzalez points out one of the more troubling claims: "Those who wished to buy an indulgence for a loved one who was deceased were promised that 'as soon as the coin in the coffer rings, the soul from purgatory springs' (*Wenn das Geld im Kasten klingt, die Seele aus dem Fegefeuer springt!*)."[46] Again, Tetzel sallied forth with yet another harangue that played upon the fears of the people: "I have here the passports . . . to lead the human soul into Paradise. . . . Who, for the sake of a quarter of a florin, would hesitate to secure one of these letters which will admit your divine, immortal soul to the celestial joys of Paradise?"[47]

In promulgating his *Ninety-Five Theses*, Martin Luther, the overly serious and even scrupulous Augustinian monk, took on both forms of theology, the popular and the official (official teaching linked indulgences with a treasury of merits that included those of the saints),[48] and reminded the hierarchy, who really did need to listen to this earnest scholar from Wittenberg, that "the true treasure of the church is the most holy gospel of the glory and grace of God."[49] Pope Leo and the curia, however, thought little of what they perceived to be simply a German upstart. The pope, in breathing the thin air of the hierarchy, which kept him at a distance from the shifting realities on the ground, bellowed at one point in exasperation: "Luther is a drunken German. He will feel different when he is sober."[50] Despite the fears and misgivings expressed in his ad hominem forays, Leo had to proceed with caution, since Frederick the Wise, who was, after all, an elector, protected his rising star at the newly founded university. Luther's fate, then, would not be the usual Roman way (remember Savonarola and Jan Hus). Excommunication by Pope Leo X in 1521 (his bull *Exsurge Domine* in 1520 helped to prepare the way) and banishment by the emperor, Charles V, would simply have to do.

The papacy tried to stem the tide of the Reformation that had finally come to the Western church through the good graces of Luther and others, who were prompted by the gracious leading of the Holy Spirit, but this anxious and fearful design of the popes proved to be impossible. Indeed, the reform of the church—not simply in terms of its troubled moral life (priestly immorality, nepotism, and simony, for instance) but also with respect to the theological difficulties and dead ends that had accreted over time in the Latin

46. Ibid., Kindle ed., locations 530–34.
47. Chamberlin, *Bad Popes*, 241.
48. Such is the case even today in Roman Catholic teaching. See *Catechism of the Catholic Church*, 2nd ed. (Mahwah, NJ: Paulist Press, 1994), 371.
49. Martin Luther, *Career of the Reformer I*, LW 31:31.
50. Roland H. Bainton, *Here I Stand: A Life of Martin Luther*, repr. ed. (Nashville: Abingdon, 2013), 72.

tradition—manifested itself not only in vibrant German expressions of renewal but also in Swiss, English, and Anabaptist ones as well.

Ascending to the papacy in 1534, Pope Paul III issued the bull *Licet ab initio* eight years later in response to all that had occurred since 1517. The language of this declaration indicates that this pope was determined not to dialogue with the Protestants at all but simply to denounce them from afar, and he therefore inaccurately referred to them as "heretics." However, to call the good members of the body of Christ "evil" or "heretical," especially if they have been raised up by none other than the Holy Spirit in the Lutheran, Reformed, Anglican, and Anabaptist traditions, is serious business indeed. This point must not be missed or misprized; it remains an important window on the papacy and its beclouded theological vision, a vision that is repeatedly self-referential and therefore continually mistakes "the Christian other." Thinking that Protestants were akin to the likes of Arians, Sabellians, or the Cathari of old, Paul III set up the Roman Inquisition by means of this oddly drawn bull and revealed his intent in its opening lines: "From the beginning of our assumption of the apostolic office we have been concerned for the flourishing of the [Roman] Catholic faith and the purging of heresy. Those seduced by diabolical wiles should then return to the fold and unity of the church."[51] Was the work of the Protestant Reformers, then, of the devil, "diabolical" as the pope put it? And what is the consequence of calling that which is good none other than "evil"? Indeed, what are the implications of *that*?

For his part, Pope Paul IV, elected in 1555, continued in the dialogue-repudiating ways of his predecessor Paul III and created yet another tool to cut off knowledge and to stifle expression: the *Index librorum prohibitorum*, quite literally an Index of Prohibited Books, which reads like a Who's Who of Protestant authors. To illustrate, among the leaders whose works were banned in the 1559 edition of this guide are all the following: Martin Luther, Philip Melanchthon, John Calvin, Ulrich Zwingli, Henry Bullinger, Thomas Cranmer, Hugh Latimer, and Nicholas Ridley. Even the name of Erasmus was thrown in to boot,[52] not because he was a Protestant, for he obviously was not, but simply because he had the temerity to criticize the papacy in his writings (shades of Savonarola), as is evident in the following selection drawn from his classic *Praise of Folly*: "Then the supreme pontiffs, who are the vicars of Christ: if they made an attempt to imitate his life of poverty, . . . who would want to spend all his resources on the purchase of their position,

---

51. Denis Janz, ed., *A Reformation Reader: Primary Texts with Introductions* (Minneapolis: Fortress, 1999), 347.

52. *Index librorum prohibitorum*, Michael Scheifler's Bible Light Homepage, accessed December 27, 2016, http://www.aloha.net/~mikesch/ILP-1559.htm.

which once bought has to be protected by the sword, by poison, by violence of every kind? Think of all the advantages they would lose if they ever showed a sign of wisdom!"[53]

The most significant reason the popes ultimately failed in their censoring efforts was technology. A new world was already in place by the sixteenth century, and the papacy was simply reluctant to acknowledge it. The printing press, operative a century before these turbulent times, aided the Reformers by spreading their message far and wide.[54] The popes of this period naturally lost some of the power that earlier pontiffs had enjoyed, especially in terms of control of the message. By now that was gone, except among the docile, ever-compliant faithful, and it would never be fully recovered.

The popes had good reason to fear scholarship and the dissemination of knowledge, as Pascal noted in the seventeenth century: "The Pope hates and fears the learned, who do not submit to him at will."[55] Though the doctrine of papal infallibility was not propounded until the nineteenth century, Pope Paul IV, during the polemical context of the Reformation of the Western church, employed the *Index* as a conversation-restricting tool, the very antithesis of critical thinking and truth seeking. Ushering in an era of official censorship, the *Index* put Roman Catholics at a distinct intellectual disadvantage, especially in terms of the early phases of the scientific revolution. By the seventeenth century the works of both Copernicus and Kepler found their way onto this infamous register (because the church was pontificating in areas well beyond its competence), though these writings were eventually removed in the early nineteenth century.[56] If the Roman church does, after all, think in terms of centuries, then this was overdue for two centuries. The *Index* represents a distinct mind-set and was not abolished until 1966, by Pope Paul VI.

The Question of Papal Infallibility and Its Aftermath

As with Germany under Bismarck, a political and social movement that would unite the separate states and principalities in Italy during the nineteenth

---

53. Desiderius Erasmus, *Praise of Folly* (New York: Penguin Classics, 2004), Kindle edition, locations 2057–61.

54. For an excellent work that shows how technology and an uncontrollable flow of information helped Martin Luther in his reforming efforts, see Andrew Pettegree, *Brand Luther: How an Unheralded Monk Turned His Small Town into a Center of Publishing, Made Himself the Most Famous Man in Europe—and Started the Protestant Reformation* (New York: Penguin, 2016).

55. Blaise Pascal, *Pascal's Pensées* (New York: E. P. Dutton, 1958; repr., Seattle: Amazon Digital Services, 2012), 229, number 872.

56. "The Congregation of the Index," The Galileo Project, Rice University, last updated 1995, http://galileo.rice.edu/chr/congregation.html.

century emerged under the early leadership of Giuseppe Mazzini and Giuseppe Garibaldi but was soon taken over by Camillo Benso, Count of Cavour. The result of this movement for unification, known as the Risorgimento (rising again), was that the Kingdom of Italy was proclaimed in 1861 under King Victor Emmanuel.[57] This reunification movement proceeded in stages, and the pope during this period, Pius IX, along with the papal states he governed (supported in the past by the forgery The Donation of Constantine), yet remained a problem. The Italian king therefore sent his emissary Conte Gustavo Ponza di San Martino to the pontiff in September 1870 to work out an agreement in which Rome would revert back to the Italian people. Sensing the impending loss of a significant swath of his temporal power, the pope responded in a way that upset the king's representative. Raffaele De Cesare recounts the episode:

> The Pope's reception of San Martino was unfriendly. Pius IX allowed violent outbursts to escape him. Throwing the King's letter upon a table, he exclaimed, "Fine loyalty! You are all a set of vipers, of whited sepulchres, and wanting in faith." He was perhaps alluding to other letters received from the King. After, growing calmer, he exclaimed: "I am no prophet, nor son of a prophet, but I tell you, you will never enter Rome!" San Martino was so mortified that he left the next day.[58]

Despite the protests and fulmination of Pius IX, the Italian armies entered Rome, and by the following year the pope had been reduced to the few acres that make up Vatican City today. The democratic movement of the Italian people had been a success. Chaffing under this turn of events, Pius called the new state "illegitimate"[59] and forbade Roman Catholics to participate in Italian elections "under the pain of excommunication."[60] By now the list of things that could get one excommunicated from the Roman Catholic Church was quite long. And, of course, Victor Emmanuel was excommunicated, for to offend the pope was deemed one of the worst sins of all.[61]

Sensing that his temporal stock had fallen considerably from 1861 forward during the Italian Risorgimento, and determined to rebalance his overall portfolio, Pius had invested in his own spiritual power once more by promulgating

---

57. De Cesare, *The Last Days of Papal Rome* (London: Archibald Constable, 1909), Kindle edition, locations 4640–42.

58. Ibid., Kindle ed., locations 5436–40.

59. Garry Wills, *Papal Sin: Structures of Deceit* (New York: Doubleday, 2000), 33.

60. Ibid.

61. The pope eventually lifted the excommunication, though it was rejected by the king. See Alister McGrath, *Christian History: An Introduction* (Hoboken, NJ: Wiley-Blackwell, 2012), 247–48.

the doctrine of papal infallibility at the First Vatican Council in July 1870. Though the idea of papal infallibility in some form or another had surfaced in the life of the church from the Middle Ages forward, it took Pius IX and Vatican I to give it a formal, dogmatic declaration, by which it was henceforth required to be affirmed by all the faithful. Indeed, denying this very doctrine could also get one excommunicated. Vatican I declared:

> We [furthermore] teach and define that it is a dogma divinely revealed: that the Roman Pontiff, when he speaks *ex cathedra*, that is, when in discharge of the office of pastor and doctor (i.e., teacher) of all Christians, by virtue of his supreme apostolic authority, he defines a doctrine regarding faith and morals to be held by the universal Church, . . . is possessed of that infallibility with which the Redeemer willed that his Church should be endowed for defining doctrine regarding faith and morals; and that therefore such definitions of the Roman Pontiff are irreformable of themselves and not from the consent of the Church. But if anyone—which may God avert—presume to contradict this our definition: let him be anathema.[62]

Before assessing what elements could possibly ground such an assertion of infallibility, we must identify several oddities in the council's declaration. To begin with, notice in this particular context the well-worn anachronistic papal habit of placing later, ever-further-reaching claims on the lips of Jesus, in which Christ is appealed to as supposedly "willing" the very thing that popes, centuries later, so eagerly desire. Even Cardinal Avery Dulles has explained the difficulties entailed in this largely ahistorical, dogmatic approach by describing what he called the "regressive method" employed by some Roman Catholic scholars: "As it became increasingly clear that scholarly criticism could not demonstrate that all these offices, beliefs, and rites were instituted by Christ, theologians were urged to study the original sources using what is called the 'regressive method'—i.e., utilizing the latest teaching of the magisterium as an indication of what must have been present from the beginning."[63] Second, notice also that the council was not content in simply propounding this teaching but felt compelled to condemn or anathematize all those of whatever theological stripe who disagree. Such a condemnation naturally included Eastern Orthodox believers, Protestants, and even some Roman Catholics, like Johann Dollinger, who in 1869 published *The Pope and the Council*, in which he took issue with the very notion of infallibility.[64]

62. "Vatican Council I: On Papal Jurisdiction and Infallibility," available at http://www .intratext.com/x/eng0063.htm.
63. Dulles, *Models of the Church* (New York: Random House, 2002), 40.
64. See Dollinger, *The Pope and the Council* (Seattle: Amazon Digital Services, 2014).

For his scholarly efforts the German church historian was condemned and excommunicated.

Today the *Catechism* expresses papal infallibility in the following way: "To fulfill this service, Christ endowed the Church's shepherds with the charism of infallibility in matters of faith and morals."[65] Such an approach has by now become formulaic: take a much later development in the life of the church (in this case from the nineteenth century) and then attribute it to Jesus. What then grounds infallibility? Well, in light of the history of the popes displayed in this current chapter, it obviously cannot be either the lives or the character of these very flawed men. Indeed, several Roman pontiffs throughout history have given little evidence of being marked by a special charism, a gift that should have made them, if anything, at least moral. As a class of human beings, several popes have simply fallen far short in terms of their basic ethics, deflected as these bishops of Rome sometimes were by a self-concerned spirit that was ever assessing shifting configurations of power and interests. Unfortunately, that's exactly the kind of environment that apex-focused hierarchies can create, an environment held in place by the repetition of a brew of superlatives that can quickly go to one's head, given the deceitfulness of human sin.

The *Catechism*'s claim to infallibility just displayed above, then, is fictive (in the eyes of both Eastern Orthodoxy and Protestantism) in that it needs a sanitized papacy, not the real one that we actually have. The pages of church history are replete with examples of morally questionable, deeply troubled, very unholy pontiffs. Moreover, in some cases popes, such as Julius II, even went so far as to be at the helm of armies that were quite literally battling and dying for the provincial papal interests then in play. Here the behavior of popes reveals itself to be not a cut above the common lot but to be all too human, in other words, nothing very special. Viewed another way, the actual history of popes is nothing like what one would expect if Jesus Christ himself had established the papacy. Several popes did not even evidence the qualifications laid out for elders in 1 Timothy 3:1–7 or for deacons in 1 Timothy 3:8–10. To be sure, the average layperson during some of the more troubled pontificates lived far better Christian lives than the supposed "Vicar of Christ" of the time. Despoiled by sin, several of the bishops of Rome quite simply lived in such a way as to strain the credibility of these Roman claims to the breaking point. Accordingly, infallibility would be the very last thing that one would expect from such a class of people. Remember the counsel of Jesus, so necessary for proper discernment: "By their fruit you will recognize them" (Matt. 7:16). So then, if there is any grounding of papal infallibility, we will simply need to look elsewhere.

65. *Catechism*, par. 890.

Conclusion: The Ultimate Grounding of Papal Claims

How can all the evils of the historical papacy, its sin and debauchery, often to the detriment of innocent others, be swept aside in one grand stroke as if they were nothing? How can infallibility be established on other, more suitable grounds? All of this would be something akin to a miracle if it could be accomplished. However, notice what can emerge in a rambling, presumptuous, and ultimately specious argument: Make the claim that infallibility is grounded not upon the person or character of any pope, hardly a suitable basis for anything, given the historical record, but upon the office that he holds. Argue that it is none other than the office itself that supposedly sanctifies the holder with a special charism regardless of how the popes in fact live. Or simply claim that the office itself is holy regardless of any other consideration. Either form will do. With such a judgment in place, the entirety of the evils perpetrated by several popes, even to the lowest depths of turpitude, can suddenly be rendered utterly irrelevant, of no consequence at all. Thus, when the Roman Catholic faithful are directed toward the papal office, they see only goodness and light, but this is surely an abstraction from a much larger and more deeply troubled whole. Such misdirection to the abstracted holiness of the office, overlooking the actual lives of popes, arises from learning the wrong lessons, once again, from church history in general and from the Donatist controversy in particular, as chapter 10 on the priesthood has already demonstrated. However, for the sake of space we will not repeat those arguments here even though they are very appropriate. At any rate, the *Catechism* grounds papal infallibility on a special, distinct office supposedly held only by the bishop of Rome (even if that office is understood in concert with his bishops, the "living Magisterium").[66] The *Catechism* states: "The Roman Pontiff, head of the college of bishops, enjoys this infallibility in virtue of his *office*."[67]

But what is that office, and by whom was it established? The answer here cannot be that Peter was supposedly made the first pope and installed in that office by none other than Jesus Christ. Such a declaration can be too easily disproved, once again, by the details of church history; it cannot walk the gauntlet of the kinds of criticisms that can be leveled against it by competent historians. Let's review: First, Peter was associated largely with Jerusalem and Antioch, was an apostle and not a monarchical bishop, and certainly was not of Rome, the place where he was murdered. Second, the apostolic succession (since it needed the monarchical episcopacy to be in place first) necessarily appeared sometime in the second century at the earliest, not the

66. Ibid., par. 889.
67. Ibid., par. 891 (emphasis added).

first century, where Rome needed it for the establishment of its papal office in Peter. In other words, the apostolic period was clearly over before the rise of the monarchical bishop. This gap is exceedingly troubling to Rome, given its historiography, but is one that, try as it may, it is unable to fill in. This leaves so many of the polity claims of the Roman Catholic Church in general and of the papacy in particular dangling in the air. Third, the whole Petrine theory, dependent as it is on a distinct interpretation of Matthew 16:16–18, is undermined by other assessments that cohere far better not only with the person and work of Christ but also with the nature of his body, the church. Thus the office of the papacy, implying infallibility and hailing from the first century with the blessing of Jesus, is undoubtedly a myth. Neither Eastern Orthodoxy nor Protestantism affirms it. Such an office is therefore hardly a suitable basis for the unity of the church, as Rome so often insists, but is actually and quite ironically an emblem of its ongoing division.[68]

A far better candidate for the grounding of the papal office upon which infallibility supposedly rests may be some of the writings of the early church fathers, such as Cyprian and Jerome, as noted earlier. Yet the best choice of all—with such significant evidence to support it, and with so many throughout the centuries of the church adding their clear voices in solemn agreement and in lengthy energetic pronouncements—is none other than the popes themselves! In short, the papal office, along with its supposed infallibility, represents little more than a self-fulfilling claim, the repetition of which unfortunately has proved to be intoxicating.[69]

68. David F. Wells has argued that at Vatican II the progressives tried to bring about a broader and more inclusive form of polity (e.g., focusing on the college of bishops) that would assist and even guide the pope in a more vigorous way, but Pope Paul VI would have none of it. Wells characterizes the tension as follows: "What really alarmed him [Paul VI] was the notion that his authority was not separate from that of any other bishop. He decided to append a Note to the Constitution of the Church which would explain the real meaning of the passages by which he felt he was threatened. The Note was added after the Council had completed its work on the Constitution, so no vote was taken and no official comment was made." Wells, *Revolution in Rome* (Downers Grove, IL: InterVarsity, 1972), 110.

69. For a critique of infallibility maintaining that this theological move on the part of the Roman Catholic Church represents a shift from canon to criterion, a shift that elevates epistemological concerns in a displacing way over the canons of the church, see Mark E. Powell's treatment of William Abraham's thesis in *Papal Infallibility: A Protestant Evaluation of an Ecumenical Issue* (Grand Rapids: Eerdmans, 2009), 8–10, 12–14. See also William J. Abraham, *Canon and Criterion in Christian Theology* (Oxford: Oxford University Press, 1998).

13

Papal (Im)Probabilities

In this brief chapter we want to articulate some of the fundamental judgments of chapters 11 and 12 in a distinctly different way, with the tools of formal probability. This chapter is somewhat technical and may be skipped with no loss of our essential argument for the reader. But this way of putting the argument may be illuminating and helpful to some. In particular, we shall focus on two broad swaths of evidence that we think significant: first, there is no mention of a monarchical bishop of Rome in early patristic sources; second, corruption and scandal have sometimes marred the papacy.

When Silence Speaks Volumes

As we have seen, one of the striking facts about the history of the papacy is the broad consensus among scholars that there is no solid evidence of a monarchical papacy in Rome until the late second century at the earliest. This is not just a claim by Protestant scholars with a polemical agenda; it is also accepted by Eastern Orthodox and even most Roman Catholics.[1] While Roman Catholic apologists contest this and still try to uphold traditional papal claims, the scholarly consensus is clear.

1. In addition to Robert B. Eno, whose views we shall sketch in this chapter, other examples of such Roman Catholic scholars are Allen Brent, "How Irenaeus Has Misled the Archaeologists," in *Irenaeus: Life, Scripture, Legacy*, ed. Sara Parvis and Paul Foster (Minneapolis: Fortress, 2012), 35–52; Eamon Duffy, *Saints and Sinners: A History of the Popes*, 4th ed. (New Haven: Yale University Press, 2015).

For an example, Roman Catholic Church historian Robert Eno acknowledges that the available evidence points "predominantly, if not decisively," in the direction of the conclusion that leadership was exercised collectively in the church at Rome until well into the second century, at which point a monarchical bishop emerged for the first time.[2] There is nothing in the Apostolic Fathers, the early patristic sources closest in time to the apostles, even remotely like the claim that Peter was the first pope or that his successors were the earthly head of the church. To the contrary, key sources one might have expected to state that there was a bishop in Rome, if there in fact was one, do not do so.

Among the key sources here are Ignatius, Hermas,[3] and Clement of Rome. As Eno points out, Ignatius discusses the importance of the bishop in ecclesiastical affairs in all his letters except one, his letter *To the Romans*. Some have explained this omission as due to the possibility that Ignatius did not know the name of the bishop at Rome. Eno thinks this is a doubtful explanation and comments: "He could have spoken to or of a bishop even if he had not known his name. More importantly, if one should presume from his other letters that a strong individual bishop-leader existed everywhere in the Church of his time, then he would have known that there was such a leader in the Roman community."[4] Hermas was also situated to know whether there was a bishop in Rome, since he was a member of the Roman Christian community. Moreover, as Eno observes, Hermas makes a number of incidental remarks about the leaders of the community, but he always refers to them in the plural, with no mention of a bishop who is singled out as the key leader.[5] Clement is interesting not only because he was a member of the community in Rome but also because he had a leadership role. But again, neither he nor anyone else is singled out as anything like the sort of bishop Ignatius had described in his letters. Eno sums up as follows: "This evidence (Clement, Hermas, Ignatius) points us in the direction of assuming

2. Robert B. Eno, *The Rise of the Papacy* (Eugene, OR: Wipf & Stock, 2008; originally published by Michael Glazier, 1990), 26.

3. Hermas was an apostolic father known only from autobiographical information that appears in the writings collectively known as the *Shepherd of Hermas*.

4. Eno, *Rise of the Papacy*, 27.

5. Cf. John Behr's observation that Hermas "addresses 'the leaders of the Church,' and those who take 'the first seats,' urging them to reform their ways. There is evidently discord and tension between them, especially 'regarding privilege and reputation.' He notes how those who have an exalted attitude, wishing to have 'the first seat,' avoid 'the assembly of righteous men' and 'shun them,' preferring to remain 'in a corner' with the 'double-minded,' giving empty speech to the empty minded. . . . Since there is no mention of a monarchical bishop for the city, as there would be in a later period, it seems that each leader or elder was responsible for the oversight and well-being of their own community." Behr, *Irenaeus of Lyons: Identifying Christianity* (Oxford: Oxford University Press, 2013), 22–23.

that in the first century and into the second, there was no bishop of Rome in the usual sense given to that title."[6]

One other significant source that figures in these discussions is Justin Martyr. He too was a member of the Roman Christian community and was one of the earliest Christian apologists. For our concerns, he joins the other three names above as someone who discussed church life in Rome, but he never mentions anything like a monarchical bishop.[7]

Now this might be dismissed as an argument from silence that should carry little, if any, weight. Even if there is no positive evidence of a monarchical bishop of Rome until well into the second century, the evidence does not absolutely rule out the possibility that there was one. However, we have not framed the argument in chapters 6, 11, and 12 on the papacy as an argument from silence; instead, we have looked at the historical evidence surrounding the papacy, and we find the Roman claims about the papacy highly implausible. Our argument is cumulative, and the factor of silence is only one of several strands of evidence.

Arguments from silence are notoriously complex and are sometimes dismissed as informal fallacies that have no evidential value whatever; often they are fallacious. Still, the reality is that they sometimes carry significant weight. The conditions for a good argument from silence are, however, rather demanding. In a careful analysis of these issues, Timothy McGrew has pointed out that there are three key questions at the heart of arguments from silence:

1. If H (the event or fact in question) were true, how probable is it that the author in question would have noticed it (N)?

2. If H were true and the author had noticed it, how probable is it that he would record it (R)?

3. If H were true, and if the author had both noticed and recorded it, how probable is it that this record would have survived and that contemporary historians would have been aware of it (S)?[8]

The H, of course, is a monarchical bishop in Rome starting with Peter and having successors continuously after that. Let us designate by E the evidence, which in this case would be a surviving account or record of such a monarchical bishop in Rome.

6. Eno, *Rise of the Papacy*, 29.

7. See, e.g., Justin Martyr, *First Apology* 67, where he describes a local Sunday service, including the Eucharist. A presider over the service is mentioned, as well as a deacon, but there is no indication of a bishop who has authority over these local leaders.

8. McGrew, "The Argument from Silence," *Acta Analytica* 29 (2014): 221–22.

McGrew goes on to explain how these three questions can enable us to calculate the probability of the evidence and what we should conclude from the silence of the sources:

> In more formal terms, these three questions amount to a request for three numbers: P(N/H), P(R/H & N), and P(S/H & N & R). Since (N & R & S) entails E, we can approximate the critical value P(E/H) by the product
>
> P(N/H) × P(R/H & N) × P(S/H & N & R)
>
> noting that this is equivalent to P(N & R & S/H), which in turn must be less than or equal to P(E/H).[9]

As he proceeds to show, one must judge the probability in each of these matters to be fairly high to move one to the judgment that H is probably false. So it is not easy to get an argument from silence that carries much force. We want to suggest, however, that there is a rather powerful argument from silence here that can meet these stringent demands.

So let us begin with the first question, which will be critical to get the argument going. Let us assign a probability to each of the four sources, recognizing that these estimates are at best approximations. We judge that it is highly probable that each of these figures would have known there was a monarchical bishop in Rome if there were one. If such a bishop had existed, starting with Peter and continuing in unbroken succession, then it is extremely probable that the existence of such a bishop would have been well known decades later in the second century by informed persons. We think the probability in the case of Clement is highest, since according to traditional Roman Catholic claims he was the bishop, so let us assign this a probability of 0.97. It is perhaps slightly less probable in the case of Hermas but still rather high, so let us say it is 0.95 probable. There is also very good reason to think Ignatius would have known this, given his clear interest in ecclesial government, so let us say it is 0.95 likely in his case. Finally, let us say that it is 0.90 probable in the case of Justin. We think the probability is actually higher in most of these cases, but we shall work with these more conservative estimates.

Now, how likely is it that each of them would record the fact of a monarchical bishop, given that there was one and he had noticed it or known about it? In the case of Clement, it seems very high, since he was involved in leadership (and again, according to traditional Roman Catholic claims,

9. Ibid., 222.

he was the bishop, indeed the fourth bishop in a succession beginning with Peter). So let us say it is 0.90 probable in his case. In the case of Hermas, let us say it is 0.80 probable, given his various observations about ecclesial government in Rome. In the case of Ignatius, it may be argued that he would be less likely to record it, given the persecution the church was facing, so let us say in his case, the probability is 0.50. And finally, let us say the probability for Justin is 0.60. Given the alleged significance of the bishops of Rome as the successor of Peter, these are modest probabilities. This is the sort of thing one should expect to be prominently recorded by interested persons if they knew of it, especially when they were talking about ecclesial government.

Now what is the likelihood that the record would have survived in each of these cases, given that these authors knew about a monarchical bishop and had recorded the fact? One might think the odds are very high, indeed, that the record would have survived in counterparts of the documents that have in fact survived. Yet perhaps for various reasons, if Ignatius had recorded the fact of a monarchical bishop in his letter to Rome, that letter would not have survived. Or perhaps he recorded it in some other document that has not survived. Similar possibilities might apply to the other sources. So let us assign to Clement the probability of 0.50. For Hermas, let us say 0.70, for Ignatius, 0.70, and for Justin, 0.50. Again, on Roman Catholic assumptions, one may think the odds are much higher, because it seems likely that God would have providentially preserved such an account if it had been recorded, given the theological significance of this claim for their ecclesiology.

Now then, what is the probability, given these numbers, that Clement knew of a monarchical bishop, recorded it, and that the record survived? Let us call this complex event CR. The probability of CR is $(0.97)(0.9)(0.5) = 0.44$. For Hermas (HR), it is $(0.95)(0.8)(0.7) = 0.53$. For Ignatius (IR), it is $(0.95)(0.5)(0.7) = 0.33$. And for Justin (JR), it is $(0.9)(0.6)(0.5) = 0.27$.

Given our assumptions, there is reasonable probability for each of these complex events. But now we can ask a further question: How should we put them together? What is the probability that at least one of them would have occurred? That is, we are now asking for the probability of their disjunction: P(CR or HR or IR or JR).

Getting a formal argument combining these various probabilities becomes a bit complicated. We can, however, get an agreeably high value for P(CR or HR or IR or JR) by making some independence assumptions that are plausible but not demonstrable. In particular, we must assume that the four events are not only causally independent but also probabilistically independent. Our judgment about the probability of CR does not depend on our judgment about the probability of HR, and so on.[10]

Given this further assumption, P(CR or HR or IR or JR) is going to be 1 minus the probability that none of them occur, that is:

P(CR or HR or IR or JR) = 1 − P(~CR & ~HR & ~IR & ~JR).[11]

Here is the key equation to calculate this probability:

$$1 - P(\sim CR \And \sim HR \And \sim IR \And \sim JR) = 1 - [P(\sim CR) \times P(\sim HR) \times P(\sim IR) \times P(\sim JR)].$$

Since

$$P(CR) = 0.44, \text{ and } P(CR \text{ or } \sim CR) = P(CR) + P(\sim CR) = 1,$$

we know that

$$P(\sim CR) = 1 - P(CR) = 1 - 0.44 = 0.56,$$

and we can conclude that

$$P(CR \text{ or } HR \text{ or } IR \text{ or } JR) = 1 - [(0.56) \times (0.47) \times (0.67) \times (0.73)] = 1 - 0.1287$$
$$= 0.87.$$

In view of this, we can reasonably assign a 0.87 probability to the claim that either Clement, or Hermas, or Ignatius, or Justin would have noticed if there had been a monarchical bishop in Rome during their time, that one of them would have recorded it, and that the record would have survived. The fact

10. Here's an example to show why causal and probabilistic independence aren't the same. Consider the following two propositions:
    F: My football team is ahead at halftime in today's game.
    R: It rains here tomorrow.
These two propositions are, in a very straightforward sense, causally independent. Yet they may be probabilistically correlated. Suppose, e.g., that it is also true that
    W: My football team tends to do well on a muddy field.
Putting F and W together raises the probability that
    T: It's raining here today.
But that, in turn, raises the probability that R. Now, it's barely possible that these factors are somehow canceled out and leave us right back where we started with respect to F and R—but that isn't the way to bet. So quite plausibly F and R are causally independent but probabilistically dependent. Thanks to Tim McGrew for this example, shared in an email to the author on July 6, 2016.
11. The tilde (~) indicates negation, or "not."

that none of them did is a powerful argument from silence, and a striking result, given the stringent standards for such arguments.

But even if we are skeptical of the independence assumption, it is worth emphasizing that the exercise has value at a more informal level. The key point is that there are multiple ways by which we might have heard about a monarchical Roman bishop if one had been acknowledged at the time. If on the one hand strict independence is difficult to prove, it is also true on the other hand that scenarios in which these avenues of information are strongly positively dependent (reducing the force of the argument) are rather far-fetched. In a worst-case scenario, the argument has some force; in a best-case scenario, it has a great deal of force. In either case, it is worth adding it to the cumulative case against the Roman Catholic position regarding the bishop of Rome.

Here it is worth reflecting on another striking fact about the history of the papacy as pointed out by Robert Eno. He observes that the first known appeal by a bishop of Rome to Peter's authority and to the disputed text in Matthew 16 did not come until the middle of the third century from Stephen, in a dispute over rebaptism with Cyprian, an African bishop, and Firmilian, a Greek bishop. It is telling that these bishops did not yield to Stephen's attempt to assert his authority over them in this controversy, nor did they accept his appeal to the authority of Peter. Perhaps even more interesting is Eno's observation, previously cited in chapter 11, that "we must note as well that Firmilian not only does not accept the claim, he seems never to have heard of it before."[12]

One might expect the Petrine claim to be widely understood and acknowledged by the middle of the third century if the claims of Rome were true. Roman apologists, however, often contend that the doctrine of the papacy required time to develop, similar to the doctrines of the incarnation and the Trinity. Yet there are major differences here that undermine the alleged analogy. Both of the latter doctrines are not only richly supported by abundant biblical material but, more relevant to the matter of development, are highly complex and intellectually profound. Indeed, they remain endlessly fascinating and mysterious despite two thousand years of earnest and devoted efforts to understand them by some of the greatest minds in history. By contrast, there is nothing conceptually challenging about the claim that Christ appointed Peter the first pope and earthly head of the church, and expected his successors to have the same role. Indeed, the Jews and other Christians in the ancient world were well aware of such ideas of succession, so it would hardly be a difficult thing for them to grasp or absorb, unlike the Trinity, which required a profound rethinking of what it meant to say that "God is one." So if Christ

---

12. Eno, *Rise of the Papacy*, 64.

indeed intended the papacy, as Roman Catholic theology contends, there is no similar reason in terms of complexity or mystery to explain why it should have taken so long to develop. There is no comparable explanation for why, in the middle of the third century, when Pope Stephen first appealed to Peter to assert his superior authority, his fellow bishop would reject his claim and, further, would appear never to have heard of the idea.

This intriguing bit of history is far less surprising, however, given that there is no good evidence of a monarchical bishop in Rome until the late second century. Indeed, these observations not only mutually reinforce each other, but they also lend considerable support to the larger point that traditional Roman claims about the papacy are on shaky historical ground.

How Probable Are Pestilent Popes?

Now let us consider a similar sort of argument that attempts to articulate in formal terms the fundamental intuitions behind the idea that the actual history of the papacy poses severe problems for the claims of Roman Catholicism. In particular, we want to focus here on the problems posed by the moral and spiritual corruption that has sometimes marred the papacy. While Roman apologists may find this sordid history somewhat embarrassing, they seem to think it does not represent a substantive difficulty for their view. Indeed, sometimes Roman apologists try to preempt these problems by trotting out, say, the Borgia popes, as if they can neutralize the difficulty by bringing up the bad popes themselves. Yet the problem is serious and cannot be so easily dismissed.

Consider the following conditional statement:

> If (A) the pope is the "chief shepherd," the "vicar of Christ," and the papacy was instituted by Christ to play the essential role of leading the Church and protecting it from doctrinal and moral error, and God has providentially secured an unbroken line from Peter to the present day, then (B) surely all popes down the ages would at the least be persons whose lives overall were marked by moral integrity and a sincere love for Christ and the gospel.

The question here is, how probable do we judge this statement to be? More exactly, the initial question we are asking is this: If we postulated that (A) is true, how likely would we expect it to be that (B) would also be true? In our judgment, (B) would be overwhelmingly likely to be true given (A). Indeed, we are inclined to think that the probability of (B), given the truth of (A), is somewhere in the neighborhood of 1, or 100 percent.

Of course, Roman Catholics will have to deny this, given the abundant evidence that (B) is false. Since the truth of (A) is essential to their faith, if they admit that (B) is highly probable, given (A), then if there is strong evidence that (B) is in fact false, that will pose serious problems for (A), as we shall see. But for those not already committed to Rome, the truth of (B) given (A) may seem enormously probable a priori. Our argument is directed at those who share this judgment. For those who do not, we readily concede that it will likely carry little weight.

First notice that this statement makes a rather modest claim. It does not insist that popes must be perfect, or even that they would all be model Christians, although the latter might be a reasonable expectation given the NT criteria and qualifications for elders and bishops (1 Tim. 3:1–7). We might reasonably expect that the "chief shepherd," the bishop of bishops, would meet the NT criteria for bishops. However, the statement does not insist on this, but merely says that they should all be persons of moral integrity, with a sincere love for Christ and the gospel. Nor are we assuming that sacraments administered by corrupt priests or clergy have no validity. The apostle Paul, after all, rejoiced when the gospel was preached even by those with bad motives, because the gospel was still being proclaimed (Phil. 1:15–18).

It might be objected that even such modest standards should not expected if we consider a biblical example, such as the actual history of the kings of Israel and Judah. While some of those kings were godly men who led with integrity, many others fell far short of this ideal. In light of this history, we should hardly be surprised at the unsavory history of the papacy.

Although this objection might have a certain initial plausibility, it is not convincing for a couple of reasons. First, the OT monarchy was instituted at least partly due to a rejection of God as King and as a concession to Israel's preference for an earthly king so that it could be like other nations. A major lesson to be learned from the story is the inevitable failure that results when God's leadership is rejected. The bigger lesson yet is our need for Christ, David's greater Son.

Second, the OT monarchy was a genetic dynasty, in contrast to the papacy, which is a charismatically chosen succession of bishops. Again, the Roman claim is that God has providentially assured an unbroken succession beginning with Peter and extending to the present. God, through the Holy Spirit, directed the choice of the popes. So the better comparison is not between the OT kings and the papacy but between the OT prophets and the papacy. When we consider the OT prophets, all who are recognized as true prophets were indeed persons of basic moral integrity and genuine love for God, even prophets like Jonah, who were less than perfect in reflecting God's love and grace. If all the prophets whom God called were persons of integrity and true faith, it hardly seems too much to think that all the "chief shepherds" of the church would meet the modest standards of our conditional statement. The papacy, after all, has the advantages not only of the coming of Christ but also the resources of Pentecost. So much more should be expected of the papacy than of OT kings, whose history is marked by greed, treachery, political intrigue, and lust for power.

Another objection might come from a different direction. It might be suggested that this argument proves too much. Given this argument, perhaps we should expect *all* clergymen to be persons of basic moral integrity and have a sincere faith in Christ. While initially plausible, this is unrealistic, and indeed, the NT contains warnings that would hardly lead us to expect this. When Paul spoke to the Ephesian elders, he emphasized that part of their role as overseers and shepherds of the church was to guard against false teachers. "I know that after I leave, savage wolves will come in among you and will not spare the flock. Even from your own number men will arise and distort the truth in order to draw away disciples after them" (Acts 20:29–30). Given the reality of sin and imperfect human discernment, it is not surprising that ambitious and dubiously motivated persons should sometimes enter the ranks of the clergy, or that some would be corrupted. But it is another matter to think that the "chief shepherd" who is uniquely chosen to lead the church, and who represents a providentially guaranteed succession beginning with Peter, should be as vulnerable and given to corruption as the history of the papacy shows it has been.

So let us assign the probability of (B) given (A) to be 90 percent, or 0.9. We think it is actually near 1, as already stated, but for the sake of this argument, we will assign it a slightly lower probability.

Next, let us consider the probability of (A). Again, Roman Catholics will likely assign this a probability of 1. Based on both exegetical and historical evidence, we think the probability of (A) is quite low, indeed, near 0. The detailed evidence carefully analyzed by Peter Lampe and others shows that Roman claims about an unbroken succession going back to the apostle Peter lack historical credibility.[13] Nevertheless, for the sake of argument, let us assign (A) a probability much higher than we actually think true: 60 percent, or 0.6.

Finally, let us consider the probability that (B) is true if (A) is false. Given human nature and the likelihood of corruption in any institution involving

---

13. For details, see chaps. 6 and 11. Of course, the argument of the first part of this chapter showed that a powerful argument from silence can be mounted against the Roman claim.

power and prestige, the probability that (B) would be true if (A) is false is extremely low, likely somewhere near 0. So let us assign the probability of (B) given (~A) to be 10 percent, or 0.1.

Now we can turn to the question that is our main concern. How does the history of papal corruption affect the plausibility of Roman Catholics' claims? In particular, how does this affect the probability that (A) is true? So let us calculate the probability that (A) is true assuming that (B) is false.

Let us imagine a whole collection of universes, and in 60 percent of them, (A) is true. Then (B) will be true in 90 percent of that 60 percent, which amounts to 54 percent.[14] Similarly, (A) will be true and (B) will be false in 10 percent of the 60 percent, which amounts to 6 percent. Then we have 40 percent of the cases where (A) is false. Of these (B) will be false in 90 percent, which amounts to 36 percent of the total.

What fraction of the time, among all the cases where (B) is false, is (A) true? Here is the answer:

$$0.06/(0.06 + 0.36) = 6/42 = 0.14$$

In other words, there is only a probability of 0.14 that (A) is true if (B) is false, if (B) given (A) has a probability of 0.9, if (B) given (~A) has a probability of 0.10, and if (A) has a probability of 0.6.

Probably a Problem (or Two) Here

We reiterate that these assigned probabilities for both of these arguments are only approximations that represent intuitive judgments, and not everyone will agree with them, although we think they are generous in the direction of Rome's claims. But for those who share these judgments, these arguments count significantly against the probability of Roman Catholic claims about the papacy.

While these are independent arguments in one sense, there is also a certain interesting connection between them. When confronted with the corruption in the papacy, the characteristic response from Roman Catholics is to dismiss it on the grounds that it does not invalidate their essential claim. The authority of the pope depends not on moral or spiritual integrity but on the fact that he is the successor of Peter, that he stands in a line of unbroken succession going back to Christ. What is essential is formal succession, and even grave moral and spiritual failures do not invalidate this objective reality.

14. $0.9 \times 0.6 = 0.54$.

Now it may seem odd that the papacy is so vital that God has acted providentially to secure an unbroken succession, beginning with Peter, but has not acted to consistently provide men with basic integrity to hold this office. In any case, it is easy to see the relevance of the first argument to this appeal to formal succession. Unfortunately for this defense, it is highly improbable that there was anything like a monarchical bishop in Rome until the late second century at best, and the first known claim by a bishop of Rome to have unique authority on the grounds of Petrine succession did not appear until the middle of the third century.

If Christ intended to make Peter the earthly head of the church by his words recorded in Matthew 16, and intended that authority to be passed on to Peter's successors down the centuries, it seems that not only would Peter certainly have appointed a successor but also that he would have made that momentous truth clear to his successor and to the church at Rome.[15] Had Peter done so, it seems that his successor would have been clearly recognized as a monarchical bishop, and that it would have been understood that this bishop had this unique authority by virtue of the fact that he was the new occupant of the chair of Peter. Moreover, given the importance of this claim, it seems that the successors of Peter would have articulated their authority in these terms from the start, and that this would have been understood and accepted decades later in the rest of the church as the definitive teaching of Christ.

The facts, however, are otherwise. Early sources familiar with the church at Rome (cited in this chapter) give no indication of a monarchical bishop in that city. Moreover, the first known claim to unique authority on the grounds of Petrine succession was not asserted by a bishop of Rome until the middle of the third century, and it was rejected at the time by his fellow bishops not only as presumptuous but as a novelty.[16] This early history of the papacy, among other things, gives us reason to think that the appeal to formal succession is a very frail staff to ward off the problem posed by pestilent popes.

---

15. Cf. these official declarations of anathema concerning papal dogma from Vatican I: "Therefore, if anyone says that blessed Peter was not appointed by Christ the lord as prince of all the apostles and visible head of the whole Church militant; or that it was a primacy of honor only and not one of true and proper jurisdiction that he directly and immediately received from our lord Jesus Christ himself: let him be anathema." First Vatican Council, session 4, chap. 1.

"Therefore, if anyone says that it is not by the institution of Christ the lord himself (that is to say, by divine law) that blessed Peter should have perpetual successors in the primacy over the whole Church; or that the Roman Pontiff is not the successor of Peter in this primacy: let him be anathema." First Vatican Council, session 4, chap. 2.

16. See Eno, *Rise of the Papacy*, 61–65.

14

Protestants in the Crosshairs

Popular Roman Catholic Apologetics

In this book our focus has been on official Roman Catholic documents and standards, along with other scholarly authors and sources. In this chapter, however, we want to look at popular Roman Catholic apologetic books. A number of such books have been written, many of them by former Protestants, which aim to convert evangelicals and other Protestants to Rome. Several of these books are conversion narratives that detail the reasons that the authors converted from evangelical Christianity to Roman Catholicism. Although many of them are not by scholars or academics, some have been endorsed and promoted by respected Roman Catholic academics. This chapter will look at a couple of these books by former Protestants, both of which have been endorsed by noted Roman Catholic scholars. The first, titled *The Protestant's Dilemma*, is by a single author, and the second, *Surprised by Truth*, contains the conversion stories of eleven different persons who are described in the foreword by Scott Hahn as "theological step-children who have finally come home."[1] The popularity of these books is suggested by the latter book's front cover, which advertises that it has sold over 250,000 copies.

Our aim in this chapter is first to get a sense of the sorts of arguments and claims that thrive in popular Roman apologetics, especially given the fact that these books apparently have a rather large circulation and are taken

---

1. Patrick Madrid, ed., *Surprised by Truth: Eleven Converts Give the Biblical and Historical Reasons for Becoming Catholic* (San Diego: Basilica, 1994), 10.

quite seriously by their many enthusiastic readers. We also want to point out not only the weaknesses of these arguments but also the problems they pose for the larger project of Christian apologetics and Christian unity. We will conclude with some advice for readers of these books, who may have contracted "Roman fever."

Protestantism Is Impossible . . .

A good place to begin to get a sense of the tone of popular Roman Catholic apologetics is the following quote from Devin Rose in his introduction to his book *The Protestant's Dilemma*, where he describes the outcome of his critical examination of his Protestant commitments. In doing so, he emphasizes that he came to his investigation with a commitment to reason and evidence, and this is what he discovered.

> I brought such an analysis with me into my newfound faith, and I discovered that Protestantism's tenets led to untenable conclusions. It was simply not possible to maintain a reasonable basis for my Christian faith while remaining a Protestant. At least one *ad hoc* leap was required—accepting a given set of books as inspired Scripture—but once I chose to endorse such a leap, I had no basis to criticize some who made a different leap (say, for instance, that the book of Mormon or the Koran was also inspired by God).[2]

Several interesting and characteristic claims here are worth noting, but we especially want to highlight his claim, "It was simply not possible to maintain a reasonable basis for my Christian faith while remaining a Protestant." This is an extraordinary claim. Does he really mean to say that no reasonable basis for Christian faith is possible on Protestant principles? It certainly sounds like it. Later on the same page, he writes that Protestant premises "result in logical absurdities." Logical absurdity is a decisive indicator of incoherence and therefore falsity.

If Rose is correct in this claim, then no Protestant who is true to Protestant premises has ever succeeded in maintaining a reasonable basis for his faith. What is "simply impossible" cannot be done, after all. None of the notable Protestant theologians, biblical scholars, or philosophers have ever maintained a reasonable basis for their faith: not John Calvin, not John Wesley, not Gottfried Wilhelm Leibniz, not Jonathan Edwards, not Thomas Reid, not C. S.

2. Devin Rose, *The Protestant's Dilemma: How the Reformation's Shocking Consequences Point to the Truth of Catholicism* (San Diego: Catholic Answers Press, 2014), 18.

Lewis, not N. T. Wright, not Wolfhart Pannenberg, not William Lane Craig, not Alvin Plantinga. Even for such brilliant and learned thinkers, doing the impossible has remained just that—impossible.

Here it might be objected that Rose is not claiming anything as strong as this. Perhaps all he means to say is something much more modest and personal. Recall that he says, "It was simply not possible to maintain a reasonable basis for *my* Christian faith" (emphasis added). Perhaps the key word here is "my," and he is merely making a claim about himself, not about the logical absurdity of Protestant faith per se.[3] Moreover, on the next page, he makes a more modest claim when he writes that his ultimate goal is "to demonstrate that the Catholic Faith is more plausible than Protestantism."

If this was all that Rose meant to claim, he should have been clearer in his language. Certainly the rhetorical force of his claim depends on taking him to be making the stronger claim. Suppose Rose had said the following: "As a relatively young believer, and as an amateur theologian and apologist, I did not have the resources to maintain a rational basis for my Protestant faith." If he had said something like this, his statement would be a trivial piece of autobiography. It would be a statement about his personal capacities or his own personal understanding of Protestantism, but it would tell us nothing whatever about whether it is possible for other Protestants to maintain a rational basis for their faith. It is a safe bet, however, that most of his readers take him to be doing something much more interesting and significant than registering an autobiographical fact about himself and his own limitations.

In any case, the remainder of his paragraph is also interesting in its own right and perhaps also telling. Notice that he thinks that an "*ad hoc* leap" is required for Protestants to accept as inspired Scripture the sixty-six books that they believe are canonical. Indeed, he suggests that there is no principled difference between accepting those books as inspired Scripture and accepting the Book of Mormon or the Qur'an. Again, this is a striking claim. Does Rose not think the intrinsic moral authority and the "divine qualities" of those books are more clearly evident than the moral authority and divinity of the Book of Mormon or the Qur'an? Since Protestants reject the claims of Rome, are they left to make a blind, arbitrary leap in the dark when it comes to discerning the true revelation of God? Does Rose think the objective historical credentials of the NT are no more substantial than the historical credentials of the Book of Mormon or the Qur'an?

If Rose really thinks this, it is not surprising that he could not maintain a rational basis for his previously Protestant faith. But again, this tells us

---

3. Rose indicated as much in a Facebook exchange involving his views.

nothing whatsoever about whether it is possible for Protestants who judge these matters differently to do so.

Canonical Caricature

Let us look a little more at Rose's account of the Protestant view of the canon. At the outset of one of his chapters on this issue, he writes: "If Protestantism is true, the canon of Scripture is subject to every Christian's personal discernment." Later on the same page, he expounds what he takes to be Calvin's theory of the self-authenticating authority of Scripture: "This theory did away with the need for trusting the corrupted early Church or for tracing the messy history of the canon's development. Instead, you as a faithful Christian simply picked up your Bible, read the books, and listened for the inner witness of the Spirit telling you that the books were inspired by God."[4] Here Rose's account of Calvin is at best a caricature of what follows from Calvin's view of the authority of Scripture. Recall from chapter 5 the sketch of contemporary Reformed theologian Michael Kruger's account of the canon, with its emphasis on understanding what Rose calls "the messy history of the canon's development" and the crucial role of the church in discerning the canon. Calvin's theory hardly dispenses with those factors as irrelevant.

Nor does Calvin's view license the sort of individualism that Rose depicts here. He goes on to quote a passage from Calvin in which the Reformer affirms the self-authenticating power of Scripture, while denying that its certainty depends on the church. Among the lines quoted are these: "It is utterly vain, then, to pretend that the power of judging Scripture so lies with the church and that its certainty depends on churchly assent. Thus, while the church receives and gives its seal of approval to Scripture, it does not thereby render authentic what is otherwise doubtful or controversial."[5] Rose proceeds to charge Calvin with presenting us with a false dilemma: "Either the Church, by discerning the canon, imagines itself in authority over Scripture, or the canon is self-evident to any Christian. Calvin replaces the belief that God guided the Church in selecting the canon with the belief that God guides me or you in selecting it. He forces the reader to choose between these options, but in fact they are both false."[6] Yet again, this is a

---

4. Rose, *Protestant's Dilemma*, 75.

5. Ibid., 76. The lines cited are from *Institutes of the Christian Religion*, ed. John T. McNeill, trans. Ford Lewis Battles, 2 vols. (Philadelphia: Westminster Press, 1960), 1.7.2 (1:76).

6. Rose, *Protestant's Dilemma*, 77.

caricature of Calvin's view. It hardly follows from the self-authenticating power of Scripture through the witness of the Holy Spirit that any given Christian has the discernment by oneself to sort out the entire canon or that every book would be "self-evident" to every Christian. Even more obviously, the absurd notion does not follow that Protestants believe "God guides me or you in selecting it."

The canon has already been determined, and Protestants do not labor under the notion that it is up to them to keep selecting it as individuals. Indeed, Protestants can readily concur that God guided the church, not in "selecting" the canon but in correctly discerning it. As Calvin remarks, the church gives its "seal of approval," but that approval is not the ultimate source of our certainty that it is true.

Consider an analogy. Suppose a math professor writes a textbook that includes many complicated proofs. The fact that they are included in the book is good reason for a student to believe the proofs are sound. However, the truth of the proofs does not ultimately reside in the fact that they are included in this book or the fact that the professor chose to include them. Rather, it resides in the very nature of mathematical truth. Students who work the proofs and come to see them for themselves know their truth more directly and certainly than do those students who accept that they are true simply because they are in the book. The role of the church is like that of the professor. His seal of approval does not make the proofs correct, nor is it the ultimate basis for the certainty that they are true.

On their own principles Protestants have perfectly good reasons, moreover, to believe that since God providentially guided the church in the formation of the canon, it is closed.[7] So again, Rose's claim is quite wide of the mark when he alleges that for Protestants, "the possibility remains that there may be future public revelation—like the Book of Mormon—leading to confusion and chaos among God's people."[8]

Silly Sola Scriptura Straw Man

The aim in challenging the Protestant account of canon is to make the case that the Roman Catholic Church gave us the Bible, so Protestants cannot consistently appeal to the authority of Scripture without acknowledging the infallible authority of the Church of Rome. Bob Sungenis puts it like this:

7. See Michael J. Kruger, *Canon Revisited: Establishing the Origins and Authority of the New Testament Books* (Wheaton: Crossway, 2012), 94–97, 280–81, 286–87.
   8. Rose, *Protestant's Dilemma*, 109.

> I found an indisputable example of the infallibility of the Catholic Church when I began to reflect on the question of the canon of Scripture—how the books of the Bible were determined, an issue often ignored by Protestants. There is no inspired "table of contents" anywhere in Scripture. . . . Since the Bible does not indicate which books belong within it, and since Protestants do not believe the Church has any authority to infallibly determine which books belong and which books don't, Protestants are left with an epistemological dilemma. . . . The issue of the canon is an unsolvable epistemological problem for Protestants.[9]

We have discussed the canon elsewhere and why Protestants have principled reasons for accepting as Scripture the books they do. But here again, we want to point out the rhetorical overkill in these claims. First, the author claims to show us an "indisputable" instance of the infallibility of the Roman church. We are then informed that the canon is "an unsolvable epistemological problem for Protestants." The problem, moreover, is unsolvable because the Bible does not give us a table of contents. The only way out is to accept the claims of Rome.

As stated previously, we readily grant the crucial role of the church in discerning the canon, and we can even agree that it had infallible guidance from the Holy Spirit in doing so. This does not, however, entail that the church was infallible, only that God infallibly directed the church in the crucial matter of receiving Scripture. Indeed, guiding the church to correctly recognize Scripture is integral to the whole purpose of inspiring it as an infallible authority in the first place. It would make little sense for God to inspire Scripture as a source of infallible teaching and moral instruction and then leave to happenstance whether it was accurately recognized as such by those for whom it was intended. But this hardly requires us to accept the infallibility of the Church of Rome in all its dogmatic pronouncements.

Nor is our only recourse to deal with this allegedly unsolvable epistemological dilemma to have a table of contents that identifies which books are canonical. Indeed, this is a curious claim, and it is not clear how it would help even if we had such a list, as Michael Kruger has observed. Suppose there were a twenty-eighth book that listed the twenty-seven books of the NT. Would this satisfy the concerns that Roman Catholics raise about sola Scriptura and convince them that we need not affirm the infallibility of the Church of Rome? Not at all, Kruger contends, for the question would just arise all over again, in this case, of how we can know that twenty-eighth book has actually come from God.

> The Catholic objection about the need for a "table of contents," therefore, misses the point entirely. Even if there were another document with such a table,

---

9. Madrid, *Surprised by Truth*, 123.

this document would still need to be authenticated as part of the canon. . . .
Such a "table of contents" would never satisfy their concerns, even if it were to
exist, because they have already determined *a priori*, that no document could
ever be self-attesting. In other words, built into the Roman Catholic model is
that any written revelation (whether it contains a "table of contents" or not)
will require external approval and authentication from an infallible church.[10]

In any case, sola Scriptura comes in for frequent attack in popular Roman
Catholic apologetics as part of this same web of arguments pertaining to canon
and the claim that the infallibility of the church is necessary to establish the
canon. Here again is Sungenis, with the same sort of overstated rhetoric: "If
Protestantism's fundamental doctrine was nowhere to be found in Scripture
the implications are devastating to Protestantism: if sola scriptura is not taught
in the Bible then it is a self-refuting proposition."[11] And then several pages
later, he characterizes his experience with those who hold to sola Scriptura as
follows: "My seventeen-year experience with Protestant biblical scholars had
made one thing clear to me: Sola scriptura is a euphemism for 'sola ego.'"[12]

A couple of comments are in order. First, sola Scriptura is not Protestantism's fundamental doctrine. The fundamental doctrine of Protestantism is
the essential claim of the gospel: that Christ died for our sins, that he was
raised from the dead, that we are saved by grace through faith, and the like.
Sola scriptura is a fundamental claim about the nature of authority, but it is
not a first-order doctrine in the same sense as the incarnation, the resurrection, and the Trinity.

Next, it is not necessary for sola Scriptura to be stated in so many words
in order for it to be found in Scripture. As John Peckham has argued, all we
need to show is that it can be derived from Scripture. In particular, we can
derive sola Scriptura from the fact that Scripture presents itself as uniquely
authoritative over other sources: reason, experience, and tradition.[13]

To be sure, sola Scriptura has been abused and misused by both its critics and its proponents, and certainly criticism is warranted when that is the
case. Roman Catholic apologists make lots of hay highlighting the diversity
within Protestantism, and indeed they seem to revel in depicting Protestants

---

10. Kruger, *Canon Revisited*, 43 (emphasis original).
11. Sungenis in Madrid, *Surprised by Truth*, 103.
12. Ibid., 119.
13. Peckham, "Sola Scriptura: Reductio ad Absurdum?," *Trinity Journal* 35, n.s. (2014):
10–13. See also John C. Peckham, *Canonical Theology: The Biblical Canon, Sola Scriptura,
and Theological Method* (Grand Rapids: Eerdmans, 2016); Kevin Vanhoozer, *Biblical Authority
after Babel: Retrieving the Solas in the Spirit of Mere Protestant Christianity* (Grand Rapids:
Brazos, 2016).

as strident individualists who concoct their own personal versions of the faith. T. L. Frazier, for instance, colorfully describes Protestants as a "bunch of individualists running around with Gideon Bibles and 'Just Me and Jesus' attitudes."[14] In a similar vein, Devin Rose alleges that "in a sense, every Protestant since the Reformation has been a new reformer: sifting, interpreting, and assembling his own potpourri of doctrines to profess."[15]

No doubt we could point to persons who would meet these descriptions. The question, however, is whether they are good representatives of the principle of sola Scriptura. Roman Catholic apologists like to suggest that they are and that they indeed are the very embodiment of what Protestantism is all about. Indeed, Rose points to heretical bishop John Shelby Spong as someone who really "gets" Protestantism.[16] As Rose sees things, for Protestants there is no principled reason why the likes of Spong "could not start a new Reformation that would do for the Christianity of today what Luther's Reformation did for the Church in the 1500s since, by Protestant acclaim, rejecting traditional doctrines can be a noble thing."[17]

Spong has proposed that his radical departures from core Christian doctrines are in the spirit of the Reformation, and Rose agrees. For Rose, there seems to be no difference between (1) Luther's biblically driven reform of a church that was undeniably corrupt in many ways and (2) Spong's radical departure from clear, consensual biblical doctrine that is agreed on by all major Christian traditions.

In chapters 2 and 5 we have argued that sola Scriptura, properly understood, does not in any way undermine classic consensual Christian orthodoxy but instead firmly undergirds it. But here is the point we want to emphasize now. These popular Roman Catholic apologetic works give readers the impression that sola Scriptura is not only a frivolous doctrine that is obviously self-defeating and incoherent but also a doctrine that leads inevitably to absurd consequences. One would never get the impression that the doctrine represents a serious option for any thoughtful person, or that countless brilliant biblical scholars and theologians have for centuries been operating with this conviction, have produced outstanding works of Christian scholarship, and continue to do so in the present. To the contrary, it is presented in cartoonish fashion in order to discredit Protestant Christianity and promote Rome as the only alternative.[18]

14. Frazier in Madrid, *Surprised by Truth*, 209.
15. Rose, *Protestant's Dilemma*, 203–4.
16. Ibid., 205.
17. Ibid., 207.
18. For a defense of sola Scriptura against popular objections, see Peckham, "Sola Scriptura." See also Michael Allen and Scott R. Swain, *Reformed Catholicity: The Promise of Retrieval for*

Simplistic History and Question-Begging

Another problem with these books is that they rely on simplistic, uncritical historical claims, as well as question-begging assertions. Such claims are frequently made about the Roman Catholic doctrine that Jesus appointed Peter as the first pope and established the bishop of Rome as the head of the church. Popular Roman Catholic apologetics often presents this as straightforward historical fact that is beyond serious dispute. Consider, for instance, the following from Devin Rose: "The Church had a pope, a visible head, from the beginning. In fact, we know the names and approximate dates of all of the popes, all the way back to the first century: Peter first, then Linus, Anacletus, and Clement I."[19]

This claim, however, is entirely lacking in terms of solid historical evidence. As we have stated in chapters 6 and 11, there is no good evidence of a monarchical bishop in Rome until the late second century. We have also examined the dubious historical credentials of this list of popes, as shown in the careful work of scholars like Peter Lampe (Protestant), John Behr (Orthodox), and Allen Brent (Roman Catholic).[20] The contrast between this careful historical analysis and Rose's breezy claims about the papacy is striking. What Rose presents as simple historical fact is judged by critical historical scholars to be simply false.[21]

Notice in particular his claim that "we know the names and approximate dates of all of the popes." Whom does he mean to include in the "we" who allegedly know these things? The phrase "we know" in a controversial context like this is typically employed when referring to something that is a matter of broad agreement or scholarly consensus. Beginning on the basis of what can be fairly said to be a matter of agreement that "we know," one proceeds to defend more disputed claims. But Rose's claim here is hardly a matter of scholarly consensus, even among Roman Catholic historians. Most Roman Catholic scholars would reject his claim as simplistic, if not outright false.[22] So it is not only misleading but question-begging as well for Rose to simply say "we know" these claims about the papacy. He is simply assuming to be true

---

Theology and Biblical Interpretation (Grand Rapids: Baker Academic, 2015), 49–93; Vanhoozer, *Biblical Authority after Babel*, 109–46.

19. Rose, *Protestant's Dilemma*, 35.

20. See chaps. 6 and 11 on the church and the papacy, respectively.

21. Indeed, Roman Catholic apologists often prooftext patristic sources with the same simplistic certainty that Protestant fundamentalists prooftext the Bible.

22. See Robert B. Eno, *The Rise of the Papacy* (1990; repr., Eugene, OR: Wipf & Stock, 2008); Allen Brent, "How Irenaeus Has Misled the Archaeologists," in *Irenaeus: Life, Scripture, Legacy*, ed. Sara Parvis and Paul Foster (Minneapolis: Fortress, 2012), 35–52.

the very claims that are at issue between Protestants and Roman Catholics, which is obviously question-begging.

For another instance of this, consider these lines from Julie Swenson: "John Henry Newman, the famous Evangelical Protestant convert to Catholicism, once said, 'Knowledge of Church history is the death of Protestantism.' He was right. My study of the early Church showed clearly that it was Catholic in its beliefs and practices—in fact, had begun calling itself 'Catholic' at least as early as the end of the first century."[23] Newman's famous line (paraphrased by Swenson) is a favorite among Roman Catholic converts, as we have noted earlier. While many Catholics may fondly imagine that Protestants can maintain their Protestant faith only if they remain blissfully ignorant of church history, the many learned church historians and historical theologians in the ranks of Protestantism should be sufficient to discredit this myth once and for all (see Irena Backus, Roland Bainton, Gerald Bray, Henry Chadwick, Owen Chadwick, Justo L. Gonzalez, Charles Hill, Michael W. Holmes, Kenneth Scott Latourette, J. B. Lightfoot, Morwenna Ludlow, George Marsden, Alister McGrath, Mark Noll, Heiko Oberman, Thomas Oden, Alec Ryrie, and Philip Schaff, for a start).[24] Indeed, one of the authors of this book is a church historian who has spent his whole career reading and researching church history and historical theology, and his years of study have only strengthened his Protestant evangelical convictions. But John Henry Newman's claim apparently remains popular and was cited several times by other authors in the book in which Swenson's essay appears.

Notice, moreover, that Julie Swenson deems it "clearly" to be the case that early church history supports the claims of Roman Catholicism, as attested partly by the fact that the term "catholic" was used to describe the church by the end of the first century. But again, this is question-begging, not least because the use of the word "catholic" in the first century hardly provides significant evidence in favor of the distinctive ecclesial claims of Rome. It is anachronistic to import into the first-century use of the term all the later developments that came to predominate in the Church of Rome, and to distinguish it not only from Eastern Orthodoxy but also from Reformation churches. The fact that the term "catholic" was used early in the history of the church does not even begin to settle the issue of whether the Roman Catholic Church of today is the "one true church" or the church that distinctively represents the contemporary embodiment of the first-century church. Indeed, it is more than a little ironic that those who cite Newman's famous line often make such simplistic historical claims.

23. Swenson in Madrid, *Surprised by Truth*, 154–55.
24. We include Anglicans since Newman appears to do so in the context of his famous remark.

Later in the same volume cited above, Frazier cites Ignatius of Antioch to make a similar point. "'Where the bishop is to be seen, there let all his people be, just as where Jesus Christ is present, there is the Catholic Church.' That Ignatius called the Church 'Catholic' had a profound psychological effect on an anti-Catholic like myself."[25] While we will not dispute that seeing the church described as "catholic" by an early church father may have a "profound psychological effect" on a self-described "'born-again' Fundamentalist,"[26] this says nothing in favor of the notion that the use of the term here supports the claims of the Church of Rome. Indeed, notice that Ignatius says the catholic church is "where Jesus Christ is present." We heartily concur with that, but that does nothing to show that Jesus Christ is distinctively present in the Church of Rome in some sense that uniquely identifies it as the "one, holy, catholic Church." Indeed, it is misleading that the word "catholic" was capitalized in the quote from Ignatius, since that identifies the "catholic" church with the Roman Catholic Church. The Greek word simply means "catholic" in the sense of "universal."[27]

For one final example, consider the claim that Protestants, in effect, do not believe the promises of Jesus that he gave to his disciples to protect the church and guide it into all truth since they reject the claims of Rome. Marcus Grodi, detailing the reasons he "could no longer remain a Protestant," cites this as a crucial consideration: "To do so [remain a Protestant] meant I must deny Christ's promises to guide and protect his Church and to send the Holy Spirit to lead it into all truth (cf. Matt. 16:18–19; 18:18; 28:20; John 14:16, 25; 16:13)."[28] Again, this is deeply question-begging. Grodi apparently identifies whatever the Church of Rome claims to be infallible teaching with the truth into which Christ promised the church would be led by the Holy Spirit. But that claim is hardly warranted unless we assume that the Church of Rome is indeed the one true church, whose magisterium truly has the unique teaching authority it claims to have.[29] And again, that is precisely what is at issue. We

25. In Madrid, *Surprised by Truth*, 197.

26. Ibid., 181.

27. The passage quoted is from the letter of Ignatius *To the Smyrnaeans* 8.2. The passage is translated by J. B. Lightfoot and J. R. Harmer as follows: "Wherever the bishop shall appear, there let the people be; even as where Jesus may be there is the universal Church." See *The Apostolic Fathers* (London: Macmillan, 1891), 158. More recently the passage has been translated: "Wherever the bishop appears, there let the congregation be; just as wherever Jesus Christ is, there is the catholic Church." See *The Apostolic Fathers*, ed. and trans. Michael W. Holmes, 3rd ed. (Grand Rapids: Baker Academic, 2007), 255.

28. Grodi in Madrid, *Surprised by Truth*, 53.

29. Converts to Rome typically ignore the claims of the Orthodox Church, and it is far from clear why they so readily accept the claims of Rome rather than those of Orthodoxy.

can certainly believe that the Holy Spirit has faithfully led the church into all truth, as Christ promised, without agreeing that everything the Church of Rome claims as infallible truth is in fact infallible truth into which it was led by the Holy Spirit.

Protestants certainly believe that the Holy Spirit has led the church into the truth that God intended, by inspiring the apostles and others not only to write the Scriptures but also to correctly discern the canonical books and accurately interpret their essential teaching. Despite the errors and corruption into which the church has undoubtedly fallen at various stages of history, including the present, God has preserved the church and the message of the gospel, and he will do so until the end of time. We need not agree on all the details of the narrative to affirm God's providential role in protecting the church and preserving the truth of the gospel. It is quite parochial to insist that Protestants cannot make these claims with integrity unless they accept the claims of Rome.

Examples of such question-begging and other simplistic arguments could easily be multiplied, but let us turn now to another sort of argument that frequently recurs in popular Roman Catholic apologetics. Indeed, this is perhaps the argument that drives all the others we have surveyed.

Cartesian Certainty Syndrome

Descartes's very name has become identified with his attempt to find an utterly secure foundation for his beliefs, a foundation so secure that it would be completely invulnerable to doubt and uncertainty. To do so, he engaged in his famous thought experiment in which he doubted all his beliefs that he could possibly doubt and even imagined that an evil demon was trying to deceive him and lead him into error. In this thought experiment, he arrived at one belief that would be invulnerable to this most extreme onslaught, his belief that he was thinking, and this led to one of the most famous lines in the history of philosophy: "I think, therefore I am."

Descartes then proceeded to rebuild the edifice of his beliefs from this secure foundation, arriving at what he believed to be an utterly certain system of knowledge. The sort of knowledge claims that achieve invulnerability to doubt thereby acquire the lofty status of "Cartesian certainty."

It is not insignificant that Descartes was a Roman Catholic who wrote his famous works in the aftermath of the Reformation, when competing truth claims by Protestants and Roman Catholics undermined the claims to certainty that were previously taken for granted by many believers. Descartes's project thus appealed to many persons whose sense of certainty had been shaken. Indeed, Descartes set the modern world on a centuries-long debate about the nature and possibilities of knowledge.

It has come to be recognized, however, that Cartesian certainty is an unrealistic standard to expect for human knowledge claims. Many things that we can rightly claim to know—such as basic sense perceptions, memory beliefs, historical beliefs, and so on—fall short of Cartesian certainty. Yet the ghost of Descartes lives on, and his quest for a guarantee of absolute certainty continues to haunt many people.

Indeed, a big part of the attraction of Rome is that many people see it as providing a degree of certainty that they did not find in Protestantism. For a characteristic instance of this, consider the following from Marcus Grodi, who was a Calvinist pastor before he converted to Rome.

> I struggled with the questions, "How do I know what God's will is for my life and for the people in my congregation? How can I be sure that what I am preaching is correct? How do I *know* what truth is?" . . . Since it was my duty and desire to teach the truth of Jesus Christ to my congregation, my growing concern was, "How do I *know* what is truth and what isn't?" . . . "Am I preaching truth or error?" I asked the Lord repeatedly. "I *think* I'm right, but how can I know for sure?" . . . I remember standing beside the hospital bed of a man who was near death after suffering a heart attack. His distraught wife asked me, "Is my husband going to heaven?" All I could do was mouth some sort of pious but vague "we-must-trust-in-the-Lord" reassurance about her husband's salvation. She may have been comforted but I was tormented by her tearful plea. After all, as a Reformed pastor I believed John Calvin's doctrines of predestination and perseverance of the saints. This man had given his life to Christ, he had been regenerated, and was confident that he was one of the God's elect. But *was* he?[30]

The italicized words in this quote are all in the original, and they highlight the intense quest for certainty that drove Grodi's conversion to Rome. Indeed, he apparently thought he should even have absolute certainty about the state of grace of persons who have died, and thought that his uncertainty in this matter was an argument against Protestantism.

Grodi apparently believes that embracing the claims of Rome solves all these issues and gives him the infallible certainty he craved. Near the end of his essay, he writes: "All this wrangling of how to interpret Scripture gets one nowhere if there is no way to know with infallible certitude that one's interpretation is the right one. The teaching authority of the Church in the

---

30. Grodi in Madrid, *Surprised by Truth*, 37, 38, 39, 40.

magisterium centered around the seat of Peter. If I could accept this doctrine, I knew I could trust the Church on everything else."[31] On the very last page of his essay, he quotes Newman's line, "To be deep in history is to cease to be a Protestant," and then goes on to state with characteristic certainty that the Church of Rome is the true church. "Newman was right. The more I read Church history and Scripture the less I could comfortably remain a Protestant. I saw that it was the Catholic Church—the Roman Catholic Church—that was established by Jesus Christ, and all other claimants to the title 'true Church' had to step aside."[32] The ease with which converts like Grodi attain "infallible certitude" about a whole host of exegetical, historical, and theological issues that are deeply contested among Anglican, Eastern, Protestant, and Roman scholars who share a deep commitment to the authority of Scripture and classic Nicene catholic Christianity is striking indeed. It is also appealing, and all the more so in a chaotic world where conflicting claims abound. Whether this "infallible certitude" is warranted or corresponds to objective truth is another matter. But the promise to resolve these disputes with a guarantee of infallible certainty is clearly a large part of the appeal in Roman apologetics.

Indeed, the quest for infallible certainty is a driving force behind the other arguments we have examined as well. The claim that it is "impossible" to maintain a rational basis for Protestant faith, the caricatures of sola Scriptura and the notion that it is obviously incoherent, the suggestion that it is a knockdown argument against Protestantism that the church gave us the canon, the simplistic historical claims, and the question-begging claims that assume the authority of Rome—all of these feed the hankering for infallible certainty and lead readers to think that they can have it if they simply accept the claims of Rome.

In all these respects, popular Roman Catholic apologetics is reflecting the worst tendencies of popular apologetics, period. We have no doubt that there is Protestant literature critical of Roman Catholicism that mirrors the worst arguments of Roman Catholic apologists. And more generally, popular Christian apologetics sometimes displays the same unfortunate tendencies.

Readers of popular apologetics are usually looking for answers; indeed, they are often looking for easy answers, and it is tempting to cater to their wishes by grossly oversimplifying the views one is criticizing and claiming easy victories over them, and to exaggerate the strength and conclusiveness of one's own arguments.[33] We do not mean to demean popular apologetics, and indeed, we believe it plays a

---

31. Ibid., 53–54.
32. Ibid., 56.
33. See Scott R. Burson and Jerry L. Walls, *C. S. Lewis and Francis Schaeffer: Lessons for a New Century from the Most Influential Apologists of Our Time* (Downers Grove, IL: InterVarsity, 1998), 239–44.

vital role. There is certainly a need for books that present apologetic arguments in a clear, engaging, and accessible fashion. But it does not serve the apologetic enterprise and, what is even more important, it serves neither truth nor charity nor Christian unity to promote books that perpetuate simplistic caricatures.

Roman Catholic Apologetics and the Broader Apologetic Enterprise

A question certainly worth asking here is how the arguments of popular Roman apologetics bear on the broader apologetic enterprise, in which evangelicals and Roman Catholics and Eastern Orthodox often cooperate in the common project of defending "mere Christianity." This is an important question because these arguments that we have been examining appeal to the authority claims of Rome and insist that Rome alone has the resources to resolve the "epistemological dilemmas" that Protestantism allegedly faces.

These arguments are variations on the all-or-nothing arguments we considered in chapter 4. In addition to the very ambitious version of this argument advanced by Newman, we examined more modest versions of the argument insisting that we have no rational warrant for believing central creedal Christian doctrines unless we accept the authority of the Roman magisterium and its other doctrinal pronouncements.

Consider again the example of the Marian dogmas, which the pope has declared to be infallibly true. In chapter 16, we cite some of the following words of Pope Pius XII from his encyclical *Munificentissimus Deus*: "We pronounce, declare, and define it to be a divinely revealed dogma: that the Immaculate Mother of God, the ever Virgin Mary, having completed the course of her earthly life, was assumed body and soul into heavenly glory. Hence if anyone, which God forbid, should dare willfully to deny or call into doubt that which we have defined, let him know that he has fallen away *completely* from the divine and Catholic Faith."[34] This is all-or-nothing reasoning with a vengeance! To deny the bodily assumption of Mary is to fall away "completely" from the Catholic faith. But the logic is straightforward: to question a Marian dogma is to question papal infallibility, and to question papal infallibility is to question the Roman claim that the magisterium "alone" has been entrusted with the task of authentically interpreting the Word of God.[35]

---

34. Pope Pius XII, *Munificentissimus Deus*, pars. 44–45, the Holy See, 1950, http://w2.vatican.va/content/pius-xii/en/apost_constitutions/documents/hf_p-xii_apc_19501101_munificentissimus-deus.html (emphasis added).

35. On the exclusive authority of the magisterium to interpret the Word of God, see *Catechism of the Catholic Church*, 2nd ed. (Mahwah, NJ: Paulist Press, 1994), par. 85.

Now the question might be raised whether the pope intends his claim to apply only to Roman Catholics or to all Christians. Does he mean to say only that if any Roman Catholic were to deny or call into the doubt the bodily assumption of Mary, he would thereby cease to be a *Roman Catholic* since this doctrine has been defined at a level of authority that obliges the faithful to "irrevocable adherence"?[36] Or does he mean to say that in so doing, a Roman Catholic would deny the whole Christian faith and thus no longer even be a Christian? Or does he mean to say that *any* Christian who considers and understands the doctrine of the assumption yet denies it, thereby denies the whole Christian faith? It is not altogether clear.[37]

But the broader question here is how Roman Catholic claims about the authority of the magisterium affect the way Roman Catholics carry out the apologetic enterprise, especially when they work together with evangelicals. Can they proceed on more ecumenical terms to defend the claim that there are good reasons to believe in "mere Christianity" whether or not one accepts the claims of Rome? Or do they believe (as many apologists contend) that we have no good grounds to believe in the NT canon, the authority of Scripture, and the classic creeds unless we accept the authority of the Roman church? Do Roman Catholics believe that acceptance of the authority of Scripture and the classic creeds commits one, rationally or logically, to the authority of the Roman magisterium? Or do Roman Catholic apologists believe reasons that support belief in "mere Christianity" are logically independent of papal infallibility and the Marian dogmas?[38] Can one be fully rationally justified in believing the catholic faith as expressed in the Nicene Creed while being fully informed of, and consciously rejecting, the claims of the Roman magisterium?

These questions point out certain tensions between the project of Roman Catholic apologetics aimed at Protestants and the more general apologetic

---

36. Ibid., 88.

37. The whole matter is complicated by the question of what is involved in "willful" denial of the doctrine. On one account, a person willfully denies something when he refuses to acknowledge what he actually recognizes to be true, which is perverse by definition. On a second understanding, a person willfully denies something when he consciously and freely rejects it because it does not seem to him to be true.

38. Here Roman Catholics may appeal to the "motives of credibility": "Thus the miracles of Christ and the saints, prophecies, the Church's growth and holiness, and her fruitfulness and stability 'are the most certain signs of divine Revelation, adapted to the intelligence of all.'" *Catechism*, par. 156, quoting *Dei Filius* (*Dogmatic Constitution on the Church*, issued by the First Vatican Council, 1870), sec. 3. Two things are worth noting: first, these "signs of divine Revelation" do not seem adequate to account for the canon or for Nicene orthodoxy; second, the appeal to the miracles of saints and the church's growth and so on seems designed to support not mere Christianity but the more specific claims of the Church of Rome. Presumably the church mentioned here is intended to be the Roman Catholic Church.

project aimed at unbelievers. If Roman Catholic apologists believe that the case for "mere Christianity" can be rationally made entirely apart from accepting the claims of Rome, then it is hard to see how they can consistently employ the all-or-nothing strategy when trying to convert their Protestant friends to Rome. On the other hand, if they believe that one cannot consistently or rationally believe "mere Christianity" on good grounds without going on to accept the claims of Rome (once fully informed of them), they should be honest about this up front. This obviously poses problems for the project of a common apologetic enterprise, one that does not commit a person to the distinctive beliefs of a specific church or theological tradition.

In the preface to *Mere Christianity*, Lewis makes it clear that it was no part of his concern to tell readers which church they should join once they had been convinced that Christianity is true. He only identified the sort of questions that one should ask in making this decision: "Are these doctrines true: Is holiness there? Does my conscience move me towards this? Is my reluctance to knock at this door due to my pride, or my mere taste, or my personal dislike of this particular doorkeeper?"[39]

As a lifelong Anglican, Lewis believed that the doctrines of his church were true, but he did not think his church was exclusively the "one true Church," and obviously he did not think the Church of Rome had exclusive rights to that title.[40] Just as obviously, he thought the case for "mere Christianity" did not hinge on accepting the claims of Rome. But what about Roman Catholics who take quite seriously the claims that their church makes about itself and who consequently believe that Protestants are at best "separated" brothers and sisters who can never be fully in communion with the "one true Church" unless they become Roman Catholics? Do they forthrightly share this as part of their apologetic message, or do they bracket their true convictions in this matter?

In short, we think one can coherently and consistently be an apologist for "mere Christianity" and make a rational case for believing it. Or one can, alternatively, accept all the claims of the Roman magisterium and consistently defend the all-or-nothing view that asserts that denying, say, one of the Marian dogmas is tantamount to "completely" falling away from the faith. But it is far less clear that one can consistently do both.

Yet the apologetic project has another whole layer of challenges if the rational grounds for believing in classic creedal Christianity depend on accepting the

39. C. S. Lewis, *Mere Christianity* (New York: HarperSanFrancisco, 2001), xvi.

40. Stewart Goetz has convincingly argued that Lewis had fundamental philosophical differences with Rome that prevented him from being a Roman Catholic, in addition to the characteristic disagreements Protestants have with Rome. See *A Philosophical Walking Tour with C. S. Lewis: Why It Did Not Include Rome* (New York: Bloomsbury, 2015).

claims of Rome. As we have explained in previous chapters, the Roman claims about the papacy, for instance, face numerous challenges exegetically and historically as well as morally. If the truth claims of the Christian faith depend on the Roman claims about the papacy, the apologetic project will require convincing answers to all these difficulties. Insofar as there are doubts about the papacy, the whole faith is on shaky grounds, and the larger apologetic enterprise is accordingly jeopardized. Fortunately, the integrity of the faith for Protestants is in no way contingent on the papacy, but for faithful Roman Catholics, it seems that it is.

This reality no doubt partly explains what we reported in earlier sections of this chapter, that Roman apologists are often determined to discredit Protestantism entirely, dismissing it as unworthy of serious belief or easily refutable if not "impossible" to rationally maintain. The very prospect that Protestantism might be rationally defensible threatens to undermine the entire faith for Roman Catholics who have bought into the all-or-nothing line of argument we examined earlier in this chapter.

Prescriptions for Roman Fever

It's likely that most people who read popular Roman Catholic apologetic books are exploring "conversion" to Rome. Indeed, they may be hanging around the banks of the Tiber and may have contracted a bad case of Roman fever, a condition that produces an alluring vision of what lies on the other side and a strong urge to plunge into the river and swim across as fast as one can, never looking back. In this final section, we offer some counsel to those in the grip of Roman fever.

First, take every care not to fall into the mind-set of comparing the best of Rome with the worst of Protestantism. One of my Roman Catholic friends, wanting to score a point for his church, quipped: "We have Dante's *Divine Comedy*, and you have the *Left Behind* series." He was, I think, only being mischievous, since he has many evangelical friends and often works closely with them on various projects. But his quip does reflect an attitude that typically comes with Roman fever. Those in the grip of it invariably tend to latch on to the worst practitioners or the most notable foibles of evangelicalism, as if they are typical, and to extol the best of Rome (which is sometimes an idealistic illusion) by way of invidious comparison. And in fact the books we examined in this chapter do this repeatedly.

Of course, Protestants do not have to look too hard to find displays of popular piety in Roman Catholicism that are hardly worthy of celebration or emulation. Carl Trueman serves up a few examples with a humorous flourish.

There are things which can be conveniently ignored by North American Roman Catholic intellectuals because they take place in distant lands. Yet many of these are emblematic of contemporary Roman Catholicism in the wider world. Such, for example, are the bits of the real cross and vials of Jesus' blood which continue to be displayed in certain churches, the cult of Padre Pio and the relics of Anthony of Padua and the like (both of whom edged out Jesus and the Virgin Mary in a poll as to who was the most prayed to figure in Italian Catholicism). We Protestants may appear hopelessly confused to the latest generation of North American Roman Catholic polemicists, but at least my own little group of Presbyterian schismatics does not promote the veneration of mountebank stigmatics or the virtues of snake-oil.[41]

Italy is rather close to the heart of Roman Catholicism, so the results of this poll mentioned by Trueman are more than a little telling.[42] Trueman also comments on the irony that Rome has managed to advertise itself as the church for intellectuals and academics. A little historical perspective, looking beyond the last few decades, reminds us that things were rather different not so long ago. Indeed, the infamous Index of Prohibited Books, first adopted in 1559, was not abolished until 1966, when Pope Paul VI finally got rid of it.

I well remember being amazed when reading the autobiography of the analytic philosopher and one-time priest, Sir Anthony Kenny, that he had to obtain special permission from the Church to read David Hume for his doctoral research in the 1950s. At the start of the twenty-first century, Rome may present herself as the friend of engaged religious intellectuals in North America but she took an embarrassingly long time even to allow her people free access to the most basic books of modern Western thought. Women in Britain had the vote, Elvis (in my humble opinion) had already done his best work and the Beatles and Rolling Stones were starting to churn out hits before Roman Catholics were free to read David Hume without specific permission from the Church.[43]

The point here is that honesty, as well as charity, requires us to recognize that both theological traditions have many strengths to celebrate, as well as embarrassing weaknesses.

Fixating on the weaknesses of either tradition while ignoring the strengths, in order to justify conversion, serves neither clarity nor charity. Indeed, as Steve

41. Trueman, "Pay No Attention to That Man behind the Curtain! Roman Catholic History and the Emerald City Protocol," *reformation21*, April 2012, http://www.reformation21.org /articles/pay-no-attention-to-that-man-behind-the-curtain-roman-catholic-history-and-the-e.php.

42. For details about the poll, see "Padre Pio Tops Saints Poll," November 1, 2006, *Italy Magazine*, http://www.italymagazine.com/italy/padre-pio-tops-saints-poll.

43. Carl Trueman, "Pay No Attention to That Man behind the Curtain!"

Long has astutely observed, "Many Protestant conversions to Catholicism are themselves *protestant* conversions. On one occasion when I was tempted to convert to Catholicism, I did so because I was angry at the silliness of activities like puppet-and-clown Eucharists."[44] A little honest perspective that recognizes silliness on both sides, as well as much to be admired, can often cool Roman fever.

The practical question here may come down to this: "Where do I go on Sunday morning?" And it's a question that needs an answer. If one is attending a church that is primarily evangelistic in focus and offers little by way of nourishment for growing and mature believers, it may be advisable to change churches. If one's spiritual needs would be better met in a more liturgical church with an emphasis on classical forms of worship and hymnology, it may be advisable to change churches. But it hardly follows that Rome is the panacea for all ills, or that Rome is the only alternative to the superficiality of some evangelical churches.

Second, keep squarely in mind that one can embrace a fully catholic faith without going to Rome. Firmly resist any attempt to drive a wedge between traditional catholic orthodoxy and Protestantism. As we have argued throughout this book, the claim of Rome to be the one true church and its identification of "catholic" with "Roman Catholic" does justice neither to the complexities of church history nor to larger ecclesial realities.

Protestants need to understand their catholic legacy, and where it has been ignored or minimized, they need to recover and celebrate it. No doubt part of what produces Roman (and Eastern) fever is a desire to be part of a great tradition, and one of the weaknesses of evangelicalism is that it has often failed to communicate this larger tradition. Protestants no less than Roman Catholics have roots that go all the way back to the apostles and the great ecumenical consensus represented in the classic creeds, and this was strongly emphasized by the great Reformers.[45]

There is another side of the coin we need to recognize as well: Roman Catholics also have Reformation roots that are very much a part of their own story. Roman Catholic historian Gary Macy expresses this point as follows:

Not a single Christian group in the west survived the Reformation unchanged. Even the Roman church emerged a very different entity than that of the medieval

---

44. D. Stephen Long, "My Church Loyalties: Why I Am Not Yet a Catholic," *Christian Century*, July 28, 2014, http://www.freerepublic.com/focus/f-religion/3186144/posts.

45. Some excellent sources here are Allen and Swain, *Reformed Catholicity*; Vanhoozer, *Biblical Authority after Babel*; and Peter J. Leithart, *The End of Protestantism: Pursuing Unity in a Fragmented Church* (Grand Rapids: Brazos, 2016).

church. . . . Different churches retained different customs of the old medieval church, to be sure, and some of the churches, especially the Roman Catholic and Anglican churches, treasured their continuity with the medieval centuries. Yet it is important to remember that none of the churches that emerged from this great upheaval can claim the past as exclusively their own. The modern Roman Catholic church started in the sixteenth century just as surely as the Lutheran or Calvinist churches.[46]

So just as it is true that Protestants have a patristic catholic heritage, it is also true in an important sense that Roman Catholics have a Reformation heritage.

The third, in keeping with the previous point, it is vital to understand that those who embrace an understanding of the church catholic that is larger than Rome can celebrate and be spiritually and intellectually nourished by the whole host of theologians, saints, martyrs, and artists who have given witness to classic Christian faith in their lives, writing, painting, and music. All these riches are gifts of God to be received with gratitude and joy by all Christians.

The attitude we are recommending here is very much at odds with that of some Roman Catholic apologists, who want to claim Christians of their tradition as their exclusive property. Indeed, Devin Rose deploys the saints in yet another variation on the all-or-nothing argument to contend that Protestants cannot claim them. He writes: "If I were drafting baseball players as a Protestant Christian, I would want Saint Augustine on my team for his great love of Scripture, the honesty of his *Confessions*, his Protestant-friendly ideas on justification and predestination, and his philosophical wisdom."[47] Rose goes on, however, to contend that Augustine also held a number of views typically rejected by Protestants, so he could not be on the Protestant team. Similarly, he argues that Athanasius, Cyprian, Thomas Aquinas, and Francis de Sales are also disqualified.

Leaving aside the anachronistic problems with this claim, we want to highlight how remarkably parochial it is. Rose does not celebrate these great saints as members of the Christian "team" who have much to teach all of us; instead, his primary concern is to draft these great saints to score points for team Rome.

The view of the church catholic we have been commending in this book recognizes that the church fathers belong to all of us, that the saints and heroes of our particular traditions are to be claimed not jealously as our exclusive

46. Macy, *The Banquet's Wisdom: A Short History of the Theologies of the Lord's Supper* (Maryville, TN: OSL Publications, 2005), 170.
47. Rose, *Protestant's Dilemma*, 196.

possession but rather as treasures to be joyfully shared for the enrichment of the whole church. C. S. Lewis, Protestant though he certainly was, is a gift to believers in "mere Christianity" of all traditions. J. R. R. Tolkien, Roman Catholic though he certainly was, is no less a gift to all Christians. The same can be said about the music of Bach; the poetry of George Herbert and Dante; the sermons of Wesley, Spurgeon, and Newman; the theological brilliance of Barth and von Balthasar; the masterful biblical scholarship of Joseph Fitzmyer and N. T. Wright; the philosophical genius of Thomas Aquinas, Thomas Reid, Alvin Plantinga, and Richard Swinburne; the missionary zeal of Francis Xavier and Amy Carmichael; the social reforming passion of William Wilberforce and Dorothy Day; the fiction of Flannery O'Connor and Marilynne Robinson; the piety of Thomas à Kempis, Catherine of Genoa, Oswald Chambers, and Dallas Willard. None of these are gifts to be hoarded as the exclusive property of any particular Christian tradition.

It surely is appropriate to take pride in the great exemplars of one's tradition even while recognizing that they were partisans of particular traditions and would defend their distinctive theological convictions. One need not agree with any of these persons on all points, even important points, in order to embrace them wholeheartedly as fellow believers in Christ and to have an open heart and mind to receive what they have to teach us about loving and following Christ more faithfully.

Fourth, think carefully about the implications for the Christian community that nurtured you before you join any church that would not recognize your current siblings in the faith as full members of the one true church. Peter J. Leithart pointedly raises the inescapable questions that need to be answered by prospective converts to Rome:

> Are you willing to start eating at a eucharistic table where your Protestant friends are no longer welcome? How is that different from Peter's withdrawal from table fellowship with gentiles? Are you willing to say that every faithful Protestant or Pentecostal saint you have known is living a sub-Christian existence because they are not in churches that claim apostolic succession, no matter that they live lives fruitful in faith, hope, and love? . . . To become Catholic, I would have to begin regarding my Protestant brothers as ambiguously situated "separated" brothers rather than full brothers in the divine Brother, Jesus. Why should I distance myself from other Christians like that? . . . To become Catholic I would have to *contract* my ecclesial world. The communion I acknowledge would become smaller, less universal. I would have to become *less* catholic—*less catholic than Jesus.*[48]

---

48. Leithart, *End of Protestantism*, 170–71 (emphasis original).

In the same vein, consider Steve Long's account of why he has not converted to Rome:

> The main reason I am not (yet) Catholic and remain a Methodist and an ordained Methodist elder is that I do not know how to become Catholic without betraying the people who taught me to love God, pray, worship, desire the Eucharist, take delight in scripture, and so on. How can I leave the people I love?
>
> I remember my pastor, Lloyd Willert, who tended to me when I had major surgery at the age of 19 and was in a body cast for three months. He visited me and prayed with me. When I went to seminary, his wife gave me books from his library. I still cherish them.
>
> Then there was Cleveland Tennyson, a self-educated African-Caribbean Methodist preacher whom I worked with in Honduras for a year. His sermons brought me into the presence of God in such a way that I felt you had to take off your shoes when he preached because you were standing on holy ground.[49]

Many evangelicals who "convert" to Rome no doubt have their own stories of those who first taught them to believe in Christ, encouraged them, nurtured them, and loved them. It is no small matter to join a church that considers those persons "separated brethren" who are not in communion with the one true church. So converting to Rome means breaking communion with those nurturing persons. While unity of a certain kind is achieved with Christians of one's new ecclesial home, spiritually significant bonds of unity are simultaneously broken with others.

Long describes such a move as "betraying" his personal mentors in the faith. That is a strong word, but perhaps it accurately conveys some of the real dynamics in these situations. Of course, potential converts may simply be convinced that the claims of Rome are true and they have no choice but to convert. We suggest that the negative implication entailed for the prospective convert's relationship to Protestant and evangelical brothers and sisters is a good reason to reconsider whether the exclusive claims of Roman ecclesiology are really true.

The larger point here is not simply about personal relationships or even about respected and admired mentors in the faith, important as these are. The larger point is about the fact that these persons are lovers of God who have been powerfully used by him as a means of grace to bring us to a saving relationship with Christ. And yet as Rome sees it, they remain separated from full membership in the body of Christ. Think of the many great Protestant evangelists and apologists whose passionate witness has won countless

---

49. Long, "My Church Loyalties."

persons to Christ and has taught them to follow him and to seek holiness: George Whitefield, John Wesley, Phoebe Palmer, Charles Spurgeon, William and Katherine Booth, C. S. Lewis, Billy Graham, William Lane Craig, and Ravi Zacharias. If we think such persons should be recognized as full members of the body of Christ and welcomed with open arms to the family table, we have reason to resist Roman fever and to embrace a larger vision of Christian unity and the church catholic.

15

Mary

Why She Matters

Tourists who visit the National Gallery of Art in Washington, DC, encounter an array of paintings, mostly from the fourteenth century forward, that celebrate the Madonna and Child. As visitors amble from room to room, they will be delighted by Giotto's *Madonna and Child*, hailing from the early fourteenth century, and by Albrecht Dürer's composition with the same title produced in the latter part of the fifteenth century. They will be thoroughly enchanted by Raphael's *The Niccolini-Cowper Madonna*, painted in the early sixteenth century right before the dawn of the Reformation. If these art lovers meander to other rooms and later centuries, in this particular gallery or elsewhere—the Metropolitan Museum of Art in New York readily comes to mind—they will quickly realize that the face of the Madonna, along with that of Jesus, has for the most part disappeared.

Despite these artistic trends, Mary the mother of Jesus remains even today a figure of ongoing interest, especially as a model for women around the world. A decade before his death in 2006, Jaroslav Pelikan, the great church historian, estimated the significance of Mary for culture in the following observation: "Because Mary is *the* Woman par excellence for most of Western history, the subtleties and complexities in the interpretation of her person and work are at the same time central to the study of the place of women in history."[1] Indeed, as Pelikan observed, "The Virgin Mary has been more of an inspiration to more

1. Pelikan, *Mary through the Centuries* (New York: History Book Club, 1996), 219.

people than any other woman who ever lived."[2] Beyond this, the magisterium of the Roman Catholic Church weighs in on this topic in the *Catechism*: "At once virgin and mother, Mary is the symbol and the most perfect realization of the Church."[3] Not surprisingly, then, in 1987 the late Pope John Paul II in his encyclical *Redemptoris Mater* proclaimed 1987–88 to be a Marian Year, and the pontiff dedicated the world to the Blessed Mother. Such a proclamation, special in many respects, was only the second of its kind. Pope Pius XII had earlier declared that 1954 would be the first Marian Year.[4]

Though Mary continues to be honored by Roman Catholics and Eastern Orthodox, for reasons that will become clear as this chapter progresses, most Protestants have not taken up the devotion. And evangelicals, for their part, have been even more reluctant when it comes to Mary. "It is like Mary hardly matters," Christian Smith exclaims, "as if the verses were not in the Bible, as if Mary deserves no theological reflection."[5] Among the passages of the NT that concern Mary, in one way or the other, and which therefore give some substance to Smith's claim are the following: Matthew 1:18–25; 12:46–50; Mark 3:20–21; 6:3; Luke 1:26–38, 39–45, 46–56; 2:34–35, 48–51; 11:27–28; John 2:1–5; 19:25–27; Acts 1:13–14; and Galatians 4:4–5.

In fact, there is theologically weighty material about Mary not only in the pages of the NT but also in the Qur'an, the major scripture of Islam, especially in sura 19, which is titled Maryam, "the only surah to bear a woman's name."[6] Accordingly, the perspective of the early church was surely correct in its judgment that teaching about Mary in a real sense is a species of Christology. Therefore, to fail to get one's doctrine of Mary right is likewise to fail, in some sense, in terms of the doctrine of Jesus Christ. At least at this level of the argument, virtual silence about Mary hardly corresponds to a suitable Christology.

Though Smith has pointed out the consequence of this evangelical neglect of Mary, he has not laid out the processes of historical and theological reasoning, the various causes that have produced such a result. He has failed to take note that such inattention to Mary, found among many Protestants, actually emerged out of numerous concerns, many of which devolved upon a consideration of the significance of revelation against the backdrop of the

2. Ibid., 2.
3. *Catechism of the Catholic Church*, 2nd ed. (Mahwah, NJ: Paulist Press, 1994), par. 507.
4. See John A. Hammes, "The Patristic Praise of Mary," Eternal Word Television Network, accessed December 28, 2016, https://www.ewtn.com/library/ANSWERS/FR90203.HTM; first published in *Faith & Reason*, Summer 1990.
5. Smith, *How to Go from Being a Good Evangelical to a Committed Catholic in Ninety-Five Difficult Steps* (Eugene, OR: Cascade, 2011), 48.
6. Pelikan, *Mary through the Centuries*, 68–69.

proper place for Scripture and tradition. As Pelikan himself has pointed out, "The contrast between the biblical evidence and the traditional material [in this area] is so striking that it has become a significant issue in the ecumenical encounter between denominations."[7]

This considerable difference in perspective can be seen in terms of how the Protestant and the Roman Catholic traditions approach the Ave Maria even today. Coming into popular usage in the twelfth century,[8] this prayer, otherwise known as the "Hail Mary," was eventually neglected by Protestants when they became increasingly cognizant of what sacred tradition, at the hands of Rome, had done to Mary herself, and as a consequence to Christ as well. Indeed, the transformation of Mary from a first-century figure, steeped in humility, to what sacred tradition ultimately made of her, often at the hands of male virginal monks (Jerome and Bernard of Clairvaux readily come to mind), provided the wherewithal, the theological substance, that admittedly resulted in an overreaction by Protestants. The important point is that such reactions clearly had prior, precipitating causes. Therefore, we will explore such causes in this present chapter in terms of the Marian doctrines of the Bearer of God (θεοτόκος, *theotokos*) and of perpetual virginity. In chapter 16 we will take up a discussion of the doctrines of the immaculate conception and assumption. Along the way, we will attempt to offer a more balanced reading of Mary, one that is both theologically sound and historically accurate and that therefore rejects any possible future proclamation of Mary as co-redemptrix. Such an approach, then, should serve as a suitable corrective to both Protestant neglect and Roman Catholic excess.

Mary as the New or Second Eve

Remarkably enough, the earliest known reference to Mary is found not in the Gospels but in the writings of Paul. In his Letter to the Galatians, for example, the apostle observes: "But when the set time had fully come, God sent his Son, born of a woman, born under the law, to redeem those under the law, that we might receive adoption to sonship" (4:4–5). Among other things, this pithy verse underscores the doctrine of the incarnation, that Christ, contrary to what

7. Ibid., 8. Continuing in this line of thought, Pelikan states: "In a striking way, therefore, the *Ave Maria* epitomized not only the irony of Mary's having become a major point of division among believers and between churches but the dichotomy between the sole authority of Scripture and the development of doctrine through tradition" (ibid., 14).

8. Everett Ferguson, *Church History*, vol. 1, *From Christ to Pre-Reformation: The Rise and Growth of the Church in Its Cultural, Intellectual, and Political Context* (Grand Rapids: Zondervan, 2009), Kindle edition, locations 8925–26.

the gnostics would claim, was truly human, "born of a woman." This very first reference, then, clearly shows the vital connection between appropriate teaching about Mary and correct doctrine about Jesus Christ.

In the following century, Irenaeus found a place for Mary as the new Eve in his theology of recapitulation, in which Christ was principally presented as the new Adam (Rom. 5:12–20), who redid human history but this time in a salvific way. In such a schema Christ undid the work of Adam; Mary, for her part, undid the work of Eve. Irenaeus explains this in a passage worth quoting in full: "Wherefore also Luke, commencing the genealogy with the Lord, carried it back to Adam, indicating that it was He who regenerated them into the Gospel of life, and not they Him. And thus also it was that the knot of Eve's disobedience was loosed by the obedience of Mary. For what the virgin Eve had bound fast through unbelief, this did the virgin Mary set free through faith."[9] Not content with this role attributed to Mary, Irenaeus enhanced it in order to view her as the very cause of redemption: "Mary, having a man betrothed [to her], and being nevertheless a virgin, by yielding obedience, became the cause of salvation, both to herself and the whole human race."[10] Or, as the *Catechism* put it succinctly much later: "Death through Eve, life through Mary."[11]

Once this typology of Mary as the new Eve emerged in the second century, it became increasingly popular. For one thing, because the "Latin name *Eva* spelled backwards became *Ave*, the greeting of the angel to Mary in the Vulgate,"[12] such a linguistic happenstance filled the popular imagination, especially during the later Middle Ages, such that the very title "Ave Maria" was now invested with mystical[13] and even paradigmatic significance well beyond any meanings that could possibly be culled from Scripture. The basic problem with the Eve → Mary relation that Irenaeus postulated is that if this typology were pressed too far (as it eventually was), it would reveal itself as inherently and theologically unstable. For one thing, the Eve → Mary relation was eventually associated, in a parallel fashion, with that of Adam → Christ, the latter one worked out by the apostle Paul himself in Romans 5. To illustrate, a recent treatment of this very same association, found in a book with an imprimatur affixed by Rome, reveals part of the ongoing problem in the by-now-enlarged claim: "Adam-Eve is *the first couple*, the evil-bearing couple who brought about the ruin of the entire human race through the joint fall

9. Irenaeus of Lyons, *Against Heresies* 22.4, in *The Apostolic Fathers with Justin Martyr and Irenaeus*, ANF 1:455.

10. Ibid.

11. *Catechism*, par. 494.

12. Pelikan, *Mary through the Centuries*, 44.

13. Ibid.

of Adam, 'sinner,' and Eve, 'co-sinner'; instead, Christ-Mary is *the second couple*, the couple bearing the blessing of universal salvation."[14]

Admittedly this is a sensitive topic, but such conjectures, driven by the myth making of an eager religious sentiment, can do genuine harm to the grace, beauty, and unsurpassed excellence of Jesus Christ. First of all, for the sake of propriety, it must be recognized that Christ and Mary are *not* a couple in the same way that Adam and Eve were. Second, the relations of the two couples (Adam and Eve; Christ and Mary), if we restrict this comparison simply to soteriological considerations (having to do with salvation), do not fall neatly, as the typology would seem to suggest, along the lines of "sources of sin" and "sources of redemption." Indeed, configuring things in this way possibly confuses the human with the divine. That is, the salvific role that Christ plays in the face of Adam's sin cannot be matched or even approached in terms of Mary's role. Mary's lack of divinity, even if we do not consider yet the question of a sinful nature, disqualifies her at the outset from precisely the kind of saving role that only the God/Human can play. Mary is not the source or origin of redemption (the Father is, who sends the gift of the Son) but the chosen instrument through which the Redeemer comes by being born of a woman, an understanding that richly affirms the significance of the incarnation. Between the two couples there is a mixing of apples and oranges, as it were, especially if redemption is in view. Actually, there is only one who is divine among the "couples." Consequently, it is the typology itself, taking on a life of its own and not any perceived biblical affirmation, that accords Mary a far loftier role than she could have ever played in the economy of salvation.

And finally, this typology over time eventually generated even more new doctrine. With its tight polarity of "sources of sin" and "sources of redemption" in play, this literary construal implies that Mary, like Christ, her salvifically coupled partner, was without sin. Mary thus basked in the salvific aura of Christ and began to take on characteristics that properly belonged to him alone. Indeed, in the early twentieth century O. R. Vassall-Phillips contended that "the doctrine of the Immaculate Conception is the development or unfolding of the doctrine that Mary is the Second Eve, in which it lay hidden as a germ."[15] Theological paradigms, then, are both powerful and generative: they give birth to so much, whether appropriate or not, whether biblical or not.

---

14. Mark Miravalle, *Mariology: A Guide for Priests, Deacons, Seminarians, and Consecrated Persons* (2008; repr., Seattle: Amazon Digital Services, 2013), Kindle edition, locations 281–83 (emphasis added).

15. Vassall-Phillips, *The Mother of Christ; or, The Blessed Virgin Mary in Catholic Tradition, Theology, and Devotion* (London: Burns, Oates & Washbourne, 1920), Kindle edition, locations 6032–35.

Theotokos (The Bearer of God)

The language that would eventually be ascribed to Mary, and that proved to be so fruitful for the generation of subsequent titles and even novel honors, was the Greek word θεοτόκος (*theotokos*), which is best translated in English by the phrase "Bearer of God." John Henry Cardinal Newman during the nineteenth century contended that the title *theotokos* (its English transliteration) was "familiar to Christians from primitive times, and had been used, among other writers, by Origen."[16] Other, more contemporary scholars, however, clearly disagree: "There is no altogether incontestable evidence that it [*theotokos*] was used before the fourth century."[17] Our own research reveals that it is inordinately difficult to make the case for this terminology specifically in the writings of Origen. However, a small piece of papyrus was discovered in a trash heap in Oxyrhynchus, Egypt, during the nineteenth century that uses the language of *theotokos* in a prayer.[18] The John Rylands Library in Manchester, England, estimates the date of this fragment at around 250, though other scholars disagree.[19] For one thing, this dump was in continual use for centuries, making dating of its shifting contents that much more difficult. At any rate, a middle-of-the-third-century use of the language of *theotokos* may be a possibility, if not in the writings of Origen, then at least in this fragment.

From our perspective, a far more interesting transition, taken up by later church fathers, has to do with the shift from *theotokos*, understood as the "Bearer of God," to the celebrated language of the "Mother of God." The terminology is not the same. The Egyptian fragment found at Oxyrhynchus, just considered, employs the Greek term θεοτόκε (*theotoke*) with reference to Mary. This word, however, is rendered as *Genetrix* (and not *Mater*, "mother") in the Latin translation, once again suggesting the idea of "Bearer of God" rather than "Mother of God."[20] Indeed, the specific use of the latter title, "Mother of God," represents a world of theological difference, and it would prove to be troubling for some in the early fifth-century church since, among other things, it evidenced a shift of attention *from* Christ *to* Mary.

16. Newman, *An Essay on the Development of Christian Doctrine* (Westminster, MA: Christian Classics, 1968), 145.

17. Pelikan, *Mary through the Centuries*, 57.

18. Untitled comments below a photograph of Papyrus John Rylands 470, *Ancient Peoples* (blog), November 5, 2012, http://ancientpeoples.tumblr.com/post/35057679168/papyrus-john -rylands-470-is-a-small-fragment-of.

19. Ben Witherington III, New Testament scholar, argues that the date is actually difficult to establish given the nature of the source of the fragment.

20. Untitled comments below a photograph of Papyrus John Rylands 470, *Ancient Peoples* (blog), November 5, 2012, http://ancientpeoples.tumblr.com/post/35057679168/papyrus-john -rylands-470-is-a-small-fragment-of.

At any rate, clear, unequivocal evidence of the use of the specific language of the "Mother of God" (in other words, evidence that this is the sense of the word *theotokos* in play) can be found in the writings of Alexander of Alexandria, who penned an encyclical in 319 as he combatted the Arian heresy.[21] Later Eusebius of Caesarea stated in his *Oration of the Emperor Constantine*, "Conception was there, yet apart from marriage: childbirth, yet pure virginity: and a maiden became the mother of God!"[22] In this same century Athanasius observed that "as the flesh was born of Mary, the Mother of God, so we say that he, the Word, was himself born of Mary."[23] Other evidence for the specific and uncontested use of this phraseology can be found in the writings of Gregory of Nyssa, Gregory of Nazianzus, and Ambrose of Milan, among others.

The specific language of *theotokos* in a real sense did not come into its own in a very large way until the fifth century, during the great christological controversy that surrounded the teaching of Nestorius, bishop of Constantinople. Studying in the Antiochian school of interpretation, Nestorius had been exposed to the teachings of Theodore of Mopsuestia, who was one of the first theologians to take issue with the title "Mother of God," as applied to Mary of Nazareth.[24] Theodore maintained that such language was theologically improper: "Mary bare Jesus, not the Word, for the Word was and remained omnipresent. . . . Thus Mary is properly the Mother of Christ (*Christotocos*) but not the mother of God (*Theotocos*)."[25] Again, "It is madness to say that God is born of the Virgin. . . . Not God, but the temple in which God dwelt, is born of Mary."[26] Mindful of his earlier instruction in the Antiochian school, Nestorius took up the language of *Christotocos* and thereby denied that Mary was properly referred to as the "Mother of God."[27] Nestorius believed that

---

21. Ibid.

22. Eusebius of Caesarea, *Oration of the Emperor Constantine* 11, in *Eusebius: Church History, Life of Constantine the Great, and Oration in Praise of Constantine*, trans. Ernest Cushing Richardson, NPNF[2] 1:569.

23. Henry R. Percival, "Excursus on the Word Θεοτόκος," in *Seven Ecumenical Councils*, NPNF[2] 14:208.

24. Ibid.

25. Ibid.

26. Ibid.

27. Though they had differed sharply in the past over christological issues, the Roman Catholic Church and the Armenian Apostolic Church signed a "Common Declaration" during the mid-1990s under the leadership of Pope John Paul II and Catholicos Karekin I: "Pope John Paul II and Catholicos Karekin I give their blessing and pastoral support to the further development of existing contacts and to new manifestations of that dialogue of charity between their respective pastors and faithful which will bear fruit in the fields of common action on the pastoral, catechetical, social and intellectual levels." See "Common Declaration of John Paul II and Catholicos Karekin I," the

God, the eternal and most glorious, the one who cannot not be, can simply have no mother, period. To think otherwise is to confuse very badly the temporal and the eternal, the finite and the infinite. So then, according to both Theodore of Mopsuestia and Nestorius, what the Alexandrian theologians were arguing with their use of the language of *theotokos*, especially in the writings of Cyril of Alexandria, for instance, was simply wrong.

Something of the strength and energy of the condemnation of this heresy at the Council of Ephesus in 431 can be seen in the forceful language of Cyril of Alexandria's denunciation of the teachings of Nestorius: "If anyone will not confess that the Emmanuel is very God, and that therefore the Holy Virgin is the Mother of God (Θεοτόκος), inasmuch as in the flesh she bore the Word of God made flesh [as it is written, 'The Word was made flesh']: let him be anathema."[28] After this judgment, however, the Nestorians did not simply go away, so this controversy not only resulted in the condemnation of heterodoxy but also issued in schism. In fact, Nestorianism continues even today in the form of the Assyrian Orthodox Church.

To appreciate more fully the orthodox condemnation of the Nestorian heresy at the Council of Ephesus—which was reaffirmed, by the way, at the Council of Chalcedon in 451—it is best to consider this whole matter as a problem not in Mariology but in Christology. Thus, in denying that Mary was the Mother of God and affirming that she could therefore only be the mother of Christ, for instance, Nestorius in effect postulated a sharp division between the natures of Christ, the divine and the human, such that Mary could be the mother of one but not of the other. Such a view, in its consequences, detracted from the very unity of the person of Christ. Indeed, if Christ is, as the orthodox formula has it, "one person with two natures," then these natures cannot be sharply separated such that Mary could be rightly called the bearer of one but not the other. That is, the very unity of Christ's personhood requires both Marian affirmations.

A Mariological Morph

But then a remarkable thing happened with the passage of time, the stuff of which church history is made. What had in reality and originally been a christological affirmation in the fifth century soon receded, and it began to

---

Holy See, December 13, 1996, http://www.vatican.va/roman_curia/pontifical_councils/chrstuni /anc-orient-ch-docs/rc_pc_christuni_doc_19961213_jp-ii-karekin-i_en.html.

28. Cyril of Alexandria, "The XII Anathematisms of St. Cyril against Nestorius," in *Seven Ecumenical Councils*, NPNF[2] 14:206 (bracketed text in original).

slowly morph into a Mariological one, front and center. The primary and secondary foci of attention in the historic doctrinal dispute changed roles. By the Middle Ages, as in the twelfth century,[29] the term *theotokos* was viewed principally as depicting a teaching about Mary, not about Christ. Its earlier historical and theological context was for the most part replaced by new burgeoning interests, many of them surrounding Mary. J. B. Mozley, in his very able response to Newman, chronicles the subtle, and at times not so subtle, shift with respect to the subsequent use of the word *theotokos*, showing the cardinal himself to be guilty of this:

> The Council [of Ephesus] had not the rank of the Virgin Mary, but the truth of the Incarnation as its object. . . .
>
> Between being used for one purpose, and being used for another, there is unquestionably a difference. . . .
>
> The whole statement of the case [by Newman] is moulded with the same view; in order to produce . . . a general impression different from what the facts of the case themselves give, an impression of the Virgin's personal rank as the primary subject of, her personal elevation as the crowning work of, the Ephesian Council.[30]

In other words, Roman Catholics have sometimes worked toward a sort of Copernican revolution that in effect makes Mary the central point of the *theotokos* doctrine instead of Christ.

There are four elements to the elevation of Mary's status in this early setting, and Rome itself clearly recognizes all of them. To illustrate, the *Catechism* states: "Called in the Gospels '*the mother of Jesus*,' Mary is acclaimed by Elizabeth, at the prompting of the Spirit and even before the birth of her son, as '*the mother of my Lord*.' . . . The Church confesses that Mary is truly '*Mother of God*' (Theotokos)."[31] However, the fourth element of this process is not so readily discerned. It only appears, as Mozley has pointed out, when the third element, the orthodox term *theotokos* (as well as the phrase "The Mother of God"), becomes untethered from its specific historical and theological context and thereby takes on decisively new meanings. This problem is compounded by some interpreters simply because the very same language

29. During the twelfth century, Mary's status as *theotokos* added strength to the idea that she was conceived without sin; it was then that her strong association with divinity came to have the cash value of quite practical moral and spiritual consequences. See Ferguson, *Church History*, Kindle ed., locations 8930–32.

30. Mozley, *The Theory of Development: A Criticism of Dr. Newman's Essay on the Development of Christian Doctrine* (New York: E. P. Dutton, 1879), 63–65.

31. *Catechism*, par. 495 (emphasis added).

can be used in remarkably different ways. Thus the medieval estimations of Mary, especially in the Latin church and precisely because they were connected to the term *theotokos* in devotional practices and popular religious life, often basked in the authority and legitimacy of the Council of Ephesus itself.[32]

In time Mary was even referred to as "the Queen of Heaven,"[33] her celestial enthronement virtually guaranteed by the theological momentum that Marian doctrines were gaining. Thus Vatican II, without any biblical warrant and instead drawing from the fecundity of what it has called Holy Tradition (although Protestants see this as tradition's ongoing generative power, at least in this particular instance), has declared that Mary is "exalted above all angels and men to a place second only to her Son, as the most holy mother of God. . . . She is rightly honored by a special cult in the Church."[34] Therefore, in terms of one of those seats that the disciples James and John had coveted, one to the right of Jesus in glory and the other to the left, and even though Jesus himself clearly stated that it was not within his authority to grant, nevertheless the Roman magisterium has apparently rushed in, emboldened by the weight of tradition, and has declared that the seat on the right, the one principal in importance, second in command, belongs to Mary alone.

Beyond this, Mary's regal status has been displayed graphically in a painting that hails from the fourteenth century, *The Coronation of the Virgin Mary in Heaven*, by Giacomo di Mino. The Marian cult was expanded even further during the sixteenth century, and Mary's regency, her rule and governance, now included as subjects patriarchs, prophets, apostles, martyrs, confessors, virgins, and all saints, as in the Litany of Loreto approved by Pope Sixtus V in 1587.[35] More recently, in October 1954, Pope Pius XII reaffirmed Mary's celestial crowning in his encyclical *Ad Caeli Reginam*. In this letter, the pope took up the by-now-common Roman practice of anachronism in his very opening words: "From *the earliest ages* of the catholic church a Christian people

---

32. Tempers were flaring at this ecumenical council, and Nestorius was condemned as a "blasphemer." Philip Schaff, e.g., writes: "The council of Ephesus, in the sentence of deposition against Nestorius, uses the formula: 'The Lord Jesus Christ, whom he has blasphemed, determines through this most holy council.'" See Schaff, *History of the Christian Church—from the 1st to the 19th Century* (n.p.: Delmarva Publications, 2014), Kindle edition, locations 38180–81.

33. The pagan use of this term can be seen in Jer. 7:18; 44:17–19, 25.

34. Pope Paul VI, *Lumen Gentium: Dogmatic Constitution on the Church*, sec. 66, in *The Conciliar and Post Conciliar Documents*, vol. 1 of *Vatican II*, ed. Austin Flannery (Vatican City: Libreria Editrice Vaticana, 2011), 421; see also the Holy See, http://www.vatican.va/archive /hist_councils/ii_vatican_council/documents/vat-ii_const_19641121_lumen-gentium_en.html.

35. "The Litany of the Blessed Virgin Mary," *Our Catholic Prayers*, accessed December 28, 2016, http://www.ourcatholicprayers.com/litany-of-the-blessed-virgin-mary.html.

. . . has addressed prayers of petition and hymns of praise and veneration to the *Queen of Heaven.*"[36]

Mary as Virgin

The title of this section is "Mary as Virgin" instead of "The Virgin Birth of Christ" simply because the issue of the virginity of Mary in Roman Catholic doctrine embraces far more than the basic, scriptural affirmation that it was a virgin who conceived Jesus of Nazareth. To be sure, the significance of Mary's virginity is often expressed by means of three Latin distinctions: (1) *ante partum*, that it was a virgin who conceived and was pregnant with Jesus; (2) *in partu*, that Mary throughout the bearing of the child and the birthing process itself remained a virgin; and (3) *postpartum*, that Mary continued in her virginal state even after the birth of Jesus, throughout her entire life. We will explore each of these forms of virginity in turn.

Ante Partum: Consensual Virginal Orthodoxy

All orthodox Christians (Roman Catholics, Eastern Orthodox, and Protestants) affirm the clear biblical declaration—as recorded in the Gospel of Matthew, for example—that Mary's pregnancy was "from the Holy Spirit" (Matt. 1:20). This salient truth of the Christian faith, associated with the incarnation of Christ, was naturally declared repeatedly in the early church. Ignatius of Antioch, for instance, wrote in his letter *To the Smyrnaeans* that Christ "was truly of the seed of David according to the flesh, and the Son of God according to the will and power of God; that He was truly born of a virgin."[37]

More recently the *Catechism* has observed that "the Fathers see in the virginal conception the sign that it truly was the Son of God who came in a humanity like our own."[38] Such a statement suggests a consideration of both the divine and the human elements in the conception of Jesus Christ. That it was in fact "the Son of God" who was born of Mary can be affirmed, on the one hand, by pointing to the virginity of Mary itself, as the church fathers and Rome do here, or it can also be declared, on the other hand, by referring

36. Pope Pius XII, *Ad Caeli Reginam*, prologue, the Holy See, 1954, http://w2.vatican.va/content/pius-xii/en/encyclicals/documents/hf_p-xii_enc_11101954_ad-caeli-reginam.html (emphasis added).

37. Ignatius of Antioch, *To the Smyrnaeans*, in *The Apostolic Fathers with Justin Martyr and Irenaeus*, ANF 1:86.

38. *Catechism*, par. 496.

to the action of God, as reflected in Luke 1:35: "The Holy Spirit will come on you, and the power of the Most High will overshadow you. So the holy one to be born will be called the Son of God." Thus, just as in terms of the doctrine of Mary as *theotokos*, the divine and human frameworks have to be considered, both a Mariological and a christological one, so too, though not quite in exactly the same way, divine and human frameworks are necessary in order to understand the full significance of the virgin birth *ante partum*. That Jesus of Nazareth was born of Mary as nothing less than the Son of God can be avowed by pointing to the virginity of Mary, its truly miraculous nature, or by underscoring the statement "The power of the Most High will overshadow you" (Luke 1:35), as just noted. As was the case with respect to the doctrine of *theotokos*, both lenses are required for a proper assessment to emerge, and care therefore must be taken in terms of how each is emphasized.

During the fourth century an important shift on this topic took place in the theology of Ambrose of Milan. At his hands, the virginity of Mary was now pressed to guarantee that Christ was without sin. Identifying the transmission of original sin with human copulation (a notion to be taken up by Augustine as well), Ambrose taught that Mary's virginity, at least in some respect, guaranteed the sinlessness of Christ.[39] So in this configuration, virginity and holiness were so strongly associated that in order for the affirmation that Jesus was free from sin to be credible, it was thought that "Christ had to be free from the normal mode of conception."[40] Such judgments—further developed in the writings of Jerome, in his *Against Jovinianus*,[41] for example—celebrated virginity to such an extent, and linked sin in some sense with human sexuality, that other theologians of the same period, such as Augustine, felt compelled to reaffirm the very goodness of marriage,[42] lest the faithful think otherwise. In his own day, John Calvin refuted the idea that the holiness of Christ was grounded in the virginity of Mary by giving the divine agency its proper role in any assessment: "We do not hold Christ to be free from all taint, merely because he was born of a woman unconnected with a man, but because he was sanctified by the Spirit."[43] Traces of a similar association of holiness and virginity set in contrast to sin and the lack of virginity can be seen in Rome's recent affirmation: "Mary is a virgin because her virginity is the sign of her

39. Pelikan, *Mary through the Centuries*, 119–20.

40. Ibid., 190.

41. Jerome, *Against Jovinianus*, in *St. Jerome: Letters and Select Works*, trans. W. H. Fremantle, G. Lewis, and W. G. Martley, NPNF² 6:346–416.

42. Augustine of Hippo, "On the Good of Marriage," in *St. Augustin: "On the Holy Trinity," Doctrinal Treatises, Moral Treatises*, trans. C. L. Cornish, NPNF¹ 3:397–413.

43. John Calvin, *Institutes of the Christian Religion*, trans. Henry Beveridge (Edinburgh: Calvin Translation Society, 1845), 2.13.4 (2:20).

faith 'unadulterated by any doubt.'"[44] One of the results of this particular teaching is that married, conjugal life, with its obvious lack of virginity, implies at least doubt and perhaps even sin. Once again the wrong things are being associated here.

In Partu: Stretching the Truth to Make Mary the Star

Current Roman Catholic teaching affirms, in the words of the *Catechism*, that Mary "remained a virgin in conceiving her Son, a virgin in giving birth to him, a virgin in carrying him, a virgin in nursing him at her breast, always a virgin."[45] Our present concern, as we consider Mary's virginity *in partu*, is the specific declaration that the mother of Jesus remained a virgin in giving birth to him. What this teaching means, then, is that Mary did not give birth to her son in the normal way, through the usual biological process of the passage of the baby through the birth canal and on through the vagina, a process that would naturally disrupt the "intact" nature of any virgin (even if she had conceived miraculously) by breaking the hymen. All these normal biological processes are denied in the *in partu* postulation. In other words, not only did Mary miraculously conceive as a virgin but she also carried her child and gave birth to him in a supernatural way, in a way unlike all other women. In the mid-twentieth century Alois Müller, a Mariologist, took this a step further and thereby removed Mary from the normal birthing experience of most mothers once more by denying that she suffered any birth pangs at all during her delivery. The thinking here was that such pain could only be seen as a consequence of sin (Gen. 3:16).[46]

The historical source of such a surprising doctrine supposedly goes all the way back to the middle or latter part of the second century, in which the *Protevangelium of James*, which was later rejected by scholars as a forgery, "launched the intact hymen on its career through Mariology."[47] Although early in the third century Tertullian specifically repudiated the idea of virginity *in partu*,[48] in the fifth century this did not stop Pope Leo the Great from energetically endorsing it. He exclaimed: "For although the LORD's nativity

---

44. *Catechism*, par. 506.

45. Ibid., par. 510.

46. Uta Ranke-Heinemann, *Eunuchs for the Kingdom of Heaven: Women, Sexuality, and the Catholic Church* (New York: Doubleday, 1990), 342. We ultimately repudiate the Marian views of Uta Ranke-Heinemann since she also denies the truth of virginity *ante partum*. See also Müller, *Ecclesia Maria: Die Einheit Marias und der Kirche* (Freiburg: Schweiz Universitatsverlag Freiburg, 1955).

47. Ranke-Heinemann, *Eunuchs for the Kingdom of Heaven*, 343.

48. Tim Perry, *The Blessed Virgin Mary* (Grand Rapids: Eerdmans, 2013), 23.

according to the flesh has certain characteristics wherein it transcends the ordinary beginnings of man's being, both because He alone was conceived and born without concupiscence of a pure Virgin, and because He was so brought forth of His mother's womb *that her fecundity bare Him without loss of virginity*: yet His flesh was not of another nature to ours."[49]

In the twelfth century Bernard of Clairvaux continued the thought of Leo in a newfangled way by strongly associating it with the whole Stella Maris myth, which goes back at least to the ninth century in the writings of Paschasius Radbertus.[50] However, both Bernard and Paschasius before him may have confused the etymology and the meaning of the word Mary and its reputed Hebrew antecedent in the form of Miryam, all of which were supposed to justify the claim that Mary is the lodestar of the Christian life, the Star of the Sea, *Stella Maris*. At any rate, Bernard's observations usher in some important new doctrinal developments, especially in terms of the manner in which he affirms the virginity of Mary *in partu*: "Let me speak a few words upon this Name, which, being interpreted, means Star of the Sea, and marvelously fits the Maiden-Mother. For most fitly may she be likened unto a star. A star sends forth its ray without any harm to itself; and *the Virgin brought forth her Son without any hurt to her virginity*. Neither does the ray lessen the brightness of the stars, nor does her Son lessen the inviolateness of the Virgin."[51] Notice in this teaching the subtle shift of framework (which we have been detecting elsewhere) that occurs at the hands of the devotional interest of Bernard. In his affirmation of virginity in the sense of *in partu*, Bernard quite literally makes Mary "the star," whereas the Son of God is relegated simply to being a ray. Again we see a sort of Copernican revolution that puts Mary at the center. Here as elsewhere, what's preeminently important for Bernard, given his celebration of virginity, as a reflection of his own course of life, is that Mary remain intact.

Though later Pope Pius XII quoted this exact same language of Bernard in his own writings, in his encyclical *Doctor Mellifluus*, promulgated in 1953,[52]

---

49. Pope Leo the Great, "Letters," in *Leo the Great, Gregory the Great*, trans. Charles Lett Feltoe, NPNF² 12a:49 (emphasis added).

50. Paschasius Radbertus writes: "We capsize amid the storm-tossed waves of the sea" without Mary's guidance as Stella Maris. See "Star of the Sea," University of Dayton: International Marian Research Institute, accessed December 15, 2016, https://udayton.edu/imri/mary/s/star-of-the-sea.php.

51. Bernard of Clairvaux, "Second Homily on Luke," in *Carmina Mariana: An English Anthology in Verse*, ed. Orby Shipley (London: Burns & Oates, 1902), iii, quoted in O. R. Vassall-Phillips, *Mother of Christ*, Kindle ed., locations 372–75 (emphasis added).

52. Pope Pius XII, *Doctor Mellifluus*, par. 31, the Holy See, 1953, http://w2.vatican.va/content/pius-xii/en/encyclicals/documents/hf_p-xii_enc_24051953_doctor-mellifluus.html.

and though Pope John Paul II employed the vocabulary of being "intact" in his own encyclical *Redemptoris Mater* in 1987,[53] this issue is by no means simply a Roman Catholic matter; it is also a Protestant one. In fact, Luther observed in his own writings, "That did not happen with this mother, for she remained a virgin during the birth and after the birth, just as she was before the conception and the birth."[54] Later on *The Formula of Concord*, which was completed in 1577 (and has served as the theological expression of the Lutheran Reformation), affirmed in a similar fashion that Mary was a virgin in the sense of *in partu*: "He demonstrated his divine majesty even in his mother's womb in that he was born of a virgin without violating her virginity."[55]

Postpartum: The Perfect Sexless Marriage?

That Mary remained a virgin even after Christ was born—that she never had sexual relations with her husband, Joseph—is taught in the *Catechism* (as well as in Vatican II documents, as in *Lumen Gentium*, sec. 52) in its declaration that "the liturgy of the [Roman Catholic] Church celebrates Mary as *Aeiparthenos*, the 'Ever-virgin.'"[56] Such a teaching would have been foreign to the ears of the first-century church and is nowhere found in the pages of the NT. It makes its earliest appearance in that forgery noted earlier, the *Protevangelium of James*, which falsely purported to have been drafted by no one less than James of Jerusalem. Judging from the content of this mid-second-century, counterfeit document, we must conclude that it was likely written by an extreme ascetic, one who viewed human sexuality as distasteful at best and perhaps a necessary evil at worst.[57] It is therefore hardly a resource for any suitable and balanced theological reflection, much less one about the *theotokos*.

Beyond this, Mary as a virgin in the sense of postpartum, that is, as ever virgin, was taught much later, in the writings of Athanasius, Cassian, and Leo the Great, and it was enthusiastically championed by Pope Martin I at the

53. John Paul II observes: "If through faith Mary became the bearer of the Son given to her by the Father through the power of the Holy Spirit, while preserving her virginity intact . . ." *Redemptoris Mater: On the Blessed Virgin Mary in the Life of the Pilgrim Church*, sec. 20, the Holy See, http://w2.vatican.va/content/john-paul-ii/en/encyclicals/documents/hf_jp-ii_enc_25 031987_redemptoris-mater.html.

54. Martin Luther, "The Second Sermon: For the Feast of the Presentation of Christ in the Temple; [On] the Gospel, Luke 2[:22–32]," in *Sermons V*, LW 58:433.

55. Theodore G. Tappert, ed., *The Book of Concord: The Confessions of the Evangelical Lutheran Church* (Philadelphia: Mühlenberg, 1959), 595.

56. *Catechism*, par. 499.

57. James Orr, ed., *The Protevangelium of James* (London: J. M. Dent, 1903).

First Lateran Council in 649.[58] However, the greatest defense of this doctrine emerged in the work of Jerome as he sought to refute the teachings of a certain Helvidius, who among other things dared to contend not only that Christ had flesh-and-blood brothers and sisters, as the NT teaches, but also—horror of all horrors—that virginity was ranked below marriage.[59] Jerome, being the good ascetic that he was (no doubt similar in sentiment, at least on this point, to the author of the *Protevangelium*) and a veritable champion of virginity, would have none of this. The Latin father's attempt at a refutation, then, can be expressed in three basic propositions:

1st. That Joseph was only putatively, not really, the husband of Mary.

2nd. That the "brethren" of the Lord were his cousins, not his own brethren.

3rd. That virginity is better than the married state.[60]

For better or for worse, the magisterium followed Jerome—who was later declared a doctor of the church—at every step along the way in his argument. Thus, in terms of the first proposition, the Roman Catholic Church contends even today, and despite significant exegetical evidence to the contrary, that Joseph was merely the legal husband of Mary and had never actually consummated the marriage.[61] Realizing the difficulty of such a teaching, especially for an understanding of marriage, Rome's theologians and canon lawyers got to work and in effect redefined marriage, retooled it to render it in harmony with just such a teaching. Indeed, Pelikan pointed out that these leaders defended the matrimony of Mary and Joseph as a true marriage, even though it had not been sexually consummated, on the basis of the putative principle that "it is consent, not sexual intercourse, that makes a marriage [*consensus, non concubitus, facit connubium*]."[62]

---

58. Roland H. Seboldt, *Christ or Mary: The Coredemption of Mary in Contemporary Roman Catholic Theology* (St. Louis: Concordia, 1963), 13.

59. Jerome, "The Perpetual Virginity of Blessed Mary, against Helvidius," in *St. Jerome: Letters and Select Works*, NPNF[2] 6:334–46.

60. Ibid.

61. According to Charles F. Pfeiffer and Everett Falconer Harrison, "One would naturally infer that the normal relationship of marriage would follow, unless one is committed to defend the perpetual virginity of Mary. Matthew betrays no such inclination." Pfeiffer and Harrison, eds., *The Wycliffe Bible Commentary: New Testament* (Chicago: Moody Press, 1962), Matt. 1:24–25. Moreover, Svendsen maintains, "The literary evidence suggests that the Greek speaker of Matthew's time would have understood the phrase ἕως οὗ [in v. 25] to imply cessation of the action of the main clause after the action of the subordinate clause." Eric D. Svendsen, *Who Is My Mother? The Role and Status of the Mother of Jesus in the New Testament and Roman Catholicism* (Amityville, NY: Calvary Press, 2001), 78.

62. Pelikan, *Mary through the Centuries*, 122.

Yet if simple consent makes a marriage, in an essential way, then perhaps many more people are married than even they themselves have imagined. Moreover, what is the effect of such a judgment on an understanding of the family itself? In contrast to this teaching, Scripture observes that Joseph did not know (in the biblical sense) Mary until she gave birth to a son: καὶ οὐκ ἐγίνωσκεν αὐτὴν ἕως οὗ ἔτεκεν υἱόν[63] (*kai ouk eginōsken autēn heōs hou eteken huion*; "But he did not consummate their marriage until she gave birth to a son"; Matt. 1:25a). The Greek text here is actually quite instructive and indicates not only that carnal knowledge is present, by the employment of the verb ἐγίνωσκεν (*eginōsken*) in this setting, but also that such knowledge did not take place *until*—the Greek word here is ἕως (*heōs*)—a specified period of time. Blaise Pascal expressed this truth succinctly in the seventeenth century: "The Gospel only speaks of the virginity of the Virgin up to the time of the birth of Jesus Christ. All with reference to Jesus Christ."[64] To claim, then, that Joseph never had normal sexual relations with his wife is unfounded. Other passages from the Bible that impugn the postpartum view are found in Matthew 1:18 and Luke 2:7, among several others.

Furthermore, an important window on just how Rome understands the relation between Scripture and tradition can be seen in how its biblical scholars interpret the following NT passage, found in Mark 6:3, which focuses on the salient issue of siblings: "Isn't this the carpenter? Isn't this Mary's son and the brother of James, Joseph, Judas and Simon? Aren't his sisters here with us?" Pre–Vatican II scholarship, for its part, hardly gives this passage a second look and simply declares that "the form of the expression in Greek, ὁ υἱὸς τῆς Μαρίας [*ho huios tēs Marias*; the son of Mary], indicates that Jesus was the *only* son of Mary."[65] However, recent scholarship is far more careful and is no doubt aware of the criticisms that some Protestant exegesis has raised. The current *Catholic Study Bible*, for example, observes that "in Semitic usage, the terms 'brother,' 'sister' are applied not only to children of the same parents, but to nephews, nieces, cousins, half-brothers, and half-sisters."[66] However, after this initial observation, the *Study Bible* itself raises the objection that "one cannot suppose that the meaning of a Greek word should be sought in the first place from Semitic usage." This work then concludes this discussion

63. Kurt Aland et al., eds., *The Greek New Testament*, 4th rev. ed. (interlinear with morphology) (Stuttgart: Deutsche Bibelgesellschaft, 1993), Matt. 1:25.

64. Blaise Pascal, *Pascal's Pensées* (New York: E. P. Dutton, 1958), 194–95, number 741.

65. J. A. O'Flynn, "The Gospel of Jesus Christ according to St Mark," in *A Catholic Commentary on Holy Scripture*, ed. Bernard Orchard and Edmund F. Sutcliffe (Toronto: Thomas Nelson, 1953), 915 (emphasis added).

66. Donald Senior, John J. Collins, and Mary Ann Getty, eds., *The Catholic Study Bible: The New American Bible*, rev. ed. (New York: Oxford University Press, 1990), 1410 (Mark 6:3).

in a remarkably forthright way: "The question of meaning here would not have arisen but for the faith of the church in Mary's perpetual virginity."[67]

Despite this helpful scholarship of late, the official documents of the Roman Catholic Church (e.g., Vatican II declarations and the *Catechism*) do not entertain any reading of Mark 6:3 other than that Mary was a perpetual virgin. Indeed, the *Catechism* contends that in reality the supposed brothers of Jesus "are the sons of another Mary, a disciple of Christ, whom St. Matthew significantly calls 'the other Mary.'"[68] The *Protevangelium of James* handled this matter somewhat differently, "presenting Joseph as a widower with children by an earlier marriage,"[69] though it ended up with the same result: Mary remained a virgin.

Virginity and Holiness: A Dubious Sexual Hierarchy

Current scholarship, both Roman Catholic and Protestant, may be in a much better place today to assess this ongoing issue in light of the biblical materials and against the larger backdrop question of the proper relation between Scripture and tradition. For one thing, current theologians, historians, and biblical scholars are far more aware of the power and influence of one's own social location in the interpretive process. Add to this the lingering effects of original sin, the ongoing self-curvature whereby we read ourselves and our own perspective into everything, and it is not surprising to learn that some of those most championing the doctrine of Mary's perpetual virginity were also eager champions of virginity as an entire course of life. Such religious leaders, in a way contrary to Scripture, painted Mary with the strokes of their own image, in terms of their own likes and dislikes, especially in terms of their broader asceticism.

Precisely because sin on some level had been associated with human sexuality in early medieval theology, this ascetic inheritance was passed on to later generations. Since Augustine taught that sin in the form of concupiscence infected nearly all sexual activity, Mary, of course, could not participate.[70] The consequence of this move, once again, was that virginity was strongly associated with holiness (though a virgin can be as rank a sinner as a nonvirgin),

67. Ibid.

68. *Catechism*, par. 500.

69. Ferguson, *Church History*, Kindle ed., locations 1207–9. The original text states: "And Joseph replied, saying, 'I have sons and am old, while she is young. I will not be ridiculed among the children of Israel.'" See https://www.asu.edu/courses/rel376/total-readings/james.pdf. See also Orr, *Protevangelium of James*, 295–96.

70. Thomas C. Fox, *Sexuality and Catholicism* (New York: George Braziller, 1995), 23.

such that it was best to renounce all sexual activity. With this linkage in place, Jerome and, later on, Bernard of Clairvaux likely reasoned in this way: since Mary, the *theotokos*, was holy in a preeminent way, she could not under any circumstances have engaged in sexual activity, with its concupiscence and lust, even after the birth of Jesus.

Moreover, when the writings of the early church fathers are read (influenced as they were by Hellenistic and even Stoic trends), along with some of the greatest spiritual classics of the Roman Catholic Church, the careful reader will eventually discern an emerging sexual hierarchy that is strongly associated with sanctity. In this problematic schema, the nearer one is to the state of virginity, the holier one supposedly is. In some respect sexual status results in a perceived soteriological status. However, sanctity does not necessarily flow along these lines. In any case, at the apex of this hierarchy of valuation, of course, is *virginity* as reflected in the writings of Jerome, for instance. But not everyone is a virgin. And so the next best thing is *celibacy*, the discipline taken up by those who, though they cherish virginity, may have nevertheless lost their own. Next in line is *continent marriage* (the forswearing of normal sexual relations with one's spouse), an ascetic move that Catherine of Genoa, for example, eventually made during the course of her own marriage. After this, if this last counsel is yet too severe and unwanted (against which even the apostle Paul warned in 1 Cor. 7:5), then there is *chaste marriage*. This form of marriage means that no unlawful sexual activity takes place within this sacred bond. This practice therefore precludes any sexual practice that is not properly ordered, that does not aim at procreation, for instance (contraception is therefore precluded), or that wallows at times in the disorder, as Thomas Aquinas put it, of masturbation. And finally there is, for want of better language, what can be termed *average marriage*, which is likely to describe the sexual practices of most Roman Catholics today, who, contrary to the teachings of the magisterium, clearly practice contraception in significant numbers, though we will not speculate at all in terms of their other sexual practices!

This is not the place to assess how the theological and ethical judgments of several leaders within the Roman Catholic tradition over the ages have helped to foster a distinct sexual ethic and way of life with virginity as their compass. It is also not the appropriate setting to consider whether such a move disrupts the gracious harmony of the proper roles of God as creator (who gives the beautiful gift of human sexuality, which is emblematic of trinitarian love) and God as a redeemer, who sets the captives free from both the guilt and the power of sin. The focus here is simply on Mary and the consequences of viewing her as ever virgin. And though some believers, both Roman Catholic and Protestant, may want to fill out the implications of such teaching for the larger church, we must content ourselves, at least at this point, simply with observations about Mary. More to the point, the championing of Mary's perpetual virginity by many in the church (Roman Catholics, Eastern Orthodox, and even some Protestants)—claiming that Mary went so far as to repudiate normal, marital, sexual relations with a living husband, thereby valuing virginity inordinately—all of this teaching has unfortunately done great harm to no one less than Mary herself. It has not only in effect robbed her of her husband; it has also taken away most of her children.

16

Mary Again

From Dogmatic Definition to Co-Redeemer?

Devotion to Mary and her cult in the Roman Catholic Church arises out of an eager imagination coupled with a pious sentiment that ever celebrates Mary herself as a more-than-worthy object of attention. This is a church-wide phenomenon that is socially and theologically validated in many ways and is therefore found among both the laity and bishops alike. From statues carved, painted, dressed, and then paraded through the streets of the faithful; to the novenas dedicated to the honor of Mary over the course of nine days; to the exuberant hymns sung at the Mass and on special occasions of veneration; and finally to the rosaries repeated both in church and at home—Roman Catholic Marian devotion appears at times to have a life all its own.

This same Marian pious sentiment is also evident, more formally, in careful theological expression in terms of some of the more popular doctrines and titles that have been attributed to Mary over time. These include the immaculate conception, the assumption, and Mary as intercessor, mediatrix, and even possibly as co-redemptrix. The careful reader will discern that these teachings at times appear to imply one another. Once a particular Marian doctrine is in place, it seems that another is already waiting in the wings for its articulate theological expression and for its more popular cult. It is to these doctrines that we now turn.

The Immaculate Conception

The recent forays of a few of the neo-atheists, such as Sam Harris, into the teachings of the Christian faith indicate just how poorly the doctrine of the immaculate conception is understood beyond the church. Thinking that he is actually engaged in a bit of serious criticism of the doctrinal heritage of the church, Harris takes up the well-worn argument that the language of Isaiah 7:14 does not specify a virgin but merely refers to a "young woman."[1] He then goes on to conclude in an observation that is stunning in both its confusion and ineptitude: "It seems all but certain that the Christian dogma of the Immaculate Conception, and much of the church's anxiety about sex, was the result of a mistranslation from the Hebrew."[2] However, contrary to the judgment of Harris, the doctrine of the immaculate conception is not about how Jesus was born (of a virgin) but about how Mary was conceived (without original sin). It's not a teaching about Christ but about Mary.

In contrast to the fumbling of Harris, the *Catechism*, taking up the language of Pope Pius IX in his encyclical *Ineffabilis Deus*, states the doctrine both clearly and succinctly: "The most Blessed Virgin Mary was, from the first moment of her conception, by a singular grace and privilege of almighty God and by virtue of the merits of Jesus Christ, Savior of the human race, preserved immune from all stain of original sin."[3] Since neither the Eastern Orthodox nor Protestants affirm the immaculate conception, certainly not in the way that Pope Pius did in 1854, the declaration of this particular teaching as dogma, that is, as one required to be believed by all the faithful, demonstrates once again that the grounding authority here in the nineteenth century is actually *sola Roma*, or Rome alone. Such a judgment does not deny that Rome tried to substantiate this teaching; it did so, and in several ways, not just one. However, the preeminent appeal here is to the present and ongoing teaching authority of the church itself, specifically in the form of the papacy, though the doctrine of papal infallibility was yet to be declared. Rome does, after all, appeal to earlier church tradition to buttress a doctrinal case that is actually made on other grounds. Thus, for example, the Roman Catholic Church has claimed that "it was customary for the Fathers to refer to the Mother of God as all holy and free from every stain of sin." Yet Schaff had already reported in his own age that the ante-Nicene fathers, for instance, made no such affirmation. In fact, "far from teaching that Mary was free from

1. Sam Harris, *The End of Faith: Religion, Terror, and the Future of Reason* (New York: Norton, 2004), 95.
2. Ibid.
3. *Catechism of the Catholic Church*, 2nd ed. (Mahwah, NJ: Paulist Press, 1994), par. 491.

hereditary sin," he observes, "[they] do not even expressly exempt her from actual sin."[4] Origen may refer obliquely to the substance of this doctrine in his *Homilies*, but this is far from enough evidence to warrant the assertion that "it was customary for the Fathers" to refer to Mary in these terms.[5] It may be helpful to ask whether the phrase "free from every stain of sin," as employed by both Ambrose and Ephraem Syrus, for instance, is a general expression of holiness that can occur in later life or a pointed reference to the manner in which Mary was conceived.[6] Moreover, if this special doctrine with respect to Mary's *conception* is so evident in the church fathers, then why has Eastern Orthodoxy by and large rejected it?[7] At any rate, as with so much else in church history, it often takes considerable time for weighty doctrines to develop and mature, and that is clearly the case here.

The teaching that Mary was conceived apart from original sin, meaning also that she was born without a carnal nature, came into its own in the Middle Ages, in the eleventh century in particular, when Anselm, the archbishop of Canterbury, became one of its more able proponents. By this point Mary had already been known in clerical life as well as in popular piety as the second Eve, *theotokos*, and ever virgin. Some of the faithful began to reflect further on these matters and to draw some conclusions that seemed obvious to them, though they were doubted by others. The teaching of Mary's "special gift" became more popular in the following century, especially since the recitation of the "Hail Mary," which affirmed that the mother of Christ was "full of grace,"[8] was introduced at this time, as noted earlier.

Such developments were not without their opposition. Both Bernard of Clairvaux in the twelfth century and Thomas Aquinas in the thirteenth (though the latter may have finally assented to this doctrine) charged that if Mary "had been conceived without original sin, she did not need redemption—which would detract from 'the dignity of Christ as the Universal Savior of all.'"[9] To illustrate, in the *Summa Theologica*, Aquinas reasoned as follows: "And thus, in whatever manner the Blessed Virgin would have been sanctified before

4. Philip Schaff, *The Creeds of Christendom*, vol. 1, *The History of the Creeds* (Grand Rapids: Baker, 1983), 116–17.

5. See Frederick Holweck, "Immaculate Conception" (under the heading "The Absolute Purity of Mary"), *The Catholic Encyclopedia*, vol. 7 (New York: Robert Appleton Co., 1910), New Advent, http://www.newadvent.org/cathen/07674d.htm.

6. Ibid.

7. Few references to Mary are evident in the Apostolic Fathers. The four that do surface are all found in the writings of Ignatius of Antioch, *To the Ephesians* 7.2; 18.2; 19.1; *To the Trallians* 9—in *The Apostolic Fathers with Justin Martyr and Irenaeus*, ANF 1:52, 57, and 69–70.

8. This phrase likely refers to Mary's current condition, not the manner of her conception.

9. Jaroslav Pelikan, *Mary through the Centuries* (New York: History Book Club, 1996), 195.

animation, she could never have incurred the stain of original sin: and thus she would not have needed redemption and salvation which is by Christ, of Whom it is written (Matt. 1:21): He shall save His people from their sins. But this is unfitting, through implying that Christ is not the Saviour of all men, as He is called (1 Tim. 4:10)."[10]

Aware of this criticism as well as the subtlety of what Aquinas had argued, Duns Scotus, for his part, contended that this special grace and honor of Mary could be understood in three different ways: "It was . . . possible for God (1) to preserve her from original sin or (2) to rescue her from it within an instant of her conception (as Thomas Aquinas taught), so that, though conceived in sin, she was born pure of sin, or (3) to purify her of it at the end of a period of time."[11] Developing a theological method known as "maximalism," Scotus reasoned that it was better to falsely attribute an honor to Mary than to possibly take a real one away.[12] However, for some in the church even back then, it was not a matter of "whether it was possible for her to be conceived without [original sin], but whether in fact she was conceived without it."[13]

In the fifteenth century, in 1439, the Council of Basel declared that the immaculate conception was "a pious doctrine, in conformity with the worship of the church, the [Roman] Catholic faith, right reason, and Holy Scripture."[14] And although the theological faculty of Paris reaffirmed this teaching in 1497,[15] Erasmus, the gifted Christian humanist, apparently had his doubts in the following century, as revealed in his satirical work *Praise of Folly*: "The apostles knew personally the mother of Jesus, but which of them proved how she had been kept immaculate from Adam's sin with the logic our theologians display?"[16]

As the Reformation of the Western church got under way—and Protestants, by the way, did not have a unified view on this topic[17]—the Council of Trent finally took up the issue of Mary and original sin in a late session and

10. Thomas Aquinas, *Summa Theologica*, trans. Fathers of the English Dominican Province (London: Burns, Oates & Washbourne, n.d.), IIIa, q. 27, a. 2, ad 2.
11. Pelikan, *Mary through the Centuries*, 196.
12. Ibid.
13. Ibid.
14. Ibid., 198.
15. Desiderius Erasmus, *Praise of Folly* (New York: Penguin Classics, 2004), Kindle edition, location 3757n109.
16. Ibid., Kindle ed., locations 1825–26.
17. Luther, e.g., wrote: "But, lest I become too involved, let me state that my position is proved in this one instance, namely, that the Roman church along with the general council at Basel and almost with the whole church feels that the Holy Virgin was conceived without sin. Yet those who hold the opposite opinion should not be considered heretics, since their opinion has not been disproved." Martin Luther, *Career of the Reformer I*, LW 31:173.

decreed: "This same holy Synod doth nevertheless declare, that it is not its intention to include in this decree, where original sin is treated of, the blessed and immaculate Virgin Mary, the mother of God."[18] However, this teaching did not achieve formal dogmatic status, whereby it would have to be affirmed by all the faithful, until as late as the nineteenth century, when Pope Pius IX proclaimed it in his encyclical *Ineffabilis Deus* in 1854, as reported earlier.

Roman Catholic folk theology eventually expressed these doctrinal developments a few years later, in 1858, when Bernadette Soubirous, a fourteen-year-old French peasant girl, claimed that a lady had spoken to her and revealed herself as the immaculate conception. The Roman Catholic hierarchy at the time was naturally delighted about the prospects of such an apparition for the ongoing cult of Mary. Not surprisingly, then, Bernadette was not only held up as a worthy example of what popular piety should look like, but she was also elevated rather quickly (given the time it often takes to be declared a saint) to the status of sainthood by Pope Pius XI on December 8, 1933.

Nevertheless, some of the most recent attempts at a defense of Mary's supposed special gift have floundered. Christian Smith, for example, the newly converted Roman Catholic, backed himself into a theological corner by attempting to defend this teaching along the following lines: "The underlying idea is that if Mary was a sinner, then Jesus would have inherited the sin of his human parent. The Incarnation therefore needed a mother preserved from the stain of original sin *to bear the Son sinless.*"[19] However, in this line of reasoning, in order for Mary to be pure, she herself would need to have been born of parents who were themselves free from the stain of original sin, and in order for that to happen, then the parents of Anna and Joachim (the names traditionally given to Mary's parents) would likewise need to have been pure themselves, and so on and on it goes in a pointless, feckless chain.

Contrary to these theological developments, both the weight of Scripture and tradition challenge the easy assumption that Mary was without original sin by pointing out possible incidences that display some of her faults and possibly even her actual sin (which would entail at some point a corrupted nature). Indeed, though we have listed above the many Scripture references that pertain to Mary, it is now appropriate to point out that not all of them are good. Take Mark 3:20–21, for example: "Then Jesus entered a house, and again a crowd gathered, so that he and his disciples were not even able to eat. When his family [which may have included Mary] heard about this,

---

18. Schaff, *Creeds of Christendom*, 2:88.
19. Christian Smith, *How to Go from Being a Good Evangelical to a Committed Catholic in Ninety-Five Difficult Steps* (Eugene, OR: Cascade, 2011), 124–25 (emphasis added).

they went to take charge of him, for they said, 'He is out of his mind.'"
Did the family of Jesus, then, so mistake his person and character that they
misjudged him to be insane? And what does such a judgment suggest about
the spiritual state of those who made it, relatives who surely should have
known better? And then there is the praise offered to Mary by a woman
in a crowd who called out to Jesus, "Blessed is the mother who gave you
birth and nursed you" (Luke 11:27). The reply of Jesus is remarkable in its
frankness: "Blessed *rather* [Greek μενοῦν, *menoun*] are those who hear the
word of God and obey it" (Luke 11:28). Why then, given Mary's supposed
immaculate conception, her lofty status, did Jesus not immediately agree
with the woman and at least mention some of Mary's greatness, a few of her
accolades? Why did he pass up this opportunity in the face of such holiness
and unique splendor? More important, why did he immediately change the
very nature of the praise and refer instead not to Mary but to those who
"hear the word of God and obey it"? In a similar vein, John Chrysostom in
the fourth century found Mary's behavior at Cana to be troubling. He attributed her conduct at this wedding feast "to undue haste, a sort of unholy
ambition."[20] And as Tim Perry points out, "Tertullian does not shy away
from including Mary among Jesus' opponents prior to the resurrection and
from indicting her as an example of unbelief."[21] These are hardly the mak-
ings of a woman who was immaculately conceived.

Just what is at stake here, theologically speaking? We take the criticism of
both Bernard of Clairvaux and Thomas Aquinas very seriously, since we, too,
believe that the elevation of Mary, declaring that she was conceived without
a carnal nature, does indeed detract from the uniqueness and the dignity of
Jesus Christ as the Savior of all humanity; nevertheless we also see something
here that is far more basic and that therefore constitutes a direct affront to any
sound Christology. That is, if Mary lacked original sin and therefore lacked
a carnal nature, then she was like no other human being who has ever lived.
In such a theological configuration, Mary is unlike Jesus because she was
not divine, yet she is unlike the rest of humanity because she lacked original
sin, a carnal nature. Thus she is not connected to Adam either as her federal
head or as her origin. She is therefore unlike all the rest of humanity, in a
class all her own.

What is being eclipsed here, in a roundabout sort of way, is the true
humanity of Mary, and along with it nothing less than the true humanity

---

20. Philip Schaff, "Prolegomena: The Life and Work of St. John Chrysostom," in *Saint
Chrysostom: On the Priesthood, Ascetic Treatises, Select Homilies and Letters, Homilies on
the Statues*, NPNF[1] 9:21.

21. Perry, *The Blessed Virgin Mary* (Grand Rapids: Eerdmans, 2013), 23.

of Christ as well.[22] Once the latter is undermined, so is the unique status of Jesus as the God/Human. Since Mariological doctrines do indeed have christological consequences, the affirmation of the immaculate conception in effect denies that Jesus was truly human simply because he was not born of a woman who herself was really human, like the rest of humanity. Set apart in a category all her own, as theologians doing constructive theology have left her, Mary approaches perhaps a demigod, a distinct class of being in significant ontological power (see below) but not a genuine human being, certainly not any human being whom we have ever known. After the fall of Adam and Eve and with its universal consequences in place, the only way one could be free from original sin would entail nothing less than being divine. Though sin is not essential to human nature but represents its corruption, Mary is still a sinner, because, like the rest of humanity, she is related to Adam, but unlike Jesus, she is by no means divine. As fully divine, Jesus is not merely human, even though he is fully human.[23] Mary, however, was merely human, and as such she was not spared the universal corruption spread by Adam. That's precisely why the God/Human had to come in the first place. So then, Jesus was not born of a demigod or of some intermediate being between God and humanity, in a special class all by herself. Rather, Christ was born of a real woman who herself needed redemption, as the Gospel of Luke clearly attests (Luke 1:47). Jesus, then, was, is, and remains the Savior of all people, Mary included.

Bodily Assumption: Deny This and the Faith Will Fall?

When the doctrine of the immaculate conception was formally articulated by the pope in the nineteenth century, there was already significant support for another Marian teaching. However, the notion of the bodily assumption of Mary into heaven was not declared dogma by the pope, in this case the later Pius XII, until November 1, 1950, on All Saints' Day. The words of his encyclical *Munificentissimus Deus* state the substance of what is now required to be affirmed by all the Roman Catholic faithful: "We pronounce, declare, and define it to be a divinely revealed dogma: that the Immaculate Mother of

22. This is not to suggest that a sinful nature is necessary to be a human being but only to affirm that all humanity, with the notable and singular exception of Jesus Christ, is marked by sin and therefore in need of a Savior (Luke 1:47). Viewed somewhat differently, Christ was born of a real, flesh-and-blood woman, not of one who was "above" the rest of humanity though "below" the Almighty.

23. For more on the difference between fully human and merely human, see Thomas V. Morris, *The Logic of God Incarnate* (Ithaca, NY: Cornell University Press, 1986), 62–70.

God, the ever Virgin Mary, having completed the course of her earthly life, was assumed body and soul into heavenly glory."[24]

What is so very odd about Pius XII's dogmatic venture (esp. for church historians) is the censure or condemnation that comes immediately after this particular Marian declaration: "Hence if anyone, which God forbid, should dare willfully to deny or to call into doubt that which we have defined, let him know that he has fallen away *completely* from the divine and [Roman] Catholic Faith."[25] Part of the difficulty here, as will be demonstrated shortly, is that not only is such a teaching not evidenced in the NT or represented in the faith of the early church, but it also lacks significant support from the ongoing ecclesiastical tradition itself, until beyond the early centuries of the church. Moreover, though Pius XII no doubt believed his proclamation to be an exercise of his infallibility, something spoken ex cathedra, nevertheless, his centering of this teaching at the very heart of the Christian faith, such that those who for the sake of their conscience, for instance, cannot affirm its substance and as a consequence have "fallen away completely" from the faith—that is simply hyperbole, to say the least. If this teaching were so important for the very substance of the faith, then why did ante-Nicene Christianity know virtually nothing of it? Indeed, even later, during the fourth century, Ambrose and Epiphanius were evidently still ignorant of this doctrine in its substantive form.[26] However, Epiphanius did indeed speculate about the possibility that Mary had never died, though he never came to a conclusion on this particular matter.[27]

If apocryphal narratives such as *The Assumption of Mary*[28] or *Liber Requiei Mariae*[29] (The book of Mary's repose), as well as forgeries, are bracketed out of consideration, then an early expression of the essential elements taught regarding the assumption of Mary may be during the fifth century in material drawn from "Coptic Christianity under marked Gnostic influence."[30] In

24. Pope Pius XII, *Munificentissimus Deus: Defining the Dogma of the Assumption*, par. 44, the Holy See, 1950, http://w2.vatican.va/content/pius-xii/en/apost_constitutions/documents/hf_p-xii_apc_19501101_munificentissimus-deus.html.

25. Ibid., par. 45 (emphasis added).

26. F. L. Cross and Elizabeth A. Livingstone, eds., *The Oxford Dictionary of the Christian Church* (Oxford: Oxford University Press, 2005), 118.

27. Stephen J. Shoemaker, *The Ancient Traditions of the Virgin Mary's Dormition and Assumption* (Oxford: Oxford University Press, 2006), 13.

28. Alexander Walker, "Apocrypha of the New Testament: Translator's Introductory Notice," in *Fathers of the Third and Fourth Centuries: The Twelve Patriarchs, Excerpts and Epistles, the Clementina, Apocrypha, Decretals, Memoirs of Edessa and Syriac Documents, Remains of the First Ages*, ANF 8:359.

29. "Assumption of Mary," in *New World Encyclopedia*, last revised April 21, 2016, http://www.newworldencyclopedia.org/p/index.php?title=Assumption_of_Mary&oldid=995437.

30. R. P. C. Hanson, *Tradition in the Early Church* (Eugene, OR: Wipf & Stock, 2009), 259n1.

Western Christianity the doctrine does not appear until the sixth century, as defended by Gregory of Tours.[31] By the eighth century a feast day in accordance with this teaching began to be celebrated throughout Europe on August 15.[32] In the East during this same period, John Damascene had associated a number of triumphalist psalms with Mary, a fact picked up by Pope Pius XII in his own encyclical.[33] Describing the honor that earlier theologians and preachers had accorded Mary on this theme, the pope wrote of the "Queen entering triumphantly into the royal halls of heaven and sitting at the right hand of the divine Redeemer," a reference to, though not the exact language of, Psalm 44(45):10–14.[34] Such an expression, drawn loosely from the OT, is similar to that employed by Sister Maria de Jesus de Ágreda in the seventeenth century in her *Life of the Virgin Mary*. In this work she tied these same psalms to a decidedly Christian perspective and exclaimed: "Mary was elevated to the right hand of her son and the true God, and situated at the same royal throne of the Most Blessed Trinity."[35] This same glorification of Mary by earlier and later writers resulted not only in the affirmation that she is "Queen over all things" but also in the claim that, to use the words of the *Catechism*, she enjoys "a singular participation in her Son's resurrection and an anticipation of the resurrection of other Christians,"[36] an honor that is nowhere found in Scripture and actually undermines some of its basic affirmations: Christ alone is the *firstfruits* of the resurrection (1 Cor. 15:20, 23), a *first* that is not shared by or parceled out to another. Second, there is no other salvific resurrection (beyond Christ's resurrection) but the one that is to come, in which all the just, not simply Mary, will be raised to glory.

Intercessor or Mediator?

As the body of Christ goes through history, that holy and blessed communion is made up of both the church militant, those who are still struggling on the earth in the face of trials and persecution, and the church triumphant, those who are in the presence of Christ in glory (2 Cor. 5:6–8). As the early church

---

31. Cross and Livingstone, *Oxford Dictionary of the Christian Church*, 118.

32. Ibid., 118–19.

33. Pope Pius XII, *Munificentissimus Deus*, par. 26, http://w2.vatican.va/content/pius-xii/en /apost_constitutions/documents/hf_p-xii_apc_19501101_munificentissimus-deus.html.

34. This parenthetical reference represents the different ways that Roman Catholics and Protestants number the Psalms in their respective Bibles. The first designation, without parentheses, corresponds to the Roman Catholic version; the number in parentheses, to the Protestant one.

35. Pelikan, *Mary through the Centuries*, 111.

36. *Catechism*, par. 966.

so clearly recognized, *the example* of the holy lives left by Mary and the saints is not only an encouragement to the church militant but also something that should be emulated. Naturally Christians of the first three centuries revered Mary and the saints, and a genuine progression can be discerned in such veneration. To illustrate, up until around the year 300, commemorations at the tombs of the saints were marked by prayers for the repose of their souls.[37] By the way, these festivities at the gravesite, especially when they involved food, marked the nearly utter gentile orientation of the church by this point, since this practice was viewed as distasteful to Jews, who for their part avoided contact with dead bodies (Num. 19:11) and therefore did not arrange for suppers to be held anywhere near them in graveyards.[38] Alister McGrath suggests that honoring the Christian dead with such meals at the tombs was actually absorbed from "Traditional Roman [pagan] religion."[39] At any rate, by the late sixth century, prayer *for* the saints had become "prayer to God *through* the saints."[40] Beyond this, in the folk theology that had emerged by the twelfth century, both Mary and the saints became the distinct objects of prayer. The faithful now prayed directly *to* them, as intercessors of course, nevertheless to them.

Lest there be misunderstanding, we are not denying that either Mary or any of the saints in glory continue to offer their prayers and supplications to the Most High on behalf of the church militant. The church is one, whether on earth or in heaven. In fact, such a form of intercessory prayer appears to be supported by Scripture in the OT in terms of reference to a cloud of witnesses (as observed in Heb. 12:1) or in the NT as those who bore testimony in the past, presently cry out in a loud voice, and will soon receive a white robe (Rev. 6:9–10; 7:14–17).[41] Moreover, both Ambrose and Augustine affirmed this basic truth that describes the nature of the church, which is active both on earth and in heaven. Augustine, for example, states: "For we cannot, they say, believe that the saints shall lose their bowels of compassion when they have attained the most perfect and complete holiness."[42] We strongly agree.

37. Earle E. Cairns, *Christianity through the Centuries: A History of the Christian Church*, 3rd rev. ed. (Grand Rapids: Zondervan, 2009), Kindle edition, locations 2987–89.

38. Rabbi Michael Katz and Rabbi Gershon Schwartz, *Swimming in the Sea of Talmud: Lessons for Everyday Living* (Philadelphia: Jewish Publication Society, 1997), 124, 143.

39. McGrath, *Christian History: An Introduction* (Hoboken, NJ: Wiley-Blackwell, 2012), 45.

40. Cairns, *Christianity through the Centuries*, Kindle ed., locations 2987–89.

41. Cross and Livingstone, *Oxford Dictionary of the Christian Church*, 1455.

42. Augustine of Hippo, *The City of God* 21.18, in *St. Augustine's "City of God" and "Christian Doctrine,"* trans. Marcus Dods, NPNF[1] 2:466. For material on Ambrose, see Philip Schaff and Henry Wace, eds., "Prolegomena to St. Ambrose," in *St. Ambrose: Select Works and Letters*, NPNF[2] 10:xiv.

It is necessary, however, to make two further distinctions on this topic for the sake of clarity. First, it is one thing for the saints in heaven, Mary of course included, to exercise their freedom and to pray for the church militant. Contemporary views on this matter, found among some Protestant fundamentalists, for instance, will not eliminate this freedom of the saints in heaven; nor can the objectors possibly limit, despite their protests, this graciously offered intercessory prayer. However, it is quite a different thing for the church militant to pray to the church triumphant directly, as if those on earth knew with certainty precisely those who are in glory: "The righteousness that is by faith says: 'Do not say in your heart, "Who will ascend into heaven?"' (that is, to bring Christ down) 'or "Who will descend into the deep?"' (that is, to bring Christ up from the dead)" (Rom. 10:6–7). With the exception of Mary, of course, whose eternal sanctity for us is beyond question, the problem of hypocrisy and even deception is very real. In the end only God knows the human heart. Thus, lacking omniscience, a trait that pertains to God alone, the faithful on earth are likely to err in naming the saints. Oddly enough, one may even find oneself praying to the damned.[43]

But even with these caveats and the one exception in mind, it is best not to approach Mary directly as an intercessor, despite her undoubted sanctity, for the reason that John Calvin had recognized in his own age: "It is a common opinion among them, that we need intercessors, because in ourselves we are unworthy of appearing in the presence of God. By speaking in this manner, they deprive Christ of his honour."[44] So although we affirm the intercessory role of Mary and the saints as they pray for the church militant, we do not uphold an intercessory role in the sense of the church on earth approaching Mary and the saints (whoever they may be) who are in heaven. Christ alone should be the object of requests for intercession in this sense. Indeed, the temple curtain has been torn in two (Matt. 27:51), and the unworthiness of any sinner should not bar the way or displace Christ's gracious and distinct mediatorial role. Only he is the perfect intercessor, a perfection that others lack quite simply because Christ alone is the God/Human. Again, he and he alone is a bridge in ways that all others cannot be.

Second, we obviously support intercession in the sense of standing alongside fellow believers. However, there is another movement, and though it has the

43. I differ from Jerry Walls on this matter. Walls is open to the idea of requesting intercession (mediation, in the view of Collins) from those who have gone before us. In his view, the communion of the saints that allows us to ask persons to pray for us in this life may allow us to ask those who have died to pray for us, despite the possibility that we may be mistaken about their state of grace.

44. John Calvin, *Commentaries on the Epistles to Timothy, Titus, and Philemon*, trans. William Pringle (Bellingham, WA: Logos Bible Software, 2010), 59.

appearance of the first, at least initially, it ends up making both Mary and the saints genuine mediators, those who are not really standing beside believers who are offering intercessory prayers so much as standing in between such believers and Christ and hence functioning as supposed intermediaries. The first role can be recognized and affirmed, underscoring the unity of the church militant and triumphant; the second, however, must be rejected as necessarily detracting from the unique office of the God/Human, Jesus Christ. It is both the humanity and the divinity of Christ, a divinity that Mary and the saints so obviously lack, that render the Messiah the one and only mediator between God and humanity.

So then, in a way that many others have not, we have distinguished between intercession and mediation, between standing alongside, which we affirm, and coming in between, which we do not. Such a differentiation is reflected, once again, in the work of John Calvin. In his *Institutes*, for example, he states: "Christ, therefore, is the only Mediator by whose intercession the Father is rendered propitious and exorable (1 Tim. 2:5). For though the saints are still permitted to use intercessions, by which they mutually beseech God in behalf of each other's salvation, . . . yet these depend on that one intercession [in reality mediation], so far are they from derogating from it."[45]

Mediatrix: Mary in the Middle

That Mary was not simply an intercessor but a genuine mediator between God and humanity apparently emerged first in Eastern theology.[46] The term "Mediatrix" is not found in Scripture, and it did not even gain currency in the West until toward the end of the eighth century.[47] A more developed use of the term can be seen in the writings of Bernard of Clairvaux, who during the twelfth century referred to Mary as "our Mediatrix, . . . the one through whom we have received thy mercy, O God."[48] Blurring the lines between intercession and mediation, the Roman Catholic Church today confounds these two very different roles (standing alongside/coming in between), as is evident in the language of the *Catechism*: "[Mary] . . . by her manifold intercession continues to bring us the gifts of eternal salvation. . . . Therefore the Blessed Virgin is invoked in the Church under the titles of Advocate, Helper,

---

45. Calvin, *Institutes of the Christian Religion*, trans. Henry Beveridge (Edinburgh: Calvin Translation Society, 1845), 3.20.19 (2:479–80).

46. Pelikan, *Mary through the Centuries*, 130–31.

47. Ibid.

48. Ibid., 132.

Benefactress, and Mediatrix."[49] This same language, by the way, was repeated at Vatican II.[50] More recently, Pope John Paul II, for his part, quickly moved from intercession to mediation in his encyclical *Redemptoris Mater*: "Mary places herself *between her Son and mankind* in the reality of their wants, needs and sufferings. She puts herself 'in the middle,' that is to say she acts as a mediatrix not as an outsider, but in her position as mother."[51] Other titles along these lines ascribed to Mary include "Mother to us in the order of grace,"[52] "Ark of the Covenant,"[53] "the Window of Paradise,"[54] and even "the Gate of Heaven."[55] Like the popes throughout much of the history of the church, Mary keeps on acquiring new titles over time, so deep is the fund of piety and religious imagination.

From the sixteenth century forward, Rome has been aware of Protestant criticism on this particular issue and has attempted to shunt aside such censure in its simple declaration that "Mary's function as mother of men [that is, as mediatrix] in no way obscures or diminishes this unique mediation of Christ, but rather shows its power."[56] However, from the Protestant perspective, obscuring and diminishing Christ's mediation are *exactly* what the title of mediatrix does. Rome's declaration, then, does not obviate a discussion on this matter but actually requires it. Thus, what the *Catechism* and Vatican II so readily assume must in the end be called into question. In fact, Rome's (again from a Protestant perspective) dismissive response here, which is supposed to shut down any possible objection, is in fact formulaic, given this theological tradition's other pronouncements in areas that are similarly contested. To illustrate, the careful reader will recall that after John Paul II had ventured into the troubled waters of the ordination of women in his *Letter to Women*, composed in 1995, and after he had in effect declared that the matter is forever closed, he then offered a statement that was supposed to make all further criticism pointless, in a

---

49. *Catechism*, par. 969.

50. Pope Paul VI, *Lumen Gentium: Dogmatic Constitution on the Church*, sec. 62, in *The Conciliar and Post Conciliar Documents*, vol. 1 of *Vatican II*, ed. Austin Flannery (Northport, NY: Costello, 1998), 419; see also the Holy See, http://www.vatican.va/archive/hist_councils /ii_vatican_council/documents/vat-ii_const_19641121_lumen-gentium_en.html.

51. Pope John Paul II, *Redemptoris Mater: On the Blessed Virgin Mary in the Life of the Pilgrim Church*, sec. 21, http://w2.vatican.va/content/john-paul-ii/en/encyclicals/documents /hf_jp-ii_enc_25031987_redemptoris-mater.html (emphasis added).

52. *Catechism*, par. 966.

53. This language appears in the "Litany of Loreto," originally approved in 1587 by Pope Sixtus V. See https://udayton.edu/imri/mary/l/litany-of-loreto.php.

54. Pelikan, *Mary through the Centuries*, 135.

55. See https://udayton.edu/imri/mary/l/litany-of-loreto.php.

56. *Catechism*, par. 970.

way remarkably similar to Rome's earlier Marian response just recounted above: "This in no way detracts from the role of women."[57] Once again, that's *exactly* what it does.

Jesus and Mary as Co-Redeemers?

With the language of "Mediatrix" well represented in the official documents of the Roman Catholic Church, it was but a small step (at least in the eyes of some) to move from that vaunted title to one of flat out co-redemption, that is, Mary as "Co-Redemptrix." Indeed, Mary's cause in terms of her supposed work as a co-redeemer or co-savior along with Jesus Christ has been championed since the 1920s with ups and downs along the way. During this early period, the Belgian leader Cardinal Désiré-Joseph Mercier got the ball rolling, so to speak, and he was aided in his efforts by Rev. Maximilian Kolbe.[58] Since that time over eight hundred cardinals and bishops have beseeched numerous popes to make an infallible declaration (and hence dogma) of Mary's special role as co-redemptrix in the economy of salvation.[59] More recently, a large box of petitions to accord Mary this title (which numbered over forty thousand) appeared on the steps of the Vatican in 1997.[60]

Those who were eager to have the so-called fifth Marian doctrine declared (beyond *theotokos*, perpetual virginity, immaculate conception, and assumption) no doubt thought that their cause would be successful under the pontificate of John Paul II. Indeed, so devoted was this popular pope to Mary and her cult that he even had the letter "M" (which stood for Mary) emblazoned on his papal, personal coat of arms. Moreover, this was the same pope who, once again in his encyclical *Redemptoris Mater*, named the second part of this work "The Mother of God at the *Center* of the Pilgrim Church."[61] Indeed, Mary at the very center of the body of Christ was precisely the theme that Pope John Paul II took up when he addressed the faithful in Guayaquil, Ecuador: "Having suffered for the Church, Mary deserved to become the Mother of all the disciples of her Son, the Mother

---

57. Pope John Paul II, *Letter of Pope John Paul II to Women*, sec. 11, http://w2.vatican.va /content/john-paul-ii/en/letters/1995/documents/hf_jp-ii_let_29061995_women.html.

58. Robert Moynihan, "Is the Time Ripe for a 5th Marian Dogma?," *Zenit*, March 1, 2009, http://www.zenit.org/en/articles/is-the-time-ripe-for-a-5th-marian-dogma.

59. Ibid.

60. Kenneth L. Woodward, "Hail, Mary," *Newsweek*, August 24, 1997, http://www.news week.com/hail-mary-172216.

61. Pope John Paul II, *Redemptoris Mater*, heading for part 2 (preceding sec. 25), http:// w2.vatican.va/content/john-paul-ii/en/encyclicals/documents/hf_jp-ii_enc_25031987 _redemptoris-mater.html (emphasis added).

of their unity. . . . In fact Mary's role as co-redemptrix did not cease with the glorification of her Son."[62]

Furthermore, though John Paul II obviously did not balk at using this particular title for Mary, and though this language repeatedly appears in Roman Catholic literature (e.g., in the book *Mariology: A Guide for Priests, Deacons, Seminarians, and Consecrated Persons*,[63] which, by the way, contains an imprimatur), there has yet to be any formal declaration of this teaching to give it the status of dogma. In fact, both the *Catechism* and the documents from Vatican II are careful to avoid the specific language of co-redemptrix, though some may argue that the idea is actually present in each. The *Catechism*, for example, states: "This *union of the mother with the Son in the work of salvation* is made manifest from the time of Christ's virginal conception up to his death."[64] And Vatican II, for its part, declared: "In celebrating this annual cycle of the mysteries of Christ, Holy Church honors the Blessed Mary, Mother of God, with a special love. She is *inseparably linked with her son's saving work.*"[65]

Despite this lack of official recognition, the doctrine of Mary as co-redemptrix, in the absence of sound biblical support, is already believed by many Roman Catholics, popes of the past included. From our perspective, it may be only a matter of time before official teaching will finally catch up with popular piety if Rome follows the same pattern of doctrinal "development" it has in the past. In fact, this trend is already beginning to happen. To illustrate, in 2009 cardinals and bishops from all around the world asked Pope Benedict XVI to declare officially that Mary is to be venerated as nothing less than "Co-Redemptrix, Mediatrix of all graces, and Advocate."[66] In January 2017, the International Marian Association, representing the voices of over one hundred bishops, priests, and theologians, published a document requesting that, during the 2017 centenary anniversary of the Marian Apparitions at Fatima, Portugal, Pope Francis "kindly grant public recognition and honor to the role of the Blessed Virgin Mary for her unique human cooperation with the one divine Redeemer in the work of Redemption as 'Co-redemptrix with

62. Pope John Paul II, quoted in Mark Miravalle, *Mariology: A Guide for Priests, Deacons, Seminarians, and Consecrated Persons* (2008; repr., Seattle: Amazon Digital Services, 2013), Kindle edition, locations 2298–300.

63. Ibid. Indeed, in the strangest of exegesis, Miravalle sees both Deborah (from the OT) and Judith (from the Apocrypha) as prefiguring Mary as co-redemptrix. See Miravalle, *Mariology*, Kindle ed., locations 543–44 and locations 573–75, respectively.

64. *Catechism*, par. 964 (emphasis added).

65. *The Constitution on the Sacred Liturgy*, par. 103, in Flannery, *Conciliar and Post Conciliar Documents*, 29 (emphasis added).

66. Moynihan, "Is the Time Ripe?"

Jesus the Redeemer.'"[67] Given the structure of authority in the Roman Catholic Church, with its pointed hierarchy, the champions of this cause only have to win once, so to speak, for once a teaching is declared as dogma, it is then for all practical purposes irrevocable (since a reversal would contradict the infallibility of the pope and undermine the authority of the papacy). And the Marian cause may just have one of its best friends in Pope Francis, devoted as he is to Mary "the Untier," the one who loosens knots and sets the captives free! We will not be surprised, then, if this dogmatic declaration happens sometime in the twenty-first century, if not with Francis then perhaps with another pope. The Marian doctrinal accretions already in place almost require it.

Mary's redemptive status was elevated through an unfortunate mistranslation of Genesis 3:15, and this error has contributed to the exaggerated claims that are sometimes made about Mary in Roman Catholic theology. That text appears in the fall narrative and is recognized as the first prophecy of the coming of Christ: "And I will put enmity between you and the woman, and between your offspring and hers; he will crush your head, and you will strike his heel." The Roman Catholic Douay–Rheims version translates this text in such a way as to suggest that it is a prophecy about Mary. Instead of "he will crush," it says "she shall crush," and instead of "his heel," it says "her heel." This famous mistranslation, which has significantly affected artistic depictions of Mary, was based on the Vulgate, the fifth-century Latin translation of the Bible.[68] Contemporary Roman apologists have acknowledged the mistranslation yet defend the Marian claim on other grounds. Indeed, the myth that Mary crushed the serpent's head is perpetuated in a number of statues and paintings and it is enshrined in the famous statue of Mary that stands atop the fabled Golden Dome at the University of Notre Dame.

Should Mary Then Be Worshiped?

By the early fourth century there was as yet little of the considerable cult that surrounds Mary in the Roman Catholic Church today. For example, during this period Basil the Great's writings lack any trace of such devotion.[69]

67. "The Role of Mary in Redemption: A Document of the Theological Commission of the International Marian Association," International Marian Association, January 1, 2017, http://internationalmarian.com/sites/marian/files/uploads/documents/the_role_of_mary_in_redemption_1.pdf.

68. For more details and critique, see David F. Wells, *Revolution in Rome* (Downers Grove, IL: InterVarsity, 1976), 133–35.

69. Blomfield Jackson, "Prolegomena: Sketch of the Life and Works of Saint Basil," in *St. Basil: Letters and Select Works*, NPNF[2] 8:lxxiii.

However, toward the end of this same century a distinct change does indeed occur in the writings of Ephraem Syrus, a Syrian theologian and sometime composer of hymns. Combining a desire to honor Mary with his own gift for expression (which shines through even in translation), the ordained deacon drafted the following hymn:

> O pure and immaculate and likewise blessed Virgin, who art the sinless Mother of thy Son, the mighty Lord of the universe, thou who are inviolate and altogether holy, the hope of the hopeless and sinful, we sing thy praises. . . . Make us worthy of the glory of thy Son, O dearest and most clement Virgin Mother. Thou indeed are our only hope most sure and sacred in God's sight to whom be honor and glory, majesty and dominion forever and ever world without end. Amen.[70]

Ephraem's poetic license here led him into the theologically troubled and confused territory of making Mary the object of the sinner's hope, something that she herself—during her own sojourn on the earth, steeped as she was in deep humility—never did for herself. Her gaze was directed toward her Son. And though the name of Mary was obviously invoked in the East during the fourth century and even earlier (though of less importance), the first Latin hymn addressing Mary did not appear until the fifth century.[71]

By the time of Augustine, who died a year before the Council of Ephesus met in 431, this bishop of Hippo recognized that the cult of Mary (and of the saints!) was growing so strongly that appropriate theological distinctions would have to be put into place. This effort was deemed necessary in order to keep veneration within the proper bounds lest it result in outright worship and therefore idolatry. In his *City of God*, for example, Augustine reasoned: "But that service which is due to men, and in reference to which the apostle writes that servants must be subject to their own masters, is usually designated by another word in Greek [δουλεία, *douleia*] whereas the service paid to God alone by worship is always, or almost always, called λατρεία [*latreia*] in the usage of those who wrote from the divine oracles."[72]

During the High Middle Ages, in the thirteenth century, Marian devotion continued apace and became so considerable that Thomas Aquinas believed

---

70. Joseph P. Christopher, *The Raccolta; or, A Manual of Indulgences* (Potosi, WI: St. Athanasius Press, 2003), 371.

71. Everett Ferguson, *Church History*, vol. 1, *From Christ to Pre-Reformation: The Rise and Growth of the Church in Its Cultural, Intellectual, and Political Context* (Grand Rapids: Zondervan, 2009), Kindle edition, locations 6117–18.

72. Augustine of Hippo, *The City of God* 10.1, in *St. Augustine's "City of God" and "Christian Doctrine,"* trans. Marcus Dods, NPNF[1] 2:180. Although Augustine did not include the Greek word δουλεία, he clearly implied it.

that the language of *douleia* and *latreia* was no longer adequate to describe the distinct honor and veneration owed to Mary. He observed: "Consequently the worship of *latria* is not due to any mere rational creature for its own sake. Since, therefore, the Blessed Virgin is a mere rational creature, the worship of *latria* is not due to her, but only that of *dulia*: but in a higher degree than to other creatures, inasmuch as she is the Mother of God. For this reason we say that not any kind of *dulia* is due to her, but *hyperdulia*."[73]

Though theologians like Aquinas could revel in tight, fine theological differentiations that supposedly kept the forces of idolatry at bay, others were not so convinced. As a moderate Christian humanist who sought the moral reform of the Roman Catholic Church, Erasmus jabbed at the "aberrations of late medieval piety" surrounding the veneration of Mary.[74] His aim, among other things, was to return Christ to his rightful place not only in the economy of salvation but also in that popular piety that had in some respects gone astray. Much more forcefully, John Calvin (employing admittedly intemperate language, typical of the controversies of his day—though he made a necessary theological point) fulminated against the scholastics with folk like Aquinas clearly in mind: "That I may omit to say that they babble through childish ignorance, how many of them do understand that rotten distinction [between *douleia*, *latreia*, and *hyperdouleia*]?"[75] The Genevan Reformer then added his theological coup de grâce: "Neither do I speak only of the common sort, *but of the chieftains*. Therefore, all their worshippings must needs be infected and corrupt with wicked superstition, seeing they unadvisedly match creatures with God."[76] Despite Calvin's rhetoric, surely Rome can recognize the substance of his point that these theological subtleties, which give such comfort to its theologians, are surely lost on many of the laity, who invariably fall into enslaving, superstitious idolatry. As shepherds of their flock, the members of the magisterium must surely take pastoral responsibility for some of the more aberrant forms of folk religion that have emerged in their midst.

Newman's Arian Marian Piety

Given this history, Roman Catholics of late, even laity, have been especially sensitive in this area—and with good reason. In a manner that some would

---

73. Aquinas, *Summa Theologica*, IIIa, q. 25, a. 5.
74. Erasmus, *Praise of Folly*, Kindle ed., locations 3550–52.
75. John Calvin, *Commentary upon the Acts of the Apostles*, trans. Henry Beveridge (Bellingham, WA: Logos Bible Software, 2010), 1:430–31.
76. Ibid. (emphasis added).

consider to be overly defensive, Christian Smith, for example, commands evangelicals (yes, he does indeed use the imperative!): "Correct your understanding of the veneration of Mary and the saints."[77] Smith, however, is apparently not appreciably aware of the interpretive dynamic surrounding Mary that has played out not simply in Protestant historically driven apologetics but also in Roman Catholic scholarship itself. Accordingly, our response in light of his demand will proceed by citing a Roman Catholic theologian, even one of its most celebrated authors from the nineteenth century. However, before concluding this chapter with the Marian observations of John Henry Newman, we observe that the great church historian Jaroslav Pelikan, in careful and evenhanded scholarship, has discerned a "methodology of amplification" that has played out in this burgeoning Mariology. Once Mary was deemed by her devotees to be "higher than the cherubim, more glorious than the seraphim,"[78] she was fair game "to be regarded as not unworthy of any of the honors and privileges that had, according to the Scriptures of both the Old and New Testament, been conferred on others."[79] With this amplification in place, which represented a distinct attitude and determination of will, the entire Bible was then sifted for any title that could possibly be applied to Mary. Thus, in quoting the church fathers and others, Newman pointed out in one of his own works, and with appreciation, that Mary was "signified by the Pillar of the cloud,"[80] according to Ambrose; by "the Rod out of the stem of Jesse,"[81] according to Jerome; by "the Eastern gate through which the High Priest alone goes in and out,"[82] according to Saint Niles; by "the Morning Star,"[83] according to Antiochus; and—perhaps the most troubling accolade of all—by "God's only bridge to man,"[84] according to Proclus.

So attracted was Cardinal Newman, this Roman Catholic convert, to the cult of Mary, so taken up was he with its defense, that in his book *An Essay on the Development of Christian Doctrine* he reached even further, well beyond any of the lofty titles that had already been ascribed to Mary by an energetic piety. Thinking that he was carefully honoring the distinctions between *douleia*, *latreia*, and *hyperdoulia*, Newman actually ended up, in his Marian ruminations, filling in a niche of veneration that was best left empty. Going back to

---

77. Smith, *How to Go*, 126.
78. Pelikan, *Mary through the Centuries*, 34.
79. Ibid.
80. Newman, *An Essay on the Development of Christian Doctrine* (Westminster, MA: Christian Classics, 1968), 146.
81. Ibid.
82. Ibid.
83. Ibid.
84. Ibid., 146–47.

the Arian controversy of the fourth century for suitable materials, the cardinal reasoned in the following fashion: The church in rightly condemning Arianism had *"discovered a new sphere, if we may so speak, in the realms of light, to which the Church had not yet assigned its inhabitant."*[85] Thus there should be little concern about filling this sphere with the proper person so long as the distinction between creature and eternal Creator is maintained, for even the highest celebration of what in fact is a creature (the problem of Arianism) does not detract from the honor and glory of God alone. In the words of Newman himself, "The highest of creatures is levelled with the lowest in comparison of the One Creator Himself."[86] So then, with these distinctions in place, Newman felt entitled, even obligated, to fill in this "new sphere" with "'the Mother of fair love, and fear, and holy hope,' . . . created from the beginning before the world in God's everlasting counsels."[87] Mary, the mother of Christ, in the estimation of Newman, now became resident in the sphere left in the wake of the heresy of Arianism. What was inappropriate for Christ has now been moved over to Mary. Every honor short of the divine, then, could be given to Mary; she was deemed to be that special.

If Newman had simply left it at this in his Marian speculations, then perhaps the situation would not have been so theologically problematic. However, in trying to bring additional glory to Mary, he continued his foray—and this move got him into all sorts of theological trouble. Carrying over his earlier observations on Arianism and fitting them now, appropriate or not, into the great christological council of Ephesus, Newman reasoned:

> I have said that there was in the first ages no public and ecclesiastical recognition of the place which St. Mary holds in the Economy of grace; this was reserved for the fifth century, as the definition of our Lord's proper Divinity had been the work of the fourth. There was a controversy contemporary with those already mentioned, I mean the Nestorian, which brought out the complement of the development, to which they had been subservient; and which, if I may so speak, *supplied the subject of that august proposition of which Arianism had provided the predicate.*[88]

Newman is doing at least three things in this passage. First of all, he is relating the work of the Councils of Nicaea and Constantinople—which together articulated "the definition of our Lord's proper Divinity"[89]—to that labor

85. Ibid., 143 (emphasis added).
86. Ibid.
87. Ibid., 144.
88. Ibid., 145 (emphasis added).
89. Ibid.

of the Council of Ephesus, which treated "the place which St. Mary holds in the Economy of grace."[90] Second, Newman maintains that Nestorianism brought out "the complement of the development" of the earlier controversies, not simply a teaching about Christ but also a proper parallel doctrine about Mary. Third, and most troubling of all, Newman contends in this passage that Arianism "provided the predicate"—meaning here the attributes, traits, titles, and honors—for the subject, meaning Mary, a subject that was provided by the Council of Ephesus.

What, then, are some of those attributes that make up the predicate that Arianism supplied and that in the judgment of Newman should rightfully be applied to Mary? The cardinal himself lists them: "having an ineffable origin before all worlds,"[91] "the Intercessor for man with God,"[92] and "the Object of worship, the Image of the Father."[93] However, next come the glorifications of Mary that even more forcefully cross the line: "God of the Evangelical Covenant"[94] and "Creator of the Universe."[95] To be sure, Arius applied all these attributes to Christ; nevertheless, they left the Lord merely a being who was brought into existence before the creation of the world. The distinction, then, between a very exalted creature (who at some point comes into being) and the eternal God, so developed by Arius in his aberrant Christology, provides no license or authority whatsoever for Newman to move such heretically supposed "christological" traits from Christ, for whom they are indeed heretical in the larger scheme of things, to Mary, for whom they are supposedly not heretical. In other words, the sphere that Arianism had created in between God and humanity, the stuff of demigods, if you will, should not be filled by Mary. Once again, this dimension is best left empty. It is the stuff of which only heresy can be made. Therefore, the imperative "Correct your understanding of the veneration of Mary and the saints"[96] is preeminently a counsel not for evangelicals or for broader Protestants but for Roman Catholics themselves.

90. Ibid.
91. Ibid., 143.
92. Ibid.
93. Ibid.
94. Ibid.
95. Ibid.
96. Smith, *How to Go*, 126.

17

Justification Roman Style

Evangelical Christianity, particularly of the Pentecostal variety, is growing by leaps and bounds in the Global South. When thinking about conversion to Christianity, Christians often call to mind the forgiveness of sins, the renewal of nature, and a sense of assurance. In short, they describe their experience with the familiar biblical terminology of being "born again." Poor peasants from Guatemala and Honduras, for example, have heard the call of Christ upon their lives in the pointed preaching of an evangelical preacher, and they have found themselves wonderfully transformed in the midst of forgiveness, tears, and renewal.[1]

Theologically speaking, the doctrines that correspond to this vibrant, life-changing experience, marked by the graces of the Holy Spirit, are better known as justification, regeneration, and assurance. Since these salient teachings are at the heart of what Christian discipleship means, it is not surprising to learn that they are deeply rooted in Scripture, embedded in the writings of the church fathers, and fleshed out in the materials of the Reformation, both Protestant and Roman Catholic. In this chapter we will consider the doctrine of justification. In chapter 19, we will take up the doctrine of regeneration and assurance, as they too relate to the larger theme of conversion, that transformation of life and character brought about by no one less than a God of holy love.

1. For more on the growth of evangelicalism in Latin America, see Henri Paul Pierre Gooren, "The Pentecostalization of Religion and Society in Latin America," *Exchange* 39, no. 4 (2010): 355–76.

We will begin this larger enterprise by laying out the official doctrinal position of the Roman Catholic Church on justification as found, for example, in Vatican II documents and in the *Catechism*. We will then explore the earlier Council of Trent and demonstrate to what extent it has served and continues to serve as a resource for such contemporary teaching.

Justification

Though the teaching on justification is amply expressed in Scripture and in the writings of the church fathers—indeed, Thomas C. Oden has produced an entire book demonstrating the significant evidence on this score found in the patristic period of the church[2]—this vital doctrine, which some have called *articulus stantis et cadentis ecclesiae* (the article by which the church stands or falls)[3] receives relatively scant attention both in the documents of Vatican II and in the more recent *Catechism*. This has been something of a surprise. In fact, the exact phrase "justified by faith" appears only two times in each, and always in a way that is strongly associated with the sacrament of baptism: "All who have been justified by faith in Baptism are incorporated into Christ."[4] Indeed, as Alister McGrath points out, "The very term 'justification' itself appears to have been gradually eliminated from the homiletical and catechetical literature of Catholicism."[5]

Though the phrase "justified by faith in Baptism" is repeated in both sets of documents, those of Vatican II and of the *Catechism*, the phrase itself is actually ambiguous. And appealing to the larger context of official Roman Catholic teaching is not as helpful here as one might initially expect, since the magisterium repeatedly identifies justification with the sacrament of baptism itself, such that there is, in effect, no justification apart from the sacrament. Indeed, it is precisely Rome's sacramental configuration of justification, conceiving it within the parameters of baptism, that has led precisely to this kind of ambiguity. So then, does "justified by faith in Baptism" mean that one has faith *in baptism*, in other words, that one has a hearty trust that *the sacrament*

2. Oden, *The Justification Reader* (Grand Rapids: Eerdmans, 2002).

3. E.g., Robert Preus, a Lutheran scholar, writes: "The article of justification—or the article of Christ (*solus Christus*), or of faith in Christ, or of Christian righteousness—was soon called the *articulus stantis et cadentis ecclesiae* by all Lutheran teachers." Preus, *Justification and Rome* (St. Louis: Concordia, 2006), 18.

4. *Catechism of the Catholic Church*, 2nd ed. (Mahwah, NJ: Paulist Press, 1994), par. 818. See also *Unitatis Redintegratio: Decree on Ecumenism*, sec. 3, in *The Conciliar and Post Conciliar Documents*, vol. 1 of *Vatican II*, ed. Austin Flannery (Northport, NY: Costello, 1998), 455.

5. McGrath, *Iustitia Dei: A History of the Christian Doctrine of Justification*, 2nd ed. (Cambridge: Cambridge University Press, 1998), 284.

itself is ever efficacious and therefore effectuates the condition of justification? Roman Catholic folk religion appears to favor just such an interpretation, and this view also accords well with the "problem" of infant baptism.[6] Or does the phrase mean that one is *justified by faith* when baptized, faith itself being the only means by which the forgiveness of sins is ever received? Indeed, justification in this second sense can be expressed by way of a sign, in the sacrament of baptism, though faith itself would remain the instrument of its reception, such that faith is absolutely required. Again, in this second view it is not baptism but faith that justifies; it, and not the sacrament, is reckoned for righteousness (Rom. 4:5). The problem here is that both interpretations just offered can be supported from Roman Catholic materials, and this, no doubt, is part of the ongoing difficulty entailed in the sacramental construal of justification.

Beyond this, there is after all a sense in which justification can be clearly distinguished from baptism: one is a saving or soteriological reality; the other is a sign as well as a means of grace. Thus the sacrament may or may not be the occasion of the reception of such saving grace, even if the ritual is performed properly, especially in the case of adults. Rome struggles to acknowledge such a truth in its observation that "the instrumental cause is the sacrament of baptism, which is the sacrament of faith, without which no man was ever justified."[7] Indeed, modern NT scholarship affirms that "in the Pauline communities believers are justified when they are baptized and receive the Spirit,"[8] yet also according to such scholarship, "This does not mean that justification is magically linked with the sacrament. This is refuted not merely by 1 Corinthians 1:17 but by the whole Pauline concept of faith."[9] In declaring that justification (and, one would suppose, the new birth as well) occurs when the baptismal ritual is performed, the Church of Rome once again demonstrates that faith in the sacrament itself (has it occurred or not?) is in effect the preferred and repeatedly acknowledged means of justification.

The Confusion of Justification with Sanctification

Vatican II's use of the word "justification" in a theological sense is indeed limited, with only a couple of references in its documents, though the *Catechism*

6. When I ask Roman Catholics, "Are you justified and born of God?" the reply I invariably receive is "Yes! I was justified and born of God in baptism."

7. Philip Schaff, *The Creeds of Christendom*, vol. 3, *The Evangelical Protestant Creeds, with Translations* (Grand Rapids: Baker, 1983), 96.

8. Gerhard Kittel and Gerhard Friedrich, eds., trans. Geoffrey W. Bromiley, *Theological Dictionary of the New Testament*, 10 vols. (Grand Rapids: Eerdmans, 1964–76), 2:206.

9. Ibid.

does employ the term along with its cognates in several places. The problem with the Roman portrayal, however, is that the basic meaning of "to justify," as found in such passages as Romans 4:3–5; Galatians 3:6; and James 2:23, is subsumed under the theme of sanctification, of "making holy." To illustrate, the *Catechism* states, "Justification is at the same time the acceptance of God's righteousness through faith in Jesus Christ. Righteousness (or 'justice') here means the rectitude of divine love. With justification, faith, hope, and charity are *poured into* our hearts, and obedience to the divine will is granted us."[10] Even more pointedly the *Catechism* goes on to state: "Justification is not only the remission of sins, *but also* the sanctification and renewal of the interior man."[11]

The difficulty with Rome's view, exegetically speaking, is that the use of the Greek word λογίζεσθαι (*logizesthai*) in Romans 4:5 and elsewhere ("However, to the one who does not work but trusts God who justifies the ungodly, their faith is *credited* as righteousness") is best rendered as *credited* or *counted for* or *reckoned as* righteousness, but not as *making* righteousness. This is something that the early church fathers such as Clement of Alexandria,[12] for example, as well as the later Protestant Reformers, both Luther and Calvin, clearly understood. Though this may seem to be a technical, exegetical issue, yet much is actually at stake. Confounding justification with sanctification, mixing these doctrines such that holiness and the impartation of love are now identified with what "to justify" essentially means, amounts to backing away from—at least in some respect, and therefore to deem "fictive"—the radical Pauline notion that God justifies not the holy but sinners. What is at stake is nothing less than the graciousness and beauty of the gospel that faith in Jesus Christ is reckoned to the sinner as righteousness. Sinners do not need to clean themselves up first before they can be forgiven. Indeed, they already are forgiven through the atoning work of Christ, though that forgiveness must be received. Thus one must not mistake the consequences of the justified life, in all manner of holiness, for its very grounding. Indeed, "the fathers of the first four centuries [developed]," as Nick Needham observes, "this major strand of justification teaching where the meaning is forensic: a not-guilty verdict, an acquittal, a declaration of righteousness, a nonimputation of sin, an imputation of righteousness."[13]

10. *Catechism*, par. 1991 (emphasis added).

11. Ibid., par. 1989 (emphasis added).

12. Clement of Alexandria, *Who Is the Rich Man That Shall Be Saved?*, in *Fathers of the Second Century: Hermas, Tatian, Athenagoras, Theophilus, and Clement of Alexandria* (entire), trans. William Wilson, ANF 2:591–604. See also Oden, *Justification Reader*, 92.

13. Needham, "Justification in the Early Church Fathers," in *Justification in Perspective: Historical Developments and Contemporary Challenges*, ed. Bruce L. McCormack (Grand Rapids: Baker Academic, 2006), 36.

Imputation and Impartation?

The sheer graciousness of the gospel, especially as it is expressed in Romans 4:5 ("However, to the one who does not work but trusts God who justifies the ungodly, their faith is credited as righteousness"), can be seen in the distinction developed by the church fathers[14] as well as by the Protestant Reformers between imputation on the one hand, and impartation on the other, especially with respect to the crucial issue of righteousness. Luther, for example, excoriated the scholastics in his own day by pointing out the error of contending that "Sacred Scripture requires us to have a supernatural quality infused into us from heaven, namely, love, which they call the formal righteousness that informs and adorns faith and makes it justify us."[15] This language of "infused" has led Darrell Bock and Mikel Del Rosario to observe, "And so in the Medieval as well as the Post-Reformation Catholic Church, grace is treated almost as if it's a substance, something that can be dispensed through various avenues of change and means through the magisterium."[16]

Bear in mind that imputation involves a forensic *relation* between God and humanity. Impartation, however, is concerned with a participatory ontology, or change in *being*, the infusion of love, as Luther rightly distinguished. Accordingly, "the notional distinction, necessitated by a forensic understanding of justification, between the external act of God in pronouncing sentence, and the internal process of regeneration," McGrath observes, "must be considered to be the most reliable *historical* characterization of Protestant doctrines of justification."[17] Not surprisingly, the Reformed theologian R. C. Sproul has pointed out, "For Protestants God both makes just and declares just—*but not in the same way*. For Rome the declaration of justice *follows* the making inwardly just of the regenerate sinner. For the Reformation the declaration of justice follows the imputation of Christ's righteousness to the regenerated sinner."[18]

As well developed as this distinction is between justification/imputation, on the one hand ("the work that God does for us"[19] in a new relation), and

---

14. Oden, *Justification Reader*, 91–94.

15. Martin Luther, *Lectures on Galatians, 1535, Chapters 1–4*, LW 26:129.

16. Bock and Del Rosario, "The Table Briefing: Seven Key Differences between Protestant and Catholic Doctrine," *Bibliotheca Sacra* 171, no. 683 (July–September 2014): 355. See also David P. Scaer, "Joint Lutheran/Roman Catholic Declaration on Justification: A Response," *Concordia Theological Quarterly* 62, no. 2 (April 1998): 89.

17. McGrath, *Iustitia Dei*, 190.

18. Sproul, *The Evangelical Doctrine of Justification* (Grand Rapids: Baker, 1995), 97–98 (emphasis original).

19. In the opening paragraph of his sermon "The New Birth," John Wesley writes, "If any doctrines within the whole compass of Christianity may be properly termed fundamental they

impartation/sanctification on the other hand ("the work that God does in us"[20] by making believers holy), it is remarkable that the exact phrase "the righteousness of Christ is imputed to believers" is nowhere to be found in the Bible, as John Wesley himself, the father of Methodism, clearly recognized in his own day: "Do not dispute for that *particular phrase* 'the imputed righteousness of Christ.' It is not scriptural; it is not necessary."[21] To be sure, Scripture clearly employs the phrase "the righteousness of God," as in Romans 1:17. According to the celebrated NT scholar Gerhard Kittel, "The δικαιοσύνη θεοῦ [*dikaiosynē theou*] is God's righteousness as a conjunction of judgment and grace which He enjoys and demonstrates by showing righteousness, by imparting it as His pardoning sentence."[22] However, the NT never utilizes the exact phrase "the righteousness of Christ," though it does employ the language of "To those who through the righteousness of our God and Savior Jesus Christ have received a faith as precious as ours" (2 Pet. 1:1).

How then did such a phrase and its associated ideas emerge even from the early annals of the church? The notion of imputation developed around the same three passages noted earlier (Rom. 4:3–5; Gal. 3:6; James 2:23) as exegetes, both ancient and modern, came to terms with what λογίζεσθαι (*logizesthai*, "to reckon") means in the context of δικαιοσύνη (*dikaiosynē*, "righteousness"). To illustrate, in the fourth century Ambrosiaster (the name given to a commentator on Paul's Letters) pointed out: "Paul says this because to an ungodly person, that is, to a Gentile, who believes in Christ without doing the works of the law, his faith is reckoned for righteousness just as Abraham's was."[23] More recently, as Kittel again explains, "What is reckoned is what is established by sovereign grace. Thus λογίζεσθαι acknowledges that thanks to God there is a full achievement of right in faith."[24] Furthermore, in reference to Romans 4:5b ("Their faith is credited as righteousness"), it was not unreasonable to ask, *in whom* had believers placed their faith? The answer, of course, was not God in general (corresponding to "the righteousness

---

are doubtless these two—the doctrine of justification, and that of the new birth: the former relating to that great work which God does *for us*, in forgiving our sins; the latter to the great work which God does *in us*, in renewing our fallen nature." Kenneth J. Collins and Jason Vickers, eds., *The Sermons of John Wesley: A Collection for the Christian Journey* (Nashville: Abingdon, 2013), 157 (emphasis original).

20. Ibid.

21. John Telford, *The Letters of the Rev. John Wesley*, 8 vols. (London: Epworth, 1931), 3:372 (emphasis original).

22. Kittel and Friedrich, *Theological Dictionary*, 2:203.

23. Gerald Bray, *Romans*, rev. ed., Ancient Christian Commentary on Scripture: NT 6 (Downers Grove, IL: InterVarsity, 1998), 108.

24. Kittel and Friedrich, *Theological Dictionary*, 2:207.

of God") but more specifically Jesus Christ. It was, after all, faith in Jesus Christ in particular that was reckoned as righteousness. This was the way, the precious path, that God the Father had established through the power of the Holy Spirit to justify the sinner; it would be through faith in the Son of God, the Lamb of God slain before the foundation of the world—and there was, is, and will never be anything "fictive" about it.[25]

Synergism (Cooperant Grace)

Rome's failure to comprehend the larger theological significance of properly distinguishing justification from the *process* of sanctification, the forensic from the participatory and ontological, results in other difficulties as well, especially in terms of the conception of grace involved in salvation. Thus operating almost exclusively within a synergistic conception of grace, entailing both divine and human working, the *Catechism* declares that "God's free initiative *demands* man's free response."[26] With cooperant grace, the problem of divine and human working—especially regarding the reception of justification as a forensic reality, a change in relation—is that such a synergistic view of grace invariably places the decisive burden on what humans do precisely because it is so readily assumed that God has already acted.

Justification, however, is not a human work but a divine one. Only God can justify the sinner. Therefore the very language of synergistic grace, of demanded and required human working, is somewhat misleading. To illustrate, the *Catechism* fails to recognize that "the free response" of humanity must also be understood in the context of sin, in the wake of the consequences of original sin (as Protestants would understand it) and of the lingering effects and powers of concupiscence (as Roman Catholics would). Thus not just any kind of freedom is being referred to here (such as the freedom to eat this or that, wear this or that, etc.) but the freedom to God, the freedom, in other words, to be redeemed, what Luther referred to as freedom *coram Deo*,[27] liberty in the sight of God.

How free, then, is the sinner in terms of this special, soteriological understanding of liberty? Lest there be misunderstanding, we are not arguing that there is not a measure of freedom in this special setting (*coram Deo*). To the

25. Gerhard Kittel notes that "Paul takes over a sacred Jewish word when he speaks of righteousness, but he turns it against the legal conception of Judaism." Kittel and Friedrich, *Theological Dictionary*, 2:202.

26. *Catechism*, par. 2002 (emphasis added).

27. Martin Luther, *Career of the Reformer III*, LW 33:234.

contrary, we affirm that a measure of freedom, in the face of the ongoing carnal nature, would have to be restored by God alone in a species of prevenient grace. Due to its sovereign restoration (that is, one without human cooperation), this freedom itself is best understood as an instance not of cooperant grace but of free grace. In other words, the very freedom whereby we can receive the gift of justification is itself a gift of God.

On the one hand, like Lutherans and Calvinists, Wesleyans freely acknowledge an Augustinian understanding of original sin that displays the utter corruption of the sinner, the distortion of will and desire, which thereby delimits freedom precisely *coram Deo*. Yet on the other hand, like Anglicans, Wesleyans affirm that God has preveniently and in some measure acted, countering such sin and human impotence, to bring about in some measure a restoration of freedom, and this is done sovereignly precisely due to the extent and reach of corruption. Article 10 of the historic *Thirty-Nine Articles* expresses this truth well: "The condition of Man after the fall of Adam is such, that he cannot turn and prepare himself, by his own natural strength and good works, to faith, and calling upon God. Wherefore we have no power to do good works pleasant and acceptable to God, without the grace of God by Christ preventing us [i.e., coming beforehand], that we may have a good will, and working with us, when we have that good will."[28] Furthermore, unlike Roman Catholics, Wesleyans view such freedom not as always having been present but as a genuine restoration in the face of the depravity of original sin. By a sovereign act of God, then, a measure of freedom is restored, an act that bespeaks not cooperant grace but free grace.

Sola Fide?

Beyond this, Rome's failure to distinguish justification as the work that God does *for us* from sanctification as the work that God does *in us* has prevented this particular theological tradition from understanding that both justification and initial sanctification (in the form of the new birth) are not human works, entailing significant human acting to get the job done so to speak, but sheer gifts of God, that is, in a very real sense the works of God alone. Rome repeatedly flinches at any suggestion of monergism. And although the *Catechism* does employ the language of grace as free in the context of justification, such freedom is immediately caught up, once again, in a synergistic context of both divine and human working, as in the following: "Grace is *favor*, the

---

28. Schaff, *Creeds of Christendom*, 3:494.

free and undeserved help that God gives us *to respond* to his call to become children of God."[29] However, what the Continental Reformers understood so clearly was that only God can forgive sins; only God can make a soul holy. In a certain sense, neither of these actions is a human work. The reception of these gifts must be comprehended not in terms of cooperant grace (for neither justification nor the new birth is given on the basis of prior human cooperation or working [Eph. 2:8–9]) but in terms of free grace, highlighting what only the Most High can do.

Like Lutherans and Calvinists, Wesleyans affirm the importance of free grace in underscoring what only God can do. Wesleyanism—informed by the rich streams of the Anglican and the magisterial Reformation, the latter largely through the influence of Moravianism—is very similar to Calvinism, for example, on the issue of justification: "I think on Justification just as I have done any time these seven-and-twenty years, and just as Mr. Calvin does," Wesley remarked. "In this respect I do not differ from him a hair's breadth."[30] However, unlike Lutherans and Calvinists (and in a way similar to Roman Catholics), Wesleyans acknowledge that these gifts of justification and regeneration must be *received* even if only with the outstretched hand of a beggar. Indeed, there is a receiving of grace before there is any responding, and this is an important step in the process of redemption that Roman Catholic theology often obscures or simply repudiates. For want of better language, there is an "openness and a receptiveness" (almost in a passive sense), best understood in terms of the integrity of the personhood and the image of God that yet remain even in the sinner (now marked by prevenient grace) and issue in a measure of freedom. The outstretching of the hand is hardly a work; instead, describing the reception of grace in this way underscores that what is so graciously granted and received is an utter gift from the Deity, representing what only God can do. Moreover, unlike Roman Catholics, Wesleyans (as noted earlier) conceive such freedom to receive saving grace as accruing from God's action in restoring the faculties of prevenient grace (a measure of freedom, conscience, etc.), which are themselves best understood as instantiations of free grace.[31]

For Wesleyans, not one of these observations just made denies that cooperant, synergistic grace has a role to play in the process of redemption. It's just

---

29. *Catechism*, par. 1996 (emphasis original, except that we have italicized *to respond*).

30. Ted A. Campbell, ed., *The Works of John Wesley*, vol. 27, *Letters III: 1756–1765* (Nashville: Abingdon, 2015), 427.

31. For more on the faculties of prevenient grace that are sovereignly restored, see Kenneth J. Collins, *The Theology of John Wesley: Holy Love and the Shape of Grace* (Nashville: Abingdon, 2007), 77–82.

that such grace is associated not with justification itself but with the divine and human working prior to justification (in receiving convincing grace) or as following justification (in the good works of a lively faith). The human working expressed in this synergistic notion of grace is not and could never be the basis upon which justification is granted. So then, it is the rich and well-developed understanding of free grace that belongs in this theological context, since it is precisely this particular grace that highlights not only what God alone can do but also that both justification and the new birth are sheer gifts of the Almighty and therefore must be received by grace through faith alone. What's so remarkable about the treatments in both Vatican II documents and the *Catechism* is that the exact phrase "free grace" (or the Augustinian "operant grace") is not mentioned at all. Little wonder, then, that the Roman Catholic tradition has balked at employing the language of *sola fide* (by faith alone). It lacks the theological wherewithal and apparently the will to affirm it.

Merit

Although the *Catechism* is clear that *"no one can merit the initial grace* of forgiveness and justification at the beginning of conversion,"[32] it nevertheless offers a different judgment in terms of what takes place afterward in the out-working of Christian discipleship, as is evident in the following claim: "Moved by the Holy Spirit and by charity, *we can then merit* for ourselves and for others the graces needed for our sanctification, for the increase of grace and charity, and for the attainment of eternal life."[33] Since it is difficult to remove from the meaning of the term "merit" the sense of obligation that comes out of a recognition of owing someone something, it therefore is best to forgo the use of this problematic term, especially in consideration of relations with the Most High, *coram Deo*. Indeed, not even those who are redeemed, who are steeped in sanctifying graces, ever put God in their debt.

A Traditional Source for Rome's View?

Before we examine the Council of Trent, revealing the broad similarity between its doctrinal conclusions and the theology of justification just displayed in the official documents of the Roman Catholic Church today and demonstrating

32. *Catechism*, par. 2010 (emphasis original).
33. Ibid. (emphasis original).

a basic continuity, it is helpful to consider the earlier historic attempt at Regensburg to overcome the important theological divide on justification between Roman Catholic and Protestant leaders.

The Colloquy of Regensburg, which met in 1541 and is also known by historians as the Colloquy of Ratisbon, was an early effort to work out the theological differences between Roman Catholics and Protestants in a way that would lead to a resolution, especially in terms of the doctrine of justification. The Roman side was represented by Johann Eck and others under the careful oversight of Cardinal Gasparo Contarini; the Reformers were led by Martin Bucer, Johann Pistorius the Elder, and Philip Melanchthon. The colloquy came to the helpful recognition that conversion is a broad term and therefore embraces both an inherent righteousness, stressed by Roman Catholics, and an imputed righteousness, championed by the Reformers. In the course of its labors, the colloquy eventually produced a joint document that could have become the instrument for a better and more peaceful theological future. However, it was not to be. The Roman Catholic theologians and bishops who had not participated in this colloquy but who were present at Trent thought that the reality of imparted, inherent grace in justification needed a far better and more able expression than what Regensburg had offered. To be sure, "the two key points of the Regensburg article—the insufficiency of our inherent righteousness and the consequent need for imputed righteousness upon which to rely," as Anthony Lane has stated, "were clearly rejected by the Tridentine fathers."[34] Here, then, was yet another opportunity lost.

The Council of Trent

With the collapse of the efforts at Regensburg, the Roman Catholic Church, through the authority of Pope Paul III, eventually called the Council of Trent into session in 1545, and this body met in an on-and-off fashion through 1563. Caught up in the polemics of the period, in its opposition to the doctrinal initiatives and clarifications of the Protestant Reformers, Trent issued judgments and decrees that are clearly marked by an oppositional flavor, and many of these statements are still in effect today. In the wake of these initial observations (above), what is especially noteworthy is that the formal doctrinal teaching of the Roman Catholic Church, expressed more recently in Vatican II documents and in the *Catechism*, is in basic harmony—especially

34. Lane, "A Tale of Two Imperial Cities: Justification at Regensburg and Trent," in *Justification in Perspective: Historical Developments and Contemporary Challenges*, ed. Bruce L. McCormack (Grand Rapids: Baker Academic, 2006), 134.

on the matter of justification—with many of the decrees propounded at Trent four centuries earlier.

Something of the reactionary flavor of the council, in the face of Protestant initiatives, can be seen in Trent's various condemnations laced throughout its doctrinal record. Canon 33, for example, fulminates: "If any one saith, that, by the Catholic doctrine touching Justification, by this holy Synod set forth in this present decree, the glory of God, or the merits of our Lord Jesus Christ are in any way derogated from, and not rather that the truth of our faith, and the glory in fine of God and of Jesus Christ are rendered [more] illustrious: let him be anathema."[35] In fact, the word "anathema" occurs more than one hundred times in the pronouncements of the Council of Trent. Regardless of content, such usage surely bespeaks a theological posture and tone.

Trent: The Confusion of Justification with Sanctification

The decrees of this northern Italian conference suggest to some, at least, a confidence in diligent theological judgment. Yet upon closer examination, when specific arguments are addressed, it appears that such confidence arises not from careful and decisive theological reflection, as if the "last word" had now been spoken, but from that old ecclesiastical and well-worn argument emerging once more: "The magisterium has spoken."

Indeed, the doctrinal teaching of Trent on justification is marked by the same theological missteps and confusions as detailed above, especially in terms of the *Catechism*. Thus Trent declared that justification is "not only a remission of sins *but also* the sanctification and renewal of the inward man,"[36] once more confounding the forensic and relational with the ontological. Even more troubling, Trent goes on to declare that the holiness of the new birth, or what some call initial sanctification, is the very basis upon which one is justified: "In that new birth there is bestowed upon them, through the merit of His passion, the grace by which they are made just."[37] In such a view an infusion of grace, in the form of charity, is poured into the heart, making the believer just. Trent declared, "In the said justification of the impious, ... the charity of God is poured forth, by the Holy Spirit, in the hearts of those that are justified, and ... [the one who is justified] receives, in the said

---

35. Schaff, *Creeds of Christendom*, vol. 2, *The Greek and Latin Creeds, with Translations* (Grand Rapids: Baker, 1983), 118.
36. Ibid., 94 (emphasis added).
37. Ibid., 91.

justification, together with the remission of sins, all these [gifts] infused at once, faith, hope, and charity."[38]

As Karla Wübbenhorst points out, "Augustine and the Catholic conciliar documents that enshrine this thought, know nothing of the cherished Reformed distinction between justification and sanctification."[39] Thus the mouth of sanctification is so broad and wide that it nearly consumes the distinct reality of what is entailed in justification. Though in many respects he appreciated the doctrinal contributions of Augustine, Calvin nevertheless insisted upon a clear distinction between these two very different works of grace. To illustrate, we may consult his *Commentary on Romans*, where he reasons as follows: "They think that these two things well agree,—that man is justified by faith through the grace of Christ,—and that he is yet justified by the works, which proceed from spiritual regeneration; for God gratuitously renews us, and we also receive his gift by faith. But Paul takes up a very different principle,—that the consciences of men will never be tranquillized until they recumb on the mercy of God alone."[40] Such an observation has led Wübbenhorst to conclude: "Calvin [became] convinced that this was a distinction worth contending for."[41] It was at the very heart of the utterly gracious good news of the gospel.[42] In fact, the doctrine of justification must be rightly distinguished, according to the Genevan Reformer, precisely because it is the "main hinge"[43] or "the principal ground on which religion must be supported."[44] As a consequence of this, "it requires greater care and attention."[45]

38. Ibid., 96.

39. Wübbenhorst, "Calvin's Doctrine of Justification: Variations on a Lutheran Theme," in McCormack, *Justification in Perspective*, 109.

40. John Calvin, *Commentary on the Epistle of Paul the Apostle to the Romans*, trans. and ed. John Owen (Bellingham, WA: Logos Bible Software, 2010), 135.

41. Wübbenhorst, "Calvin's Doctrine of Justification," 109.

42. The Finnish school of interpretation in Luther studies has maintained that the German Reformer's understanding of justification was quite broad and in fact embraced the Eastern Orthodox notion of theosis (Greek *theōsis*). However, we find this reading of Luther's works somewhat problematic, especially since it is overly dependent on his early writings. That is, it cannot embrace Luther's mature understanding of this crucial matter. For more on this topic, see Carl Trueman, "Simul Peccator et Justus: Martin Luther and Justification," in McCormack, *Justification in Perspective*, 73–97.

43. John Calvin, *Institutes of the Christian Religion*, ed. John T. McNeill, trans. Ford Lewis Battles, 2 vols., Library of Christian Classics 20–21 (Philadelphia: Westminster, 1960), 3.11.1 (1:726).

44. John Calvin, *Institutes of the Christian Religion*, trans. Henry Beveridge (Edinburgh: Calvin Translation Society, 1845), 2:302. We have quoted two different translations of Calvin's *Institutes* to show the differences.

45. Ibid.

Trent: Imputation and Impartation?

Since Trent readily mixed the distinct works of justification and regeneration, thereby making holiness in some sense the heart or very substance of what justification means, it consequently left little room for the imputation or reckoning-as-righteousness that is such an important part of the apostle Paul's teaching on justification, especially in the prominent passages of Romans 4:3–5; Galatians 3:6; and James 2:23, as noted earlier. In fact, Trent specifically denies that faith imputed for righteousness (Rom. 4:5b) is the very substance, on one level, of justification. Instead, it insists on the *impartation* and infusion of love as necessary to the basic meaning of justification. For example, canon 11 states: "If any one saith, that men are justified, either by the sole imputation of the justice of Christ, or by the sole remission of sins, to the exclusion of the grace and the charity which is poured forth in their hearts by the Holy Ghost, and is inherent in them; or even that the grace, whereby we are justified, is only the favor of God: let him be anathema."[46]

In light of such reasoning, what has happened to the Pauline notion that faith is credited for righteousness? Here as elsewhere in Roman Catholic materials, both ancient and modern, the Pauline understanding of imputation has been washed out in a theology that is admittedly uneasy about considering any justification of the sinner apart from the ontological reality of holiness. Justification conceived forensically and relationally is simply not enough; it must be "infused" with holiness and love to bear its proper sense. However, this substantival, reified conception of grace, more particularly the notion of *gratia infusa* and *gratia habitualis* (infused grace and habitual grace),[47] so important to the Roman Catholic view here, has "no basis in Scripture,"[48] according to some. Indeed, in crafting its position Trent interweaved streams of earlier scholastic theology to offer a "consistent metonymical understanding of . . . [justification]" and thereby confused, once again, an effect for a cause.[49] Perhaps even more damaging to Trent's scholastic view is the recognition that the term "forensic" does not mean "as if he were righteous,"[50] as Kittel once again observes, "since the sovereign sentence of God is *genuinely* pronounced."[51]

46. Schaff, *Creeds of Christendom*, 2:112–13.
47. Preus, *Justification and Rome*, 54.
48. Ibid.
49. Ibid., 46.
50. Kittel and Friedrich, *Theological Dictionary*, 2:202.
51. Ibid. (emphasis added).

Trent: Synergism (Cooperant Grace)

In the eyes of Trent, justification is received on the basis of prior human co-operation, a working together with God that is deemed absolutely necessary for the reception of forgiveness. That is clear from the language of the sixth session of the council, which concluded: "So they, who by sins were alienated from God, may be disposed through his quickening and assisting grace, *to convert themselves to their own justification*, by freely assenting to and co-operating with that said grace."[52] Even understood in its best sense and in a most charitable way, such language is obviously unguarded, given all that has to be factored into any such pronouncement. It therefore calls for greater and more careful theological articulation.

Beyond this ongoing fault, Trent has the same emphasis on human freedom *coram Deo* as does the *Catechism*, as if the issue of liberty were not a problem at all in this very special context. The key difference, however, is that in this earlier setting, due to the contrarian nature of so many of Trent's judgments, an anathema was attached to any view that differed from that of the magisterium: "If any one saith, that man's free-will moved and excited by God, by assenting to God exciting and calling, nowise co-operates towards disposing and preparing itself for obtaining the grace of Justification; . . . let him be anathema."[53] However, the question that plagued Luther, the erstwhile Augustinian monk, still troubles sinners even today: "Have I done enough?" This larger theological issue, then, is far more complicated than the council allowed, in terms of both its soteriological and psychological dimensions. Its proper assessment, therefore, should have entailed both theological nuance and greater care, especially in terms of the supernatural, uncanny, and numinous graces under review. Moreover, Rome even in the sixteenth century had something of a theological partner on this issue of liberty (at least conceived as a prevenient restoration in the face of the debilitating effects of original sin) in Anglicanism. However, the polemical nature of this period and the constant falling back to a particular ecclesiology would not allow for precisely such a dialogue.

Trent: *Sola Fide?*

It is clear from a consideration of the scholarship now available through the publication of the Ancient Christian Commentary on Scripture series that the

---

52. Schaff, *Creeds of Christendom*, 2:92 (emphasis added).
53. Ibid., 111.

early church fathers heartily affirmed the teaching of sola fide. As Thomas Oden has pointed out, such a doctrinal expression was not a Protestant innovation: "The major Reformers' appeals to sola scriptura, sola gratia, and sola fide are found abundantly in the patristic interpreters of scripture."[54] To illustrate this basic truth, we can point to Origen in the third century, who in his commentary on Romans 3:28 states: "It remains for us who are trying to affirm everything the apostle says, and to do so in the proper order, to inquire who is justified by faith alone, apart from works."[55] Ambrosiaster reasoned as follows: "How then can the Jews think that they have been justified by the works of the law in the same way as Abraham, when they see that Abraham was not justified by the works of the law but by faith alone? Therefore there is no need of the law when the *ungodly* is justified before God by faith alone."[56] What then was Trent's assessment of this early church teaching that was carefully expressed and reappropriated by the Reformers of the sixteenth century? Canon 9 of the sixth session reveals its judgment, yet again marked by polemics and anathema: "If anyone says that the sinner is justified by faith alone, meaning that nothing else is required to cooperate in order to obtain the grace of justification, and that it is not in any way necessary that he be prepared and disposed by the action of his own will, let him be anathema."[57] Bear in mind also that here Rome's claim to speak for the universal church, in a purported ecumenical council, belies the ongoing significance not only of Protestantism but also of Eastern Orthodoxy.

Trent: Merit

Though the Protestant Reformers such as Martin Luther carefully argued for an abundance of good works in an active life of Christian discipleship, as evidenced in his *Treatise on Good Works*,[58] he nevertheless cautioned that the whole matter of good works must be understood properly and in a way that does not devolve upon the issue of merit. In his *Lectures on Galatians*, for instance, Luther exclaimed: "With Paul, therefore, we totally deny the 'merit of congruity' and the 'merit of condignity.' . . . For God has never given anyone grace and eternal life for the merit of congruity or the merit of condignity."[59] The Council of Trent, however, was of an entirely different

54. Oden, *Justification Reader*, 162.
55. Bray, *Romans*, 100.
56. Ibid., 108 (emphasis added).
57. H. J. Schroeder, *Canons and Decrees of the Council of Trent* (Rockford, IL: TAN Books, 1978), Kindle edition, locations 1327–29.
58. Luther, *Treatise on Good Works*, trans. Scott H. Hendrix (Minneapolis: Fortress, 2012).
59. Martin Luther, *Lectures on Galatians, 1535, Chapters 1–4*, LW 26:125–26.

mind on this specific issue. For example, canon 26 of the sixth session of the council declares: "If anyone says that the just ought not for the good works done in God to expect and hope for an eternal reward from God through His mercy and the merit of Jesus Christ, . . . let him be anathema."[60] Interestingly enough, "The authority with which Thomas [Aquinas] was invested [on this and other issues]," as McGrath observes, "may be judged from the fact that he was cited more than any theologian—other than Augustine—during the course of the Tridentine debate on justification."[61]

Not content with this pronouncement on works, the council continued to insist upon mixing the theologically dubious notion of "merit" with such labors, thereby undermining, at least in some sense, the grace-infused nature of these charitable acts, a nature that surely bespeaks their gifted source, the empowering presence of the Holy Spirit within. Indeed, in contending that such works also merit eternal life, the council departed from some of the dimensions of the graciousness of the gospel. Canon 32, for instance, opines: "If any one saith, that the good works of one that is justified are in such manner the gifts of God, that they are not also the good merits of him that is justified, . . . [that person] does not truly merit increase of grace, eternal life, and the attainment of that eternal life; . . . let him be anathema."[62]

Just as it is now evident that the Council of Trent shines through the teachings of Vatican II as well as the *Catechism*, so too does it inform, interestingly enough, many of the theological judgments expressed in a more recent document, the *Joint Declaration on the Doctrine of Justification*. We will explore this work in considerable detail in the following chapter.

60. Schaff, *Creeds of Christendom*, 2:116.
61. McGrath, *Iustitia Dei*, 251.
62. Schaff, *Creeds of Christendom*, 2:118.

18

Justification

The Joint Declaration *and Its Aftermath*

By the twentieth century the Roman Catholic Church had begun to throw off some of its earlier triumphalist approaches to move in a direction in which genuine dialogue with Protestant theological traditions could at least now be possible. An important step in this regard occurred at Vatican II, in which key Protestant leaders were invited as observers, including Karl Barth, Oscar Cullmann, and George Lindbeck.

Though Roman Catholic apologists are reluctant to admit it,[1] the Vatican is, after all, influenced in some sense by broader cultural and theological changes. In 1959, for example, in calling for the Second Vatican Council, Pope John XXIII, the most ecumenical pope of the century, recognized that the Roman Catholic Church was clearly in need of updating, or what has often been referred to as *aggiornamento*. By way of contrast, during the nineteenth century Pope Pius IX, in his "Syllabus of Errors," had railed against a host of errors, eighty to be exact (hardly the climate for ecumenical dialogue). Here

---

1. For a contemporary, triumphalist, and utterly dogmatic approach to ecumenical "conversation," see Devin Rose, *The Protestant's Dilemma: How the Reformation's Shocking Consequences Point to the Truth of Catholicism* (San Diego: Catholic Answers Press, 2014). Indeed, in this book Rose starts from the assumption that an unchanging, dogmatic Rome is always correct in any of its many judgments as well as ever being the center of any supposed "dialogue," as is evidenced in his following observation: "But it is not dialogue for dialogue's sake. It is dialogue with an end in mind of bringing all involved in the dialogue to the fullness of truth that the Catholic Church alone possesses in fullness. That is what authentic dialogue in the conciliar sense is all about." Ibid., Kindle edition, locations 55–57.

is one example of a statement that Pius IX condemns as an "error": "18. Protestantism is nothing more than another form of the same true Christian religion, in which form it is given to please God equally as in the Catholic Church."[2] However, by the mid-twentieth century these older divisive pronouncements, though still held by many traditionalists in the church in the name of keeping "the faith," were seen as more or less embarrassing to the more ecumenically minded.

As important as Vatican II is and though its judgments did affect Protestants, it nevertheless was largely an internal conversation within the Roman Catholic tradition itself. Moreover, as explained in chapter 17, the crucial doctrine of justification was hardly considered in this groundbreaking venue. That conversation, in which Protestants would indeed be included, took place only in the wake of this historic council. Indeed, it would not be until the closing days of the twentieth century that an agreement on this salient doctrine was eventually hammered out.

The *Joint Declaration* on Justification by Faith

With much fanfare, though not all were celebrating, the Roman Catholic Church, more specifically its Pontifical Council for Promoting Christian Unity, and the Lutheran World Federation signed the *Joint Declaration on the Doctrine of Justification* in the historic city of Augsburg, known for the famous Augsburg Confession, on October 31, 1999, the anniversary of the Reformation. Naturally with an event of this magnitude, earlier conversations among a variety of theologians and ecclesiastical figures helped to prepare the way, including the following reports:

- *The Gospel and the Church* (1972) and *Church and Justification* (1994), by the Lutheran–Roman Catholic Joint Commission
- *Justification by Faith* (1983), of the Lutheran–Roman Catholic dialogue in the USA
- *The Condemnations of the Reformation Era: Do They Still Divide?* (1986), by the Ecumenical Working Group of Protestant and Catholic theologians in Germany.[3]

2. Pope Pius IX, "Syllabus of Errors," December 8, 1864, Papal Encyclicals Online, http://www.papalencyclicals.net/Pius09/p9syll.htm.
3. Lutheran World Federation and the Pontifical Council for Promoting Christian Unity, *Joint Declaration on the Doctrine of Justification*, English ed. (Grand Rapids: Eerdmans, 2000), 9–10, par. 3.

Moreover, it will no doubt be helpful for readers, giving them a sense of orientation, to view the basic outline of this *Joint Declaration*. Its parts, which are not equally weighted in the task of interpretation, are displayed in the following structure:

Preamble
1. Biblical Message of Justification
2. The Doctrine of Justification as Ecumenical Problem
3. The Common Understanding of Justification
4. Explicating the Common Understanding of Justification
5. The Significance and Scope of the Consensus Reached
Sources for the Joint Declaration on the Doctrine of Justification
Official Common Statement
Annex to the Official Common Statement

Embedded in the preamble is both a Roman Catholic understanding of the weight of tradition and its own preferred ecclesiastical judgments in the form of an unerring hierarchy and magisterium. On the one hand, it is stated that "the remaining differences in its explication are no longer the occasion for doctrinal condemnations"[4] and, on the other hand, in a very traditional way that "the churches neither take the condemnations [e.g., of the Council of Trent] lightly nor do they disavow their own past."[5] For its part, Rome has dealt with this apparent contradiction, which can strike at its own ecclesiastical authority, by affirming (to cite just one example) the correctness of Trent in its pronouncements (for by definition that "ecumenical council" cannot have erred) but softening the offense (to Protestants) by maintaining that in the present, in a far less polemical context, "new understandings" have emerged in terms of this earlier yet continually affirmed history: "On the contrary, this Declaration is shaped by the conviction that in their respective histories our churches have come to *new insights*."[6]

JD: The Confusion of Justification with Sanctification

Although the theological contributions of the Lutherans expressed in an earlier report supported the appropriateness of "the distinction between justification

4. Ibid., 11, par. 5.
5. Ibid., 11, par. 7.
6. Ibid. (emphasis added).

and sanctification,"[7] the Roman Catholic centuries-old habit of mixing these two distinct works of grace became the preferred language of the *Joint Declaration* itself. Thus paragraph 11 of this historic document observes: "Justification is the forgiveness of sins (cf. Rom. 3:23–25; Acts 13:39; Luke 18:14), *liberation from the dominating power of sin and death* (Rom. 5:12–21) and from the curse of the law (Gal. 3:10–14)."[8] Even more pointedly, paragraph 27 reveals that the Roman Catholic conception of the relation between justification and sanctification brought to bear in this ecumenical setting is utterly in line with the earlier pronouncements of the *Catechism* and the Council of Trent. Indeed, the *Joint Declaration* emphasizes that "the justification of sinners is forgiveness of sins *and* being made righteous by justifying grace, which makes us children of God."[9] When the Lutheran and Roman Catholic voices eventually merged at points in the *Joint Declaration*, to speak in unison, they evidently spoke with a very Roman Catholic accent: "We confess together. . . . When persons come by faith to share in Christ, God no longer imputes to them their sin and through the Holy Spirit effects in them an active love."[10]

Something of a concession on the part of Rome on this critical issue can perhaps be discerned not so much in the formal part of the *Joint Declaration* itself as in the "Sources Section." Thus the earlier report *The Condemnations of the Reformation Era: Do They Still Divide?* expresses the Roman Catholic position in the following manner:

> Catholic doctrine knows itself to be at one with the Protestant concern in emphasizing that the renewal of the human being does not "contribute" to justification, and is certainly not a contribution to which he could make any appeal before God. Nevertheless it feels compelled to stress the renewal of the human being through justifying grace, for the sake of acknowledging God's newly creating power; although this renewal in faith, hope, and love is certainly nothing but a response to God's unfathomable grace.[11]

Rome's concern, demonstrated above, for real, imparted transformation in the form of holiness is undoubtedly important in considering the constitution of the Christian life. It's just not very helpful to state that "the renewal of the human being [takes place] through justifying grace,"[12] thereby mixing the relational and forensic language of Scripture with its participatory and

7. Ibid., 33, sources for sec. 4.3.
8. Ibid., 13, par. 11 (emphasis added).
9. Ibid., 20, par. 27 (emphasis added).
10. Ibid., 18, par. 22.
11. Ibid., 33.
12. Ibid.

ontological articulation. In effect, and in a way similar to Trent, "the Roman view," as Robert Preus has aptly pointed out, "subsumes the article of justification under the articles of sanctification, renewal, and grace, and does so by divesting it of its meaning and identifying it with its effects so that cause and effect coalesce in the process."[13] In our judgment it would be far better and much more theologically appropriate—especially in consideration of the larger process of conversion, of which justification is ever a vital part—to distinguish this crucial justifying work of grace from that of sanctification. Again, it is necessary to clearly state that initial sanctification or regeneration, and not justification itself, is that salvific grace that actually makes one holy. Why then balk at this? Why be limited to a single theological idiom when another is so clearly called for, especially when the inclusion of such would go a long way in clearing up theological confusion, especially between Protestants and Roman Catholics? Indeed, having justification do all the heavy lifting here, in what amounts to the larger process of sanctification and conversion, is precisely the problem. What then, in the face of all of this, has become of the Lutheran concern, expressed in the earlier report, to distinguish justification from sanctification? It has fallen away.

JD: Imputation and Impartation?

In a manner that epitomizes the Roman Catholic theological posture toward how λογίζεσθαι (*logizesthai*) is to be understood in terms of its usage, as for instance found in Romans 4:5 ("God who justifies the ungodly"), the *Joint Declaration* has but one single statement (as difficult as this is to believe) that expresses a theological understanding of the term "imputation." It appears, then, that the Lutheran World Federation, once again, has simply acceded to the Roman view, neglecting an important part of its own theological heritage: "We confess together . . . [that] God no longer imputes to them their sin and through the Holy Spirit effects in them an active love."[14] To be sure, the overarching problem here is that such a statement embraces only about half of what's actually entailed in the theological substance of imputation, a point that Luther himself readily acknowledged. To illustrate, the German Reformer observed in his *Lectures on Galatians*, "It is not in vain, therefore, that so often and so diligently we inculcate the doctrine of the forgiveness of sins *and* of the imputation of righteousness for the sake of Christ."[15] More

---

13. Preus, *Justification and Rome* (St. Louis: Concordia, 2006), 69–70.
14. Ibid., 18.
15. Martin Luther, *Lectures on Galatians, 1535, Chapters 1–4*, LW 26:133 (emphasis added).

recently Preus has written about the *twofold movement* of imputation, not simply about the nonimputation of sin, as Rome would have it, but also, and more positively, in terms of what he calls "Christ's 'blessed exchange'"[16] with us, whereby "He took upon Himself our personal sins *and* gave to us His personal innocence and victory."[17] In other words, in the Lutheran tradition, from Luther forward, imputation was conceived not in a monological sense but in a twofold way: "1) forgiveness, or the non-imputation of sin, *and* 2) the imputation of a righteousness outside of us."[18] Simply put, that God no longer imputes sin to sinners is simply not enough. Such a reduction of the blessed nature of imputation cannot even explain all that is theologically present in Paul's 2 Corinthians: "God made him who had no sin to be sin for us, so that in him we might become the righteousness of God" (5:21).

JD: Synergism or Cooperant Grace

It is in this specific area of the nature of justifying grace—that is, in what sense grace entails synergism, or divine and human cooperation (even if only to be "prepared" to receive justifying grace), and in what sense grace is freely given by God, thereby underscoring the work of God alone—that perhaps the greatest advance has been made in the *Joint Declaration* beyond both the *Catechism* and Trent. The Lutherans take pains to articulate their position clearly and to acknowledge Roman Catholic concerns about its implications. Thus, in the section of the document titled "Explicating the Common Understanding of Justification," they point out first that "a person can only receive (mere passive) justification, . . . thereby . . . exclud[ing] any possibility of contributing to one's own justification."[19] Second, they assert that "justification remains free from human cooperation and is not dependent on the life-renewing effects of grace in human beings."[20] They caution that these two statements will be properly understood only in light of the following: "The strict emphasis on the passivity of human beings concerning their justification never meant, on the Lutheran side, to contest the full personal participation in believing."[21]

In a similar fashion, after the Roman Catholic contributors to the *Joint Declaration* affirm "that persons 'cooperate' in preparing for and accepting

16. Preus, *Justification and Rome*, 62 (emphasis added).
17. Ibid. (emphasis added).
18. Ibid., 59 (emphasis added).
19. Lutheran World Federation and the Pontifical Council for Promoting Christian Unity, *Joint Declaration*, 17, par. 21.
20. Ibid., 18, par. 23.
21. Ibid., 31, sources for sec. 4.1.

justification by consenting to God's justifying action," they go on to declare in a later paragraph, and in a helpful manner, that "they do not thereby deny that God's gift of grace in justification remains *independent of human cooperation,*"[22] something that Luther had insisted upon all along. Does this mean, then, that Roman Catholic theology can actually embrace a full-orbed notion of free grace (operant grace) and the sovereignty of God, in conjunction with cooperant grace, as a part of its larger theological whole? If so, then it would be considerably helpful to state this explicitly.

JD: Sola Fide?

A careful reading of the *Joint Declaration* shows that the Lutheran and the Roman Catholic statements on the role of faith in salvation are markedly different. On the one hand, the Lutherans affirm that the doctrine of justification by faith is not just any doctrine, but that it "stands in an essential relation to all truths of faith, which are to be seen as internally related to each other. It is an indispensable criterion that constantly serves to orient all the teaching and practice of our churches to Christ."[23] In fact, during the sixteenth century Melanchthon had arranged the articles of faith in the Augsburg Confession around "Article IV on justification and Article XX on 'Faith and Good Works.'"[24]

The Roman Catholics, on the other hand, when they do show interest in the doctrine (justification was not directly addressed at Vatican II), consider themselves bound by several criteria and not by one chief orienting concern, though they do admit something of "the special function of the message of justification."[25] Remarkably enough, an earlier draft of the *Joint Declaration* (the June 1996 version) contained the Lutheran preference on the issue of criterion, but this was eventually overturned by the Roman Sacred Congregation for the Doctrine of the Faith. As Eberhard Jüngel put it at the time: "Cardinal Ratzinger corrected Cardinal Cassidy to the effect that the *Pontifical Council for Promoting Christian Unity* may concede only that 'the doctrine of justification is an indispensable criterion.'"[26] Jüngel went on to observe: "By the addition of the indefinite article 'an' justification was demoted from

22. Ibid., 18–19, par. 24 (emphasis added).
23. Ibid., 16, par. 18.
24. Preus, *Justification and Rome*, 15.
25. Lutheran World Federation and the Pontifical Council for Promoting Christian Unity, *Joint Declaration*, 16, par. 18.
26. David P. Scaer, "Joint Lutheran/Roman Catholic Declaration on Justification: A Response," *Concordia Theological Quarterly* 62, no. 2 (April 1998): 88.

its position of unique, overarching criterion to one among others."[27] Thus it was not *the* criterion but *a* criterion.

Moreover, the *Joint Declaration* reveals that the Lutherans in their contribution to the document readily employed the language of sola fide but that the Roman Catholics did not. Compare the two very different statements: "According to Lutheran understanding, God justifies sinners in faith alone (sola fide). In faith they place their trust wholly in their Creator and Redeemer and thus live in communion with him."[28] This first statement, then, takes into account the two very practical reasons why sola fide was so important to the Lutheran tradition: "First, God wants us to be sure of the forgiveness of our sins (Rom. 4:16). Second, God wants us to glory not in ourselves but in His grace (Eph. 2:9)."[29] However, the Roman Catholic affirmation simply considers faith as "fundamental in justification. For without faith, no justification can take place."[30] Yet it never once mentions sola fide. Granted, the idiom sola fide does indeed emerge in the *Annex to the Official Common Statement*, but even here there is no specific Roman Catholic ownership. And why couldn't such language have been made a part of the *Official Common Statement* instead of being pushed off to the side in an *Annex*? Indeed, if Roman Catholic theologians dislike the language of "alone" or "*sola*" in this context, then let them, to use the words of Preus, "remove the other exclusive terms from Paul, too, like 'freely,' 'not of works,' 'it is a gift,' etc., for these terms are also exclusive."[31] Moreover, in a concluding observation this Lutheran leader notes: "The whole thrust of the Book of Galatians is to show that justification before God is by faith alone."[32]

JD: Merit

Several of the *Joint Declaration*'s paragraphs go a long way in clearing up any misunderstanding that today Roman Catholicism teaches justification to be merited by the proper use of prevenient grace. For its part, Rome maintains that justification is due to the grace and mercy of God. To illustrate, paragraph 15 of section 3, "The Common Understanding of Justification," states:

27. Ibid.
28. Lutheran World Federation and the Pontifical Council for Promoting Christian Unity, *Joint Declaration*, 19, par. 26.
29. Preus, *Justification and Rome*, 97.
30. Lutheran World Federation and the Pontifical Council for Promoting Christian Unity, *Joint Declaration*, 20, par. 27.
31. Preus, *Justification and Rome*, 99.
32. Ibid., 101.

"Together we confess: By grace alone, in faith in Christ's saving work and not because of any merit on our part, we are accepted by God and receive the Holy Spirit, who renews our hearts while equipping and calling us to good works."[33] Again, paragraph 17 affirms that the message of justification "tells us that because we are sinners our new life is solely due to the forgiving and renewing mercy that God imparts as a gift and we receive in faith and never can merit in any way."[34] Beyond this, paragraph 25 declares: "But whatever in the justified precedes or follows the free gift of faith is neither the basis of justification nor merits it."[35]

Why, then, has the question of merit remained a contentious issue (see below) even after the pronouncements of the *Joint Declaration*? For one thing, Rome has insisted on a place for merit, especially in terms of those works that follow justification. Thus, when "Catholics affirm the 'meritorious' character of good works, they wish to say that . . . a reward in heaven is promised to these works."[36] However, in a way much more in line with a biblical idiom, the Lutherans, for their part, have declared that they "view the good works of Christians as the *fruits and signs* of justification and *not as one's own 'merits.'*"[37] What compounds this difficulty even further is that the Lutheran sense of the matter had already been specifically condemned by Trent. Recall the language of this council cited earlier: "If any one saith, that the good works of one that is justified are in such manner the gifts of God, that they are not also the good merits of him that is justified . . . [and that he] does not truly merit increase of grace, eternal life, and the attainment of that eternal life, . . . let him be anathema."[38] Since this teaching has not been put aside by the *Joint Declaration*, because it contains a "salutary warning," we are now in a better position to understand just why controversy over this terminology yet remains.

Even today Rome contends that by the use of such "meritorious" language it is only underscoring the value of responsibility in the ongoing Christian life—an emphasis that, by the way, goes back to Augustine[39]—nevertheless such a concern could have been better held in place by an appeal to the necessity of

33. Lutheran World Federation and the Pontifical Council for Promoting Christian Unity, *Joint Declaration*, 15, par. 15.

34. Ibid., 16, par. 17.

35. Ibid., 19, par. 25.

36. Ibid., 25, par. 38.

37. Ibid., 25, par. 39 (emphasis added).

38. Canon 32 of the Council of Trent, in Philip Schaff, *The Creeds of Christendom*, vol. 2, *The Greek and Latin Creeds, with Translations* (Grand Rapids: Baker, 1983), 117–18.

39. Lutheran World Federation and the Pontifical Council for Promoting Christian Unity, *Joint Declaration*, 38, sources for sec. 4.7.

cooperant, responsible grace, if there be time and opportunity, precisely after justification has occurred. This would have been a better, less problematic course to pursue, especially since cooperant, responsible grace is already very much a part of the array of Roman Catholic theological resources. To be sure, the language of merit was, is, and remains burdened with an enormous capacity for misunderstanding. What truth it attempts to preserve can be suitably expressed in far better and less ambiguous language. As Michael Root has so ably revealed in an important article on this very topic, "No matter how one may wish to affirm the reality 'merit' seeks to describe, the concept 'merit' brings with it more problems than it solves."[40]

JD: The "New Perspective" to the Rescue?

The key differences between Roman Catholics and Protestants on the issue of justification turn, in large measure, on a proper interpretation of the writings of the apostle Paul. Some in the church therefore hoped that the "new perspective" on Paul (and on justification)—as found, for example, in the earlier work of E. P. Sanders in his *Paul and Palestinian Judaism* (1977) and the more recent contributions of N. T. Wright in his *Justification: God's Plan and Paul's Vision* (2009)—would save the day. But alas, it was not to be. There are many good reflections in Wright's work on the topic of justification, which we receive in deep appreciation, especially in terms of trying to overcome the Jewish/Christian divide; yet also a few problems are indicated in the following observations: (1) Wright underscores a single covenant, to the loss of the full worth and distinctiveness of the new covenant; (2) he views justification simply as acquittal, a courtroom act, and therefore as "the granting of a status,"[41] in terms of this single covenant; and (3) he considers saving faith more along the lines of what medieval theologians referred to as *fides* (belief or faith) rather than *fiducia* (confidence or trust).[42] In Wright's interpretive hands, then, redemptive faith is apparently belief that Jesus is Lord and that God raised him from the dead. Although the Letter to the Romans does indeed make such a statement (e.g., 10:9), Paul is no doubt assuming that such a belief is emblematic of a much larger whole. In the Pauline context, such usage is actually informed by many things, some of which would imply

40. Root, "Aquinas, Merit, and Reformation Theology after the Joint Declaration on the Doctrine of Justification," *Modern Theology* 20, no. 1 (January 2004): 18–19.
41. Wright, *Justification: God's Plan and Paul's Vision* (Downers Grove, IL: IVP Academic, 2009), 90.
42. Ibid., 251.

other dimensions of redemptive faith such as a vibrant personal trust and relation—aspects that, in our judgment, Wright leaves underdeveloped.[43]

But there is even a far greater problem here, and this constitutes the principal reason why a discussion of the "new perspective" has been relegated, in this present context, simply to a few paragraphs. Consider this: the language, idioms, and basic meanings of justification discussed and at times disputed at Trent and much later by both Roman Catholics and Protestants in the *Joint Declaration* were nevertheless far more similar to each other (largely Augustinian or Thomistic in approach), despite the differences in play at the time, than the offerings of the new perspective itself were to either the current Roman Catholic perspective or the Protestant one. Many of the terms surrounding justification have been redefined in special new-perspective ways whose meanings were not employed either at Trent or in the context of the *Joint Declaration*. After all, that's the whole point of the project of the new perspective, is it not, to celebrate the "new"? Therefore, it is precisely that newness or redefinition that must make up a conversation (and no doubt an interesting one) for another day. It simply does not belong here.[44]

Is the Common Understanding of Justification Theologically Sufficient?

Section 3 of the *Joint Declaration*, better known as "The Common Understanding of Justification," contains a number of joint, ecumenically minded statements made by both the Lutheran World Federation and the Roman Catholic Church that are supposed to express the substance of the teaching on justification as revealed in the following numbered (and slightly edited) paragraphs:

14. This common listening, together with the theological conversations of recent years, has led to a shared understanding of justification. This *encompasses a consensus in the basic truths....*[45]

43. To be sure, Wright criticizes along the following lines: "It is of course popular to say that, since the language of 'righteousness' is essentially 'relational,' 'justification' actually means 'the establishment of a personal relationship,' a mutual knowing, between the believer and God, or the believer and Jesus. But this is extremely misleading." Ibid., 149.

44. For a book that takes issue with Wright's "New Perspective" in significant and cogent ways, see John Piper, *The Future of Justification: A Response to N. T. Wright* (Wheaton: Crossway, 2007).

45. Lutheran World Federation and the Pontifical Council for Promoting Christian Unity, *Joint Declaration*, 15, par. 14 (emphasis added).

15. In faith we together hold the conviction that justification is the work of the triune God. . . . Justification thus means that Christ himself is our righteousness. . . . Together we confess: By grace alone, in faith in Christ's saving work and not because of any merit on our part, we are accepted by God and receive the Holy Spirit, who renews our hearts while equipping and calling us to good works.[46]

16. All people are called by God to salvation in Christ. *Through Christ alone are we justified*, when we receive this salvation in faith. *Faith is itself God's gift through the Holy Spirit* who works through word and sacrament in the community of believers. . . .[47]

17. We also share the conviction [that] . . . *our new life is solely due to the forgiving and renewing mercy that God imparts as a gift and we receive in faith, and never can merit in any way.*[48]

18. Therefore the doctrine of *justification . . . is more than just one part of Christian doctrine*. It stands in an essential relation to all truths of faith, which are to be seen . . . as internally related to each other. . . . *When Catholics see themselves as bound by several criteria*, they do not deny the special function of the message of justification.[49]

In these numbered paragraphs, observe the following difficulties: (a) the ongoing confusion of justification with the ontological work of heart renewal in the process of sanctification; (b) the absence of a robust, bidirectional sense of imputation as a "blessed exchange"; (c) little room made for free grace: the idiom is by and large displaced by the Roman Catholic preference for synergistic grace; (d) no specific mention of sola fide or faith alone, though the question of merit admittedly is more carefully treated here than elsewhere.

In light of these pointed observations, it should come as no surprise that many, not just a few, theologians from diverse theological backgrounds have found the above common affirmations of the *Joint Declaration* far from satisfactory. "The JD does have a number of clear and helpful statements of positive consensus," R. R. Reno observed, "but are they, strictly speaking, statements about justification? Or, are they more accurately statements of trinitarian and christological consensus, affirmations, in a word, of the common Augustinian heritage of western Christianity?"[50] Beyond this, Reno, citing

46. Ibid., 15, par. 13.
47. Ibid., 16, par. 16 (emphasis added).
48. Ibid., 16, par. 17 (emphasis added).
49. Ibid., 16, par. 18 (emphasis added).
50. Reno, "The Joint Declaration on the Doctrine of Justification: An Outsider's View," *Pro Ecclesia* 7, no. 4 (Fall 1998): 431.

Inge Lonning, pointed out that "the positive statements of consensus, both
the general statement . . . and the statements pertinent to areas of historical
controversy . . . are not formulated in the vocabulary of the Lutheran doctrine of justification or in terms which might be equivalent."[51] In fact, Preus,
who was critical of the prior theological conversations that took place in
preparation for the *Joint Declaration*, observed in terms of his own Lutheran
tradition that it has become very different from what it was in the sixteenth
century. This transformation, not all of it good, was due in large measure
to the "intellectual climate [that] took hold in the nineteenth and twentieth centuries,"[52] in which an "identity crisis"[53] along with "doctrinal drift"[54]
emerged among the Lutheran churches. Even in the wake of such drift, Preus
nevertheless concluded that "the differences on the doctrine of justification
between the Lutheran Church and the Roman Catholic Church still exist on
such topics as original sin, concupiscence, bondage of the will, human passivity in conversion and justification, grace, *sola fide* and good works, and the
assurance of salvation."[55] And yet Roman Catholic theologians themselves
complained that "at key points JDDJ appears to favor the Lutheran perspective over that articulated at the Council of Trent."[56] Indeed, the late Avery
Cardinal Dulles remarked that there are "two languages of salvation"[57] here.
Such an observation has led Ted Dorman to conclude: "Specifically, Catholic
and Lutheran theological statements differ at many points because they reflect
different 'thought-forms.'"[58]

Although different theological idioms are clearly present in the *Joint Declaration*, careful observation reveals that the language employed in section 3,
"The Common Understanding of Justification," is general enough that each
tradition can see something of the larger complex of its own theological meaning displayed. Nevertheless general expressions in relation to such a crucial
doctrine of the Christian faith—that is, a doctrine like justification, which
evidences subtlety and therefore requires careful theological nuance—also

51. Inge Lonning, "Lifting the Condemnations: Does It Make Sense?," in *By Faith Alone:
Essays on Justification in Honor of Gerhard O. Forde*, ed. Joseph A. Burgess and Marc Kolden
(Grand Rapids: Eerdmans, 2004), 177, cited by Reno, "Joint Declaration," 434.

52. Preus, *Justification and Rome*, 104.

53. Ibid.

54. Ibid.

55. Ibid., 24.

56. See the observations of Avery Dulles as found in Ted M. Dorman, "*The Joint Declaration on the Doctrine of Justification*: Retrospect and Prospects," *Journal of the Evangelical
Theological Society* 44, no. 3 (September 2001): 422.

57. As quoted in Dorman, "*Joint Declaration*," 430.

58. Ibid.

raise the specter of ambiguity and even outright equivocation for the sake of the common, ecumenical enterprise. The phrase employed by Gottfried Martens that may capture what is actually at work in these distinct theological contexts that yet seek a common affirmation is "differentiated consensus."[59] For instance, when Lutherans think about justification, do they have the elements of the consensus in mind, or do they have in view the factors that make up the differentiations of their own particular tradition? The same question must also be posed to Roman Catholics in order to unveil this same ambiguity and even possible equivocation.

In light of these significant criticisms, the key question to raise at this juncture and one that was posed in my own earlier work on this topic over a decade ago is "Do the common statements on justification [above] actually reveal a sufficient and full-bodied doctrine, one commensurate with the life and witness of the historic church, or is it a doctrine that unfortunately has been eviscerated due in some measure to the ecumenical enterprise itself?"[60] Perhaps the *Joint Declaration*, in light of this overarching question, is not after all making so much a theological statement, given the general nature and the ambiguity of so much of its language, but an ecumenical statement, one offered to ease the tensions of these two quite different theological traditions. But if in the end an ecumenical document is being offered, then it obviously has not satisfied over two hundred European Lutheran theologians who have argued that the *Joint Declaration* "promulgates an essentially Catholic view of justification."[61] We heartily agree.

A common mistake of some contemporary theologians, bespeaking the methodical preferences of academia itself, is to become overly analytical in handling any particular theological doctrine. Those who employ such an approach mistakenly believe that they have comprehended the substance of "justification" or some other doctrine simply by analyzing its parts, critically examining the elements that make up that doctrine. Although this analytic work is clearly necessary, a synthetic approach, considering doctrines as parts of a much larger theological whole, must also be employed. Therefore, the doctrine of justification as affirmed by Rome must also be assessed in terms of the larger array of its other doctrinal affirmations, which would include such things as the necessity of confessing one's sins to a priest in the sacrament

59. Martens, "Inconsequential Signatures? The Decade after the Signing of the Joint Declaration on the Doctrine of Justification," *Lutheran Quarterly* 24, no. 3 (Autumn 2010): 320.

60. Kenneth J. Collins, "The Doctrine of Justification: Historic Wesleyan and Contemporary Understandings," in *Justification: What's at Stake in the Current Debates*, ed. Mark Husbands and Daniel J. Treier (Downers Grove, IL: InterVarsity, 2004), 202.

61. Dorman, "*Joint Declaration*," 422.

of penance, praying to Mary as a mediatrix, the mediation of the saints, the employment of indulgences to diminish the duration of purgatory, the requirement that a temporal satisfaction for sins be made even after they are forgiven, and so on. Thus the chief question becomes, Does the doctrine of justification, carefully explored in terms of its biblical and larger traditional theological context, actually cohere with these other teachings of the Roman Catholic Church just mentioned? Or do such teachings, at least to some extent, undermine the graciousness and freedom entailed in justification itself? Synthetic questions such as these were hardly addressed in the *Joint Declaration*, and that is indeed part of the ongoing problem. This stubborn fact, then, helps to explain why "no fewer than 255 Protestant professors came out against the signing of the OCS," the Official Common Statement related to the declaration.[62]

Though the Methodists, in the form of representatives from the World Methodist Council, were present at the historic signing of the *Joint Declaration* on October 31, 1999, many of their number, as Geoffrey Wainwright reports, expressed a "desire to explore whether Methodists might in some way become associated with the original achievement and benefit from it."[63] Indeed, as German theologian Christoph Raedel points out, the Methodists "publicly hailed the ecumenical progress of the *Joint Declaration*."[64] Not surprisingly, given this large ecumenical interest, in July 2006 "the *Joint Declaration* was affirmed by the executive committee of the World Methodist Council,"[65] even though parts of the document clearly departed from the teaching of John Wesley on the doctrine of justification. In fact, Wesley's own views on the matter were far more in line with those of Wittenberg and Geneva than with those of Rome.[66]

The Aftermath

A year after the *Joint Declaration* was promulgated, the Congregation for the Doctrine of the Faith of the Roman Catholic Church issued a declaration titled *Dominus Iesus: On the Unicity and Salvific Universality of Jesus Christ*

62. Martens, "Inconsequential Signatures?," 312–13.

63. Wainwright, "The Lutheran–Roman Catholic Agreement on Justification: Its Ecumenical Significance and Scope from a Methodist Point of View," *Journal of Ecumenical Studies* 38, no. 1 (Winter 2001): 20.

64. Raedel, ed., *Als Beschenkte miteinander unterwegs: Methodistisch-Katholische Beziehungen auf Weltebene* (Göttingen: Ruprecht, 2011), 110. See also my (Kenneth J. Collins) review of this book in *The Wesleyan Theological Journal* 46, no. 1 (Spring 2011): 198–201.

65. Ibid., 124.

66. See Kenneth J. Collins, *The Theology of John Wesley: Holy Love and the Shape of Grace* (Nashville: Abingdon, 2007), 160–65, 176–81.

and the Church. Upon reading this document, the leaders of the Evangelische Kirche in Deutschland (The Protestant Church in Germany, the EKD) were stunned.[67] They feared that whatever had been achieved in 1999 was now being squandered away in yet another iteration of Roman triumphalism, buoyed high by a distinct ecclesiology. What was the specific language in *Dominus Iesus* that had so roiled the German Protestant church? It was the phrasing of paragraph 17, part of which reads as follows: "On the other hand, the ecclesial communities which have not preserved the valid Episcopate and the genuine and integral substance of the Eucharistic mystery, are not Churches in the proper sense; however, those who are baptized in these communities are, by Baptism, incorporated in Christ and thus are in a certain communion, albeit imperfect, with the Church."[68]

Naturally, the EKD responded to *Dominus Iesus* in its own declaration titled *Kirchengemeinschaft nach evangelischem Verständnis* (*KneV*—A Protestant understanding of ecclesial communion),[69] in which it befittingly pointed out that "the Roman Catholic understanding of church and ecclesial communion is 'not compatible' with the understanding presented in this [current] declaration."[70] Clearly the Lutheran and the Roman Catholic conceptions of the church are and remain very different even after 1999.

In light of such ecclesiastical declarations with weighty, not insignificant, theological implications, we are compelled to connect the dots, so to speak, and thereby to point out that not only is *Dominus Iesus* not compatible with the *Kirchengemeinschaft nach evangelischem Verständnis*, but it is also not consonant with the theology of justification expressed in the *Joint Declaration on the Doctrine of Justification* itself. Here then is the analytic/synthetic problem in yet another troubling manifestation. This time, however, it is expressed specifically in terms of the integration (or lack thereof) of theological and ecclesiological frameworks. Viewed another way, in the proclamation of *Dominus Iesus* Rome has backed away, once more, from some measure of the ecumenical spirit that was present in the *JDDJ* by separating itself (yet another version of Rome alone) decisively from other theological traditions, especially at the Communion table by barring justified believers from participation. How then is justification rightly understood in the wake of such

---

67. Martens, "Inconsequential Signatures?," 318.

68. Joseph Cardinal Ratzinger, *Dominus Iesus*, par. 17, the Holy See, 2000, http://www.vatican.va/roman_curia/congregations/cfaith/documents/rc_con_cfaith_doc_20000806_dominus-iesus_en.html.

69. Martens, "Inconsequential Signatures?," 318.

70. Ibid. For more on the EKD response, see "Das evangelische Verständnis der Bezeugung der Einheit des Leibes Christi als Kirchengemeinschaft," *Evangelische Kirche in Deutschland*, http://www.ekd.de/international/6422.html.

actions? Such a division has been engineered and put in place by the Roman Catholic magisterium simply because other Christian theological traditions do not affirm (a) an unbroken succession of bishops that supposedly goes back to Peter and (b) the theology of transubstantiation. And though Brad Gregory in his *The Unintended Reformation* likes to pretend that Protestants are at the heart of all schism[71]—indeed, his use of the word "fissiparous" is excessive, detracting even from a suitable literary style—the language of *Dominus Iesus* actually proves otherwise. Perhaps, then, the *JDDJ*, when all is said and done, is not even an ecumenical document.

Surrounding all such claims as those found in the ecclesiology offered in *Dominus Iesus*, in which Rome offers itself as "the Church," around which all the other theological communions are supposedly imperfectly related, there remains an air of unreality, especially in light of the ongoing strength of Eastern Orthodoxy. For what it's worth, such an ecclesiology appears to pervade everything, as we have observed in earlier chapters, and it may therefore actually be the metanarrative of the Roman Catholic Church, to which virtually all other theological doctrines must conform, including the pivotal doctrine of justification. Clearly the doctrine of justification encompasses such vital, essential teachings of the Christian faith as the atoning work of the Mediator, the reconciliation of God and humanity so freely offered in Christ, the good news of the forgiveness of sins, and the cleansing of consciences along with measures of assurance. All these precious gifts of justification, some of the very staples of salvation itself, are so heartily affirmed by German Lutherans and other Protestants and are lived out in vibrant Christian witness, but not even this vigorous embrace is apparently enough for them to gain admission, in the Spirit of grace and love in which they abide, to a Roman Catholic Communion table. In such a view, in which the Roman Catholic Church is ever at the center, even the precious doctrine of justification by faith, as great and glorious as it is, must bow the knee before the Roman hierarchy; it too must genuflect before the wishes of the magisterium. This is yet another iteration of Rome alone. In the end, ecclesiology trumps everything.

---

71. Gregory, *The Unintended Reformation: How a Religious Revolution Secularized Society* (Cambridge, MA: Harvard University Press, 2012). Though Gregory charges the Reformation with the modern faults of pluralism and secularism, he is about two centuries too late. The status of universals had preoccupied the Middle Ages at least from the time of Anselm, with an ebb and flow of realism, moderate realism, and nominalism in the offing. Then in the fourteenth century William of Ockham led a revival of nominalism that in its emphasis on the individual and the particular prepared the way not only for Martin Luther (who was trained in nominalism) but also for the rise of science. For a better analysis of the same area covered by Gregory, and with much better judgment, see Michael Allen Gillespie, *The Theological Origins of Modernity* (Chicago: University of Chicago Press, 2008).

19

Regeneration, Assurance, and Conversion

A Minor Chord in Roman Catholic Theology?

Protestants often consider conversion to include the contents of both this chapter (regeneration and assurance) and the preceding two chapters (justification). In other words, many Protestants today, especially evangelicals and Pentecostals, often have in mind a theological complex when they think of the reality of conversion. They bring together three specific doctrines under conversion: justification, regeneration (or the new birth), and a measure of assurance. This engaging transformation flowers in the recognition that such believers are nothing less than the children of God, the beloved of the Lord.

Since the doctrine of justification has already been treated in chapters 17 and 18, this chapter will fill out the remaining elements of a theology of conversion: the crucial new birth, of which Jesus spoke (John 3:3), and the blessing of Christian assurance, of which the apostle Paul wrote (Rom. 8:16). After these vital teachings of the Christian faith are considered in light of the public doctrine of the Roman Catholic Church, we will observe how two very different theologies of conversion, that of Rome on the one hand, and that of evangelical Protestantism in the form of Pentecostalism on the other hand, are currently playing out in Latin America with some very remarkable results. We will conclude by raising (and answering) the question of whether the Roman Catholic Church itself is able to articulate a robust doctrine of the new birth, one that is so eagerly being embraced by the Hispanic community around the world and especially in Latin America.

The New Birth (or Regeneration)

Since no one less than the Savior Jesus Christ underscored the importance of regeneration or the new birth ("Very truly I tell you, no one can see the kingdom of God unless they are born again" [John 3:3]), it is something of a surprise to learn that the table of contents of the *Catechism* contains neither the specific word (much less the topic) "regeneration" nor the exact phrase (again, much less the topic) "the new birth." There are significant sections on other important theological teachings, such as the themes of sin and the virtues, law and grace, and even justification itself, but no topic or section can be found that even mentions the new birth in its title.

Careful analysis reveals that the term "new birth" does not occur until paragraph 169 of the *Catechism*, well beyond the table of contents. In this initial setting, the new birth is immediately described in terms of what has become a distinct Roman Catholic fingerprint, with respect to the ongoing and apparently preferred narrative of ecclesiology: "We believe the Church as the mother of our new birth, and not *in* the Church as if she were the author of our salvation."[1] In this setting, then, the magisterium is teaching that the Roman Catholic Church is not the agent or author of redemption (only God can make a soul holy) but the means through which the grace of the new birth is received. That such an interpretation is accurate is made clearer in a later section of the *Catechism*: "By preaching and Baptism she [the Church] brings forth sons, who are conceived by the Holy Spirit and born of God, to a new and immortal life."[2]

Beyond this, the first employment of the specific word "regeneration" is much later, in paragraph 556, where the *Catechism* states: "Jesus' baptism proclaimed 'the mystery of the first regeneration,' namely, our Baptism; the Transfiguration 'is the sacrament of the second regeneration': our own Resurrection."[3] By this point what was once cloudy has now become clear. The reason why the words "new birth" and "regeneration" do not appear in the table of contents of the *Catechism* is not that they do not receive any treatment at all in this manual of doctrine and practical Christian living but

---

1. *Catechism of the Catholic Church*, 2nd ed. (Mahwah, NJ: Paulist Press, 1994), par. 169 (emphasis original).
2. Ibid., par. 507.
3. Ibid., par. 556.

because such a treatment is, by and large, subsumed under Rome's teaching on baptism!

Such an approach means that much of what the Roman Catholic Church has to say about being born again devolves upon those who receive the sacrament of baptism, this initiatory rite of the church. "Baptism is the sacrament of regeneration through water and in the word,"[4] the *Catechism* proclaims. Put another way, baptism ever brings the grace of the new birth along with it if the ritual is properly performed. Tethering its sacramental theology, which took literally centuries to develop, to the Johannine biblical account that expresses the requirement uttered by Jesus himself, the *Catechism* continues: "This sacrament [baptism] is also called 'the washing of regeneration and renewal by the Holy Spirit,' for it signifies and *actually brings about* the birth of water and the Spirit without which no one 'can enter the kingdom of God.'"[5]

With such regenerating power and efficacy in mind, one can only conclude that what Jesus was actually requiring in John 3:3 and following was not something so uncanny and numinous as to be wrapped in inscrutability in terms of both its source and goal ("You cannot tell where it comes from or where it is going," John 3:8), but something far more distinct, even tangible, and therefore eminently more manageable: the reception of a sacrament offered by the institutional church. In such a view the free and mysterious agency of the Holy Spirit in bringing about the new birth has in some sense been made concrete in both space and time, a genuine concrescence, in the sense that one can *now* announce that the Spirit has acted decisively in this particular place and time. By way of analogy, a comparison with the quantum realm may be instructive here: Like the presence of an electron whose location is unknown until measured, the Holy Spirit's presence and agency in bringing about the new birth itself, marked by mystery and uncanny freedom, is not affirmed (or even acknowledged) until the sacrament is duly administered.

At any rate, the validity of this particular sacrament is *not* guaranteed by an appeal to either priestcraft (the usual sacerdotalism that plays out in the sacraments of the Eucharist, penance, and the anointing of the sick) or the vaunted apostolic succession that supposedly places Rome ever at the center of the church. Here, for once at least, the sacrament as celebrated by many Protestants is good enough and is indeed accepted by Rome, though it does reject the Anabaptist view (and claims that those baptized as infants do not need to be *rebaptized* if the sacrament was performed in a proper, trinitarian

4. Ibid., par. 1213.
5. Ibid., par. 1215 (emphasis added).

way). The ritual of the Baptist congregation, if it is not a rebaptism, in the end counts for something.

Many of the theological descriptions of the sacrament of baptism that play out in the *Catechism* and elsewhere are shared by many (though clearly not all) Protestants as well: Lutherans, Anglicans, Methodists, and Presbyterians among them. To illustrate, like Rome, these Protestant traditions affirm the theological propriety of baptizing children, even infants, as abundant evidence of the grace and mercy of a sovereign God. Thus, in facing some of his critics in the sixteenth century, Luther confessed: "I know that infant baptism pleases God; I know that I was baptized as a child; I know that I have the Holy Spirit, for this I have the interpretation of the Scriptures themselves."[6] Moreover, Calvin insisted, "If any account of this is made, it will be evident that baptism is properly administered to infants as something owed to them."[7] Compare this with the teaching of Rome today: "Born with a fallen human nature and tainted by original sin, children also have need of the new birth in Baptism to be freed from the power of darkness and brought into the realm of the freedom of the children of God, to which all men are called."[8]

Beyond this, Rome makes the relation between baptism and the new birth explicit, and then it gathers them both under the larger umbrella of "conversion" in a pithy, parenthetical statement. The *Catechism* elaborates: "Conversion to Christ, the new birth of Baptism, the gift of the Holy Spirit and the Body and Blood of Christ received as food have made us 'holy and without blemish.'"[9] Like several other Christian theological traditions that practice infant baptism, the Roman Catholic Church also maintains that this sacrament is suitably followed by the rite of confirmation, a sacrament performed as early as seven years old or as late as sixteen, whereby the faithful are strengthened by the Holy Spirit.[10] With these relations in place, the *Catechism* then moves in a slightly different theological direction, and it now postulates that the two sacraments of baptism and confirmation, together, signify the reality of regeneration! "In *Baptism* and *Confirmation*, the handing on (*traditio*) of the Lord's Prayer," the *Catechism* affirms, "signifies new birth into the divine life."[11] If we bring together these two doctrinal affirmations side by side, the theological situation looks like this:

6. Martin Luther, *Sermons I*, LW 51:186.
7. John Calvin, *Institutes of the Christian Religion*, ed. John T. McNeill, trans. Ford Lewis Battles, Library of Christian Classics 20–21 (Philadelphia: Westminster, 1960), 4.16.5 (2:1328).
8. *Catechism*, par. 1250.
9. Ibid., par. 1426.
10. Ibid., par. 1212.
11. Ibid., par. 2769 (emphasis original).

First Affirmation: Baptism + New Birth = Conversion
Second Affirmation: Baptism + Confirmation = New Birth

So then, if the new birth of the second statement above contains the sacrament of confirmation, is the new birth of the first declaration thereby rendered in some sense lacking, and conversion along with it, simply because they both are not informed by confirmation? In light of such considerations Rome (and some Protestant traditions as well) has little difficulty in viewing the new birth (and conversion) as a lifelong process punctuated at key points along the way by sacramental graces that mirror the human journey, as evident in the following declaration: "For the Christian the day of death inaugurates, at the end of his sacramental life, the fulfillment of his new birth begun at Baptism."[12] However, a new birth that is a lifelong sacramental process, that waits for the completion of regeneration on one's deathbed, may be far too late. The new birth is, after all, the beginning of the Christian life, not its end.[13]

The New Birth and Assurance

One way that Roman Catholicism's teaching on conversion differs markedly from that of Protestant traditions, especially evangelicalism and Pentecostalism, involves the whole matter of assurance. The theological complex of conversion for many Protestants contains the realities of justification and the new birth (however it is sacramentally "configured"), yet it also embraces a third element, the vital component of Christian assurance. This apostolic teaching, evident in the life of the early church, also has the generous warrant of Scripture attesting to its truth. The clearest explication of what some like John Wesley[14] have called "the direct witness of the Holy Spirit," for example, can be found in the apostle Paul's engaging description, found in the book of Romans. The particular passage on this head is worth quoting at length:

> For those who are led by the Spirit of God are the children of God. The Spirit you received does not make you slaves, so that you live in fear again; rather, the Spirit you received brought about your adoption to sonship. And by him we cry, "*Abba*, Father." The Spirit himself testifies with our spirit that we are

12. Ibid., par. 1682.
13. We affirm that the new birth is followed by the process of sanctification. In other words, a qualitatively distinct grace (from sin to initial sanctification in the new birth) is followed by incremental grace, changes in degree, whereby one becomes increasingly holy.
14. Kenneth J. Collins and Jason Vickers, eds., *The Sermons of John Wesley: A Collection for the Christian Journey* (Nashville: Abingdon, 2013), 207.

God's children. Now if we are children, then we are heirs—heirs of God and
co-heirs with Christ, if indeed we share in his sufferings in order that we may
also share in his glory. (Rom. 8:14–17)

Accordingly, not only is the Holy Spirit the One who leads the children of
God and is the cause of their adoption, but also this same Spirit bears witness with their spirit that they are the children of God, the beloved of the
Most High, and as such co-heirs with Christ, a glorious testimony, indeed!
Why then has not Rome (or "Constantinople" for that matter) energetically
endorsed such an apostolic declaration? To answer this question, a little historical background is necessary.

The Council of Trent

It is well known that when Martin Luther was an Augustinian monk in Erfurt,
one of his major struggles was to find consolation and peace in God through
Christ. Schooled in a medieval notion that Christ was more of an almighty
Judge than a Redeemer (Christ as Pantocrator), Luther suffered bouts of
anxiety and distress, the most notable one being when he was saying his first
Mass. When he finally came to peace and reconciliation by grace through
faith, after his tower experience, he was left with a deep and abiding appreciation for the biblical doctrine of Christian assurance. In 1535 in his *Lectures
on Galatians*, for example, Luther took issue with the pope for repudiating
this comforting as well as illuminating grace of the Most High: "I did this in
order that you might utterly repudiate the wicked idea of the entire kingdom
of the pope, the teaching that a Christian man must be uncertain about the
grace of God toward him. If this opinion stands, then Christ is completely
useless."[15] With such a bold statement Luther went on record, distinguishing
his theology from the confines of the Western medieval consensus, which
taught "the impossibility of such assurance."[16] In his *Lectures on Romans*
Luther forthrightly declared: "For it is the Spirit Himself, the Holy Spirit, who
is given to us, who bears witness, by strengthening our faith in God, with our
spirit that we are the children of God."[17]

By the time the Council of Trent met years later (1545–63), there was a
significant contrast on the topic of Christian assurance between the Reformers

15. Martin Luther, *Lectures on Galatians, 1535, Chapters 1–4*, LW 26:385.
16. Alister McGrath, *Iustitia Dei: A History of the Christian Doctrine of Justification*, 2nd
ed. (Cambridge: Cambridge University Press, 1998), 264.
17. Martin Luther, *Lectures on Romans*, LW 25:71.

on the one hand, and the magisterium on the other. The council, therefore, could not let the matter simply go unnoticed.[18] Thus, after some reflection on this by-now-controversial issue, those assembled at Trent condemned the Lutheran teaching on assurance as "an assertion contrary to proper Christian humility."[19] Add this judgment to the one expressed at the sixth session (in its chap. 9) of this same council, and a remarkably odd theological picture emerges: "So each one, when he considers himself and his own weakness and indisposition, may have fear and apprehension concerning his own grace, since no one can know with the certainty of faith, which cannot be subject to error, that he has obtained the grace of God."[20]

Two significant theological problems are evident in Trent's response to Luther's affirmation of the scriptural teaching of Christian assurance. First of all, to assert that the assurance of believers by the grace of God, as well as the serenity it brings, can only detract from Christian humility is a judgment that involves a distorted view of what genuine Christian humility actually looks like. In the Tridentine view it seems as if sin, and the lack of assurance that it invariably leaves in its wake, are somehow "required" to keep believers humble. However, who was more humble than Jesus Christ, and yet who was as sinless as he was? Second, claiming that believers cannot know that they are accepted as the beloved of the Lord, are redeemed, and have "obtained the grace of God"[21] involves in some sense repudiating the work of the Holy Spirit and the salvific operations of grace that bear witness to the integrity and soundness of the believer's relationship with God. The judgment of Trent is thus powerless to stop the superintending agency of the Holy Spirit through which believers come to know in whom they have believed, with the measure of assurance that it brings, and through which they therefore cry out, as no doubt the apostle Paul did in his own day, "Abba, Father." Indeed, that cry bears witness to the very substance of Christian assurance. Doctrinal pronouncements, even by the magisterium, cannot stop it. All would do well, then, to recognize it.

The *Joint Declaration* Weighs In

Fortunately the twentieth-century *Joint Declaration on the Doctrine of Justification* emerged out of a far less polemical context than that of the Council

18. Ibid.
19. Ibid., 265.
20. H. J. Schroeder, *Disciplinary Decrees of the General Councils: Text, Translation, and Commentary* (St. Louis: Herder, 1937), 35.
21. Ibid.

of Trent in the sixteenth century. However, despite the passing of the centuries, and despite a much better tone, little progress was made on the specific doctrine of assurance by the Roman Catholic participants, who mostly overshadowed the greatly reduced effort of the modern Lutherans, an effort that hardly approached Luther's own more vigorous offering. Such a turn of events led *Christianity Today* to cite Rolf Hille, the chair of the German Evangelical Alliance: "The *JDDJ* falls short in that it does not stipulate that faith includes the assurance of salvation. 'What is, then, grace? What is faith? All of this remains unclear.'"[22]

The accuracy and cogency of Hille's judgment are abundantly evident as the separate Lutheran and Roman Catholic contributions are examined. In terms of the former, the *JDDJ* affirms: "This [Christian assurance] was emphasized in a particular way by the Reformers: in the midst of temptation, believers should not look to themselves but look solely to Christ and trust only him. In trust in God's promise they are assured of their salvation, but are never secure looking at themselves."[23] Compare this Lutheran declaration with that of Roman Catholicism as found in this same document: "Catholics can share the concern of the Reformers to ground faith in the objective reality of Christ's promise, to look away from one's own experience, and to trust in Christ's forgiving word alone."[24] Though each statement focuses on the promise of God (the Lutheran contribution) or Christ (the Roman Catholic one) and turns away from believers' looking in a subjective manner at themselves, nevertheless the role afforded the believing self in each instance (the self-drawing assurance from the promises of God and Christ) is actually a far different one than that described by the apostle Paul in Romans 8:16. Believers being assured by, or taking comfort in, the "objective" promises of God actually entails a far more active role for the self (despite the cautions) than that described by Paul in his own observation, "*The Spirit himself testifies* with our spirit that we are God's children" (Rom. 8:16, emphasis added).

Beyond this, the common statement of Lutherans and Roman Catholics in the *JDDJ* directs believers, for what assurance they may have, to the Word of God itself, thereby drawing strength and comfort once more from the promises of God, but this time around, interestingly enough, believers are

22. Richard Nyberg, "Germany: Protestant Theologians Object to Lutheran-Catholic Accord," *Christianity Today*, June 15, 1998, http://www.christianitytoday.com/ct/1998/june15/8t7012.html.

23. Lutheran World Federation and the Pontifical Council for Promoting Christian Unity, *Joint Declaration on the Doctrine of Justification*, English ed. (Grand Rapids: Eerdmans, 2000), 24, par. 35.

24. Ibid., 24, par. 36.

also directed to the sacramental ministrations of the institutional church. The common statement declares: "We confess together that the faithful can rely on the mercy and promises of God. In spite of their own weakness and the manifold threats to their faith, on the strength of Christ's death and resurrection they can build on the effective promise of God's grace in Word and Sacrament and so be sure of this grace."[25]

The Seoul Report Weighs In

Roman Catholic and Methodist leaders have been meeting in ecumenical dialogue since 1967. These meetings became more formal, and reports were issued on a regular cycle of every five years beginning with the Denver assembly in 1971. The work of what came to be known as the International Commission for Dialogue between the Roman Catholic Church and the World Methodist Council is especially valuable in revealing both Methodism's and Rome's understanding of the doctrine of assurance. The contribution of each theological tradition on this important topic was fleshed out in the meeting that took place in Seoul in 2006, and the report generated by that meeting is known as *The Grace Given You in Christ: Catholics and Methodists Reflect Further on the Church*.

Among other things, *The Grace Given You in Christ*, also called more simply the Seoul Report, revealed that "the experience of assurance has been a treasured feature of Methodist piety."[26] In fact, John Wesley, as the father of Methodism, underscored two distinct witnesses under the larger heading of assurance. First, the witness of our own spirit is evident in such things as conscience, obedience to Christ through the moral law, and the fruit of the Spirit.[27] Here, then, is vital indirect evidence pointing to the reality of a child of God. Second, the direct witness of the Holy Spirit to believers' hearts attests that they are indeed the children of God. This is the very same witness that Paul wrote about in Romans 8:16, as cited above.[28]

As the Seoul Report considered the Roman Catholic understanding of Christian assurance, a marked shift took place from the personal dimensions

---

25. Ibid., 23, par. 34.

26. International Methodist-Catholic Dialogue Commission, *The Grace Given You in Christ: Catholics and Methodists Reflect Further on the Church*, par. 120, the Holy See, 2006, http://www.vatican.va/roman_curia/pontifical_councils/chrstuni/meth-council-docs/rc_pc _chrstuni_doc_20060604_seoul-report_en.html.

27. See Wesley's sermon "The Witness of Our Own Spirit," in Collins and Vickers, eds., *Sermons of John Wesley*, 226–32.

28. Ibid., 194–213.

of the Methodist explication to the corporate and institutional features of Rome's view. "Catholics have an instinct for the whole and an emphasis upon the confident actions of the Church as Church,"[29] the report declared. What, then, makes up the heart of assurance so understood? First, assurance now consists in the confidence that believers have as they embrace "certain authoritative acts of teaching"[30] of the church. What supposedly provides the faithful with this fund of confidence is none other than the magisterium along with the authority of the papacy in general and the doctrine of infallibility in particular. But does the pope's declaration, for example, that Mary was bodily assumed into heaven make it so? Is there not considerable room for doubt about such supposedly grounding elements of this teaching as the office of the papacy (a doubt growing out of a careful historical investigation), the preferred epistemology embedded in a doctrine of infallibility (a doubt growing out of a painstaking biblical, theological, and philosophical analysis), and all of this on top of the particular concerns about Mary herself? Given the nature of this appeal, does it not, all things considered, actually increasingly detract from assurance?

Beyond exploring Christian assurance in terms of "certain authoritative acts of teaching,"[31] Rome takes up a second theme and in doing so turns once more to the usual ecclesiastical dogma that pervades practically every one of its doctrinal affirmations. That is, assurance, so reconfigured in a way that we do not find in Scripture, consists in the surety of knowing that the Roman Catholic Church has a rightly ordained ministry in apostolic succession, which offers valid sacraments. Indeed, the Roman Catholic delegation at Seoul raised the question "Can the church not have a *corporate assurance* in terms of the liturgical actions of its ordained ministers?"[32] Again, notice that Rome has changed the very nature of the discussion. The Methodists had begun by talking about the witness affirmed by the apostle Paul in Romans 8:16, that is, about what the Holy Spirit does. Rome responded to this by appealing to the well-worked teaching of the magisterium and its preferred doctrine of the church. However, the appeal to ecclesiology should not displace or minimize in any way the precious and gracious role of the Holy Spirit. Indeed, the assurance that God brings is far greater than what the magisterium has to offer. To be rightly focused surely is part of what assurance is all about.

29. International Methodist-Catholic Dialogue Commission, *Grace Given You in Christ*, par. 99.
30. Ibid., par. 136.
31. Ibid., par. 92.
32. Ibid., par. 133 (emphasis added).

The New Birth and the Challenge of Pentecostalism

No Christian theological tradition today, especially in the wake of the information revolution, lives in a vacuum. Each communion of faith is known by others as the task of a global mission is undertaken by all. In his book *The Next Christendom: The Coming of Global Christianity*, Philip Jenkins has revealed the rise of the Global South as well as the prospering of the Christian faith in Latin America, especially among Pentecostals.[33] Not surprisingly, tensions have emerged in this part of the world between differing theological traditions. On the one hand, Pentecostal evangelicals reveal the strengths and weaknesses of the Roman Catholic tradition in a remarkable way (and laypeople readily understand this), just as Rome on the other hand returns the favor in kind to Pentecostalism. In some important respects these two vital, global traditions are "mirror" communions of faith. What is a strength in one is sometimes a weakness in the other. Take the doctrine of the new birth, for example, or what some Latin American Pentecostals refer to as the born-again experience. Pentecostalism, unlike Rome, has little difficulty affirming the reality of the new birth apart from water baptism (the converted are, of course, urged to be baptized) though never apart from the superintending agency of the Holy Spirit. Indeed, according to many Pentecostals, people are born of God in many different circumstances: in hearing the Word of God proclaimed, during times of prayer and fasting, and in serving the poor. What is more, it doesn't always happen at the baptismal font or even in a church. This tradition, again unlike Rome, has become especially known for emphasizing the direct role of the Holy Spirit not only in bringing about the new birth when and where the Spirit sees fit but also in generating the assurance, the direct witness of the Spirit, that normally accompanies this salvific work of grace.

In an important article on ecumenical relations in Latin America, Peter Hocken has listed a number of challenges that Pentecostals pose to the Roman Catholic Church, including "belief in direct access to God, to Jesus and the Father, through the Holy Spirit; faith in God speaking and God acting; expectation of visible results; a vision for every-member ministry; [and] the reality of spiritual opposition."[34] What's at stake here, then, in the words of Ralph Del Colle, is "the authenticity of conversion along with the necessity in ecumenical dialogue of discerning how the work of the Spirit is operative

---

33. See Jenkins, *The Next Christendom: The Coming of Global Christianity* (New York: Oxford University Press, 2002), 95–100.

34. Hocken, "What Challenges Do Pentecostals Pose to Catholics?," *Journal of the European Pentecostal Theological Association* 35, no. 1 (April 2015): 49.

in other ecclesial traditions."[35] Though Hocken readily admits that Roman Catholic Charismatics would have little difficulty in affirming such things as those just enumerated, nevertheless these believers remain a minority in a very large church that embraces theological liberals as well, those who are found especially among the well educated, the knowledge class, who "have been influenced by secular tendencies that deny such [possibilities]."[36]

With a model of baptism that goes back to the time of Tertullian,[37] but hardly before then, many Latin Americans are baptized into the Roman Catholic Church as infants. Whether their participation in the sacramental life of the church, along with the mediation afforded by a priestly class, is sufficient to move them much beyond nominal Christianity is a much-debated question. What is clear, however, is that their attraction in later life to the pneumatological power and freedom, the gifts and graces, so evidently displayed in the Pentecostal community poses a genuine crisis for these Latin Americans on several levels. For one thing, to covert to the evangelical faith is "by definition inseparable from a decision to leave the [Roman] Catholic church."[38] And many are indeed departing. In fact, according to Larry Ortiz, Latinos are leaving the Roman Catholic Church at the rate of 600,000 annually,[39] and "for every one (Latino) who comes back to the [Roman] Catholic Church, four leave it."[40] Some scholars are even beginning to write about the "Pentecostalization of religion in Latin America,"[41] so strong are current trends. To illustrate, Henri Gooren, in considering developments in South America as well, points out the early successes of Pentecostalism in Chile, Brazil, and Peru during the 1960s and 1970s;[42] in Guatemala, Costa Rica, El Salvador, Honduras, and Nicaragua during the 1980s;[43] and in Argentina during the 1990s;[44] and this Holy Spirit–led movement continues today in Paraguay,

---

35. Del Colle, "On Becoming a Christian: Commentary on the Fifth Phase Report of the International Catholic/Pentecostal Dialogue," *One in Christ* 43, no. 1 (2009): 120.

36. Hocken, "What Challenges?," 50.

37. As Gerald Bray observes: "All we know for sure is that by AD 200 infant baptisms were taking place, and that Tertullian (who tells us this) disapproved of the practice." Bray, *The Church: A Theological and Historical Account* (Grand Rapids: Baker Academic, 2016), 53.

38. M. Daniel Carroll R., "The Evangelical–Roman Catholic Dialogue: Issues Revolving around Evangelization: An Evangelical View from Latin America," *Trinity Journal* 21, no. 2 (Fall 2000): 199.

39. Ortiz, "Latino Migration to Protestantism: A Historical, Socio-Cultural, Ecclesiastical Analysis," *Journal of Sociology and Social Welfare* 41, no. 3 (September 2014): 24.

40. Ibid.

41. Henri Paul Pierre Gooren, "The Pentecostalization of Religion and Society in Latin America," *Exchange* 39, no. 4 (2010): 359.

42. Ibid., 356.

43. Ibid.

44. Ibid., 357.

Venezuela, and Bolivia.[45] According to Thomas Rausch, "It is estimated that some 8,000 to 10,000 [Roman] Catholics leave their church every day to join Pentecostal churches."[46] Putting the larger picture into focus, this scholar goes on to observe that "Pentecostal Christians grew from 74 million in 1970 to an estimated 497 million by 1997, an increase of 670 percent."[47] And the trend continues.[48]

Beyond the obvious spiritual motivations, many Latinos are "migrating to Protestant churches,"[49] as Ortiz points out, because not only do they have "an increased opportunity to participate in the polity of the church"[50] but also their women are given "opportunities not usually available in other Christian denominations, and certainly not in the RCC."[51] Though some would like to take comfort in the notion that Pentecostalism is simply embracing the sluffed-off lower classes of the region, evidencing a kind of "classism," the demographics, according to Rodney Stark, actually tell a much different story. In a passage worth quoting in full, he argues thus: "To sum up our findings, the prevailing notions about who in Latin America is especially prone to becoming a Protestant and why are unfounded. Instead, Protestantism seems to appeal fairly equally across the demographic spectrum. If people are turning to Protestantism to escape their deprivations, these deprivations are evidently not of the standard material variety."[52] These huge demographic shifts have created some bad feelings on both sides of the equation. On the one hand, many evangelicals, in the words of Daniel Carroll, "consider the institution, theology, and everyday practice of Latin American Catholicism as unbiblical."[53] In fact, they are even reluctant to be involved "in a common witness with the Roman Catholic Church at a formal level"[54] because such action could be viewed as "in some measure a betrayal of Christian faith";[55] that's how

---

45. Ibid.

46. Rausch, "Catholics and Pentecostals: Troubled History, New Initiatives," *Theological Studies* 71, no. 4 (2010): 933.

47. Ibid., 926.

48. Ibid., 933. Rausch cites Allan Anderson, who predicted that "present growth rates indicate that some Latin American countries could have a majority of 'evangelicals,' mostly Pentecostals, by 2010." Ibid., citing Allan Anderson, *An Introduction to Pentecostalism: Global Charismatic Christianity* (Cambridge: Cambridge University Press, 2013), 307–8.

49. Ortiz, "Latino Migration," 36.

50. Ibid.

51. Ibid., 41.

52. Stark, "Conversion to Latin American Protestantism and the Case for Religious Motivation," *Interdisciplinary Journal of Research on Religion* 6, no. 7 (2010): 9.

53. Carroll, "Evangelical–Roman Catholic Dialogue," 200.

54. Ibid.

55. Ibid.

strained relations at times can be. On the other hand, the Roman Catholic hierarchy in Latin America, enjoying centuries of unopposed advance, has been reluctant to embrace an "irreversible trend toward pluralism,"[56] which the Pentecostal evangelical growth so clearly represents. In fact, the late John Paul II was so disturbed by the evangelical gains, which looked like they were coming at Roman Catholic expense, that in a very uncharacteristic move, he even began to rail against the "sects" at a bishops' conference held in Santo Domingo in 1992, calling them "rapacious wolves."[57]

Precisely because the theological and ecclesiastical diversity of both the Roman Catholic and the evangelical Protestant traditions will undoubtedly be an ongoing reality in this part of the world in the years ahead, the best course of action will be to embrace those policies, attitudes, beliefs, and practices that ever mark dedicated disciples of Jesus Christ, those who are, as Jesus put it, known for their love of one another (John 13:35). One small step in this direction is that both theological traditions should be encouraged to put aside the recriminations and name-calling that despoil the Christian love and fellowship that can remain even between these very different traditions. We need a new kind of apologetics from both sides. Granted, things look very different from an evangelical perspective than they do from a Roman Catholic one, but we are nevertheless convinced that genuine progress can be made in both ecumenical relations and Roman Catholic effectiveness in this shifting, increasingly pluralistic, and at times perplexing environment. Motivated by genuine goodwill, which affirms Roman Catholics as our brothers and sisters in Christ (an affirmation that some Protestant radicals are loath to accept), we as evangelicals recognize that many elements of holiness and of truth are to be found in the Roman Catholic witness. In an ecumenical spirit we therefore offer a number of recommendations that from our perspective seem likely to go a long way in resolving some of the challenges posed by the exuberant growth of evangelical Pentecostalism in Latin America. Both traditions can thrive in this area to the larger good of the glory of God. If we were Roman Catholic bishops, a part of the magisterium, this is what we would propose to do as the way forward in the twenty-first century. And all these proposals, in one way or another, touch upon the vital reality of the new birth, or conversion, more broadly speaking.

First of all, we would not give way to fear or name-calling in the face of Pentecostal advances. All Christians, of whatever theological communion, can and should rejoice that the kingdom of God is moving forward, bondages are

56. Ibid., 203.
57. Ibid.

being broken, forgiveness is being received, and lives are being healed through the power of the Holy Spirit. Thus as a part of a rich theological tradition, we would be marked by a spirit of gracious and generous confidence and would therefore rejoice in this obvious movement of the Holy Spirit. We therefore would strengthen the charismatic movement that is already in our own midst. This renewing movement, which hails from the 1960s, has underscored "the foundational experience of baptism in the Spirit as a personal submission to the lordship of Jesus Christ."[58] More to the point, the theological emphases here will not only make Roman Catholicism more attractive to a broader population but also help to improve relations with Pentecostals, even acting as a bridge to this community of faith. Thus, exploring some of the very good consequences of a more concerted move in this direction, Hocken points out: "As someone blessed to have contact with both evangelical-Pentecostal and charismatic Catholic patterns of formation, I am convinced that a greater interaction between the two can only be an enrichment for all concerned."[59] Moreover, Rausch has weighed in here and contends that "the Catholic Charismatic Renewal (CCR) forms a potential bridge between Pentecostals and Roman Catholics."[60] We heartily agree.

Second, we would encourage our fellow bishops and theologians of the Roman Catholic Church to articulate a full-bodied doctrine of the new birth, one that will have its own section in the *Catechism*. Such a teaching will be able not only to embrace the conjunction of sacramental water and the Holy Spirit, and even infant baptismal regeneration for that matter, as some Protestant traditions already do (such as Methodism),[61] but also to acknowledge the reality of the new birth more broadly as the Spirit freely leads. Such a theology would be able to recognize the new birth present at the sacrament of baptism as well as the reality of regeneration, which can so often happen apart from the baptismal waters. Naturally everyone will be encouraged to receive the sacrament of baptism, in line with the clear teaching of Scripture, regardless of how the graces of the new birth are received. Remember Cornelius, someone who first was born of God and only later was baptized. Such a generosity of recognition, of acknowledging the freedom of the Holy Spirit to move as the Spirit wills, is what a robust doctrine of the new birth is all about, something that the Pentecostal faithful already know.

58. Peter Hocken, "New Patterns of Formation in the Roman Catholic Church and the Role of Catholic Charismatic Renewal," *Asian Journal of Pentecostal Studies* 9, no. 1 (January 2006): 129.

59. Ibid., 141.

60. Rausch, "Catholics and Pentecostals," 938–39.

61. See the discussion on John Wesley's full-orbed understanding of baptism, reflective of both his Anglican and evangelical heritage, in Kenneth J. Collins, *The Theology of John Wesley: Holy Love and the Shape of Grace* (Nashville: Abingdon, 2007), 262–65.

In order for this second counsel to be implemented in Roman Catholic life, certain attitudes and even prejudices about the term "born again" may have to be cleared away. As Arthur Canales points out, "Quite frankly, the phrase being 'born-again' causes *most* Roman Catholics to become uneasy and uncomfortable, and in fact, most Catholics might be appalled if someone were to call them a 'born-again' Christian."[62] However, a Roman Catholic second look in this area is clearly warranted in the face of the following two considerations: First, the authority behind the salience of the new birth is none other than that of Jesus Christ himself. It is he who employed the language of "born again" or "born from above." Second, Christ also revealed that the new birth is required of everyone in order to enter the kingdom of heaven. Does the Roman Catholic association of baptism and the new birth (born of water; born of the Spirit) exhaust what Christ was referring to in his teaching? We think not, and what is more, millions of others agree.

With the background of a parish youth minister and university campus minister under his belt, Canales has reflected upon the importance of the new birth precisely as a Roman Catholic: "I find both the terminology and the pericope of being 'born again' most satisfying. . . . In ten years of youth ministry, this text has served me in more ministerial success than any other biblical text in terms of bringing high school students to a fuller and richer appreciation of their faith-life in Jesus Christ."[63] What is so helpful about the work of Canales is that his thought moves in the direction of what a generous doctrine of the new birth, appropriate to the domain under review, should look like. To that end he makes a very helpful distinction between a sacramental understanding of the new birth (which at times appears to be the only suit in the Roman Catholic deck of cards) and a pastoral view that grew out of his Christian experience in ministry to youth amid the warp and woof of life. He affirms both views, a sacramental one and a pastoral one, without any sense of the one contradicting or overthrowing the other. On this second distinction, he elaborates: "Pastorally, the phrase 'born-again' is extremely rich and highly appropriate for Catholic renewal."[64] After this initial observation Canales points out that "when a person professes to be 'born-again' it is a declaration of accepting Jesus of Nazareth by faith as the Christ, the Risen One, and this is primarily the *direct invitation of God* and the communication of the Holy Spirit."[65]

62. Canales, "A Rebirth of Being 'Born Again': Theological, Sacramental and Pastoral Reflections from a Roman Catholic Perspective," *Journal of Pentecostal Theology* 11, no. 1 (October 2002): 99.

63. Ibid., 113.

64. Ibid., 112.

65. Ibid. (emphasis added).

After laying out his case for a renewal of Roman Catholic theology, at least in this particular area, Canales concludes his work with an affirmation utterly in harmony with the truth of Scripture so broadly affirmed by Pentecostal evangelicals today: "Theologically, sacramentally and pastorally, then, in a tangible way, everyone has to become 'born-again' if a person truly wants to encounter Jesus the Christ—the Risen One."[66] Again, Canales observes: "Make no mistake, Catholics *must* be 'born-again' in order to experience the Christian conversion process, which is ultimately a journey of discovery with God."[67] With a balanced conclusion that could be embraced by so many theological traditions today, this pastoral observer declares, in a way that may clear up some reluctance in this area: "Make no mistake [Roman] Catholics *must* be 'born-again.'"[68]

At this point in the argument, let's conduct a little thought experiment. If this call for theological renewal in the crucial area of regeneration were actually carried out by the magisterium, such that Rome would now affirm both a sacramental and a so-called pastoral understanding of the new birth, would Roman Catholic theology then begin to unravel? Would it start to topple under an alien weight? We think not. Indeed, there is nothing in the latter view that necessarily undermines the reality and the significance of the former. In our judgment, the embrace of the second understanding would entail the very helpful recognition of how the Holy Spirit works in the lives of believers with the result that it would only serve to strengthen the overall purpose of Roman Catholic theology, which is the inculcation of holiness.

Let's entertain a different question here: Is the failure to embrace the larger reality of the new birth (and conversion, for that matter), which is so evident in the sacramental-only view, a genuine theological deficiency, one that therefore needs to be corrected in a process of transformation and renewal? We think so. Indeed, we are reminded of the ministry of John Wesley, Church of England priest in eighteenth-century England, who as a good Anglican embraced the reality of sacramental infant baptism, yet also recognized the significance and the need for regeneration beyond the baptismal font. Consider Wesley's advice to his contemporary sinful adults who contended that they did not need to be born again since they had already been baptized. Wesley, as a good pastoral counselor, cautioned:

I tell a sinner, "You must be born again." "No," say you. "He was born again in baptism. Therefore he cannot be born again now." Alas! What trifling is

66. Ibid., 118.
67. Ibid., 119 (emphasis original).
68. Ibid. (emphasis original).

this? What if he was *then* a child of God? He is *now* manifestly a "child of the devil!" For the works of his father *he* doth. Therefore do not play upon words. He must go through an entire change of heart.[69]

Moreover, in a fusillade of pointed, pungent questions, Wesley challenged the presumptuous bromide that all was well simply because current sinners, steeped in their sins, had, after all, been baptized as infants. "How many are the baptized gluttons and drunkards, the baptized liars and common swearers, the baptized railers and evil-speakers, the baptized whoremongers, thieves, extortioners?"[70] he asked. "What think you? Are these now the children of God?"[71] Wesley then brought the matter to a head in his concluding observation: "To say, then, that ye cannot be born again, that there is no new birth but in baptism, is to seal you all under damnation, to consign you to hell, without help, without hope."[72]

Conclusion

As a visible sign of an inward grace, the sacrament of baptism does indeed depict the reality of the new birth, in which holiness is imparted to the soul. Therefore this sacrament, commanded by Jesus (Matt. 28:19), is a means of grace, a sign that points to one of the early goals of religion: holiness. Behind the visible sign of water is the promise of God to redeem as expressed, for example, in the Lutheran *Book of Concord*, which states: "For without the Word of God the water is merely water and no Baptism. But when connected with the Word of God it is a Baptism, that is, a gracious water of life and a washing of regeneration in the Holy Spirit."[73]

Though, as we have seen, scriptural accounts do urge those who have already received the Holy Spirit to be baptized with water subsequently, the emphasis throughout the Bible is on the goal of the restoration of God's holy image, in which humanity has been created. Evangelicals, Pentecostals among them, have underscored the truth (highlighting the freedom of the Holy Spirit, as Jesus attested) that the new birth may take place apart from sacramental

69. Wesley, "A Farther Appeal to Men of Reason and Religion, Part 1," in *The Works of John Wesley*, bicentennial ed., vol. 11, *The Appeals to Men of Reason and Religion and Certain Related Open Letters*, ed. Gerald R. Cragg (Nashville: Abingdon, 1975), 107.

70. Wesley, "The Marks of the New Birth," in *The Works of John Wesley*, bicentennial ed., vols. 1–4, *Sermons*, ed. Albert C. Outler (Nashville: Abingdon, 1984–87), 1:429.

71. Ibid.

72. Ibid.

73. Theodore G. Tappert, ed., *The Book of Concord: The Confessions of the Evangelical Lutheran Church* (Philadelphia: Mühlenberg, 1959), 349.

waters but never apart from either holiness or the presence of the Holy Spirit within. This evangelical emphasis of being born again in the strength of salvific graces is undoubtedly a challenge to those theological traditions, like Rome, that so identify the new birth with the sacrament of baptism that they fail to see clearly the regenerating power and work of the Holy Spirit beyond the ministrations of the institutional church and its ordained hierarchy. Here we find the old ecclesiastical problem once more. Future dialogue on this particular head is therefore clearly warranted not only for the sake of the church's broader mission but also for fostering sound ecumenical relations.

In addition, the marks of the new birth—the theological virtues of faith, hope, and love—should provide abundant evidence of a qualitatively distinct life of holiness that is in harmony with the liberties expressed in Romans 8 and 1 John. Unfortunately, such evidence is not always present in the lives of the baptized, even when the sacrament was properly administered. Accordingly, the difference between a sacramental grace once received and what adherents to the faith are in fact today in their practical Christian lives may give all, both Roman Catholic and Protestant alike, cause for concern. Such care may be heightened in the face of the abiding truth of the scriptural witness—passed along from age to age, as a rich part of the testimony of the church that must ever be affirmed—that "without holiness no one will see the Lord" (Heb. 12:14).

20

The Deeply Divided Church of Rome

The World's Largest Pluralist Christian Denomination?

Much of the appeal of Roman Catholicism for many people, no doubt, is due to the claim that it provides rock-solid, uncompromising commitment to unchanging truth. A common refrain of Roman apologists and converts is that Protestantism, by contrast, is hopelessly divided, unstable, and confusing. Often this includes the claim that Protestantism is composed of thousands of denominations and sects.[1] Consider these words from former evangelical pastor and Gordon-Conwell Seminary graduate Steve Wood, describing some of the questions he was wrestling with before he converted to Rome. "How could Protestantism be his [Christ's] 'church' when Protestant is nothing but disintegration, splintered, not unified, a frightening proliferation of squabbling, competing denominations, many masquerading under the title 'non-denominational.' The disunity and doctrinal chaos [within] Protestantism became deeply unsettling to me."[2]

---

1. A popular claim by Roman Catholic apologists is that there are thousands of Protestant denominations: the specific number 33,000 is often cited. For an incisive critique and refutation of this popular myth, see Glenn Peoples, "The Protestant Bogeyman of Thousands of Churches," *Right Reason* (blog and podcast), September 10, 2007, http://rightreason.org/2007/the-protestant-bogeyman-of-thousands-of-churches/. Roman Catholic apologist Scott Eric Alt acknowledges that Peoples's analysis is correct and urges his fellow Catholics to stop making this "outlandishly false" claim: "We Need to Stop Saying That There Are 33,000 Protestant Denominations" (blog post), *National Catholic Register*, February 9, 2016, http://www.ncregister.com/blog/scottericalt/we-need-to-stop-saying-that-there-are-33000-protestant-denominations.

2. Steve Wood, "A Prodigal's Journey," in *Surprised by Truth: Eleven Converts Give the Biblical and Historical Reasons for Becoming Catholic*, ed. Patrick Madrid (San Diego: Basilica, 1994), 89.

Wood's internal struggle came to a head one Sunday morning when he was deeply disturbed about giving the sacrament of Communion to members of his church who were divorced and remarried. "My heart was flooded with conviction and sorrow. I felt God was telling me I had no right to administer the Lord's Supper in this situation. I realized that as a pastor, I couldn't continue to overlook the unbiblical marriages in my congregation."[3]

He was so distressed by these feelings that he walked to the Communion table and, to the shock and confusion of his congregation, announced that he was unprepared to administer the Lord's Supper that day. Not long afterward, he converted to Rome, which held out the promise of silencing the cacophony of conflicting voices and contradictory theological claims by providing a clear and palpable display of unity. "The Catholic Church has bishops who claim apostolic succession, and can back it up biblically and historically; the Catholic Church, unlike Protestantism, possesses visible doctrinal unity."[4]

Leaving aside Wood's remarkably simplistic claims about the biblical and historical grounds for the claims of Rome, it is hard to see how anyone who is even reasonably informed can maintain such an idealistic picture of its unity. Anyone who has ever compared, say, the claims asserted by Pope Pius IX's "Syllabus or Summary of the Main Errors of Our Age" with Vatican II knows that the Church of Rome is a dramatically different church than it was in the nineteenth and early twentieth centuries. More important, those very changes did not come about by seamless "development" or easy consensus. Rather, they were due to significant internal divisions and the desire to come to terms with them.

Even with all the dramatic changes that Rome has undergone, it still often projects a powerful image of unshaken consistency and singular unity. This image, however, is largely an illusion when examined more closely. In the following pages, by highlighting some important facts about the Church of Rome's actual nature, we will show that its unity is not what it appears to be. Specifically, we will show that the Church of Rome is in reality more like a pluralist Protestant denomination than the bulwark of unbroken consistency that its popular apologists purport it to be.

Are Most Roman Catholics Functional Protestants?

I (Jerry) want to begin to make this case by drawing on personal experience. As I noted in the introduction, my time at the University of Notre Dame as a graduate student provided me with not only a great philosophical

3. Ibid., 94.
4. Ibid., 90.

education but also something of an education about Roman Catholicism. I had had relatively little direct interaction with Roman Catholics before that time, so my three years there gave me at least something of a window into American Catholicism. While my data here was naturally piecemeal, anecdotal, and informal, I did come to some interesting impressions about American Catholics from my conversations with fellow students, faculty, and so on. In short, I concluded that most of them were not much different from Protestants.

Indeed, I argued this case briefly in an article I wrote for the student newspaper, *The Observer*. In that article, I identified three different kinds of Catholics I had encountered. First, there were a fair number of conservatives, whom I described as follows: "Those who belong to this group like to characterize themselves as thoroughly Catholic. They stress the teaching authority of the Church and are quick to defend the official Catholic position on all points. For such persons, papal encyclicals are not to be debated; they are to be accepted and obeyed."[5] I met a number of students who were actively involved with Opus Dei[6] and met this description, as well as several others.

I also encountered some rather liberal Catholics, who were openly skeptical about not only the distinctive claims of their church but even basic creedal orthodoxy. They would be as skeptical of the virgin birth as of the immaculate conception (if they even knew the difference), but they would still identify as Catholic, even proudly so.

But my impression at the time was that most Roman Catholics fit into a third group somewhere between these two, a group I called "functional Protestants." I wrote: "When I say most Catholics are functional protestants I simply mean that most Catholics do not accept the authority claims of their Church. In actual belief and practice, they are much closer to the protestant view."[7] Many of the Catholics I knew at Notre Dame did not accept papal infallibility and were skeptical of one or more of the Marian dogmas. Moreover, many of them rejected their church's stance on birth control. They were fundamentally orthodox in the classic creedal sense and took their faith in Christ seriously, but the same could not be said for many of the distinctive

5. Jerry Walls, "Reformational Theology Found in Catholicism," *Observer*, April 23, 1987, 8. My title for the article, as I recall, was "Are Most Catholics Functional Protestants?," but the editors changed it.

6. Opus Dei (whose name means "Work of God") is a lay organization within the Roman Catholic Church. The organization's website says that its mission is "to spread the Christian message that every person is called to holiness and that every honest work can be sanctified." See "Frequently Asked Questions about Opus Dei," Opus Dei, accessed December 3, 2016, http://www.opusdei.org/en-us/faq/#what-is-opus-dei.

7. Walls, "Reformational Theology Found in Catholicism," 8.

claims of their church. Although they still had a certain loyalty to their Roman Catholic heritage, and very much identified themselves as Catholic, their theological views were pretty much the same as mine.

The reaction to my article was telling. My conservative Catholic friends applauded me and agreed that many of their fellow Catholics did not deserve the name. Others thought my conclusions were off target because I was defining Catholicism in traditional terms that were not true to the diversity in the contemporary church. (Rumor had it this was the reaction in the theology department.) Still others essentially agreed with my analysis but thought I was operating with too narrow an understanding of what is involved in being a faithful Catholic.[8]

One of the most interesting reactions to my article came from Professor Ralph McInerny, the distinguished medieval scholar and philosopher. In addition to teaching at Notre Dame and writing both scholarly and popular books, as well as detective novels, Professor McInerny had, with Michael Novak, cofounded *Crisis Magazine*, which described itself as "a voice for the faithful catholic laity." In one of his articles in that magazine, McInerny not only agreed with my claims but also saw them as further evidence that illustrated his concerns about the direction of his church. In the second paragraph of that article, he wrote: "It was not clear to me four and a half years ago, when Mike Novak and I began this journal, how deep the divisions among Catholics were nor how much deeper they were destined to become. Nowadays, the very term 'Catholic' has become equivocal."[9] A few paragraphs later McInerny summarized my article, then commented:

> Now if Walls has a point, and surely he does, things have come to a pretty pass among us Catholics. As often before, I am reminded of Newman's "A Form of Infidelity of the Day." The most insidious enemy is the enemy within, and the heretic who claims to be a Catholic. It is such people, we are told, who are now in charge—readers will remember Thomas Sheehan's triumphalist victory statement on behalf of what he calls the liberal consensus.
>
> Wasn't it Karl Rahner who said that it had become necessary to think of Hans Küng as a Protestant in order to make sense of him?
>
> A few years ago I would never have described the foe in terms he now uses of himself. The days are far darker than once dreamed.[10]

8. See the letter to the editor by Margaret E. Payne in response to my article in *Observer*, April 28, 1987, 5.

9. McInerny, "Quodlibets: On Protesting Too Much," *Crisis Magazine*, May 1, 1987, http://www.crisismagazine.com/1987/quodlibets-on-protesting-too-much.

10. For more on "the liberal consensus," see Ralph McInerny, "The Liberal Consensus," *Crisis Magazine*, July 1, 1984, http://www.crisismagazine.com/1984/the-liberal-consensus.

Particularly striking here are McInerny's confession that he had underestimated the depth of the divisions within his church when he first founded *Crisis Magazine* and his assessment that things were "far darker than once dreamed." Moreover, the only way to make sense of some "Catholics" is to think of them as Protestants. McInerny was not an extremist but rather a highly sophisticated Catholic intellectual, who was very gracious and likable. I remember him fondly from my days at Notre Dame. But it is most telling that he judged the Roman Catholic Church in 1987 to be much farther down the road toward liberalism than he had imagined only four or five years earlier.

Similarly, as I have now concluded, my judgment in 1987 that most Roman Catholics are "functional Protestants" was far too optimistic. I had the sense then that most Roman Catholics were rather firmly committed to core Christian orthodoxy and conservative moral convictions and could be counted on as evangelical allies on these matters. As I have continued to assess the matter, I have concluded that most Roman Catholics are functional *liberal* Protestants, and that the Church of Rome is functionally the world's largest pluralist Protestant denomination.

Putting the matter this way is somewhat provocative, but we think it is not inaccurate. To see why, let us say more about what we mean by a pluralist Protestant denomination. For an example, let us consider the United Methodist Church. Several decades ago the Methodist Church was vibrantly growing, the largest Christian denomination in the United States, and thoroughly orthodox and evangelical in its theological commitments. This began to change in the late nineteenth century, and especially in the twentieth, when various forms of liberal theology gained acceptance and even dominance in Methodist seminaries. As a result, more and more clergy were trained in liberal schools of thought, and the Methodist theological identity became confused and equivocal. By the 1960s, this was so much the case that when the United Methodist Church was formed in 1968 by merging the Methodist Church and the Evangelical United Brethren, the church in reality was radically pluralist in terms of the theological diversity within the ranks of the clergy and the theological seminaries. At its General Conference in 1972, the church made the move to affirm "theological pluralism" within its ranks as a "principle," thereby explicitly endorsing what had been the reality for several decades.

Fortunately, this experiment that many hailed as a bold harbinger of vitality and growth was soon recognized as a disastrous mistake.[11] In 1988 the United Methodists repudiated the pluralism they had embraced sixteen years

---

11. See Jerry L. Walls, *The Problem of Pluralism: Recovering United Methodist Identity*, rev. ed. (Wilmore, KY: Good News Books, 1988).

earlier by adopting a new theological statement that reaffirmed the classic orthodoxy represented in their official doctrinal standards. And indeed, the United Methodist Church has been moving in the same direction ever since, as was made clear in the 2016 General Conference, when the church not only reaffirmed its traditional stance on sexuality, but also adopted more conservative positions on abortion and other social and moral issues. At stake in these recent developments is the identity of the United Methodist Church as a global orthodox Christian church, a topic that is significant in its own right, though it is not our concern in this chapter.

But here is an important point to make clear what we mean by a pluralist Protestant denomination. Throughout the time when radical theological pluralism had been tolerated within the ranks of United Methodist clergy, even during those sixteen years when it was explicitly endorsed as a principle, the official doctrinal stance of the church remained quite orthodox. All along if one wanted to know the doctrine of the United Methodist Church, the official answer could be found by consulting *The Book of Discipline*, the *Articles of Religion*, and Wesley's *Standard Sermons*, which affirm not only the substance of classic creedal orthodoxy but also distinctively Reformed and Wesleyan claims about justification, sanctification, and the like. So a pluralist denomination is not necessarily one that officially gives up its orthodox doctrinal standards. To the contrary, they may retain and continue to affirm those standards.[12]

What then does characterize a pluralist denomination? We suggest three things. First, there is large divergence between official doctrine and the actual beliefs and practices of significant numbers of that denomination's members. Second, pluralist denominations are marked by tolerating clergy and academics who ignore or even deny the official teachings of their church and espouse theological views that are radically at odds with their doctrinal standards. The seminaries and other schools of pluralist denominations have no binding confessional requirements for their professors. Third, members of these denominations, particularly clergy, not infrequently ignore church law and engage in practices that are officially prohibited.

Consider again the United Methodist Church. Not only do many of its clergy and seminary professors espouse views contrary to official doctrine, but they also ignore church law. The most controversial instances involve homosexual behavior and marriage. Despite the official teaching and policy

---

12. So the official doctrinal and moral standards in the *Book of Discipline* of the United Methodist Church play a role similar to that of magisterial doctrinal statements in the Roman Catholic Church. But in both cases, official teaching is one thing, and actual belief and practice may be quite another.

of the church, a number of United Methodist clergy have performed gay weddings, and most of the time they do so with impunity. So there is a glaring gap between official doctrine and policy on the one hand, and in many cases actual belief and practice on the other hand.

With regard to these three characteristics, the Roman Catholic Church may be functionally the world's largest pluralist Protestant denomination. So let us turn now to explore this claim in more detail.

Comparing Catholic Convictions

We can make some initial headway by comparing the beliefs of Roman Catholics with the beliefs of mainline Protestants, who are the epitome of pluralist denominations, and evangelicals, who are more orthodox and conservative in their convictions. A good place to begin is with a Pew Research poll from 2014 that compared the beliefs of various religions, including different Christian traditions.[13]

For a start, consider how these three groups answered when queried about absolute standards for beliefs about right and wrong. They were asked whether there are clear standards for right or wrong, or whether right and wrong depend on the situation. Of Roman Catholics 30 percent said there are clear standards, while 67 percent said that it depends on the situation. Of mainline Protestants 32 percent said that there are clear standards, while 65 percent said that it depends on the situation. There is a marked difference with evangelicals, with 50 percent saying that there is a clear standard, while 48 percent said that it depends on the situation.

These broad differences also appear when we consider more-specific moral beliefs. Consider first abortion, where there is a significant gap between Roman Catholics and mainline Protestants: 48 percent of Roman Catholics said abortion should be legal in all or most cases, and 47 percent said it should be illegal in all or most cases, compared to 60 percent of mainline Protestants who said it should be legal in all or most cases, while 35 percent said it should be illegal in all or most cases. Again, evangelicals returned the most conservative numbers, with 33 percent saying it should be legal in all or most cases, and 63 percent saying it should be illegal in all or most cases.[14]

13. The statistics that follow are from Pew Research Center, *Religious Landscape Study* (Washington, DC: Pew Research Center, 2014), http://www.pewforum.org/religious-landscape-study. See also "U.S. Catholics Open to Non-Traditional Families," Pew Research Center, September 2, 2015, http://www.pewforum.org/2015/09/02/u-s-catholics-open-to-non-traditional-families.

14. A significant majority of Roman Catholics voted for the most proabortion president in American history, Barack Obama, in 2008: 54 percent of Roman Catholics voted for him,

When we turn to what is perhaps the most volatile moral issue in contemporary America, we see Roman Catholics again aligning more with mainline Protestants than with evangelicals. When asked about homosexuality (the exact choice on the questionnaire was between "homosexuality should be accepted by society" and "homosexuality should be discouraged by society"), 70 percent of Roman Catholics said it should be accepted, while 23 percent said it should be discouraged. This is slightly more liberal than mainline Protestants, 66 percent of whom said homosexuality should be accepted, while 26 percent said it should be discouraged. Evangelicals were considerably more conservative, with 36 percent saying it should be accepted, compared to 55 percent who said it should be discouraged. On the issue of same-sex marriage, Roman Catholics and mainline Protestants are virtually identical: 57 percent of Roman Catholics favor or strongly favor same-sex marriage, and 34 percent oppose or strongly oppose it, compared to 57 percent of mainline Protestants who favor or strongly favor it, while 35 percent oppose or strongly oppose it. Again, the numbers for evangelicals are significantly different: 28 percent favor or strongly favor same-sex marriage, whereas 64 percent oppose or strongly oppose it.

There is one interesting matter of traditional doctrine where the Pew Research poll found Catholics to be very close to evangelicals, and that is belief in heaven. When asked if they believed in heaven, 85 percent of Catholics said they did, while 10 percent said they did not. This compares to 88 percent of evangelicals who affirmed belief in heaven, while 5 percent did not. Mainline Protestants are somewhat less confident of heaven, with 80 percent affirming belief in it, while 12 percent did not. However, when we turn to the less popular doctrine of hell, once again we see Roman Catholics more in line with mainline Protestants than with evangelicals: 63 percent of Catholics affirm belief in hell, and 29 percent do not, while 60 percent of mainline Protestants said they believed in it, compared to 29 percent who said they did not. In contrast 82 percent of evangelicals said they believed in hell, while 11 percent did not.

Here we emphasize that these reported liberal convictions are held not only by Roman Catholics in the United States, but also by many other parts of the church as well. While Catholics in some parts of the world are much more conservative than they are in the American church, in other parts of the world many Catholics are even more liberal than those in the United States. A dramatic example of this was on display recently in the Republic of

---

compared to 45 percent of Protestants overall. Only 26 percent of Protestant evangelicals voted for Obama in 2008. Pew Research Center, "How the Faithful Voted" (Washington, DC: Pew Research Center, 2008), http://www.pewforum.org/2008/11/05/how-the-faithful-voted.

Ireland, one of the most traditionally Roman Catholic countries in the world, with one of the highest percentages of Roman Catholics on the planet. In a national referendum on same-sex marriage in 2015, the Republic became the first country to legalize it through a popular vote, and it did so overwhelmingly, with 62 percent of the population supporting it.

A recent worldwide poll of Roman Catholics was also telling, showing not only the liberal beliefs of many Catholics but also the extreme diversity in the church.[15] While same-sex marriage is supported by a significant majority in several countries, it is opposed by 99 percent of African Catholics. The poll also found that 78 percent of Catholics overall support the use of contraceptives, but over 90 percent do so in Argentina, Colombia, Brazil, Spain, and France.

Another issue of particular interest given recent developments in the Church of Rome is the question of whether divorced and remarried persons should be permitted to receive Communion. The official teaching is that they should not. The survey found that only 19 percent of European Catholics and 30 percent of South American Catholics agree with this; 75 percent of African Catholics do, however.

These statistics tell an interesting story. A significant majority of Roman Catholics are at odds with the teaching of their church on important issues. On some of these matters, they may be aligned with conservative Protestants (and Eastern Orthodox). Many conservative Protestants and Orthodox believe that contraception is morally acceptable. Likewise, many conservative Protestants (and Orthodox) believe that there are biblically justified reasons for divorce and remarriage.[16] To this extent, then, many Roman Catholics are functionally Protestant.

However, there is more to the story. Many or even most Roman Catholics also hold views that are more in line with liberal Protestants, as the Pew Research Poll demonstrated.[17] Over and over again, we saw that Roman Catholic

15. Michelle Boorstein and Peyton M. Craighill, "Pope Francis Faces Church Divided over Doctrine, Global Poll of Catholics Finds," *Washington Post*, February 9, 2014, https://www.washingtonpost.com/national/pope-francis-faces-church-divided-over-doctrine-global-poll-of-catholics-finds/2014/02/08/e90ecef4-8f89-11e3-b227-12a45d109e03_story.html.

16. The Orthodox Church excommunicates divorced persons for a time to emphasize that divorce is a serious sin. After that, they may be restored to full participation in the community, including receiving the sacrament of Communion. Such persons may then be remarried with the blessing of the church.

17. Readers might wonder whether educational differences account for the more liberal views of Roman Catholics. This does not appear to be the case since the differences in education between evangelicals and Roman Catholics are negligible. For Catholics, 46 percent only graduated from high school or less, compared to 43 percent of evangelicals; 27 percent of Catholics had some college, compared to 35 percent of evangelicals; 16 percent of Catholics graduated from college, compared to 14 percent of evangelicals; 10 percent of Catholics had a postgraduate

views on various moral and religious issues align very much with mainline Protestants and diverge from the majority of evangelicals. This is one good reason, then, to suggest that many or even most Roman Catholics are not only functional Protestants but indeed functional liberal Protestants.

Birth Control and Papal Authority

The fact that Roman Catholics overwhelmingly reject their church's teaching on birth control is, in more ways than one, emblematic of the fact that most Catholics are functional Protestants. It reflects the deeper reality that many Roman Catholics reject the distinctive authority claims that characterize their church, claims that are clearly at the heart of the divisions between Protestants and Roman Catholics.

To understand the connection between birth control and papal authority, we need to look back to the momentous events of Vatican II. As many analysts have observed, a majority of delegates supported the "progressive" theology that was having a growing influence in the church, even as a conservative minority represented the traditional theology favored by the pope and the curia (the power structure in Rome). The documents of Vatican II were thus crafted, as much as possible, to satisfy both sides. Sometimes this resulted in language that was ambiguous enough for both sides to assent to it; at other times both views were presented in such a way that it was not clear how they could be mutually consistent.

A famous instance of this occurs in the very first document of Vatican II, *Lumen Gentium: Dogmatic Constitution on the Church*, specifically in its chapter 3, "On the Hierarchical Structure of the Church and in Particular the Episcopate." This chapter, while asserting traditional claims about the papacy and episcopal authority, also emphasized a strongly collegial view of the relationship between the pope and the college of bishops and of the power they shared. Pope Paul VI, however, thought the document had compromised papal authority and made an unusual move to rectify the situation. After the document had already been passed, he inserted a "Note of Explanation" that asserted a stronger view of papal authority than the document seemed to support.

> It is up to the Supreme Pontiff, to whose care Christ's whole flock has been entrusted, to determine, according to the needs of the Church as they change

degree, compared to 7 percent of evangelicals. Mainline Protestants were slightly more educated than both Catholics and evangelicals: 37 percent only had high school or less; 30 percent had some college; 19 percent had a college degree; and 14 percent had a postgraduate degree.

over the course of centuries, the way in which this care may be best exercised—whether in a personal or a collegial way. The Roman Pontiff, taking account of the Church's welfare, proceeds according to his own discretion in arranging, promoting, and approving the exercise of collegial activity.

As Supreme Pastor of the Church, the Supreme Pontiff can always exercise his power at will, as his very office demands.[18]

Since this "Note of Explanation" was added after the council had completed its work, it was not voted on like other parts of the document.

This clash of authority came to the fore after Vatican II on birth control, an issue that many hoped the council would resolve. In 1963, Pope John XXIII had appointed a commission to study the issue. After the death of John, Paul VI increased the Pontifical Commission on Birth Control to seventy-two members, including several theologians and medical professionals. In its 1966 report, the commission concluded that artificial birth control is not inherently evil and that Roman Catholics should be permitted to use it. Their recommendation was rejected, however, and the minority report prevailed, resulting in the 1968 papal encyclical *Humanae Vitae*, a document that reaffirms the traditional Roman Catholic view that artificial birth control is sinful.

What is most telling about this episode is that the arguments for the minority report at times seemed less concerned with the morality of birth control than with the concern that accepting it would undermine magisterial and papal authority. Given the many times the church had condemned birth control in very strong terms, to accept it now would be an admission that the magisterium had been mistaken in the past. Consider these lines from the minority report:

> If contraception were declared not intrinsically evil, in honesty it would have to be acknowledged that the Holy Spirit in 1930 (Encyclical, *Casti Connubi*), 1951 (Address of Pius XII to midwives) and 1958 (Address to the International Congress of Haematologists in the year of Pius XII's death), assisted Protestant Churches, and that for half a century Pius XI, Pius XII and a great part of the hierarchy did not protest against a very serious error, one most pernicious to souls; for it would be suggested that they condemned most imprudently, under pain of eternal punishment, thousands upon thousands of human acts which are now approved. Indeed, it must be neither denied nor ignored that these acts would be approved for the same fundamental reasons which Protestantism alleged and which they (Catholics) condemned or at least did not recognize.[19]

18. *The Documents of Vatican II: Vatican Translation* (Staten Island, NY: Paulist Press, 2009), 76.

19. Cited in Hans Küng, *Truthfulness: The Future of the Church* (New York: Sheed & Ward, 1968), 132–33. The original appeared in *The Tablet*, London, April 29, 1967.

Particularly interesting for our concerns is the recognition that to acknowledge the use of artificial birth control as morally acceptable would not only call into question previous papal pronouncements but would also legitimize Protestantism over against Rome.

Even though the conservative position prevailed officially, the decision by Paul VI hardly went uncontested, and those who took issue with the pope's decision thought he should have called a meeting of the bishops and the matter should have been resolved by collegial action. This claim goes back to the document on the church at Vatican II and the pope's decision to insert his "Note of Explanation" asserting his authority to act alone. Apparently not all bishops agreed with the claims he made in that "Note." David Wells describes what happened later:

> When the bishops eventually got together in Rome after Pope Paul's encyclical had been issued, they took him to task for not consulting with them. Leo Suenens, the Belgian cardinal and leader of the progressives, was most forthright in this matter, letting the pope know that he had acted unconstitutionally. Whether this was so, of course, depends on how the document is interpreted. There are two ways of looking at it. From one perspective, Pope Paul acted quite within his power, while from the other perspective, he did not.[20]

In any case, our key point here is that the overwhelming majority of Roman Catholics side with Protestants on the issue of birth control, and that their doing so is emblematic of the fact that most Catholics reject the claims to papal authority that Paul VI tried to reassert at Vatican II. While conservatives rightly feared that accepting birth control would both undermine papal authority and give credence to Protestantism, the reality is that papal authority as Rome wanted to maintain it had already been lost.

The Bewildering Variety of Roman Catholic Theology

The larger reality, however, is that Roman Catholics have far bigger theological fish to fry than any worries they may have about birth control. Recall again McInerny's admission in 1987 that it was not clear to him "how deep the divisions among Catholics were nor how much deeper they were destined to become" when he and Michael Novak founded *Crisis Magazine* four years earlier. What had become clear to McInerny has become all the more evident in the years since then: the Roman Catholic Church is not only

20. David Wells, *Revolution in Rome* (Downers Grove, IL: InterVarsity, 1972), 111.

deeply divided but also radically pluralistic in the range of theological views represented in the church. It is not putting it too strongly to say that every theological novelty spawned by liberal Protestantism has been replicated or reproduced within Roman Catholic theology. And now Catholics have invented some of their own.

If I may draw on my Notre Dame experience again, my conservative friends complained that the theology department there represented the liberal sort of approach to the discipline that they thought destructive to Catholic orthodoxy. A good measure of the pluralism represented at Notre Dame is *Catholicism*, a widely used textbook by Richard P. McBrien, who was chairman of the theology department there for many years. His book, a "classic" that sold over 150,000 copies in its first edition, was intended by the author to be a "bridge between the Church of yesterday and the Church of today, and between conservative, traditionally minded Catholics, on the one hand, and progressive, renewal minded Catholics, on the other, even if some in the former group seem determined to resist and depreciate such an effort."[21]

The enormous popularity of McBrien's book suggests that the picture he paints of Catholicism resonates with many contemporary members of his church. The book has been controversial, however, and has drawn criticism from church officials, both in its earlier editions and in the 1994 version. In 1996 the National Council of Catholic Bishops Committee on Doctrine released a critical review of the book, after expressing disappointment that McBrien had not corrected the defects they had pointed out in earlier editions. The review was published because the bishops judged that the book posed pastoral problems, so that a review identifying those problems would be of value to the larger Roman Catholic community, as well as an expression of concern to McBrien. The review identified three broad areas of concern with the book. "First, some statements are inaccurate or at least misleading. Second, there is in the book an overemphasis on the plurality of opinion within the Catholic theological tradition that makes it difficult at times for the reader to discern the normative core of that tradition. Third, *Catholicism* overstates the significance of recent developments within the Catholic tradition, implying that the past appears to be markedly inferior to the present and obscuring the continuity of the tradition."[22] Particularly interesting for our concerns here is the "overemphasis on the plurality of opinion within the Catholic theological tradition." The bishops were

---

21. Richard P. McBrien, *Catholicism* (New York: HarperOne, 1994), xli.

22. Committee on Doctrine of the National Council of Catholic Bishops, "Review of Fr. McBrien's *Catholicism*," April 9, 1996, http://www.catholicculture.org/culture/library/view.cfm ?id=541&CFID=121743&CFTOKEN=22026492.

especially concerned that the book would be confusing when used as a college textbook for beginners, or by Roman Catholic laypersons. Here is part of what they said about the concern with plurality: "The book gives an overview of the theological scene in all of its variety and presents numerous brief summaries of many positions. . . . The book requires the reader to find his or her own way through what is sometimes a bewildering number and variety of positions."[23]

To be sure, this does pose a pastoral problem, as the bishops claim. But the deeper problem for the Church of Rome resides in the fact that there is a "bewildering number and variety of positions" in Roman Catholic theology to begin with. The reality is that McBrien's book simply reflects the deep division and radical diversity that prevails in contemporary Roman Catholic theology.

A Clear Account of Jesus's Resurrection?

Even apart from the diversity of options in contemporary Roman Catholic theology, much of that theology is bewildering because it is so equivocal and ambiguous. For a good example of this, consider the foundational Christian doctrine of the resurrection of Jesus as presented by the eminent theologian Edward Schillebeeckx, who was prominently involved in Vatican II. The classic Christian claim as expressed by the apostle Paul is rather straightforward: "that he was raised on the third day according to the scriptures, and that he appeared to Cephas, and then to the twelve" (1 Cor. 15:4–5). This is the essential basis for belief in Jesus's resurrection.

According to Schillebeeckx, however, faith in the resurrection was not generated by actual appearances of Jesus to his disciples after his death, along with the empty tomb, as traditional theologians and biblical scholars have contended. Rather, "in the development of the tradition it appears that the resurrection *kerygma* was already present even before the traditions about the tomb and appearances had arisen."[24]

So the question remains how faith in the resurrection arose in the first place. According to Schillebeeckx's reconstruction of the historical evidence, it was produced by a conversion experience the disciples had when they were gathered after the death of Christ and felt that they were forgiven for their cowardice

---

23. McBrien, *Catholicism*, also surveys various Protestant views in some of his chapters, yet the "bewildering" variety remains even when only Catholic positions are included.

24. Schillebeeckx, *Jesus: An Experiment in Christology*, trans. Hubert Hoskins (New York: Vintage Books, 1981), 333–34.

and lack of faith when he was crucified: "May it not be that Simon Peter—and indeed the Twelve—arrived via their concrete experience of forgiveness after Jesus' death, encountered as grace and discussed among themselves (as they remembered Jesus' sayings about, among other things, the gracious God) at the 'evidence for belief': the Lord is alive? He renews for them the offer of salvation; this they experience in their own conversion; he must therefore be alive."[25] This sentence is rather complex, but Schillebeeckx is claiming that this experience of grace, this sense that Christ was offering the disciples forgiveness as they recalled and discussed his teaching, led them to believe "he must therefore be alive." They later articulated this experience in terms of a vision of Christ appearing to them.[26]

This certainly is a complete reversal of how traditional theologians view the matter. Roman Catholic theologian Gerald O'Collins, who taught for many years at the Gregorian University of Rome, finds this suggestion incredible and pointedly comments as follows: "Were the evangelists such confused and confusing writers that they really intended to say that the disciples first believed in the risen Christ, were converted and later expressed this conversion-experience 'in the form of an appearance vision'? Surely the ordinary conventions of language indicate the evangelists meant to say that the appearances to the disciples effected their conversion, and not that their conversion was later verbalized by reporting appearances of the risen Christ."[27] O'Collins's critique of Schillebeeckx, though pointed, is also charitable. Despite his recognition that the famous theologian "rejects any actual appearances in the sense of meeting Jesus alive after his death and burial," he begins his critique by remarking that "it would confuse matters not to note that Schillebeeckx clearly accepts the personal, bodily resurrection of Jesus."[28]

A number of O'Collins's fellow Roman Catholics are skeptical of his claim here, as suggested by the fact that Schillebeeckx was called to Rome more than once to defend his writings. His views, however, were never officially condemned. Still, the point here is that contemporary Roman Catholics can hardly be blamed if they are bewildered that views like those of Schillebeeckx now count as "clear" affirmations of the bodily resurrection of Jesus at the highest levels of academic theology in their church.

25. Ibid., 391.

26. For details, including Schillebeeckx's account of the origin of the empty tomb tradition, see ibid., 320–97.

27. O'Collins, *Interpreting Jesus* (London: Geoffrey Chapman, 1983), 123, quoting Schillebeeckx, *Jesus*, 390.

28. O'Collins, *Interpreting Jesus*, 121, 120.

Inventing Tradition in a New Tune

Let us turn now to consider a more recent work that perhaps poses even more fundamental challenges to conservative Roman Catholic theology: the title *Inventing Catholic Tradition* is a telling indicator of what its author, Terrence W. Tilley, believes. In short, Tilley is quite skeptical of the view that Christian truth is "given" in divine revelation in anything like the sense in which conservative theologians have used terms such as "given" and "revelation." Rather, it is constructed or invented as much as it is given, and its content is accordingly fluid and open-ended.

Tilley's account of tradition is philosophically subtle as well as elusive, yet it seems clear that he rejects any sort of propositional "given" in divine revelation that provides us direct knowledge of ontological reality and enables us to make stable truth claims about it. Faithfulness to tradition, if his account of tradition is accepted, may accordingly require us to give it content that is very different from traditional formulations, even if we retain the same verbal formulas. Given the fluidity of tradition, there can be no certainty of how things may develop as the tradition is carried on. Tilley puts this point poetically on the last page of his book: "We may sing a different tune than our forebears, and our successors will sing yet differently. Not in spite of but because of these differences we can engage faithfully in *traditio*."[29] Tilley distinguishes between *traditia*, by which he means that which is passed down, and *traditio*, "the actual process or practice of passing on the tradition."[30] It is precisely the reality of what is involved in the process or practice of passing it on that makes tradition the fluid thing that it is, according to Tilley.

It is not our purpose here to critically assess Tilley, but it is worthwhile to notice the sort of variations that Catholic doctrine may assume while remaining true to Catholic tradition, as he construes it.[31] Consider what he says about the Roman Catholic doctrine of the real presence of Christ in the Eucharist. Transubstantiation, he contends, was developed in medieval times with multiple meanings and "linguistic practices" that do not connect with contemporary meanings and practices. Thus even if the term "transubstantiation" is retained, it does not mean today what it meant in medieval times, even if church authorities "impose" it or require the use of the term. "It may well remain practically meaningless as a theology for and of eucharistic practice. It may even acquire a new meaning hardly connected to the traditional

29. Tilley, *Inventing Catholic Tradition* (Maryknoll, NY: Orbis Books, 2000), 186.
30. Ibid., 25.
31. For a critical assessment of Tilley by a conservative Catholic theologian, see Matthew Levering, *Engaging the Doctrine of Revelation* (Grand Rapids: Baker Academic, 2014), 146–58.

sense, for example, that transubstantiation refers to the transformation of the worshiping assembly into the body of Christ in and through reception of the Eucharist."[32] Tilley does not mean to deny the doctrine of transubstantiation as Protestants do. Rather, he is explaining what the doctrine may actually mean for contemporary Catholics, even if that meaning is "hardly connected to the traditional sense." As he sees it, Catholics who understand the term this way are merely engaging in faithful *traditio*.

But Tilley's doctrinal revisions that are "hardly connected" to the traditional sense of the terms are not confined to matters distinctive to Roman Catholics. Indeed, Tilley insists that even the very core of consensual orthodoxy is open to such change of meaning in the ongoing process of inventing tradition.

> The Church has had numerous Christologies operative in particular times and places. The introduction of the definitive *homoousios* to define Jesus' relation to the Father is not only unscriptural (as opponents of the definition pointed out in the disputes leading up to the Ecumenical Council of Nicea in 325) but also problematical for theories of salvation, as it was unclear how someone "one in being" with the Father could indeed be like enough to humanity to be the savior of humanity.[33]

Given his doubts about propositional revelation, it is hardly surprising that he does not believe Nicene Christology represents an unchanging truth that must be clearly maintained in order to be faithful to the Christian revelation and the very heart of the gospel. Nor is it surprising that later in the book he shows little interest in philosophical defenses of the incarnation that try to show how the doctrine represents a coherent truth claim. Rather, he seems to think that exploration of the doctrine with the tools of logical analysis is a Protestant project that is "profoundly un-Catholic."[34]

The reality is that traditional Roman Catholics, no less than orthodox Protestants, have a deep investment in the claim that the doctrine of the incarnation is rationally coherent. This is hardly to deny that the doctrine is a mystery surpassing our full understanding; rather, it is to insist that the classic creedal orthodoxy is not logically incoherent, and this is essential to recognizing it as a serious truth claim.

But for now the point to emphasize is that Tilley is not a fringe figure in the Roman Catholic Church. To the contrary, he is the Avery Cardinal Dulles

32. Tilley, *Inventing Catholic Tradition*, 72.
33. Ibid., 32–33.
34. Ibid., 132. As an example of the attempt to show the incarnation to be a coherent doctrine, Tilley cited Thomas V. Morris, *The Logic of God Incarnate* (Ithaca, NY: Cornell University Press, 1986).

Professor of Theology at Fordham University and a past president of the Catholic Theological Society of America. His views are far from eccentric in contemporary Catholic theology.[35]

On a personal note, I found Tilley's book most interesting partly because I had the privilege of getting to know Cardinal Dulles through my participation in the Dulles Colloquium, as I noted in the introduction to this book. In view of this, I found particularly fascinating Tilley's claim that his views and those of Dulles on the doctrine of revelation "are not only compatible but mutually elucidating."[36] At first blush, I was inclined to doubt this claim, but I am not an expert on the work of Dulles, so I may be mistaken. Given Tilley's views on the nature of Catholic tradition and in the fluid nature of its ongoing development, the claim is entirely plausible.

A Mandate for Theologians?

Before moving on from the state of theology in Roman Catholicism, we recall that Pope John Paul II in 1990 issued the document *Ex Corde Ecclesiae* (From the heart of the church) in an attempt to call Catholic colleges and universities to some basic standards of accountability in order to preserve their identity as Catholic schools. Among the requirements of the document was the following: "In ways appropriate to the different academic disciplines, all Catholic teachers are to be faithful to, and all other teachers are to respect, Catholic doctrine and morals in their research and teaching. In particular, Catholic theologians, aware that they fulfill a mandate received from the Church, are to be faithful to the Magisterium of the Church as the authentic interpreter of Sacred Scripture and Sacred Tradition."[37] Of particular interest here is the claim that theologians have a mandate from the church, and the passage ends with a note that refers to a number of church documents and quotes canon law 812: "It is necessary that those who teach theological disciplines in any institute of higher studies have a mandate from the competent ecclesiastical authority."

Given the state of contemporary Roman Catholic theology, it is hardly necessary to comment that this requirement for Roman Catholic theologians to have a mandate from the "competent ecclesiastical authority" and to "be faithful to the Magisterium of the Church" has not been widely followed. Indeed, Anne Hendershott described the reaction to the document as follows:

35. See Levering's comment on "how widely his [Tilley's] views are shared," in *Engaging the Doctrine of Revelation*, 114n15.

36. Tilley, *Inventing Catholic Tradition*, 177.

37. Pope John Paul II, *Ex Corde Ecclesiae*, art. 4, par. 3.

Defiant from the earliest days of the release of *Ex Corde Ecclesiae*, many Catholic college presidents have refused to implement it. Notre Dame's then-president Fr. Edward Malloy, along with Fr. Donald Monan, chancellor of Boston College, responded to the release of the document by publishing an article in *America* calling the document "positively dangerous." Warning of "havoc" if it were adopted, the faculty senate at Notre Dame voted unanimously for the guidelines to be ignored.[38]

What we have seen, then, is that not only is the Roman Catholic Church marked by extreme pluralism among its theologians, but official efforts to hold them accountable to magisterial teaching also have little force or effect. In both respects, the Church of Rome very much resembles pluralist Protestant denominations.

Ignoring Church Law

Another defining marker of pluralist Protestant denominations is that liberal clergy frequently disregard church law with little if any disciplinary action from church leaders. As reported early in this chapter, the most notorious example of this reality pertains to official church teaching about homosexuality and same-sex marriage. Some pluralist denominations have officially changed their policy on this controversial issue; others have maintained their traditional position but have been lax in enforcing it. Here again, the Church of Rome is not exempt from this difficulty.

A high-level instance of this recently played out in Germany. In April 2015 a Roman Catholic woman who headed a Caritas day-care center in Bavaria had been asked to resign because she had announced that she was going to marry a woman. The decision was then reversed with the blessing of church officials. William Oddie explains: "Cardinal Reinhard Marx, Archbishop of the Diocese of Munich, has agreed to implement immediately new regulations approved by the German Bishops' Conference at the end of April 2015, drastically liberalising the Catholic Church's disciplinary rules in Germany. In the past, employees who deliberately and persistently did not live according to the Church's moral teaching would (as at first happened in this case) have

38. Hendershott, "A New Front in the Catholic Campus Culture Wars," *First Things*, August 24, 2012, http://www.firstthings.com/web-exclusives/2012/08/a-new-front-in-the-catholic-campus -culture-wars. See also Jeff Mirus, "*Ex Corde Ecclesiae* in America," CatholicCulture.org, January 21, 2011, http://www.catholicculture.org/commentary/articles.cfm?id=482; Richard P. McBrien, "Why I Shall Not Seek a Mandate," *America: The National Catholic Review*, February 12, 2000, http://americamagazine.org/issue/275/article/why-i-shall-not-seek-mandate.

been asked to leave their position in institutions of the Church."[39] Oddie then cites the opinion of the German cardinal Reinhard Marx, who expressed the view that the German church is not simply a branch of Rome. "Each conference of bishops is responsible for pastoral care in its cultural context and must preach the Gospel in its own, original way." Oddie is incredulous of this claim, insisting that all Catholics are members of churches that are branches of Rome, which is why they are called "Roman Catholics." "And all this talk of being responsible for care of its own part of the Church 'in its pastoral context' is a weasely way of saying that the German bishops have a right to determine what their own version of Catholic DOCTRINE is: when Marx says the German church 'must preach the gospel in its own, original way' he is unambiguously declaring unilateral doctrinal independence from the teaching authority of the Church."

Oddie then gives vent to the wish—which many conservative Roman Catholics no doubt share—that the pope would fire and replace all dissenting bishops. He concedes, however, that even if the pope were so disposed, he lacks the authority to do so. To resort to that measure or anything like it would lead to open schism. To make matters worse, Oddie realizes that lay opinion runs heavily in a liberal direction even in many parts of the church where conservative bishops are trying to remain faithful to official doctrine and policy.

We could easily belabor this point with other examples and illustrations, but there is no need. The hard reality is that a significant majority of the Church of Rome's membership is so far out of step with its official views that any hope of consistently enforcing church doctrine and policy is at best a conservative's pipe dream. And there are numerous clergy, including bishops, who share and promote the liberal agenda.

The Pope Will Keep Things Straight

Many Roman Catholics may grant all this but still be inclined to dismiss it as not having any sort of force. Yes, they may say, shenanigans like this go on at Notre Dame and in Germany and in other pockets of the church. But Rome still has a safeguard that Protestantism lacks: the papacy. Indeed, for many Roman Catholics and converts, the pope is the very embodiment of

39. Oddie, "The German Bishops Have Declared Independence from Rome on Same-Sex Marriage: How Far Will the Rot Spread Now?," *Catholic Herald*, August 6, 2015, http://www .catholicherald.co.uk/commentandblogs/2015/08/06/the-german-bishops-have-declared-indepen dence-from-rome-on-same-sex-marriage-how-far-will-the-rot-spread-now/.

the stability and the guarantor of the unbroken continuity that Rome claims to represent.

While it is instinctive for Roman Catholics to pivot to the pope when pressed with the realities we have discussed in this chapter, it is far from clear how this move will help them. The truth is that the authority of the papacy faces the same sort of problems that Roman Catholics think Protestants uniquely face because of their reliance on the authority and perspicuity of Scripture. In a response to Brad Gregory's critique of Protestantism along these lines, Carl Trueman wrote as follows:

> Further, if Dr. Gregory wants to include as part of his general concept of Protestantism any and all sixteenth century lunatics who ever claimed the Bible alone as sole authority and thence to draw conclusions about the plausibility of the perspicuity of scripture, then it seems reasonable to insist in response that discussions of Roman Catholicism include not simply the Newmans, Ratzingers and Wotjylas [sic] but also the Kungs, Rahners, Schillebeeckxs and the journalists at the *National Catholic Reporter*. And why stop there? We should also throw in the sedevacantists and Lefebvrists for good measure. They all claim to be good Roman Catholics and find their unity around the Office of the Pope, after all. Let us not exclude them on the dubious grounds that they do not support our own preconceived conclusions of how papal authority should work. At least Protestantism has the integrity to wear its chaotic divisions on its sleeve.[40]

"Sola pope," we might say, has been no more successful in keeping everyone in line than sola Scriptura! To make matters even worse, the credibility of appealing to the pope varies significantly, depending on who occupies the chair of Peter. Consider historian Robert Eno's telling observation that his fellow Roman Catholics are very much inclined to pick and choose which popes they will fully honor and follow. "Catholics in fact professing unconditional loyalty to Rome can be remarkably selective in what or in whom they choose to support or extol. Hans Küng continually cites John XXIII as his ideal pope. On the other side, some radical conservative groups refuse to acknowledge any legitimate pope after Pius XII."[41] As I write these lines, we are living in a period when many Roman Catholics are demonstrating this tendency to be "remarkably selective" in their support for their pope. I refer to the irony

---

40. Carl Trueman, "Pay No Attention to That Man behind the Curtain: Roman Catholic History and the Emerald City Protocol," *reformation21*, April 2012, http://www.reformation 21.org/articles/pay-no-attention-to-that-man-behind-the-curtain-roman-catholic-history -and-the-e.php.

41. Robert B. Eno, *The Rise of the Papacy* (Eugene, OR: Wipf & Stock, 2008; first published by Michael Glazier, 1990), 12–13.

that it is precisely conservative Roman Catholics who have been most vocal in showing this tendency in their attitude toward Pope Francis.

Conservatives are not without their reasons for concern insofar as they believe that the traditional views of their church must be carefully maintained. Francis has undeniably not only supported a number of leftist political views but also attempted to moderate his church's position on a number of controversial issues. Indeed, from the standpoint of some conservative Roman Catholics, he is a dangerous threat to the church.[42] In old-fashioned polemics, it was a common charge from Protestants that the pope was the antichrist. Nowadays it is almost as if some conservative Catholics seem to think that!

Many of these concerns came to a head in the reaction to the highly publicized Synod on the Family that met in 2014 and 2015 and to the papal document that came out after the Synod in 2016, *Amoris Laetitia* (The joy of love). The hot-button issue that generated the most controversy, however, was not homosexuality but the matter of divorce and remarriage.

The traditional Roman view is starkly clear. "Contracting a new union [after divorce], even if it is recognized by civil law, adds to the gravity of the rupture: the remarried spouse is then in a situation of public and permanent adultery."[43] Adultery is a mortal sin, so to be in a state of permanent adultery is to be in a state of permanent mortal sin. To freely remain in mortal sin is to remain in a state that leads to damnation if the sin is not repented of and forgiven. Such persons accordingly are unable to receive the sacrament of Communion so long as they remain in this situation.[44]

There is, however, a remedy for persons in these adulterous marriages that allows them to be reconciled to the community: the sacrament of penance. What this penance requires, however, is rather severe. "Reconciliation through the sacrament of Penance can be granted only for those who have repented for having violated the sign of the covenant and of fidelity to Christ, and who are committed to living in complete continence."[45] The couple can remain married and be welcomed again to receive the sacrament of Communion so long as they are totally committed to a sexless marriage. The only way to be restored to the community and to escape the state of perpetual mortal sin is to live together thereafter in perpetual continence, the way Roman Catholics believe Joseph and Mary did.

42. "We Deserve Francis," Rorate Caeli, see http://rorate-caeli.blogspot.com/2016/06/we-deserve-francis.html. See numerous other examples at this website.
43. *Catechism of the Catholic Church*, 2nd ed. (Mahwah, NJ: Paulist Press, 1994), par. 2384.
44. Some evangelicals share this view.
45. *Catechism*, par. 1650.

What is also starkly clear is that the overwhelming majority of Roman Catholics reject their church's teaching on this matter, as indicated by statistics cited at the beginning of this chapter. More telling, however, is that apparently a significant number of Roman Catholic priests, including those in the hierarchy, also think the church's stance on this issue is too stringent. The document *Amoris Laetitia* gives us good reason to infer that the pope also thinks it is too strict.

The most controversial passages of this document appear in its chapter 8, "Accompanying, Discerning and Integrating Weakness," particularly in the section "The Discernment of 'Irregular' Situations." The opening line of the chapter sets the stage for what follows: "The Synod Fathers stated that, although the Church realizes that any breach of the marriage bond 'is against the will of God,' she is also 'conscious of the frailty of many of her children.'"[46]

What follows is not so remarkable unless read through the lens of Rome's stringent stance on divorce and remarriage. Indeed, Protestant and Eastern Orthodox readers will likely see the chapter as simply a wise and sensitive piece of pastoral direction for dealing with the many broken people in our world today. But for Roman Catholics who are keenly aware of what their Church teaches and are committed to maintaining it, the document is laced with a number of potentially explosive lines.

Consider just one passage, the one that has perhaps elicited the most controversy.

> Because of forms of conditioning and mitigating factors, it is possible that in an objective situation of sin—which may not be subjectively culpable, or fully such—a person can be living in God's grace, can love and can also grow in the life of grace and charity, while receiving the Church's help to this end. Discernment must help to find possible ways of responding to God and growing in the midst of limits. By thinking that everything is black and white, we sometimes close off the way of grace and of growth, and discourage paths of sanctification which give glory to God.[47]

This passage comes in the larger context of a number of other passages that urge priests not simply to resort to rules, which can be used as stones to throw at broken people, but to use personal discernment in their pastoral choices.

46. Pope Francis, *Amoris Laetitia*, par. 291, the Holy See, 2016, https://w2.vatican.va/content/francesco/en/apost_exhortations/documents/papa-francesco_esortazione-ap_20160319_amoris-laetitia.html. The quotes within the quote come from *Relatio Synodi*, the final report of the Synod of Bishops on *The Vocation and Mission of the Family in the Church and in the Contemporary World*.
47. Pope Francis, *Amoris Laetitia*, par. 305.

The extent of this discernment is suggested in the much-discussed and much-debated footnote 351 that appears in the text:

> In certain cases, this can include the help of the sacraments. Hence, "I want to remind priests that the confessional must not be a torture chamber, but rather an encounter with the Lord's mercy" (Apostolic Exhortation *Evangelii Gaudium* [November 24, 2013], 44: AAS 105 [2013], 1038). I would also point out that the Eucharist "is not a prize for the perfect, but a powerful medicine and nourishment for the weak" (*ibid.*, 47:1039).[48]

Again, for Protestants and Eastern Orthodox, this footnote is nothing remarkable; it is simply an expression of God's grace, which is at the heart of the gospel. Indeed, it may even be read as a highly qualified and constrained expression of grace, if that is not a contradiction in terms. But for conservative Roman Catholics keenly aware of church dogma, the footnote is explosive. Why? Because it threatens to undermine the official Roman position by allowing that divorced and remarried persons can receive the sacrament while maintaining a normal marriage.

Rome cannot officially change its position because of the larger ramifications. The situation here is quite reminiscent of the birth-control controversy after Vatican II. On both issues Rome alone has taken an absolute stand that not only goes beyond what the Orthodox and most Protestants believe is the clear teaching of Scripture but also is contrary to what the overwhelming number of its members believe.[49] And in both cases, Rome cannot reform its position in the direction of Protestantism and Orthodoxy without undermining its claims to authority and indeed without seriously damaging the very coherence of Roman theology.[50]

A Conservative Catholic Critique

Consider the analysis of conservative Roman Catholic Ross Douthat. He observes that his church has managed to remain officially united despite its deep divisions by a sort of truce between conservatives and liberals. "That coexistence depends on a tension between doctrine and practice, in which the church's official teaching remains conservative even as the everyday life of

---

48. Ibid., n. 351.

49. On this issue, Collins's view is close to that of Rome. He thinks remarriage is only acceptable in clear cases of adultery. See Matt. 19:9.

50. Of course, many critics note that Rome deals with this issue by annulments, which some refer to as "Catholic divorce."

Catholicism is shot through with disagreement, relativism, dissent."[51] This arrangement, he claims, allows conservatives to feel reassured even as it allows liberals to remain in the church as they wait for it to "evolve" even more in their direction. Douthat thinks, however, that the terms of the truce have now changed with *Amoris Laetitia*. While the document does not provide a *formal* path for the divorced and remarried to receive Communion (without committing to total continence), it still marks a significant new policy. In effect, it endorses what is already "the existing practice in many places—the informal admission of remarried Catholics to communion by sympathetic priests."[52]

The new document represents a highly significant development because it is essentially "a teaching *in favor of the truce itself.*" Instead of merely tolerating the profound split between actual practice and official doctrine for the sake of formal unity, the split "now has a papal imprimatur."[53] Douthat sees this new variation on the truce as even shakier than the earlier one between conservatives and progressives. "In effectively licensing innovation rather than merely tolerating it, and in transforming the papacy's keenest defenders into wary critics, it promises to heighten the church's contradictions rather than contain them."[54] He concludes his article with these words:

> Francis doubtless intends this language as a bridge between the church's factions, just dogmatic enough for conservatives but perpetually open to more liberal interpretations. And such deliberate ambiguity does offer a center, of sorts, for a deeply divided church.
>
> But not one, I fear, that's likely to permanently hold.[55]

Rome-Colored Glasses: Visible Unity or Deep Division?

Anyone who understands the deep divisions in the Church of Rome that have been growing ever deeper since the pre–Vatican II era also understands that the image of unity Rome projects is just that, an image. I fully concur with Douthat in doubting that the "deliberate ambiguity" that comprises the center of his church will hold in decades to come.[56]

---

51. Douthat, "The New Catholic Truce," *New York Times*, April 9, 2016, http://www.nytimes.com/2016/04/10/opinion/sunday/the-new-catholic-truce.html.
52. Ibid.
53. Ibid. (emphasis original).
54. Ibid.
55. Ibid.
56. As I write, controversy continues to mount about these and related issues: Nicole Winfield, "Conservative Criticism Intensifies against Pope Francis," *Star Tribune*, February 4, 2017, http://www.startribune.com/pope-gives-delegate-all-needed-powers-for-knights-of-malta/412770093;

As I have followed these recent controversies, I could not help but think about the story of Steve Wood and his conversion that I sketched at the beginning of this chapter. Recall his crisis of conscience because divorced and remarried persons were invited to receive the sacrament of Communion in his church. I wonder what Wood thinks of the recent developments in his new church. Does he support his pope and believe that what he found so troubling in his church decades ago is now okay decades later if the pope approves of it? Or does he hold fast to the official teaching of his church and think (like Douthat and many other conservatives) that the changes Francis has subtly embraced generate deep inconsistencies in official teaching?

Either way, the point is clear. Protestant converts to Rome who imagine they are joining a church that is free of the divisions and disagreements that plague Protestantism are quite mistaken. Indeed, far from escaping those problems of Protestantism they disdain, they are in fact joining a church that is functionally a radically pluralist Protestant denomination.

Evangelical Protestantism, with all its denominational diversity, actually represents a far more impressive model of true unity than does the Church of Rome. The National Association of Evangelicals is composed of some forty different evangelical churches. Despite their differences on secondary issues, there is genuine agreement and substantial unity on classic orthodox catholic doctrine. Most of these churches, moreover, are in communion with each other. In the same vein, it is a safe bet that there is far more genuine agreement about catholic Christianity among the members of the Evangelical Theological Society than there is among, say, members of the Catholic Theological Society of America.

Curiously, when these sorts of facts are pointed out, converts to Rome often dismiss them with little more than a wave of a hand. As Gerald Bray has observed, "Intellectual Protestant converts [to Roman Catholicism or Orthodoxy] either ignore these unpleasant facts or make excuses for them in a way that they would never do for the Protestant denominations they have left."[57] This is more than a little telling. Regardless of how they try to excuse it, and regardless of the double standard that may be at work here, the hard truth is that the permanence and unity that Roman apologists and converts like to project over against Protestantism is at best an idealistic illusion.

Phil Lawler, "Pope Francis Has Become a Source of Division," *Catholic Culture*, January 27, 2017, http://www.catholicculture.org/commentary/otn.cfm?id=1199; Pete Baklinski, "Vatican Cardinal: Catholics in Adulterous Unions 'Must Be Given' Communion," *LifeSite*, February 14, 2017, https://www.lifesitenews.com/news/canonical-cardinal-clashes-with-doctrinal-cardinal-over-communion-for-adult; William Doino Jr., "Pope Francis's Achilles Heel," *First Things*, March 27, 2017, https://www.firstthings.com/web-exclusives/2017/03/pope-franciss-achilles-heel.

57. Bray, *The Church: A Theological and Historical Account* (Grand Rapids: Baker Academic, 2016), 236–37.

CONCLUSION

A Come to Jesus Moment

The title *Roman but Not Catholic* epitomizes three major themes that the book has developed. First, it highlights the exclusivity of the Roman Catholic Church in bringing forth many of its claims. Such affirmations, repeated throughout the centuries, pertain to Rome alone and not to other theological traditions. Examples of this first theme are evident in the following observations: "This Church, constituted and organized as a society in the present world, subsists in (*subsistit in*) the [Roman] Catholic Church, which is governed by the successor of Peter and by the bishops in communion with him."[1] Here the Roman Catholic Church not only is supposedly a part of a proper succession that goes back to the apostle Peter (giving validity to its orders and sacramental life) but also evidences a proper hierarchical order, with the pope at the apex, that all other Christian communions so obviously lack. Another variation on this theme of exclusivity can be seen in the declaration that Jesus Christ established or founded the Roman Catholic Church—and by implication no other. Indeed, this claim not only was a part of a recent North American TV campaign but also is one that has been repeated by apologists.[2] And finally it has been argued by the magisterium that all churches or so-called ecclesiastical

---

1. *Catechism of the Catholic Church*, 2nd ed. (Mahwah, NJ: Paulist Press, 1994), par. 816.
2. One Roman Catholic apologist claims, "The Church that Christ founded is the [Roman] Catholic Church which has a formal earthly structure established by Christ and which continues under His authority and protection." Fritz Tuttle, "Jesus Christ Established a Visible Church on Earth," Eternal Word Television Network, accessed January 2, 2017, https://www.ewtn.com/faith/teachings/churb1.htm.

communions must be properly related to the bishop of Rome.[3] In this thinking only Rome is properly the center. Summing up, then, this first theme underscores that the Roman Catholic Church has authority, powers, and privileges that other Christian communions lack—at least it is so argued.

Second, the title *Roman but Not Catholic* underscores the separation created by the Roman Catholic Church precisely in making many of its exclusive claims. Thus, in developing a particular ecclesiology predicated upon an apostolic succession of bishops that putatively goes back to the apostle Peter, Rome has looked askance at the ministerial orders of Protestants and has judged them to be deficient, with implications for sacramental life as well. As a result of this ecclesiological move, Rome not only bars Protestants from its Communion table but also forbids its own flock from the sacramental life of a Protestant table. Another variation on this theme of separation is that the magisterium has been invested with such authority, supposedly over the universal church, that it ends up propounding doctrines (such as the immaculate conception) that only Rome itself affirms in their fullness. This too constitutes a separation. And finally, the Roman Catholic Church keeps this division, this disunity, very much alive by arguing that all other theological traditions, Eastern Orthodoxy included, must acknowledge the universal leadership of the bishop of Rome. Ironically enough, what is claimed as a basis of unity for the church—the papacy—actually becomes one of the central reasons for its ongoing division and continuing separation.

Third, *Roman but Not Catholic* emphasizes the authoritative basis upon which so many Roman Catholics, especially conservative ones, actually build their lives of belief, discipleship, and Christian service. Criticizing Protestants for their affirmation of sola Scriptura and sola fide, Roman Catholic apologists, interestingly enough, have been oblivious to their own "sola" tendencies, which are well developed. They are epitomized in the language of *sola Roma* and are expressed in dogmatic pronouncements. In other words, the magisterium of the Roman Catholic Church, though it acknowledges the authority of Scripture, has nevertheless made itself such an awesome power—buttressed by appeals to sacred tradition, which itself is given the same reverence as Scripture—that *sola Roma* quickly becomes the basis, the reason, why many Roman Catholics believe as they do. This too detracts from the genuine catholicity of the church. Recall the language of the *Catechism* from chapter 3 that touches on this very point: "'The task of giving an authentic

---

3. The *Catechism* states: "For the Roman Pontiff, by reason of his office as Vicar of Christ, and as pastor of the entire Church has full, supreme, and universal power over the whole Church, a power which he can always exercise unhindered." Par. 882.

interpretation of the Word of God, whether in its written form or in the form of Tradition, has been entrusted to the living, teaching office of the Church *alone*. Its authority in this matter is exercised in the name of Jesus Christ.' This means that the task of interpretation has been entrusted to the bishops in communion with the successor of Peter, the Bishop of Rome."[4] And though the role of the magisterium supposedly consists simply in the interpretation of Scripture, nevertheless that interpretation is virtually all that is heard by those in the pews. Why do you believe as you do? Because the hierarchy says so or because the pope says so. In fact, the magisterium has encouraged this large role, this particular ecclesiology, at every step along the way. Consider once more how *The Catechism of the Council of Trent* put it much earlier: "This knowledge is nothing else than faith, by virtue of which we hold that as fixed whatsoever the authority of our Holy Mother the Church teaches us to have been revealed by God."[5] Here then is a foundational appeal not to either Scripture, faith, or even the Holy Spirit, but to a particular ecclesiology, the authority of "our Holy Mother the Church," which is so readily affirmed in practical Roman Catholic life, at least by conservatives and traditionalists.

Death and the Last Things

Now let us raise a question with far-reaching implications and practical consequences: Does the troika of exclusivity, separation, and grounding authority continue to play out on the deathbed itself, as faithful Christians are departing this world? Moreover, is all this teaching, with its distinctions and separations, carried into the next life, into the world to come? To answer these significant and perhaps problematic questions, it is helpful to look at the NT practice of anointing the sick, as found in James 5:14–15 and Mark 6:12–13, and then to compare it with the Roman Catholic sacrament of the same name, hitherto known as extreme unction.

The passage from James reads as follows: "Is anyone among you sick? Let them call the elders of the church to pray over them and anoint them with oil in the name of the Lord. And the prayer offered in faith will make the sick person well; the Lord will raise them up. If they have sinned, they will be forgiven" (5:14–15). Notice the general nature of this grace: "Is *anyone* among you sick?"

4. Ibid., par. 85 (emphasis added); the internal quotation is from Pope Paul VI, *Dei Verbum: Dogmatic Constitution on Divine Revelation* (1965), sec. 10, of which a translation may be found at http://www.vatican.va/archive/hist_councils/ii_vatican_council/documents/vat-ii_const_19651118_dei-verbum_en.html.

5. Theodore Alois Buckley, *The Catechism of the Council of Trent* (Oxford: Aeterna, 2014), Kindle edition, locations 173–74.

If this is the case, then one should call for the elders. Mark's passage is even more instructive along these lines: "They went out and preached that people should repent. They drove out many demons and anointed many sick people with oil and healed them" (6:12–13). In this second setting, with its strong evangelistic note, it appears that the disciples, whom Jesus sent out two by two, were anointing not the sick of the church but a much more general population: those who had responded to the preaching of the disciples and who were therefore now in a state of repentance. However, what is common in both passages is that the anointing of the sick is a wonderful demonstration of the love and mercy of God toward those in very tangible, bodily need. R. T. France considers such anointing as nothing less than a "symbol of God's care for . . . restoration."[6]

With respect to its own sacramental life, the Roman Catholic Church maintains that the anointing of the sick was instituted by Christ, in light of the passages of James and Mark just cited, and more specifically in terms of the Savior's command, "Heal the sick!"[7] The change from the earlier name of the sacrament, extreme unction, to its present designation, the anointing of the sick, has cleared up some misunderstandings. Earlier some laity mistakenly believed that the sacrament could not be repeated or that such a ritual constitutes the "last rites" of the faithful who are about to depart, in other words, that it was to be the very last ritual performed before death. Indeed, since Rome believes that the Eucharist is the very center of its ecclesiastical life, this sacrament, and not the anointing of the sick, should be the viaticum, food for the journey, and as such the very last one. The *Catechism* states: "As the sacrament of Christ's Passover the Eucharist should always be the last sacrament of the earthly journey, the 'viaticum' for 'passing over' to eternal life."[8] Indeed, in many instances at the deathbed not one but three sacraments are offered to the faithful, in the following order: penance, the anointing of the sick, and finally Eucharist.

Bishops and priests perform this sacrament of gracious unction and in doing so utter the following words only once: "Through this holy anointing may the Lord in his love and mercy help you with the grace of the Holy Spirit. May the Lord who frees you from sin save you and raise you up."[9] All this language looks as if it could have been drawn from the pages of the NT itself. But when the question is raised, "To whom is this sacrament rightly administered?" once more we encounter the Roman accretions spawned over

---

6. France, *The Gospel of Mark: A Commentary on the Greek Text, New International Greek Testament Commentary* (Grand Rapids: Eerdmans; Carlisle, UK: Paternoster, 2002), 251.

7. *Catechism*, par. 1509.

8. Ibid., par. 1517.

9. Ibid., par. 1513.

time by tradition (now in contrast to the graciousness and mercy of the NT rite), through which a particular ecclesiology invariably reigns with its exclusivity and inevitable separation. This troubled narrative, which we have encountered earlier, also plays out at the deathbed itself.

Though some Roman Catholic bloggers[10] believe that Vatican II opened up the administration of this particular sacrament to all Christian believers, Protestants included, the basic position taken at this council was actually one of denial as its set point, to which allowances (if a number of conditions were met) could then be made. Admittedly, it would be rare for a Protestant to lack the services of a minister at the deathbed and therefore request anointing by an available Roman Catholic clergy. At any rate, the answer to the question, "Can 'separated brethren' receive the sacrament of the anointing of the sick?" is not a simple and straightforward "Yes," as some would have it. It's actually far more complicated than that. Vatican II explains: "Where this unity of sacramental faith is deficient, the participation of the separated brethren with Catholics, especially in the sacraments of the Eucharist, penance and anointing of the sick, is forbidden."[11] Remarkably enough, the number of conditions that must be met to receive this sacrament of mercy and grace are different depending upon the particular theological tradition in question. Since Eastern Christians, for example, are separated from the Roman Catholic Church, they cannot receive this sacrament simply as a matter of course unless they "ask of their own accord and have *the right dispositions.*"[12] The requirements for Protestants, however, are far more considerable. Vatican II enumerates them as follows: "The Church can for adequate reasons, allow access to those sacraments to a separated brother. This may be permitted in danger of death or in urgent need (during persecution, in prisons) if the separated brother has no access to a minister of his own communion, and spontaneously asks a Catholic priest for the sacraments—so long as he declares a faith in these sacraments in harmony with that of the Church, and is rightly disposed."[13]

Vatican II documents go on to stipulate that in other cases in which there is some doubt as to the proper fulfillment of the conditions above, "the judge of

10. Monsignor M. Francis Mannion states, "The answer to this question is yes. Before the Second Vatican Council, this was not possible; however, as a result of the council, the Catholic Church made some modifications in its outlook and practice on this matter." "Anointing of Non-Catholics," *OSV Newsweekly,* June 16, 2010, https://www.osv.com/OSVNewsweekly /ByIssue/Article/TabId/735/ArtMID/13636/ArticleID/7694/Anointing-of-non-Catholics.aspx.

11. *Directory concerning Ecumenical Matters,* part 1, sec. 55, in *The Conciliar and Post Conciliar Documents,* vol. 1 of *Vatican II,* ed. Austin Flannery (Vatican City: Libreria Editrice Vaticana, 2011), 499.

12. Ibid., sec. 27, in Flannery, *Conciliar and Post Conciliar Documents,* 450 (emphasis added).

13. Ibid., sec. 55, in Flannery, *Conciliar and Post Conciliar Documents,* 499.

this urgent necessity must be the diocesan bishop or the episcopal conference."[14]
This means, then, that Protestants who are dying and who have, for example,
spent a life of selfless missionary service to the poor do not receive the balm of
the grace and mercy of God on the deathbed but instead are interviewed, and
if that doesn't go well, then they are subject to the judgment of the bishop (if
he can even be quickly consulted), and failing that, their "case" is put before
the bureaucracy of an episcopal conference. Clearly what should have been
a means of grace as well as a demonstration of the love and mercy of God
toward genuine, baptized members of the body of Christ—Christian brothers
and sisters who are clearly marked by the Holy Spirit—has instead become
something remarkably different. Moreover, when Vatican II documents go on
to stipulate that "a Catholic in similar circumstances may not ask for these
sacraments [such as the anointing of the sick] except from a minister who has
been validly ordained," then such a teaching can only reveal that once again
a particular ecclesiology, which itself is dubious and repeatedly challenged
by historians, has caused a division, a separation, on the very deathbed itself,
where there should have been grace and mercy in abundance.

A Come-to-Jesus Moment

If Protestants and Roman Catholics are separated at the deathbed in a genuine
schism of love and mercy—and all of this done not by Protestant choice but by
those who adhere to Roman Catholic teaching, the will of the magisterium—
then is this division, this schism, to be carried into the future, into the very wedding supper of the Lamb itself? Recall the language of the book of Revelation:

> Then I heard what sounded like a great multitude, like the roar of rushing
> waters and like loud peals of thunder, shouting:
>
> > "Hallelujah!
> > For our Lord God Almighty reigns.
> > Let us rejoice and be glad
> > and give him glory!
> > For the wedding of the Lamb has come,
> > and his bride has made herself ready.
> > Fine linen, bright and clean, was given her to wear."
>
> (Fine linen stands for the righteous acts of God's holy people.)

14. Ibid. In this same section it is affirmed: "A Catholic in similar circumstances may not
ask for these sacraments except from a minister who has been validly ordained."

Then the angel said to me, "Write this: Blessed are those who are invited to the wedding supper of the Lamb!" (Rev. 19:6–9)

If we can assume that both Roman Catholics and Protestants believe those from the other theological tradition will indeed be in heaven (and we think that is a safe assumption), then it is eminently reasonable to pose the question, How could Protestants on the one hand be rejected at the deathbed (or at the Communion table, for that matter) and yet on the other hand be sitting around the table at the great wedding feast of the Lamb? Put another way, how are the divisions among Christians in this life overcome in a glorious unity in the next? In order not to beg the question here (in other words, simply to assume that which is actually at stake), we will conclude with two basic scenarios: one that we believe is consistent with Roman Catholic teaching, the other with Protestant doctrine.

The first scenario answers this key question of the transition from disunity to unity in the following fashion: Protestants, as separated brethren, will at some point after death realize the error of their ways—their aberrant ecclesiology along with their deficient views of the ordained and sacramental life—and will quite simply repent. This change will be brought about by an overwhelming illumination (overcoming invincible ignorance) upon entrance into the world to come, or perhaps they will receive some sort of instruction in Roman Catholic ecclesiology and sacramental theology in purgatory. At any rate, as a consequence of this transformation, however it occurs, Protestant brothers and sisters will be invited by Christ to fellowship with Roman Catholic saints who are already sitting at the wedding supper in full communion. Simply put, all impediments will have been removed, purged away.

The second scenario is much different from the first. It recognizes, for one thing, the considerable difference between this life and the next. Accordingly, this second view recognizes first of all, that the one High Priest Jesus Christ, himself, reigns at the supper of the Lamb. Second, there are no rabbis or teachers in heaven ("But you are not to be called 'Rabbi,' for you have one Teacher, and you are all brothers" [Matt. 23:8]) but the one teacher, who is Christ, for all eternity. Third, there is no ecclesiastical hierarchy in heaven and certainly not among those who as brothers and sisters are seated around the table at the feast, in the unity of holy love resplendent under Christ's lordship.

In this second scenario, then, belief in and the affirmation of a past and particular ecclesiastical order, affirmed only by Rome, so important to the first scenario, is deemed unnecessary. Thus the kind of illuminating process depicted in the first view (in terms of valid orders and proper sacramental life) is pointless. In fact, it has been rendered obsolete by Christ, who reigns at the supper with his bride, the church, composed of all those of whatever Christian theological tradition who have received both the forgiveness of sins and the washing by the blood of the Lamb in the power of the Holy Spirit. Protestants are sitting at the great wedding feast, then, not because they have been purged of deficiencies in the eyes of the Roman magisterium but because the Holy Spirit reigns in their hearts. All those artificial impediments that caused division on earth, even at the table of the Lord, have no weight in heaven. The wedding garment is not a particular ecclesiology or view of the sacraments but holiness!

We are pleased to learn that Pope Francis has been thinking about this ongoing ecumenical issue as well. On November 15, 2015, for example, he responded to a question at Christuskirche, the Lutheran church in Rome, posed by a Protestant woman, who asked if she would be permitted to receive Holy Communion along with her Roman Catholic husband.[15] The Pope's reply, cited below, is not altogether clear, and the reason, we suspect, is that Pope Francis ran into a conflict of both heart and mind on this issue; he seems to be pulled in two very different directions. Readers can judge for themselves. The pope replied as follows:

> Thank you, Ma'am. Regarding the question on sharing the Lord's Supper, it is not easy for me to answer you, especially in front of a theologian like Cardinal Kasper! I'm afraid! I think the Lord gave us [the answer] when he gave us this command: "Do this in memory of me." And when we share in, remember and emulate the Lord's Supper, we do the same thing that the Lord Jesus did. And the Lord's Supper will be, the final banquet will there be in the New Jerusalem, but this will be the last. Instead on the journey, I wonder—and I don't know how to answer, but I am making your question my own—I ask myself: "Is sharing the Lord's Supper the end of a journey or is it the viaticum for walking together?" I leave the question to the theologians, to those who understand. It is true that in a certain sense sharing is saying that there are no differences between us, that we have the same doctrine—I underline the word, a difficult word to understand—but I ask myself: don't we have the same Baptism?[16]

Up until this point it appears as if the pope was about to grant the woman's request. But then, for whatever reason, he abruptly changed his mind and concluded with the following observation: "I would never dare give permission to do this because I do not have the authority. One Baptism, one Lord, one faith. Speak with the Lord and go forward. I do not dare say more."[17]

15. Sandro Magister, "Communion for All, Even for Protestants," July 1, 2016, *Chiesa*, http://chiesa.espresso.repubblica.it/articolo/1351332?eng=y.

16. Ibid.

17. Ibid.

We find both telling and encouraging the recent comments of Pope Francis toward more inclusive practices in celebrating the sacrament of Holy Communion, even if such statements were expressed in the midst of lingering doubt and ambiguity. The larger picture here shows Francis recognizing that the spiritual and substantial doctrinal agreement uniting faithful Protestants and Roman Catholics is far more significant than their disagreements about ecclesiology and sacramental theology. And yet, because of the official doctrinal commitments of Rome, he cannot fully and straightforwardly affirm that Protestants and Roman Catholics should share the sacrament.[18] In this book, we have commended a robust vision of Christian unity and the church catholic that allows us consistently and forthrightly to recognize each other fully as brothers and sisters in Christ and to celebrate that reality by sharing the sacrament of Christian unity. Perhaps the pope will take further steps in this same direction, during the pivotal 2017 year, to allow us to celebrate the fundamental reality that we are all characterized by one Lord, one faith, one baptism. We surely hope so. The advance of world Christianity on that occasion and its witness to the world would be epic.

Until that time, however, or until some other ecumenical breakthrough moment comes, we are humbly aware that both Roman Catholics and Protestants will continue to disagree about the how of the transition from disunity in this life to unity in the next. Yet at least we can find agreement in recognizing that the future the Lord has prepared for us all is one of unsurpassed communion, beauty, and truth. Indeed, we are all getting closer to that glorious reality by God's grace as we live out our Christian lives from decade to decade, walking in the obedience of faith, encouraged by hope and empowered by love. May that future, then, become our reality in a deeper and richer way, in a "realized

18. We realize the difficulties entailed in Roman Catholics and Protestants sharing the sacrament of the Eucharist. It is perhaps easier for Protestants to share in the Lord's Supper with Roman Catholics, for Protestants can affirm Roman Catholics fully as brothers and sisters in Christ on the basis of a common faith in Nicene orthodoxy, while Roman Catholics qualify that by designating Protestants as "separated brethren." Protestants often readily agree that Roman Catholics believe everything that is necessary for salvation, even as they also think Roman Catholics require as essential belief *more* than is necessary. Similarly, Protestants believe that our common faith in Christ and our belief that Holy Communion is a sacrament Christ commanded us to observe unite us, even as they reject some of Rome's claims about the nature and meaning of the sacrament. Protestants may thus be able to share the sacrament more easily with their Roman Catholic brothers and sisters, even as they recognize that those brothers and sisters are unable to join in Protestant celebrations of the sacrament. Recognizing this reality, the pope may be willing as an initial step to welcome to the table Protestants who are willing to share the sacrament despite points of disagreement. It must also be recognized that many Protestants disagree with Roman Catholic views of the sacrament so strongly that they could not in good conscience take Communion in a Roman Catholic service.

eschatology," whereby last things become present ones, possibilities become actualities. May knowledge of the world to come transform our hearts now, in a flush of graces, in order that we may see the Christian "other" in fresh and engaging ways. And finally, may the unity of heaven above become realized on the earth below such that the words of Christ might receive a grand and glorious fulfillment in the church, for the salvation of the whole world and to the utter glory of God:

> My prayer is not for them alone. I pray also for those who will believe in me through their message, that all of them may be one, Father, just as you are in me and I am in you. May they also be in us so that the world may believe that you have sent me. (John 17:20–21)

Amen!

Author Index

Scripture and Ancient Writings Index

Subject Index